The Taxation of Pensions

CESifo Seminar Series
Edited by Clemens Fuest

Global Interdependence, Decoupling and Recoupling
Yin-Wong Cheung and Frank Westermann, editors

The Economics of Conflict
Karl Wärneryd, editor

Climate Policy and Nonrenewable Resources
Karen Pittel, Frederick van der Ploeg, and Cees Withagen, editors

Taxation and Regulation of the Financial Sector
Ruud de Mooij and Gaëtan Nicodème, editors

The Mobility of Students and the Highly Skilled
Marcel Gérard and Silke Uebelmesser, editors

Political Economy and Instruments of Environmental Politics
Friedrich Schneider, Andrea Kollmann, and Johannes Reichl, editors

Emissions Trading Systems as a Policy Instrument
Marc Gronwald and Beat Hintermann, editors

The Economics of Infrastructure Provisioning
Arnold Picot, Massimo Florio, Nico Grove, and Johann Kranz, editors

Public Sector Economics and the Need for Reforms
Apostolis Philippopoulos, editor

The Economics and Political Economy of Energy Subsidies
Jon Strand, editor

The Economics of Language Policy
Michele Gazzola and Bengt-Anne Wickström, editors

Demographic Change and Long-Run Development
Matteo Cervellati and Uwe Sunde, editors

Social Economics: Current and Emerging Avenues
Joan Costa-Font and Mario Macis, editors

International Currency Exposure
Yin-Wong Cheung and Frank Westermann, editors

Energy Tax and Regulatory Policy in Europe
Ian Parry, Karen Pittel, and Herman Vollebergh, editors

Developments in Global Sourcing
Wilhelm Kohler and Erdal Yalcin, editors

See http://mitpress.mit.edu for a complete list of titles in this series.

The Taxation of Pensions

Robert Holzmann and John Piggott, editors

with support by Bernd Genser

CESifo Seminar Series

The MIT Press
Cambridge, Massachusetts
London, England

This book was set in Palatino by Westchester Publishing Services. Printed and bound in the United States of America.

Library of Congress Cataloging-in-Publication Data

Names: Holzmann, Robert, editor. | Piggott, John (John R.), editor.
Title: The taxation of pensions / edited by Robert Holzmann and John Piggott, with support by Bernd Genser.
Description: Cambridge, MA : MIT Press, [2018] | Series: CESifo seminar series | Includes bibliographical references and index.
Identifiers: LCCN 2018001227 | ISBN 9780262038324 (hardcover : alk. paper)
Subjects: LCSH: Pensions—Taxation.
Classification: LCC HJ4653.P5 T39 2018 | DDC 336.24/28—dc23
LC record available at https://lccn.loc.gov/2018001227

10 9 8 7 6 5 4 3 2 1

Contents

Series Foreword

This book is part of the CESifo Seminar Series. The series aims to cover topical policy issues in economics from a largely European perspective. The books in this series are the products of the papers and intensive debates that took place during the seminars hosted by CESifo, an international research network of renowned economists organized jointly by the Center for Economic Studies at Ludwig-Maximilians-Universität, Munich, and the Ifo Institute for Economic Research. All publications in this series have been carefully selected and refereed by members of the CESifo research network.

Acknowledgments

This publication is the result of transcontinental cooperation between the Sydney-based Australian Research Centre of Excellence in Population Ageing Research (CEPAR), University of New South Wales, and the Munich-based CESifo company, a research group consisting of the Center for Economic Studies—an independent institute within the Faculty of Economics of Ludwig-Maximilians-Universität, Munich—and the Ifo Institute–Leibniz Institute for Economic Research at the University of Munich.

The volume originated with two workshops (in Sydney on November 17–18, 2014, and in Munich on September 3–4, 2015). First drafts of selected papers were presented at the first workshop, with a focus on the Australian perspective. Revised and additional papers focused on Europe were presented at the second workshop. A few more papers were commissioned after the second workshop; we are grateful for the commitment and participation of their authors. All papers were internally and externally peer reviewed—sincere thanks go to Viktor Steiner (Humboldt University Berlin) and Bernd Genser (University of Constance) for their contributions. The final revision of the full manuscript profited very much from the pertinent comments and suggestions by an anonymous reviewer as part of the MIT manuscript review process.

The distributed production process was only made possible by the committed participation of all the authors in the volume over a long period of time; their engagement was exceptional. Likewise, the support of collaborators across the globe was essential for the organization of the workshops. We were blessed with great administrative support in Sydney from Amy Brushwood, Annabella McHugh, and Alexi Phelps, as well as from Karin Fournier, Deirdre Weber, and Daniela Wech in

Munich. Special thanks go to Amy Gautam, who was an outstanding copyeditor.

The conference hosting, accommodations, and travel to the workshops were financed by the respective research institutions. All authors in this volume provided their time ad honorarium. We are extremely thankful for their dedication and support.

I Setting the Stage

1 The Taxation of Pensions under Review: Motivation, Issues, and Directions

Robert Holzmann and John Piggott

1.1 Motivation and Background

The quest for better-designed pension schemes and effective pension system reforms has preoccupied policy makers and academic researchers for the last several decades. The debate has swept across the globe, at times generating strong theoretical and policy arguments and creating reform leaders and followers. The notions of systemic and parametric pension reform that emerged with the debate suggest the depth of proposed reforms and the willingness to explore new ones.

By contrast, the topic of taxation of pensions, and retirement income provision more broadly, has been much more limited. Taxation of pensions did receive some country-specific attention within much broader tax reform discussions and sporadic interest from the research community, but no new paradigms were proposed; changes in pension tax regulations happened mostly at the margin; and apart from some modeling efforts, academic research was very sparse. The relative neglect of this topic is surprising, as a number of developments came to the forefront during recent decades that impact the taxation of pensions, and public finance more generally. The most important of these trends call for a broader policy and research response:

1. Population aging has advanced worldwide and commands ever greater attention from policy makers, international organizations, and researchers. Population aging makes the tax base(s) of retirement income even more important. Individuals' expected delays in retiring combined with continued increases in life expectancy postretirement lengthen the span between pension contribution payments and receipt of benefits and make the timing of tax revenues more sensitive to front- or back-loaded arrangements for taxing pensions. The trend toward

replacing public and private annuities during the drawdown stage with phased withdrawals or individual portfolio management renders choices among retirement savings instruments more sensitive to taxation regimes and their changes.

2. Globalization now encompasses not only the movement of goods and services but also the flow between countries of people, both as workers and as retirees, and of capital. This makes tax revenues more sensitive to the way pension contributions, and retirement savings more generally, and their returns are treated by work and residence countries during the saving, accumulation, and withdrawal phases.

3. The tax treatment of retirement income provision is highly complex, variable over time, and highly diverse across savings alternatives within and between countries. This creates potential distortions and invites arbitrage activities on retirement income programs that by themselves are already complex; arbitrage activities on the selection of countries of work, investment, and retirement residence; and greater rent seeking on the part of the tax advice industry.

4. The aforementioned developments affect the distribution of tax expenditures and tax revenues of retirement income schemes along individuals' life cycles, but the increasing mobility of the labor force and retirees also affects the distribution of tax expenditures and revenues between countries. Existing double-taxation treaties do not address interpersonal or intercountry inequities, and little consensus exists among policy makers and researchers about how to coordinate the taxation of retirement income provision across the World Bank's "five pension pillars" (discussed below) and between countries.

5. Most of the discussion on approaches to taxing pensions still centers heavily on the type and scope of tax preferences and the timing of taxation. However, developments in the academic literature over recent decades provide an analytical base suggesting that taxing wage and capital income at the same rate may not be welfare-optimal; lower capital income tax rates may lead to long-run welfare improvements; age-based taxes may have the potential to significantly improve welfare; and the design of pension systems and tax systems should be better coordinated.

This volume aims to shed some light on these issues by doing three things: (1) documenting how pension systems are subject to various forms of taxation, (2) analyzing how economic theory can explain what is observed both qualitatively and quantitatively, and (3) asking the normative question of whether the observed interactions of taxation and pensions may or may not be efficient. The goal is to provide a platform for further research; this volume is not intended to deliver a unified vision of pension taxation in the twenty-first century.

This publication is the result of cooperation between CEPAR (ARC Centre of Excellence in Population Ageing Research, based at the University of New South Wales, Sydney) and CESifo (Center for Economic Studies & Ifo Institute, based in Munich), and demonstrates the power of this kind of international institutional cooperation. These organizations held two consecutive workshops, in Sydney in late 2014 and in Munich in late 2015, to begin the discussion. The workshop papers were then developed, reviewed internally and externally, and revised into the chapters of this volume. Some of the papers were invited after the workshops to augment content and depth.

The rest of this chapter is organized as follows. Section 1.2 offers a selective view of some of the research questions and policy issues raised in the volume. Section 1.3 provides an overview of the chapters and their results, and how they fit together. Finally, section 1.4 outlines key research questions on topics suggested for priority attention going forward.

1.2 Framing of Research Questions and Policy Issues

This section aims to frame key questions and highlight selective answers on the topic of taxing pensions. Its purpose is to provide alternative perspectives on the topic against the assessment that economic theory currently offers some limited specific guidance for policy makers, while the country realities are very complex and difficult to reconcile with such guidance. To this end, the following questions and issues were selected: (1) How can the tremendous diversity of tax treatment of pensions within and across countries and time be explained? (2) What does recent academic literature imply for the direction of pension taxation? (3) What conceptual guidance is available for taxing the different pillars of retirement income policy? (4) What possible directions exist for incremental or major reforms by key country groups? (5) Should and can taxation and pensions be treated jointly or separately from a policy viewpoint? (6) What are the implications for analysis when moving from a closed economy to an open one, taking into account population aging?

1.2.1 Explaining the Complexity and Diversity of Pension Taxation

Taxation of pensions differs substantially within and between countries and over time. Several chapters in this volume offer deeper country-specific insights on both the rationales and reforms. Reasons for this diversity include differentiated legal structures and the differences between wage-based contributions to an unfunded scheme as withheld earnings and funded contributions as financial savings; the lack of policy coordination between agencies in charge of pensions and those in charge of taxation policy at the national and international levels; the fiscal policy cycles that expand and curtail tax advantages accorded to pension saving; and the incomplete establishment of income taxation oriented toward personal consumption (see Genser and Holzmann, chapter 15, this volume). Here, the focus is on the last point.

While the Schanz-Haig-Simons (SHS)[1] concept of comprehensive income taxation was the intellectual bedrock of personal income taxation for almost 100 years, it has rarely been applied to organized retirement saving. The administrative advantages generated by the comprehensive definition of income have mostly been waived in the pension domain, with little articulation of the reasons why but with notable consistency. Among possible reasons that might be offered *ex post* for this policy position are: (1) under a progressive schedule, it penalizes individuals with highly fluctuating annual incomes over their life cycle; and (2) the taxation of saving distorts intertemporal consumption decisions, as income spent on savings is subject to double taxation—once when income is saved and again when these savings earn returns. When saving for retirement is considered, compound interest makes this distortion large, but even as the actual treatment of pension savings approximated the consumption tax base, public accounting of these tax arrangements typically espoused a comprehensive income tax basis. Arguments for a general consumption-oriented income taxation structure (Fisher 1930; Kaldor 1955) were ignored or rejected by tax policy makers and their advisers, so pension saving (and to a lesser extent owner-occupied housing) was treated as an income tax concession in many countries.

From an academic perspective, consumption-type tax treatment became more established with the development of the theory of optimal tax policy in the 1970s, which rejected the optimality of equal tax rates for capital and labor. The approach gained political traction when its operational feasibility was enabled by exempting normal returns on capital (Atkinson and Stiglitz 1976; Institute for Fiscal Studies 1978; US Department of Treasury 1977). The advantages of consumption-oriented income taxation were stressed again recently by the two volumes of the Mirrlees Review (Mirrlees et al. 2010, 2011), but no industrialized country has yet implemented a fully consumption-oriented personal income tax (Auerbach 2009). Instead, this kind of treatment is reserved for life cycle saving in many but not all countries, for most but not all pension pillars, and often but not always for owner-occupied housing. The variation in these tax arrangements has not yet stabilized, nor have the contributions from economic theory provided new and stabilizing conceptual benchmarks.

1.2.2 Implications of Recent Developments in the Academic Literature

As indicated, it would be fair to say that in the last half century, the academic literature has established that there is no reason why labor income and capital income should be taxed at the same rate. This is the first and most important of several developments in the relevant literature. Early on, Pigou (1928) argued for the efficiency of a personal expenditure tax over an income tax in a two-period model recognizing only current and future consumption. Later work on optimal taxation in the 1970s developed this idea by including an untaxed good (leisure) in such models, leading to results that were less clear-cut. Atkinson and Stiglitz (1976), however, showed that a zero capital income tax was optimal when certain separability properties of utility functions were met—that is, that an income tax with a saving deduction remained optimal under these conditions.

The idea of the desirability of a zero capital income tax also received support from analysis using a different modeling framework. In the 1980s, a number of papers (Judd 1985; Chamley 1986) adopted a Ramsey-type growth framework to argue that it is inefficient to tax capital in the long run. In the Ramsey model, agents in the economy choose consumption and investment to maximize their overall welfare. Two mechanisms account for this result. First, the additional investment financed by the extra saving induced by removing capital taxation would eventually increase wages, and thus the labor income tax base, to a point where a labor tax would raise the same revenue without increasing the tax rate. Second, in a dynastic model, the price distortion between present and future consumption eventually becomes extreme. The zero capital income tax result thus comes from alternative modeling frameworks.[2]

However, this result was qualified in subsequent literature that used life cycle or incomplete market models. First, if a life cycle framework is used rather than the dynastic infinite horizon framework adopted by Chamley and Judd, and age-specific taxation is not available, some capital income taxation may be a second-best solution. In particular, Erosa and Gervais (2002), using a standard life cycle model, show that it is optimal for a government to tax or subsidize interest income, at least when age-dependent tax schedules are not available. This is because individuals' optimal consumption and work plans are not constant over the life cycle. As a result, it would be efficient for government to use age-varying capital and income tax rates. If it is not possible to condition tax rates on age, a nonzero capital income tax rate can be a substitute. Second, literature beginning with Hubbard and Judd (1986) showed that if incomplete credit or insurance markets are present, so that individuals are liquidity constrained or face uninsurable idiosyncratic income risk, then the optimal capital tax rate will not typically be zero, since substituting capital taxes for labor taxes will reduce the impact of these constraints.

An important paper by Conesa, Kitao, and Krueger (2009) quantitatively characterized the optimal capital and labor income taxes using an overlapping-generations model in which individuals face uninsurable idiosyncratic income shocks and permanent productivity differences. The authors found that the optimal capital income tax rate is significantly positive, at 36 percent, which is surprisingly high.

Commentary on Conesa, Kitao, and Krueger (2009) shows how sensitive their capital tax result is to generalizations of the model. Nakajima (2010) extended the Conesa, Kitao, and Krueger work by adding housing into the model to compare whether and how the optimal capital tax rate differs between models with and without housing. He showed that the optimal capital tax rate in the model with tax-exempt owner-occupied housing is 1 percent. This result stems primarily from the interasset distortion introduced between housing and nonhousing capital when one is taxed and the other is not, a recasting of the Hamilton and Whalley (1985) result discussed later. Peterman (2013) changed two critical assumptions in a canonical model of the Conesa type to demonstrate the sensitivity of the optimal capital tax rate to model assumptions. He modified the utility function such that it implies an agent's Frisch labor supply elasticity is constant, as opposed to increasing, over the agent's lifetime, and he allowed the government to tax accidental bequests at a separate rate from ordinary capital income. These two changes led the optimal tax on capital to drop by almost half. Kuklik (2011) extended the Conesa, Kitao, and Krueger (2009) model by adding two additional elements—a nonlinear mapping between hours worked and wages and *inter-vivos* transfers—and showed that the optimal capital income tax rate in the United States is 7.4 percent. Fehr and Kindermann (2015) found that adding transitional dynamics reduced the tax rate so that it was close to zero, while Peterman (2016) found that different approaches to modeling human capital accumulation had different impacts on the optimal capital tax rate. Kumru and Piggott (2017) found that combining social security and tax regimes reduced the optimal capital income tax rate.

This volume's judgment is that, on balance, while the literature since the 1980s has qualified the zero capital income tax result, the desirability of lower capital income tax rates, relative to labor income tax rates, is probably the most important conclusion from the academic literature as it currently stands (Mankiw, Weinzierl, and Yagan 2009).

A second important development relates to age-based taxation. The idea that tax rates on both capital income and labor income should depend on age was developed in recent decades (Alvarez et al. 1992 is the earliest reference found, although the most influential is Erosa and Gervais 2002). As in the case of traditional optimal tax literature, clear policy implications are hard to find. The additional flexibility introduced by allowing tax instruments to be conditioned on age does lead to welfare improvements, however, and numerical analysis suggests that these can be substantial.

While age-based programs do exist—the US Medicare program is one example—the literature on age-based taxes has not been developed in a policy setting. Woodland (2016) discussed the literature on age-based taxes in some detail, and Bateman (chapter 7, this volume) offers specifics on motivation and policy changes.

A third recent development is a series of papers that treat the income tax system and the pension system as an integrated whole, consistent with the suggestion by Cremer and Pestieau (chapter 2, this volume). These use a range of theoretical approaches and sometimes deal explicitly with retirement age as a policy instrument. Examples include Cremer, Lozachmeur, and Pestieau (2004), Shourideh and Troshkin (2013), and Kumru and Piggott (2017).

Finally, the "new dynamic public finance" (NDPF) literature embodies recent developments in public finance analysis that offer new guidance on how the taxation of savings and labor supply should differ from the traditional Ramsey-type approach. This literature builds on Mirrlees (1971), but in a dynamic incarnation with heterogeneity of agents (e.g., by skill) and private information. The NDPF approach considers the form of fully optimal taxes given the informational structure in the system. In this modeling framework, new results of NDPF include (1) that it is optimal to introduce positive distortions in savings that implicitly discourage saving, (2) perfect labor tax smoothing as in typical Ramsey models may not be optimal with uncertain and evolving skills, and (3) the time consistency problem is very different, as capital is not directly at the root of the problem. The NDPF result arises essentially through learning and using acquired information rather than taxing sunk capital (Golosov, Tsyvinski, and Werning 2007). Kocherlakota, the coiner of the notion of NDPF, states that "the ultimate goal of the NDPF is to provide relatively precise recommendations as to what taxes should be … and not be side-tracked or irritated how [*sic*] the current provisions actually look like and how they are motivated" (Kocherlakota 2010, 15). The NDPF approach is probably best seen as a complement to the alternative approaches already discussed.

These recent strands in the academic literature bear directly on pension taxation. Prefunded pensions involve accumulations of capital—in most economies, pensions represent the largest personally held pool of assets, along with owner-occupied housing. Pensions are by their nature age based. The taxation of labor and skills is relevant for labor supply decisions, which in many countries include formal versus informal participation and thus the presence or absence of acquired rights to future benefits. However, the lack of clear-cut policy guidance and potential operationalization that emerges from the age-based literature makes age-based considerations only a useful reference for *ex post* rationalization of design decisions, not an intellectual benchmark to inspire new taxation approaches. In addition, the NDPF initiative has not yet been broadly embraced or matured to a point where its insights may be translated into implementable policy proposals. All these strands, however, provide a rich foundation for future research on retirement income.

Last but not least, two major gaps remain in the analytical public finance literature as it relates to pension taxation. First, as Cremer and Pestieau (chapter 2, this volume) point out, behavior may not reflect rational life cycle expectations, and considerable evidence suggests that most people do not respond rationally to price changes in this context (Chetty et al. 2014). Subsection 1.2.3 expands on this. Second, it is worth noting that very little research undertaken to date models taxation policy explicitly in the presence of changing demographics. This is surely an area for future research, since much current interest in pension policy and pension taxation is generated by the aging population.

1.2.3 Academic Guidance on the Different Components of Retirement Income Policy

Throughout this volume, "pensions" should be thought of as encompassing not only occupational or personal pensions but also basic provision financed by general revenues (i.e., social pensions) and contributory social security schemes (i.e., public pensions). The rather disparate literature on the impacts of all these policies on behavior, especially labor market and saving choices, is thus relevant.

All these interventions bring with them price distortions that impact consumer choice. They do so at multiple points in an individual's life cycle—at the very least, when the benefit is received and when the tax required to finance it is levied. Furthermore, the overall effects of these interventions are mediated through government-provided or regulated programs for health, long-term care, and related services.

To see how policy and practice relate to this literature, it is convenient to revert to the World Bank's "five-pillar" system of retirement policy (Holzmann and Hinz 2005). The "zero" pillar encapsulates social pensions: noncontributory instruments for which eligibility is based on age, perhaps other income or assets, and some residency criterion. The first pillar captures schemes such as social security, either traditional pay-as-you-go-financed defined benefit schemes or more recent nonfinancial defined contribution schemes. The second and third pillars refer to pension saving that is prefunded, either occupational or personal, and either mandated or voluntary, respectively. The fourth pillar refers to nonpension assets and entitlements, including cohabitation of the elderly, owner-occupied housing, and access to public health and long-term care programs.

1.2.3.1 The zero pillar Most zero-pillar systems are means tested. Targeted or means-tested programs, also referred to as social pensions, base eligibility and the level of benefits on individual or family resources. By their nature, means-tested programs have a redistributive role and are funded from general taxation. Means testing provides an inexpensive way of ensuring a minimum level of retirement income. The means test is often criticized for creating disincentives to work and save, but such distortions are dwarfed by disincentives from much larger earnings-related pensions with associated payroll taxes or social insurance premiums (Chomik et al. 2015; Kumru and Piggott 2017).

While some form of targeting exists in most countries, it is rarely exploited to its full potential. Often, means testing is deployed in programs that address destitution, such as the US Supplemental Security Income program. Such policies can, however, also be used to reduce the liability of large publicly financed pension or social security promises by excluding the affluent. Comprehensive policies of this kind are in place in only a few developed economies (e.g., Australia, Canada, Chile, and Denmark) but have recently been advocated to address both fiscal pressure and inequality issues, notably by the International Monetary Fund (2014).

A common concern about means testing is how it affects incentives and distorts economic activity. Yet recent analytical insights reveal that means-tested programs can enhance economic efficiency because they cost less and distort fewer decisions than alternative arrangements. Furthermore, means-tested retirement programs, in particular, may be interpreted as an age-based capital income tax (Kumru and Piggott 2017). While little is known about the relative merits of alternative withdrawal schedules, the interpretation of the means test as an age-based tax should ameliorate concerns about very high effective marginal tax rates that are frequently brought to bear. The "effective" taxation introduced by means testing requires much more analysis.

1.2.3.2 The first pillar In most countries, mandated and unfunded public schemes from the very beginning had an expenditure tax treatment of a consumption-oriented income tax—deferred taxation whereby no taxes are levied at the stages of contributions and returns on assets, while full income taxation takes place at the stage of benefit disbursement (EET: exempt, exempt, taxed).[3] This consumption-type tax treatment had little to do with theoretical guidance but instead was driven by operational considerations: under the then-universal nonfinancial defined benefit schemes, the implicit rate of return was impossible to calculate and thus to tax. Perhaps more importantly, however, in the past, wage-based contributions were considered withheld wages to be taxed when disbursed. While the original consumption neutrality of taxing public pensions thus arose more by accident than by design, today it is the guiding principle for reforms, including the guidance for neutrality between alternative retirement arrangements. The 2005 retirement income tax reform in Germany falls into this category (see Börsch-Supan and Quinn, chapter 8, this volume).

Yet the neutrality of unfunded systems is violated (as in the zero pillar) by distributive considerations, in particular the earnings test under traditional nonfinancial defined benefit schemes, which often continue to include strong redistributive components. An earnings test is motivated by a desire to prevent "double dipping" by workers—drawing a pension at an early age while continuing to receive wage earnings. In its extreme form, an earnings test amounts to a tax on the supply of mature labor.

It is the redistributive structure of a nonfinancial defined benefit scheme that creates the very rationale of an earnings test. Under a nonfinancial defined contribution scheme, individuals get out only what they pay in, as this mimics an actuarially fair scheme (up to the difference between the financial interest rate and the notional rate of return, which is germane to the natural rate of growth). This pseudo-actuarial structure renders an earnings test unnecessary and allows any combination of benefit receipt and continued wage earnings, as is done in Sweden. Redistributive interventions then take place in a separate and transparent manner.[4]

1.2.3.3 The second and third pillars A recent authoritative policy document covering this issue, the Mirrlees Review, recommended a consumption-oriented income tax treatment of all saving, citing both the legal complexity of differentiating different forms of saving and the need to encourage pension saving (Mirrlees et al. 2011). While the Mirrlees Review suggests a broader consumption tax implementation via rate-of-return allowances, thus taxing capital returns and profit above a risk-free rate, it is open to other consumption tax approaches for retirement saving (i.e., immediate payment and thus the earnings tax variant TEE, meaning taxed, exempt, exempt, or deferred payment and thus the expenditure tax variant EET). This flexibility and self-selected combinations should smooth the effects of a progressive tax schedule. A consumption tax basis is appealing from an economic efficiency perspective because it eliminates both intertemporal and interasset price distortions. This latter effect is given less attention in the literature but is potentially equally important (Hamilton and Whalley 1985).

Here, owner-occupied housing is crucial, especially in those countries with high owner-occupancy rates, as is human capital investment. We return to this topic in subsection 1.2.3.4, when we discuss the fourth pillar.

Strong relevant evidence shows that households react to pension tax breaks in different ways. Chetty et al. (2014) analyzed some 41 million observations in Denmark over a 15-year period and concluded that pension tax breaks did not have a large impact on aggregate household saving. They split the sample into "active" and "passive" savers and found that only active savers (around 15 percent of the population) responded to variations in the pension tax breaks. However, they did so mainly by shifting savings between different saving vehicles. The remaining, "passive" savers (85 percent of the population) appeared not to alter their behavior. It is also possible that tax incentives may induce firms to offer workplace pensions. This leads back to the notion discussed earlier in this chapter that workplace-linked pension institutions can (1) provide affordable access to the capital market for households that otherwise would not participate, (2) operate in an environment where peer effects can be influential, and (3) act as a commitment device for long-term saving.

This evidence, if supported by other studies, raises the question of the efficacy of removing the intertemporal price distortion, particularly if these efforts go beyond what is called for by consumption taxation. If households do not react to expensive tax incentives, why provide them? Perhaps one response is that pension plans within these pillars operate as a commitment device. People save within them because they are there, and people around them do the same. It is unlikely that employers would offer such plans in the absence of a tax advantage (Mitchell and Piggott 2016). Nevertheless, other cheaper devices may achieve voluntary retirement saving, as the burgeoning literature on behavioral finance suggests (Mitchell and Utkus 2004; Benartzi and Thaler 2007, 2013). However, portfolio distortions created by different treatments of retirement saving instruments (including housing) may still call for neutrality.

Consumption tax treatment of these pillars returns the discussion to Pigou's (1928) analysis of "neutrality" between consumption in working life and in retirement. Pragmatically, a good deal can be said for such a position. Combined with the judgment that the weight of modern public finance analysis still indicates a lower rate of taxation for capital income than for labor income, the considerations raised here suggest that a pension tax structure generating neutrality between present and future consumption, and among alternative saving vehicles, is a good tax design to aspire to.

1.2.3.4 The fourth pillar Optimal financial retirement saving is also determined by the scope, pricing, and taxation of services highly relevant in old age, in particular cohabitation (i.e., living with children and family), owner-occupied housing, health care, and long-term care. The availability or absence of these services substantially changes the value of retirement income required to smooth lifetime consumption, as does their pricing and taxation. For this reason, these provisions are summarized as a memorandum under the fourth pension pillar.

For example, the availability of free health care at old age, or health care financed during active life and actually or notionally presaved through premiums above period expenditures when younger, has a bearing on how much cash income and precautionary saving are needed in retirement. The same applies to long-term care, a topic where guidance for good financing arrangements is still missing (CEPAR 2014). Consistent and preferably neutral taxation of those publicly and privately provided services may be called for to avoid costly arbitrage games or confusion.

Consumption tax treatment and thus consumption neutrality eliminate an important interasset price distortion between the two major life cycle assets—pensions and owner-occupied housing. Owner-occupied homes in many countries receive (approximate) expenditure tax treatment (OECD 2010). Treating housing and pensions very differently leads to asset misallocations. Estimates of efficiency costs associated with this distortion are somewhat dated but are substantial (Hamilton and Whalley 1985).

1.2.4 Possible Directions for Tax Reform by Country Groupings

Despite the heterogeneity of the taxation of retirement income provision across countries, four groups of country approaches can be broadly distinguished. Their path dependency with regard to both pension and taxation arrangements suggests both constraints and options and offers some limited perspectives for smaller- and larger-scale improvements.

1. In the first group of countries, such as Australia, the United Kingdom, and the United States, unfunded public retirement provision is more limited while broadly offering consumption-oriented income taxation

to funded retirement income provision (within limits), mostly in the form of EET, as well as to savings in residential housing, mostly in the form of TEE. With retirement income accumulations (for social security, occupational, and personal retirement provision) and housing property, these countries cover most long-term individual savings under a consumption-type tax provision that is, however, complex and often inconsistent. Simplicity and consistency could be achieved by a full move toward a consumption-oriented income taxation approach. The Mirrlees Review suggested (a) establishing neutrality for all saving efforts and (b) completing the move toward consumption taxation of income (in addition to a single-rate value-added tax). The latter would allow for a mixture of front- and back-loaded consumption taxation but is essentially based on a rate-of-return allowance approach that keeps the normal rate of return (as well as the normal rate of profits) untaxed (see Mirrlees et al. 2012 for a summary). As life cycle saving becomes tax-free and the border to other savings becomes porous, this approach may require taxation of intergenerational transfers of bequests received or donated to avoid intergenerational inequities.

2. Many countries with very large unfunded schemes and limited supplementary funded provision (such as in Central and Southern Europe) offer some limited consumption-oriented treatment of income taxation for their funded pillar, with no intention of a complete move toward such a taxation approach. Their most important tax structure remains the personal income tax. As various country chapters in this volume document, these exceptions included new tax preferences to incentivize personal retirement saving given reduced public and occupational pension payments. These were often reversed to address the budgetary fallout of the 2008–2009 global financial crisis. Such selective tax preferences for retirement saving would profit from more consistency of exemptions among retirement income provisions and clearer differentiation from other forms of nonretirement savings. To this end, it is important to work out very clearly the objectives for deviation from the standard income taxation approach and whether the expected effects on savings and other outcome variables can be or have been achieved. A crucial empirical question is the effect of tax preferences on the individual and aggregate retirement saving volume and the net effect on national saving once the tax expenditure over the life cycle is taken into account. Chomik and Piggott (chapter 11, this volume) critically review the concept of tax expenditures as applied to pension taxation.

3. A number of countries have recognized that critical economic arguments exist for taxing labor earnings and capital income differently, and thus they have established a dual income tax (DIT) regime. The DIT is a particular form of schedular tax that applies a separate (generally lower) tax rate to capital income and applies a progressive tax schedule to the sum of the taxpayer's income from other sources (e.g., labor and pension income), with the lower capital tax rate typically set equal to the entry rate of the progressive tax schedule. Tax credits and deductions are used to enhance horizontal and vertical equity. This approach is at times considered a compromise between the comprehensive income tax and the consumption-oriented income tax approaches. The DIT is often linked with the Nordic tax approach, having originated in Scandinavia (Sørensen 1994). Schedular taxation of a share of capital income (such as from dividends and savings accounts) also advanced in a number of OECD countries without moving toward a full DIT, albeit no Nordic country has introduced a DIT in its pure form.[5] While the DIT offers a compromise for issues of capital and labor taxation and in principle taxes all savings the same way, this approach harbors no consistent approach to the tax treatment of retirement income and other savings, or more generally between life cycle and non–life cycle saving (Bravo, chapter 6, this volume). As a result, DIT systems typically have a variety of tax preferences toward retirement income provision that are country specific and ad hoc. Thus, as in the case of the comprehensive income tax system, a move toward a more equitable and efficient design of pension taxation requires clear objectives and rigorous evaluation of deviations from the standard approach.

4. Finally, about 50 countries worldwide have introduced a low-rate income tax at a single rate above an exemption—a so-called flat tax. Various former transition economies in Central, Southern, and Eastern Europe have done so, as have many developing and emerging economies.[6] The flat-tax proposal is or has been under discussion in developed countries such as the United Kingdom and the United States; a flat tax has in fact been enacted in some US states. Having chosen such an approach, these countries voted for a lower rate to encourage entrepreneurial activities and induce lower labor tax distortions at the expense of permanent sizable distortions in intertemporal consumption prices. Thus, little room remains for special preferences for retirement income provision under a flat personal income tax approach

except to move toward a flat consumption tax (Hall and Rabushka 2007) or a multirate version that Bradford (1986) called the "X tax" (Auerbach 2013). Both are based on a subtraction-method value-added tax but with labor income taxed at the individual level to facilitate a progressive rate structure (one positive rate above a threshold under the flat tax, three under the X tax). Thus far, neither of these options has been implemented anywhere.

1.2.5 Establishing Consistency between Taxation and Pension Policy

The formulation of government policies on taxation and on retirement income provision is happening largely as parallel processes, with very limited coordination. This contrasts with the view of many economists who strive for a theoretically underpinned and unified conceptualization of both government programs. Theoretical economists argue that the policy instruments of taxation and public (i.e., social security–type) pension provision cannot actually be separated (Diamond 2009; Cremer, Lozachmeur, and Pestieau 2008). Cremer and Pestieau (chapter 2, this volume) claim that "the desirable approach consists of combining the optimal design of [public] pensions and taxes in a single model." This view of (nonlinear) income tax policy and pension policy as complementary instruments that can be or need to be productively combined to achieve minimum distortions and envisaged distributive outcomes also underpins the work by Bastani, Blomquist, and Micheletto (chapter 3, this volume).

An alternative welfare-based approach is to view public (or social insurance) pensions as an instrument to substitute for incomplete financial markets of intertemporal resource exchange and annuity provision (Holzmann 1990). The contribution and benefit design of a public scheme should thus imitate the ideal private sector scheme with regard to work and retirement incentives, as promised by nonfinancial (or notional) defined contribution schemes (Holzmann and Palmer 2006; Holzmann, Palmer, and Robalino 2012, 2013). Income redistribution and social policy objectives would be handled outside a nonfinancial defined contribution scheme and be financed by general revenue. Adding a social wing (i.e., social pensions) to address poverty issues and a funded wing (i.e., occupational and/or voluntary individual provision) to supplement the mandated public provision for the higher income strata creates a sound retirement income system in which pension taxation and pension provision are connected but remain separate instruments. Nevertheless, these would profit from a coordinated but not integrated approach. Areas of overlap and joint interest between these two policy areas are explored by Feher and Jousten (chapter 4, this volume). Which of these approaches ultimately offers higher social welfare through fewer distortions on skills acquisition, labor supply, and savings decisions and better-targeted redistribution has not yet been fully explored.

Regarding the coordination of taxation and pension policy, the limited experience available on this deeply understudied topic is not encouraging. The Swedish tax reform of the early 1990s, part of a major reform effort in the aftermath of the country's economic and financial crisis, contained some relevant changes in taxing retirement income provision (Agell, Englund, and Sødersten 1995), but there was no direct coordination with the major pension reform that followed in the mid-1990s, which introduced the nonfinancial defined contribution scheme plus an additional and mandated financial defined contribution pillar. The tax reform's main contribution to pension reform was the message that major reforms supported by all key political parties in the country were possible.

The experience from other countries where major tax and pension reforms have taken place—such as Australia—also suggests that little direct coordination has occurred. Participants in these reforms believe that trying to coordinate across two already very complex policy fields may be too ambitious.[7] At the same time, however, pensions as an institution would be unlikely to exist without income tax preferences. Thus, a natural question is, which tax treatments best facilitate this under alternative general income tax designs?

1.2.6 Expanding the Analysis toward International Labor Mobility and Aging Populations

Even the most recent analytical and policy work in the area of the taxation of pensions was conducted essentially under traditional assumptions reflecting a closed economy and stable demography. Nevertheless, despite some current pushback on globalization and lip service regarding the aging population, these phenomena are important pieces of today's economic reality. This requires the review and adjustment of traditional concepts and the exploration of new ideas on the topic of taxing pensions.

Population aging is driven both by birthrates below the replacement rate and ever-increasing life expectancies for all ages, from lower infant mortality to longer life spans for the aged. These trends are projected to continue for at least several more decades. This has implications for pension design across all pension pillars and for the design of retirement income taxation schemes—at both the analytical and policy levels. Conceptually, population aging and later retirement increase the gap between the points at which contributions are paid and benefits are received. Similarly, the uncertainty of future gains in life expectancy across socioeconomic groups and the currently observable increase in heterogeneity across cohorts further scatter the equivalence of front- and back-loaded taxation, with implications for both equity and government revenues.

Globalization is moving well beyond capital, goods, and services and increasingly affects individual workers across their life cycle, including where they retire. While in 2015 only about 3.3 percent of the world's population resided outside their home country, a much larger and increasing share will spend at least part of their working life in other countries in the future, often acquiring rights to public and private pensions that will be consumed in a different jurisdiction upon retirement.[8] This raises the seldom-explored issue of how best to tax internationally portable pensions and what international guidelines on the taxation of cross-border pension payments need to be revisited or newly established. These issues question the equivalence of front- and back-loaded consumption taxation, put into doubt the current dominant residency principle of income taxation, and stress additional differences between defined benefit and defined contribution schemes (Genser and Holzmann, chapter 15, this volume).

1.3 Volume Structure and Overview of Chapters

1.3.1 Overview of Part I: Setting the Stage—Chapters 2–4

Part I sets the stage for the rest of the volume. In addition to this opening chapter, three more contributions offer specific theoretical and broader policy perspectives on the topic of pensions and taxation. These chapters do not claim to cover the full range of theoretical and policy perspectives on the topic, but the theoretical angles explored are claimed to be the most developed tax guidance on pensions.

Chapter 2, by Helmuth Cremer (Toulouse School of Economics) and Pierre Pestieau (University of Liege), reviews key issues regarding the taxation of pensions and uses an elegant, simple, two-period model to analyze various policies. A critical aspect of their approach is the clear distinction between the tax treatment of private retirement savings (via pension funds) and of public (i.e., social security–type) pensions. The first set of issues concerns the taxation approaches of a comprehensive income tax (taxed, taxed, exempt: TTE), which implies double taxation of savings, versus a front-loaded consumption-oriented income tax (TEE), which does not tax capital income. The latter prescription for private pension fund savings emerges under a set of assumptions where the only source of heterogeneity is labor productivity. If this assumption is dropped, then the optimal tax on retirement capital is not zero. However, while the authors refute the zero taxation of capital in general, they offer a number of arguments, including behavioral restrictions, for why back-loaded consumption taxation (EET) may prove welfare-enhancing. The second set of issues turns to the taxation of public pensions, for which the authors propose an integrated approach that builds on the recent literature on age-related (optimal) taxation. Based on their own and other recent work, the authors suggest that the desirable approach for taxing public pensions is to combine the optimal design of pensions and taxes in a single model. They illustrate the approach and implications for varying income tax rates across active and retirement periods, again using a two-period model.

Chapter 3, by Spencer Bastani (Linnaeus University), Sören Blomquist (Uppsala University), and Luca Micheletto (University of Milan), provides an innovative approach to integrating taxation and pensions, advocated, inter alia, by Cremer, Lozachmeur, and Pestieau (2008), Diamond (2009), and Choné and Laroque (2014). The authors use an overlapping-generations model with skill uncertainty and private savings to investigate whether an optimally designed set of public pension transfers can usefully supplement a nonlinear labor income tax as a welfare-enhancing policy instrument. They consider a Mirrleesian setting where agents' skills are private information, and they highlight that even though pensions adversely affect achievement of the golden rule (i.e., the savings rate which maximizes steady state level or growth of consumption) by crowding out private savings, they can be used as a mimicking-deterring device that makes it easier for the government to achieve its desired redistributive goals.

Chapter 4, by Csaba Feher (International Monetary Fund) and Alain Jousten (University of Liege), provides an overview of the factors influencing the interplay of pension and tax policies from a fiscal and welfare perspective, and identifies areas where both topics can materially impact one another. The authors find that while strong arguments arise for coordinating tax (especially income tax) policy and pension policy, these areas are still rarely treated as components of the same interpersonal and intertemporal distributional framework. Policy makers are therefore urged to harmonize the objectives and instruments of tax policy and pension policy. While the efficiency of both tax policy and pension policy can be improved by synergies between these areas, and may result in more adequate and equitable pensions, the authors question whether the current tax treatment of contributions and prospective tax treatment of pension payouts can materially influence behavior in terms of coverage, compliance, and labor mobility. For reasons of equity and efficiency, the authors argue for taxing pensions similarly to all other income, while making sure that income streams are not taxed more than once. They also support reforms that downscale or eliminate the preferential tax treatment of mandatory pensions. Given the fiscal and welfare impacts of aging, the authors advise that tax and pension reforms that jointly improve pension systems' fiscal sustainability, adequacy, and equity be introduced before the progression of electoral demographics makes these reforms even more politically costly.

1.3.2 Overview of Part II: Country Issues and Research Questions—Chapters 5–11

Part II offers individual country chapters on how the complex taxation of retirement income provision across the key pillars is actually done, and it embeds the information in select historical, empirical, and policy analyses for the country under review. This type of information typically is not easily available, and rarely in a broadly comparable structure. The countries reviewed include Australia, Denmark, Germany, Portugal, Sweden, the United Kingdom, and the United States. These chapters exhibit some cross-country commonality in the search for a consistent and well-funded policy approach to the taxation of pensions. However, they indicate quite different and country-specific policy concerns regarding the topic of tax preferences, their size, and their effects on saving, equity, and efficiency. Consumption-type tax treatment considerations play a mostly limited role, and more recent theoretical developments do not seem to have made a mark on actual policy considerations.

In chapter 5, Torben Andersen (Aarhus University) discusses conceptual questions within the context of two Scandinavian countries (Denmark and Sweden). These include: How should pensions be taxed (in many cases, pension savings are taxed more leniently than other forms of savings)? What is the rationale for this? Are those concerns best targeted via taxation or mandatory pension savings? Denmark and Sweden provide interesting case studies because, on the one hand, both have extended welfare states but quite different pension systems, and, on the other hand, both (mainly) pursue an ETT taxation regime regarding pensions. It is argued that the incentive structure related to pension savings and retirement cannot be seen independently from how private pensions (and savings more generally) affect public pensions via means testing. The effective rates of taxation may thus differ significantly from the nominal rates. For Denmark and Sweden, Andersen shows that the effective tax rates on pension savings can be rather high—for low- and medium-income groups, close to 100 percent.

In chapter 6, Jorge Bravo (Universidade Nova de Lisboa) evaluates the potential for a semidual income tax for taxation of pensions in Portugal. Such a tax typically combines a progressive tax schedule for labor and pension income with low and often flat and differentiated nominal tax rates on some forms of capital (personal or corporate) income. The Nordic countries took the lead in implementing a dual income tax system in the early 1990s, but in reality it is hard to find a country that uses a pure comprehensive, expenditure, or dual income tax system. This chapter motivates and reviews the current tax treatment of Portuguese pensions and other retirement income, highlights its particularities, and discusses whether it can contribute to creating an adequate, affordable, sustainable, equitable, and efficient pension system. The arguments for and against adoption of a semidual income tax for the taxation of occupational and private pensions and other retirement income are assessed, with particular emphasis on the effects of pension taxation on the level and composition of saving, horizontal and vertical equity, intergenerational risk sharing, economic growth, and labor market outcomes.

In chapter 7, Hazel Bateman (University of New South Wales) presents the Australian experience with taxation of pensions and explores the conceptual and political issues of recent decades. While most countries exempt contributions and pension fund earnings, and tax benefits at personal marginal tax rates under a postpaid expenditure tax regime, Australia imposes flat-rate taxes on contributions and pension fund earnings, and exempts retirement benefits for most people under a comprehensive income tax regime. To address equity issues and emulate progressivity of pension taxation, governments across the world introduce time-varying floors and ceilings, rebates, deductions, co-contributions, and other measures. This chapter describes and critically assesses the Australian approach, which differs from international practice. Benefits include the bringing forward of tax revenue and protecting the tax base in the face of international labor mobility. Reforms legislated in 2016 will improve the targeting of superannuation tax concessions. However, in the absence of a direct link with personal marginal tax rates, the author predicts that taxation of superannuation will remain vulnerable to policy instability, which will continue to increase the complexity of life cycle decisions, challenge public confidence in retirement income arrangements, and increase political risk.

Chapter 8, by Axel Börsch-Supan (Max-Planck-Institute for Social Law and Social Policy, Munich) and Christopher Quinn (University of Bayreuth), motivates and describes the tax treatment of German retirement benefits and pensions after the 2005 reform initiated by the German Federal Constitutional Court. The 2005 reform responded to the unequal and complex tax treatment within and across mandated, occupational, and personal pension provision in existence at that time. It led to a broadly, but not fully, uniform consumption-oriented deferred income taxation approach. The main question is whether this reform will produce a "level playing field" among the many providers of retirement income in Germany by the time it is fully implemented in 2040 and during the transition period. To this end, the chapter briefly outlines principles for the taxation of retirement benefits and pensions, explores the principles of neutrality, and compares these with the current (reformed) practice in Germany. Based on their own stylized calculations, the authors conclude that the 2005 reform flattened the playing field somewhat, but it is still not completely level. Moreover, substantial transition costs are imposed on retirement income savers in the form of double taxation.

Chapter 9, by Carl Emmerson and Paul Johnson (both of the Institute for Fiscal Studies), explores the taxation of pensions in the United Kingdom. Private pension saving is hugely important in the United Kingdom, and the taxation of pensions has traditionally been relatively stable and rather generous, beyond the treatment offered by an expenditure tax regime. Recently, though, substantial changes were made. Annual and lifetime allowances were cut dramatically, largely as a way of increasing tax revenues. At the same time, the requirement to annuitize defined contribution pension wealth was abolished, boosting revenues in the near term and making saving in these pensions look much more similar to other forms of saving. Meanwhile, the tax treatment of other important forms of saving was made more generous. The motivation for many of the reforms enacted was largely one of increasing tax revenues. The authors argue that the recent changes were encouraged by a misunderstanding of the purpose, and cost, of the current system. The changes do not deal with elements that are overgenerous, while limiting opportunities for receiving "neutral" treatment of savings. Consequently, the chapter argues that the United Kingdom now faces great uncertainty about the future tax treatment of pensions.

Chapter 10, by Gary Burtless and Eric Koepcke (both of the Brookings Institution), offers an overview of taxation of the main pension pillar in the United States before digging into the intricacies of tax expenditures for private pensions in this country. To encourage workers to save privately for retirement, the US government offers favorable tax treatment on money withheld from wages and saved inside a pension plan. The private retirement system built around this tax preference has accumulated assets amounting to 1.33 times gross domestic product, a fivefold increase since the mid-1970s. The chapter offers a brief description of the workplace retirement system and the regulatory and cost considerations that led to a shift away from defined benefit pensions and toward defined contribution ones. The authors show how the value of the tax preference for pension savings can be modeled and measured, and how it varies among workers. The chapter demonstrates that the value of the preference varied widely in recent decades not because of a change in the pension tax preference but because of changes in tax preferences conferred on equity investments held outside a pension account. The chapter concludes with a brief analysis of the most glaring shortcomings of the system, including the wildly unequal accumulations of retirement savings in the tax-preferred system.

Chapter 11, by Rafal Chomik and John Piggott (both of CEPAR, University of New South Wales), investigates the concept of tax expenditures on pensions, both the concerns such expenditures raise and the misconceptions produced by the concept. Pension savings commonly attract lower taxes to encourage self-provision or to maintain neutrality between current and future consumption. As a result, in countries where funded pensions are prominent, tax costs appear large and poorly targeted, while benefits of such treatment seem unsubstantiated. Nevertheless, the authors argue that much of the criticism of tax arrangements is misconceived. The chapter explains the basic concepts, tackles concerns related to the scale and fairness of tax expenditures, and presents policy reform proposals. The authors provide illustrative examples of saving over the life cycle and across the earnings distribution based on the Australian retirement income system. This yields an instructive case, since it has significant prefunding and high levels of measured tax expenditures that, in turn, have attracted considerable political interest.

1.3.3 Overview of Part III: Country-Calibrated OLG/CGE Models—Chapters 12–14

Part III explores issues of pension taxation through the application of country-calibrated computational general equilibrium (CGE) models for Switzerland, Finland, and Australia. All CGE models have an unquestioned consumption-type treatment of retirement income programs as the core approach of pension taxation. Each chapter has a special focus, but interesting differences and commonalities emerge regarding the topic of front- and back-loaded pension taxation.

In chapter 12, Christian Keuschnigg (University of St. Gallen) raises the issue of demographic shifts in Switzerland, which include a doubling of the old-age dependency ratio until 2050. To quantify the effects of this trend on pensions, taxes, and social contributions, the author uses an overlapping-generations model with five aspects of labor supply: labor market participation, hours worked, job search, retirement, and on-the-job training. The chapter highlights that a passive fiscal strategy that merely adjusts labor taxes and contribution rates to balance budgets would be very costly. Total labor taxes would rise by 21 percent, and per capita income would fall by roughly 20 percent. In contrast, comprehensive reform, including an increase in the effective retirement age to 68 years, may limit the tax increases to 4 percent of the value-added tax and reduce the decline in per capita income to less than 6 percent. The author argues that the present rules of deferred taxation of pension income support social security and labor market reform by shifting tax revenue to the future, when it is needed most in an aging society.

Chapter 13, by Jukka Lassila and Tarmo Valkonen (both of the Research Institute of the Finnish Economy), investigates the implications of a revised timing of pension taxation on government finances and economic outcomes. This is motivated by the observation that while problems of fiscal sustainability led many countries to consider ways to cut expenditures and increase tax revenues, one policy option is rarely used—changing the timing of the taxation of pensions. Currently, taxation typically follows an EET regime, and longer lifetimes reduce current tax revenues and increase future ones, but not enough to be revenue-neutral. Switching from an EET regime to a TEE one would increase current tax revenues and, despite reducing them in the future, could enhance public finances. The authors simulate this transition under a defined benefit pension scheme with a numerical overlapping-generations model, using stochastic mortality projections as inputs. Under a traditional pension scheme with no automatic longevity rules, such as life expectancy adjustment of pensions or a link between life expectancy and retirement age, the tax regime shift can be used to improve public finances. Under an automatically adjusting pension scheme, the tax regime shift is not as efficient, but neither is it that necessary. An important element in sustainability effects comes from lower public wage costs. Diminished private savings and weaker labor supply incentives are among the downsides. The latter especially makes the reform welfare-reducing if the improvement in state finances is not used to relieve the taxation of labor.

Chapter 14, by George Kudrna and Alan Woodland (both of CEPAR, University of New South Wales), provides a quantitative analysis of hypothetical replacements of existing tax arrangements applied to superannuation (Australia's term for private pensions) with traditional EET and TEE regimes. These taxation regimes exempt pension fund earnings from any taxation and tax either benefits or contributions progressively as regular income. By contrast, superannuation taxation features concessional flat tax rates on contributions and pension fund earnings, with benefits generally tax-free. Using an overlapping-generations model calibrated for Australia, the authors find that these hypothetical superannuation tax reforms have positive implications for vertical equity, as indicated by larger relative welfare gains and income improvements experienced by lower-income households. The simulation results also show positive long-run effects of the reforms on domestic assets as well as reduced pension expenditures.

1.3.4 Overview of Part IV: Cross-Border Taxation of Pensions—Chapter 15

Part IV enters new territory, exploring the taxation of cross-border pensions. Very little economic analysis has been done in this area to date, although the topic has garnered some attention from legal scholars. Two chapters were planned for this part of the volume, one written by economists and one by legal scholars, but only the economics chapter was completed.

Chapter 15, by Bernd Genser (University of Konstanz) and Robert Holzmann (CEPAR and CESifo), explores the taxation of internationally portable pensions—a topic that is still terra incognita for economists. This chapter highlights the huge differences in old-age pension taxation within and across OECD countries and spells out the fiscal equity and efficiency issues that emerge under the current complex and inconsistent taxation of cross-border pensions in a world of internationally mobile workers and pensioners. It offers explanations for this heterogeneity, shows why deferred pension taxation under a residence principle is not sustainable, and proposes a switch from deferred taxation to front-loaded taxation of old-age pensions. The three policy options proposed share the same timing of when the tax liability is established but differ in the timing of when the tax liabilities are settled: immediately, delayed, or phased across accumulation, when returns are received, and at the disbursement phase. All options are claimed to be superior to single-country measures taken to uphold deferred pension taxation or to rely on renegotiations of bilateral double-taxation treaties.

1.4 Research Needs

This volume offers valuable information on the analysis of pension taxation—at the theoretical, country, and empirical levels. It provides some guidance for policy makers and as a reference source for researchers interested in but not yet involved in the topic. The topic itself remains seriously underresearched. The process of workshops, conferences, and paper preparation that culminated in this volume crystallized a menu of research needs. This chapter thus closes with a brief discussion of the most important research needs.

1.4.1 Refining the Analysis of Consumption-Oriented Income Taxation for Pensions

Most economists favor a consumption-oriented income taxation approach for the tax treatment of retirement income provision across the key pension pillars. It is in essence an income tax with a retirement savings deduction. Not all theoretical and empirical issues are resolved, however. Perhaps most topical is the timing of tax collections under this rubric. It is possible to tax either contributions or benefits under this tax design—either front- or back-loaded taxation of retirement income provision. Both are variations of the way consumption-oriented income taxation can be implemented—as earnings taxation if contributions (or other retirement savings) are paid out of taxed income or as expenditure taxation when benefits are taxed when disbursed.

Many pension economists claim that the different versions of the consumption-type approach to pension taxation (TEE and EET) are essentially equivalent up to second-order effects on economic outcomes (see, for example, Kingston and Piggott 1993). This theoretical equivalence, however, holds only under very strict conditions that are typically violated in reality. How important these deviations are for individual and societal outcomes is not clear, and research is required to determine what their impact might be. This is of particular importance in the current global economy, because governments under fiscal stress will be tempted to move revenue collection from the future to the present, as exemplified by recent changes in the United Kingdom. Three brief examples provide more context.

1. *Ricardian equivalence and the timing of tax collections* Under the assumption of Ricardian equivalence, whether taxation is front- or back-loaded will not matter for public finance as the intertemporally optimizing government would be able to establish neutrality by appropriate borrowing and saving behavior, and households would recognize and take account of this. However, this requires both households and governments to have very long foresight. When Ricardian equivalence is violated, what are the implications of choosing between EET and TEE?

2. *Progressive income tax* It is well known that, under a progressive income tax, TEE-EET neutrality is violated, and individuals with fluctuating earnings are penalized. The Mirrlees Review (Mirrlees et al. 2011) suggested that offering a variety of front- and back-loaded tax savings options would smooth many of the differences, also through self-selection. But does any analytical evidence exist for this statement?

3. *Excess returns taxation* The Mirrlees Review (Mirrlees et al. 2011) argued that while in general excess returns on investment should be taxed (but not normal returns), for pension taxation the excess returns tax should not be invoked. Others (Genser and Holzmann, chapter 15, this volume) argue for its inclusion in pension tax design. Excess returns might be earned through innovation or alternatively through rent seeking. This unresolved issue could be clarified with a more intensive and focused research program.

1.4.2 Analyzing and Comparing Large-Scale Model Results on Pension Taxation

The macroeconomic impacts of pension taxation can best be analyzed using large-scale models that capture the general equilibrium effects of price changes and have some representation of passing time, either through a dynastic or an overlapping-generations structure. These models, however, while steadily proliferating, do not adhere to standard assumptions regarding expectations, the treatment of revenue equivalence through time, and other model features and parameters that can be critical in determining results over a long time frame. A serious research effort is needed to understand the implications of possible alternative benchmark model assumptions for pension tax policy analysis. Such research would better leverage the considerable time investment in the highly skilled work these models require. An early step in this direction might be to run simulations of equivalent reform options in different country-calibrated CGE models and to explore and identify the differences resulting from different modeling designs and parameter values.

An important application of large-scale modeling in the context of pension taxation is a comprehensive investigation of the macroeconomic and welfare impacts of coordinating pension and tax policies. A few estimates referenced in this volume's chapters offer magnitudes from ad hoc calibrations, but executing well-reasoned simulations with full-fledged and country-calibrated CGE models should offer deeper insight.

1.4.3 Assessing the Impact of Tax Preferences on Behavior and Behavioral Alternatives

An important motivation for income tax breaks for pension savings concerns encouraging saving for retirement, but how effective is this design in achieving this end? The international evidence suggests limited effects of tax preferences on the size of savings, but some research signals relevant and often sizable (distortionary) effects of heterogeneous tax preferences on the composition of savings. Widespread and well-established workplace-linked pensions are observed around the world, however, and firms are not likely to offer these in the absence of a tax break (Mitchell and Piggott 2016).

Very recent country research suggests that only a subset of retirement savers are sensitive to any tax preferences at all. Finally, a burgeoning body of literature is emerging on the role of behavioral economics in improving scheme participation as an effective and cheaper alternative to incentivize retirement saving. Much research on this issue still needs to be done to establish a firm evidence base one way or the other.

1.4.4 Determining the Implications of Population Aging and Globalization on Pension Taxation

Both population aging and globalization are anticipated to be major forces in the world economy for decades to come. Both phenomena create various challenges for pension taxation, including the timing of expenditures and tax revenue receipts, and where these financial flows are going—to the source country or the residence country. These topics have received little attention from either tax or pension economists so far, possibly because a sophisticated treatment of demographic dynamics immensely complicates the structure and solution of large-scale models. Issues of strategy and international cooperation inherent in the international mobility of workers and retirees have hardly been analyzed at all. The first indications of issues and possible solutions are offered in this volume, but much more research is needed.

1.4.5 Operationalizing Age-Based Taxation

Age-based taxation and the linking of pensions and taxation is a promising avenue for reducing labor supply and savings distortions and thus creating measurable individual welfare effects. This idea has been around for 25 years, and various valuable contributions have been produced, but no move to operationalize it has occurred. The potential operationalization of consumption-oriented income taxation in the 1960s and 1970s provided the dynamism for the related policy discussion. A similar operationalization breakthrough is needed to move this approach from a curiosity in optimal tax theory to actual policy relevance.

Notes

This chapter was inspired by the outstanding contributions to this volume and profited from intensive interactions with the authors throughout the long process of preparing it for publication. Special thanks go to Bernd Genser, who was a great source and supporter for conceptualization of the workshops and this volume's preparation; he also offered important comments and suggestions on this opening chapter. The revision of this chapter profited very much from the pertinent comments and suggestions by Cagri Kumru and by an anonymous reviewer during the MIT manuscript review process. Rafal

Chomik offered a range of drafting suggestions; John Whalley's overview conference comments also informed our thinking. Any remaining errors are our own.

1. The concept was first advocated by German public finance scholar Georg von Schanz (Schanz 1896) and was further developed by two American economists, Robert Haig (Haig 1921) and Henry Simons (Simons 1938).

2. Recently, however, this has been reconsidered by Straub and Werning (2014), who argue that in a Ramsey context, substantial capital taxation may be optimal for a long period of time. Others (e.g., Chari, Nicolini, and Teles 2016) have responded.

3. The letters *E* and *T* refer respectively to *exempt* or *taxed* in the three stages of retirement income provision: contribution payment or saving effort, return on pension wealth, and disbursement.

4. See the papers on nonfinancial defined contribution by Holzmann and Palmer (2006) and Holzmann, Palmer, and Robalino (2012, 2013) for a comprehensive overview of theoretical, empirical, and policy issues. This approach has been implemented by eight countries so far (including Italy, Norway, Latvia, Poland, and Sweden), borrowed in part by various others (including Brazil), and is under discussion in many others (including China). The forthcoming third conference (Rome 2017) and the planned 2018 volume on the topic aim at addressing the challenges of marginalization and polarization to the design of the scheme; this may reintroduce issues of earnings test and taxlike distortions.

5. For summary articles on the dual income tax system in theory and practice and select country proposals, see the contributions by Boadway and by Eggert and Genser in *CESifo DICE Forum*, no. 3 (2004).

6. The best up-to-date source on these flat-tax countries is Wikipedia, http://wikipedia.org/wiki/Flat_tax, available in various languages.

7. Based on personal interviews and correspondence with reform committee members.

8. For the European Union, it is estimated that of those who entered the labor market after the 1990s, 15–25 percent will have spent at least one spell of their working life outside their home country (Holzmann 2015).

References

Agell, Jonas, Peter Englund, and Jan Södersten. 1995. "The Swedish Tax Reform: An Introduction." *Swedish Economic Policy Review* 2:219–228.

Alvarez, Yvette, John Burbidge, Ted Farrell, and Leigh Palmer. 1992. "Optimal Taxation in a Life-Cycle Model." *Canadian Journal of Economics* 25:111–122.

Atkinson, Anthony, and Joseph Stiglitz. 1976. "The Design of Tax Structure: Direct versus Indirect Taxation." *Journal of Public Economics* 6 (1–2): 55–75.

Auerbach, Alan J. 2009. "Direction in Tax and Transfer Theory." In *Australia's Future Tax and Transfer Policy Conference: Proceedings of a Conference*, edited by the Melbourne Institute, 63–71. Melbourne: University of Melbourne.

Auerbach, Alan J. 2013. "Capital Income Taxation, Corporate Taxation, Wealth Transfer Taxes and Consumption Tax Reforms." Paper prepared for the conference "The Empirical

Foundations of Supply-Side Economics," Becker Friedman Institute, University of Chicago, September 27, 2013. Mimeo, University of California, Berkeley.

Benartzi, Shlomo, and Richard Thaler. 2007. "Heuristics and Biases in Retirement Savings Behavior." *Journal of Economic Perspectives* 21 (3): 71–104.

Benartzi, Shlomo, and Richard Thaler. 2013. "Behavioral Economics and the Retirement Savings Crisis." *Science* 339:1152–1153.

Boadway, Robin. 2004. "The Dual Income Tax System: An Overview." *CESifo DICE Report* 2 (3): 3–8.

Bradford, David F. 1986. *Untangling the Income Tax*. Cambridge, MA: Harvard University Press.

CEPAR. 2014. "Aged Care in Australia: Part I—Policy, Demand and Funding." Research Brief No. 2014/1, ARC Centre of Excellence in Population Ageing Research, University of New South Wales, Sydney, Australia.

Chamley, Christophe. 1986. "Optimal Taxation of Capital Income in General Equilibrium with Infinite Lives." *Econometrica* 54 (3): 607–622.

Chari, V. V., Juan Pablo Nicolini, and Pedro Teles. 2016. "More on the Taxation of Capital." Mimeo. https://www.bde.es/f/webpi/SES/seminars/2016/files/sie1614.pdf.

Chetty, Raj, John N. Friedman, Søren Leth-Petersen, Torben Heien Nielsen, and Tore Olsen. 2014. "Active vs. Passive Decisions and Crowding-Out in Retirement Savings Accounts: Evidence from Denmark." *Quarterly Journal of Economics* 129 (3): 1141–1219.

Chomik, Rafal, John Piggott, Alan Woodland, George Kudrna, and Cagri Kumru. 2015. "Means Testing Social Security: Modelling and Policy Analysis." Report on Project UM15-14, November 2015. CEPAR Working Paper No. 2015/35, ARC Centre of Excellence in Population Ageing Research, University of New South Wales, Sydney, Australia.

Choné, Philippe, and Guy Laroque. 2014. *Income Tax and Retirement Schemes*. Publ. No. 2014–06. Paris: Sciences Po Publications.

Conesa, Juan Carlos, Sagiri Kitao, and Dirk Krueger. 2009. "Taxing Capital? Not a Bad Idea After All." *American Economic Review* 99 (1): 25–48.

Cremer, Helmuth, Jean-Marie Lozachmeur, and Pierre Pestieau. 2004. "Social Security, Retirement Age and Optimal Income Taxation." *Journal of Public Economics* 88 (11): 2259–2281.

Cremer, Helmuth, Jean-Marie Lozachmeur, and Pierre Pestieau. 2008. "Social Desirability of Earnings Tests." *German Economic Review* 9:114–134.

Diamond, Peter A. 2009. "Taxes and Pensions." *Southern Economic Journal* 76 (1): 2–15.

Eggert, Wolfgang, and Bernd Genser. 2004. "Dual Income Taxation in EU Countries." *CESifo DICE Forum*, no. 3:41–47.

Erosa, Andres, and Martin Gervais. 2002. "Optimal Taxation in Life-Cycle Economies." *Journal of Economic Theory* 105 (2): 338–369.

Fehr, Hans, and Fabian Kindermann. 2015. "Taxing Capital along the Transition—Not a Bad Idea After All?" *Journal of Economic Dynamics and Control* 51:64–77.

Fisher, Irving. 1930. *The Theory of Interest*. New York: Macmillan.

Golosov, Mikhail, Aleh Tsyvinski, and Ivan Werning. 2007. "New Dynamic Public Finance: A User's Guide." *NBER Macroeconomics Annual 2006*, edited by Daron Acemoglu, Kenneth Rogoff, and Michael Woodford, 317–387. Cambridge, MA: MIT Press.

Haig, Robert M. 1921. "The Concept of Income—Economic and Legal Aspects." In *The Federal Income Tax*, edited by Robert M. Haig, 1–28. New York: Columbia University Press.

Hall, Robert E., and Alvin Rabushka. 2007. *The Flat Tax*. Stanford, CA: Hoover Institution Press.

Hamilton, Bob, and John Whalley. 1985. "Tax Treatment of Housing in a Dynamic Sequenced General Equilibrium Model." *Journal of Public Economics* 27 (2): 157–175.

Holzmann, Robert. 1990. "The Welfare Effects of Public Expenditure Programs Reconsidered." *IMF Staff Papers* 37 (2): 338–359.

Holzmann, Robert. 2015. "Taxing Pensions of an Internationally Mobile Labor Force: Portability Issues and Taxation Options." CEPAR Working Paper No. 2015/22, ARC Centre of Excellence in Population Ageing Research, University of New South Wales, Sydney.

Holzmann, Robert, and Richard Hinz, eds. 2005. *Old-Age Income Support in the 21st Century: An International Perspective on Pension Systems and Reform*. Washington, DC: World Bank.

Holzmann, Robert, and Edward Palmer. 2006. *Pension Reform: Issues and Prospect for Non-Financial Defined Contribution (NDC) Schemes*. Washington, DC: World Bank.

Holzmann, Robert, Edward Palmer, and David Robalino. 2012. *NDC Pension Schemes in a Changing Pension World*, Vol. 1, *Progress, Issues, and Implementation*. Washington, DC: World Bank.

Holzmann, Robert, Edward Palmer, and David Robalino. 2013. *NDC Pension Schemes in a Changing Pension World*, Vol. 2, *Gender, Politics, and Financial Stability*. Washington, DC: World Bank.

Hubbard, Glenn R., and Kenneth L. Judd. 1986. "Liquidity Constraints, Fiscal Policy, and Consumption." *Brookings Papers on Economic Activity* 1:1–50.

Institute for Fiscal Studies (IFS). 1978. *The Structure and Reform of Direct Taxation*. London: Allen and Unwin.

International Monetary Fund (IMF). 2014. "Fiscal Policy and Income Inequality." IMF Policy Paper, International Monetary Fund, Washington, DC.

Judd, Kenneth. 1985. "Redistributive Taxation in a Simple Perfect Foresight Model." *Journal of Public Economics* 28 (1): 59–83.

Kaldor, Nicholas. 1955. *An Expenditure Tax*. London: Allen and Unwin.

Kingston, Geoffrey, and John Piggott. 1993. "A Ricardian Equivalence Theorem on the Taxation of Pension Funds." *Economics Letters* 42:399–403.

Kocherlakota, Narayana. 2010. *The New Dynamic Public Finance*. Princeton, NJ: Princeton University Press.

Kuklik, Michael. 2011. "Optimal Taxation and Labor Supply." In PhD diss., "Essays in Macroeconomics and Health Economics," University of Rochester, Rochester, NY. Mimeo.

Kumru, Cagri, and John Piggott, 2017. "Optimal Capital Taxation with Means-Tested Benefits." *Scottish Journal of Political Economy* 64 (3): 227–262.

Mankiw, N. Gregory, Matthew Charles Weinzierl, and Danny Ferris Yagan. 2009. "Optimal Taxation in Theory and Practice." *Journal of Economic Perspectives* 23 (4): 147–174.

Mirrlees, James, Stuart Adam, Tim Besley, Richard Blundell, Stephen Bond, Robert Chote, Malcolm Gammie, Paul Johnson, Gareth Myles, and James Poterba. 2012. "The Mirrlees Review: A Proposal for Systematic Tax Reform." *National Tax Journal* 65 (3): 655–684.

Mirrlees, James A. 1971. "An Exploration in the Theory of Optimum Income Taxation." *Review of Economic Studies* 38 (2): 175–208.

Mirrlees, James A., Stuart Adam, Timothy Besley, Richard Blundell, Stephen Bond, Robert Chote, Malcolm Gammie, Paul Johnson, Gareth Myles, and James Poterba, eds. 2010. *Dimensions of Tax Design: The Mirrlees Review—Volume 1*. Oxford: Oxford University Press.

Mirrlees, James A., Stuart Adam, Timothy Besley, Richard Blundell, Stephen Bond, Robert Chote, Malcolm Gammie, Paul Johnson, Gareth Myles, and James Poterba, eds. 2011. *Tax by Design: The Mirrlees Review—Volume 2*. Oxford: Oxford University Press.

Mitchell, Olivia S., and John Piggott. 2016. "Workplace-Linked Pensions for an Aging Demographic." In *Handbook of the Economics of Population Aging*, edited by John Piggott and Alan Woodland, 865–904. Amsterdam: Elsevier.

Mitchell, Olivia S., and Stephen Utkus. 2004. "Lessons from Behavioral Finance for Retirement Plan Design." In *Pension Design and Structure: New Lessons from Behavioral Finance*, edited by Olivia S. Mitchell and Stephen Utkus, 3–42. Oxford: Oxford University Press.

Nakajima, Makoto. 2010. "Optimal Capital Income Taxation with Housing." Working Paper No. 10-11, Federal Reserve Bank of Philadelphia, Philadelphia, PA.

OECD (Organisation for Economic Co-operation and Development). 2010. *Tax Policy Reform and Economic Growth*. Paris: OECD Publishing.

Peterman, William. 2013. "Determining the Motives for a Positive Optimal Tax on Capital." *Journal of Economic Dynamics and Control* 37:265–295.

Peterman, William B. 2016. "The Effect of Endogenous Human Capital Accumulation on Optimal Taxation." *Review of Economic Dynamics* 21:46–71.

Pigou, Arthur Cecil. 1928. "An Analysis of Supply." *Economic Journal* 38:238–257.

Schanz, Georg von. 1896. "Der Einkommensbegriff und die Einkommensteuergesetze." *Finanzarchiv* 13:1–87.

Shourideh, Ali, and Maxim Troshkin. 2013. "Providing Efficient Incentives to Work: Retirement Ages and the Pension System." Working paper. Mimeo.

Simons, Henry. 1938. *Personal Income Taxation: The Definition of Income as a Problem of Fiscal Policy*. Chicago: University of Chicago Press.

Sørensen, Peter Birch. 1994. "From the Global Income Tax to the Dual Income Tax: Recent Reforms in the Nordic Countries." *International Tax and Public Finance* 1:57–79.

Straub, Ludwig, and Iván Werning. 2014. "Positive Long Run Capital Taxation: Chamley-Judd Revisited." NBER Working Paper No. 20441, National Bureau of Economic Research, Cambridge, MA.

US Department of Treasury. 1977. *Blueprints for Basic Tax Reform*. Washington, DC: US Government Printing Office.

Woodland, Alan. 2016. "Taxation, Pensions, and Demographic Change." In *Economics of Population Aging*, edited by John Piggott and Alan Woodland, vol. 1B, 713–780. Amsterdam: Elsevier.

2 Taxing Pensions: Theoretical Considerations

Helmuth Cremer and Pierre Pestieau

2.1 Introduction

A wide variety of tax treatments of pensions exist across the world, but the reasons for such a range of regimes are not clear. This chapter reviews the general principles of pension taxes and analyzes specifically the theoretical foundations of why pension incomes should be taxed. At first sight, the issue at hand could be restricted to the way pension benefits should be taxed at the time they are paid out. The question would then be whether those pensions should benefit from a tax break relative to other types of income, as is the case in a number of countries. Another related question pertains to the possibility of combining pensions and labor income. For a long time, earning labor income while receiving a public pension was not allowed. This is part of the earnings test issue (Cremer, Lozachmeur, and Pestieau 2008b). Combining earnings and private pensions was never a problem.

Focusing on the stage at which pension benefits are paid out gives only a partial view of the underlying issues. It is more relevant to consider the different stages at which pensions are involved: the stage of contribution, for funded schemes; the stage of capital income accruals; and finally the stage of paying out. It is also essential to study the relationship between pension systems and the labor market or, more specifically, the retirement decision.

As far as public pensions (social security in US terminology) are concerned, it is not conceivable to separate the benefit side from the revenue side. Actually, benefits can just be seen as negative taxes, and vice versa for revenues. Both social security benefits and contributions influence the whole life cycle of individuals, particularly their saving, working, and retirement decisions. Furthermore, the issue of taxation of social security benefits is rather artificial. What matters for retired persons is their net income, which can be determined as part of the optimal allocation. The separation into gross income and taxes is purely a matter of implementation and is of no relevance for optimal policy design.

2.2 Taxation of Private Pension Funds

Three transactions constitute the process of saving, each of which provides an opportunity to collect taxes: (1) when part of the income is saved, (2) when investment income and capital gains accrue, and (3) when benefits are received.

Given these three points at which it is possible to levy tax, several basic tax policy combinations arise. Some are more common and characterize theoretical ideals for the tax system. The taxation regime of standard precautionary saving is represented by the triplet of letters TTE: taxation (T) at the first two stages and tax exemption (E) at the third one. In other words, savings are not tax-exempt, and capital income is taxed when it accrues. Once the savings plus interest is withdrawn, this is not considered taxable income. On the other hand, forced saving through a pay-as-you-go (PAYG) scheme is denoted as EET, even though the second stage is a bit particular, as the return is notional and equal to the growth of the economy. Finally, in most countries, private pensions are subject to the EET regime, thus benefiting from an edge relative to standard precautionary saving. Money contributed by employers and employees, as well as investment income and capital gains accrued to the fund, are not taxed.

From an economic perspective, the discussion on the ideal triplet is not very instructive. What matters are the rates of taxation and, in the final analysis, the overall tax burden. Historically, these regimes emerged for a variety of reasons, mostly related to issues of tax law. For instance, the income tax exemption of an employer's contribution to a pension fund on behalf of an employee is justified by the fact that it is not considered "income" under tax law. This view relies on different arguments. For instance, it is not considered income because employees have no discretion on how to spend it.[1] Furthermore, tax laws often require that income be taxed at the time it is effectively perceived.

In the public economics literature, favorable tax treatment of pension savings has been questioned from two standpoints. The first concerns the efficacy of such favorable provisions at stimulating saving and ensuring adequate and sustainable levels of retirement income. The second pertains to the economic rationale of those provisions.

This chapter focuses on the latter perspective, which leads to two questions. First, why is standard saving subject to TTE, namely to double taxation, and then why is retirement pension saving exempt from double taxation? Furthermore, why is its taxation often deferred to the third stage of the process? The first question refers to the literature on tax expenditures versus income taxation. The second question is about the suitability of introducing distortions between various savings products. What makes retirement saving different from precautionary saving or saving for one's children's education? These two issues are analyzed in turn.

2.2.1 TEE or TTE

The choice between TEE and TTE amounts to the choice between an expenditure tax and a comprehensive income tax. With TTE, capital income is taxed, and future consumption is taxed more heavily than current consumption. Under TEE, capital income is not taxed. The expenditure taxation versus income taxation issue is an old and prominent one in optimal tax theory.

Historically, this question was first dealt with in a Ramsey setting where all taxes are linear (Atkinson and Sandmo 1980). The main insight can be explained in the simple case in which there are two periods and labor is supplied only in the first. The optimal tax results then imply that if first- and second-period consumption were equally substitutable for leisure, a consumption tax would be efficient (capital income should not be taxed). If second-period consumption is more complementary with leisure, it should bear a higher tax. In that case, the tax on capital should be positive. However, this does not in general imply that capital and labor incomes should be taxed at exactly the same rate. To summarize, the optimal policy is in general neither TEE nor TTE, and it is not clear which of these regimes is preferable.

Things become clearer when the assumption that all taxes are restricted to being linear is dropped and the Atkinson and Stiglitz (1976) approach is adopted, which allows for nonlinear taxation of income. Then, if both present and future consumption are separable from leisure, a consumption tax will be optimal, and no capital income taxation is needed. However, besides the assumption of separability, this result assumes that the only source of heterogeneity is labor productivity. If instead individuals differ in other characteristics such as their survival probability, time preference, or initial endowment, then the tax on capital income is not in general equal to zero (Cremer, Pestieau, and Rochet 2003; Cremer 2003). Diamond (2009) listed a number of cases under which capital income should be taxed, thus departing from the Atkinson-Stiglitz theorem. These include nonseparable preferences, heterogeneous preferences, uncertain future earnings, the difficulty in distinguishing capital income from entrepreneurial earnings, borrowing constraints, different initial wealth, and limited tax tools.

To illustrate this point, consider a simple two-period model with two agents ($i=1,2$) who differ in their productivity w and their survival probability π. Assume that the agent with the higher productivity is also the one with the higher probability of surviving through the second period ($w_1<w_2$; $\pi_1<\pi_2$). The efficient structure of taxation has to be self-selecting. Consequently, the government has to make sure that the individual with the higher income and higher survival probability does not mimic the other individual, who will benefit from the tax policy.[2]

The expected utility of individual i is given by

$$U_i=u(c_i)-v(\ell_i)+\pi_i u(d_i),$$

where c_i is first-period consumption, d_i second-period consumption, l_i labor supply, and π_i survival probability. In the absence of government intervention, with a zero interest rate, and with perfect annuity markets implying an annuity rate of return of $1/\pi_i$, the individual's budget constraint is given by

$$c_i+\pi_i d_i=w_i\ell_i=y_i.$$

The functions u and v are strictly concave and convex, respectively. The problem of the government is to maximize the Lagrange expression

$$\begin{aligned}\pounds = &\sum_{i=1}^{2} n_i\left[u(c_i)-v\left(\frac{y_i}{w_i}\right)+\pi_i u(d_i)+\mu(y_i-c_i-\pi_i d_i)\right]\\ &+\lambda\left[u(c_2)-v\left(\frac{y_2}{w_2}\right)+\pi_2 u(d_2)-u(c_1)+v\left(\frac{y_1}{w_2}\right)-\pi_2 u(d_1)\right],\end{aligned}$$

where μ is the multiplier associated with the revenue constraint and λ the multiplier associated with the self-selection constraint.

From the first-order conditions with respect to c_2, y_2, and d_2, one obtains the optimal conditions: $u'(c_2)=u'(d_2)=v'\ (y_2/w_2)/w_2$. These are the famous nondistortions at the top conditions. Differentiation with respect to $c_1, y_1\ c_1, y_1$, and d_1 yields the following first-order conditions:

$$u'(c_1)-\mu-\frac{\lambda}{n_1}u'(c_1)=0,$$

$$u'(d_1)-\mu-\frac{\lambda\pi_2}{n_1\pi_1}u'(d_2)=0,$$

$$-v'\left(\frac{y_1}{w_1}\right)/\,w_1+\mu+\frac{\lambda}{n_1}v'\left(\frac{y_1}{w_2}\right)/\,w_2=0.$$

Rearranging these conditions and using $\pi_1<\pi_2$ yields

$$\frac{u'(d_1)}{u'(c_1)}=\frac{1-\dfrac{\lambda\pi_2}{\mu n_1\pi_1}}{1-\dfrac{\lambda}{\mu n_1}}<1,$$

and

$$\frac{v'(y_1/w_1)}{u'(c_1)}=\frac{\mu w_1+\dfrac{\lambda}{n_1}v'(y_1/w_2)w_1/w_2}{\mu+\dfrac{\lambda}{n_1}u'(c_1)}<w_1.$$

The single crossing property is used to obtain the last inequality.[3] In words, these expressions imply a tax on both savings and earnings of individuals of type 1. Consequently, it is not desirable to exempt savings from taxation in this context.

Arguments in favor of capital income taxation, namely in favor of TTE, were summarized by Banks and Diamond (2011). Their survey paper also covered the so-called new dynamic public finance (NDPF), which generally supports the need to tax capital income in addition to labor income.

2.2.2 The Exception of Pension Saving

If one grants that saving should be taxed twice at rates to be determined, the question remains: Why make an exception for pension saving? In other words, why depart from neutrality among the different saving motives? Is there something special in retirement that does not exist in the need to finance long-term care, children's education, or any lifetime risks? One should keep in mind that private pensions' tax expenditures represent huge amounts of government revenue and are redistributively regressive, because low-income individuals do not contribute to private pensions or at best contribute very little. The costs in terms of forgone tax revenue are also not negligible. In Australia, Canada, and the United Kingdom, pensions' tax incentives cost about 4.5 percent of total tax revenues (Whitehouse 2009).

Among the arguments in the literature, the following are retained (Dilnot 1993). First, pensions would cover the risk of mortality in the absence of annuities. Second, pension funds would be invested in long-term projects, which are essential for steady growth. Third, tax breaks on private pensions would be a substitute for the progressive withdrawal of governments in financing public pensions for the middle class.

These arguments are not convincing. If the concern were to protect retirees against the risk of mortality, a more effective policy would be to directly target the organization of annuity markets, which are dramatically lacking currently. This is a problem at a time when most pensions are of the defined contribution type. As to the second argument, it is not clear that pension funds are invested in longer-term or riskier ventures than other savings products. Finally, the last argument is one of political economy. For this argument to be relevant, one has to show that the amounts of these tax expenditures would not have been better used keeping the public pensions at their previous levels.

2.2.3 Rationale for Tax Deferment

One behavioral argument could justify not taxing pensions in the first two stages but just in the last one. Empirical and experimental studies have shown that individuals tend to undersave for retirement. The reasons are multiple: myopia, underestimation of survival probabilities, and a duality that makes individuals favor immediate gratification over long-term concerns. To address those behaviors, the government may choose to subsidize and not tax pension savings at the first two stages and to catch up at the third stage. This argument could explain the triplet EET. Recent research has underlined various inadequacies of the standard discounted utility model as a descriptive representation of behavior.

Agents report a gap between their long-run goals and their short-run behavior. This has important implications for their economic choices and leads to phenomena such as procrastination and undersaving. This gap between long-run and short-run preferences leads to the important conceptual question of whether the government should give priority to long-run time preferences at the expense of instant tastes. In other words, should the present individual's choices be corrected to make them time consistent? It is widely agreed that the government should paternalistically give priority to long-term concerns.

Not surprisingly, individuals will *ex post* be grateful to the government for having forced them to act according to their long-run concerns. A two-period static model illustrates this idea, whereby individuals work in the first period and retire in the second. The technology is linear, so both interest and wage rates are given. Individuals save part of their earnings for their consumption in retirement. First, look at the case of identical individuals, whose utility can be written as

$$U = u(c) - v(\ell) + \beta\pi u(d),$$

where c is first-period consumption, d second-period consumption, l labor supply, β a time preference factor, and π a survival probability. The functions u and v are strictly concave and convex, respectively.

Assume that in period 1 an individual uses a value of $\beta = \bar{\beta} < 1$ even though truly preferring 1. The individual thus maximizes

$$U = u(w\ell - s) - v(\ell) + \bar{\beta}\pi u\left(\frac{Rs}{\pi}\right),$$

where w is the wage rate, R the interest factor, s saving, and R/π is the return of an annuity. The first-order conditions of this problem are

$$u'(c) - \bar{\beta}\pi u'(d)R = 0,$$

$$u(c)w - v'(\ell) = 0.$$

These laissez-faire conditions have to be distinguished from those of the first-best case:

$$u'(c) - \pi u'(d)R = 0,$$

$$u(c)w - v'(\ell) = 0.$$

Comparing these expressions shows that $d^{FB} > d^{LF}$; in the laissez-faire situation, second-period consumption is too small. Two alternative policies can decentralize the first-best situation: (1) simply transfer resources from the first period to the second in a lump-sum way, which is close to a public pension scheme, or (2) impose a subsidy on savings at rate $(1 - \bar{\beta})$, which is financed by a lump-sum tax.

This model can easily be extended to a setting where individuals differ in productivity and in their degree of shortsightedness (discount factor). Those two characteristics are not observable. Shortsighted individuals may not save "enough" for their retirement because their "myopic self" emerges when labor supply and savings decisions are made. The optimal policy will consist of a nonlinear earnings tax and a nonlinear capital income subsidy that achieves two objectives: reaching the second-best optimal level of saving and redistributing income among individuals with different characteristics.

2.2.4 EET or TEE

Section 2.2.3 showed that EET can be preferred over TEE in the case of myopia. Other arguments favor TEE. For example, Romaniuk (2013) showed that the TEE regime is neutral on risk taking, while the EET system can affect risk taking, at least in the case of defined contribution funds. Another benefit of the TEE regime is that it allows the government to collect revenue earlier (Auerbach 2012). These two arguments call for broadening the use of the TEE regime.

At this point, recall that in reality the choice is not between TEE and EET but between TtE and EET, where the lowercase t means that the tax rate, though positive, is lower than that of the income tax.[4] In that respect, the Mirrlees Review recommended TtE or the Rate of Return Allowance (RRA) method, which taxes annual returns to capital as they occur, but in this case only partially, allowing a deduction for the normal rate of return, thus leaving only supernormal returns in the tax base.

2.3 Public Pensions and Taxation

Whereas the literature regarding the optimal regime for taxing private pensions is relatively old, the literature studying the relation between (public) pensions and taxation is much more recent. This literature is closely related to work on age-related taxation and on the impact of the retirement decision on social security design. The starting idea behind this literature is that nonlinear taxes and pensions are two instruments that closely interact and should be combined. For a long time, they were studied in quite different settings. Optimal income taxation was developed in a rather static framework with rather sophisticated tools, whereas the design of optimal pension schemes was analytically simple but relied on temporal dimensions, specifically the career profile and the age at retirement. As noted by Diamond (2009), Cremer, Lozachmeur, and Pestieau (2008b), and Choné and Laroque (2014), the desirable approach consists of combining the optimal design of pensions and taxes in a single model.[5]

To illustrate this view, consider a two-period model in which individuals work and save in the first period. They also pay an earnings tax that finances redistribution and public pension benefits. The tax impacts their intensive margin, which is their weekly labor supply. In the second period, they work a certain number of years and then retire. While individuals are working, their weekly labor supply is endogenous. In other words, they face both an intensive margin and an extensive margin labor supply decision. Furthermore, the pension benefit may depend on the length of retirement (retirement age). If it does not, an additional year of work does not increase the pension level, which discourages prolonging work. In words, in the second period, the combined effect of taxation and the pension rule is to discourage both the length of the workweek and the age of retirement. Henceforth, the tax level and the pension have to be adjusted accordingly. With such a setting, following Lozachmeur (2006) and Cremer, Lozachmeur, and Pestieau (2008a), the result is that the income tax will be higher in the first period than in the second.

As shown by Gruber and Wise (1999) and many others, existing pensions along with income and payroll taxes generate an implicit tax on prolonged activity that has to be taken into account when designing an optimal social security system. This can be illustrated by the example of an individual who in the second part of his life has to choose his age of retirement, z.

Consider again a two-period model with identical individuals maximizing their utility:

$$U = u(c) + u(d) - v(z) = u(w(1-\tau) - s) + u(Rs + wz(1-\tau) + (1-z)a(z)) - v(z),$$

where $a(z)$ is the pension benefit, which depends on retirement age. One normally expects that $a'(z) > 0$. The first-order conditions are

$$u'(c) = Ru'(d),$$

$$v'(z) = u'(d)w(1-\Theta),$$

where

$$\Theta = \tau + \frac{a(z) - (1-z)a'(z)}{w}.$$

In the literature (Gruber and Wise 1999), Θ is called the implicit tax on prolonged activity. The previous expression shows that a downward distortion on retirement comes not only from the payroll tax τ but also from the incentive toward early retirement that underlines some pension systems. Let $\bar{a}$ denote a positive constant. Consider three canonical regimes:

1. $a(z)=\bar{a}$ so that $\Theta=\tau+\frac{\bar{a}}{w}$,

2. $a(z)=\frac{\bar{a}}{1-z}$ so that $\Theta=\tau$,

3. $a(z)=\frac{\tau w z}{1-z}$ so that $\Theta=0$.

Regime 1 implies that the distortion comes not only from the tax but also from the nonactuarial neutrality of the pension system. As shown by Gruber and Wise (1990), this is a feature of many social security systems. In regime 2, the pension system is actuarially neutral, but Θ continues to be positive because second-period labor income is taxed. Finally, regime 3 corresponds to an earnings-related benefit pension that is fully neutral. This distinction can be applied to private pensions as well. Typically, defined contribution pensions tend to correspond to regime 3, and defined benefit pensions comprise features inducing early retirement. Cremer, Lozachmeur, and Pestieau (2004, 2008a) showed that full neutrality is generally not optimal in a second-best setting. Even with a nonlinear tax, informational asymmetries call for a non-optimal (distorted) retirement age, as long as the social objective implies some redistribution.

The examples until now have just described the impact of a given pension scheme. The next example looks at policy design. Assume that the government can use two different tax rates: τ in the first period and θ in the second period. Consider a utilitarian social welfare function

$$\Sigma_i n_i[u(w_i(1-\tau)-s_i)+u(Rs_i+w_i z_i(1-\theta)+(1-z_i)a(z_i))-v(z_i)]$$

subject to the revenue constraint

$$\Sigma_i n_i[w_i(\tau+\theta z_i)-(1-z_i)a(z_i)]=0.$$

Cremer, Lozachmeur, and Pestieau (2004, 2008a) showed that (1) $\tau>\theta>0$ and (2) $a(z_i)$ is a combination of regimes 2 and 3. In words, property (1) says that the tax rate on labor income is larger in the first period than in the second one but both rates are strictly positive.

Clearly, in the first-best case, one should have $\Theta_i = 0$, but in the second-best case with linear taxes and a liquidity constraint, or alternatively with nonlinear taxes and limited information, some distortion is unavoidable. People have to retire earlier than they would in the first-best case or in a pure laissez-faire setting.

2.4 Conclusions

This chapter reviewed the general principles of pension taxes. It analyzed the theoretical foundations of why pension income should be taxed specifically and how contributions to private pensions should be treated. To do this, one has to distinguish between public and private pensions. The chapter reviewed and discussed the various private pension regimes observed in reality. Historically, these regimes emerged for a variety of reasons, mostly related to issues of tax law; little attention has been devoted to their economic foundations. The chapter also showed that the key issue is whether savings should be taxed in general and whether pension saving should be treated differently from other forms of saving. While the taxation of capital income is subject to debate, even among economists, a number of recent contributions have shown that from an optimal tax perspective it is generally not desirable to fully exempt the returns of savings from taxation. The main arguments rely on multidimensional heterogeneity and/or uncertainty. However, the optimal tax rate on capital income typically differs from that on labor income.

Turning to the need for a specific regime for pension savings, the arguments traditionally given for their full tax exemption are not convincing. However, a tax deferment may well be desirable, mainly for paternalistic reasons. It is well known that individuals tend not to save enough for their retirement unless forced to do so by the pension system. This is in line with recent insights achieved in behavioral economics that show that intertemporal choices may by tainted by various types of myopia.

The design of public pensions cannot be separated from that of taxation. Both systems must be designed jointly, and, as in any optimal tax problem, informational asymmetries are of crucial importance. The distortions implied by pension systems depend on the benefit formula and the age-specific taxation of labor income. These occur at both the extensive margin (early retirement) and the intensive margin. While these distortions and, in particular, the "implicit tax on continued activity" are often criticized, they may be unavoidable in a second-best setting.

Notes

This chapter was presented at the CEPAR-CESifo workshop "Taxation of Pensions," held in Munich, September 3–4, 2015. We thank Louis Kaplow for a helpful discussion and Robert Holzmann for his insightful comments. Financial support from the "Chaire Marche des risques et creation de valeur" of the FdR/SCOR is gratefully acknowledged.

1. The same argument applies to employers' health insurance contributions.

2. The example concentrates on the case where this incentive constraint is binding. Roughly speaking, this occurs when productivity is the dominant source of heterogeneity.

3. Which implies

$$\frac{v'(y_1/w_1)}{w_1} < \frac{v'(y_1/w_2)}{w_2}.$$

4. TtE can be interpreted as a variant of the dual income taxation system, which is common in Nordic countries.

5. This is the approach of Bastani, Blomquist, and Micheletto (chapter 3, this volume) in a dynamic setting with skill uncertainty.

References

Atkinson, Anthony B., and Agnar Sandmo. 1980. "Welfare Implications of the Taxation of Savings." *Economic Journal* 90:529–549.

Atkinson, Anthony B., and Joseph Stiglitz. 1976. "The Design of Tax Structure: Direct versus Indirect Taxation." *Journal of Public Economics* 6 (1–2): 55–75.

Auerbach, Alan. 2012. "The Mirrlees Review: A US Perspective." *National Tax Journal* 65:685–708.

Banks, James, and Peter Diamond. 2011. "The Base for Direct Taxation." In *Dimensions of Tax Design: The Mirrlees Review*, edited by The Institute for Fiscal Studies (IFS), 548–648. Oxford: Oxford University Press for The Institute for Fiscal Studies (Oxford).

Choné, Philippe, and Guy Laroque. 2014. *Income Tax and Retirement Schemes*. Publ. No. 2014–06. Paris: Sciences Po Publications.

Cremer, Helmuth. 2003. "Multi-dimensional Heterogeneity and the Design of Tax Policies." *Baltic Journal of Economics* 4:35–45.

Cremer, Helmuth, Jean-Marie Lozachmeur, and Pierre Pestieau. 2004. "Social Security, Retirement Age and Optimal Income Taxation." *Journal of Public Economics* 88 (11): 2259–2281.

Cremer, Helmuth, Jean-Marie Lozachmeur, and Pierre Pestieau. 2008a. "Social Security and Retirement Decision: A Positive and Normative Approach." *Journal of Economic Surveys* 22:213–233.

Cremer, Helmuth, Jean-Marie Lozachmeur, and Pierre Pestieau. 2008b. "Social Desirability of Earnings Tests." *German Economic Review* 9:114–134.

Cremer, Helmuth, Pierre Pestieau, and Jean-Charles Rochet. 2003. "Capital Income Taxation When Inherited Wealth Is Not Observable." *Journal of Public Economics* 87:2475–2490.

Diamond, Peter A. 2009. "Taxes and Pensions." *Southern Economic Journal* 76 (1): 2–15.

Dilnot, Andrew. 1993. *The Taxation of Private Pensions*. London: Institute for Fiscal Studies.

Gruber, Jonathan, and David Wise, eds. 1999. *Social Security and Retirement around the World*. Chicago: University of Chicago Press.

Lozachmeur, Jean-Marie. 2006. "Optimal Age-Specific Income Taxation." *Journal of Public Economic Theory* 8:697–711.

Romaniuk, Katarzyna. 2013. "Pension Fund Taxation and Risk-Taking: Should We Switch from the EET to the TEE Regime?" *Annals of Finance* 9 (4): 573–588.

Whitehouse, Edward. 2009. "The Tax Treatment of Funded Pensions." OECD (Organisation for Economic Co-operation and Development), http://www.oecd.org/finance/private-pensions/2391559.pdf.

3 Public Pensions in a Multiperiod Mirrleesian Income Tax Model

Spencer Bastani, Sören Blomquist, and Luca Micheletto

3.1 Introduction

A key feature of Mirrleesian models of optimal nonlinear income taxation is that, given asymmetric information (individual skills are private information of agents and are not directly observable by the government), the government must design the income tax subject to a set of self-selection (incentive-compatibility) constraints. This means that the income tax must be chosen in such a way that agents find it in their own interest to choose the pretax income and after-tax income bundle that the government wishes them to select rather than to act as "mimickers" by choosing a bundle intended for a different type of agent.

In a static setting where agents supply labor in a single period and where there are N types of agents, differing only in terms of market ability, the government will aim at offering N different bundles in the pretax income and after-tax income space, one for each skill type. More generally, in dynamic settings where agents supply labor in several periods, the government would like to differentiate the pretax income and after-tax income bundles offered to agents not only on the basis of the specific skill type of an agent at a given period but also on the basis of the agent's past history of skill realization. This is because in a dynamic setting one has as many different types of agents as there are different lifetime skill-realization histories. However, the possibility of screening among agents with the same current skill but different skill-realization histories is severely limited under a history-independent nonlinear income tax (i.e., a nonlinear income tax that only depends on current earned income). This is because when choosing the pretax income and after-tax income bundles to be offered to agents, the government faces a very large set of incentive-compatibility constraints (hereafter, IC constraints) since in every period agents can choose any of the bundles defined by the income tax schedule.

Under a history-dependent income tax, on the other hand (i.e., an income tax that is allowed to be a general function of an agent's current and past earned incomes), screening becomes easier, since the government has a more powerful tool for punishing agents who adopt mimicking strategies.[1] This implies that the set of IC constraints faced by the government is smaller under a history-dependent income tax than under a history-independent income tax.[2] Moreover, as has been documented by some recent contributions, the stronger screening power of a history-dependent income tax generates sizable welfare gains compared to an ordinary, history-independent, nonlinear income tax (Farhi and Werning 2013; Weinzierl 2011).

As pointed out by Diamond and Saez (2011), however, the structure of an optimal fully history-dependent tax is likely to be too complex to be relevant for actual public policies. This observation spurred interest in exploring alternative, but less complex, instruments that might allow achievement of a substantial share of the welfare gains attainable via fully history-dependent taxes. One such device that has received considerable attention in the optimal tax literature is tagging by age (i.e., the possibility of making the tax schedule a function of both earned income and the age of the taxpayer).[3]

This chapter focuses on the welfare-enhancing role of a different policy instrument, public pensions, and looks at the mechanisms by which it can usefully supplement an optimal nonlinear labor income tax. It thus contributes to the relatively small body of normative literature that considers the interaction between nonlinear taxes and pension schemes in second-best settings characterized by asymmetric information between the government and private agents.[4] While most of the contributions in this area (Cremer, Lozachmeur, and Pestieau 2004; Choné and Laroque 2014; Shourideh and Troshkin 2017) emphasize how individuals' extensive margin of choice (when to retire) should be optimally distorted, the retirement decision is neglected herein, assuming that there is a fixed mandatory retirement age. The focus is instead on how public pensions can allow improvement of the social optimum achieved by relying only on (annual) nonlinear labor income taxation and linear interest income taxation.

The vehicle for the analysis is a three-period overlapping-generations (OLG) economy with heterogeneous agents in which individuals work for two periods and then retire, and young workers face uncertainty about their second-period skill realization.

The chapter highlights that even though public pensions adversely affect achievement of the golden rule of capital accumulation by crowding out private savings, they can be used as a mimicking-deterring device that makes it easier for the government to achieve the desired redistributive goals. As will be seen, the welfare effects of public pensions depend, in general, on the assumptions made about the possibility for agents to borrow against their future pension entitlements. When agents are free to borrow against their future pension entitlements, public pensions can be used as an instrument to (almost) replicate the optimal allocation that would have been implemented had the labor income tax schedule been allowed to be history dependent. When agents cannot borrow against their future pension entitlements, this might no longer be the case, but, on the other hand, an optimally designed set of pension transfers can relax some IC constraints that could not have been affected if agents were unrestricted in borrowing against their future pension entitlements. In particular, the pension system can be designed to relax those binding IC constraints where mimickers plan to save less for retirement than the agents they plan to mimic.

Simulations based on US data shed light on the potential magnitude of the welfare gains arising from using public pensions as an additional policy tool (assuming that agents cannot borrow against their future pension transfers). As a benchmark system for computing welfare gain measures, the solution to the government's problem is considered under an optimal age-independent (AI) nonlinear labor income tax with zero public debt, no pensions, and an optimally chosen interest income tax. The main results are summarized as follows.

For a utilitarian social welfare function, when the nonlinear labor income tax is AI and the government has no access to public debt policy, the possibility of introducing pension transfers generates a sizable welfare gain, equivalent to about 2.48 percent of aggregate gross domestic product (GDP). If instead it is assumed that the government faces no constraints in managing public debt policy, the welfare gains from pensions amount to 4.73 percent. Once the government is unrestricted in its use of debt policy and pension transfers are optimally chosen, the welfare gains that could be achieved by moving from an optimal AI nonlinear labor income tax to an optimal age-dependent (AD) income tax are virtually nil. In particular, an optimal AD nonlinear income tax coupled with optimally chosen pensions and an optimal interest income tax delivers a welfare gain of 6.18 percent over the benchmark system, implying a 0.01 percent welfare gain in moving from an AI labor income tax to an AD labor income tax. However, when the government has no access to public debt policy, in moving from an optimal AI labor income tax to an optimal AD labor income tax, large welfare gains remain (about 3 percent), even with pensions being used as an additional policy instrument. Finally, when the nonlinear income tax is AD, the welfare gains from optimally choosing pensions are about 4 percent (irrespective of the assumptions about the availability of debt policy).

Qualitatively similar results are obtained under a max-min social welfare function. Two main differences arise between the utilitarian and the max-min cases. One is that whereas under a utilitarian objective function debt policy is always (both with and without pensions) a redundant instrument for the government when the labor income tax is AD, this is no longer the case under a max-min objective function. Specifically, when public debt is constrained to be nonnegative and pensions are optimally chosen, the economy does not reach the golden rule even if the nonlinear income tax is AD. However, even though this implies that when debt policy is unconstrained, public pensions are more generous and most agents only rely on them to finance consumption during retirement, the welfare gain arising from the availability of debt policy is negligible, about 0.04 percent. The other difference between the utilitarian and the max-min cases is that whereas in the former case public pensions tend to mostly favor the agents who were of intermediate skill type when young, in the latter case pensions favor the agents who were of the lowest skill type when young.

The chapter is organized as follows. Section 3.2 presents the main ingredients of the model, while the government's problem is described in section 3.3. Section 3.4 provides a discussion of the mechanisms by which public pensions can represent a welfare-enhancing policy tool. Section 3.5 provides a description of the calibration used in the numerical simulations. Section 3.6 presents the results of the numerical simulations. Finally, section 3.7 offers some concluding remarks.

3.2 The Model

Consider a three-period OLG economy where agents, heterogeneous in terms of productivity (skills), work in the first two periods and retire in the third. Agents are indexed by their skill and age and start their lives as one of m^y possible productivity types. Let a young agent's productivity be denoted by θ_i, with $i \in \{1,\ldots,m^y\}$, and let π_i denote the proportion of young agents of type i, with $\sum_{i=1}^{m^y} \pi_i = 1$. With probability π_{ij}, an agent who is of productivity i when young has productivity θ_{ij}, with $j \in \{1,\ldots,m^o\}$, when middle-aged, where $\pi_{ij} \geq 0\ \forall\ (i,j) \in \{1,\ldots,m^y\} \times \{1,\ldots,m^o\}$ and $\sum_{j=1}^{m^o} \pi_{ij} = 1$. Denoting the sets $\{1,\ldots,m^y\}$ and $\{1,\ldots,m^o\}$ by I and J, respectively, θ_σ is interpreted as referring to the productivity of a middle-aged agent if σ is a tuple $(i,j) \in I \times J$ and as referring to the productivity of a young agent if σ is a single index $i \in I$.

Labor supply and consumption of a young agent of type i born in period t are denoted by $\ell_{i,t}$ and $c_{i,t}$, respectively, whereas $\ell_{ij,t}$ and $c_{ij,t}$ denote the labor supply and consumption at time t of a type j middle-aged agent (born in $t-1$) who was of type i when young. In the third period of life, labor supply is zero, and $c_{ij,t}^R$ denotes consumption in period t of a retiree who was of type i when young and of type j when middle-aged. Starting from an initial size N_0, population grows at rate n, so that the size of the cohort born at time t is $N_t = (1+n)^t N_0$. Labor in efficiency units and consumption are defined as

$$\tilde{L}_t = \sum_{i=1}^{m^y} \pi_i \theta_i \ell_{i,t} + \frac{1}{1+n} \sum_{i=1}^{m^y} \pi_i \left(\sum_{j=1}^{m^o} \pi_{ij} \theta_{ij} \ell_{ij,t} \right) \tag{3.1}$$

and

$$\tilde{C}_t = \sum_{i=1}^{m^y} \pi_i c_{i,t} + \frac{1}{1+n} \sum_{i=1}^{m^y} \pi_i \left[\sum_{j=1}^{m^o} \pi_{ij} \left(c_{ij,t} + \frac{1}{1+n} c_{ij,t}^R \right) \right], \tag{3.2}$$

whereas total effective labor and consumption in the economy are given by $L_t = N_t \tilde{L}_t$ and $C_t = N_t \tilde{C}_t$.

Firms operate a constant returns to scale (CRS) technology $F(K_t, L_t)$ admitting zero equilibrium profits. The capital depreciation rate, the interest rate, and the wage rate per efficiency unit of labor are denoted, respectively, by δ, r_t, and ω_t. With perfectly competitive markets, factors earn their marginal products such that $r_t = f'(k_t) - \delta$ and $\omega_t = f(k_t) - k_t f'(k_t)$, where $k_t \equiv K_t / L_t$ and $f(k_t) = F(K_t / L_t, 1)$. An agent's labor income is defined as the product of labor in efficiency units and the equilibrium wage rate: $y_{i,t} = \omega_t \theta_i \ell_{i,t} \equiv w_{i,t} \ell_{i,t}$ and $y_{ij,t} = \omega_t \theta_{ij} \ell_{ij,t} \equiv w_{ij,t} \ell_{ij,t}$.

In each period, individual preferences are represented by a twice differentiable, strictly quasiconcave utility function $u(c_t, \ell_t)$, where $u_c > 0$ and $u_\ell < 0$. Denoting a time-preference parameter by β, the expected lifetime utility of an agent with productivity i when young is given by

$$EU_{i,t} = u(c_{i,t}, \ell_{i,t}) + \sum_{j=1}^{m^o} \pi_{ij} \left[\beta u(c_{ij,t+1}, \ell_{ij,t+1}) + \beta^2 u(c_{ij,t+2}^R) \right]. \tag{3.3}$$

Two alternative systems of labor income taxation are considered. One is represented by an AI nonlinear labor income tax where the same tax schedule applies to both young and middle-aged workers. The other is a system of AD taxation where the government chooses two different nonlinear tax schedules, one for the young and one for the middle-aged. Thus, consider tax systems of the form $\{T_1(y_i), T_2(y_{ij})\}$, where $T_1(\cdot)$ is the tax function that applies to young agents, $T_2(\cdot)$ is the tax function for middle-aged agents, and $T_1(\cdot)$ is constrained to be equal to $T_2(\cdot)$ under an AI tax. With respect to capital income taxation, the analysis maintains the assumption that interest income can only be taxed at a proportional rate. However, it also allows for the possibility that the interest tax rate can be made AD.[5] This will enable numerical simulations to explore whether large welfare gains would arise in moving from a system of AI interest income taxation to a system of AD interest income taxation.

Finally, as a further policy instrument at the government's disposal, the analysis allows for the possibility of running a pay-as-you-go (PAYG) pension system where agents get a pension transfer in the third period of their life that is a (general) function of their lifetime labor earnings profile. When allowing for this additional policy instrument, it is assumed that in each period the pension transfers paid to current retirees are entirely financed by a proportional, AI, social security contribution rate α on the labor income of current workers.[6]

Denoting after-tax labor income when young and when middle-aged by, respectively, $b_i = y_i - T_1(y_i) - \alpha y_i$ and $b_{ij} = y_{ij} - T_2(y_{ij}) - \alpha y_{ij}$, and denoting savings in the first and second periods by $s_{i,t}$ and $s_{ij,t+1}$, respectively, (3.3) can be rewritten as

$$EU_{i,t} = u\left(b_{i,t} - s_{i,t}, \frac{y_{i,t}}{w_{i,t}}\right) + \beta \sum_{j=1}^{m^o} \pi_{ij} u\left(b_{ij,t+1} + (1 + r_{t+1}(1 - \tau_{1,t+1}))s_{i,t} - s_{ij,t+1}, \frac{y_{ij,t+1}}{w_{ij,t+1}}\right) + \beta^2 \sum_{j=1}^{m^o} \pi_{ij} u((1 + r_{t+2}(1 - \tau_{2,t+2}))s_{ij,t+1} + P(y_{i,t}, y_{ij,t+1})),$$

where $\tau_{1,t+1}$ denotes the interest income tax rate that applies to the return on savings made by young agents, $\tau_{2,t+2}$ denotes the interest income tax rate that applies to the return on savings made by middle-aged agents, and $P(y_{i,t}, y_{ij,t+1})$ represents the pension transfer received in the third period.

For given values of $b_{i,t}$, $y_{i,t}$, $b_{ij,t+1}$, $y_{ij,t+1}$, $\tau_{1,t+1}$, $\tau_{2,t+2}$, $P_{ij,t+2}$, an individual chooses first- and second-period savings to maximize expected lifetime utility. When a young agent makes plans for second-period savings, these plans are contingent on the realization of the agent's productivity when middle-aged.

The aggregate savings of generation t is given by $N_t s_t = N_t \sum_{i=1}^{m^y} \pi_i s_{i,t}$, and the aggregate savings in period t of the generation born in period $t-1$ is given by $N_{t-1}s_{t-1} = N_{t-1} \sum_{i=1}^{m^y} \pi_i \left(\sum_{j=1}^{m^o} \pi_{ij} s_{ij,t} \right)$. Agents invest either in government bonds D_t or in physical capital. The capital stock in period $t+1$ is equal to that part of investment that goes into physical capital in period t:

$$K_{t+1} = N_t s_t + N_{t-1} s_{t-1} - D_t. \tag{3.4}$$

Dividing (3.4) by $L_{t+1} = N_{t+1}\tilde{L}_{t+1}$ and defining $d_{t+1} \equiv D_t / N_{t+1}$ gives

$$\tilde{L}_{t+1}(1+n)k_{t+1} = s_t + \frac{s_{t-1}}{1+n} - d_{t+1}(1+n). \tag{3.5}$$

Denoting the quantity $N_t s_t + N_{t-1} s_{t-1}$ by S_t, the resource constraint of the economy is

$$(1-\delta)K_t + F(K_t, L_t) = C_t + S_t. \tag{3.6}$$

Dividing (3.6) by L_t gives

$$(1-\delta)k_t + f(k_t) = C_t / L_t + S_t / L_t. \tag{3.7}$$

Combining (3.5) and (3.7) with the private budget constraints relating before-tax income to after-tax income, and using the definitions of C_t and L_t, one obtains the government's budget constraint

$$\begin{aligned}
&\sum_{i=1}^{m^y} \pi_i \left[T_{1,t}(w_{i,t}\ell_{i,t}) + \alpha_t w_{i,t}\ell_{i,t} \right] \\
&\quad + (1+n)^{-1} \sum_{i=1}^{m^y} \pi_i \left[\sum_{j=1}^{m^o} \pi_{ij} (T_{2,t}(w_{ij,t}\ell_{ij,t}) + \alpha_t w_{ij,t}\ell_{ij,t}) \right] \\
&\quad + (1+n)^{-1} r_t \left[\tau_{1,t} \sum_{i=1}^{m^y} \pi_i s_{i,t-1} + (1+n)^{-1} \tau_{2,t} \sum_{i=1}^{m^y} \pi_i \left(\sum_{j=1}^{m^o} \pi_{ij} s_{ij,t-1} \right) \right] \\
&\quad + (1+n) d_{t+1} = (1+r_t) d_t + (1+n)^{-2} \sum_{i=1}^{m^y} \pi_i \sum_{j=1}^{m^o} \pi_{ij} P_{ij,t},
\end{aligned}$$

where $P_{ij,t} \equiv P_{ij,t}(w_{i,t-2}\ell_{i,t-2}, w_{ij,t-1}\ell_{ij,t-1})$ denotes the pension transfer paid in period t to a retiree who was of type i when young and of type j when middle-aged.

The following section describes the government's problem. To simplify the analysis, it focuses on stationary equilibria where prices, tax and debt policy, and all per capita quantities are constant. Formally, a stationary equilibrium is defined as follows.

Definition 3.1 A stationary equilibrium is a competitive equilibrium with the property that, for all periods $t \geq \bar{t}$, $\{T_{1,t}(y_i), T_{2,t}(y_{ij}), \tau_{1,t}, \tau_{2,t}, P_{ij,t}\} = \{T_1(y_i), T_2(y_{ij}), \tau_1, \tau_2, P_{ij}\}$, $\{r_t, \omega_t\} = \{r, \omega\}$, $d_t = d$, $\{\tilde{C}_t, \tilde{L}_t\} = \{\tilde{C}, \tilde{L}\}$, and $k_t = k$.

3.3 General Structure of the Government's Problem

The government knows the skill distribution at each age and the Markov probabilities relating these distributions. Moreover, it can observe pretax incomes, $y = \omega\theta\ell$, whereas neither individual skills θ nor labor supplies ℓ are publicly observable. The government has at its disposal a nonlinear labor income tax schedule that can be conditioned on the age of the taxpayer (assumed to be observable). Agents maximize expected utility based on the link between pretax earnings and after-tax earnings implied by the tax schedules. Thus, the government's problem can equivalently be stated as choosing the allocations $\{b_i, y_i\}_{i \in I}$ and $\{b_{ij}, y_{ij}\}_{(i,j) \in I \times J}$ subject to a set of IC constraints and a public budget constraint.

Instead of choosing a single income point as in a static optimal tax problem, in a dynamic setting agents choose a strategy. A strategy specifies which income point is chosen by an agent in each period of work and for each state of the world (i.e., for each skill realization in the second period of life). Agents' strategies are independent of each other, and there is no aggregate uncertainty. Each strategy implies (unique) savings decisions consistent with the chosen income points and the agent's first-order conditions for savings. The IC constraints require that each agent (weakly) prefers to choose the strategy intended for his or her type rather than to behave as a mimicker by choosing a deviating strategy.

Formally, a strategy corresponding to a young agent of type i is, under an AD tax, a plan $\sigma^i = (\sigma_1^i, \sigma_2^i)$, where $\sigma_1^i \in I$ is the reported type when young and σ_2^i is a functional $\sigma_2^i : J \to I \times J$ determining the income point chosen when middle-aged as a function of the second-period skill realization $j \in J$. The set of all strategies available to a young agent of type i is denoted by Γ_i. Truth telling implies that a young agent of type i chooses the income point (b_i, y_i) in the first period and the income point (b_{ij}, y_{ij}) in the second period if j is his skill realization when middle-aged. The truthful strategy for an agent of type i is denoted by $\tilde{\sigma}^i = (\tilde{\sigma}_1^i, \tilde{\sigma}_2^i)$ with $\tilde{\sigma}_1^i = i$ and $\tilde{\sigma}_2^i(j) = (i, j)$, $\forall j \in J$. Under an AI tax, a strategy corresponding to a young agent of type i is instead a plan $\sigma^i = (\sigma_1^i, \sigma_2^i)$, where $\sigma_1^i \in (I \times J \cup I)$ is the reported type when young and σ_2^i is a functional $\sigma_2^i : J \to (I \times J \cup I)$ determining the income point chosen when middle-aged as a function of the second-period skill realization $j \in J$.

Assuming that the government maximizes a concave social welfare aggregator $W(\cdot)$ whose arguments are the steady-state expected lifetime utilities of the m^y types of agents forming a representative cohort,[7] the government's problem can be described as

$$\max_{d, \tau_1, \tau_2, \{b_i, y_i\}_{\in I}, \{b_{ij}, y_{ij}\}_{(i,j) \in I \times J}, \{P_{ij}\}_{(i,j) \in I \times J}} W(V_1(\tilde{\sigma}^1), \ldots, V_{m^y}(\tilde{\sigma}^{m^y}))$$

subject to the set of IC constraints

$$\forall i \in I : V_i(\tilde{\sigma}^i) \geq V_i(\sigma^i), \forall \sigma^i \in \Gamma_i, \tag{3.8}$$

the government's (per period) budget constraint

$$\sum_{i=1}^{m^y} \pi_i (y_i - b_i) + \frac{1}{1+n} \sum_{i=1}^{m^y} \pi_i \left(\sum_{j=1}^{m^o} \pi_{ij} (y_{ij} - b_{ij}) \right)$$
$$+ \frac{1}{1+n} r \left[\tau_1 \sum_{i=1}^{m^y} \pi_i s_i + \frac{1}{1+n} \tau_2 \sum_{i=1}^{m^y} \pi_i \left(\sum_{j=1}^{m^o} \pi_{ij} s_{ij} \right) \right]$$
$$+ (1+n)d = (1+r)d + (1+n)^{-2} \sum_{i=1}^{m^y} \pi_i \sum_{j=1}^{m^o} \pi_{ij} P_{ij},$$

and the capital market equilibrium condition

$$(1+n)k\tilde{L} = s + (1+n)^{-1} s_{-1} - d(1+n), \tag{3.9}$$

where $\tilde{L} \equiv \sum_{i=1}^{m^y} \pi_i (y_i / \omega) + (1+n)^{-1} \sum_{i=1}^{m^y} \pi_i \left(\sum_{j=1}^{m^o} \pi_{ij} (y_{ij} / \omega) \right)$, and

$$V_i(\tilde{\sigma}^i) \equiv u\left(b_i - s_i, \frac{y_i}{w_i} \right) + \beta \sum_{j=1}^{m^o} \pi_{ij} u\left(b_{ij} + (1 + r(1-\tau_1)) s_i - s_{ij}, \frac{y_{ij}}{w_{ij}} \right)$$
$$+ \beta^2 \sum_{j=1}^{m^o} \pi_{ij} u((1 + r(1-\tau_2)) s_{ij} + P(y_i, y_{ij})),$$

$$V_i(\sigma^i) \equiv u\left(b_{\sigma_1^i} - s_{\sigma_1^i}, \frac{y_{\sigma_1^i}}{w_i} \right) + \beta \sum_{j=1}^{m^o} \pi_{ij} u\left(b_{\sigma_2^i(j)} + (1 + r(1-\tau_1)) s_{\sigma_1^i} - s_{\sigma_2^i}(j), \frac{y_{\sigma_2^i(j)}}{w_{ij}} \right)$$
$$+ \beta^2 \sum_{j=1}^{m^o} \pi_{ij} u\left((1 + r(1-\tau_2)) s_{\sigma_2^i}(j) + P\left(y_{\sigma_1^i}, y_{\sigma_2^i(j)} \right) \right),$$

with $s_{\sigma_1^i}$ denoting the savings chosen in the first period by a type i agent who adopts the strategy σ^i and $s_{\sigma_2^i}(j)$ denoting the savings prescribed by strategy σ^i in the second period conditional on the agent's skill realization when middle-aged being j.

Having described the structure of the government's problem, it is worth summarizing how, in the absence of public pensions, a nonlinear AD labor income tax enables the policy maker to Pareto-improve the optimum achieved through an AI tax. As highlighted in Bastani, Blomquist, and Micheletto (2013), the potential gains of an AD nonlinear labor income tax as compared to an AI one are twofold. First, by shutting down some mimicking strategies, such a tax reduces the number of IC constraints faced by the government.[8] Second, in a general equilibrium environment with endogenous capital accumulation and constraints on the management of public debt policy, only an AD tax can always achieve the golden-rule level of capital without interfering with the government's redistributive goals.[9]

Section 3.4 analyzes how public pensions can be used as an additional welfare-enhancing policy instrument. For simplicity, the discussion provided is based on the assumption that, conditional on the skill type of an agent when young, two possible skill realizations exist when middle-aged: an agent experiences either an unfavorable skill shock or a favorable one. Notice that this terminology is used even though it is not assumed that if an agent is hit by an unfavorable skill shock, the wage rate in the second period is necessarily lower than the wage rate in the first period.

3.4 Public Pensions as a Welfare-Enhancing Device

Introducing public pensions as an additional policy instrument requires the government to optimally choose how they are related to the labor income earned by agents during their working years. Formally, the government has to optimally select the set of transfers $P(y_i, y_{ij})$, where y_i refers to labor income earned in the first period and y_{ij} to labor income earned in the second period, and where no restriction is placed *ex ante* on the shape of the $P(y_i, y_{ij})$ function, except that $P(y_i, y_{ij}) \geq 0$.

Consider first how pensions can play a role as a welfare-enhancing device when used as a policy tool that supplements an optimal nonlinear labor income tax (with or without interest income taxation). Given that the calibrated wage process considered in the numerical simulations is such that, in the solution to the government's tax problem in the absence of public pensions, the steady-state optimum is dynamically efficient under both an AD tax and an AI tax, it is clear that pensions cannot generate welfare gains that are related to capital-accumulation effects. By providing agents with a transfer in their retirement period, pensions will lessen the need for agents to save for retirement purposes. Thus, in terms of capital-accumulation effects, pensions will not be desirable, since they hinder achievement of the golden rule.[10] This also means that if pensions can have a role as a welfare-enhancing device, such a role must be traced back to mimicking-deterring effects. With respect to these kinds of effects, two cases need to be distinguished, depending on whether one assumes that agents are free to borrow against their future pension entitlements. In discussing these two cases, it is assumed for simplicity that the government faces no restrictions on its debt policy, so it can control an independent policy instrument that allows the economy to reach a steady state where the golden rule is achieved.[11]

In the former case, the pension transfers can be combined with a reform in the labor income tax schedule such that one makes nonbinding all the IC constraints associated with deviating strategies where a mimicker does not perfectly match the lifetime labor income profile of a nondeviating agent.

Intuitively, suppose that, at an optimum without pensions, one of the binding IC constraints is associated with the following deviating strategy: a young type 2 agent chooses the income point (y_2, b_2) intended for him in the first period and then plans to select either the point (y_{11}, b_{11}) or the point (y_{12}, b_{12}) in the second period, depending on his realized productivity shock (i.e., he plans to choose in the second period one of the income points intended for a middle-aged worker who was of type 1 when young).[12] To relax this IC constraint, one could supplement taxation of labor income and interest income with a set of pension transfers and implement the following reform: keep y_{11} and y_{12} fixed at the prereform values and lower b_{11} and b_{12} by $db_{11}<0$ and $db_{12}<0$, respectively, while at the same time introducing pension transfers $P(y_1, y_{11})= -[1+r\ (1-\tau_2)]db_{11}$ and $P(y_1, y_{12})=-[1+r\ (1-\tau_2)]db_{12}$ (while no pension is paid out to agents who earn y_{11} or y_{12} but earned y_2 in the first period; i.e., $P(y_2, y_{11})=0$ and $P(y_2, y_{12})=0$). If middle-aged agents are unrestricted in borrowing against future pension entitlements, one can keep replicating the type of reform described, raising $P(y_1, y_{11})$ and $P(y_1, y_{12})$ while at the same time lowering b_{11} and b_{12}, in a way that is both welfare-neutral for agents of type 1 and welfare-reducing for a type 2 agent contemplating adoption of the assumed deviating strategy.[13]

An optimally designed set of pension transfers can then be used, both under an AI labor income tax and under an AD labor income tax, as an instrument to (almost) replicate the allocation that, absent a pension system, would have been implemented by a history-dependent labor income tax system.[14] As a consequence, if the government has the possibility of optimally selecting the set of transfers $P(y_i, y_{ij})$, moving from an optimally designed AI labor income tax to an optimally designed AD tax might be of second-order importance in terms of welfare gains resulting from mimicking-deterring effects.[15] It is worth noticing, however, that with agents unrestricted in borrowing against their future pension entitlements, the pension system cannot be used as an instrument to relax binding IC constraints associated with deviating strategies where a mimicker perfectly replicates the lifetime labor income profile of a nondeviating agent (for instance, the case of a type 2 agent choosing y_1 in the first period and either y_{11} or y_{12} in the second period).

Next, consider the case where agents have limited or no ability to borrow against future pension transfers. In this case, the pension system might be less effective in slackening the IC constraints associated with deviating strategies when a mimicker does not replicate the lifetime labor income profile of a nondeviating agent. This is because there is now a limit to how much the government can exploit the mimicking-deterring reforms outlined (i.e., raising the pension transfer and lowering the after-tax labor income when middle-aged) without lowering the utility of a nondeviating agent. In fact, when a nondeviating agent becomes borrowing constrained in the second period of life, a further increase in his pension transfer, combined with a present-value neutral reduction in his after-tax labor income in the second period, makes him worse off.[16] The extent to which this represents a serious hindrance for the government will in general vary according to the specific parameterization of the model considered (e.g., distribution of skills in the first and second periods, transition probabilities, proportion of different types of agents).[17]

On the other hand, when agents have limited or no ability to borrow against future pension transfers, an optimally designed set of pension transfers may relax IC constraints that could not be affected if agents were unrestricted in borrowing against their future pension entitlements. This is the case for the IC constraints associated with lifetime labor income profiles that perfectly mimic those of nondeviating agents. Consider, for instance, the case of a binding IC constraint associated with a deviating strategy where a type 2 agent fully mimics a type 1 agent by choosing the income point (y_1, b_1) in the first period and either the point (y_{11}, b_{11}) or the point (y_{12}, b_{12}) in the second period. If both a type 1 agent and a type 2 mimicker had the same probability of getting an unfavorable skill shock or a favorable one, then their saving behavior in both the first and second periods would be identical, and it would not be possible to rely on the pension transfers to alleviate this IC constraint. However, if they faced different probabilities of getting a favorable or unfavorable skill shock, then their saving behavior would be different in both the first and the second periods. In this case, if in the absence of pensions a type 2 mimicker would save less when middle-aged (for retirement) than a type 1 agent, the government could rely on a proper choice of pension transfers to alleviate this IC constraint.[18] That is because by providing pensions the government can push a mimicker into a corner solution where he is forced to underconsume when middle-aged and overconsume during retirement.[19]

To summarize, when agents have limited or no ability to borrow against future pension entitlements, an optimally designed set of pension transfers may relax IC constraints that could not have been affected otherwise. However, this requires that, at an optimum in the absence of pensions, middle-aged mimickers would like to save less than the agent they mimic. In turn, this condition is more likely to be met when the probability of getting a favorable skill shock in the second period is higher for the potential mimicker than for the agent being mimicked.

As a final remark, one should always take into account that when the government faces constraints on the management of debt policy, the mimicking-deterring effects highlighted here will in the end need to be traded off against the adverse capital-accumulation effects generated by the PAYG system.

Having discussed the channels by which a PAYG system can affect the government's problem, in section 3.5 we present some results based on numerical simulations aimed at illustrating the potential welfare gains that could be obtained by using an optimally designed set of pension transfers as an additional policy instrument. In performing the simulations, it is assumed that agents cannot borrow against their future pension transfers.[20]

3.5 Calibration

3.5.1 Parameterization

The simulations use the same parameterization and skill process that were used in Bastani, Blomquist, and Micheletto (2013). Each period corresponds to 20 years. Based on an annual depreciation rate of 8 percent and a population growth rate of 1.1 percent, the 20-year analogues are calculated, which yields $n=(1.011)^{20}-1$ and $\delta=1-0.92^{20}$. The individual rate of time preference β is set to $\beta=0.988^{20}$. Production is Cobb-Douglas (i.e., $F(K_t, L_t)=AK_t^{\alpha}L_t^{1-\alpha}$), and the share of capital in production is $\alpha=1/3$. The production scale factor A is chosen such that the equilibrium rental price for one efficiency unit of labor is equal to 1 when the golden rule is satisfied. Agents maximize their expected lifetime utility given an instantaneous utility function defined as $u(c,\ell)=\frac{c^{1-\gamma}}{1-\gamma}-\frac{\ell^{\kappa}}{\kappa}$ with $\kappa=3$ (implying a Frisch elasticity of 0.5) and $\gamma=2$.

3.5.2 Skill Process

The skill process consists of three parts: the skill distributions in the first and second periods and the transition probabilities linking these distributions.

The distribution of skills is inferred from the distribution of market wage rates. Since the focus is on a zero-productivity-growth stationary state, the skill distribution for young and middle-aged agents is calibrated using wage distributions obtained from the same year t. In particular, the 2003 wave of the Current Population Survey (CPS) is used to obtain the skill distributions for both young and middle-aged agents.

To capture how agents' skills evolve over the life cycle, it is necessary to adopt a procedure that is based on wage distributions taken from two separate periods in time. Because the period length is 20 years and the analysis is interested in how individuals' wages change over time, a panel dataset spanning a long period of time is needed. For this reason, the National Longitudinal Study of Youth (NLSY79) is used to retrieve the transition probabilities. Since the model abstracts from productivity growth, it is likely to overestimate the increase in skills that occurs over time by computing transition probabilities based on cohort-specific wage distributions in years t and $t+20$. This problem is handled by looking at how over time agents change their relative position in their cohort-specific wage distribution.[21] The analysis focuses on agents who were 25 years old during the period 1982–1988 and determines how they move in the wage distribution by calculating their wages 20 years later during the period 2002–2008 (when they are 45). Since the number of IC constraints severely limits the number of types that can be handled in the numerical simulations, the wage distribution for the young is divided into three groups and the wage distribution for the middle-aged into four groups. Some of the transition probabilities are also restricted by assuming $\pi_{ij}>0$ for $0\leq j-i\leq 1$. The wage rates and the transition matrix are given in table 3.1.

The numbers in the matrix show the proportion of agents belonging to a given group in the first period who move to a particular group in the second period. However, these numbers are consistent with different assumptions about how individuals perceive their wage process.

Table 3.1
Transition matrix and hourly wages.

	Middle-aged				
Young	1	2	3	4	Wages
1	0.41	0.59	0	0	8.19
2	0	0.43	0.57	0	12.38
3	0	0	0.59	0.41	19.58
Wages	9.67	15.42	21.40	34.75	

Note: Wages expressed in 2003 US dollars.

The assumption is that individuals perceive these proportions as probabilities. Thus, if a proportion p_{ij} moves from group i in the first period to group j in the second period, the assumption is that individuals who belong to group i in the first period regard π_{ij} as the probability that they will end up in group j in the second period.

3.6 Results

The results presented are obtained assuming that the government maximizes either an *ex ante* utilitarian social welfare function or an *ex ante* max-min social welfare function.[22] To obtain a revenue-based measure of the welfare gains attainable under different assumptions about the set of policy instruments available to the government, the analysis considers an equivalent-variation welfare gain measure, taking as a benchmark the solution to the government's problem under an AI nonlinear labor income tax with zero public debt, no pensions, and an optimally chosen (AI) interest income tax rate. The model first calculates the minimum amount of extra revenue that should be injected into the government's budget in the benchmark optimal AI tax problem to achieve the same social welfare level as under a different policy regime. Once this minimum amount of extra revenue is determined, it is divided by aggregate GDP at the AI tax benchmark to get a revenue-based measure of the welfare gains. All results are displayed in tables 3.2–3.5.

First, consider the results obtained for a utilitarian social welfare function (see the fifth column of table 3.2, and table 3.3).[23] It can be seen that when the nonlinear labor income tax is AI, public debt is fixed at zero, and the interest income tax is optimally chosen; allowing the government to optimally choose the set of pension transfers generates a sizable welfare gain, equivalent to about 2.48 percent of aggregate

Table 3.2
Overview of welfare gains (WG).

Labor tax	Debt	Capital tax	Pensions	WG utilitarian	WG max-min
AI	Zero	AI	No	Benchmark	Benchmark
AI	Zero	AI	Yes	2.48%	4.94%
AI	Free	AI	No	1.44%	2.24%
AI	Free	AI	Yes	6.17%	8.26%
AD	Zero	AI	No	2.19%	3.35%
AD	Zero	AI	Yes	6.18%	8.27%
AD	Free	AI	Yes	6.18%	8.31%

GDP under the benchmark tax system. It is worth noting that such a large welfare gain is obtained with quite small pension transfers: the equilibrium contribution rate is just 4.62 percent.[24] The reason the optimal pension transfers in this case are so low is that without access to an unrestricted debt policy (in particular, a negative public debt), making the pension transfers more generous entails a trade-off between relaxing IC constraints and moving the economy even further away from the golden rule.[25] Finally, it can be seen that, based on the computed equilibrium contribution rate, the implicit rates of return on social security contributions vary a lot, depending on the realized lifetime labor-earning trajectory of an agent, and tend to be higher for agents who experienced a favorable skill shock when middle-aged.

If besides allowing the government to optimally choose the set of pension transfers it is also assumed that the government faces no constraints in managing public debt policy, the welfare gain, compared to the benchmark system, amounts to 4.73 percent (calculated from table 3.2, column "WG utilitarian," as the difference between 6.17 percent and 1.44 percent). In this case, pensions can be used for the sole purpose of slackening binding IC constraints, without the need to worry about adverse consequences on capital accumulation (the golden-rule condition is satisfied, with the reduction in private savings more than compensated by the increase in public saving; i.e., negative public debt).[26] The equilibrium contribution rate increases to 12.17 percent;[27] once again, the implicit rates of return on social security contributions, even though they increase compared with the case when public debt was fixed at zero, vary a lot and are always larger for agents who experienced a favorable skill shock when middle-aged.

Table 3.3
Utilitarian social welfare function with pensions.

Instruments		Pension transfers	Implicit rate of return
AI T, $d=0$, AI τ	$r=79.28\%$	P11=0.10	–61%
	$\tau=93.81\%$	P12=2.19	190%
	$\alpha=4.62\%$	P21=0.41	–22%
		P22=0.48	–20%
		P31=0.03	–93%
		P32=2.24	60%
AI T, d free, AI τ	$r=24.46\%$	P11=0.11	–83%
	$\tau=16.22\%$	P12=2.27	33%
	$\alpha=12.17\%$	P21=1.69	–3%
		P22=6.06	101%
		P31=2.55	–7%
		P32=4.91	18%
AD T, $d=0$, AI τ	$r=24.46\%$	P11=0.01	–97%
	$\tau=21.32\%$	P12=1.90	30%
	$\alpha=10.52\%$	P21=2.99	58%
		P22=6.83	140%
		P31=0.12	–91%
		P32=3.63	5%

One can also notice that once the government is unrestricted in its use of debt policy and pension transfers are optimally chosen, the welfare gains that could be achieved by moving from an optimal AI nonlinear labor income tax to an optimal AD income tax would be virtually nil. An optimal AD nonlinear income tax, coupled with optimally chosen pensions and an optimal AI interest income tax, delivers a welfare gain of 6.18 percent over the benchmark system, implying a 0.01 percent welfare gain in moving from an AI labor income tax to an AD labor income tax.

It is also worth noting that for a utilitarian social welfare function, when the nonlinear labor income tax is AD, it does not matter whether the government has access to debt policy.[28] This implies that, at least for the case where the government has no access to public debt policy, large welfare gains remain (3.7 percent, calculated as the difference between 6.18 percent and 2.48 percent in the "WG utilitarian" column of table 3.2), even with pensions being used as an additional policy instrument, in moving from an optimal AI labor income tax to an optimal AD labor income tax. Regarding the set of optimal pension transfers under a nonlinear AD income tax, it resembles fairly closely the one obtained under a nonlinear AI income tax with unrestricted debt policy.[29]

Finally, when the nonlinear income tax is AD, the welfare gains from optimally choosing pensions are quite large, close to 4 percent (calculated as the difference between 6.18 percent and 2.19 percent in the "WG utilitarian" column of table 3.2). This number is larger than the corresponding gain (2.48 percent) calculated under a nonlinear AI income tax with debt restricted to zero. This is because, as emphasized earlier, under a utilitarian social welfare function, debt policy is redundant under a nonlinear AD tax both when pensions are used and when they are not (in both cases, the economy reaches the golden rule). On the contrary, under a nonlinear AI tax, a zero public debt constraint hinders the government because of the trade-off that arises between the pursuit of redistributive goals and achievement of the golden rule. In this case, if pensions provide a source of welfare gain because of the mimicking-deterring effects that they exert, they also move the economy further away from the golden rule.

Now, briefly consider how results change under a max-min social welfare function. The main difference pertains to the case of a nonlinear AD income tax. It is now no longer true that the availability of debt policy is irrelevant when the nonlinear labor income tax is AD and pension transfers are provided by the government. Specifically, when public debt is fixed at zero and pensions are optimally chosen, the economy does not reach the golden rule even if the nonlinear income tax is AD.[30] However, even though this implies that, when debt policy is unconstrained, pensions are more generous and most agents only rely on pensions to finance consumption during retirement, the welfare gain arising from the availability of debt policy is negligible, about 0.04 percent (calculated as the difference between 8.31 percent and 8.27 percent in the last column of table 3.2). Compared with the case when pensions are not provided, under a nonlinear AD income tax the welfare gain of using pensions amounts to about 5 percent.

Once again, with the government unrestricted in its use of debt policy and pension transfers optimally chosen, the welfare gains that could be achieved by moving from an optimal AI nonlinear labor income tax to an optimal AD income tax would be virtually nil (0.05 percent, calculated as the difference between 8.31 percent and 8.26 percent in the last column of table 3.2). If instead debt were restricted to zero, there would still be significant welfare gains, 3.3 percent (calculated as the difference between

Table 3.4
Max-min social welfare function with pensions.

Instruments		Pension transfers	Implicit rate of return
AI T, $d=0$, AI τ	$r=84.36\%$	P11=0.41	5%
	$\tau=89.87\%$	P12=0.92	36%
	$\alpha=6.72\%$	P21=2.87	126%
		P22=3.23	114%
		P31=0.23	–78%
		P32=1.02	–47%
AI T, d free, AI τ	$r=24.46\%$	P11=1.20	74%
	$\tau=14.64\%$	P12=2.33	112%
	$\alpha=9.23\%$	P21=1.25	5%
		P22=4.22	107%
		P31=0.45	–71%
		P32=3.21	2%
AD T, $d=0$, AI τ	$r=27.09\%$	P11=0	–100%
	$\tau=46.65\%$	P12=0.92	–100%
	$\alpha=14.91\%$	P21=5.01	96%
		P22=6.04	91%
		P31=1.68	–42%
		P32=8.86	51%
AD T, d free, AI τ	$r=24.46\%$	P11=4.64	126%
	$\tau=34.37\%$	P12=5.20	94%
	$\alpha=23.39\%$	P21=1.55	–37%
		P22=6.09	38%
		P31=6.52	8%
		P32=7.91	0%

8.27 percent and 4.94 percent in the last column of table 3.2), in moving from an AI income tax (with pensions) to an AD income tax (with pensions).

Comparing tables 3.3 and 3.4, another difference between the utilitarian and the max-min case is that in the former case pensions tend to mostly favor those agents who were of the intermediate skill type when young (at least when the solution to the government's problem is such that the economy reaches the golden rule), while in the latter case pensions definitely favor those agents who were of the lowest skill type when young.

Before concluding, two more issues are briefly discussed, one related to the welfare effects of interest income taxation and the other related to

Table 3.5
Optimal interest income tax rates and welfare gains.

				Utilitarian		Max-min	
T	*d*	τ	**Pensions**	τ	**Welfare gain**	τ	**Welfare gain**
AI	Zero	Zero	No	$\tau_1 = \tau_2 = 0$	−2.91%	$\tau_1 = \tau_2 = 0$	−1.20%
AI	Zero	AI	No	$\tau_1 = \tau_2 = 73\%$	—	$\tau_1 = \tau_2 = 84\%$	—
AI	Zero	AD	No	$\tau_1 = 51\%$ $\tau_2 = 82\%$	0.4%	$\tau_1 = 56\%$ $\tau_2 = 96\%$	0.1%
AI	Zero	Zero	Yes	$\tau_1 = \tau_2 = 0$	1.11%	$\tau_1 = \tau_2 = 0$	2.9%
AI	Zero	AI	Yes	$\tau_1 = \tau_2 = 81\%$	2.48%	$\tau_1 = \tau_2 = 89\%$	3.64%
AI	Zero	AD	Yes	$\tau_1 = 5\%$ $\tau_2 = 91\%$	2.55%	$\tau_1 = 11\%$ $\tau_2 = 97\%$	3.67%

the relative merits of taxing private savings according to a TTE (taxed, taxed, exempt) scheme or an EET (exempt, exempt, taxed) scheme.[31] Regarding the first issue, the solution to the government's problem was considered, with and without pensions, under various assumptions regarding the tax treatment of interest income: no taxation, AI proportional taxation, and AD proportional taxation. The results indicate that the only cases where there would be some nonnegligible welfare gains in moving from an AI interest income tax to an AD interest income tax are when the nonlinear labor income tax is AI and debt policy is unavailable (see table 3.5). In these cases, under a utilitarian social welfare function, the welfare gains of moving from an AI interest income tax to an AD interest income tax are about 0.4 percent when pensions are not provided and about 0.7 percent when pensions are optimally chosen. Under a max-min social welfare function, the corresponding figures are 0.1 percent and 0.3 percent. In each of these cases, an optimal AD interest income tax would require a higher tax rate on the savings of middle-aged workers.

Regarding the second issue (i.e., the relative merits of taxing private savings according to a TTE scheme or an EET scheme), the first thing to notice is that throughout the analysis the informational assumption that savings transactions could only be observed anonymously, not at an individual level, was maintained, thus preventing the tax authority from nonlinearly taxing the returns on savings.[32] Consistent with this informational assumption, the analysis only considered tax schemes of the TTE type. However, if one assumes that private savings are publicly observable at an individual level, another possibility is to tax them according to a consumption-type EET scheme.[33] The question then arises whether, being informationally more demanding, an EET scheme welfare dominates a TTE scheme. To answer this question, the solution to the government's problem was also computed assuming that private savings are publicly observable and subject to an EET scheme where they are taxed at the consumption stage, together with the earned interest, according to an optimally chosen proportional tax rate.

The results show that in the absence of public pensions, the EET scheme is better than the TTE scheme either when the nonlinear labor income tax is AI and the social welfare function is utilitarian or when the nonlinear labor income tax is AD. Instead, a TTE scheme welfare-dominates an EET scheme either when the government uses public pensions as a supplementary policy tool or when, in the absence of public pensions, the nonlinear labor income tax is AI and the social welfare function is max-min.

3.7 Conclusions

Using an OLG model with skill uncertainty and private savings, this chapter investigated whether an optimally designed set of public pension transfers can usefully supplement a nonlinear labor income tax as a welfare-enhancing policy instrument in a Mirrleesian setting where agents' skills are private information. The chapter highlighted that even though pensions, by crowding out private savings, adversely affect achievement of the golden rule, they can be used as a mimicking-deterring device that makes it easier for the government to achieve the desired redistributive goals. It also emphasized that the welfare effects of pensions depend, in general, on the assumptions made about the possibility for agents to borrow against their future pension entitlements. When agents are free to borrow against their future pension entitlements, public pensions can be used as an instrument to (almost) replicate the optimal allocation that would have been implemented had the labor income tax schedule been allowed to be history dependent. When instead agents cannot borrow against their future pension entitlements, this might no longer be the case, but, on the other hand, an optimally designed set of pension transfers can relax some IC constraints that could not have been affected if agents were unrestricted in borrowing against their future pension entitlements. In particular, the pension system can be designed to relax those binding IC constraints where mimickers plan to save less for retirement than the agents they plan to mimic.

To shed light on the potential magnitude of the welfare gains arising from using public pensions as an additional policy tool, and assuming that agents cannot borrow against their future pension transfers, numerical simulations based on US data were conducted.

The results confirm that if the government faces no constraints on the management of debt policy, using pensions as a policy instrument implies that the welfare gains that could be achieved by moving from an optimal AI nonlinear labor income tax to an optimal AD income tax are virtually nil. If instead the government has no access to debt policy, significant welfare gains would still remain in moving from an AI labor income tax to an AD one, even when pensions are used as an additional policy instrument. Depending on the social welfare function being maximized, the welfare gains arising from supplementing a nonlinear labor income tax with an optimal set of pension transfers range between 2.5 percent and 6 percent in the case of a nonlinear AI labor income tax and between 4 percent and 5 percent in the case of a nonlinear AD labor income tax.

To conclude, some of the many limitations of the analysis should be emphasized. Apart from considering only a very limited number of types in the numerical simulations, attention was restricted to steady-state equilibria, and the possibility for agents to decide when to retire based on the incentives created by the pension system was neglected.[34] It was assumed that the government can commit to its future tax and pension policy. Moreover, it was assumed that all agents are fully rational. However, myopia is often regarded as a standard justification for public pension systems and might also influence the effectiveness of public pensions as a mimicking-deterring device, especially if the degree of myopia is heterogeneous across agents.[35] Finally, it was implicitly assumed that agents cannot misreport their true earned income to the tax authority; if misreporting were possible, the scope for using pension transfers as a mimicking-deterring device would be weakened.

Notes

We thank Pierre Pestieau for a helpful discussion and Robert Holzmann for insightful comments.

1. As an illustrative example, consider the case where there is an agent of skill type j who plans to earn at period t the same pretax income intended by the government for a different type (who can be different either because he is of skill type $i \neq j$ at period t or because he has a different history of past earned incomes) to get the same tax treatment. Under a history-independent income tax, if the two agents earn at period t the same pretax income, they will also pay the same income tax. Under a history-dependent tax,

instead, for the tax liability at period t to be the same, it is not enough that the two agents earn the same income. It must also be the case that their past record of earned incomes is the same. This stricter requirement can be exploited by the government to make mimicking less appealing.

2. The desirability of using history-dependent income taxes is at the heart of the so-called new dynamic public finance literature. See, for example, Golosov, Tsyvinski, and Werning (2006), Kocherlakota (2010), and Golosov and Tsyvinski (2015).

3. Akerlof (1978) is the seminal contribution exploring the idea of using observable, and hard to manipulate, individual characteristics as "tags" to lower the efficiency costs of redistributive programs. Subsequent contributions on tagging and income taxation include Boskin and Sheshinski (1983), Immonen et al. (1998), Cremer, Gahvari, and Lozachmeur (2010), Mankiw and Weinzierl (2010), Bastani (2013), and Kanbur and Tuomala (2016). Blomquist and Micheletto (2008) provided the first analysis considering tagging by age in the context of a Mirrleesian setting. The idea of age-dependent taxation is described in Banks and Diamond (2010) as one of the most promising avenues for improving the tax system. Recent contributions by Farhi and Werning (2013) and Weinzierl (2011) seem to suggest that age-dependent taxes can capture a substantial share of the total welfare gains achievable through more sophisticated fully history-dependent tax schemes.

4. As Diamond (2009) stated, "Apart from some simulation studies, theoretical studies of optimal tax design typically contain neither a mandatory pension system nor the behavioral dimensions that lie behind justifications commonly offered for mandatory pensions. Conversely, optimizing models of pension design typically do not include annual taxation of labor and capital incomes."

5. Linearity of interest income taxation is usually justified based on the assumption that savings transactions can only be observed anonymously, not at an individual level, preventing the tax authority from taxing the returns on savings nonlinearly. Notice that this informational assumption would also represent a hindrance to any attempt by the government to implement an AD interest income tax. Thus, allowing for the possibility of AD interest income taxation requires relaxing the assumption that savings can only be observed anonymously.

6. Given that it is assumed that the social security contribution rate is proportional and AI, and that the labor income tax is nonlinear, it does not matter whether or not one assumes that social security contributions are subtracted from the base of the nonlinear labor income tax.

7. This is equivalent to maximizing the discounted sum of the expected lifetime utilities of all agents of all subsequent generations.

8. Under an AD tax, an individual cannot choose an income point intended for an agent belonging to a different age group.

9. This implies that under an optimal AD nonlinear tax the economy reaches a steady state where the golden-rule capital to labor ratio is achieved even if debt policy is unavailable. Notice that under an AD nonlinear tax one can always marginally change the after-tax labor incomes of the young, and at the same time adjust the after-tax labor incomes of the middle-aged, in such a way that the present-value lifetime tax payment of all agents is left unaffected, all young agents change their savings by the same amount, the public budget is kept balanced, and all the IC constraints continue to be satisfied if they were initially satisfied (see appendix A.2 in Bastani, Blomquist, and Micheletto 2013). For instance, marginally increasing all the after-tax labor incomes assigned to the

various young workers b_i and decreasing by $1+r(1-\tau_1)$ all the after-tax labor incomes b_{ij} assigned to the various middle-aged workers would not affect the IC constraints faced by the government (since under an AD tax middle-aged workers are prevented from choosing a bundle on the income tax schedule for the young), but it would imply that all young workers respond by marginally raising their savings in the first period to keep consuming the same amount of material goods and leisure in all periods and possible states of the world. In this sense, one can claim that the absolute level of private savings does not matter for self-selection purposes; savings can be controlled (by a proper choice of the labor income taxes when young and when middle-aged) with the sole purpose of achieving the golden-rule capital stock and without interfering with the redistributive goals of the government. Instead, under an optimal AI tax, the economy does not necessarily reach a steady state where the golden rule is satisfied. Whether it does depends crucially on the assumptions about debt policy. If debt policy is fully unrestricted, it can be used by the government to achieve the golden rule, while the tax policy can be chosen with the sole purpose of fulfilling the intragenerational redistributional objectives. However, if there are restrictions on the use of debt policy, the tax instruments are burdened with the pursuit of two objectives, achieving the golden rule and redistributing among agents of a given cohort, which are not necessarily coherent. For instance, there is no guarantee that trying to boost private savings by marginally increasing all the after-tax labor incomes assigned to the various young workers b_i and decreasing by $1+r(1-\tau_1)$ all the after-tax labor incomes b_{ij} assigned to the various middle-aged workers would not violate the IC constraints faced by the government (since under an AI tax middle-aged workers can choose a bundle on the single income tax schedule).

10. This is true both when the underlying nonlinear labor income tax is AI and when it is AD. In particular, when pension transfers are provided to retired agents, it is no longer true that an AD tax can always achieve the golden-rule level of capital accumulation without interfering with the redistributive goals of the government, at least if one assumes that all the elements in the set $\{b_{ij}\}$ are constrained to be nonnegative (which is equivalent to assuming that the average tax rate on the labor income earned by a middle-aged agent cannot exceed 100 percent). If pension transfers are sufficiently generous, the savings by middle-aged workers will eventually become nil. At that point, the only source of private savings will be savings made by the young for the purpose of supplementing their after-tax labor income when middle-aged. By reallocating the income tax burden from young workers to middle-aged ones (lowering the after-tax labor income of the middle-aged and raising it for the young), the government can provide a boost to private savings, but this effect might not be strong enough to allow the economy to reach the golden rule in the steady state. Savings by the young can be boosted, without affecting the IC constraints faced by the government, by marginally increasing all the after-tax labor incomes assigned to the various young workers b_i and decreasing by $1+r(1-\tau_1)$ all the after-tax labor incomes b_{ij} assigned to the various middle-aged workers, but such a savings-increasing intertemporal reshuffling of the income tax burden can be replicated, without affecting the IC constraints faced by the government, only until a point is reached where one of the elements in the set $\{b_{ij}\}$ becomes equal to zero. Once this happens, and under a constraint that all the elements in the set $\{b_{ij}\}$ must be nonnnegative, the element that has reached the lower bound cannot be adjusted further downward, and then there is no guarantee that a further reshuffling of the tax burden from the young to the middle-aged will not violate one of the IC constraints faced by the government.

11. This is done to focus attention on the effects of pensions on the IC constraints faced by the government.

12. In accordance with the notation introduced in section 3.3, the income point (y_{11}, b_{11}) denotes the bundle intended for a middle-aged agent who was of type 1 when young and who experienced an unfavorable skill shock in the second period. The income point (y_{12}, b_{12}) denotes the bundle intended for a middle-aged agent who was of type 1 when young and who experienced a favorable skill shock in the second period.

13. The mimicking-deterring effect would obviously be even stronger if one were to remove the constraint that $P(y_i, y_{ij}) \geq 0$ so that $P(y_2, y_{11})$ and $P(y_2, y_{12})$ could take large negative values.

14. With an unrestricted debt policy at one's disposal, and if one did not impose the restriction that $P(y_i, y_{ij}) \geq 0$, an optimally designed set of pension transfers would enable the government, under both an AI labor income tax and an AD labor income tax, to perfectly replicate the allocation that, absent a pension system, would have been implemented by a history-dependent labor income tax system. That is because without the restriction $P(y_i, y_{ij}) \geq 0$ there would be no limit to the punishment that could be inflicted on an agent who planned to adopt a deviating strategy that does not perfectly match the lifetime labor income profile of a nondeviating agent. With $P(y_i, y_{ij}) \geq 0$ there is instead an implicit upper bound on the penalty. In this case, the allocation implemented by supplementing the nonlinear labor income tax with public pensions might not perfectly replicate the one that could be achieved using an unconstrained history-dependent tax function.

15. The welfare gain by moving from an optimally designed AI labor income tax to an optimally designed AD tax would be nil if one were to remove the restriction that $P(y_i, y_{ij}) \geq 0$. With the constraint $P(y_i, y_{ij}) \geq 0$ in place, there might still be (some small) welfare gains in moving from an AI labor income tax to an AD tax.

16. Reconsidering the example sketched here, once a type 1 nondeviating agent becomes borrowing constrained in the second period, one can no longer keep raising $P(y_1, y_{11})$ and $P(y_1, y_{12})$ while at the same time lowering b_{11} and b_{12} in a way that is welfare-neutral for the agent.

17. Moreover, if one did not impose the restriction that $P(y_i, y_{ij}) \geq 0$, the government would have another instrument for imposing an indefinitely large penalty on the mimicker without affecting the utility of nondeviating agents. Thus, without the restriction that $P(y_i, y_{ij}) \geq 0$, it would still be true, even when agents have limited or no ability to borrow against future pension entitlements, that the government could implement the allocation that, absent a pension system, would have been achieved by a history-dependent labor income tax system.

18. If instead, at the optimum without pensions, a type 2 mimicker would like to save more when middle-aged (for retirement) than a type 1 agent, pension transfers could not be used as an instrument to alleviate this IC constraint.

19. Starting from an initial equilibrium without pensions and where the nonlinear income tax is optimally chosen, this can be done by implementing the following reform. Keep y_{11} and y_{12} fixed at the prereform value and lower b_{11} and b_{12} by, respectively, $-c_{11}^R/[1+r(1-\tau_2)]<0$ and $-c_{12}^R/[1+r(1-\tau_2)]<0$, where c_{11}^R and c_{12}^R denote consumption during retirement, at the income tax optimum without pensions, of, respectively, a type 1 agent who was hit by an unfavorable skill shock when middle-aged and a type 1 agent who was hit by a favorable skill shock when middle-aged. At the same time, introduce pension transfers $P(y_1, y_{11}) = c_{11}^R$ and $P(y_1, y_{12}) = c_{12}^R$. Clearly, the expected well-being of a

young type 1 agent who does not plan to enact a deviating strategy would be unaffected by the reform (the agent would no longer save when middle-aged but would continue to work and consume in all periods and states of the world as in the prereform equilibrium). But suppose that at the prereform equilibrium with no pensions a type 2 mimicker, when choosing in the second period either the point (y_{11}, b_{11}) or the point (y_{12}, b_{12}), was saving less for retirement than the corresponding nondeviating agent choosing the same income point. Under the assumption that agents are not free to borrow against their future pension entitlements, the reform would make the mimicker worse off by preventing him from achieving his preferred intertemporal consumption profile.

20. This seems the most realistic case to consider. Moreover, the assumption that $P(y_i, y_{ij}) \geq 0$ is maintained.

21. That is, in both the first and second periods, each individual's percentile position in the wage distribution is calculated. How individuals move between percentiles in the wage distribution over time can then be seen.

22. In the first case, the government maximizes the sum of the lifetime expected utilities of the three different types of young agents; in the second case, the government maximizes the expected lifetime utility of the least-skilled young agents.

23. In tables 3.3 and 3.4, the column "Pension transfers" P_{i1} with $i=1, 2, 3$ denotes the pension paid to an agent who was of skill type i when young and who experienced an unfavorable skill shock when middle-aged. P_{i2} with $i=1, 2, 3$ denotes instead the pension paid to an agent who was of skill type i when young and who experienced a favorable skill shock when middle-aged. The implicit rates of return are calculated based on the equilibrium value of the contribution rate α. For a given labor-earning trajectory and corresponding pension entitlement, the implicit rate of return (IRR) was calculated by solving the equation

$\alpha\,[y_i\,(1+IRR)^2 + y_{ij}\,(1+IRR)] = P(y_i, y_{ij})$.

24. The share of consumption during retirement that is financed through public pensions ranges from a minimum of 0.5 percent (for type 3 agents who experienced an unfavorable skill shock when middle-aged) to a maximum of 45.9 percent (for type 1 agents who experienced a favorable skill shock when middle-aged).

25. Under the golden-rule condition, the equilibrium interest rate is equal to the population growth rate, which in this setting is about 24 percent. In the benchmark AI system without pensions and with no public debt, the equilibrium interest rate is 63 percent. With an optimally chosen set of pension transfers, the equilibrium interest rate is raised to 79 percent and the capital to labor ratio falls from 30 percent to 25 percent.

26. Under the golden rule, the capital to labor ratio is 47.48 percent.

27. The maximum share of consumption during retirement financed through public pensions increases to 92 percent (for type 2 agents who experienced a favorable skill shock when middle-aged).

28. As discussed in section 3.4, this result, which Bastani, Blomquist, and Micheletto (2013) showed generally holds in a setting without pensions, does not necessarily generalize to the case where pensions are used as an additional policy tool. However, at least for the case of a utilitarian social welfare function, the simulations show that even when optimally choosing pensions and having no access to public debt policy, a nonlinear AD labor income tax enables the government to move the economy to the golden rule.

29. The equilibrium contribution rate is 10.52 percent, and the maximum share of consumption during retirement financed through public pensions increases to 100 percent (for type 2 agents who experienced a favorable skill shock). The implicit rates of return on social security contributions are always larger for agents who experienced a favorable skill shock when middle-aged.

30. The equilibrium interest rate is 27.1 percent, slightly higher than that prevailing under the golden rule (24.46 percent).

31. A TTE scheme involves saving out of taxed income (T), taxing on an accrual basis the fund's investment return (T), and tax-free withdrawal of pension benefits (E). Under an EET scheme, savings are deductible against the labor income tax (E) and are then taxed (T), together with the interest earned, in the period when the funds are used for consumption purposes.

32. This assumption is relaxed when considering the possibility for the government to implement an AD interest income tax.

33. One should also note that when private savings are publicly observable at an individual level, the government could do better than using the available information to implement an EET scheme. It could implement a nonlinear AD tax function that depends, in a nonseparable way, on both labor income and interest income.

34. For an optimal tax model where the age of retirement is a choice variable for agents (but where for each agent the labor supply is constant across periods during the working years), see Cremer, Lozachmeur, and Pestieau (2004). See also the discussion contained in Cremer and Pestieau (2016).

35. Myopia as a rationale for the existence of social security systems has been widely analyzed in the literature. See, among many contributions, Feldstein (1985), Tenhunen and Tuomala (2010), Andersen and Bhattacharya (2011), and Cremer and Pestieau (2011).

References

Akerlof, George A. 1978. "The Economics of Tagging as Applied to the Optimal Income Tax, Welfare Programs, and Manpower Planning." *American Economic Review* 68:8–19.

Andersen, Torben, and Joydeep Bhattacharya. 2011. "On Myopia as Rationale for Social Security." *Economic Theory* 47 (1): 135–158.

Banks, James, and Peter Diamond. 2010. "The Base for Direct Taxation." In *Dimensions of Tax Design: The Mirrlees Review*, edited by The Institute for Fiscal Studies, 548–648. Oxford: Oxford University Press for The Institute for Fiscal Studies (Oxford).

Bastani, Spencer. 2013. "Gender-Based and Couple-Based Taxation." *International Tax and Public Finance* 20 (4): 653–686.

Bastani, Spencer, Sören Blomquist, and Luca Micheletto. 2013. "The Welfare Gains of Age-Related Optimal Income Taxation." *International Economic Review* 54:1219–1249.

Blomquist, Sören, and Luca Micheletto. 2008. "Age-Related Optimal Income Taxation." *Scandinavian Journal of Economics* 110:45–71.

Boskin, Michael J., and Eytan Sheshinski. 1983. "Optimal Tax Treatment of the Family: Married Couples." *Journal of Public Economics* 20:281–297.

Choné, Philippe, and Guy Laroque. 2014. "Income Taxes and Retirement Schemes." CREST Working Paper No. 2014-07, CREST, Paris.

Cremer, Helmuth, Firouz Gahvari, and Jean-Marie Lozachmeur. 2010. "Tagging and Income Taxation: Theory and an Application." *American Economic Journal: Economic Policy* 2:31–50.

Cremer, Helmuth, Jean-Marie Lozachmeur, and Pierre Pestieau. 2004. "Social Security, Retirement Age and Optimal Income Taxation." *Journal of Public Economics* 88 (11): 2259–2281.

Cremer, Helmuth, and Pierre Pestieau. 2011. "Myopia, Redistribution and Pensions." *European Economic Review* 55 (2): 165–175.

Cremer, Helmuth, and Pierre Pestieau. 2016. "Theoretical Foundations of the Taxation of Pensions." CESifo Working Paper No. 5930, May, CESifo, Munich.

Diamond, Peter A. 2009. "Taxes and Pensions." *Southern Economic Journal* 76 (1): 2–15.

Diamond, Peter, and Emmanuel Saez. 2011. "The Case for a Progressive Tax: From Basic Research to Policy Recommendations." *Journal of Economic Perspectives* 25:165–190.

Farhi, Emmanuel, and Ivan Werning. 2013. "Insurance and Taxation over the Life Cycle." *Review of Economic Studies* 80:596–635.

Feldstein, Martin 1985. "The Optimal Level of Social Security Benefits." *Quarterly Journal of Economics* 100:303–320.

Golosov, Mikhail, and Aleh Tsyvinski. 2015. "Policy Implications of Dynamic Public Finance." *Annual Review of Economics* 7:147–171.

Golosov, Mikhail, Aleh Tsyvinski, and Ivan Werning. 2006. "New Dynamic Public Finance: A User's Guide." In *NBER Macroeconomics Annual 2006*, edited by Daron Acemoglu, Kenneth Rogoff, and Michael Woodford, 317–387. Cambridge, MA: MIT Press.

Immonen, Ritva, Ravi Kanbur, Michael Keen, and Matti Tuomala. 1998. "Tagging and Taxing: The Use of Categorical and Income Information in Designing Tax/Transfer Schemes." *Economica* 65:179–192.

Kanbur, Ravi, and Matti Tuomala. 2016. "Groupings and the Gains from Tagging." *Research in Economics* 70:53–63.

Kocherlakota, Narayana. 2010. *The New Dynamic Public Finance*. Princeton, NJ: Princeton University Press.

Mankiw, N. Gregory, and Matthew Weinzierl. 2010. "The Optimal Taxation of Height: A Case Study of Utilitarian Income Redistribution." *American Economic Journal: Economic Policy* 2:155–176.

Shourideh, Ali, and Maxim Troshkin. 2017. "Incentives and Efficiency of Pension Systems." Working Paper, Cornell University, Ithaca, NY.

Tenhunen, Sanna, and Matti Tuomala. 2010. "On Optimal Lifetime Redistribution Policy." *Journal of Public Economic Theory* 12:171–198.

Weinzierl, Matthew. 2011. "The Surprising Power of Age-Dependent Taxes." *Review of Economic Studies* 78:1490–1518.

4 Taxation and Pensions: An Overview of Interplay

Csaba Feher and Alain Jousten

4.1 Introduction

Public pensions reallocate income across periods, individuals, and generations. Taxation permits the state to pool resources for the sake of scale economies, to address market failures, to create the regulatory and infrastructural foundations of economic activity, and also to redistribute consumption capacity. The state's objectives for intragenerational and intergenerational redistribution, as well as consumption smoothing along individuals' life cycles, can be served by both of these policy areas.[1] The following question naturally arises: can tax policy be expected to impact—either advance or hinder—the realization of pension policies' objectives and vice versa?

Tax policy influences people's old-age income in two genuinely different ways. Tax regimes can have a direct impact on the absolute and relative sizes of benefits through the effect they have on contribution-liable income, net returns, and net pension benefits. At the same time, taxes may have an indirect, behavioral effect by providing incentives or disincentives to participation, compliance, and under- or overinsurance relative to adequate or optimal old-age income levels.

Pension policy may also play a role in tax policy. Among wage taxes and social insurance contributions, pension contributions are special in that only they create exclusively long-term individual entitlements.[2] Thus, the observance of pension promises by the state, or lack thereof, is one of the indicators through which taxpayers subjectively assess whether the state is a credible partner to the social contract as collector of taxes and distributor of benefits, goods, and services. Tax and social security contribution liabilities are typically established on the basis of the same sets of accounting records. Therefore, compliance with the two sets of rules goes hand in hand, be it explicit (by means of common bases and joint collection) or implicit (through mutually beneficial measures to tackle evasion and fraud). This has another important implication for the labor market and the extent of informality: pension contributions and the returns on these contributions as implied by benefit promises are an integral part of the (dis)incentives to formalize labor relations and to comply with income-reporting regulations. Thus, the design and parameters of public pension systems may impact the formal labor supply, depending on their perceived actuarial characteristics: negative implicit returns on pension contributions and the lack of perceived credibility of future pension promises (e.g., inflation risk, pension reform risk) decrease incentives for formalization.

Another important relationship between pension policy and tax policy arises when a state's capacity to levy and collect taxes and contributions is hampered. Pension reforms mostly—although not exclusively—enter the policy agenda because of an imminent or expected future revenue shortfall relative to liabilities already accrued or expected to arise in the future. The capacity to fulfill pension promises is—except for extreme cases of major economic or political crises—relative and depends on a government's priorities regarding possible reductions of pensions versus other public expenditures, generating additional revenues, and how far a government's policy horizon stretches beyond its mandate. Notably, the discrepancy between the growth of benefit liabilities and the capacity to collect commensurate revenues may emerge not only as a result of steeper than expected expenditure dynamics. In many cases, such as in numerous European transition economies, it was the steep and persistent decline in tax collection capacity that forced states to consider parametric—and often structural—pension reforms.

This chapter provides an overview of the factors that may influence the interplay of pension and tax policies in both directions and identifies areas where a material impact can be expected. Section 4.2 reviews the conceptual links between pension policy and tax policy, while section 4.3 discusses the taxation of pensions. Section 4.4 raises the issue of whether pension benefits should be taxed differently from other income. The chapter closes with conclusions in section 4.5.

4.2 The Relationship between Pension Policy and Income Tax Policy

The conceptual links between public pensions and income tax policy are well established, as both represent tools for reallocating resources among individuals, thereby altering income distributions as well as intertemporal consumption patterns. Cremer and Pestieau (2016, chapter 2, this volume) even claim that the differentiation between tax payments and public pension transfers is irrelevant from the perspective of optimal policy design, arguing that only net lifetime income matters to individuals. Such results clearly have to be read with caution, as the strong underlying assumptions of the theoretical framework are unlikely to be met by real-world conditions. These assumptions include a perfect overlap of taxpayer and pensioner populations, the absence of work disincentives, intertemporal stability of tax regimes, homogeneous time preferences of consumption among individuals, and a lack of bequest motives, among others. The differences between theoretical models and the real-life impact of tax and pension policies notwithstanding, the basic conclusion remains valid: both taxes and public pensions are transfers and should not be seen as completely separate from each other in the policy-making process. Indeed, tax and benefit policies should be viewed as components of an overarching welfare strategy in terms of design, effectiveness, and efficiency, as pointed out by various authors, including those of the seminal Mirrlees Review. This section presents a brief review of the objectives and constraints of pension and tax policies as well as some aspects of their interaction.

4.2.1 Basic Features of Pension Policy: Consumption Smoothing and Redistribution

What are the reasons for mandating or at least promoting participation in pension schemes? Two key motivations stand out. First, pensions provide a means of consumption smoothing (and insurance) to life cycle consumers faced with the uncertain time of death (Yaari 1965)—at least insofar as these pensions are paid out as annuities and not as lump sums. This motivation clearly highlights the importance of distinguishing pensions from mandatory savings products with lump-sum payouts or phased withdrawals, since lifelong consumption smoothing can only be realized by annuities, as shown by Jousten (2001). Second, public pensions are typically designed to redistribute income among individuals to protect people with insufficient pension savings and entitlements against old-age poverty. Different motivations for redistribution translate into different social preference specifications (Vickrey 1945; Harsanyi 1955; Rawls 1971) and system designs. However, they all share a common overarching theme in an intragenerational setting: that the observed distribution of skills and/or resource endowments should be seen not as accruing strictly to individuals but rather as collective claims that can be redistributed according to a society's underlying values.

This also holds for systems that moved toward defined contribution arrangements, as such schemes (1) typically introduce life cycle redistribution in the form of annuities and, occasionally, rate-of-return guarantees (both of which imply intentional redistribution) and (2) are usually augmented by explicitly redistributive schemes (e.g., basic pensions, downsized defined benefit social insurance schemes, social assistance for the elderly). Thus, "funded reforms" do not imply eliminating redistribution; instead, they may reduce redistribution and may also segregate the policy objectives of ensuring horizontal and vertical equity into clearly differentiated rules and institutions.

Intergenerational redistribution is also an integral part of public pension systems, as demonstrated by Samuelson (1975). The strong intergenerational link between contributors and pensioners is most obvious in a pay-as-you-go (PAYG) system, but the use of the accrued savings (of current retirees) by the current young in a fully funded system also establishes such a link, although through more indirect channels. Old-age poverty prevention can also be linked to such redistributive aims, ensuring at least a minimum income for the elderly, whose earning capacity and ability to absorb financial shocks are severely limited. Poverty prevention among the elderly is not strictly limited to redistribution within the pension system. It can also increase or limit reliance (both in terms of uptake and benefit levels) on other social assistance and insurance schemes.[3]

Pension regulations have also proved useful in addressing labor market tensions by allowing labor supply to be adjusted to changing demand.[4] As Gruber and Wise (1999, 2004) have documented for various countries, many public pension systems provide strong incentives for retirement at an age that is well below the normal retirement age. Also, early- retirement rules as a means of freeing up jobs for young workers have long played an important role in the retirement policy debate. In this respect, however, it should be noted that both theoretical and empirical studies—including Gruber and Wise (2010)—provide extensive evidence that labor demand is generically not a fixed quantity, and the substitution of young workers for old ones only holds over short horizons or under special circumstances. In addition to old-age pensions, the uptake of disability pensions responds to labor market conditions, too, indicating that this segment of public pension systems can also function as a safety valve, relieving labor market pressures.

In addition to insuring against longevity risk, Diamond and Mirrlees (1978) pointed out social security's capacity to insure against the uncertainty of the length of working life. Separate schemes (e.g., sickness, disability, workplace accident insurance) may exist for dealing with these concerns, but the model mentioned here shows the inseparable nature of pensions and other social protection schemes (see also Diamond and Sheshinski 1995). At a more general level, Gruber and Wise (1999, 2004) documented the strong interlinks between social insurance programs that translate into some nonpension programs effectively serving as retirement routes (e.g., unemployment insurance in Belgium and France and disability insurance historically in the Netherlands) and retirement incentives dominated by nonpension rules (e.g., labor market exits well before the early entitlement age applicable to pensions).

Finally, it is important to point out that pension policy is constrained by the availability of resources, including the extent to which intra- and intergenerational distributional characteristics can be maintained. In practice, this means that when overall budgetary and/or demographic challenges put pressures on the revenue side of the pension system, the system's average generosity and degree of redistribution can be severely affected. This, in turn, may impact incentives for coverage, compliance, overall labor market formality, and labor mobility as well as the financial viability of the system.

Ultimately, the relative weight of the consumption smoothing and poverty alleviation objectives, as well as the prevailing budgetary and legal constraints, translate into specific choices in terms of key pension system parameters, including PAYG financing versus full prefunding, contribution versus general revenue financing, benefit origination and risk sharing according to defined benefit versus defined contribution paradigms, universal versus segregated rule sets, compulsory versus voluntary participation, and worker benefits only versus extended survivor and/or spousal benefits.

4.2.2 Basic Features of Tax Policy: Optimal Revenue Generation and Redistribution

What are the reasons for having taxes? The first is to generate sufficient revenues to finance the functioning of the state and all its subdivisions. A second objective is to generate this revenue at minimal explicit and implicit economic costs, be they under the form of behavioral distortions or administrative and compliance costs. A third objective—particularly present in the income tax literature—is to affect the distribution of income among individuals along the same principles already discussed for pensions. In this setting, one of the primary roles of tax policy is to devise the best possible tax structure to collect a given amount of revenue in a socially acceptable way. One of the key differences between the literature on optimal taxation—and also on tax policy—and the pension literature is that it is predominantly focused on static settings, often relying on the calendar year as a time frame rather than the entire life cycle. In his seminal paper on optimal income taxation, Mirrlees (1971) introduced this simplification. Diamond (2009) convincingly argued that the complexity of real-world environments is such that it is perfectly acceptable to approach static issues separately from dynamic considerations insofar as analysts are aware of the limitations of their own models and conscious of others' contributions in reaching an overall policy conclusion.

What are the main messages on income taxation from the tax policy literature? Two key messages of the classical optimal tax literature—and of relevance to the pension sphere—stand out: first, tax systems should respect horizontal and vertical equity concerns; and second, there should be no taxation of capital income (and, consequently, earnings on pension savings, where applicable). A classical reference is by Atkinson and Stiglitz (1976), who showed that in a world of "first best" with full information on capital income and savings, no room exists for differential intertemporal consumption taxation and hence no scope for taxes on savings and capital. Chamley (1986) and Judd (1985) further proved the optimality of no taxation on savings in an infinite horizon model. Diamond (2009) argued that these (and other) classical optimal tax results have to be nuanced in the real world, as some of the underlying assumptions are not satisfied. For example, taxing savings might be (second-best) optimal in a world where savings are not distributed equally across the population. In such cases, taxing savings might contribute to an increase in social welfare through redistribution even if this occurs at an efficiency cost in terms of capital accumulation.

Diamond (2009) and Slemrod and Gillitzer (2014) also argued that inflation and other real-world limitations might play an important role in outlining a second-best optimal tax system. For example, the imperfect inflation indexing of tax systems, administrative and compliance costs, and enforcement considerations are important ingredients that impact the design of an optimal tax system in a second-best sense. Expressed differently, tax policy formulation that is excessively based on a current (and often annual) income basis and that relies on the basic optimal tax results might be far off the mark in terms of maximizing social well-being. There might be substantial room for other tax structures on a current income basis as well as reasons to go beyond current income when determining optimal tax structures. With strongly progressive tax systems on an annual basis, more erratic earnings patterns are treated less favorably than more steady ones—keeping lifetime earnings constant.[5] Similarly, periods of formal education or temporary absences from the labor market affect the length of the working period and hence influence the number of taxable periods and the progressivity within each one of them (again keeping lifetime income constant).

4.2.3 The Relationship between Pension and Tax Policy: From Common Goals to Contradictions

As discussed at the beginning of this section, pensions and (income) taxes are intrinsically linked—up to a point where they are viewed as perfectly equivalent in some highly abstract situations. Nonetheless, or maybe precisely because of these differences between theory and practice, understanding the interactions between these fields is of prime importance. As the first step, it is useful to expand the discussion of Diamond (2009) on the key dimensions in which taxes and pensions differ.

Income taxes are generally levied on income of a recent period, often the current or the preceding year. Financial incentives are straightforward to understand, even for myopic individuals, as they concern current events. Tax rates and all other tax system attributes are generally set in an age-independent way for each taxable period. Tax systems are also often based on a distinction between residence and source countries, with residence countries generally retaining the residual taxing power. Interactions (and conflicts) between national tax systems are typically addressed through bilateral tax treaties.[6] Tax systems often rely on individual or household-level taxation—with the relevant household unit being the fiscal household. Furthermore, taxes are always compulsory and are levied on behalf of the state.

In contrast to taxes, pensions are generally based on a much longer reference period, often several decades (possibly the individual's entire residence, earnings, and insurance history), and benefits generally depend on age (e.g., in terms of benefit entitlement and benefit generosity). Financial incentives generated by pension systems are difficult to understand, as they involve a substantial degree of forward-looking perspective and analysis under very high degrees of uncertainty concerning future governments' policy stances as well as the stability and credibility of current policies. In addition to age, date of birth ("calendar effect") is an important criterion—particularly in times of increasing or decreasing generosity.

In terms of jurisdiction, social and basic pensions are largely residence based, whereas contributory social insurance pensions are mostly source (or country-of-work) based[7] and treated as an earned right, enjoying high levels of legal protection. Interactions between national pension systems are mostly dealt with in bilateral treaties, but with a substantially smaller treaty network than for taxes.[8,9] In most social insurance pension systems, the relevant contributory unit is an individual, whereas the relevant beneficiary unit can be either the individual or a household—though the latter notion is generally defined in a different way than the one used for tax purposes. Other social insurance programs that sometimes play the role of pensions (e.g., disability, workplace accident, and formal early-retirement schemes) often rely on yet another set of conditions to determine financing, eligibility and generosity, applicable legislation, and the specific nature of beneficiary units. Pensions can be compulsory or voluntary, private or public, and individuals may have a say in their pension package.

Given imperfect (and asymmetric) information and market imperfections, tax and pension systems can also benefit from each other—although in a manner difficult to incorporate into policy making. Cremer and Pestieau (2016, chapter 2, this volume) illustrated that in the presence of myopia, the timing of tax easements granted to pensions could bring individual (or household) savings decisions more closely in line with socially desirable levels. Diamond (2009) took a broader perspective and recognized the key role of voluntary pensions as tools that help bridge the gap between the relative uniformity of public tax and benefit systems and the very different person-specific needs of individuals and families, as well as surmounting fiscal limitations of public pension schemes (e.g., high public debt levels preventing system expansion) and bypassing institutional limitations (e.g., thin capital and annuity markets) by creating dedicated pension savings products.

The basic design of pension schemes also has implications on tax policy. In contributory schemes, the rate of return on these contributions—the relative generosity of pension promises—has a profound impact on both pension policy and tax policy. This effect is particularly important in contributory defined benefit schemes: if taxpayers view pension, health, and other contributions tied to well-defined benefits as incommensurably higher than the value of promised benefits, it will have an impact on compliance—and not only on contribution compliance but over the entire spectrum of wage taxes.[10] It is important to note that because of the long-term nature of pension entitlements, the subjective rate of return on pension contributions depends heavily on discount rates—which, in turn, reflects not only standard economic assumptions but also the credibility of the state. Thus, pension reforms must take into account the total impact they may have on incentives to voluntarily comply with contribution—and, by extension, income tax—rules.

Noncontributory universal benefits (such as citizens' basic pensions) raise tax policy issues, too. The role of basic ("zero pillar") pensions conditioned solely on age—and, possibly, residence—is to prevent old-age poverty. Thus, households above some income threshold may need to be excluded from receiving benefits to maintain the scheme's targeting efficiency[11] and lower its fiscal costs. This may be achieved by *ex ante* or *ex post* targeting. *Ex ante* targeting is the standard approach of means testing through proxies or direct income and asset tests. In the case of pensioners, the *ex ante* means test is often reduced, for the sake of administrative facility, to pension testing (i.e., making transfers conditional on whether the beneficiary receives any other form of pension but irrespective of other income and wealth). It is *ex post* targeting where tax policy may play a role: income tax bases and rates can be calibrated such that universal basic pensions are "clawed back" gradually, ensuring that at some predetermined threshold the net transfer becomes zero.

In addition to the capacity to improve or damage the credibility of the state to honor its long-term commitments, the reform of public pension schemes is intimately linked to tax policy through a country's fiscal stance. It is the current or projected absolute or relative insufficiency of revenues that triggers pension reforms—even in cases where the argument applied is equity. It is worth noting here that the perceived lack of equity—regardless of how fairness is conceived in a given social and historical context—eventually also translates into declining compliance and coverage and a discrepancy between expected benefits and contributions. The design and reform of public pension schemes must consider the state's capacity to tax—in terms of both the tax base and the administrative capacity to enforce compliance. While we are unaware of any such situations where a pension system was launched without sufficient resources to pay for concurrent benefits, numerous cases exist where policy makers did not take into consideration the system's

Box 4.1
Tax incidence and equity

The term "unfunded pension liability" refers to the accrued liabilities in excess of existing and expected resources (reserves plus contributions) measured over the same time horizon and scope of people as the liabilities. If the scheme is to stay solvent, the underwriter of pension entitlements behind the liabilities needs to provide extra resources. In the case of public pension schemes, the underwriter is the state and the extra resources are mostly taxes or nontax revenues, which could otherwise be applied toward other public expenditures or debt reduction. However, the incidence of these forgone expenditures does not coincide with that of pension benefits. It is this discrepancy that gives rise to intergenerational redistribution (from future to current beneficiaries) but also to intragenerational redistribution between taxpayers who are full public pension scheme members and those not covered to the same extent or not covered at all.

Two important and common cases of such redistribution are social pensions and noncontributory public sector schemes; both arrangements imply very different tax and benefit incidences. In the case of social pensions, the resulting redistribution is progressive: benefit incidence is higher in lower-income groups than tax incidence (on account of these individuals' lower income and consumption but relatively higher weight of pension benefits in their total income). At the same time, noncontributory public sector pensions typically represent regressive (perverse) redistribution, especially in low-income countries where public employees already enjoy stable and often generous wages, access to services, and other privileges not available to the majority.

What are the policy implications of these issues? First, it is important to match the incidence of financing instruments with that of benefits: earnings-related pensions should be financed from contributions as much as possible and ensure full funding to reduce the fiscal burden inherited by future generations. Second, public sector (occupational) pension schemes should rely on contributions collected from employees and the state as employer (as opposed to the state as underwriter). Third, in cases where contributions and direct taxes are—or have become—difficult to collect or where coverage is partial or declining, replacing earnings-related defined benefit schemes with universal basic or social pensions may sometimes represent a more equitable option than using general revenues to supplement contribution revenues.

future resource requirements (under a scenario of no policy change) or where the state's capacity to collect taxes collapsed. These developments can also serve as catalysts for pension reforms.

In sum, while tax and pension systems could theoretically be based on the same set of life cycle criteria to achieve a common overall social objective function taking into account a person's complete life cycle, in practice they are not. Their interaction can even lead to contradictory and inefficient outcomes. Interactions of progressive annual tax systems and public pension rules could result either in wholly undesired outcomes (e.g., by redistributing resources from the poor to the lifetime rich) or merely disputable outcomes (e.g., where the same person is taxed and subsidized at various stages across the life cycle, beyond any risk and insurance considerations), such as mentioned in Diamond (2002).

A commonly occurring policy issue is work incentives for older or low-wage workers. It is not uncommon that the implicit taxes imposed on continued work through the pension system are so large as to outweigh any work-friendly income tax treatment (Gruber and Wise 1999, 2004). Similarly, cases abound of tax rules essentially annulling pension rules.[12] In the case of Scandinavian countries, Andersen (2015, chapter 5, this volume) argued that it is the overall package of taxes and transfers that matters when judging the sustainability and feasibility of a system rather than the mere individual components (as characterized by indicators such as the marginal income tax rate). Similarly, Purcell (2015) illustrated the large potential impact of the current uncoordinated approach to pension and tax indexation rules in the United States.

However, even in strongly earnings-related systems such as the German public pension system, situations will inevitably arise of unintended taxation of some categories of pension scheme participants. In practice, the degree of taxation will depend on such things as household composition, earnings level, and caps and ceilings in the pension and contribution rules. In light of this, Börsch-Supan and Quinn (2015, chapter 8, this volume) point out that all these rules imply effective taxation of pension benefit components going beyond what is actuarially justified on the basis of contributions. De facto, such deviations from actuarial fairness create another implicit income tax system, with a different taxpayer population, different rules, operating without the benefit of tax treaties, and other differences compared to regular income tax regimes.

More strikingly, the real-world decoupling of pension and tax policies and the associated implicit tax component is further reinforced by the recent trend in numerous countries to "strengthen" the financial position of public pension schemes by means of alternative financing—usually with earmarked consumption tax revenues or other types of dedicated budgetary transfers. Insofar as such restructuring partially shifts the burden of financing pensions to a set of current and future taxpayers—including current pensioners—who may or may not benefit from the improved sustainability of the public pension scheme, these transfers introduce new and heterogeneous effective implicit taxes.

4.3 Taxation of Pensions

This section provides a brief overview of theoretical considerations in the taxation of pensions and how they are applied in practice. It also weighs the pros and cons of granting special tax treatment to pension benefits (i.e., whether pensions are special enough to enjoy the preferential tax status they receive in many countries).

4.3.1 Pension Taxation in Theory

The conceptual discussion revealed a multitude of links between tax and pension policies. In practice, the most common typology used to summarize the tax treatment of pensions is the one that reflects the three stages in a pension product's life cycle: (1) the contribution phase, (2) the capital buildup phase, where capital returns are accrued, and (3) the benefit payout phase. A label of "T" (taxation) or "E" (exemption) is attributed to each stage. The main advantage of this typology is to allow a quick classification of real-world pension systems into broad categories. For example, classical savings accounts would be classified as TTE: savings are accumulated out of taxed income, equivalent to taxing contributions (T_ _); interest is taxed as it accrues (_ T _); and withdrawals from savings accounts are not taxable (_ _ E). Despite the absence of a capital accrual phase, PAYG systems can also be described in the same schematic way. It should be noted, however, that the emergence of notional defined contribution pension schemes poses a new problem for the tax treatment of PAYG pension schemes: the notional returns credited to notional defined contribution accounts are indistinguishable from ordinary capital gains in a defined contribution scheme and could be subject to similar tax treatment. Following the same train of thought, the difference between the benefit resulting from an actuarially fair and sustainable replacement rate in a defined benefit scheme and the higher or lower benefit based on a legislated replacement rate could also be perceived as an accrued gain or loss realized during the accumulation phase and taxed accordingly.[13]

Numerous pension plans benefit from an "exemption" during the buildup phase. The favorable tax treatment of capital gains during the accrual phase is linked to the idea that pensions are deferred consumption and thus their allocation over time should not be distorted by generating tax liabilities (Atkinson and Stiglitz 1976). Most pension plans also benefit from an exemption at the contribution and/or the benefit stage, and while cases of EEE systems do indeed exist, the large majority of plans fall into the EET and TEE categories. In a world of perfect foresight, political stability, and perfect (and riskless) capital markets as well as flat taxes, EET and TEE systems can easily be shown to be equivalent: the question of front- or back-loading of tax stimuli for pensions is merely an issue of timing both for pension plan participants and for the state. As soon as one of these assumptions is relaxed, the situation becomes more intricate.

With progressive taxation, individuals might prefer an EET system, as it allows shifting taxable income to periods when income is lower (as characterized by less work), resulting in lower marginal and effective income tax rates. This trend might be further reinforced in the case of lump-sum payouts of pension benefits, which often are not subject to the usual progressive annual rate structure of taxes but rather to some (lower) rates. A lower tax burden for the individual obviously correlates with lower (and later) government revenues—at least as a result of first-round effects.

Different incentives may arise when other assumptions are relaxed. With a less credible or stable tax system, or even in a system with a perceived upward risk in terms of tax pressure, individuals might have a preference for TEE over EET.[14] The threat of future tax increases may more than compensate contributors for the difference between higher immediate taxes and lower taxes promised for future pension payments. Similarly, a government may have preferences among systems: faced with binding deficit and budget rules, governments should prefer TEE over EET to soften the per-period budget constraint.

Other considerations may matter, too. For example, Romaniuk (2013) showed that the choice between TEE and EET might have consequences for the risk-taking behavior of pension funds themselves. While EET tax treatment in a defined contribution framework is shown to bias risk taking, TEE defined contribution schemes as well as EET and TEE defined benefit schemes do not suffer from the same distortion.

4.3.2 Public Pension Taxation in Practice

The overwhelming majority of mandatory, publicly managed pension schemes are PAYG-financed defined benefit schemes, which reduces the number of theoretically possible periods of taxation from three to two: contribution and payout. In this respect, three observations need to be made before reviewing the tax treatment of public pension schemes in selected countries (table 4.1). First, contributions are typically split between employer and employee, with employer contributions often representing the larger share within total contributions. At the same time, employer contributions are accounted for not as personal (wage) income but as a deductible cost of the employer's operations. Thus, even in cases where contributions are taxed (i.e., are not deducted from the individual's income tax base), a large share of pension contributions reduces the relevant tax base. Second, in cases where pension benefits themselves are tax-exempt, they may still count toward the income tax base, increasing an individual's tax burden in the case of progressive income tax schedules.[15] Finally, in addition to pension income, pensioners often enjoy preferential tax treatment whereby their total income (not only their pension) falls under reduced tax rates.

Of those member states of the Organisation for Economic Co-operation and Development (OECD) and European Union (EU) with readily available information about the tax treatment of pensions and pensioners, the majority employ an EET regime, where benefit payments are subject to income taxation, at least in principle. This picture is misleading, however.

With a few exceptions (such as Denmark, Sweden, and Poland), practically all countries observed offer preferential tax treatment to pensioners. These may take the form of tax-exempt pension income brackets, lower tax rates, or full exemption of certain types of benefits. While preferential taxation is often limited to low pensions, in some countries (e.g., Slovenia and the Czech Republic) tax easements practically exempt the majority of pensioners from paying income taxes. These systems would probably best be described as EEt, alluding to the preferential tax treatment of pension payouts.

Whereas tax easements granted to elderly people with low incomes may be viewed as a legitimate alternative to means-tested income support (using tax rules as targeting instruments), the OECD's relevant

Table 4.1
Taxation of public pensions in selected countries, 2015.

Country	Public pension tax scheme	Benefits	Easements?	Types of easements
Australia	EET	Taxed	Yes	Tax relief for pension income
Austria	EET	Taxed	No	n/a
Belgium	EET	Taxed	Yes	Exemption based on number of children, level of disability; no taxes on social/minimum pensions
Bulgaria	EEE	Exempt	No	n/a
Canada	EET	Taxed	Yes	Tax relief for pension income
Chile	EET	Taxed	Yes	Special income tax rate for pensioners
Croatia	EET (EEE)	Taxed	Yes	Tax allowances exempting most pensions from income tax
Cyprus	EET	Taxed	No	n/a
Czech Republic	EET (EEE)	Taxed	Yes	Only pensions at least 36 times the minimum wage are taxed
Denmark	EET	Taxed	No	n/a
Estonia	EET	Taxed	Yes	Private scheme withdrawals are exempt if paid as annuity
Finland	EET	Taxed	Yes	Income tax credit for first EUR 12,610 per year
France	EET	Taxed	Yes	Low-income pensioners pay no health contributions; occupational disability pensions are exempt
Germany	TEE → EET	Exempt → Taxed	No	n/a
Hungary	EEE	Exempt	No	Pension benefits count toward taxable income
Ireland	EET	Taxed	Yes	PRSI exemption above 66 years
Italy	EET	Taxed	Yes	Pensions under €7,500 per year are exempt
Japan	EET	Taxed	Yes	Tax relief for pension income
Korea	EET	Taxed	Yes	Tax relief for pension income

(continued)

Table 4.1 (continued)

Country	Public pension tax scheme	Benefits	Easements?	Types of easements
Latvia	EET	Taxed	Yes	Disability pensions are mostly exempt; low pensions (below €2,820 per year) are exempt; withdrawals from voluntary private schemes are exempt
Malta	EET	Taxed	Yes	Minimum pension is exempt; pensioners in part-time employment are levied a preferential income tax rate
Netherlands	EET	Taxed	Yes	Preferential tax rates apply to pensioners; survivor benefits are exempt; minimum pension is exempt
Norway	EET	Taxed	Yes	Low pensions are exempt
Poland	EET	Taxed	No	n/a
Portugal	EET	Taxed	Yes	First €4,104 per year is exempt; special tax rates for disability pensioners
Romania	EET	Taxed	Yes	First RON 1,000 is exempt
Slovakia	EEE	Exempt	No	n/a
Slovenia	EET	Taxed	Yes	Various tax reliefs, including tax allowances and lower tax rates
Sweden	EET	Taxed	No	n/a
UK	EET	Taxed	No	n/a

Sources: OECD (2015); European Commission (2015).

studies point to the poor targeting and leakages inherent in these arrangements. As shown in figure 4.1, people receiving pensions equal to the average wage tend to pay substantially lower taxes than average wage earners—or no taxes at all (as in Hungary, Slovakia, and Turkey).

Finally, it is worth pointing out that changing the tax status of pensions and pensioners—by subjecting them to standard income tax rules and reducing or eliminating tax easements—is a reform measure rarely used compared to other pension reforms (such as increasing the retirement age, revisions to accrual schedules, or amended indexation rules). On the one hand, this is understandable from a political perspective: pensioners are the largest single-issue block of voters in all developed

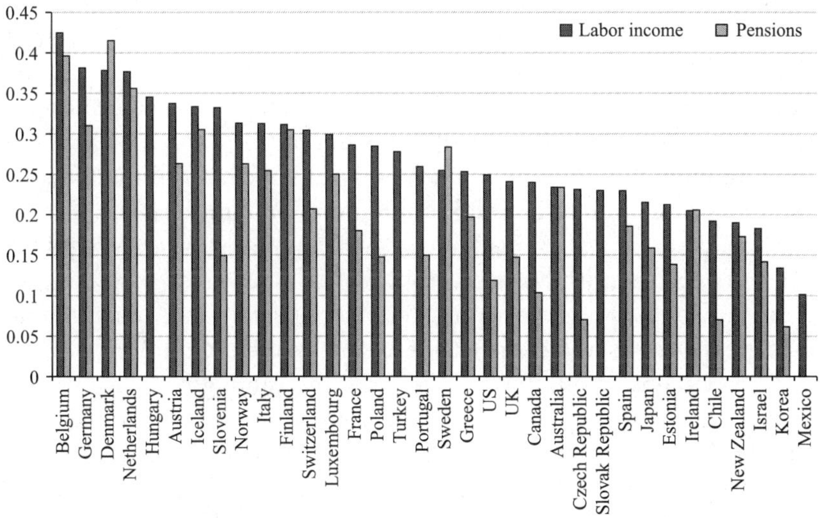

Figure 4.1
Taxation of public pensions in selected countries, 2015. *Source*: OECD (2015).

and middle-income countries. On the other hand, with continued aging, the introduction of tax reforms negatively impacting pensioners but positively influencing fiscal sustainability and the equitable treatment of different incomes will become increasingly more difficult and therefore merits attention at present.

4.4 Do Pensions Merit Special Income Tax Treatment?

Do pensions—and other benefits effectively serving as pensions—actually merit the special tax treatment they often benefit from in the real world as documented in section 4.3? On balance, the answer is likely to be negative, though arguments can clearly be made both in favor of and against it. This section elaborates on some of these dimensions in light of the general interlinks between tax and pension policies highlighted in section 4.2. It first explores some general considerations before getting to second-best and voluntary pension applications.

One of the most immediate conceptual arguments against special treatment applies to compulsory public pensions and can be summarized as follows: taxing pensions is a priori a futile exercise, as it merely shifts money from one pocket to another. In its most stylized form, assuming that the populations of taxpayers and pension members are perfectly overlapping, having (costly) pension taxation causes inefficiency. While not entirely applicable to real-world settings in its purest form, this approach raises an issue in terms of accounting for pension expenditures. For example, countries that exempt both contributions to and benefits from public pensions will appear in international statistics to have a smaller government sector than countries that pay the exact same net benefit but subject the gross amount to taxes. Ceteris paribus, the nontaxation leads to an artificial reduction in recognized pension expenditures that is exactly offset by an equal-sized tax expenditure (lower than otherwise possible tax revenues)—thus understating the true degree of involvement of the state in the economy.

A second argument, this time in favor of granting pensions preferential tax status, is a proxy for "lack of ability to respond in old age" and/or "poverty in old age." These arguments may be convincing at first sight but are less so upon closer inspection—similar to their use as tools for redistribution of resources.[16] Conceptually, preferential tax treatment for pensions is similar to indiscriminate price subsidization in the energy sector, which has been shown to be badly targeted and to have substantial revenue and efficiency costs (Clements et al. 2013). Not all aged are poor or unable to respond to shocks, and hence it is not clear whether targeting the old is the best possible use of public resources. In addition, not all pensioners are old, as pension systems often include early-retirement options (e.g., for special professional groups) as well as coverage for risks other than retirement (e.g., survivor, spousal, or children's benefits).

Third, could preferential tax treatment be favorable to the labor market, including aspects of job and locational mobility? Although taxes could be conceptually modeled to work either way, it is rather likely that, in the real world, negative effects prevail for average workers—in addition to those imposed by the pension systems themselves.[17] For example, an individual who benefited from tax-deductible contributions early in life might have limited ability to relocate to a different tax jurisdiction (or face hefty exit taxation) later on. Similarly, preferential tax rules for pensions and other social benefits effectively serving as early-retirement programs (e.g., unemployment, disability) might make continued work after the onset of benefit receipt impossible or not worth it (e.g., through a categorical earnings or benefit test).

Other arguments focus the preferential tax treatment of voluntary pensions along the savings dimension. At the macro level, the results of Chamley (1986) and Judd (1985) hinted at the desirability of not taxing savings (and thus also retirement pensions) for growth reasons.

However, Diamond (2009) cautioned about the overreliance of these results on essential underlying assumptions that probably are not satisfied in a real-world setting. Arguments for granting pensions special tax treatment—as compared to other forms of savings—are even weaker. Cremer and Pestieau (2016, chapter 2, this volume) argued that granting private pensions preferential tax treatment on the basis of the nonexistence of private annuity markets, on grounds of shrinking compulsory public pensions, and because of a need for long-term investments are all unconvincing, as it is unclear (1) whether private pensions are the best response to such issues and (2) whether preferential tax breaks are the most efficient tool for achieving these objectives. Similarly, the longstanding issue of whether pension tax breaks generate net increases in retirement savings (Engen, Gale, and Scholz 1994 versus Poterba, Venti, and Wise 1995) remains unsettled. The case for preferential tax treatment is further weakened when considering pensions in an open economy, where saved amounts might and should (at least partially) be invested abroad, if only for risk management reasons—de facto breaking the link between the pension tax incentive and the investment outcome of the economy.[18]

More generally, does preferential tax treatment lead to more coverage, adequacy, equity, and sustainability? An affirmative answer is far from obvious. Various contributors to Holzmann, Robalino, and Takayama (2009) argued that (generally tax-favored) voluntary and compulsory contributory pension programs are insufficient at addressing these challenges and need to be supplemented by social pensions to address the coverage gap. In numerous countries, tax-favored systems have very openly failed on several of these fronts, such as purely general revenue–financed, tax-free civil servant pensions favoring high-earning civil servants and unlimited contributions to voluntary pension savings plans favoring groups in the population with more discretion on savings amounts (e.g., high earners, the self-employed).

Lessons from behavioral economics also matter. Using a rich administrative dataset from Denmark, Chetty et al. (2014) showed that the large majority of individuals do not respond to tax incentives, because—among other reasons—they are myopic. In such situations, the authors argued that automatic (default) options are a more efficient policy tool than preferential taxes. Cremer and Pestieau (2016, chapter 2, this volume) showed that in the case of myopia it might be preferable to front-load an otherwise equivalent tax favor to the contribution stage rather than the benefit phase to induce a better alignment of private pension savings with socially desired levels.[19]

4.5 Conclusions

The literature on the taxation of pensions is limited, although the issue merits attention. Tax and pension policies need to be designed in view of each other. This poses a different challenge than cross-referencing tax and social policies governing benefits based on short-term or immediate eligibility criteria. To effectively reinforce each other—or at least limit contradictory consequences—tax and pension policies need to be stable. However, even in the presence of reasonable stability—and it must be noted here that even if introduced with the best of intentions, tax and pension reforms imply instability—the tax treatment of current pensions should be expected to impact economically active cohorts' decisions concerning labor supply, choices between varying levels of informality, and social security compliance only to the degree that they severely impact their current and future living conditions, with more acuity in periods closer to retirement.

Given that even significant structural reforms (such as introducing mandatory funded schemes or augmenting earnings-related schemes with antipoverty, basic pensions) have had no discernible and documented impact on labor force participation or tax compliance, it is reasonable to assume that a secondary issue—the tax treatment of pensions—will make little tangible difference in active workers' decisions. In other words, it is not because of the tax treatment of pensions that a working-age person decides to seek employment or to move between sectors or jurisdictions.[20]

Although we could find no proof that the taxation of pensions could in any way alter behavior in active years (coverage or compliance), it is clearly important in determining absolute and relative (net) pension levels. Governments' views on what constitutes equitable, "fair" income distribution and desirable or acceptable levels of redistribution and taxation may differ; they may assign different importance to vertical and horizontal equity or may interpret intergenerational equity in more than one way. Regardless of their views on these issues, three policy prerogatives need to be observed.

First, different types of income should be treated in a similar manner. This implies that all income should be subject to income tax once. Currently, pension taxation fails to observe this principle in many countries.

Second, tax and pension policies should be designed in a manner that reinforces synergies and addresses distributional concerns through the most effective instruments. If, for instance, a pension system's governing principle is strongly correlating pensions to contribution performance, then the tax system may not be the most effective instrument for dealing with the welfare issues resulting from inadequate pension benefits at the lower end of the career-earning distribution, and policy makers may need to rely on nonpension cash transfers.

Finally, with the aging of all societies, political economy and electoral demographics will render the reform of pension systems—including the taxation of pensions and the critical review of tax exemptions and easements—more difficult and therefore more urgent.

Notes

1. Obviously, other areas of economic and social policy also substantially impact income distribution—such as social assistance schemes and access to and quality of public education and health care—but these systems fall outside the scope of this analysis.

2. Unemployment insurance generates shorter-term entitlements with little capacity to prove governments' ability and willingness to honor long-term legal or contractual commitments. Health insurance contributions share features of generating both short- and long-term entitlements, although the short-term one dominates, as contributions typically create concurrent eligibility.

3. Other reasons for having or promoting pensions exist. Fully funded pensions are sometimes viewed as vectors of industrialization, economic growth, and financial market development (see Holzmann 1997 on Chile); PAYG defined benefit elements are sometimes cited as vectors of formalization since they create the conditions to reward participation and compliance through higher-than-normal returns for the starting generation—though strong causal evidence on both dimensions is lacking (see Melguizo 2015 for a recent review).

4. It should be noted, however, that using permanent pension benefits to address temporary labor market tensions is fiscally costly and affords permanent withdrawal from the labor market to workers who could otherwise find employment in many cases.

5. In practice, such situations strengthen incentives to strategically relocate to low- or no-tax jurisdictions.

6. Unilateral and multilateral instruments play a more limited role.

7. Residence-based contributory pensions also existed but only in federated or confederated states where constituent entities' pension schemes were similar and financial balancing mechanisms existed (as in the Soviet Union and Yugoslavia).

8. Unilateral measures and multilateral frameworks also play an important role. European Union regulations EC 883/2004 and EC 987/2009 are likely the most far-reaching ones and deal with public pensions.

9. The scope and limits of bilateral taxation treaties for pensions are discussed in Genser and Holzmann (chapter 15, this volume).

10. In defined contribution schemes, even publicly managed ones, poor investment performance can be better separated from the overall efficiency of providing public goods and services.

11. It may sound contradictory to mention targeting efficiency with regard to a universal benefit; however, the choice of making these benefits universal is usually based on administrative considerations (i.e., the limited gain and high administrative cost of making them means tested or pension tested *ex ante*) and not because policy makers wish to support all income groups to the same extent.

12. In Belgium, the preferential tax treatment of pension payments is conditional on not having any form of non–social security income. This rule renders the option of partial retirement unattractive to most workers.

13. These are theoretical considerations; we are not aware of public pension schemes where notional returns or the marginal benefit above the actuarially fair level would be taxed.

14. Clearly, any such credibility- or stability-induced preference is also a function of the real-world ability of the state to collect other compulsory levies at the entry or exit stage.

15. This is only relevant for people who enjoy more than one source of income after retirement, and even then only in the presence of a progressive income tax scale.

16. The discussion in section 4.2 already pointed out the general difficulty of understanding redistribution patterns when confronted with (lifetime-based) pension systems and annual tax systems—with nontrivial interactions through the government's intertemporal budget constraint and implicit and explicit debt.

17. The various contributors to Gruber and Wise (1999, 2004) showed that changes in future pension entitlements are the biggest contributors to the implicit tax on continued work.

18. Andersen (2015, chapter 5, this volume) has argued that mandatory pensions could be a better tool than tax favoring, at least insofar as mandated pensions do not fully crowd out voluntary pensions.

19. Clearly, other reasons for choosing the applicable tax model matter. From a fiscal point of view, the very different timing of government revenues (and the associated impact on public debt) is of prime importance.

20. International empirical work on migrants' decisions is still in the early phase, but a very recent work in this area suggests that the skill composition of migrants is sensitive to bilateral tax treaties, bilateral social security agreements, and the marginal tax rates on high-income groups (Czaika and Parsons 2016).

References

Andersen, Torben M. 2015. "How Should Pensions Be Taxed? Theoretical Considerations and the Scandinavian Experience." CESifo Working Paper Series No. 5660, CESifo, Munich.

Atkinson, Anthony B., and Joseph E. Stiglitz. 1976. "The Design of Tax Structure: Direct versus Indirect Taxation." *Journal of Public Economics* 6 (1–2): 55–75.

Börsch-Supan, Axel H., and Christopher Quinn. 2015. "Taxing Pensions and Retirement Benefits in Germany." CESifo Working Paper No. 5636, CESifo, Munich.

Chamley, Christophe. 1986. "Optimal Taxation of Capital Income in General Equilibrium with Infinite Lives." *Econometrica* 54 (3): 607–622.

Chetty, Raj, John N. Friedman, Søren Leth-Petersen, Torben Heien Nielsen, and Tore Olsen. 2014. "Active vs. Passive Decisions and Crowding-Out in Retirement Savings Accounts: Evidence from Denmark." *Quarterly Journal of Economics* 129 (3): 1141–1219.

Clements, Benedict, David Coady, Stefania Fabrizio, Sanjeev Gupta, Trevor Alleyne, and Carlo Sdralevich, eds. 2013. *Energy Subsidy Reform: Lessons and Implications*. Washington, DC: International Monetary Fund.

Cremer, Helmuth, and Pierre Pestieau. 2016. "Taxing Pensions." IZA Discussion Paper No. 9821, IZA, Bonn.

Czaika, Mathias, and Christopher R. Parsons. 2016. "The Gravity of High-Skilled Migration Policies." KNOMAD Working Paper No. 13, World Bank, Washington, DC.

Diamond, Peter. 2002. *Social Security Reform*. Oxford: Oxford University Press.

Diamond, Peter A. 2009. "Taxes and Pensions." *Southern Economic Journal* 76 (1): 2–15.

Diamond, Peter, and James Mirrlees. 1978. "A Model of Social Insurance with Variable Retirement." *Journal of Public Economics* 10 (3): 295–336.

Diamond, Peter, and Eytan Sheshinski. 1995. "Economic Aspects of Optimal Disability Benefits." *Journal of Public Economics* 57:1–23.

Engen, Eric M., William G. Gale, and John Karl Scholz. 1994. "Do Saving Incentives Work?" *Brookings Papers on Economic Activity* 1:85–151.

European Commission. 2015. *The 2015 Aging Report*. Brussels: European Commission.

Gruber, Jonathan, and David A. Wise, eds. 1999. *Social Security and Retirement around the World.* Chicago: University of Chicago Press and NBER.

Gruber, Jonathan, and David A. Wise, eds. 2004. *Social Security and Retirement around the World: Micro-estimation*. Chicago: University of Chicago Press and NBER.

Gruber, Jonathan, and David A. Wise, eds. 2010. *Social Security Programs and Retirement around the World: The Relationship to Youth Employment*. Chicago and Cambridge, MA: University of Chicago Press and NBER.

Harsanyi, John C. 1955. "Cardinal Welfare, Individualistic Ethics, and Interpersonal Comparisons of Utility." *Journal of Political Economy* 63:309–321.

Holzmann, Robert. 1997. "Pension Reform, Financial Market Development, and Economic Growth: Preliminary Evidence from Chile." *Staff Papers (International Monetary Fund)* 44 (2): 149–178.

Holzmann, Robert, David A. Robalino, and Noriyuki Takayama, eds. 2009. *Closing the Coverage Gap: The Role of Social Pensions and Other Retirement Income Transfers*. Washington, DC: World Bank.

Jousten, Alain. 2001. "Life-Cycle Modelling of Bequests and Its Implications for Annuity Valuation." *Journal of Public Economics* 79:149–177.

Judd, Kenneth L. 1985. "Redistributive Taxation in a Simple Perfect Foresight Model." *Journal of Public Economics* 28 (1): 59–83.

Melguizo, Angel. 2015. "Pensions, Informality, and the Emerging Middle Class." *IZA World of Labor* 169. doi: 10.15185/izawol.169.

Mirrlees, James. 1971. "An Exploration in the Theory of Optimum Income Taxation." *Review of Economic Studies* 38 (2): 175–208.

OECD (Organisation for Economic Co-operation and Development). 2015. *Pensions at a Glance: OECD and G20 Indicators*. Paris: OECD Publishing.

Poterba, J. M., S. F. Venti, and D. A. Wise. 1995. "Do 401(k) Contributions Crowd Out Other Personal Saving?" *Journal of Public Economics* 58:1–32.

Purcell, Patrick J. 2015. "Income Taxes on Social Security Benefits." Social Security Issue Paper No. 2015-02, Social Security Administration, Washington, DC.

Rawls, John. 1971. *A Theory of Justice*. Cambridge, MA: Harvard University Press.

Romaniuk, Katarzyna. 2013. "Pension Fund Taxation and Risk-Taking: Should We Switch from the EET to the TEE Regime?" *Annals of Finance* 9 (4):573–588.

Samuelson, Paul. 1975. "Optimum Social Security in a Life-Cycle Growth Model." *International Economic Review* 16 (3): 539–544.

Slemrod, Joel, and Christian Gillitzer. 2014. *Tax Systems*. Zeuthen Lecture Series. Cambridge, MA: MIT Press.

Vickrey, William S. 1945. "Measuring Marginal Utility by Reactions to Risk." *Econometrica* 13:319–333.

Yaari, Menahem E. 1965. "Uncertain Lifetime, Life Insurance, and the Theory of the Consumer." *Review of Economic Studies* 32 (2): 137–150.

II Country Issues and Research Questions

5 How Should Pensions Be Taxed? Theoretical Considerations and the Scandinavian Experience

Torben M. Andersen

5.1 Introduction

A primary savings motive is to ensure consumption possibilities postretirement. Any type of savings will, in principle, serve this purpose with proper account taken of returns and risks. However, pension savings often have a particular status, including more lenient taxation or subsidies, than other forms of savings. Many countries also have mandatory elements in pension savings. This raises a fundamental question: What is the rationale for treating pension savings differently from other forms of savings?

The taxation of pension savings is a specific question within the more general area of capital income taxation. Vast literature exists on whether capital income should be taxed (see Diamond 2009 for a discussion). The focus here is not a normative analysis of the optimal taxation of capital income but instead a positive analysis of the relevant tax wedges arising from taxation and how they may be of importance for pension savings and retirement. The starting point is the empirical fact that capital income is taxed, and the prime question is whether taxation of pension savings should differ from other forms of savings and hence capital income.

The purpose of this chapter is twofold: to discuss some of the principal issues in the taxation of pensions and to consider the specific way of taxing pension savings in the Nordic countries (Denmark and Sweden).[1] Besides the interest in the Nordic countries for their own sake, Denmark and Sweden are interesting for having extended welfare models but very different pension systems. The welfare state perspective is interesting since the taxation of private savings and its interaction with public pension schemes raise crucial questions about incentives, insurance, and redistribution. Denmark and Sweden are, moreover, among the few countries with a so-called ETT (exempt, taxed, taxed) scheme for pension savings.

The Nordic countries[2] have been front-runners in applying a dual income tax system; that is, a system that separates labor income and capital income taxation, where the former is progressively taxed and the latter is proportionally taxed. One key argument in support of this tax system is that it reconciles low capital income tax rates to avoid capital mobility with the possibility of maintaining higher and more progressive labor income tax rates (Sørensen 2010).

While the Nordic countries are usually clustered together under the heading of the Nordic welfare model, their pension schemes are very different from one another (Andersen, Määttänen, and Valkonen 2014). Denmark's pension system is organized around funded occupational pension funds along with pay-as-you-go (PAYG) public pensions, while Sweden adopted a notionally defined pension scheme that is largely a PAYG-based system in which pensions stand in relation to labor income earned during the worker's career.[3] The pension systems of Norway and Finland include both PAYG pensions and funded pensions.

These differences underline a more general point concerning the Nordic countries. Even though they share some overriding objectives reflected in extended welfare states, the design of specific policies differs in significant ways. This points to the overall objectives and packaging of policies and institutions as being important rather than the specific policy instruments applied.

The chapter is organized as follows. Section 5.2 discusses some principal aspects related to the tax treatment of pensions. Section 5.3 presents and discusses various taxation regimes. The specificities of pension taxation in Denmark and Sweden are covered in section 5.4, while section 5.5 considers some macro aspects of how pensions are taxed. Concluding remarks are given in section 5.6.

5.2 Principal Aspects

Many reasons arise for public intervention in pension savings, including both the behavioral aspects related to savings decisions by households and the market side (available savings instruments) (Barr and Diamond 2006). The following discussion focuses on intervention aimed at ensuring a socially desirable savings level. Intervention via tax incentives or mandated saving requirements is often motivated by a concern that voluntary savings are insufficient.

The pension economics literature features "present bias" as a key reason why agents do not attach sufficient weight to future consumption and therefore tend to save too little.[4] Present-biased decisions can result either from too high subjective time preferences (myopia/quasi-hyperbolic preferences) or self-control problems. A straightforward case is myopia, where decisions are made under a higher subjective discount rate than that associated with true preferences (Feldstein and Leibman 2002; Cremer and Pestieau 2011). A particular form of this is quasihyperbolic discounting, where all future periods are given insufficient weight relative to the present[5] (Laibson 1996). An alternative approach assumes that agents suffer from self-control problems and are therefore tempted to increase current consumption at the cost of reduced future consumption (St-Amant and Garon 2014). For the present purpose, these different approaches are essentially observationally equivalent in predicting a suboptimal level of voluntary pension savings.

Insufficient voluntary savings for pensions motivate intervention,[6] but what form should invention take? Should savings incentives be strengthened via the taxation system, or should pension saving (up to some level) be mandatory? Both forms of intervention are used by most OECD countries (OECD 2013).[7] Finding a rationale for intervention in savings decisions does not settle the question of the appropriate form of intervention. The literature on pension economics has not considered this issue in much detail. A number of studies argue why mandatory pension savings can be welfare-improving. Even if a public pension of the PAYG type is return dominated in a dynamically efficient economy, it may be associated with welfare gains if agents are sufficiently present biased.[8] Mandated pension saving in a funded scheme is in general justified if some present bias exists (Andersen and Bhattacharya 2011, 2016). Krusell, Kuruscu, and Smith (2010) analyzed an interest rate subsidy in the case of households suffering from self control problems and found that it can be welfare-improving.

But what mode of intervention (price versus quantity control) should be used? If the motivation for intervention is present-biased preferences, it may be argued that interest rate subsidies are imprecisely targeted, since such subsidies are also available to (or predominantly used by) individuals not suffering from present-biased preferences and who therefore save adequately. This implies a deadweight loss from this form of intervention.[9] This problem can be partly circumvented by setting a cap for the interest subsidy (e.g., maximum annual contribution for which the subsidy applies). A mandatory savings level would have no or only a small effect on those who do not suffer from present-biased preferences and hence save enough from a social point of view. For individuals suffering from a present bias, a mandatory savings requirement will generally affect their net savings.[10] Based on this reasoning, pension saving is better targeted via mandated saving than by interest rate subsidies.

An important caveat should be added concerning mandatory pension savings, since they do not eliminate incentive questions. A key question is whether mandated savings contributions are considered a tax.[11] To address this question, assume that the returns on voluntary and mandatory savings are the same, in which case mandatory savings increase net savings only if voluntary savings are driven to zero.[12] If households are borrowing constrained, a further increase in mandated savings distorts the allocation of consumption over time, which in turn distorts labor supply. Hence, the effective taxation of pension savings matters and may affect labor supply along both the intensive and extensive margins (Kaplow 2015). Savings also affects retirement decisions, and hence the incentives underlying savings and retirement have to be considered equally.

The argument for intervention in pension savings decisions is intimately related to constraints on the possibilities for claiming these savings. The constraint is that savings are available only after reaching a certain age or upon retirement.[13] Similarly, there may be constraints on tax-favored forms of pension benefits. Pension benefits can be structured as (1) a lump-sum installment (capital pension), (2) a rate pension (payments of a given amount for a fixed number of years, say 10 years), or (3) a lifetime annuity. The thrust of the argument for intervention is that agents tend to front-load consumption, leaving insufficient consumption possibilities in old age. This provides an argument for why a major part of mandated pensions should be in the form of annuities[14] to ensure consumption throughout life. This is related to the so-called annuity paradox, according to which individuals tend to place too low a share of savings in annuities (Davidoff, Brown, and Diamond 2005). Such a phenomenon may reflect a present bias, a failure to understand annuity products, or market failures (e.g., imperfect competition) in annuities markets. A requirement that subsidized or mandatory pension savings predominantly apply to life annuities may thus also address the problem of insufficient annuitization.[15]

In a welfare state, a particular moral hazard problem may arise.[16] Welfare arrangements such as public pensions and health and housing subsidies are implicit life annuities in the sense that eligibility applies throughout life. Hence, if savings are not in the form of life annuities, asymmetric risk sharing arises between the individual or heirs and the welfare state. If the individual passes away early, the heirs benefit from the bequest (if savings are not in annuities), but if the individual lives long, the welfare state automatically steps in to provide support. Thus, extended welfare arrangements may be a separate reason for "insufficient" demand for life annuities. It should be added that arguments can be made that less than 100 percent of mandated pension savings should be paid out as life annuities. Consumption needs may be age dependent, and a lump-sum payment upon retirement may provide a precautionary buffer.

5.3 Pension Taxation Regimes and Tax Wedges

5.3.1 Overview

Pension schemes have three basic dimensions: contributions, returns, and benefits. Any of these dimensions can be subject to taxation (T) or exempt from taxation (E). This leaves eight possible pension taxation regimes (EEE, TEE, EET, ETE, TTE, TET, ETT, TTT) (Yoo and de Serres 2004). Sixteen possible regimes exist when including both explicit taxation and implicit taxation via possible means testing of public pensions.

In comparing these regimes, two key questions arise: (1) Does the timing of tax payments have a separate role from that of tax rates? (2) What are the tax wedges affecting savings and retirement decisions? In general (capturing all possible regimes outlined), the individual faces the following tax and pension scheme: Labor income is taxed at the rate τ_y, contributions to funded pension schemes are deductible from labor income at the rate τ_d, while benefits from funded pensions are taxed at the rate τ_p. The return on pension savings is taxed at the rate τ_r. All tax rates belong to the interval [0,1], and proportional taxation is assumed for simplicity. When retired, the individual is entitled to a public pension b that is means tested against private pensions (wealth) at the tapering rate $m \in [0,1]$.

Considering a contribution d to the pension scheme at time t, the value at time T can be written as

$$(1-\tau_y+\tau_d)(1-r(1-\tau_r))^T(1-\tau_y)(1-m)^d,$$

where r is the rate of return on the savings (which for simplicity is assumed to be time invariant). If $\tau_d = \tau_y$, it follows that contributions are fully exempt from taxation; if $\tau_r > 0$, returns are taxed; and if $\tau_p > 0$, benefits are taxed.

Several points are worth making. First, there is an important equivalence result.[17] A (T,E/T,E) system has $\tau_d = 0$ and $\tau_p = 0$, while an (E,E/T,T) scheme has $\tau_d = \tau_y$ and $\tau_p = \tau_y$. Hence, in either case—for the same tax rates τ_y and τ_p—the tax wedges are the same, so behavior is the same in the two regimes. This implies that the present value of taxes paid is the same, and therefore the allocation between current and future consumption is the same. Thus, for the same tax rates, the timing of tax payments does not have any behavioral consequences.[18] It is a corollary that postponement of taxation as in a (T,E/T,T) regime does not favor pension saving when agents do not suffer from tax illusion.

In the case where $\tau_d = \tau_y$ and $\tau_p < \tau_y$, there is a tax subsidy to pension savings. This situation may arise in an (E,E/T,T) scheme if income taxation is progressive, since most people would have a higher income when working than when retired (implying $\tau_p < \tau_y$).

The equivalence result discussed presumes rational behavior.[19] A question is whether there is some tax illusion in the sense that tax deductions are interpreted as tax rebates, disregarding the later taxation of the benefits. Advertisements by pension funds often emphasize the tax deduction without highlighting the later taxation. Contributions into voluntary pension savings arrangements also tend to peak toward the end of the year, which may reflect attempts to reduce the tax payment.[20]

It follows from the expression given earlier that if the return on pension savings is taxed more leniently than other forms of savings, then clearly the value of the lower taxation is larger the longer the investment period, because of a compound return effect. Pension contributions made close to retirement may thus be less favorable than contributions made early in life, particularly if $(1 - \tau_y)(1 - m)$ is low. This fact is important for retirement decisions, especially if pension contributions are mandatory. If the implicit tax on savings made close to retirement is high, the incentive to postpone retirement is correspondingly low.

On the taxation of returns, two more points are worth noting. First, the tax is often levied on the nominal return, so the effective taxation of the real return exceeds the tax rate on the nominal return. Second, annuities have a higher return via the insurance mechanism related to survival, and this "mortality premium" is not taxed when the tax on returns is levied on the market return.

One argument for an (E,E/T,T) regime is the global income principle that all incomes are treated equally, and therefore only the sum matters for the total tax payment. In the Scandinavian countries, this principle is applied for all earned income and social transfers (including pensions). Accordingly, all social transfers are gross amounts and taxable income. The key argument in support of this system is that it provides a better basis for redistribution (including progressive elements in taxation), and it is based on the premise that disposable income determines current consumption possibilities. Moreover, it allows the individual a possibility of smoothing marginal tax rates so as to make them more dependent on lifetime income.

The choice of taxation scheme also raises issues in relation to portability and competition (Genser and Holzmann 2016, chapter 15, this volume). In the TEE regime, this is not an issue, but in any ETT regime there is an issue both in relation to competition between pension product providers and in relation to portability of pensions in the case of migration.[21] From a taxation point of view, there is a risk of tax evasion. Clearly, both issues are related to EU regulations and especially the Single Market. To illustrate this, consider the case of Denmark, where the taxation of pensions was changed in 2007 to admit tax deductibility for contributions into a pension fund in any EU country. This was done since the earlier principle of only allowing deductibility for contributions into Danish pension funds was contested by the EU court. The foreign pension fund shall, however, be approved by the Danish tax authorities, and the arrangement offered shall correspond with Danish pension arrangements. Moreover, the fund shall agree to pay the tax on both the return and benefit payments to the Danish tax authorities. Only six foreign pension funds have been approved so far. Special rules exist for migrant workers, who, within a period of up to 60 months, can use a foreign pension fund with full deductibility for contributions and no return taxation, and the benefits (if received in a foreign country) are not taxable in Denmark.

5.3.2 Means Testing

The role of means testing is already apparent from the preceding discussion. To assess the overall incentive structure, it is crucial to consider the implicit taxation via means testing on a par with explicit taxation.

In general, means testing can involve different treatments of various types of assets and incomes, but here a very stylized setting is considered as a basis for discussing the implications.[22]

The overall division of labor in pension schemes is that public pensions[23] are targeted distribution objectives, while private (funded) pensions target the consumption-smoothing objective. While this logic appears clear, the actual design is somewhat more complicated, since it is not possible to completely separate the different roles or objectives. The problem is that it is not possible to combine the two without creating incentive problems. To see this, consider the basic question of how to design public pensions such that they are targeted to the economically weakest pensioners. This could be achieved by providing a minimum guaranteed, publicly financed pension for all old people; that is, if private pensions do not meet this target, the difference will be made up by public supplements (figure 5.1a). In this way, the distributional objective is achieved—there are no "poor" old people. The flipside, however, is that any increase in private pensions (as long as it is below the minimum level) is effectively taxed at 100 percent, since higher private pensions in this interval do not increase the total pension but only its relative composition between private and public pensions ($m=1$). This clearly has adverse incentive effects on private savings. In response to this, the public pension may be phased out more gradually (via an offset rate or taper rate $m<1$) (figure 5.1b). This implies a lower implicit tax rate, which may be conducive to savings and later retirement. However, this is achieved at the cost of a higher public expenditure on pensions, which in turn must be financed by (distortionary) taxes. A flat-rate pension for all is the limiting case, where all receive the same public pension (zero taper rate). Clearly, this leaves a zero implicit tax rate in the pension system but a higher public expenditure and thus higher explicit tax rates. Thus, a trade-off between distribution and incentives arises in deciding the division of labor between private and public pensions.

Since in most cases means testing implies a threshold above which no pension is received,[24] it follows that the effect on the tax wedge arises for low and medium levels of income (pensions). For higher levels of income (pensions), a marginal increase in income (pension) has no effect on public pensions received, and the marginal tax wedge is thus lower; that is, a regressive bias arises from the combined effect of taxes and means testing.

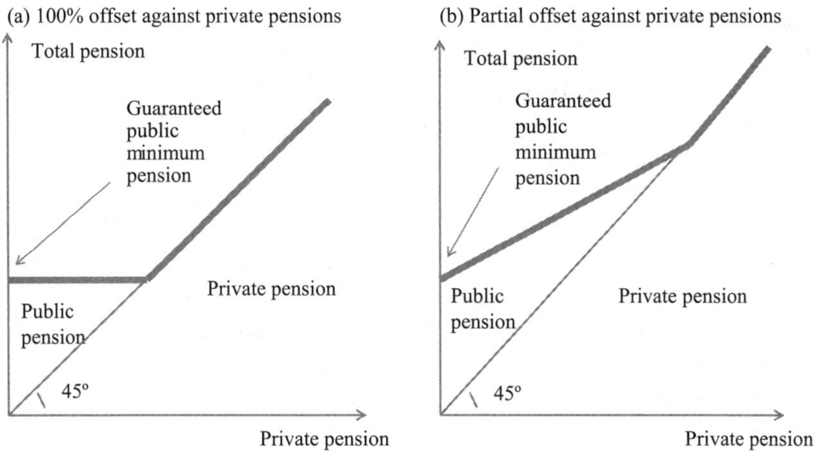

Figure 5.1
Public pensions, distribution, and means testing.

The preceding discussion points to the possible adverse incentive effects of the interplay between public and private pensions via means testing of the former (and taxation in general). However, it is worth pointing out that means testing also has an insurance effect. All changes in private pension savings beyond individual control, such as involuntary unemployment or variations in the return on pension savings, are shared or absorbed via public pensions.[25] Since means testing applies for relatively low incomes and pensions, there is an asymmetry in the insurance mechanism. Households ending up with low private pensions receive more from the public system. In the case of a higher private pension, means testing ceases at some point, implying that further increases in private pensions are to the benefit of the individual (low effective tax). The implicit insurance created via means testing and taxation is thus mainly an insurance against downside risks.

5.4 Taxation of Pensions and Capital Income in Denmark and Sweden

This section discusses taxation of pensions and capital income in Denmark and Sweden. The two countries are similar in having an extended welfare state and mainly following an ETT taxation regime. However, the two countries differ significantly in the design of their pension systems.

5.4.1 Denmark

Denmark's public pension[26] includes a basic amount (flat-rate pension)[27] and means-tested supplements. A number of age-dependent supplements also exist. These pension entitlements are of the defined benefit type and are tax financed. Public pensions are indexed to wages.

By law, all wage earners and recipients of transfer income contribute to the supplementary labor market pension (ATP), a defined contribution scheme to which all contribute the same monthly amount (depending on working hours). The contribution rates are relatively small, so this scheme cannot by itself ensure sufficiently high replacement rates.

Labor market pensions are agreed on as part of an employment relationship or through collective agreements between the social partners.[28] The development of labor market pensions took off in 1989–1991, and the arrangements were subsequently extended to a large part of the labor market; until recently, contribution rates were increasing. Today, contribution rates vary between 12 percent and 18 percent, with rates tending to be higher for high-income groups. Private pension savings comprise other forms of savings (voluntary savings) as well as savings in pension savings schemes in banks and insurance companies (the return is taxed more leniently, but the funds are tied to retirement). Figure 5.2 illustrates the structure of public pensions in Denmark and shows the interaction between public and private pensions (means testing).

Statutory ages in the pension system (for public pensions, early retirement, and age limits for payment of funds from pension schemes) are established by legislation. Recent reforms—the welfare reform of 2006 and the retirement reform of 2011—will increase these ages considerably to cope with an aging population. The first part of the reform includes the following discretionary changes: (1) increases in the early-retirement age from 60 to 62 years over the period 2014–2017; (2) shortening of the early-retirement period from five to three years over the years 2018–2019 to 2022–2023, implying an early-retirement age of 64 in 2023; and (3) increasing the pension age from 65 to 67 years over the period 2019–2022. The second element (to start in 2025) is an indexation of the early-retirement age and pension age to the increase in life expectancy at the age of 60 in order to target the expected pension period to 14.5 years (17.5 including early retirement) in the long run (currently about 18.5 and 23.5 years).

Figure 5.3 shows the replacement rates across the income distribution and their composition. Replacement rates are high for low-income

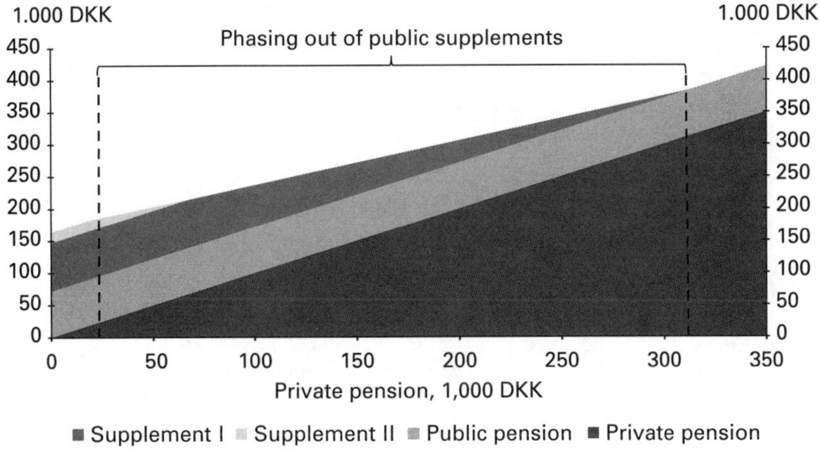

Figure 5.2
Structure of public pensions, Denmark, 2015. *Source*: Pensionskommissionen (2015). *Note*: The figure is a stylized illustration of the public pension system (Supplement I: Pensionstillæg; Supplement II: Særlig pensionsydelse) in Denmark in 2015. Supplements to the old (including housing) other than the direct pension supplements are disregarded. Pensions are taxable income. 1 DKK is approximately US$0.15 (July 2015).

groups, reflecting the public pension's distributional objective (basically ensuring that low-income individuals never experience an income drop upon retirement; hence the replacement rates are close to 100 percent). The composition of the replacement rate is also seen to vary across incomes, reflecting that public pensions via means testing are targeted to low- and medium-income groups. As a result, poverty among pensioners is very rare in Denmark (figure 5.4).

The overall structure of pension taxation in Denmark is summarized in table 5.1. The most important types of pensions—life annuities and so-called rate pensions with installments paid over 10 to 25 years—are of the ETT type and are included in the base for means testing. However, the rate pension has a cap on the annual deduction. A more recent scheme, called an "old-age pension," is of the TTE type and is not included in the base for means testing (there is also a cap on the annual contribution). For all pension types, the return is taxed at the rate of 15.3 percent.

As noted, the tax value of the tax deduction for contributions (τ_d) may differ from that of the taxation of pension benefits (τ_s), because of progressive elements in the taxation system. Figure 5.5 illustrates this by giving the tax rates for contributions (labor income) and pension

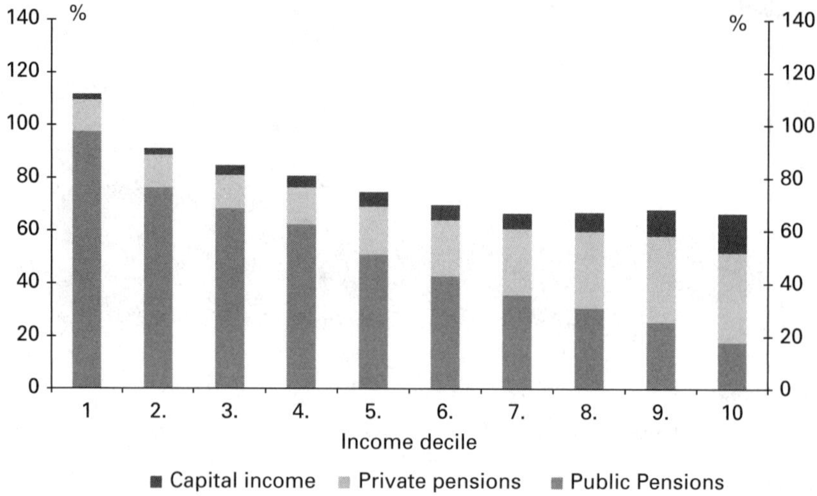

Figure 5.3
Average replacement rates at the age of 66 across income deciles, Denmark, 2012. *Source*: Pensionskommissionen (2015). *Note*: Replacement rates are computed for individual disposable income at age 66 relative to the disposable income at ages 55–57 (the same incomes used for the construction of income deciles). The disposable income at ages 55–57 is adjusted to the 2012 level by using the index for the general wage development. Among the age 66 group, only persons without market income are included.

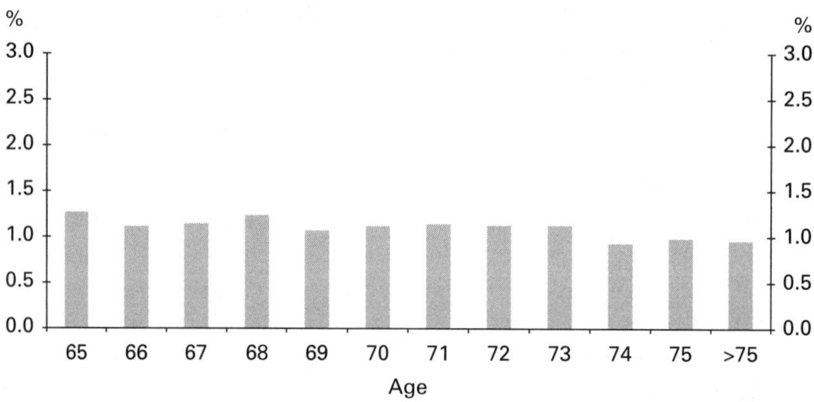

Figure 5.4
Share of persons above age 65 in the low-income group, Denmark, 2012. *Source*: Pensionskommissionen (2015). *Note*: The low-income group is defined as having a disposable income below 50 percent of the median income for the entire population.

Table 5.1
Taxation of pensions, Denmark, 2016.

	Limit (DKK)	Deduction	Return tax (%)	Benefits	Means testing
Life annuity	None	Marginal tax rate	15.3	Marginal tax rate	Yes
Rate pension	52,400	Marginal tax rate	15.3	Marginal tax rate	Yes
Old-age pension	28,900	No	15.3	No	No

Source: www.skm.dk.
Notes: Contributions to a so-called capital pension are (since 2013) no longer tax deductible, and payments into the scheme have ceased. All rates and amounts apply to 2016. For an old-age pension (alderspension), there is no means testing if the payout is a lump-sum payment. Marginal taxes applicable for contributions (the wage income tax) and for pension benefits are shown in figure 5.5.

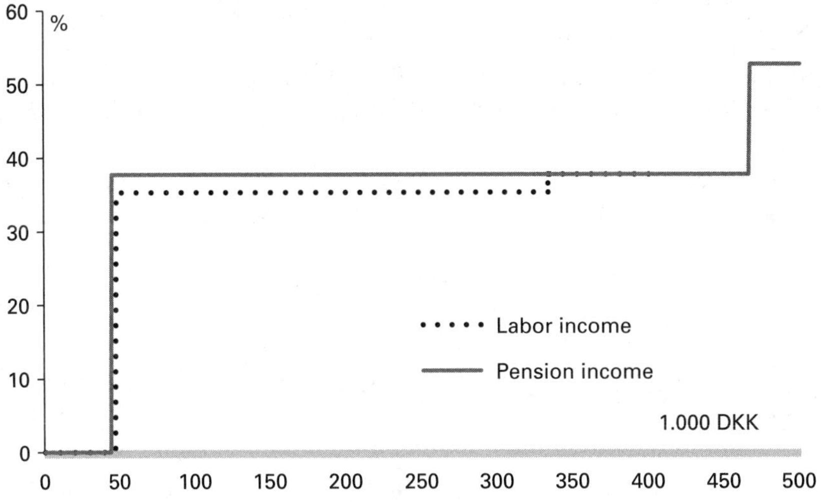

Figure 5.5
Marginal tax rates, labor income, and pension income, Denmark, 2016. *Note*: Tax values computed for an average municipal tax of 24.9 percent, excluding church tax. Labor market contribution and earned income tax credit are taken into account, at 2016 values and rates.

benefits. Two main points arise. First, the value of the tax deduction may be larger than the taxation of the pension benefit. This is the case for those facing the top marginal tax rate of about 53 percent when working and a tax of about 38 percent on the pension benefit; the difference leaves a tax incentive for pension savings for groups with high earnings when working. Second, for some middle-income groups, the value of deductions may fall short of the taxation of benefits. This arises because of the earned income tax credit, which only applies when working. This tends to lower the savings incentive.

To assess the effective tax rates relevant for savings (and retirement), it is necessary to take means testing into account. Because of the many details in both the taxation and pension schemes, it is difficult to summarize the effective tax rates on pension savings and retirement decisions in a few numbers. Figure 5.6 illustrates the effective tax rates on pension savings for a single person living in a rented apartment. Two points are worth observing. First, low- and middle-income groups face higher effective tax rates than high-income groups. The reason is means testing, as explained earlier. Second, the complexity and implied lack of transparency are illustrated by the huge variations in effective tax rates.

The current system has very different tax rates on different types of savings (figure 5.7). This is problematic since it distorts asset allocation.

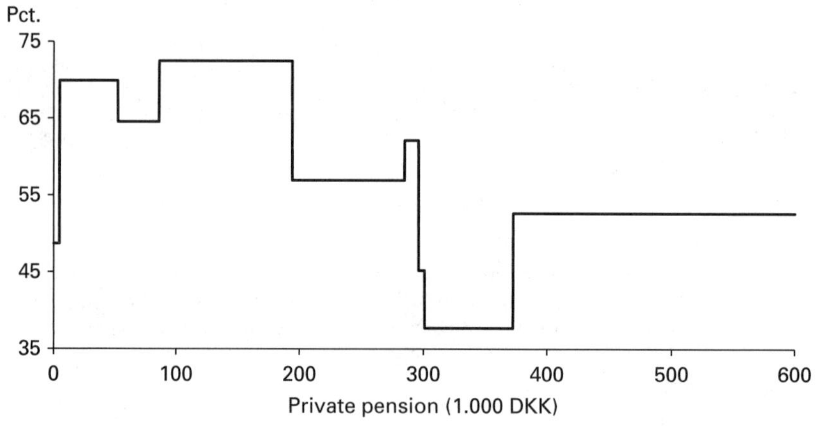

Figure 5.6
Effective tax rates on pension savings, Denmark, 2015. *Source*: Pensionskommissionen (2015). *Note*: Stylized case for a single pensioner living in a rented accommodation and thus receiving a means-tested rent subsidy.

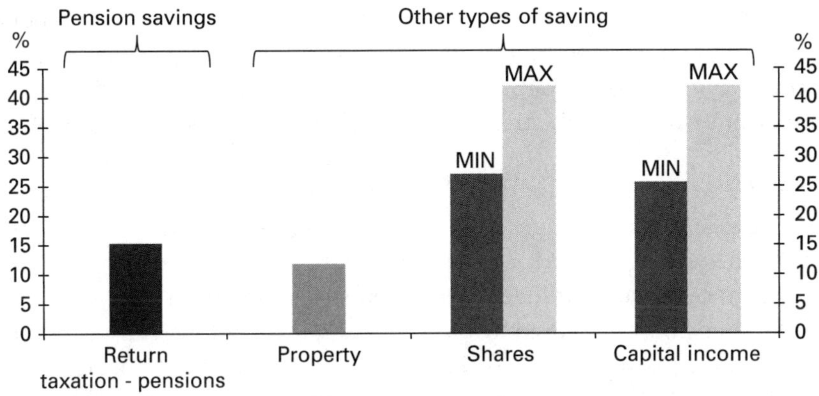

Figure 5.7
Tax rates on different types of savings, Denmark, 2015. *Source*: Pensionskommissionen (2015).

The lower taxation of the return on pension savings is motivated by the fact that these savings are held for release only upon retirement. The favorable taxation of housing is partly related to a nominal freeze on property taxes since 2002.

A particular question is whether the tax structure provides incentives for so-called balance expansion for households. A person contributing to pension savings (with a return tax of 15.3 percent) and at the same time borrowing (with interest rates deductible at a rate of 25–33 percent) effectively receives a tax subsidy by expanding the balance. Denmark stands out by having households with a high gross debt ratio, although the average household is a net creditor. Furthermore, a persistent surplus in the current account also indicates that Denmark does not have a general savings problem. However, the liquidity of assets and liabilities is very different, which may create a systemic risk factor with implications for macroeconomic stability. One may also ask why the tax system should give incentives in this direction.

5.4.2 Sweden

The Swedish pension system was radically reformed in the 1990s, with changes going into effect in 1999 (Palmer 2000; Pensionsmyndigheten 2011, 2014). The public system has three elements: the guaranteed pension, the income pension, and the premium pension. The guaranteed pension is tax financed, and the two others are financed by contributions.

In addition to the public schemes, occupational pensions are common (covering about 80 percent of workers). There are four pension funds, and, as an example, for the SAF-LO area, the contribution rate is 4.5 percent for incomes below some threshold (7.5 prisbasbelopp, approximately SEK 335,000 in 2016) and 30 percent for incomes above this level.

For the income plus premium pension, the contribution rate is 18.5 percent of earnings, split between 16 percent for the income pension and 2.5 percent for the premium pension. The contribution rate has employer and employee components. The premium pension is an individualized defined contribution system and is thus fully funded. The income pension is a PAYG scheme that is termed a notional defined contribution scheme since pensions are proportional to individual contributions, while the overall level of pensions is determined in a PAYG manner.

The income base on which pension contributions are levied is earned income (also for the self-employed, based on tax-declared income), social transfers, unemployment benefits, and other sources of income. There is even an imputed income in case of child care (for children below the age of four) and education (post–high school), with contributions financed by the state. Pension contributions are made for incomes above a certain threshold (0.423 indkomstbasbelopp, approximately SEK 25,000 in 2016), with some upper income limit (7.5 indkomstbasbelopp, approximately SEK 445,000 in 2015). For income above that level, employers still pay contributions, but they are credited not to the individual accounts but to the state (i.e., the contribution is effectively a tax). The core of the pension system is the notional defined contribution scheme, implying that pensions are dependent on lifetime earnings. Pensions are actuarially adjusted to the retirement age and longevity (for the cohort to which the individual belongs). A minimum age for eligibility exists for the guaranteed pension (65 years) and for withdrawal of income pensions (61 years).

The replacement rate for pensions displays a U-shaped path; that is, the replacement rate is high for low-income groups (above 100 percent), falls to about 60 percent for middle-income groups, and increases to about 80 percent for high-income groups (Finansdepartementet 2016). Sweden is the only OECD country with higher replacement rates for high-income groups than for middle-income ones. The Swedish taxation regime, like the Danish one, is an ETT scheme but is much simpler (table 5.2).

Table 5.2
Taxation of pensions, Sweden, 2016.

	Limit (SEK)	Deduction	Return tax (%)	Benefits	Means testing
Occupational private pensions	35% of income Max SEK 445,000	Marginal tax	15	Marginal tax	Yes

Source: www.skatteverket.se.
Notes: A deduction for individual pension savings was abolished in 2016 (in 2015, the maximum deduction was SEK 1,800). Marginal taxes applicable for contributions (the wage income tax) and for pension benefits are shown in figure 5.8.

The return tax[29] has as its basis the imputed return given as the average rate of return on government borrowing in the previous year times net assets (assets less financial debt). Since the government borrowing rate is typically lower than the rate of return on pension funds, the effective tax rate is below 15 percent. Other types of capital income are taxed at the rate of 30 percent, but the tax on insurance arrangements (kapitalförsäkringar) is 27 percent.

The marginal tax rate applied to deductions and pension benefits is given in figure 5.8. The tax structure has increasing marginal tax rates on income, implying that the tax value of tax deductions is larger than the tax applied to pensions for individuals with high incomes during their working lives. Also, in Sweden, the earned income tax implies that the tax value of deductions may fall short of marginal taxes on pensions.

Means testing arises both via the design of the guaranteed pension and from other supplements (housing). Figure 5.9 shows the sum of guaranteed and income pensions. The guaranteed pension is the floor of the system available from age 65. The pension is means tested against the income plus premium pension, and there is a residence requirement (minimum 3 years; the full amount requires 40 years of residence). For pensions below a certain level (1.26 pbb if single and 1.14 pbb if married), the taper rate is 100 percent, and it is 48 percent in the interval up to an upper threshold of 3.07 pbb if single and 2.72 pbb if married.[30] The guaranteed pension is price indexed. In 2014, about 2 percent of those in the age group 65+ received the full guaranteed pension, and about one-third received some fraction of the full amount of the guaranteed pension.

In addition, a housing supplement is available for pensioners (bostadstillägg för pensionärer). Eligibility applies from the age of 65 and

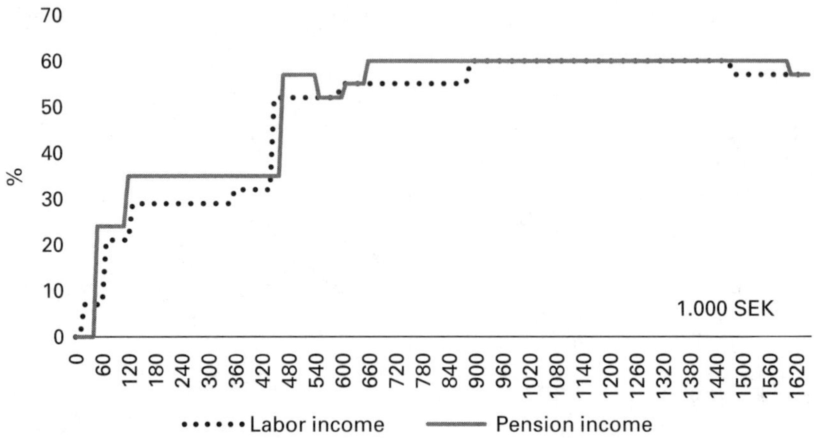

Figure 5.8
Marginal tax rates, labor income, and pension income, Sweden, 2016. *Source*: www.skatteverket.se. *Note*: Marginal tax rate for income is the marginal tax for a person with labor income only, and including earned income tax credits. For pension income, it is the marginal tax for a person with pension income only.

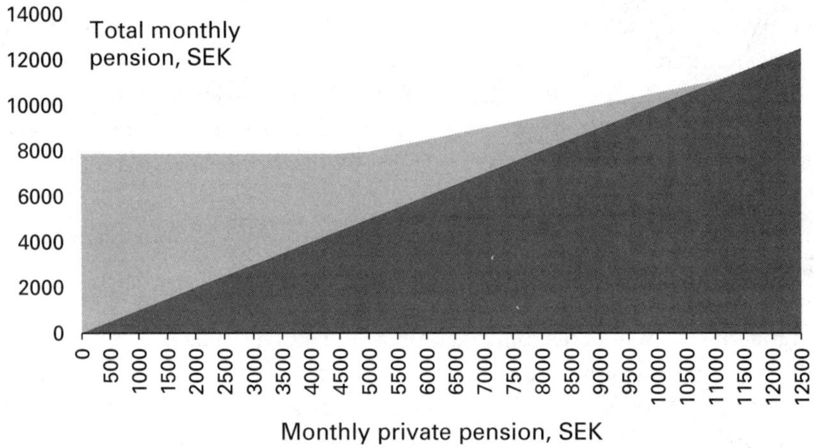

Figure 5.9
Guaranteed and income pensions, Sweden, 2016. *Source*: Author's calculation based on data from www.pensionsmyndigheten.

above. It is required that the income plus premium pension be claimed. The supplement applies for all forms of housing (e.g., rented, owner-occupied). The supplement has an upper cap on the amount of housing expenses that can be subsidized. The supplement is 95 percent of housing costs less a reduction based on a weighted income-wealth concept. This income concept weighs public pensions, capital income, and a wealth addition (15 percent of net wealth above some threshold, not including housing wealth) by 100 percent, other forms of pensions by 80 percent, and earned income (also by the self-employed) by 50 percent. This composite income concept determines the housing cost supplement.

The ultimate floor in the social safety net for the elderly is a special transfer (äldreförsörjningsstöd) for people aged 65 with insufficient means. The transfer is means tested and ensures that a minimum living standard can be maintained (the transfer is below the guaranteed pension).

The combined effect of the means testing and the direct taxes is that the effective marginal tax rates can be rather high, especially in the case of a low private pension (figure 5.10). This typically arises for low- or medium-income groups. As seen in figure 5.10, the effective tax rates are close to 100 percent for low levels of pensions and fall to about 30 percent for high levels.

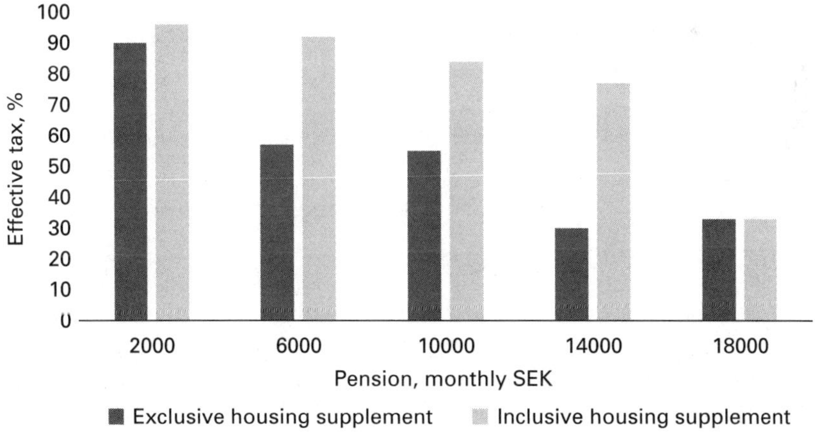

Figure 5.10
Effective marginal tax rates, single pensioner, with and without housing supplement, Sweden, 2014. *Source*: Pensionsmyndigheten 2014. *Note*: Effective tax rate depending on the level of private pension for a single pensioner. Civil servants' pensions are included.

Denmark and Sweden thus share a similar structure for the effective taxation of pensions because of the combined effect of direct taxation and means-tested benefits to pensioners with low incomes. This brings forth the dilemma illustrated in figure 5.1 of reconciling distributional goals with the incentive structure to save and to postpone retirement.

5.5 Macro Implications

As noted in section 5.3, the choice of taxation regime (for a given overall tax burden) has crucial implications for public finances. Consider for the sake of argument the schemes (T,T/E,E) and (E,T/E,T) for given tax rates (proportional and equal). For the same level of savings, the (T,T/E,E) regime front-loads tax revenue, and the opposite occurs for the (E,T/E,T) regime.[31] In a setting where pension savings are on an upward trend because of demographic trends and the expansion of mandatory (occupational) pension schemes (as in both Denmark and Sweden), this has crucial implications.

Figure 5.11 illustrates the development of pension wealth in Denmark. The upward trend reflects the strengthening of pension savings (mainly occupational pensions) and demographic trends. The trend implies intertemporal shifting of tax revenue because of contributions being tax-exempt, while pension benefits are taxable income. Hence, roughly 40 percent of pension wealth is deferred taxes. The timing of tax revenue has no implications for fiscal sustainability provided the rate of return on pension savings equals the relevant public discount rate. In practice, there may, however, be effects to the extent that economic policy responds to the actual budget position. In the buildup phase, the budget position is worsened by this taxation regime, and vice versa in the withdrawal phase.

However, a credibility or commitment aspect to the choice of taxation regime also exists. With deferred taxation, there is effectively a substantial presaving of public funds, which to some extent may match the upward expenditure drift caused by changing demographics. In this way, the deferred taxes may be considered a partial prefunding of the upward expenditure pressure caused by a change in the age structure of the population. Whether this is an optimal strategy clearly depends on intergenerational distribution aspects. The temptation under this regime, especially if public finances are under pressure for other reasons, is to front-load some of the tax revenue to improve the current

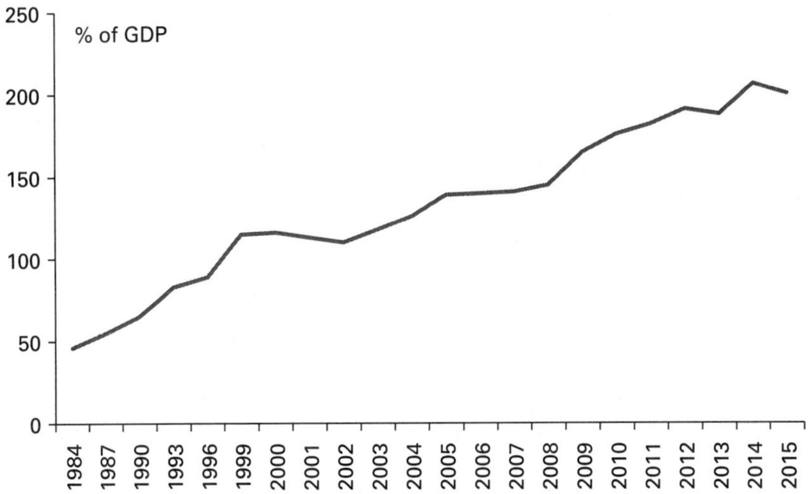

Figure 5.11
Total pension assets as a percentage of GDP, Denmark, 1984–2015. *Source*: Danish Ministry of Taxation, www.skm.dk. *Note*: Gross pension wealth in pension funds.

budget position and thus make it possible to meet budget norms. This is not a theoretical discussion, as recent Danish experience shows. Some pension schemes were changed from ETT to TTE, with the prime motivation being to improve the budget position relative to budget norms.[32]

Return taxation creates an additional aspect for public finances. Figure 5.12 shows the revenue from taxation of returns in Denmark. It shows that the tax is a significant revenue source but also that this revenue is rather volatile, reflecting developments in the financial markets. The return tends to be procyclical, which introduces a procyclical element into the budget on top of the traditional automatic stabilizers. However, this does not contribute to stabilization of income and hence demand in the same way as the automatic stabilizers, but it introduces a significant random element into the budget. This may create problems in relation to budget norms [in particular, the budget limit that actual budget deficits cannot exceed 3 percent of gross domestic product (GDP)]. Figure 5.12 shows that volatility in the revenue from taxing pension returns itself may bring the budget from a position of balance to close to the 3 percent limit. This is in itself a control problem, but it may also constrain the degrees of freedom for countercyclical policies.

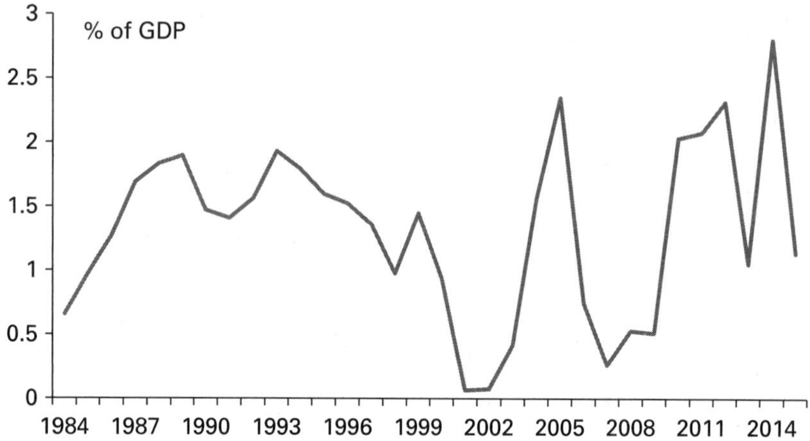

Figure 5.12
Revenue from taxation of returns in pension funds as a percentage of GDP, Denmark, 1984–2015. *Source*: Statistics Denmark.

5.6 Concluding Remarks

While pension savings receive favorable tax treatments, both Denmark and Sweden rely on mandatory savings as the key approach for ensuring adequate savings levels and thus for reaching acceptable replacement rates. In Denmark, social partners have taken on the responsibility, implying that occupational pensions are the outcome of bargaining among labor market organizations, while pension saving is a legal requirement in Sweden. The former system may have the advantage of building on the support of the social partners but also the problem that the system does not comprise the entire population.

Denmark and Sweden chose very different routes in the design of their pension systems, but some of the key issues and dilemmas are the same. Both countries have strong distributional objectives, and poverty among pensioners is not accepted. This is reflected in public base/guaranteed pensions. Means testing is used to target these pensions to the economically least well off pensioners. This reduces public expenditures to reach these distributional goals, but at the same time it introduces high effective marginal tax rates on savings and retirement decisions. This fundamental problem is without a perfect solution, but one may question whether marginal tax rates have reached levels where they jeopardize the overall objective of strengthening savings incentives and inducing later retirement (alongside increases in longevity).

Both Denmark and Sweden basically follow an ETT tax regime. While theory implies equivalence with other taxation regimes (for unchanged tax rates), the deferred taxation of pensions implies postponement of tax revenue. It can be seen as prefunding future expenditure drifts because of an aging population, but there is an inherent temptation to front-load revenue. Taxation of returns contributes significant revenue but also substantial volatility in tax revenues when the tax base is current returns, as in Denmark, rather than a more smoothed model, as in Sweden.

Notes

Paper presented at the CEPAR-CESifo workshop "Taxation of Pensions," Munich, September 3–4, 2015. Comments by seminar participants, Bernd Genser, and Robert Holzmann are gratefully acknowledged.

1. For a discussion of Finland, see Lassila and Valkonen (2016, chapter 13, this volume).

2. The dual income tax system in Denmark is not applied purely since positive net capital income above a threshold level is taxed on a par with labor income. Finland also recently introduced a moderate progressive element in capital income taxation.

3. In addition, funded labor market pension arrangements exist.

4. Insufficient savings (or inadequate portfolio composition) can also arise, for example, because of information problems or lack of financial literacy (Lusardi and Mitchell 2013). However, this leads to consideration of other types of interventions, such as education and framing, which are not the topic of this chapter.

5. Time inconsistency arises because there is a difference in the marginal rate of substitution between periods t and $t+1$ and that between $t+1$ and $t+2$ (and all future periods). With the passage of time, agents change behavior relative to what is planned in period t.

6. This involves a question of paternalism in the sense that the policy maker "knows better" what is truly in the best interest of the individual.

7. PAYG pensions are by nature mandatory. Pillar II occupational pension schemes are also usually mandatory at the individual level but can be negotiated between the labor market parties.

8. If mandatory and voluntary savings offer the same rate of return, mandatory pension savings will on a one-to-one basis crowd out voluntary savings. Mandatory savings will thus only increase net savings if voluntary savings are driven to zero and borrowing is either ruled out or is possible only at an interest rate higher than the savings rate (Andersen and Bhattacharya 2016).

9. If present-biased preferences are related to socioeconomic factors such that there is a lower prevalence of present bias among high-income groups, an interest rate subsidy may be regressive.

10. Evidence for Denmark points to relatively low crowding out (25–30 percent) of voluntary savings (Arnberg and Barslund 2012; Chetty et al. 2014).

11. If mandated (occupational) pensions are the outcome of negotiations between the social partners, the taxation of pension savings may affect the negotiated contribution rates.

12. Present-biased households try to evade the mandatory savings by reducing voluntary savings. In the case of a borrowing constraint, the crowding out continues until voluntary savings are driven into a corner (Andersen and Bhattacharya 2016). Increasing mandatory savings thus reduces present consumption, which, as seen from the household perspective, has a higher marginal utility than discounted future consumption, and hence mandatory savings have a distortion cost, although lower than that of general income taxation.

13. Eventual withdrawal may be possible a few years earlier than the statutory retirement age. Usually there are penalties for earlier withdrawal but also exceptions; for example, in the case of critical illness.

14. An annuity is not uniquely defined, the payment may be nominal or indexed, and there may be contingencies for changes in longevity at the cohort level.

15. As an example, occupational pensions may simultaneously mandate that agents save for pensions and create annuities within the risk class defined by the members; that is, a double inefficiency is addressed.

16. This may also be a reason for undersaving. Agents expect the welfare state to provide for them in old age and therefore do not save enough (Cremer et al. 2008; Fenge and von Weizsäcker 2001).

17. Yoo and de Serres (2004) present some examples illustrating this.

18. Statements to the contrary are often made; for example, "The Commission supports this system of deferred taxation since contributions to pension funds diminish a person's ability to pay taxes and since it encourages citizens to save for their old age. In addition, it will help Member States to deal with the demographic time-bomb, as they will be collecting more tax revenues at a time when more elderly people may call on the State for care." See http://ec.europa.eu/taxation_customs/taxation/personal_tax/pensions/index_en.htm.

19. Note that present-biased decision makers act rationally but based on a "biased" objective function.

20. It may also reflect greater certainty about the earnings within the year.

21. The Faroe Islands recently changed to a TTE regime to avoid loss of tax revenue caused by emigration of pensioners. Greenland is considering a similar move.

22. In general, means testing implies a nonconvex budget set, which complicates the analysis considerably and may imply bunching (many individuals being at the corner) (Fehr and Uhde 2014).

23. This is seen most clearly in the case of a flat-rate public pension. Even in systems where pensions are in some way related to some measure of lifetime income, there is some "guaranteed pension" for low-income groups for distributional reasons (see subsection 5.4.2 for Sweden).

24. There may also be a threshold such that contributions above a certain level do not imply higher pensions; that is, the contribution rate at this kink becomes a tax (see subsection 5.4.2 on Sweden).

25. The Money and Pension Panel Expert Group (2012) presented a number of cases for Denmark showing an implicit insurance effect in the sense that total pensions vary less than private pensions in the case of various events.

26. See also Andersen (2015a, 2015b) and Pensionskommissionen (2015).

27. To be eligible for the full amount, residence in Denmark for 40 years after the age of 15 is required; otherwise, the amount is reduced in proportion to the period of residence. To be eligible for the full amount, labor income cannot exceed DKK 310,000 (2016). It is possible to postpone claiming public pensions with some premium.

28. One implication is that these schemes do not include a "residual group," who are therefore more dependent on public pensions (Andersen 2015b).

29. The tax on returns was introduced in the mid-1980s because of exceptionally (unexpected) high real rates of return. However, a tax on the real return was not introduced; after some temporary measures, the current system was implemented, and the tax on returns has been 15 percent since 1995 (Bergström, Palme, and Persson 2010).

30. The lower threshold is 1.26 pbb for single persons and 1.14 ppb for married ones, and the upper thresholds are 3.07 and 2.72 pbb, respectively. The pbb was SEK 44,300 in 2016.

31. In a stationary steady state, this would not matter. In a situation with changing demographics and a higher level of contributions than benefits, there is a systematic tendency to postpone tax revenue.

32. Some recent examples of front-loading of tax revenue from pension arrangements can be found. A tax reform in 2012 made it possible to transfer a capital pension into a so-called old-age pension with some tax subsidy (2.7 percent of the amount transferred). The scheme was later prolonged to the end of 2015. For the old-age pension, there is no tax deductibility when paid in but therefore also no tax payment at payout, and the payout is not subject to means testing. A similar change (including a tax rebate) was made with the so-called LD pension to front-load tax revenue. About DKK 200 billion in tax revenue was front-loaded in this way (corresponding to about 20 percent of the deferred tax).

References

Andersen, Torben M. 2015a. "Robustness of the Danish Pension System." CESifo DICE Report No. 2/2015, 25–30, CESifo, Munich.

Andersen, Torben M. 2015b. "The Danish Pension System—Properties, Outcomes and Challenges." Invited paper for the CLAPES UC seminar "Financiamiento de las Pensiones: Capitalización vs. Reparto," Santiago, Chile, July 14.

Andersen, Torben M., and Joydeep Bhattacharya. 2011. "On Myopia as Rationale for Social Security." *Economic Theory* 47 (1): 135–158.

Andersen, Torben M., and Joydeep Bhattacharya. 2016. "Mandatory Pension Saving in a Life-Cycle Perspective." Working Paper, Aarhus University, Aarhus, Denmark.

Andersen, Torben M., Niku Määttänen, and Tarmo Valkonen. 2014. "Pension Reforms: Longevity and Retirement." In *The Nordic Model—Challenged but Capable of Reform*, edited by T. Valkonen and V. Vihriälä jointly with Tema Nord, 111–142. Nordic Councils of Ministers, Copenhagen.

Arnberg, Søren, and Mikkel Barslund. 2012. "The Crowding-Out Effect of Mandatory Labour Market Pension Schemes on Private Savings: Evidence from Renters in Denmark." Working Paper No. 2012-1, Danish Economic Council, Copenhagen.

Barr, Nicholas, and Peter A. Diamond. 2006. "The Economics of Pensions." *Oxford Review of Economic Policy* 22 (1): 15–39.

Bergström, Åsa-Pia J., Mårten Palme, and Mats Persson. 2010. "Beskattning af privat pensionssparande." Rapport till Expertgruppen för Studier i Offentlig Ekonomi 2010:2, Finansdepartementet, ESO.

Chetty, Ray, John N. Friedman, Søren Leth-Petersen, Torben Heien Nielsen, and Tore Olsen. 2014. "Active vs. Passive Decisions and Crowding-Out in Retirement Savings Accounts: Evidence from Denmark." *Quarterly Journal of Economics* 129 (3): 1141–1219.

Cremer, Helmuth, Phillippe de Donder, Dario Maldonado, and Pierre Pestieau. 2008. "Forced Saving, Redistribution and Nonlinear Social Security Schemes." CESifo Working Paper No. 2325, CESifo, Munich.

Cremer, Helmuth, and Pierre Pestieau. 2011. "Myopia, Redistribution and Pensions." *European Economic Review* 55 (2): 165–175.

Davidoff, Thomas, Jeffrey R. Brown, and Peter A. Diamond. 2005. "Annuities and Individual Welfare." *American Economic Review* 95 (5): 1573–1590.

Diamond, Peter A. 2009. "Taxes and Pensions." *Southern Economic Journal* 76 (1): 2–15.

Fehr, Hans, and Johannes Uhde. 2014. "Means-Testing Retirement Benefits in the UK: Is It Efficient?" Netspar Discussion Paper No. 02/2014-006, Tilburg.

Feldstein, Martin, and Jeffrey Leibman. 2002. "Social Security." In *Handbook of Public Economics*, vol. 4, edited by Alan Auerbach and Martin Feldstein, 2245–2324. Amsterdam: Elsevier.

Fenge, Robert, and Jakob von Weizsäcker. 2001. "Compulsory Saving: Efficiency and Redistribution—On the Interactions of Means-Tested Basic Income and Public Pensions." *International Tax and Public Finance* 8:637–652.

Finansdepartementet. 2016. "Ålderspensionssystemet vid sidan av statens budget." Supplement to Budgetpropositionen, prop. 2016/17:1, Stockholm.

Genser, Bernd, and Robert Holzmann. 2016. "The Taxation of Internationally Portable Pensions: Fiscal Issues and Policy Options." CESifo Working Paper No. 5702, CESifo, Munich.

Kaplow, Louis. 2015. "Myopia and the Effects of Social Security and Capital Taxation on Labor Supply." *National Tax Journal* 68 (1): 7–32.

Krusell, Per, Burhanettin Kuruscu, and Anthony A. Smith Jr. 2010. "Temptation and Taxation." *Econometrica* 78 (6): 2063–2084.

Laibson, David. 1996. "Hyperbolic Discount Functions, Undersaving, and Savings Policy." NBER Working Paper No. 5635, National Bureau of Economic Research, Cambridge, MA.

Lassila, Jukka, and Tarmo Valkonen. 2016. "Longevity Risk and Taxation of Public Pensions." CESifo Working Paper No. 5640, CESifo, Munich.

Lusardi, Annamaria, and Olivia S. Mitchell. 2013. "The Economic Importance of Financial Literacy: Theory and Evidence." NBER Working Paper No. 18952, National Bureau of Economic Research, Cambridge, MA.

Money and Pension Panel Expert Group. 2012. "Basic Pensions—The Default Option for Labour-Market Pensions." Report by the Committee of the Money and Pension Panel, Copenhagen.

OECD (Organisation for Economic Co-operation and Development). 2013. *Pensions at a Glance*. Paris: OECD Publishing.

Palmer, Edward. 2000. "The Swedish Pension Reform Model: Framework and Issues." Social Protection Paper No. 12, World Bank, Washington, DC.

Pensionskommissionen. 2015. "The Danish Pension System—Internationally Praised but not without Problems (Det danske pensionssystem—international anerkendt, men ikke problemfrit)." Pensionskommissionen, Copenhagen.

Pensionsmyndigheten. 2011. "Det svenska pensionssystemet." Pensionsmyndigheten, Stockholm.

Pensionsmyndigheten. 2014. "Från fattigvård till ekonomisk trygghet vid ålderdom—beskrivning af grundskyddet i det svenska pensionssystemet." Pensionsmyndigheten, Stockholm.

Sørensen, Peter B. 2010. "Dual Income Taxes: A Nordic System." In *Tax Reform in Open Economies,* edited by I. Claus, N. Gemmell, M. Harding, and D. White, 78–107. Cheltenham: Edward Elgar.

St-Amant, Pier-André B., and Jean-Denis Garon. 2014. "Optimal Redistributive Pensions and the Costs of Self-Control." *International Tax and Public Finance* 22:723–740.

Yoo, Kwang-Yeol, and Alain de Serres. 2004. "Tax Treatment of Private Pension Savings in OECD Countries." *OECD Economic Studies* 39:73–110.

6 Taxation of Pensions in Portugal: Is There a Rationale for a Semidual Income Tax System?

Jorge Miguel Bravo

6.1 Introduction

Portugal's personal tax reform in 1989 established a comprehensive, progressive, and unitary personal income tax system. Since then, a number of tax reforms have gradually moved Portugal toward a semidual income tax (SDIT) system with certain categories of income exempt from taxation and/or subject to flat nominal withholding tax rates. The Portuguese income tax system combines a highly progressive tax schedule for labor and pension income with low and flat nominal tax rates on some forms of capital (personal and corporate) income.

Despite numerous parametric reforms undertaken in recent decades, the Portuguese pension system continues to be dominated by a public pay-as-you-go (PAYG), earnings-related, defined benefit scheme. The country was hit particularly hard by the 2008–2009 global financial crisis and was compelled to cut pension payments and to reduce available income for older people. Pension reforms adopted in the last decade will significantly reduce PAYG pension benefits for both current and (particularly) future pensioners. Tax relief for some retirement savings vehicles was either capped by some amount or simply eliminated. Some of the major occupational pension schemes were incorporated into the social security system. Recent studies demonstrate that public schemes, already running considerable funding deficits, continue to be unsustainable and will deliver inadequate income in retirement unless a significant increase in the coverage and funding levels of private pension schemes takes place (Bravo, Afonso, and Guerreiro 2013, 2014).

The majority of countries in the Organisation for Economic Cooperation and Development (OECD) offer favorable tax treatment to retirement savings made through private pension plans and other retirement savings vehicles. Pension taxation should contribute toward creating an adequate, affordable, sustainable, equitable, and efficient pension system, comprising mechanisms for individuals and households to smooth consumption over time, to ensure against economic, financial, and biometric risks, and to protect against the risk of poverty in old age. The question that naturally emerges is whether there is a taxation model for public, occupational, and personal pensions that (1) complies with national constitutions and international tax agreements, (2) contributes to delivering adequate retirement income, (3) generates neutral and equitable outcomes within generations, and (4) is financially sustainable in the long term.

This chapter critically analyzes the reform path Portugal has taken toward its current SDIT system in the taxation of public, occupational, and personal pensions and other retirement income, and discusses whether this variant of a dual income tax (DIT) could provide a blueprint for reforms in other countries. Arguments for and against adoption of an SDIT in the taxation of occupational and personal pensions are assessed. The chapter highlights the key advantages and disadvantages of moving to an SDIT regime for pensions versus alternative tax regimes. The relative costs and benefits from recent pension tax reforms in Portugal are discussed, including their macroeconomic implications. Although other countries face economic, political, social, and tax environments very different from those of Portugal or the Nordic countries, the SDIT may be an appropriate solution to the many challenges involved in the taxation of pensions.

The chapter is organized as follows. Section 6.2 provides an overview of the Portuguese pension system. Section 6.3 summarizes the characteristic features of an SDIT system and offers a detailed analysis of the current tax treatment of public, occupational, and personal pensions and retirement benefits in Portugal and how it compares in international terms. Section 6.4 discusses whether a theoretical or operational rationale exists for an SDIT in the taxation of pensions, portrays the particularities of its implementation in Portugal, and analyzes the extent to which this option fits the long-term goals and challenges of the Portuguese pension system. Section 6.5 summarizes the findings.

6.2 A Brief Overview of the Portuguese Pension System

The Portuguese pension system is based on three pillars of differing importance (figure 6.1): the dominant state pension system (first pillar), the occupational pension provision (second pillar), and the personal pension provision (third pillar). The first pillar combines an earnings-

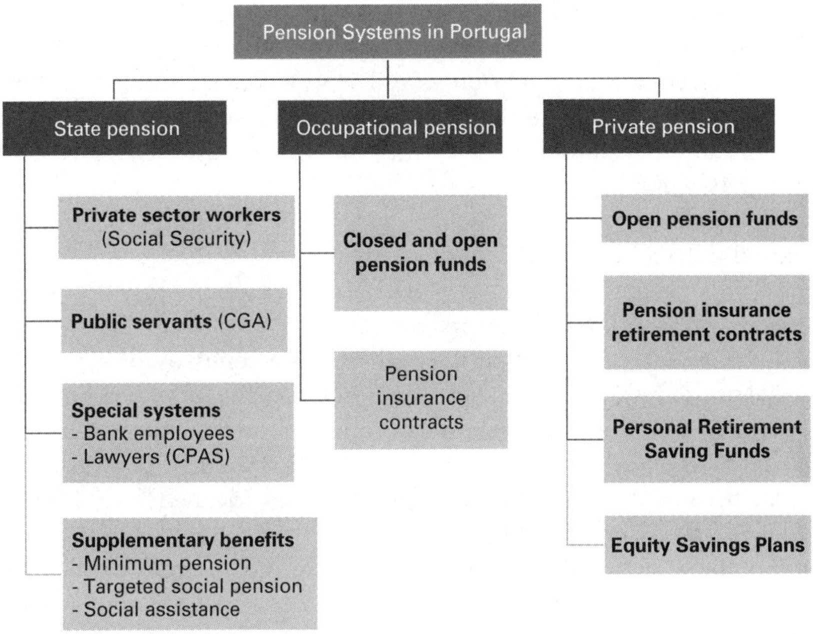

Figure 6.1
Structure of retirement income provision in Portugal. *Source*: Author's preparation based on Portuguese legislation.

related, defined benefit, mandatory public scheme, comprising two separate but convergent schemes for private sector workers (Subsistema Previdencial da Segurança Social) and public servants (Regime de Protecção Social Convergente—CGA), with minor special systems for lawyers and solicitors (CPAS) and older bank employees. Contributory state pensions are financed on a PAYG basis by social contributions paid by both the employer and employee, complemented by a small fraction of the value-added tax (social VAT). Additionally, the state system includes noncontributory means-tested pension benefits, top up minimum contributory benefits, and several targeted assistance programs, fully funded by general taxes, aimed at reducing old-age poverty. The state pension scheme comprises old age, early retirement, disability, and survivors' pensions. Together with supplementary benefits, it was designed to guarantee maintenance of an appropriate standard of living after retirement and in the event of disability or death.

In 2014, there were 3,627,000 contributory state pensions. Total pension expenditures accounted for 15.7 percent of gross domestic product (GDP) and almost 75 percent of all social security expenditures. The average annual old-age pension amounts to €5,098 for those in the private sector and €16,111 for those in the public sector. The current (2014) benefit ratio is 70.8 percent for male pensioners and 54.9 percent for female pensioners but is projected to decline significantly as a result of recent pension reforms and pension indexation rules that do not fully recognize productivity gains.

Occupational pension schemes and accident insurance form the second pillar. Occupational pensions are not very widespread in Portugal. The coverage rate is still very low: currently no more than 3.7 percent of Portugal's workforce is covered by second-pillar schemes. By law, they may be set up voluntarily at the initiative of a company or groups of social or professional associations, and they take the form of closed and open pension funds or pension insurance contracts (collective insurance). Pension schemes funded through collective membership in an open pension fund may be of different types (defined contribution, defined benefit, or hybrid schemes) and may also be contributory. Contributions to occupational pension plans are mostly from employers. Employee contributions to these plans are not impossible but are not common. Benefits are in the form of lump-sum (maximum one-third) and annuity payments.

The third pillar, personal pension provision, is voluntary and aims to close any gaps that exist in a person's pension coverage or to fulfill other ambitions at retirement. Although the household savings rate in Portugal is quite low (3.9 percent of disposable income in 2015), personal pension schemes exist in the form of individual acquisition of open pension units (Fundos de Pensões Abertos), pension insurance retirement contracts (Fundos Poupança Reforma), Personal Retirement Saving Funds (financed through insurance contracts, pension funds, or investment funds), and Equity Savings Plans (Fundos Poupança Acções). Contributions to second- and third-pillar schemes are elective and are separate from the regular social contribution. In 2013, second- and third-pillar schemes counted 190,000 participants, equivalent to approximately 1.8 percent of the total population. A Social Security Trust Fund (FEFSS), currently managing around €14.1 billion in assets, is financed through a fraction of social security contributions and would be activated should the social security treasury come under stress.[1]

In recent years, Portugal has implemented numerous (temporary and permanent) parametric pension reforms aimed at reducing public pension expenditures, with little margin for addressing income adequacy concerns in an already highly aged society. The main policy initiatives were driven by the short-term need for fiscal consolidation rather than by a long-term prospect for the design of pension systems. Parametric reforms include (1) the introduction of a sustainability factor in the pension formula, (2) an increase in the statutory retirement age, (3) moving from best years to lifetime average earnings, (4) a new indexation mechanism linked to prices and real GDP growth, (5) the introduction of bonuses for late retirement and penalties for early retirement, (6) suspension of early-retirement regimes, (7) nominal pension cuts, and (8) means testing for noncontributory benefits.

At the fiscal level, the main changes include both permanent measures (e.g., higher personal income withholding tax rates and a decrease in specific deductions within the income tax applying to pension income) and temporary measures (e.g., the Extraordinary Solidarity Surcharge—CES—and the Personal Income Extraordinary Surcharge). Despite all of the restrictive parametric measures implemented in recent years, long-term independent projections show that Portugal's systems will continue to exhibit permanent deficits and that the level of pension expenditures will remain unsustainable and will deliver inadequate income in retirement (Bravo, Afonso, and Guerreiro 2013, 2014).

6.3 The Taxation of Pensions in Portugal

This section provides a detailed analysis of the current tax treatment of pensions and retirement benefits in Portugal and how it compares in international terms. It describes separately the tax treatment of contributions, returns on investments, and accumulation of funds and pension income in public and private (personal and occupational) pension schemes, life insurance contracts, mutual funds, and alternative vehicles for retirement saving. Special attention is paid to social contributions levied on pension income and to a special personal income taxation regime for nonregular residents, particularly retirees. To highlight the special features of the SDIT system, the main alternative approaches to taxing pension income are briefly presented from a normative position.[2]

6.3.1 Basics of Pension Taxation Regimes

The taxation of pensions involves three cash flows that can be taxed and their timing of taxation. Pensions can be (totally or partially) taxed (T) or exempt (E) (1) at the point when employees and employers contribute or save to the pension scheme or savings vehicle, (2) when asset returns (interest, capital gains, or the equivalent gains in a PAYG system or distributable profit) arise, or (3) when pension income is withdrawn (Cremer and Pestieau 2016, chapter 2, this volume; Piggott and Chomik 2015, chapter 11, this volume). In addition, corporate income tax, regional taxes, inheritance taxes, regular or extraordinary surcharges, and other taxes (e.g., property taxes, stamp duties) may directly or indirectly affect pension returns. Consideration therefore needs to be given as to whether the tax treatment of pensions at the personal level should reflect this.

In a pure Schanz-Haig-Simons (SHS) comprehensive income tax system, all (or most) net cash (labor, pension, and capital) income is added up and subjected to a common (usually) progressive tax schedule. The SHS system is based on the idea that all of the taxpayer's income should be taxed once (and only once) and in the same manner. This is in contrast to a "schedular" tax system, where different types of income are taxed separately.[3] Accordingly, savings made out of taxed earnings and accrued returns on accumulated funds (including the revaluation of pension entitlements in PAYG schemes) are subject to an income tax. In return, the withdrawal of assets from such savings vehicles is fully exempt from taxation. Such arrangements are known as "taxed-taxed-exempt" (TTE) schemes. Schanz-Haig-Simons tax systems ensure horizontal equity (taxpayers with the same level of annual income are taxed equally), and properly graduated tax scales ensure vertical equity (taxpayers with higher incomes are taxed more heavily). This method of taxation discriminates in favor of current consumption, particularly in high-inflation scenarios—that is, it is not neutral with regard to present and future consumption and acts as a disincentive to (particularly long-term) saving.

In a pure Fisher-Kaldor-Meade expenditure (consumption, cash-flow) tax regime, only consumption (not saving and capital income) is taxed. Accordingly, both funds contributed and investment income and capital gains accrued in the savings vehicle are exempt from taxation. In return, the benefits are treated as taxable income upon withdrawal; thus, taxation is deferred to the payout phase. This is known as an EET (exempt, exempt, taxed) regime or tax-deferral regime (tax is deferred until people withdraw benefits). An EET base can be thought of as giving tax relief for saving up front and is thus equivalent to saving in a tax-deferred account. Contrary to SHS tax systems, in which present consumption is taxed at a lower rate when compared to future consumption, EET systems achieve fiscal neutrality between current and future consumption. An EET system allows taxpayers more freedom to smooth consumption over their life cycle. This is the most common tax treatment for savings in PAYG and funded private pension plans at the personal level in industrialized countries (Yoo and de Serres 2004; Wellisch et al. 2008; OECD 2015). The higher the returns generated by the savings vehicle, the greater the amount of tax paid on pension income. An EET regime allows tax-rate smoothing over the individual's lifetime and may create incentives to save for retirement. Specifically, under a pure EET system, individuals who pay higher income taxes during their working life but who expect to pay lower income taxes in retirement face a stronger incentive to save for retirement and vice versa.

As a compromise between the progressive comprehensive income tax and the expenditure tax, several countries have adopted a DIT. The key distinction in a DIT system is that it is a particular form of schedular tax that applies a separate (generally lower[4]) flat tax rate to capital income and a progressive tax schedule to the sum of the taxpayer's income from other sources (e.g., labor and pension income). Tax credits and deductions are used to enhance horizontal and vertical equity.[5] Under a pure DIT, capital income includes interest, dividends, and capital gains from financial assets, imputed rent on housing, accrued returns on pension savings, and profits from personal businesses. Corporate and personal income tax rates are fully integrated using imputation or some other method.[6] Given the large difference in the marginal tax rates on capital and labor income, the DIT provides medium- and high-income self-employed individuals with large incentives to participate in tax-minimizing income shifting.

Against these normative benchmarks of pension taxation, a number of residual categories have been proposed and implemented worldwide, including semidual and semicomprehensive income tax systems, the prepaid expenditure tax model, and a flat tax system. Semidual and semicomprehensive income tax systems are those in which different nominal tax rates are levied on different types of income. Unlike the DIT, an SDIT system is a particular form of schedular tax that applies different flat rates to some forms of capital (personal or corporate) income while maintaining a progressive tax schedule on other sources of income. SDIT systems tax most types of capital income at rates that deviate from the progressive tax rates on labor and pension income. Semicomprehensive income tax systems tax most types of capital income at high and often progressive rates that are levied on labor income as well. A dual progressive income tax (DPIT) system taxes capital income separately from labor income, but capital income is taxed at modestly progressive tax rates.

Under a prepaid expenditure tax model, pension contributions are paid (totally or partially) out of after-tax income, no income tax or capital gains tax is levied on returns as they accrue in the savings vehicle, and withdrawals from the pension scheme or savings vehicle are not subject to income tax. This is known as a TEE regime, or tEE when contributions are partially exempt (t) (through tax deductions or tax credits). This system provides a distortion toward future consumption among those individuals who are expected to be able to generate high returns from investment, since they will pay no further tax. The tax incentive to save for retirement provided by EET and TEE regimes over TTE and ETT regimes comes from the nontaxation of the returns on investments.

Finally, under a flat tax system, a proportional (flat) tax rate is levied on all net income (capital income, labor income, and other income minus all deductions). Labor and capital incomes are taxed equally, and the value of the tax allowances is independent of the income level, thus limiting the scope for a fair sharing of the tax burden. Given that most countries levy social security contributions only on labor income, if the system delivers a flat pension benefit, the uniformity of the system is undermined and actuarial fairness is not guaranteed. Progressivity in these types of systems is accomplished by providing basic income. If the same flat rate is introduced for personal and corporate income taxes, tax incentives for income shifting are reduced.

6.3.2 Taxation of Public Pensions in Portugal

The general taxation regime of public pension schemes in Portugal may be classified as EET for employees and employers. Employer and employee contributions to public pension schemes are not taxed. Employer contributions are considered part of the payroll and are therefore deductible in computing the corporate income tax (CIT), whereas employee contributions are deductible for personal income tax purposes. Tax relief is unlimited and is applied at the individual or family marginal income tax rate. Public pensions are funded on a PAYG basis and partially financed from the general government budget (noncontributory benefits); hence, there are no returns on investment that could be subject to or exempt from taxation. Notional capital (i.e., increases in pension entitlements through the revalorization mechanism of contributions, indexed to productivity gains and inflation) is entirely tax-free.

Public pensions are considered deferred labor income and are treated as pension income and taxed at the individual's marginal income tax rate. The first €4,104 of pension income is tax-exempt regardless of its source. However, an extraordinary solidarity contribution called CES (Contribuição Extraordinária de Solidariedade), introduced in 2011 and expanded as part of the Memorandum of Understanding signed with the Troika,[7] is paid on pensions above a certain amount. It also applies to private pensions and annuities paid by occupational pension plans. According to the Portuguese Personal Income Tax (PIT) system, Portuguese residents are taxed on their worldwide income through the Internal Revenue Service (IRS) on a self-assessment basis, while nonresidents are subject to Portuguese tax on their Portuguese-sourced income at the applicable rates. Total taxable income is split into six categories and subject to highly progressive tax rates, but the scheme contains a substantial zero-bracket amount, which results in only relatively high levels of labor income being subject to the higher progressive tax rates.[8] This version of a DIT is equivalent to a flat tax on all income, with a surcharge on labor income above a certain threshold. Tax-deductible expenses (e.g., contributions to retirement savings vehicles) are capped by an income-related global tax-deduction amount. An apportionment or splitting procedure applies to married couples. This means the ability-to-pay principle is sensitive to family circumstances. Figure 6.2 represents the current Portuguese PIT marginal tax rates by taxable income.

As of 2015, there were five income bands, with tax rates ranging from 14.5 percent to 48.0 percent (11.6 percent to 38.4 percent in the Azores Islands). A 3.5 percent additional surcharge for PIT introduced in September 2011 is levied on the family's aggregate annual taxable income exceeding the annual national minimum salary (€7,070). For taxpayers in the top bracket, a 2.5 percent to 5.0 percent additional solidarity surcharge is also levied on income above €80,000. The progressivity of the tax system and the overall tax burden of households, particularly retirees, increased significantly in recent years as a result of the 2013 PIT tax reforms. Since 2015, labor income and pension income are treated equally, with the same PIT rates and deductions. Portugal's income threshold for the top bracket is one of the three highest in OECD countries (together with Sweden and Denmark), and the marginal tax rate at that income level is close to the highest among OECD countries (see OECD Tax Database). With an average tax on labor income of 42.06 percent in 2015, Portugal is still well above OECD

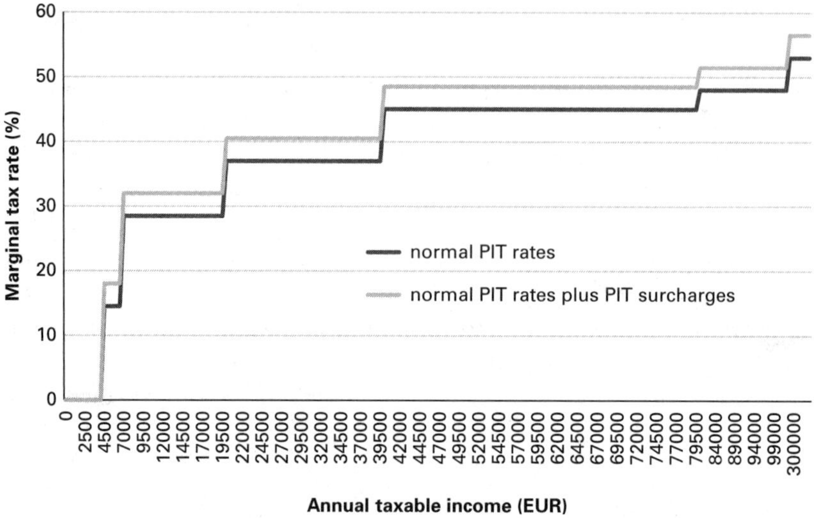

Figure 6.2
Marginal income tax rates by taxable income in Portugal. *Source*: Author's preparation based on Portuguese legislation. *Note*: Surcharges excluding CES.

(35.87 percent) and EU (38.4 percent) averages, with little room for further tax increases.

Recent tax reforms, by using a common proportion tax, promoted systematically different treatment of investment income compared to income derived from other sources. To enforce horizontal equity, tax rules were simplified and systematized by using proportional rates. To create a unified system that respects differences in the international mobility of income, tax rates applicable to income earned by residents and nonresidents were made equal, with the exception of the regime for nonhabitual tax residents detailed in subsection 6.3.7. For nonresidents, labor, business, and professional income are taxed at a uniform rate of 25 percent. Interest, dividend, capital gains on the sale of shares, and rental income are taxed at a uniform rate of 28 percent but can be exempt in particular circumstances. Pension income and capital gains on the sale of real estate are taxed progressively at the marginal rate up to 48 percent but can be exempt in some cases. The semidualization of the system aims to promote simplicity and stability. Table 6.1 provides an overview of the taxation of public pensions in OECD countries.

As can be seen, the general taxation regime of public pension schemes in Portugal is the common taxation regime. Many OECD and

Table 6.1
Overview of the taxation of public pensions in OECD countries.

Tax regime	Country	Pension taxation regimes
EET	Austria, Belgium, Cyprus, Czech Republic, Denmark, Estonia, Finland, Greece, Italy, Latvia, Luxembourg, Poland, Portugal, Slovenia, Spain, Sweden, Switzerland	Fisher/Kaldor expenditure tax, pension benefits treated as "deferred labor income"
tET	Canada, France, Ireland, Malta, Netherlands, United Kingdom	Deferred comprehensive income tax (CIT) with double-taxation relief
tEt	Germany, United States	Fragmented expenditure tax model
TEE	Lithuania	Tax-free savings accounts, prepaid expenditure tax model
tEE	Hungary	Tax-free savings accounts, "reduced prepaid expenditure tax model"
EEE	Slovakia	Full income tax exemption
TTE	None	Comprehensive income tax model (CIT)

Source: Adapted from OECD (2011, 2015); Wellisch et al. (2008, table 2, p. 27). A similar table can be found in Genser and Holzmann (2016, table 4, p. 7).

EU countries apply a variant of the EET regime to public pensions, with contributions and returns on (real or notional) investment totally or partially taxed.

6.3.3 Taxation of Occupational and Personal Pensions in Portugal

The general taxation regime of voluntary occupational and personal pension schemes in Portugal may be classified as TET for employee or individual contributions and EET for employer contributions. The tax treatment for direct insurance schemes is the same as for pension funds. Employer contributions are fully deductible in computing the CIT if the plan provides individualized acquired rights benefits. If the pension plan's benefits are "mere expectations" and a number of conditions are fulfilled,[9] employer contributions are deductible when computing the CIT, up to 15 percent of the annual total costs of wages and salaries.[10] If the contributions exceed this limit, the portion above the limit is not deductible for CIT purposes unless the amount is included in the employee's taxable income. Social contributions are not levied on employer pension contributions. A flat CIT rate of 21 percent is levied on the global taxable income realized by companies resident for tax purposes in Portugal (and is also applicable to Portuguese foreign permanent establishments).[11]

If the plan provides individualized acquired rights benefits, 20 percent of overall employee contributions to private pension plans (both occupational and personal) made before retirement are tax-deductible, up to a limit that varies according to the individual's age. In addition, the abovementioned income-related global tax-deduction amount applies. If the pension plan delivers benefits that are considered mere expectations, there are no tax deductions and a tax-deferral regime applies. The general rule is that income generated by private pension assets is tax-exempt. Dividends, rental income, interest, and other capital income are VAT-exempt. Pension funds are also partially exempt from property taxes, municipal taxes, and stamp duties. Concerning the tax treatment of accumulation of funds, there is no ceiling on the lifetime value of private pension funds. No tax applies on accumulation of funds.

The tax treatment of private pension income depends on whether contributions were exempt and on the type of payout option chosen (annuity, lump sum). Taking benefits as programmed withdrawals is not allowed in Portugal. If the plan provides individualized benefits and the payout option is in the form of an annuity, pension income is taxed at the individual's PIT rate.[12] If contributions were exempt and pensioners choose to take accumulated capital as a lump sum, as of December 31, 2014, there is no tax exemption. Capital gains and other returns on the investment component are taxed at an autonomous rate of 4 percent or 8 percent depending on whether the contributions from which such income originated were made before or after January 1, 2006, respectively. If contributions were taxed and the payout option is in the form of an annuity, the contribution component of the accumulated pot is exempt, and only the capital gain and other returns on the investment component are taxed at the marginal PIT rate. If the contributions were taxed and pensioners choose to take accumulated capital as a lump sum, the contribution component is exempt, whereas capital gains and other returns on the investment part are taxed at an autonomous rate of 4 percent or 8 percent, depending on whether the contributions from which such income originated were made before or after January 1, 2006, respectively. The preferential treatment of lump-sum withdrawals in the latter case represents significant tax relief for high-income earners, which may no longer be justified as part of the effort to boost retirement savings. With the exception of CES, social contributions are not levied on pension income.

Table 6.2
Tax treatment of occupational and personal pensions in EU and non-EU countries.

Tax regime	Occupational pensions		Personal pensions	
	EU	Non-EU	EU	Non-EU
EET	Croatia, Estonia, Finland, Germany, Greece, Ireland, Latvia, Malta, Netherlands, Poland, Portugal, Romania, Slovenia, Spain, United Kingdom	Canada, Chile, Iceland, Israel, Japan, Korea, Norway, Switzerland, United States	Croatia, Finland, Greece, Ireland, Latvia, Netherlands, Poland, Romania, Slovenia, Spain, Sweden, United Kingdom	Canada, Chile, Iceland, Japan, Norway, Switzerland, United States
TEE	Czech Republic, Hungary, Lithuania		Czech Republic, Estonia, Finland, Hungary, Lithuania	Mexico, United States
ETE	Cyprus		Cyprus	
TET	Austria, Belgium, France, Luxembourg, Portugal	Korea	Austria, Belgium, France, Germany, Luxembourg, Malta, Portugal	Israel, Korea, Norway
ETT	Denmark, Italy, Sweden		Italy	
TTE		Australia, New Zealand, Turkey	Denmark	Australia, Mexico, New Zealand, Turkey
EEE	Bulgaria, Slovak Republic	Mexico	Bulgaria, Slovak Republic	
TTT			France	

Source: Author's preparation based on OECD (2015).

Table 6.2 demonstrates that while Portugal applies a TET regime for employee or individual contributions and EET for employer contributions, many EU and non-EU countries apply a variant of the EET regime (see Genser and Holzmann 2016, chapter 15, this volume; and Bravo 2016 for a related analysis). However, at least six other tax regimes can be found internationally. Most countries apply different regimes to occupational and personal pensions. Returns on investment are taxed in seven countries. In Denmark, Italy, and Sweden, returns on investment are not subject to progressive income tax rates but rather to flat tax rates. In Italy, returns on investment are not subject to double taxation during the accumulation and withdrawal phases. In the Slovak Republic and Bulgaria, mandatory contributions to personal pension plans into which a part of social security contributions are paid enjoy an EEE tax regime.

6.3.4 Social Security Contributions Levied on Pension Income in Portugal

A fundamental shift in the perceived role of pension benefits occurred in the post–World War II period. From providing a limited insurance function to old workers unable to work and providing low benefits designated to supplement other income (part-time or lower-paid labor), pension programs were transformed into public savings schemes, particularly in countries with an earnings-related pension benefit design. Removal of the incapacity to work as an eligibility criterion and provision of more generous benefits initiated a new era, where individuals should not work after reaching a certain age, irrespective of their health condition, because their lifetime contributions give them the "right" to a work-free period of retirement and, in most cases, a period free of contributions to social security systems. Pension systems were transformed from pure social insurance mechanisms into public savings schemes.

In Portugal, health care systems are not included in social security. As such, as in most OECD countries, social security contributions are levied only on gross labor income and are used to finance pensions (old-age, survivors', disability), unemployment, sickness and death insurance, or family and maternity benefits. Before 2011, pension income (public and private) was exempt from social contributions. However, the Portuguese government was under pressure to consolidate the budget; in 2011, it was forced to adopt reforms with significant short-term effects, one of which was the introduction of an extraordinary (social) solidarity contribution, the CES, levied on public and private pensions above a certain amount. The measure soon became one of the main issues in the national political debate focusing on the question of whether there were legal boundaries to how much pension reforms could impact the "acquired rights" of pensioners, on whether CES took into account the principle of progressivity and proportionality in the PIT code, and on the extent to which CES, being a social surcharge to PIT rates, could constitute a second tax on the same pension income.

In reality, this extra contribution for pensioners was simply a way to nominally reduce pension benefit payments, similar to what would have been obtained through direct cuts, temporary freezes, and/or permanent reduction of the indexation of benefits, or through extra or higher taxes. Starting in 2011, a 10 percent levy was placed on public and private pensions above €5,000. Despite serious Constitutional Court remarks, the contribution was reformulated many times during this period to increase both the taxable base and the number of tax brackets, with marginal CES rates of up to 50 percent. For some groups of pensioners, CES actually imposed a ceiling on pension benefits.[13]

The majority of EU countries do not charge any social security contributions on public and private pension benefits, and those that do mostly apply it to health, sickness, or long-term care insurance coverage (OECD 2015). The current relevant exceptions are Portugal, France, Belgium, Norway, and Italy. Recent experience in these countries breaches pensioners' expectations about living standards in retirement and the perception of pension schemes as savings devices.

In Portugal, lump-sum payments from occupational pension plans are exempt from CES and preferentially treated via low tax rates. If the lower tax rates can be explained by the political goal of stimulating long-term saving for retirement, the exemption of lump-sum payments from CES fiscally discriminates against annuitization compared to other payout options and offers significant tax relief for high-income earners. Moreover, personal pension funds and savings schemes are exempt from CES. The contribution was supposed to be temporary and part of the Troika bailout program, but although the universe of taxpayers was reduced in 2015, the contribution was only finally eliminated in 2017. In 2014, the Portuguese government submitted a reform package that included a permanent sustainability contribution on pension income intended to replace CES, together with a small increase in social contributions and VATs to increase the funding of pension schemes, but the Constitutional Court found these measures unconstitutional and overruled them.

6.3.5 A Place in the Sun and a Tax-Free Pension: A PIT Regime for Nonregular Residents

In 2009, Portugal implemented a PIT system for nonregular residents, with the purpose of attracting professionals qualified for activities with high added value, intellectual or industrial propriety, or know-how, as well as beneficiaries of pension schemes granted abroad, offering a more beneficial tax burden. The nonregular resident tax regime is available for citizens deemed resident on Portuguese territory for tax purposes in the year to be taxed as a nonregular resident but who have not been deemed resident on Portuguese territory during the prior five years. Once granted, the regime applies for 10 years. For pensioners, the main advantage of this regime is that it offers tax exemption on pension income provided that (1) income is taxed in the country of its source based on the double-tax treaty rules or (2) that income cannot be considered as income from Portuguese sources under Portuguese domestic rules. This special regime offers Portugal a significant competitive advantage in the cross-border taxation of pension income but raises problems of international tax equity and neutrality, particularly when retired emigrants are exempt from income tax on their old-age pension saving in their home country.

6.4 Is There a Rationale for a (Semi)dual Income Tax in Pension Taxation?

The taxation of pensions directly affects consumption, saving, work, leisure, and asset-allocation decisions, and public finances. It therefore has direct implications in key areas such as capital accumulation, productivity, economic growth, capital markets, and welfare. The adoption of a specific taxation regime should be aligned with the pension system's key objectives, recent reform trends, and severe constraints on enabling environments. The implications of a given taxation regime for income and wealth distribution and public revenue should not be neglected. Important issues such as tax neutrality and tax equity (horizontal and vertical), risk sharing between governments and households, opportunistic behavior, or the need to simplify the tax system and increase transparency should also be taken into consideration.

The DIT was introduced in the Nordic countries in the early 1990s as a compromise between an SHS tax and an expenditure tax. Under the DIT system, the taxpayer's total tax bill depends not only on aggregate income but also on the split between capital and other forms of income. This is not in accordance with the philosophy of SHS or Fisher-Kaldor-Meade taxes. The Nordic countries walked away from progressive taxation of capital income as a means of redistributing income because they concluded that such taxation was ineffective at achieving progressivity and may even have unintended effects. Since then, Portugal and other EU countries (e.g., Austria, Belgium, Italy, and Lithuania) have gradually moved toward a variant of the DIT, where different nominal tax rates apply to capital and noncapital (including pension) income. Against this background, the questions that naturally emerge are:

1. Why was a schedular SDIT implemented in Portugal?
2. To what extent is a DIT (and variants) system better suited than a TTE or EET system to address the personal and policy goals of a pension scheme and the economy?
3. Does a theoretical or practical rationale exist for a DIT of occupational and personal pensions and other retirement income?[14]
4. Should capital income be taxed at a comparatively lower marginal rate(s)?

This discussion assumes that an open economy faces four main competing considerations in designing a pension taxation regime. At the domestic level, the first goal is tax progressivity (i.e., addressing vertical equity concerns). The second goal is comprehensiveness (i.e., equal and joint treatment of all income sources, addressing horizontal equity, and, in conjunction with tax progressivity, taxing individuals in accordance with ability-to-pay principles). The third goal is symmetry (i.e., ensuring all types of capital income are subject to the same tax regime). This goal addresses concerns of allocative efficiency as well as tax-induced distortions in investment and savings decisions (Ganghof 2001).

At the international level, the main goal is competitiveness or international efficiency, but topics such as the portability of pension entitlements and discriminatory tax treatment in the European Single Market can run counter to all four freedoms laid down in the European Commission Treaty. This goal addresses international tax competition on capital (and, in some cases, labor and pension) income. Discriminatory tax treatment with respect to domestic and foreign recipients or providers of old-age pensions is a source of potential restrictions for free mobility of services, labor, and capital and may deter free mobility of workers.

In a closed economy, an SHS tax can in principle satisfy the progressivity, comprehensiveness (in a life cycle perspective), and symmetry objectives. However, when domestic and international tax policy goals are taken into consideration, countries may not be able to deliver on all of them, chiefly because cross-border mobility of capital varies both between types of capital and economic regions and because globalization has significantly increased the intensity of tax competition.

Adoption of a DIT on pensions involves sacrificing comprehensiveness and symmetry but offers a flexible and scalable route for addressing international tax competition that is compatible with statutory progressive tax rates for labor income. Sacrificing comprehensiveness may be justified by the central role of savings taxation in the tax treatment of pensions. The sacrifice of symmetry objectives is mostly dictated by international tax-competitiveness considerations and the desire (or requirement) to maintain significant labor income tax progressivity to address redistributive considerations, but fiscal revenue and labor market constraints may ultimately influence the design of the system.

Adoption of a DIT also has the potential to improve tax neutrality over the timing of consumption, between savings vehicles and payout options, and at the international level. It may contribute to enhancing horizontal equity in a life cycle perspective and offer better (intra- and intergenerational) risk-sharing properties. Although the Portuguese experience may suggest that country-specific factors ultimately determine the balance between the multiple goals of pension tax reforms and the path toward a given tax regime, it is argued that adoption of an SDIT in the taxation of pensions may improve existing PIT schemes and potentially serve as a blueprint for more fundamental tax reform.

6.4.1 Sacrificing Comprehensiveness to Address the Central Role of Savings Taxation

Countries that adopted DIT systems abandoned comprehensiveness in an attempt to maintain "symmetry" while at the same time responding to strong tax competition pressures. By taxing all accruals to income, an SHS tax discriminates in favor of current consumption, is not neutral with regard to present and future consumption, and acts as a disincentive to (particularly long-term) saving.[15] Savings, particularly contributions to pension schemes, are not a normal commodity; for most individuals, savings are a way to finance deferred consumption.

The taxation of savings has a central role in the tax treatment of pensions. Pension taxation can affect both the total amount of savings in the economy and how those savings are allocated across different assets. This can directly affect the amount of capital invested and how efficiently. Under an SHS tax, saving out of current income is taxed twice: once when the income is earned and again when the return on investment is earned. Stated in a life cycle perspective, this means that horizontal equity is violated under an SHS tax. Applying a lower capital income tax rate in an SDIT can mitigate the bias against future consumption and alleviate the impact of taxing nominal (and not real) rates of return.[16] The marginal tax rate during retirement is typically lower than during working life, making pension savings more attractive under the EET regime. An EET system offers taxpayers an extra degree of freedom to smooth consumption over their life cycle. A TEE system shifts the tax burden to working-age agents and away from retirees, reducing the after-tax income that workers can allocate between consumption and savings.

Additional arguments could justify a more favorable fiscal treatment of capital income and retirement savings in pension taxation. Among them is the desire to increase the number of people who save to finance their retirement or to increase the amount saved, increasing the supply of long-term funds to capital markets that promote investment and economic growth.[17] Other relevant issues include bounded rationality and bounded willpower problems, the desire to reduce the currently high number and significance of those who are likely to fall into the safety net when in retirement, thereby increasing the already too high fiscal pressure, or the illiquidity of pension rights. Saving for retirement is particularly low in Portugal and will need to increase significantly in the future to address both sustainability and adequacy problems in PAYG systems.[18] In a scenario in which individuals will increasingly be responsible for their financial security in retirement, recent surveys show that Portuguese citizens are not well equipped to make saving decisions, with many reporting that they are unable to plan for retirement. Low financial literacy levels and misconceptions about the sustainability and generosity of public PAYG schemes weaken precautionary savings and savings motivated by life cycle considerations.

Another justification for favoring retirement savings concerns the effects of taxation on the composition of savings. Retirement savings have the potential to increase the demand for long-term securities and promote the institutionalization of asset management. The distinctive characteristics of vehicles for saving for retirement[19] imply that the portfolio composition is likely to include a significant fraction of long-term debt, equities, and real estate, while the amount of liquid assets tends to be small. To the extent that a high demand for these types of assets has positive effects on investment, productive capital formation, and growth,[20] there may be a case for providing tax incentives for channeling savings into retirement vehicles. In addition, a more favorable fiscal treatment of retirement savings is expected to increase the supply of long-term funds to capital markets, thus notably improving the function of transferring resources.[21]

Another justification for favoring retirement savings vehicles is the contribution of contractual savings institutions to the development of financial markets by promoting the concentration of asset management in large institutions.[22] However, this does not necessarily justify a special taxation regime. On the contrary, the link between effective tax rates and distortions to the pattern of saving has been clearly established, particularly in countries like Portugal, in which retirement savings vehicles are sold primarily because of their more favorable tax treatment. This means distortionary effects on the structure of the financial services industry induced by taxation regimes must be balanced with the ability of capital markets to channel savings into the most efficient investments, and with distributional considerations, since the value of tax incentives usually increases with taxpayers' marginal rates, and retirement wealth tends to be concentrated in high-income households.

A specific efficiency argument for proportional taxation of capital income is that the after-tax returns to savings will differ among taxpayers when their marginal PIT rates are not identical. This means progressivity causes the marginal rate of substitution between present and future consumption among taxpayers to be different, implying intersectoral distortions of capital allocation and an inefficient allocation of the overall level of savings (Sørensen 2005). Finally, the loss of vertical equity resulting from applying a proportional (and usually lower) rate on capital income may be largely offset by efficiency gains.

6.4.2 Sacrificing Symmetry to Account for International Capital Mobility and Other Constraints

Small open economies with perfect international capital mobility critically depend on foreign saving to counterbalance existing public and private indebtedness levels. If tax competitiveness is perceived as essential, and if political or constitutional requirements mandate significant income tax progressivity (as in Portugal), different types of capital income have to be taxed at widely different rates. This option sacrifices symmetry objectives. In recent years, global tax-competition concerns in developed and developing countries have prompted legislative proposals to reduce CIT rates significantly below tax rates under the PIT system. The option pursued in Portugal to differentiate tax rates on capital income was determined largely by the elasticity of the tax base. The most sensitive types of capital income (e.g., dividends) are taxed at lower flat rates, while others are taxed at higher flat withholding tax rates or, optionally, kept within the ambit of progressive income taxation. Compared to immobile domestic factors such as labor, capital has become increasingly mobile across international borders. Therefore, a significant risk exists that a high and progressive domestic capital income tax rate will induce taxpayers to costlessly escape domestic taxation by moving their wealth to foreign low-tax jurisdictions. In the absence of effective information exchange, even those countries that tax their residents on their worldwide income have limited capacity to tax their residents' foreign-source income effectively.

Recent banking failures and financial market distress have also contributed to undermining the attractiveness of investing in countries like Portugal. In this context, adopting an SHS tax and increasing taxes on capital income would likely lead to capital flight, an increase in the tax burden carried by the immobile domestic sectors, and reduced investment, capital intensity of production, and potential growth. Portugal's adoption of an SDIT, with the separation of the several flat capital income tax rates from the labor and pension income tax schedule, allowed policy makers to levy comparatively lower capital tax rates, reduce the risk of capital flight, and increase the attractiveness of foreign direct investment in Portugal.

In pension taxation, defining the capital income component is a problem. Some forms of capital income are simple to define in principle (e.g., interest income, dividends, royalties, and rents), and Portugal decided to tax them (by default) at a flat rate under a final withholding regime. The application of final common withholding taxes to these payments, whether to domestic or foreign recipients, is expected to improve efficiency by increasing the symmetry of tax treatment of capital income and simplify administration.[23]

Another question refers to how to tax net capital gains on corporate shares or real estate property at the individual level. In the past, the option was simply to exempt capital gains from taxation. Competitiveness considerations were behind this option, together with incentives for capital market development, and the argument that under an SDIT with full integration of distributed earnings and interest payments, any remaining gains on corporate shares largely reflect inflation. Then, for some years, the option was to tax net capital gains only for shares held for less than one year. This approach was deemed to create incentives for long-term (retirement) capital market investment, support privatization processes, and prevent taxpayers from engaging in schemes to avoid or reduce taxes on labor income by selling their shares. The current practice is to tax net capital gains at the individual level at a flat rate of 28 percent. Since gains are taxed when realized, individual taxpayers are allowed to adjust the cost basis of their shares or property to reflect any taxed, but undistributed, earnings at the corporate level or depreciation and improvement costs. Taxing capital gains based on the realization principle may lead to asset retention and lock-in effects, which hampers the optimal allocation of resources. For capital gains realized from fixed assets such as real property, only 50 percent of the capital gains will be taxable if they are reinvested in fixed assets such as real property during the year the sale occurred, the previous year, or within two years after the sale. This creates an incentive for housing savings schemes during the accumulation phase of pensions, leveraged by the existence of housing tax deductions, but challenges the withdrawal phase because of the nonexistence of equity-release mechanisms in Portugal.

The adoption of separate tax rates for labor and capital income has both revenue and progressivity implications. In recent years, the Portuguese response to both fiscal pressure and international tax competition was to reduce CIT rates, increase flat withholding taxes on interest income, and significantly increase the current tax revenue generated from labor income, augmenting both the level and progressivity of the system. Contrary to the pure form of the DIT, the capital income tax rate in Portugal is almost double that of labor income in the first bracket and is well above the CIT rate. This means that the fiscal revenue constraint is likely to prevent further significant reductions in capital income tax rates.[24] Additionally, the Portuguese economy faced difficult challenges during the last decade, particularly during the "Troika" bailout period. Substantial concerns exist about the current record-high level of unemployment (from a 3.9 percent unemployment rate at the beginning of the millennium, unemployment reached a maximum of 17.8 percent during 2013). These concerns helped to provide political support for reducing the tax burden on capital income, particularly rate cuts for CIT taxes, as a means to increase economic activity. The country faced critical choices in reforming its income tax system: increase tax rates for all income to generate sufficient tax revenue to support social programs and reduce the debt burden, undermining economic recovery efforts, or bifurcate the tax regime and apply lower rates to some forms of capital income while increasing the level and progressivity of labor and pension income taxes. Portugal chose the latter approach.[25] The choice of a specific pension taxation regime has relevant current and intertemporal implications in terms of fiscal sustainability. While under a TEE system the government gives up the possibility of taxing part of citizens' future income, under an EET system it acquires a share in the retirement assets.[26]

The SHS tax tends to discriminate against financial and physical investment compared to investment in human capital. Because an SHS tax taxes labor and pension incomes as they are earned, the cost of human capital investment (e.g., forgone wages and leisure, other cost items) implies an immediate deduction of a similar amount from taxable income. In this sense, while the costs of acquiring physical capital are only allowed to be capitalized and depreciated over the life of the asset, human capital investment benefits from "full expensing" under an SHS tax. The progressivity of the labor income tax is then justified as a way to mitigate the private return to human capital investment, thereby offsetting the tendency of a proportional comprehensive income tax to discriminate in favor of such investments. The truth is that significant positive externalities arise from education, and human capital is crucial for long-term economic growth, which means the argument against "tax subsidies" on human capital investments implicit in SDIT regimes is weakened.

6.4.3 Improving Equity and Neutrality and Offering Better Incentives for Risk Sharing

An SHS tax ensures horizontal equity, and properly graduated tax scales guarantee vertical equity. However, when stated in a life cycle perspective, horizontal equity is violated under an SHS tax, since those who choose to consume later in life are taxed more heavily. In Portugal and other countries, it is very often argued that aggravating the taxation of (retirement) savings and capital income is an effective way to pursue redistributive goals, since taxing capital income is a sort of presumptive way of taxing inheritances and gifts. The truth is that individuals with large savings are not wealthy by definition and are not necessarily better off over their lifetime than individuals without savings. They might simply earn and spend similar amounts over their lifetimes but at different moments. By taxing the interest income from savings, wealthier individuals are not being taxed; rather, those who spend their money tomorrow rather than today are taxed, and because of the compound interest effect, the longer the investment horizon involved, the greater the tax.[27]

Neutrality over the timing of consumption should only be a reasonable starting point for tax design for pensions and retirement income.[28] The taxation of savings affects individuals' decisions on how much to save, when to save, and how to allocate savings across different assets given their risk and return profile. It therefore directly affects their welfare. In principle, tax policy should not determine savings vehicles or a given asset allocation. In reality, strong reasons justify deviating from this form of neutrality when it comes to treating pensions more generously than other forms of savings in the SDIT. This is because it is important to offer incentives to save for retirement to individuals who are shortsighted and otherwise may not plan for their long-term financial needs.

Neutrality at the international level or between alternative payout options at retirement is also crucial in pension taxation. In a standard SHS tax, capital gains and other forms of income from savings are taxed on accrual. In an inflationary context in which nominal interest rates accommodate maintaining the real return on investment, taxing nominal returns increases the effective tax rate on real returns to interest-bearing assets. This means SHS taxation of savings is unable to guarantee neutrality over time, and providing some tax relief on capital income is justified under the DIT.

The appropriate treatment of retirement savings and pension income should not neglect the impact of a given taxation regime on portfolio composition and risk taking. The taxation of returns from assets discriminates against risk taking through its lowering of the expected rates of return. In EET regimes, in addition to taking a share of the expected return, the government shares in the risk, so it becomes co-investor. The risk exposure is total if there are perfect loss-offset provisions, in which case the government will carry the same share of a possible loss as it takes in a gain, or a partial share if there is no loss offset. A tax-deferral regime has better (intra- and intergenerational) risk-sharing properties than a prepaid expenditure tax model.[29] By exploiting the benefits of intergenerational risk sharing, more risk can be taken, which results in higher expected returns.

Moving now to the payout phase, important welfare effects can justify sharing longevity risk between annuitants and annuity providers and adoption of a tax-deferral regime and lower rates on some disbursement options. First, longevity risk involves very long time horizons. For instance, for an individual buying an annuity at age 50 and living to 100, 50 years of mortality uncertainty are involved in the contract. Second, longevity risk has aggregate components (e.g., medical breakthroughs may change aggregate longevity) that cannot be diversified and are best managed when shared over a larger pool. Finally, the net exposure to longevity risk varies across cohorts, which differ in their ability to respond or self-insure.

6.4.4 Arbitrage Opportunities and the Erosion of Social Contributions' Taxable Base

In Portugal, the move from an SHS tax to an SDIT offered significant tax planning (or tax evasion) opportunities by converting labor income from self-employment or from wages of owner-employees of closely held corporations into income from capital. For medium- and high-income classes, large differences in the marginal tax rates on capital income and labor income provided incentives for income shifting. Starting in 2013, the combined reduction in the number of PIT tax brackets, the increase in PIT marginal rates and surcharges, and the ongoing reduction in CIT rates created a strong incentive to characterize income from labor as income from capital. Given that under the Portuguese (and most countries') tax system labor income is subject to social security taxes, the move toward an SDIT substantially increased the effective marginal tax rates for labor income but left tax rates for capital income unchanged. As a consequence, the number of those registered as self-employed dropped substantially in recent years while the number of new small and medium-sized enterprises (SMEs) grew exponentially. For pension schemes, the immediate consequence was a decline in both the taxable base for social contributions and the contribution revenue.

To avoid such uneven tax treatment and to reduce the scope for tax avoidance, it is necessary to align the CIT rate with the PIT rate on capital income and to equalize marginal capital income tax rates across taxpayers. In the short to medium run, this objective is considered improbable given both international tax-competitiveness considerations and the need to strengthen SMEs' capital structure. Moreover, in Portugal a large percentage of corporate tax revenue comes from a relatively small number of taxpayers, which means that increasing CIT rates would likely contribute to reducing the tax base. This motivated the introduction of presumptive tax regimes that seek to tax micro- and small businesses based on gross revenue. Alternatively, it is necessary to split the income of the self-employed and the wages of owner-employees into a labor income component and a capital income component.[30]

6.5 Conclusions

This chapter critically analyzed the Portuguese reform path toward its current semidual system in the taxation of public, occupational, and personal pensions and other retirement income and discussed whether this variant of a DIT could provide a blueprint for reforms in other countries. The Portuguese income tax system combines a highly progressive tax schedule for labor and pension income with low and flat nominal tax rates on some forms of capital income. Moving to an SDIT offers both advantages and disadvantages in addressing the pension system's long-term goals and challenges and represents a compromise between the many competing domestic and international considerations an open economy faces in designing a tax regime. Retaining a progressive tax on labor income is not only a legislative and political requirement but also a way to provide some progressivity, particularly in countries like Portugal that exhibit high inequality in income and wealth.

Adoption of a DIT on pensions involves sacrificing comprehensiveness and symmetry but offers a flexible and scalable route to address international tax competition that is compatible with statutory progressive tax rates for labor income. The option to abandon comprehensiveness is justified by the attempt to reduce the discrimination against saving (future consumption) implicit in an SHS tax and to alleviate the impact of taxing nominal (and not real) rates of return. Additionally, adoption of an SDIT may contribute to boosting savings for retirement, increasing the supply of long-term funds to capital markets that promote investment and economic growth, and increasing the demand for long-term securities that promote the institutionalization of asset management and expand the role of contractual savings institutions.

The sacrifice of symmetry objectives is dictated mostly by international tax-competitiveness considerations and the desire (or requirement) to maintain significant labor income tax progressivity to address redistributive concerns, but the need to increase the attractiveness of foreign direct investment and fiscal revenue and labor market constraints may ultimately influence the design of the system.

The decision on how to differentiate tax rates among the distinct types of capital income will be determined largely by the elasticity of the tax base, with the most sensitive types of capital income normally being taxed under lower flat rates, while the remaining types are taxed under higher flat withholding tax rates or, optionally, kept within the ambit of progressive income taxation. This decision can also be influenced by problems in defining the capital income component, the desire to create incentives to long-term capital market investment, or the need to support privatization processes.

Contrary to the pure form of DIT, in which the PIT rate on capital income is aligned with both the CIT rate and the marginal tax rate on labor income in the first bracket, in Portugal capital income tax rates in the SDIT were largely determined by fiscal revenue constraints, international tax-competition pressure, unemployment and tax wedge considerations, and inequality and progressivity concerns.

Adoption of a DIT has the potential to improve tax neutrality over the timing of consumption, between savings vehicles and payout options, and at the international level. It may also contribute to enhancing horizontal equity in a life cycle perspective and may offer better (intra- and intergenerational) risk-sharing properties.

Adoption of an SDIT in pension taxation affects individuals' decisions on how much to save, when to save, and how to allocate savings across different assets. This departure from neutrality is justified by the need to encourage saving for retirement for individuals who are shortsighted and otherwise may not plan for their long-term financial needs.

Adoption of any specific taxation regime should be aligned with the pension system's key objectives, recent reform trends, and severe constraints on enabling environments, such as the need to attract foreign direct investment, the challenges of economic integration and globalization, offshoring and disintermediation, or simply difficulties in assessing taxpayers' real incomes.

On the other hand, the move to an SDIT regime offers significant tax-planning opportunities by converting labor income from self-employment or from wages of owner-employees of closely held corporations into income from capital, eroding the social contributions' taxable base and offering nonnegligible tax-arbitrage opportunities. Elimination of these tax-arbitrage opportunities may be difficult if aligning the CIT rate with the PIT rate on capital income and equalizing marginal capital income tax rates among taxpayers conflicts with both international tax-competitiveness considerations and the need to strengthen SMEs' capital structure. Conversely, tax-induced distortions (over the level and timing of saving and between different types of savings vehicles or assets) and arbitrage opportunities for income shifting between categories should not be neglected.

The Portuguese reform path toward its current pension taxation regime was not determined solely by a clear tax reform agenda. It was influenced by the specific economic, demographic, political, and social circumstances the country faced in recent years. Although other countries face economic, political, social, and tax environments very different from those of Portugal or the Nordic countries, an SDIT is a promising alternative for the many challenges involved in the taxation of pensions.

Notes

I would like to thank Robert Holzmann, Bernd Genser, and participants at the CEPAR and CESifo workshop "Pension Taxation, Population Ageing, and Globalisation" (Part 2, Munich, September 2015) for their valuable comments and suggestions, which helped to focus and improve the chapter.

1. Based on the most recent projections (Bravo, Afonso, and Guerreiro 2014), the fund will be depleted by 2024 unless additional tax transfers are made from the general budget to cover current and future expected deficits, something that has happened since 2012.

2. For a detailed analysis of the main approaches to taxing personal income, see OECD (2006).

3. This type of tax system involves significant tax allowances and tax exemptions, whose value to taxpayers increases with income.

4. In the pure form of the DIT, the personal tax rate on capital income is aligned with both the corporate income tax rate and the marginal tax rate on labor and pension income in the first bracket.

5. The introduction of a lower proportional tax rate on capital income might undermine the vertical equity, especially because income from capital tends to be concentrated in the upper income brackets.

6. For capital losses, there are two main options: offsetting capital losses against positive labor income in the same period or offsetting capital losses by using a tax credit that can be deducted from the labor tax bill.

7. In May 2011, Portugal agreed with the European Union and the International Monetary Fund on a far-reaching reform program to restore financial markets' confidence and raise potential growth. The program was successfully concluded in mid-2014.

8. Families with an annual income below €8,480 (about 83 percent of the total in 2015) are PIT-exempt.

9. At least two-thirds of the benefits must be annuitized, and the provisions of the general social security scheme are accompanied with regard to retirement age; the pension plan assets are not managed by the sponsor; and the pension plan covers exclusively benefits in the case of retirement, health (postwork), disability, or survivorship.

10. The limit is 25 percent if employees are not covered by social security.

11. A lower CIT rate of 18.4 percent applies to companies that are tax resident in the Autonomous Region of Azores. A reduced CIT rate of 17 percent applies to small and medium-sized companies on the first €15,000 of taxable income.

12. A maximum deduction of €4,104 applies to total pension income. However, if the compulsory contributions to social protection schemes and to legal health subsystems exceed that limit, the deduction will be equal to the total amount of contributions.

13. To give an idea of the fiscal burden on retirement income, pensioners in the top deciles in 2015 paid a marginal tax rate of 91.5 percent on the amount exceeding €7,126.74.

14. For detailed discussions on the merits and drawbacks of a DIT, see Sørensen (1994, 2005), Boadway (2004), and Bird and Zolt (2011).

15. The tax treatment of savings is a critical determinant of the extent to which the tax system recognizes interpersonal differences in lifetime income, as opposed to considering annual income only.

16. Whitehouse (1999) suggests that under strict (and unrealistic) assumptions, a consumption-type TEE and EET are equally optimal. Both confer an after-tax rate of return to savings equal to the pretax rate of return and are neutral between consumption now and consumption in retirement. However, there would be no general equivalence for a pension or tax policy change that would be unanticipated by households and where tax rates would differ over the life cycle.

17. Empirical evidence shows that the effects of tax incentives on national saving may be either positive or negative. If the evidence on taxing pensions more favorably suggests that it can contribute to higher private saving, the consequence for national saving depends on the response of governments and individuals (see, e.g., Feldstein 1974; Kohl and O'Brien 1998; Attanasio and Brugiavini 2003; Pfau 2005).

18. Additionally, the country has the highest combined debt level in the Eurozone, at over 360 percent of GDP.

19. Inflows and outflows are comparatively more stable and predictable; asset allocation is set up to maximize the return on investment in a long-term perspective; liabilities are generally nontradable, with lower lapse risks; lower transactions costs; comparatively lower costs charged for managing contributions and assets; regulatory constraints; and comparative advantage in compensating for the increased risk by pooling and diversifying across assets whose returns are imperfectly correlated.

20. By providing more risk capital to firms, by reducing long-term interest rates, by diminishing the cost of equity and debt to equity ratios, by reducing the dependence on bank finance, and by providing more stable financing.

21. This is particularly important in countries like Portugal, in which capital markets have struggled in recent years because of the global financial crisis of 2008, the 2011–2014 bailout program, high risk premiums, increased competition at the EU level, excessive dependence on the banking channel, recent bank restructuring and failure episodes, lack of trust in financial institutions, comparatively low liquidity levels, and no major recent initial public offerings (IPOs). Besides the quantitative effects noted, the development of retirement savings vehicles is also likely to trigger qualitative developments in financial markets (financial innovation, increased competition to the banking sector, modernization of the infrastructure of securities markets) that will facilitate in particular the functions of managing uncertainty, controlling risk, and providing price information.

22. Collective savings management has the potential to be superior to individual management because of the economies of scale in pooling risk, in collecting and managing information, in terms of transaction costs, in promoting a liquid market structure, in increasing the demand for capital market instruments, in promoting financial innovation, in improving corporate governance, and in providing more and better-quality information to shareholders. Catalan, Impavido, and Musalem (2000) argued that, among institutional investors, contractual savings institutions (pension funds and life insurance companies) are the most effective at developing capital markets.

23. Flat tax rates have increased significantly in recent years, from 20 percent to 28 percent. This counters both the goal of encouraging people to save more and the objective of allowing individuals to take personal responsibility for adequate income in retirement. The adoption of final withholding regimes expanded the tax base and is likely to enhance the progressivity of the tax system.

24. The significant budgetary pressures in Portugal and the recent signs from the government in office that it will relax or abandon fiscal consolidation triggered the discussion on a potential shift from TET to TEE in the taxation of occupational and private pension schemes and retirement savings and on the creation of a wealth tax on real and financial wealth.

25. The extent to which a low flat-rate tax on capital has contributed to increased investment and tax revenue has yet to be demonstrated since it is difficult to isolate the effect of tax changes on the cost of capital from the effect of other fiscal reforms.

26. This means, for instance, that under EET a government is exposed to increases in interest rates that raise the cost of public debt if the rate of return on pension assets does not follow. On the contrary, by shifting from EET to TEE (a proposal currently under discussion in the United Kingdom), a government can improve its current budgetary perspectives if it does not relax its budgetary stance and the interest on public debt is higher than the return on pension assets. Even if the one-time revenues related to the shift from EET to TEE are not used by a government to relax its fiscal stance, in an aging society, a shift from EET to TEE might increase revenues at the first stage and reduce them afterward, when age-related expenditures will put more pressure on budgets.

27. This is an option that is both unfair and inefficient. The only exception would be if people's savings decisions tell us something more about their underlying resources and earning capacity than just about their preferences for current versus future consumption. The main way to redistribute is to make the tax rate scale applied to earnings (money at its source) or expenditures (money when it is finally used for consumption) more progressive.

28. For a related discussion, see Börsch-Supan and Quinn (2015, chapter 8, this volume).

29. See Romaniuk (2013) and Chen et al. (2014) for a discussion on intergenerational risk sharing through both private funded pensions and the public debt.

30. For an overview of alternative methods of income splitting, see Sørensen (2005).

References

Attanasio, Orazio, and Agar Brugiavini. 2003. "Social Security and Households' Saving." *Quarterly Journal of Economics* 118 (3): 1075–1119.

Bird, Richard, and Eric Zolt. 2011. "Dual Income Taxation: A Promising Path to Tax Reform for Developing Countries." *World Development* 39 (10): 1691–1703.

Boadway, Robin. 2004. "The Dual Income Tax System: An Overview." *CESifo DICE Report* 2 (3): 3–8.

Börsch-Supan, Axel H., and Christopher Quinn. 2015. "Taxing Pensions and Retirement Benefits in Germany." CESifo Working Paper No. 5636, December, CESifo, Munich.

Bravo, Jorge M. 2016. "Taxation of Pensions in Portugal: A Semi-dual Income Tax System." *CESifo DICE Report—Journal for Institutional Comparisons* 14 (1): 14–23.

Bravo, Jorge M., Lourdes Afonso, and Gracinda Guerreiro. 2013. "Avaliação Actuarial do Regime de Pensões da Caixa Geral de Aposentações: Formulação actual e impacto das medidas legislativas." Ministry of Finance, Lisbon.

Bravo, Jorge M., Lourdes Afonso, and Gracinda Guerreiro. 2014. "Avaliação Actuarial do Sistema Previdencial da Segurança Social e Prestação Única da Segurança Social: GEP." Ministry of Solidarity, Labour and Social Security, Lisbon.

Catalan, Mario, Gregorio Impavido, and Alberto Musalem. 2000. "Contractual Savings or Stock Market Development: Which Leads?" Social Protection Discussion Paper Series No. 20, World Bank, Washington, DC.

Chen, Damiaan, Roel Beetsma, Eduard Ponds, and Ward Romp. 2014. "Intergenerational Risk-Sharing through Funded Pensions and Public Debt." CESifo Working Paper No. 4624, CESifo, Munich.

Cremer, Helmuth, and Pierre Pestieau. 2016. "Theoretical Foundations of the Taxation of Pensions." CESifo Working Paper No. 5930, May, CESifo, Munich.

Feldstein, Martin. 1974. "Social Security, Induced Retirement, and Aggregate Capital Accumulation." *Journal of Political Economy* 82 (5): 905–926.

Ganghof, Steffen. 2001. "Global Markets, National Tax Systems, and Domestic Politics: Rebalancing Efficiency and Equity in Open States' Income Taxation." Max-Planck-Institute Discussion Paper No. 09-2001, Max-Planck-Institute, Munich.

Genser, Bernd, and Robert Holzmann. 2016. "The Taxation of Internationally Portable Pensions: Fiscal Issues and Policy Options." CESifo Working Paper No. 5702, CESifo, Munich.

Kohl, Richard, and Paul O'Brien. 1998. "The Macroeconomics of Ageing, Pensions and Savings: A Survey." OECD Economics Department Working Paper No. 200, OECD Publishing, Paris.

OECD (Organisation for Economic Co-operation and Development). 2006. "Fundamental Reform of Personal Income Tax." OECD Tax Policy Studies No. 13, OECD Publishing, Paris.

OECD (Organisation for Economic Co-operation and Development). 2011. "Tax Treatment of Pensions and Pensioners." In *Pensions at a Glance 2011: Retirement-Income Systems in OECD and G20 Countries*, 122–123. Paris: OECD Publishing.

OECD (Organisation for Economic Co-operation and Development). 2015. "Stocktaking of the Tax Treatment of Funded Private Pension Plans in OECD and EU Countries." OECD Publishing, Paris.

Pfau, Wade. 2005. "The Effects of Social Security on Private Savings: A Reappraisal of the Time Series Evidence." MPRA Paper No. 19032, Munich Personal RePEc Archive, Munich.

Romaniuk, Katarzyna. 2013. "Pension Fund Taxation and Risk-Taking: Should We Switch from the EET to the TEE Regime?" *Annals of Finance* 9 (4): 573–588.

Sørensen, Peter. 2005. "Dual Income Taxation: Why and How?" *Public Finance Analysis* 61 (4): 559–586.

Sørensen, Peter Birch. 1994. "From the Global Income Tax to the Dual Income Tax: Recent Tax Reforms in the Nordic Countries." *International Tax and Public Finance* 1:57–79.

Wellisch, Dieter, Sven-Oliver Lenz, Kersti Thiele, and Rasmus Gahl. 2008. *Besteuerung der Altersvorsorge*. Baden-Baden: Nomos.

Whitehouse, Edward. 1999. "The Tax Treatment of Funded Pensions." Social Protection Discussion Paper Series No. SP 9910. Washington, DC: World Bank.

Yoo, Kwang-Yeol, and Alain de Serres. 2004. "Tax Treatment of Private Pension Savings in OECD Countries." *OECD Economic Studies* 39:73–110.

7 Taxing Pensions: The Australian Approach

Hazel Bateman

7.1 Introduction

The increasing prevalence of funded private pension systems worldwide raises questions about how retirement savings and benefits should be taxed. The three most important questions in pension taxation are: (1) At what point should pension savings be taxed? (2) Should the tax regime for pensions be integrated with personal income taxes or be separate? (3) How preferential should the taxation of pensions be? Australia's experience with the tax treatment of private retirement savings (known in Australia as superannuation) brings considerable insight to these questions.

Pension savings can be taxed at one or more of three points—at the time of contribution, as fund earnings accrue, and/or at the time benefits are received. Most countries exempt (E) contributions and fund earnings from taxation and tax (T) benefits under a postpaid expenditure tax (EET) regime. In most cases, the benefits are treated as ordinary income and taxed progressively under the personal income tax schedule. Some countries tax contributions and fund earnings under a comprehensive income tax (TTE) regime. Alternatives include a prepaid expenditure tax (TtE) under which contributions are taxed, fund earnings are exempt (except for excess returns),[1] and benefits are exempt, or a hybrid approach (TTT) whereby pension savings are taxed at all three points.

Contributions and fund earnings can be taxed either in the hands of the contributor, which allows individual differentiation, or in the hands of the fund, which does not. Tax rates may be linked with the personal income tax schedule or not—and if not this adds to potential complexity. Whether integrated or stand-alone, taxes may be imposed at "full" or "concessional" rates. The choice of tax regime has implications for incentives, fairness, administrative efficacy, political risk and policy stability, and individual decisions and engagement with retirement saving.

Over the past 30 years, superannuation in Australia has been taxed under all three regimes, starting with a very concessionary postpaid expenditure tax regime (EET) in the early 1980s; moving to a hybrid TTT regime between 1988 and 2007, when contributions, fund earnings, and benefits were all taxed; and finally remaining under a comprehensive income tax (TTE) regime since 2007.[2] Taxes at each point have been both specific pension taxes and taxes linked to the personal marginal income tax schedule and have been applied at both full and concessional rates.

The current taxation of superannuation in Australia is separate from the personal income tax schedule and features a flat-rate tax on contributions and fund earnings, with benefits generally tax-free. While the system is concessional in comparison with personal income taxation for many income earners, the distribution of tax concessions (and the net fiscal impact after accounting for the public Age Pension) is skewed toward higher-income earners (Commonwealth Treasury 2012, 2016a). This flat-rate tax structure is largely responsible for the frequent and piecemeal changes to the superannuation tax rules to address equity concerns, which have affected public confidence in the retirement income arrangements and resulted in increased complexity for both individuals and superannuation funds. An important observation is that while superannuation saving and withdrawal is managed by private financial institutions, it is not completely insulated from political risk.

The chapter proceeds as follows. Section 7.2 describes the current taxation of superannuation in Australia and compares it with international arrangements. Section 7.3 traces the changes in the taxation of superannuation in Australia over the past 35 years and links them to the evolution in retirement income policy settings. Section 7.4 evaluates the current tax arrangements using the standard criteria for tax analysis—efficiency, equity, and simplicity—and highlights implications for political risk. Section 7.5 concludes with observations and lessons for countries contemplating similar reforms.[3]

7.2 How Does Australia Currently Tax Superannuation?

Superannuation in Australia is generally taxed under a comprehensive income tax (TTE) regime with a flat-rate tax on contributions (adjusted for people with low or very high incomes), a flat-rate tax on superannuation fund earnings, and (generally) tax-free benefits.[4,5] The taxes on contributions and fund earnings are concessional (relative to personal income tax rates) for most people. While slightly different tax arrangements apply to some defined benefit funds and as a result of the application of grandfathering, the emphasis in this chapter is on the most common defined contribution arrangements as applied under Australia's mandatory Superannuation Guarantee.[6] In this context, the current taxation of superannuation (incorporating revisions legislated to commence in July 2017) is illustrated in table 7.1.

7.2.1 Contributions

Contributions are taxed, but their tax treatment differs depending on the type of contribution, the amount of the contribution, and the income of the individual for whom the contribution is made. The main distinction is between contributions made before tax (known as concessional contributions) and those made from after-tax income (known as nonconcessional contributions).

Concessional contributions comprise employer contributions (including those under the compulsory Superannuation Guarantee), voluntary salary sacrifice contributions[7] (which are made out of pretax income), and voluntary personal contributions where a tax deduction is claimed. Concessional contributions are taxed at the 15 percent flat-rate superannuation tax while in the hands of the superannuation fund and are tax-deductible. Until recently, only the self-employed were eligible to receive a tax deduction for voluntary contributions;[8] however, by virtue of changes announced in the 2016–2017 budget and later legislated, access to tax deductibility was extended to all voluntary contributions beginning in July 2017, subject to the concessional contributions cap.

Nonconcessional contributions include employee or personal contributions made from net (after-tax) income, contributions above the concessional contribution limit, spouse contributions, and, for small business owners, proceeds from the sale of assets.[9] Nonconcessional contributions are not subject to the 15 percent contribution tax and are not tax-deductible. However, a tax offset of 18 percent (i.e., up to A$540 per year) is available for contributions on behalf of a spouse (spouse contributions) if the spouse's income is less than A$13,800 per year. This threshold increased to A$40,000 per year beginning in July 2017.[10]

When first introduced in 1988, the 15 percent contribution tax applied to all concessional contributions irrespective of the income of the contributor. Since that time, a variety of different arrangements and tax

Table 7.1
Taxation of superannuation (2016–2017).

Contributions	Fund earnings	Benefits[f]
Concessional contributions	**Fund earnings in accumulation phase (excl. capital gains)[g]:** 15% (less imputation credits in dividend income)	**Individuals aged 60 and over**
Employer, self-employed, salary sacrifice, and other tax-deductible contributions: 15% (up to annual contribution cap of A$25,000[a]), then marginal income tax rates apply[c]	**Capital gains:** Tax discount of 1/3 (tax rate of 10%) when asset held for > 1 year	**Income stream:** exempt from tax
Extra tax on concessional contributions for individuals with income[d] > A$250,000: 15%	**Fund earnings in withdrawal phase:** 0%[h] (from July 2017, 15% for balances in excess of A$1.6 million)	**Lump sum:** exempt from tax
Nonconcessional contributions		**Individuals between preservation age and age 60**
Personal contributions from take-home pay, spouse contributions: Not taxed (up to annual contribution cap of A$100,000[b]), then marginal income tax rates apply[c]		**Income stream:** marginal income tax rate less 15%
Low-income super contribution (for individuals with income < A$37,001): Not taxed		**Lump sum:** 15% above tax-free threshold of A$195,000
Super co-contribution[e]: Not taxed		

Sources: Commonwealth Treasury (2016a); O'Dwyer (2016); https://www.ato.gov.au/Super/.

[a] The current cap is A$30,000 per year for members under 50 and A$35,000 per year for members 50 or over. The annual cap of A$25,000 per year commenced in July 2017.

[b] A$300,000 over a three-year period, but only when the account balance is less than A$1.6 million.

[c] Plus an excess contributions charge.

[d] Income is defined as taxable income (plus any adjustments, such as reportable fringe benefits and investment losses) plus pretax superannuation contributions. This tax is known as the Division 293 tax. The "income" threshold was A$300,000 per year but fell to A$250,000 per year beginning in July 2017.

[e] The super co-contribution is a contribution made by the government of up to A$500 per year when individuals have made a personal super contribution of A$1,000 in that year.

[f] Below the preservation age, income streams are taxed at marginal income tax rates and lump sums are subject to a 20 percent tax rate. However, benefits are available before the preservation age in exceptional circumstances.

[g] Since July 2017, superannuation fund earnings include earnings on assets supporting transitional super income streams (also known as transition to retirement pensions).

[h] Subject to minimum "age-based" annual drawdown requirements, ranging from 4 percent of assets at age 60 to 14 percent of assets at age 95.

rates have been applied to individuals at the bottom and very top of the income distribution to address the regressive nature of flat-rate taxes. Individuals at the very top of the income distribution are now subject to an additional 15 percent tax (known as the Division 293 tax) on concessional contributions made on income above A$300,000. In July 2017, this threshold was reduced to A$250,000. Individuals at the bottom end of the income distribution (that is, with taxable income of A$37,000[11] or less) are effectively refunded the contribution tax paid on concessional contributions under the Low Income Super Contribution (LISC).[12] The LISC is not taxed.

In addition, low-income earners may be eligible for a "matching" government contribution (called the "super co-contribution"). The maximum super co-contribution of A$500 is available when an individual makes a personal (nonconcessional) contribution of A$1,000 in that year and has income (in 2016–2017) of A$36,021 or less. A partial super co-contribution is available to individuals with annual income between A$36,021 and A$51,021. The super co-contribution is not taxed.

Contribution caps apply to concessional (employer, salary sacrifice, and voluntary deductible) contributions and nonconcessional contributions (personal contributions from take-home pay), and excess contribution taxes apply to contributions made above these caps. For 2016–2017, the annual contribution cap for concessional contributions is A$30,000 for people under 50 and A$35,000 for people aged 50 and over. In July 2017, this was reduced to a flat A$25,000 but accompanied by a provision allowing "catch-up" contributions (resulting from unused caps from the previous five years) for people with account balances below A$500,000.[13]

Nonconcessional contributions had been subject to an annual cap of A$180,000, or A$540,000 over three years.[14] In July 2017, the annual cap was reduced to A$100,000 (or A$300,000 over three years) and an account balance cap of A$1.6 million was introduced. Contributions in excess of the contribution caps are taxed at marginal income tax rates.

7.2.2 Fund Earnings

The statutory tax rate on income earned by Australian superannuation funds is 15 percent, but because of specific arrangements by asset type, the effective tax rate depends on the chosen or default asset allocation of fund members. More specifically, interest income is taxed at 15 percent, Australian dividends are taxed at 15 percent less imputation credits (i.e., credit for company tax already paid), overseas dividends are taxed at 15 percent less foreign tax credits (i.e., credit for foreign tax already paid), and income from capital gains receives a one-third discount (i.e., taxed at 10 percent) if the asset has been held for more than one year. As a result, the effective tax rate on the earnings of a typical Australian superannuation fund that invests a large proportion of its assets in Australian equities could be significantly less than the 15 percent statutory rate. Superannuation funds with a "balanced" asset allocation (with around 65–70 percent in growth assets) would typically be subject to an effective earnings tax rate of around half the statutory rate.

The fund earnings tax applies to all assets in the accumulation phase, and most assets in the retirement phase accumulate tax-free. That is, the fund earnings tax does not apply to assets in the withdrawal phase if minimum "age-based" drawdown limits are followed, ranging from 4 percent of assets for 60-year-olds to 14 percent of assets for those aged 95 and over. The concessional treatment of superannuation fund assets in the withdrawal phase was initially applied only to assets supporting lifetime annuities (as an incentive to encourage the takeup of these products) but was gradually extended to all retirement benefit products. Since July 2017, a lifetime cap has applied, such that only the first A$1.6 million of retirement assets will be exempt from the fund earnings tax. Earnings on excess balances will be taxed at 15 percent.

7.2.3 Benefits

Retirement benefits may be taken as a lump sum, as an account-based pension (i.e., a phased withdrawal product), or as term or lifetime annuities. Two important ages arise for the taxation of retirement benefits. The first is the preservation age, the age at which superannuation savings can be accessed. The preservation age is in the process of being increased from age 55 to age 60 by 2024 (and for the 2016–2017 fiscal year is 56). The second is age 60 since, as a result of the Simpler Super reforms of 2007 (Commonwealth Treasury 2006), almost all superannuation benefits taken after age 60 are tax-free.[15] For those taking their superannuation benefits between the preservation age and age 60, different tax rates apply, depending on the amount and type of benefit. Income streams are taxed at marginal income tax rates less a tax offset of 15 percent, and lump-sum benefits are tax-free up to a threshold of A$195,000 and thereafter are taxed at a flat rate of 15 percent.

Slightly different rules apply to a particular type of superannuation benefit known as a transition to retirement pension (or a transitional super income stream). Transition to retirement pensions were introduced as a means of lifting the labor force participation rate of older workers; they allow recipients (who have reached their preservation age but are under 65 and not retired) to access part of their superannuation savings as a noncommutable income stream while still working. Under current rules, the earnings on assets supporting transition to retirement pensions are exempt from tax. However, since July 2017, the 15 percent earnings tax has applied to assets supporting transitional super income streams, irrespective of drawdown patterns.

7.2.4 International Comparisons

As illustrated in table 7.2, Australia's approach to the taxation of superannuation differs from the taxation of private pensions in most developed countries.[16] Besides Australia, only New Zealand and Denmark tax superannuation/private pensions under a comprehensive income tax (TTE) regime where contributions and fund earnings are taxed and benefits are exempt.

Among the countries listed in table 7.2, the most common approach is the postpaid expenditure tax (EET), although pension fund earnings are taxed in specific circumstances in Sweden and Italy. Under the EET approach adopted by most developed countries, retirement benefits are (generally) taxed progressively as ordinary income at an individual's marginal tax rate and contributions and fund earnings are tax-exempt. A key benefit of the EET approach is that by not taxing fund earnings it avoids the impact of inflation on effective real rates of return, while taxing benefits at marginal tax rates in retirement facilitates income smoothing.

The TEE approach, whereby contributions are taxed progressively at an individual's marginal tax rate and fund earnings and benefits are exempt from tax, is less popular, with the United States providing the only example in table 7.2. In the United States, the standard approach to the taxation of retirement savings accounts (individual retirement accounts, IRAs) and private pensions (401[k] plans) is under an EET postpaid expenditure tax; however, related products called Roth IRAs and Roth 401(k) plans are taxed under the TEE approach, whereby contributions are made out of after-tax income and fund earnings and benefits are exempt from tax. This variation was introduced to expand access to tax concessions and is attractive to those who may anticipate that their marginal tax rate in retirement will exceed their rate at the time of contribution (Bateman and Kingston 2007). Whether contributions are taxed or not, almost all countries impose contribution caps,

Table 7.2
Taxation treatment of private pensions—international comparison.

Country	Type of plan/ contribution	Source of contribution	Contributions	Earnings	Benefits
Australia	Concessional	All	T	T	EE
	Nonconcessional	Individual	T	T	
Canada	All	All	E	E	T/PE
Chile	All	Individual	E	E	T
Denmark	"Age Savings" plans	All	T	T	E
	Other plans	All	E	T	T
France	Occupational plans	Employer	T/PE	E	T/PE
	"Perco" plans	Individual	T	T/PE	T/PE
	Other plans	Individual	T/PE	E	T/PE
Germany	Private pension insurance	Individual	T	E	T/PE
	Other plans	All	E	E	T
Italy	All	All	E	T	T/PE
Japan	All	All	E	E	T/PE
Korea	Occupational plans	Employer	E	E	T/PE
	All	Individual	T/PE	E	T/PE
Netherlands	All	All	E	E	T
New Zealand	All	Individual	T	T	E
	All	Employer	T	T	E
Norway	All	Individual	T/PE	E	T
	Occupational plans	Employer	E	E	T
Sweden	Premium pension	Individual	E	E	T
	Other plans	All	E	T	T
Switzerland	All	All	E	E	T
United Kingdom	All	All	E	E	T/PT
United States	Roth	Individual	E	E	T
	Other	All	T	E	E

Source: OECD (2015a).
Note: T = taxed, E = exempt, T/PE = taxed but partially exempt.

and excess contributions are generally taxed progressively at marginal tax rates.

Kingston and Piggott (1993) showed the equivalence of the two expenditure tax approaches (postpaid EET and prepaid TtE) in terms of the present value of tax paid for a given single tax rate and in the absence of excess returns (i.e., where $t = 0$). However, in reality, the prepaid approach would impose a higher tax burden on higher-income earners, since taxation under marginal income tax rates would be higher in peak earning years than in retirement, when incomes are lower. Furthermore, in the event of excess returns, equivalence between front- and back-loaded taxation would only apply when the excess return on fund earnings is taxed. In this regard, the Australian TTE approach (where the "T" on fund earnings is very concessional) could be considered broadly equivalent to the typical international EET approach.

Whether taxes are front-loaded or back-loaded has other implications relating to incentives to participate, complexity, risk sharing, and the timing and protection of revenue. The up-front tax concessions under the back-loaded EET approach would be more likely to encourage participation in superannuation/pension plans and encourage higher voluntary contributions and delay retirement. It is also administratively simpler to tax retirement benefits in the hands of individuals at their marginal tax rates than to tax contributions from different sources. Furthermore, a back-loaded EET approach facilitates risk sharing between individual retirees and the government in the event of fluctuations in financial markets. However, the front-loaded TEE approach generates revenue up front and protects this tax base in the event of increasing international labor mobility (Genser and Holzmann 2016, chapter 15, this volume).

As indicated in table 7.2, the comprehensive income tax approach has been adopted by a minority of countries (Australia and New Zealand apply TTE, and Denmark, Italy, and Sweden apply ETT). Under this approach, intertemporal distortions arise because of the taxation of fund earnings, affecting allocative neutrality with respect to consumption decisions. However, with the exception of New Zealand, fund earnings are taxed at concessional flat rates rather than progressively at an individual's marginal tax rate, thereby minimizing possible distortions.

A further point of difference is whether the tax rates on superannuation/pension savings are linked to the personal income tax schedule or are in fact a separate regime, and whether taxation applies at full or concessional rates. For the countries listed in table 7.2, in almost all cases the tax rates are linked to personal income tax rates. The main exception is New Zealand, where personal marginal income tax rates apply to contributions and fund earnings.

In sum, most countries tax superannuation/private pensions under a postpaid expenditure tax approach (EET), with a small but growing number of countries (including Australia) bringing forward the taxation of retirement savings and benefits by taxing contributions and fund earnings at full or concessional rates (OECD 2015a; Genser and Holzmann 2016, chapter 15, this volume).

7.3 Evolution of Australia's Approach to Superannuation/Pension Taxation

Thirty-five years ago, the coverage of superannuation was low, restricted to full-time workers in the public sector and white-collar workers, and the taxation of superannuation was extremely concessional. The evolution of superannuation taxation since then can be represented in three phases: pre-1988 (phase 1), when superannuation was voluntary and coverage was low; 1988 to 2007 (phase 2), during which superannuation coverage expanded through inclusion in industrial awards and compulsion and the Superannuation Guarantee; and post-2007 (phase 3), which saw the maturation of mandatory arrangements, resulting in almost universal coverage and growing account balances. Over this time, Australia's system for the taxation of superannuation also evolved from the pre-1988, postpaid expenditure tax (EET), to the hybrid (TTT) regime between 1988 and 2007, to a form of comprehensive income arrangement (TTE) since 2007, as summarized in table 7.3. Subsection 7.3.1 summarizes Australia's retirement income arrangements; subsequent subsections then describe these three phases in the evolution of superannuation taxation.

7.3.1 Retirement Income Provision in Australia

Australia operates a multipillar retirement income arrangement comprising a means-tested Age Pension financed from general tax revenues; a mandatory, employer-financed, defined contribution scheme known as the Superannuation Guarantee; and tax incentives to encourage voluntary superannuation contributions and other forms of private savings.[17] The "first pillar" Age Pension is paid at a rate of around 28 percent of average male full-time earnings for singles and 41 percent for couples and is currently indexed to keep up with wages in the rest of the economy. The Age Pension is available from age 65 (it will gradually increase to 67 between 2017 and 2023)[18] and is paid subject to income and asset (means) tests, which have the effect of excluding the top 25–30 percent of the wealth distribution from the Age Pension. In 2016, around 60 percent of age pensioners received the full rate of the Age Pension, with the remainder on a partial pension (Australian Department of Social Services 2016). The means tests are comprehensively defined, although the asset test excludes owner-occupied housing.

The "second pillar" Superannuation Guarantee (mandatory private retirement savings) commenced in 1992 and requires all employers to make contributions on behalf of their employees into the employee's superannuation fund of choice (or a default superannuation fund chosen by the employer in the absence of individual choice). The mandatory employer contribution gradually increased from 4 percent to 9 percent between 1992 and 2002 and, following a decision to increase it to 12 percent over a number of years, currently stands at 9.5 percent.[19]

The first two pillars are supplemented by "third pillar" voluntary, long-term savings that include voluntary superannuation contributions, currently made by around one-third of super fund members (Australian Bureau of Statistics 2009), and shares, financial assets, managed funds, property, and home ownership.

Benefits from superannuation savings can be taken at the preservation age (currently age 56, increasing to age 60 by 2024), and individuals are free to choose how they take their benefits from a menu that includes lump sums, account-based pensions (i.e., phased withdrawal products), and life and term annuities. Almost all retirees take nonannuitized benefits, although the number of life annuity policies sold recently increased sharply, from less than 20 in 2010 to over 5,000 in 2016 (Plan for Life 2016).

Around 95 percent of employees are covered by the mandatory superannuation arrangements, and compliance is high, with only those who are too young (under 18) or too poor (earning less than A$450 per month or less than 7 percent of average earnings) excluded from the arrangements. The self-employed are not covered by the compulsory arrangements, but around 75 percent make regular contributions to superannuation accounts (Australian Bureau of Statistics 2009). Including Age Pension eligibility, the Australian Commonwealth Treasury estimates that a fully mature Superannuation Guarantee can be expected to deliver a net replacement rate of around 90 percent for a worker on median earnings and 78 percent for a worker on average earnings (Australian Government 2014).

7.3.2 Superannuation Taxation Phase 1 (Pre-1988)

Traditionally, Australians relied on the Age Pension and voluntary superannuation for retirement income provision. While tax deductibility for superannuation contributions was introduced in 1915 and tax concessions for lump-sum benefits in 1936, preservation of benefits was poor and coverage was low. In the early 1980s, only about one-third of workers in the private sector and less than half of all workers were covered by superannuation arrangements; for those who were

Table 7.3
Evolution of the taxation of superannuation in Australia.

	Contributions	Earnings	Benefits	Regime
Phase 1				
Pre-1983	0%	0%	**Income stream:** Personal tax rates **Lump sum:** 5% of amount at personal tax rates	EEt
1983–1988	0%	0%	**Income stream:** Personal tax rates **Lump sum:** <A$50,000 taxed at 15% >A$49,999 taxed at 30%	EET
Phase 2				
1988	**Employer (and self-employed):** 15% (+15% surcharge for high-income earners between 1997 and 2005) **Employee:** Paid out of after-tax income Age-based contribution caps apply	**Super fund earnings in the accumulation and limited super fund earnings in retirement phase (excl. capital gains)**: 15% (reduced by imputation credits on dividend income) **Capital gains:** 10%	**Income stream:** Personal tax rates less 15% rebate **Lump sum:** <threshold (tax-free) Threshold to reasonable benefit limit (taxed at 15%) >Reasonable benefit limit (taxed at personal tax rates)	TTT

Phase 3				
Post-2007	**Employer (and self-employed)**: 15% (30% if income > A$300,000 (threshold A$250,000 from 2017–2018) and effective rate of 0% if income < A$37,001)	**Accumulation phase**	**Income stream:** Exempt (aged 60 and over)[a] **Lump sum:** Exempt (aged 60 and over)[a]	TTE
	Employee: Paid out of after-tax income	**Super fund earnings (excl. capital gains):** 15% (reduced by imputation credits on dividend income)		
	Refund of contribution tax if low income	**Capital gains**[a]: 10%		
	Flat-rate contribution caps apply	**Retirement phase**		
		Super fund earnings (and capital gains): 0% (from July 2017, 15% if balance > $1.6 million)		

Sources: Commonwealth Treasury (2016a); O'Dwyer (2016); https://www.ato.gov.au/Super/; Nielsen (2010).
[a] Different tax rates apply to people who take their benefits before age 60 (see table 7.1).

covered, retirement payouts were compromised by limited vesting and an absence of portability. Unlike in many other OECD countries, public earnings–related or employment-related pensions had never been introduced in Australia, despite several broadly supported attempts to do so. As a result, as recently as the first half of the 1980s, Australia operated a two-pillar retirement income system, with the public Age Pension supported by voluntary superannuation (Bateman and Piggott 1997).

During this period of low coverage, superannuation was taxed only lightly. Employee contributions were paid from after-tax income, employer contributions were not taxed, and superannuation fund earnings accumulated tax-free. At retirement, benefits could be taken as lump sums or annuities. Most people took lump sums, which were very generously taxed, with only 5 percent of the amount of the lump sum included in taxable income in the year of payment, resulting in an effective tax rate of no more than 3 percent, depending on the individual's personal tax rate.[20] Annuities did not receive concessions and were taxed as ordinary income. These arrangements resembled post-paid expenditure taxation (EET), with a very concessional "t" for benefits taken as lump sums.

From the early to mid-1980s, as retirement income policy in Australia started to change and coverage started to increase, so did the taxation of superannuation. In 1983, significant changes were made to the taxation of superannuation benefits: a tax on lump-sum benefits was introduced (representing the initial break with marginal income tax rates), and some tax relief was provided for benefits taken as income streams. The lump-sum tax was applied at a rate of 15 percent up to a threshold and thereafter at 30 percent. The concessions for income streams applied only to life annuities and included exemption from tax of the earnings of supporting assets (which was later extended to all retirement benefits) and the exclusion from taxable income of that part of the regular payment (income) representing the return of capital (known as the deductible amount).

The mid-1980s heralded the beginning of widespread and then mandatory coverage of superannuation. At this time, a system of centralized wage determination operated in Australia, and the 1986 national wage case included a requirement that employers (covered by industrial awards) provide workers with superannuation contributions in lieu of wage increases. This became known as productivity award superannuation (as the superannuation contributions were offered in return for productivity improvements) and was the beginning of the expansion of superannuation coverage from mainly full-time white-collar and public sector workers to the entire workforce.

By the beginning of 1988, the taxation of superannuation could still be characterized as EET, with a less generous "T" on lump sums and a more generous "T" on benefits taken as life annuities.

7.3.3 Superannuation Taxation Phase 2 (1988–2007)

The 1980s were a decade of economic reform in Australia. Key reforms included the floating of the exchange rate, the reduction and removal of tariffs, financial market reform, and tax reform. In the second half of the 1980s, Australia introduced a range of taxes, including a capital gains tax, a foreign tax credit system, a fringe benefits tax, and an imputation system. At the same time, inflation was high relative to Australia's trading partners, the current account was growing, and concerns arose about long-term fiscal deficits. In 1988, initiatives introduced to address these and other macroeconomic concerns included a dramatic change to the taxation of superannuation (Keating 1988, 2007). In effect, revenue was brought forward by reducing the taxation of benefits (by around 15 percentage points) and imposing a new 15 percent tax on employer contributions and superannuation fund earnings. The 15/30 tax on lump sums (15 percent up to a threshold and thereafter 30 percent) was reduced to 0/15, and income from lifetime annuities received a 15 percent tax rebate. The concessional tax rates on both lump sums and income streams were capped by reasonable benefit limits (RBLs), above which marginal income tax rates applied.[21]

As a result, Australia moved from an EET (postpaid expenditure tax) to a TTT (comprehensive income tax) approach to the taxation of retirement savings, which was out of sync with international practice. Not only was the taxation of superannuation brought forward, the new "superannuation taxes" were applied at a flat rate that was not linked in any way to the marginal personal income tax schedule.

Following commencement of the mandatory Superannuation Guarantee in 1992, superannuation coverage increased from around 80 percent of workers (under the productivity award arrangements) to close to 95 percent, with only the very young and very poor excluded. In addition, increases in the mandatory contribution rate (from 3–4 percent to 9 percent over the next decade) and strong asset markets resulted in steady growth in superannuation assets.

The compulsory nature of the Superannuation Guarantee, in conjunction with the growing importance of superannuation as a household asset, contributed to growing awareness of the inequities associated with imposition of the flat-rate superannuation tax on contributions and fund earnings and to considerable political pressure to address these concerns. As a result, the next decade and a half (1992–2007) saw many piecemeal and ad hoc changes to the taxation of superannuation, all with the goal of addressing these equity concerns. Initiatives included the introduction of contribution caps to supplement the lifetime limits (i.e., RBLs), a 15 percent superannuation surcharge on the contributions of high-income earners, and a government co-contribution scheme that provided matching contributions for low-income earners. Changes were also made to the taxation of income streams, with the tax concessions initially provided only to life annuities extended first to term annuities and later to account-based pensions.

By 2006, Australia's TTT approach to the taxation of superannuation had been overlaid by a variety of measures designed to provide differential taxation of contributions by income of the contributor and differential taxation of benefits by type of benefit (and, by implication, differential means-test treatment in the context of Australia's public Age Pension).

7.3.4 Superannuation Taxation Phase 3 (post-2007)

While the overall taxation of superannuation was concessional to the majority of superannuation fund members (Australia's Future Tax System 2010), it was becoming increasingly complicated, and the frequent tinkering to address equity issues created a perception of constant policy change. This culminated in a decision by the government to "simplify" the taxation of superannuation through the Simpler Super reforms announced in the 2006–2007 budget (Commonwealth Treasury 2006). The most important change was the removal of all taxes on superannuation benefits for people 60 and over (subject to "age-based" minimum drawdown requirements). RBLs were abolished, age-based concessional contribution caps were replaced with flat-rate caps, and the exclusion from tax of the earnings on assets supporting selected retirement benefits was extended to all retirement benefits. The tax regime for superannuation moved from TTT to TTE.

However, piecemeal changes to the taxation of superannuation continued over the next decade as successive governments responded to public debate about the fairness of the superannuation tax concessions (Australian Council of Social Services 2015; Association of Superannuation Funds of Australia 2014; Australia Institute 2009; Daley, Coates, and

Wood 2015), often coinciding with the annual release of tax expenditure estimates (see, for example, Commonwealth Treasury 2016b) and expedited by the election cycle. This period saw six changes to the flat-rate contribution caps, (re)introduction of an additional 15 percent contribution tax for high-income earners (the Division 293 tax), and introduction of a system to refund the contribution tax of low-income earners (the Low Income Super Contribution).

7.3.5 Henry Tax Review Recommendations

Besides actual changes to the taxation of superannuation, numerous instances exist of changes proposed or recommended but not implemented. The most comprehensive are the recommendations of the Review of Australia's Tax System—known as the Henry Tax Review (Australia's Future Tax System 2010).

In its final report, the Henry Tax Review recommended that the 15 percent tax on concessional contributions be abolished and that all contributions (employer, personal, self-employed) be taxed at marginal personal income tax rates less a flat-rate refundable tax offset that would be set so the majority of taxpayers would not pay more than 15 percent tax on their contributions. This approach would integrate the taxation of superannuation contributions with the personal tax system (thus ensuring progressivity) and would reduce complexity by removing the tax distinction by contribution type and the need for equity-enhancing add-ons. Also recommended was a halving of the tax rate on superannuation fund earnings to 7.5 percent and an extension of its application to superannuation accounts in both the accumulation and withdrawal phases. After allowing for imputation credits, the effective tax rate on superannuation fund earnings would be close to zero. Benefits would remain tax-exempt since consideration of the taxation of retirement benefits was specifically excluded by the terms of reference for the review.

This approach to reform was largely supported by main superannuation lobby groups and industry associations, and subsequently by the recent Financial System Inquiry (Australian Government 2014). However, because of political influences at the time of the release of the final report, its recommendations were largely ignored by the government. Had these changes been implemented, Australia's taxation of superannuation would resemble TtE (a prepaid expenditure tax), with the "T" on contributions explicitly linked to the personal marginal income tax schedule and the "t" on fund earnings very concessional.

Using a model-based analysis, Kudrna and Woodland (2015, chapter 14, this volume) showed that the Henry Tax Review approach to the taxation of superannuation would lead to improvements in vertical equity, an increase in national savings, and lower public pension outlays.

7.3.6 2016–2017 Budget Reforms to the Taxation of Superannuation

The most recent reforms to the taxation of superannuation were announced in the 2016–2017 budget (Commonwealth Treasury 2016a) and legislated in 2016 for commencement in 2017 and 2018. The stated aim was to improve the equity and sustainability of the superannuation tax arrangements (O'Dwyer 2016). These reforms include a reduction in the annual age-dependent concessional (largely employer) contribution cap to a flat A$25,000; a reduction in the annual nonconcessional (personal) contribution cap from A$180,000 to A$100,000; and initiatives to better target the contribution tax concessions, including confirmation of the continuation of the scheme to refund the contribution taxes of low-income workers, a reduction in the threshold for the application of the additional 15 percent contribution tax on superannuation contributions of high-income earners from A$300,000 to A$250,000; and an extension of access to tax deductions for voluntary personal contributions. Also, the fund earnings tax exemption in the retirement phase was restricted to the first A$1.6 million of retirement assets and was removed for transition to retirement income stream products.

This latest set of changes will enhance the sustainability of the superannuation tax arrangements, and it attempts to better target the tax concessions on superannuation contributions. Overall, the TTE approach to taxation of superannuation has been moderated, with the result that the "T" on contributions applies more progressively and the "E" in the retirement phase is "capped" and less vulnerable to exploitation through tax planning. However, the reforms fall short of explicitly linking the taxation of superannuation with personal income taxes.

7.4 Evaluation of Australia's Approach to the Taxation of Superannuation/Pensions

The taxation of superannuation/pensions can be evaluated by reference to the three standard criteria for tax analysis—efficiency, equity, and administrative simplicity. Also important are policy stability, the impact on individual decision making, and the vulnerability to political risk.

7.4.1 Efficiency

When considering the implications of alternative tax arrangements for economy-wide efficiency, one needs to consider which tax arrangements generate the least-damaging tax distortions, measured in terms of the cost of the resulting inefficient allocation of resources. In terms of the alternative regimes for the taxation of superannuation/pensions, efficiency would be enhanced under an expenditure tax approach where the taxes on consumption are neutral with respect to time, as opposed to a comprehensive income tax (or hybrid) approach where the returns to saving are taxed. Furthermore, those regimes that do not tax the return on assets avoid issues associated with the impact of inflation on net-of-tax real rates of return on long-term saving; that is, with positive inflation, the longer an asset is held, the higher the real effective tax rate. Efficiency would also be enhanced in jurisdictions where alternative assets were taxed similarly, thereby minimizing interasset distortions.

In this context, three main "efficiency" concerns arise with the current Australian TTE approach to the taxation of superannuation:

1. By taxing both contributions and fund earnings and exempting benefits, the Australian approach does not ensure neutrality between present and future consumption. This effect is partially addressed by the low effective tax rate on fund earnings, because of the combination of the 15 percent flat-rate tax and the impact of imputation credits, and initiatives to enhance progressivity of contribution taxes, which likely bring the arrangements closer to allocative neutrality with regard to intertemporal consumption decisions.

2. By imposing any tax on superannuation fund earnings, the Australian arrangements do not address the impact of inflation on the after-tax real rate of return on long-term (superannuation) savings.

3. Different tax rates are applied to saving through superannuation and alternative assets. For example, interest income is taxed at marginal tax rates; dividend income from domestic shares is taxed at marginal tax rates less imputation credits; dividend income from foreign shares is taxed at marginal tax rates less foreign tax credits; income from investment property benefits from tax deductibility of interest payments and other expenses and access to negative gearing (which allows a loss from owning an investment property to be offset against unrelated income for tax purposes); and home ownership is particularly tax effective, since Australia does not tax imputed rents and the family home is exempt from the capital gains tax. In general, superannuation

saving is taxed more favorably than financial assets but less favorably than property investments, which (including home ownership) dominate the household portfolio. It is often argued that tax preference for investment and owner-occupied housing has led to an overemphasis of this asset class in household portfolios at the expense of superannuation and other long-term assets.

7.4.2 Equity

The common interpretation of equity in tax analysis is the "capacity to pay." In this regard, tax regimes that tax progressively—such as arrangements where the taxation of pensions is the same as, or in some way linked to, the personal income tax schedule—are more likely to better address equity concerns. This does not mean that the equity of superannuation/pension taxation should itself be an independent objective. What is relevant is the net fiscal impact of all taxes and transfers. However, a superannuation/pension tax regime that is consistent with broader tax-related equity objectives is likely to be more resistant to political interference on equity grounds.

In this context, two main "equity" concerns have driven most of the public discussion and policy changes. First, taxes on superannuation contributions and fund earnings apply at a flat rate that is not linked to the personal marginal income tax schedule; and second, different types of contributions are taxed differently, and access to favorably taxed contributions (such as through salary sacrifice) has been limited for some people.

7.4.2.1 Flat-rate contribution taxes The main concern associated with taxing contributions at a flat rate of 15 percent is that this is unfair to low-income earners, who would pay less tax (or even no tax) if the contributions were paid as wages, and overly generous to high-income earners, who would pay considerably more tax were the contributions paid as wages. When the contribution tax was first introduced in 1988, it applied at a flat rate of 15 percent to all concessional (mainly employer) contributions. Since then, a variety of adjustments have been introduced (and varied, abolished, and reintroduced) in an attempt to deliver progressivity. The current differences in the tax rates applied to personal income and concessional superannuation contributions are summarized in figure 7.1 and table 7.4.

Figure 7.1 shows a comparison between personal marginal tax rates (the black line), the statutory 15 percent tax on concessional superannua-

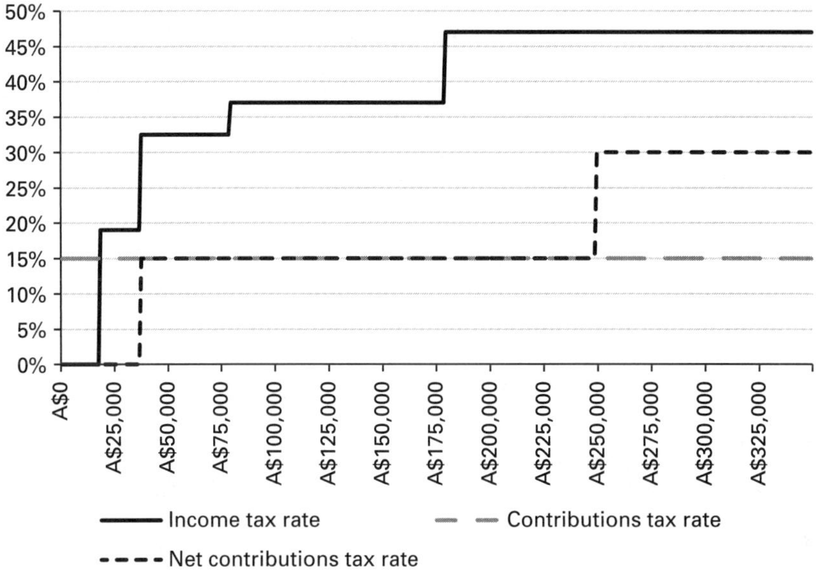

Figure 7.1
Tax on super contributions compared with marginal tax rates on income. *Source*: Author's construction using information on income tax rates from https://www.ato.gov.au/rates/individual-income-tax-rates/ and information on superannuation tax rates from https://www.ato.gov.au/Individuals/Super/Super-and-tax/. *Notes*: Tax rates as of July 1, 2017, excluding the Medicare Levy and the Temporary Budget Repair Levy (on taxable income over A$180,000); the net contribution tax rate is calculated as the 15 percent contributions rate adjusted for the Low Income Super Tax Offset (LISTO), which refunds the contribution tax for people with "income" below A$37,000 and the additional 15 percent tax on "income" in excess of A$250,000; "income" includes reported fringe benefits and employer superannuation contributions; the vertical line indicates full-time adult average weekly earnings (around A$80,000 per year in 2016).

tion contributions (grey dashed line), and the net tax on superannuation contributions after accounting for the Low Income Super Tax Offset (LISTO) (a refund of contribution tax for low-income earners) and the additional 15 percent tax applied to high-income earners (black dashed line). Because of the myriad of policy changes over the past three decades, supplemented by the most recent changes announced in the 2016–2017 budget, the tax concessions on superannuation contributions apply more evenly across the income distribution than when first introduced in 1988, peaking in the income range A$180,000 to A$250,000, with a 32 percentage point tax advantage for superannuation contributions. For most taxpayers, superannuation contributions receive a tax benefit of between 17 and 22 percentage points.

Table 7.4
Tax rates applying to personal income, concessional superannuation contributions, and superannuation earnings.

	Personal income	Concessional superannuation contributions			Fund earnings[a]	
Taxable income (A$)	Marginal tax rate	Tax rate	Net tax rate	Tax concession	Tax rate	Tax concession
< 18,201	0%	15%	0%	0%	15%	–15%
18,201–37,000	19%	15%	0%	19%	15%	4%
37,001–80,000	32.5%	15%	15%	17.5%	15%	17.5%
80,001–180,000	37%	15%	15%	22%	15%	22%
180,001–250,000	47%	15%	15%	32%	15%	32%
> $250,000	47%	15%	30%	17%	15%	32%

Note: Tax rate on superannuation earnings is as of July 1, 2016. Excludes Medicare Levy and Temporary Budget Repair Levy (on taxable income over A$180,000). The actual tax rate on superannuation fund earnings is lower than the statutory rate to the extent that the superannuation assets are invested in domestic equities and receive imputation credits. The overall net tax rate on superannuation fund earnings is around half the statutory rate.
[a] Tax concession assumes statutory tax rates, which would be lower to the extent that the assets are invested in domestic equities.

However, when it comes to taxation of superannuation fund earnings, considerable differences remain in the relative tax concessions across the income distribution (far right column of table 7.4). Earners with very low incomes (i.e., those with incomes below A$18,201 per year) are subject to a significantly higher tax rate on their superannuation fund earnings (15 percent statutory rate, reduced by imputation credits to around half that) than on their income (0 percent), while those earning the highest incomes (i.e., those with incomes above A$180,000 per year) receive a 32 percentage point tax advantage.

Finally, as a result of the changes implemented in 2007 under the Simpler Super reforms, superannuation benefits are tax-exempt for most people (irrespective of the size of the retirement accumulation), and, subject to minimum annual drawdown requirements, earnings on retirement accounts (including transitional super income streams) are tax-free. The 2016 reforms reduced this generosity through better targeting of the tax concessions, including a cap of A$1.6 million of retirement assets eligible for the earnings tax exemption[22] and removal of the earnings tax exemption for transitional super income streams. Combined, these changes reintroduce a global cap on superannuation tax concessions and limit opportunities for tax planning.

7.4.2.2 Differential access to favorably taxed contributions Another equity concern has been that different types of superannuation contributions are taxed differently. In particular, concessional contributions (which include employer contributions, salary sacrifice contributions, and contributions from the self-employed) are taxed at 15 percent (with variations for low- and high-income earners as described earlier), while employee contributions are fully taxed as income (supplemented by a government co-contribution for those with low incomes).[23] Both issues were addressed in the superannuation tax changes announced and legislated in 2016 that (subject to the concessional contributions cap) extend tax deductibility for personal superannuation contributions to all superannuation fund members.[24]

7.4.2.3 Distribution and cost of the superannuation tax concessions As previously noted, the appropriate measure of the equity (or fairness) of the superannuation tax arrangements is net fiscal impact. Figure 7.2

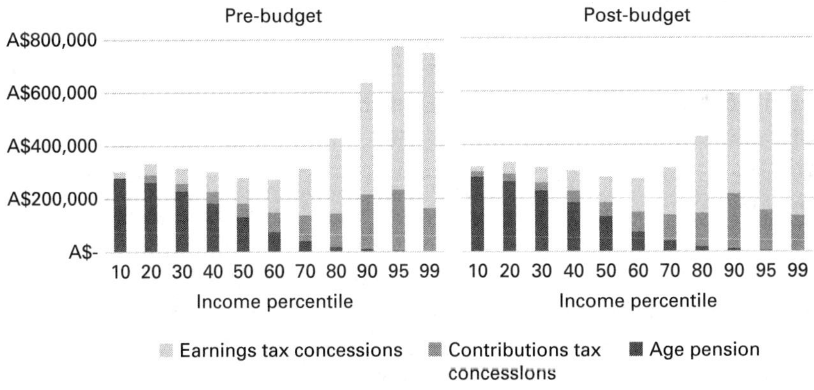

Figure 7.2
Net fiscal impact of superannuation taxes plus the Age Pension in 2016. *Source*: Commonwealth Treasury (2016a). *Note*: Individuals are assumed to commence work in 2016 at age 30 and work until age 70, with a predicted life expectancy of 92. Accumulated superannuation assets are invested in an account-based pension, and individuals are assumed to draw down their assets at the current age-based minimum drawdown rates. The level of tax assistance and Age Pension entitlements are discounted by 5 percent per year to calculate a net present value in 2016 dollars. Annual incomes are calculated for each percentile based on the distribution of earners at each single year of age. No after-tax contributions are assumed.

presents Commonwealth Treasury estimates of the net present value of total government support over a lifetime from the superannuation tax concessions and the means-tested Age Pension before (left panel) and after (right panel) the 2016 reforms. Both figures show a distinct skewness of net government support toward earners with higher incomes but a distinct reduction in this as a result of the recent initiatives.

Such analysis raises questions about the sustainability of the superannuation tax concessions. Recent estimates place Australia highest in the OECD for the cost of tax concessions for superannuation/private pensions (OECD 2015b), and the latest estimates for Australia indicate a continuation of that trend (Commonwealth Treasury 2016b). While arguments can be made regarding the appropriateness of the benchmark and the failure to account for behavioral effects, Australia's approach of flat-rate taxes plus equity-enhancing initiatives is clearly an imperfect substitute for a progressive tax schedule.

Overall, the Australian experience suggests that equity would be easier to achieve if superannuation contributions, earnings, or benefits (under whichever tax regime applies) were taxed at or closely linked to personal marginal tax rates.

7.4.3 Simplicity

For the taxation of superannuation/pensions, administrative simplicity is enhanced where there are fewer tax points and where tax rates are aligned with personal marginal tax rates, thereby requiring fewer add-ons to ensure progressivity. Simplicity would be enhanced under a tax regime where retirement savings were taxed at one point (rather than one, two, or three points) and the same tax rules were applied at each point (for example, to all types of contributions). It is also easier to apply the personal marginal income tax schedule when taxing contributions and benefits than when taxing fund earnings. As the Australian arrangements clearly show, simplicity is compromised where taxes apply at multiple points (i.e., on combinations of contributions, fund earnings, and benefits) and where flat-rate superannuation/pension taxes are supplemented by additional taxes, rebates, deductions, co-contributions, and caps (as described throughout this chapter) to mimic progressivity.

Under the current Australian approach, where a flat 15 percent tax applies to contributions and fund earnings, complexity has arisen not only from the equity-enhancing add-ons but also from political pressure to amend, abolish, and reintroduce over time many of these initiatives and the grandfathering rules. Furthermore, the perception of ever-increasing complexity is perpetuated through constant revision of new initiatives as they proceed through the consultation and legislative process and through the frequent use of regulatory jargon in the public domain.

Little mention has been made of the complexity of benefits taxation, largely because the Simpler Super reforms of 2007 removed the tax on superannuation benefits for most people aged 60 and over (subject to grandfathering arrangements). However, at the same time, this reform removed the ability to use taxes to influence the purchase of particular income stream products (such as lifetime annuities), which is a useful policy option in the absence of compulsion or defaults. Overall, the Australian approach to the taxation of superannuation/pensions clearly performs poorly in terms of "simplicity."

7.4.4 Other Criteria for Evaluation

7.4.4.1 Policy stability As documented in this chapter, the Australian arrangements for taxation of superannuation/pensions have been the subject of constant change over the past three to four decades. This can be partially explained by the evolution from low-coverage, voluntary superannuation to a broad-coverage, mandatory system and partially by the constant search for a set of initiatives that added progressivity to flat-rate contributions and earnings taxes. This policy design dilemma was exacerbated by successive governments that sought to build and maintain electoral support.

As documented in this chapter, numerous initiatives introduced to enhance progressivity have been amended, abolished, and reintroduced. For example, an extra 15 percent contribution tax for high-income earners was introduced as the superannuation surcharge in 1997, abolished in 2005, and then reintroduced as the Division 293 tax in 2012; the annual concessional contribution cap was first introduced in 1988 as an age-based cap, was changed to a flat-rate cap in 2007, and has since varied six times; and the idea of a lifetime limit on access to superannuation tax concessions was first introduced in the form of RBLs in 1988, which were abolished in 2007 and then reappeared as the A$1.6 million limit on retirement phase accounts to apply from July 1, 2017.

7.4.4.2 Impact on life cycle saving and withdrawal decisions Another issue to consider is that superannuation/pension taxes are not just a source of revenue; they also influence individual decisions and behavior. While Australia's Superannuation Guarantee mandates participation in a superannuation plan and a minimum contribution rate, individuals are left with the responsibilities of choosing the super fund in which their superannuation savings are managed and accumulate (or to opt for the default), the investment option for their contributions (or opt for the default), whether to make or increase voluntary contributions, and how to manage the drawdown of assets in retirement. These decisions are complex, and individuals need to take account of many factors, including expected time at work and in retirement, future wages, asset returns, expected longevity, changes in family makeup and health status, eligibility for the public pension and other public support, and the relevant tax rules. Recent studies have identified that a large proportion of the population lacks the appropriate financial and tax knowledge and skills to make these decisions (Agnew, Bateman, and Thorp 2013a, 2013b), and it is well known from the behavioral literature that policy complexity inhibits decision making (Bateman 2016).

7.4.4.3 Political risk A major advantage of mandatory private retirement saving is the long-term political insulation it provides relative to public provision. However, governments are still able to compromise this independence by changing pension taxation. As described in this chapter, the separation of superannuation taxes from personal income taxation under the Australian arrangements clearly shows that while superannuation accumulations are managed by private superannuation funds, and therefore are not part of the government budget, they are not completely insulated from political risk.

7.5 Conclusions

As documented in this chapter, Australia's approach to the taxation of pensions differs from that of most of the developed world. While most countries exempt contributions and fund earnings and tax benefits at personal marginal tax rates under a postpaid expenditure tax regime (EET), Australia imposes flat-rate taxes on contributions and fund earnings and (for most people) exempts retirement benefits. While at first glance this may appear to resemble a comprehensive income tax regime (TTE), the increasing progressivity of the taxation of contributions and the concessional taxation of fund earnings brings it closer to

TtE, the conceptual equivalent of a postpaid expenditure approach. The extent to which this is the case depends on whether the flat-rate taxes plus add-ons replicate the personal income tax schedule and whether the concessional treatment of fund earnings matches the taxation of excess returns.

The key lessons from the Australian experience are summarized as follows:

- Taxation of superannuation has been subject to constant change as successive governments sought combinations of design features to add onto the flat-rate contributions and fund earnings taxes to enhance progressivity. This resulted in policy complexity, policy instability, and the politicization of superannuation taxation and affected public confidence in overall retirement income arrangements. A better approach is to align pension taxes with the personal marginal income tax schedule. While this would be possible for contribution taxes, it would be administratively challenging for earnings taxes.
- It is clear from estimates of the net fiscal impact of the superannuation taxes plus the means-tested Age Pension that the flat-rate taxes plus add-ons are an imperfect substitute for the marginal income tax schedule and that the long-term sustainability of the tax concessions needs to be closely monitored.
- The increasing complexity of the Australian arrangements for taxation of superannuation affects both the superannuation funds and individuals—the former because of the administrative costs associated with constant change and the latter by compounding already complex life cycle saving and drawdown decisions.
- The front-loading in the Australian arrangements has the benefit of bringing forward tax revenue and ensures the protection of the tax base in the event of increased international labor mobility.
- Private retirement savings arrangements are not completely insulated from political risk.

Reforms legislated in 2016 will improve the targeting of the superannuation tax concessions. However, in the absence of a direct link with personal marginal tax rates, taxation of superannuation will remain vulnerable to policy instability, which will continue to increase complexity and to challenge public confidence in the retirement income arrangements.

Notes

Comments and feedback from Robert Holzmann, John Piggott, and participants at the CEPAR/CESifo conferences of November 2014 in Sydney and September 2015 in Munich are gratefully acknowledged.

1. A prepaid expenditure tax is also often referred to as TEE, for which no excess returns would be assumed.

2. Although, with the low effective tax rate on superannuation fund earnings, it could also be argued that the current arrangements are closer to a prepaid expenditure tax (TtE).

3. This chapter draws on Bateman, Kingston, and Piggott (2001, chap. 6) and Bateman, Chomik, and Piggott (2016).

4. As noted earlier, the arrangements could also be viewed as a form of prepaid expenditure tax.

5. The discussion in this chapter focuses on the taxation of superannuation in "taxed" superannuation funds. These generally are defined contribution plans and privately managed defined benefit plans. For constitutional reasons, some public defined benefit plans must be taxed under an EET regime. Grandfathering arrangements are ignored.

6. The Superannuation Guarantee is Australia's mandatory superannuation (private pension) scheme. Employers are required to contribute at least 9.5 percent of an employee's earnings to a privately managed superannuation/pension fund on behalf of just about all of their employees.

7. Under a salary sacrifice arrangement, an employer agrees to make an employee contribution from pretax income.

8. For the purpose of superannuation taxation, the self-employed are defined as individuals whose salary and/or wage is less than 10 percent of their income from work.

9. Small business owners can contribute up to A$500,000 from the sale of assets to their superannuation account.

10. Spouse contributions can only be made if the spouse is younger than 65 or is 65–70 and working.

11. This covers people in the bottom two marginal income tax ranges. It is noted that average weekly ordinary time earnings in 2016 were around A$80,000.

12. The Low Income Super Contribution (LISC) was renamed the Low Income Super Tax Offset (LISTO) in July 2017. Under both schemes, the government makes a contribution of up to A$500 per year (in effect, a refund of the 15 percent tax on the mandatory employer contributions under the superannuation guarantee) to their superannuation account.

13. Catch-up contributions will commence in July 2018.

14. That is, people under 65 can bring forward contributions for three years.

15. Retirement benefits are tax-free provided they are paid from a "taxed" fund. A "taxed" fund is one that has paid taxes on contributions and fund earnings. A small

number of public defined benefit funds are constitutionally protected from paying contributions and fund earnings taxes.

16. The tax treatment of private pensions is more complex than table 7.2 suggests, and even within a given country, the taxation of pensions may differ between public pensions, occupational pensions, voluntary and mandatory private pensions, funded and unfunded pensions, and defined contribution and defined benefit pensions.

17. The discussion in this chapter focuses on defined contribution arrangements. While some defined benefit plans still exist in Australia, most are closed to new members.

18. In its 2014–2015 budget, the government announced plans to further increase the Age Pension eligibility age to 70 by 2035, but this has not been legislated.

19. The mandatory employer contribution is scheduled to rise to 12 percent by 2026.

20. The highest marginal tax rate was 65 percent.

21. RBLs operated to limit the tax concessions. The "pension" RBL was double the "lump-sum" RBL (as an incentive for lifetime annuity purchase) and applied when at least 50 percent of the retirement accumulation was annuitized.

22. Excess retirement balances can be held in an accumulation account, and earnings thereon will be subject to the 15 percent fund earnings tax. Note that the A$1.6 million limit does not place a cap on the size of retirement accumulations but sets a cap on the amount retirees can have before paying any tax on their retirement account earnings.

23. Contributions made on behalf of a low-income spouse are fully taxed as income but receive an 18 percent rebate.

24. In addition, the income threshold for a low-income spouse will increase from A$13,800 per year to A$40,000 per year.

References

Agnew, Julie R., Hazel Bateman, and Susan Thorp. 2013a. "Financial Literacy and Retirement Planning in Australia." *Numeracy* 6 (2): 1–25.

Agnew, Julie R., Hazel Bateman, and Susan Thorp. 2013b. "Superannuation Knowledge and Plan Behaviour." *JASSA*, no. 1:45–50.

Association of Superannuation Funds of Australia (ASFA). 2014. "The Equity and Sustainability of Government Assistance for Retirement Incomes in Australia." Association of Superannuation Funds of Australia, Sydney.

Australia Institute. 2009. "The Great Superannuation Tax Concession Rort." Research Paper No. 61, Australia Institute, Canberra.

Australian Bureau of Statistics (ABS). 2009. "Employment Arrangements, Retirement and Superannuation, Australia." Cat. No. 6361.0, April–July 2007 (Reissue). Australian Bureau of Statistics, Canberra.

Australian Council of Social Services (ACOSS). 2015. "Budget Statement Priorities." Australian Council of Social Services, Sydney.

Australian Department of Social Services. 2016. *Annual Report 2015–16*. Canberra: Australian Department of Social Services.

Australian Government. 2014. "Financial System Inquiry, Final Report." Commonwealth of Australia, Canberra.

Australia's Future Tax System (AFTS). 2010. "Final Report." Commonwealth of Australia, Canberra.

Bateman, Hazel. 2016. "Retirement Income Strategies for an Ageing Population." In *Population Ageing and Australia's Future*, edited by Hal Kendig, Peter McDonald, and John Piggott, 233–260. Canberra: ANU Press.

Bateman, Hazel, Rafal Chomik, and John Piggott. 2016. "Australia's Retirement Income Policy." In *Ageing in Australia: Challenges and Opportunities*, edited by Kate O'Loughlin, Colette Browning, and Hal Kendig, 149–172. New York: Springer.

Bateman, Hazel, and Geoffrey Kingston. 2007. "Superannuation and Personal Income Tax Reform." *Australian Tax Forum* 22 (3): 137–163.

Bateman, Hazel, Geoffrey Kingston, and John Piggott, eds. 2001. *Forced Saving: Mandating Private Retirement Incomes*. Cambridge: Cambridge University Press.

Bateman, Hazel, and John Piggott. 1997. "Private Pensions in OECD Countries—Australia." Labour Market and Social Policy Occasional Papers No. 23, OECD, Paris.

Commonwealth Treasury. 2006. "A Plan to Simplify and Streamline Superannuation." Commonwealth of Australia, Canberra, May 9.

Commonwealth Treasury. 2012. "Recent Distributional Analysis of Superannuation Tax Concessions." Commonwealth of Australia, Canberra.

Commonwealth Treasury. 2016a. "Budget 2016–17—Making Our Tax System More Equitable." Commonwealth of Australia, Canberra.

Commonwealth Treasury. 2016b. "Tax Expenditures Statement 2015." Commonwealth of Australia, Canberra.

Daley, John, Brendan Coates, and Danielle Wood. 2015. "Super Tax Targeting." Grattan Institute, Melbourne.

Genser, Bernd, and Robert Holzmann. 2016. "The Taxation of Internationally Portable Pensions: Fiscal Issues and Policy Options." CEPAR Working Paper No. 2016/09, CESifo, Munich.

Keating, Paul. 1988. "Reform of the Taxation of Superannuation." Australian Government Publishing Service, Canberra.

Keating, Paul. 2007. "The Story of Modern Superannuation." Presentation to the Australian Pensions and Investment Summit, October 31, Sanctuary Cove, Queensland.

Kingston, Geoffrey, and John Piggott. 1993. "A Ricardian Equivalence Theorem on the Taxation of Pension Funds." *Economics Letters* 42:399–403.

Kudrna, George, and Alan Woodland. 2015. "Progressive Changes to Superannuation in a Lifecycle Framework." CESifo Working Paper Series No. 5645, CESifo, Munich.

Nielsen, Leslie. 2010. "Chronology of Superannuation and Retirement Incomes in Australia." Canberra: Department of Parliamentary Services, Parliament of Australia.

O'Dwyer, Kelly. 2016. "Turnbull Government Delivers on Fairer More Sustainable Super." Media Release with the Hon. Scott Morrison MP (Treasurer), November 23.

OECD (Organisation for Economic Co-operation and Development). 2015a. "Stocktaking of the Tax Treatment of Funded Pension Plans in OECD and EU Countries." OECD Publishing, Paris.

OECD (Organisation for Economic Co-operation and Development). 2015b. *Pensions at a Glance 2015*. Paris: OECD Publishing.

Plan for Life. 2016. "Detailed Annuity Statistics." Plan for Life, Asset International Australia, Mount Waverley.

8 Taxing Pensions and Retirement Benefits in Germany

Axel Börsch-Supan and Christopher Quinn

8.1 Introduction

Germany used to have a largely monolithic pension system dominated by the public pay-as-you-go (PAYG) retirement insurance scheme (GRV—Gesetzliche Rentenversicherung). This has changed in recent decades, after a string of reforms precipitated by the aging of the German population. These reforms reduced the benefits of the PAYG system through various mechanisms and strengthened funded pension schemes in general (Börsch-Supan and Wilke 2005). More specifically, three developments took place:

- In 2001, the so-called Riester pensions were introduced. These heavily subsidized and regulated voluntary personal pension plans are based on individual accounts. The main idea was to introduce a funded pension vehicle that allows households to close the "pension gap" created by the reduction of the public PAYG system's pension benefits (Börsch-Supan 2004).
- Occupational pensions were strengthened by excluding contributions from social security taxation and forcing employers to provide at least some form of occupational pension plan whenever at least one employee demanded it.
- In the wake of the general awareness of population aging and a decline in the PAYG benefits, unsubsidized private pension plans (investments in pension funds, whole life insurance with a deferred annuity, and similar vehicles) also increased their coverage.

Figure 8.1 shows how funded pension plans in Germany have increased their coverage. In 2030, an estimated one-third of retirement income will be generated by funded pensions (Kommission für die

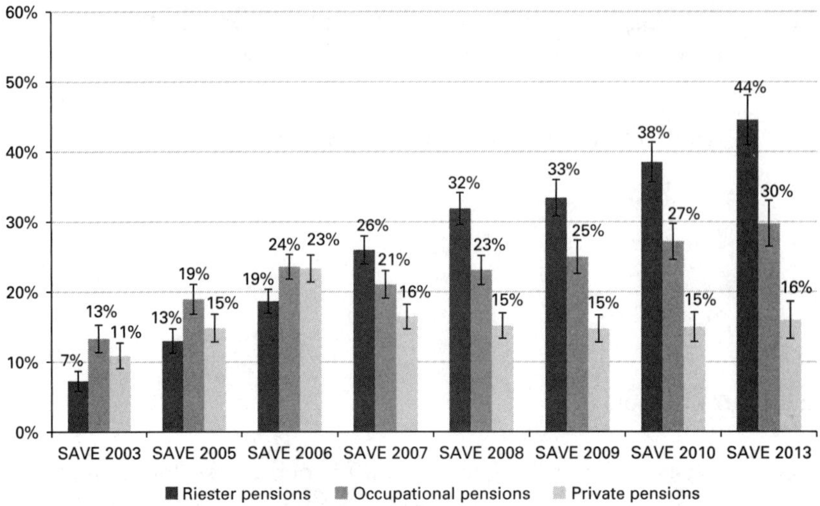

Figure 8.1
Uptake rates of supplementary pensions, Germany, 2003–2013. *Source*: Authors' calculations based on the SAVE data, waves 2003–2013 (Börsch-Supan, Coppola, and Reil-Held 2012).

Nachhaltigkeit in der Finanzierung der Sozialen Sicherungssysteme 2003). Notably, Riester, occupational, and nonsubsidized personal pensions increased their coverage in parallel; there was apparently no crowding out among these products and even some evidence for crowding in (Coppola and Reil-Held 2009; Börsch-Supan, Coppola, and Reil-Held 2012). As a result, the percentage of households that relied only on the public PAYG system for their retirement income decreased dramatically, from 73 percent to 39 percent in just 10 years, after the introduction of Riester pensions (figure 8.2).

Figure 8.1 classifies the supplementary retirement income vehicles into three categories: Riester pensions, occupational pensions, and unsubsidized personal pension plans. In fact, many different financial instruments were created within each of these broad categories, a process that happened without much coordination. Financial instruments designed to deliver retirement income are therefore subject to many different capital market regulations, liability requirements, and taxation rules. As a result, cleaning up the tax treatment of contributions to and capital gains from these various old-age pension institutions and the taxation of the ultimate retirement benefits generated from these instruments has become an increasingly important topic.[1]

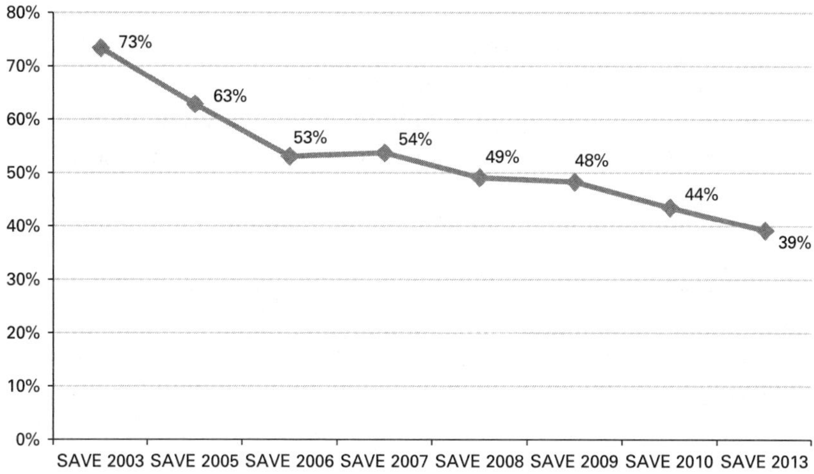

Figure 8.2
Fraction of households without supplementary pensions, Germany, 2003–2013. *Source*: Authors' calculations based on the SAVE data, waves 2003–2013 (Börsch-Supan, Coppola, and Reil-Held 2012).

Differential taxation generates important signals. First, the preferential tax treatment or subsidization of old-age pension provision beyond that accorded to other savings measures could obviate the need for mandatory supplementary old-age provision with all the ensuing negative psychological consequences (compulsory pensions) and economic side effects this would entail. Second, capital is highly mobile, so even a slight shift away from a "level playing field"—relative taxation disadvantages for one type of investment compared with another—is likely to trigger substitution movements into other forms of savings.

In an earlier study very much in the spirit of this chapter, Börsch-Supan and Lührmann (2000)[2] compared the tax treatments of various vehicles for retirement income and simulated their after-tax retirement benefits based on strictly comparable contribution and rate of return histories in several stylized scenarios of economic environments. They pointed out that the taxation of retirement benefits and pensions in Germany has been grossly inconsistent and inherently contradictory. The situation at that time was anything but a level playing field. For example, contributions to the public pension system could be partially deducted from taxable income and most of the benefits from that system were tax-free, while the mandatory system for civil servants featured full taxation of benefits. The authors' main simulation result, expressed as the ratio of after-tax benefits divided by pretax lifetime contributions, was that public PAYG pensions enjoyed after-tax benefits that were 184 percent of pretax lifetime contributions, while this ratio was 125 percent for a general purpose pension fund (Altersvorsorge-Sondervermögen) in spite of identical contribution histories and rates of return.

The differential taxation led to several lawsuits and finally to a judgment by the Federal Constitutional Court in March 2002 demanding that the Bundestag change the taxation of retirement benefits and pensions within three years to create a level playing field (Bundesverfassungsgericht 2002). The court primarily addressed the different tax treatments of private sector workers and civil servants but broadened its view on all retirement benefits and pensions.

In addition to legal pressures, there were other reasons for reform. European integration and globalization exerted additional pressure for more transparent tax treatment. First, increasing mobility within the European Union dictated that clear rules be defined about when and which forms of old-age provision are tax-deductible and when and which forms of pension benefits are subject to taxation to prevent distortions in mobility or dual and erroneous taxation. Second, the globalization of capital markets compelled harmonization of the taxes levied on capital, since capital flows to those locations where it can earn the greatest after-tax return. Countries levying higher rates of tax on capital are therefore forced to offer a higher gross yield, which, in turn, makes them less attractive, an unsustainable situation in the long term.

A commission put into place in March 2003 not only recommended deferred taxation for both civil servants and private employees in the mandatory public PAYG systems but also cleaned up taxation of occupational and personal pension plans (Commission to Reform the Taxation of Pension Contribution and Benefits 2003). Almost all of its recommendations were put into several laws that became effective in 2005 (e.g., the 2005 Retirement Income Act).

A major challenge of this reform was to specify transition rules. Changing from immediate to deferred taxation would create a double burden if the reform were implemented without transition rules, since the retirement benefits of those workers who paid contributions out of after-tax income would be taxed again when benefits were received. The 2005 reform therefore introduced a complex system of transition rules that made many compromises between economic principles and existing institutions. The final steady state will be reached in the year

2040. Several papers have analyzed the effects of these transition rules and computed the extent of remaining double taxation and the impact on economic welfare for young and old cohorts (Brall, Bruno-Latocha, and Lohmann 2003; Kambeck and von Löffelholz 2003; Grub 2004; Ruland 2004; Schnabel 2004; Krause-Junk 2006; Fehr and Jess 2007; Wernsmann 2012; Scholtz 2013; Siepe and Siepe 2016).

This chapter focuses on the final outcome of the reform and looks only briefly at the problem of double taxation during the transition process. It outlines the principles for the taxation of retirement benefits and pensions that inspired the Reform Commission's work 12 years ago, describes the reformed taxation regime, and evaluates the extent to which this regime corresponds to these principles. Section 8.2 presents the basic tax approaches and discusses important practical issues relating to taxation of retirement benefits and pensions during the contribution and benefit payment phases. Section 8.3 defines the meaning of "neutrality" in the context of taxes levied on retirement benefits and pensions and the taxation principles implied by this concept. It then discusses the reasons why, and to what extent, it would be appropriate to give preferential tax treatment to old-age provision. Sections 8.2 and 8.3 draw on parts of Börsch-Supan and Lührmann (2000). Section 8.4 describes the tax treatment of the various pension plans in Germany in great detail. Section 8.5 computes the after-tax benefits as a percentage of pretax contributions and the (implicit) rate of return after taxes to assess whether the 2005 reform's goal of a level playing field will actually be reached when it is fully implemented.

8.2 Taxation of Retirement Income

Raising taxes on income earmarked for retirement can be done in many ways, each with theoretical and practical advantages and disadvantages. This section first discusses basic taxation principles and the real-world complications that must be addressed by a tax reform such as in Germany in 2005.

8.2.1 Stages of Taxation

Income dedicated to financing retirement benefits may be taxed at three stages during the life cycle:

• Stage 1 (taxation of contributions): Contributions to a pension scheme may be taxed. In practice, this means that contributions must be financed from taxed income and cannot be deducted from taxable income.

- Stage 2 (taxation of returns): Capital returns in a funded pension system or their equivalent returns in a PAYG system may be subject to taxation during the contribution phase. This includes taxes on interest and dividend income as well as on realized (funded system) and notional (PAYG system) capital gains.
- Stage 3 (taxation of benefits): Taxes may be levied on retirement benefits and pension payments when they are paid out in old age; for example, retirement benefits and pension payments may be treated like any other form of income at the time of payout.

These tax options generate numerous taxation variants, in particular if at each stage taxes are levied only partially, because of exemptions and deductions, as was and still is the case in Germany. Double taxation occurs if those benefits taxed at stage 3 (old age) are based on contributions paid from income after taxes at stage 1 or were generated from capital gains that underwent taxation at stage 2. This was the case for certain cohorts during the reform transition in Germany. In turn, retirement income can escape taxation over the entire life cycle, as was the case with large parts of the German PAYG benefits before 2005, since contributions from employers were untaxed at stage 1, notional gains from productivity and population gains were not taxable while they accrued at stage 2, and public pension benefits were taxed only partially at old age during stage 3 (section 8.4).

Going back to principles, two polar cases arise. In the pure case of deferred taxation, contributions are made from untaxed income (i.e., they are deductible from income tax) and capital returns are tax-free during the accumulation phase; on the other hand, the resulting benefit payments bear the full weight of taxation. This is termed "EET," where the triplet refers to the form of taxation during each of the three taxation stages: tax-exempt (E), tax-exempt (E), and taxable (T). Deferred taxation clearly corresponds to the principle of consumption taxation (section 8.3).

The classic form of comprehensive income taxation, on the other hand, is effective during the first and second stages. Contributions must be made from taxed income, and capital gains—but not pension benefits—are subject to taxation. This taxation variant is abbreviated "TTE"—taxable, taxable, tax-exempt.

Since the immediate taxation of a comprehensive income tax reduces the effective amount of contributions and therefore also the capital gains that accumulate in the retirement account, the after-tax benefit is substantially larger under a consumption tax (EET) than under a comprehensive income tax (TTE), although, if computed correctly, the nominal amount of taxes paid is exactly the same. It is paid substantially later, however.

8.2.2 Taxation of Contributions

If taxes are to be levied during the contribution phase, the same tax rate must apply to contributions paid by employees and those paid by employers on behalf of their employees. If this is not the case, substitution will take place in the direction of the form of contribution subject to the lowest tax rate. As elucidated later, this is usually to the disadvantage of employees subject to lower tax rates. This consideration is important for occupational pensions and proves to be a major obstacle for this taxation variant.

The principle of equal treatment can be upheld as long as the contributions paid by employers on behalf of their employees can be clearly assigned to individual employees such that they are included in the tax levied on employees in a similar way as other benefits with respect to their money's worth. Problems arise, however, if employer contributions are either not clearly attributable to individual employees or if the amount of such contributions cannot be precisely determined. The first instance occurs if flat-rate contributions are paid into a fund for a group of employees that, for example, is managed by an industry organization. Flat-rate transfers of this type are made, inter alia, when the employer's contributions are based solely on the number of employees working for the company and not on their actual level of income. Flat-rate taxation would then have to be based on the average actual income tax paid by the employees; in other words, subsequent to annual wage tax assessment or income tax return—an entirely impractical proposition. This approach would also be to the disadvantage of employees with a below-average marginal rate of taxation and would favor higher-income employees.

Similar problems arise when reserve accounts are set up to cover (sometimes only partially) pension promises. In this case, the employer's contributions are derived implicitly from the value of the pension promise. This is usually calculated on the basis of an employee's expected salary upon retirement, however. This final salary is not known at the time the tax is levied, and it is therefore impossible to arrive at an indisputable quantification of the appropriate taxation.

8.2.3 Taxation of Returns

Capital returns in funded pension systems include income from interest and dividends as well as realized capital gains. It is important to clarify that taxation of income from capital does not constitute a form of double taxation; this only occurs if the underlying assets themselves are taxed. Capital income results from current factor income, which increases gross national product and, like every other form of factor income, is fundamentally subject to income taxation.

The problems begin with unrealized capital gains, the amount and distribution of which are indeterminate. The issue becomes even more problematic if pension funds are managed for whole groups of employees rather than for individuals. The problems that apply to the taxation of contributions then reappear: a common tax rate will disadvantage lower-income employees and favor employees with an above-average marginal tax rate.

Levying tax on the basis of nominal income is also problematic. It is especially important to make adjustments for inflation-based losses of value when taxing capital returns, as only real capital gains and interest have the character of factor income. The continued use of the nominal value principle in Germany is a source of considerable distortions (subsection 8.3.2).

In a PAYG system, returns are represented by productivity and population growth. This "implicit" or "natural" return is best visible in a notional defined contribution system as implemented in Sweden or Italy, where the annual (notional) individual account statement shows the accumulated contributions and the (notional) capital gains (Börsch-Supan, Härtl, and Leite 2017). Taxation then resembles taxation in funded systems. In a conventional PAYG system, taxation of returns during the contribution phase is much less practical. In Germany, such taxation has been mimicked by the taxation of the "profit share" of PAYG pensions (section 8.4).

8.2.4 Taxation of Benefit Payments

Taxation of benefit payments is much simpler from a technical standpoint. This is another reason why the deferred taxation of retirement benefits and pensions is by far the most common approach adopted in countries of the Organisation for Economic Co-operation and Development (OECD) (World Bank 1999; Börsch-Supan 2004). When benefits are paid out, the distribution of capital assets among the owners (pensioners) is clearly defined and the allocation problems referred to in subsections 8.2.2 and 8.2.3 are nonexistent.

Practical problems arise with regard to the treatment of lump-sum payments in comparison with life annuities. The correct systematic treatment of life annuities is sufficiently clear; they are taxed as recurring, regular benefit payments in the same way as for any other income. If the accumulated capital is paid out as a lump sum, however, a progressive tax system would create a very high marginal tax burden that becomes all the more critical the steeper the tax rate schedule. In this case, one may want to spread out the tax burden over several years, although any specific form of distribution is bound to be arbitrary.[3]

Leaving aside the problem of how to tax lump-sum payments, deferred taxation based on the consumption tax principle proves to be the most practical method of taxing retirement income and pensions from a technical point of view. This is true for both PAYG and funded pensions.

8.3 Neutrality Concepts

Governments must finance their budgets from taxes imposed on the productive factors of labor and capital as well as taxation of consumption expenditures. This should, in principle, also apply to the income and expenditures of pensioners. Economic and legal principles (maximizing the economic well-being of society and the principle of equal treatment anchored in the German constitution) require that taxes be as neutral as possible. The word "neutrality" is used here in a very general sense: taxes should not prejudice or benefit one form of economic activity over any other activity.

This is easier said than done. Strict neutrality is actually an elusive aim, since the imposition of a tax on a particular activity will almost always result in a reduction of such activity. This is just as true of taxes on labor income, which tend to reduce the supply of labor; of taxes on capital returns or wealth, which create disincentives to invest; and of taxes on consumption expenditures, which tend to reduce the demand for the taxed consumer goods.

Being neutral on the induced demand and supply changes requires a quantitative calculation of the many disincentive effects. Such calculations are far from straightforward. Hence, it is infeasible in practice to determine the economic activity to which tax rates should be applied to ensure that the burden of taxation remains the same across all forms of economic activities.

The literature has pointed out two concrete meanings of "neutrality," derived from the principles of "comprehensive income taxation" and "consumption taxation," as discussed in subsection 8.3.1. Other aspects of neutrality are reviewed in subsections 8.3.2 and 8.3.3. Last but not least, good reasons exist for deviating from neutrality (subsection 8.3.4). This chapter does not advocate any specific form of neutrality but instead conditions policy recommendations on the aims that policy makers may want to pursue.

8.3.1 Two Common Principles of Neutrality

Two schools of thought contend that taxes levied on retirement benefits and pensions should be neutral. The first argues that consumption and savings should be taxed equally. This would appear to make immediate sense given that the state is not supposed to influence how individuals use their income (i.e., the balance between consumption and savings). If one accepts this principle, taxes should be levied evenly on all forms of income (i.e., comprehensive income taxation). It implies, for instance, that income from capital be taxed equally to earnings.

The second school of thought, especially among economists, points out that savings is not an end in itself but merely a form of deferred consumption. If the principle of neutrality is applied to lifetime consumption, this would require that the state make no distinction between current and future consumption. The state should therefore levy taxes on spending rather than on income. The actual act of consumption itself should be the focus of taxation. This is consequently referred to as the principle of consumption taxation. In practice, this usually means that expenditures for capital formation are deductible from taxable income.

A comparison of both principles clearly demonstrates that a comprehensive income tax has a relatively greater discriminatory impact on the formation of savings than a consumption tax. The former discriminates in favor of current consumption and, as such, is not neutral with regard to present and future consumption and acts as a disincentive to saving, particularly on individual personal provision for old age. If one wants to strengthen old-age provision, the key norm for taxing retirement benefits and pensions should therefore be based on the consumption tax principle (Diamond 2009; Barr and Diamond 2006). On the other hand, if one believes that savings are sufficient or even too much for old-age consumption, one may prefer the comprehensive income tax approach.[4] "Neutrality" is clearly a view specific to the beholder.

8.3.2 The Role of Inflation and Progressive Taxation

The picture is even more complicated if different tax rates apply during the earnings and retirement stages of life and if inflation alters the impact of taxation. Table 8.1 demonstrates this using a simple example, in which €10,000 (in real terms) is invested over a period of 37 years at a 3 percent rate of effective interest, or a nominal rate of 5.5 percent where annual inflation is assumed to be 2.5 percent. The final amount saved is paid out as a lump sum once retirement age is reached. Under a proportional tax, employees and pensions are taxed at 22 percent; under a progressive tax, pensioners are taxed at only 12 percent, while employees are taxed at 22 percent. Table 8.1 displays after-tax benefits as a percentage of pretax contributions in real terms.

In the case of comprehensive income taxation where returns are subject to taxation, inflation results in lower net benefit payments because fictitious capital gains are now subject to taxation ("fictitious" because taxation is based on nominal rather than real values). Hence, increases in the capital stock's nominal value underlie taxation even if its real value remains constant. These lower net benefit payments are the outcome of interest on nominal amounts, which leads to attributed capital gains higher than those actually generated in real terms. In the less advantageous case represented by the immediate income tax, fictitious gains account for around one-third of the real capital gains.

Table 8.1
The influence of tax principle, inflation, and progressivity.

	EET	TTE
Taxation principle	Consumption	Comprehensive income
Timing of taxation	Deferred	Immediate
	After-tax benefits as a percentage of pretax contributions:	
Proportional tax system, no inflation	144%	125%
Progressive tax system, no inflation	162%	125%
Proportional tax system, 2.5% inflation	144%	112%
Progressive tax system, 2.5% inflation	162%	112%

Taxation of these fictitious gains results in a significant drop in net benefit payments; deferred and immediate income taxes in particular become less attractive than the two consumption tax variants. Inflation has the opposite effect if the rising nominal incomes that accompany inflation put taxpaying retirees and pensioners in a higher tax bracket and reduce the advantage that tax progression offers them.

Basically, in the case of a progressive tax system and under inflationary conditions, deferred taxation appears to result in higher net benefit payments than is the case with immediate taxation, and a consumption tax has a less distorting impact than a comprehensive income tax.

8.3.3 Other Aspects of Neutrality

Neutrality proves to be a multifaceted concept when looked at in greater detail. To begin with, there is the principle of equivalence in PAYG-financed pensions. If the requirements of this principle are met, PAYG contributions are equivalent to PAYG benefits: contributions to public retirement insurance and contributions to private (personal and occupational) pensions should both be regarded as an investment into the future. If the principle of equivalence does not hold, in particular if the public PAYG system includes components of redistribution, then contributions to the public retirement insurance schemes assume the character of a tax, at least partially. In the latter case, part of the contribution is thus deemed to be "lost" and neutrality between statutory and personal old-age provision no longer holds. The principle of equivalence of pension insurance contributions in Germany has, to date, managed to limit these negative effects for the most part. However, the principle of equivalent contributions is systematically undermined by mixed financing (e.g., in Germany, revenues from the energy tax and value-added tax that are earmarked for the public retirement insurance scheme); redistribution (e.g., the new elements introduced by the 2014 pension reform, which reintroduces early retirement at age 63 for certain groups and extends retrospective benefits for child raising; Börsch-Supan et al. 2015); and the falling implicit rate of return offered by public retirement insurance (Schnabel 1998). A "level playing field" in the tax treatment of old-age provision should therefore be seen in the context of other deviations from neutrality in the pension system and, moreover, in the context of other taxes and subsidies (Diamond 2009). Such a comprehensive analysis would require a microsimulation model of all taxes and subsidies in the tax and social system, which is far beyond the aims of this chapter.

Neutrality also needs to be achieved on the international level. Employees who change their residence and place of work within the European Union should experience neither tax advantages nor disadvantages with regard to existing private pension schemes; this applies analogously to state social insurance. To date, the portability of retirement benefits and pensions is still limited. Occupational pensions and personal savings for old age in particular are subject to different taxation regimes when transferred from one country to another.

A third important aspect of neutrality relates to the distribution over time of retirement income from capital. The principle of neutrality requires that benefit payments be given the same tax treatment, regardless of whether the accumulated capital is paid out in a lump sum or as an annuity that delivers a stream of predetermined income for the remainder of the beneficiary's life. Subsection 8.3.4 discusses why this aspect of neutrality is contentious.

8.3.4 Reasons for Diverging from the Principle of Neutrality

A number of reasons explain why many economists go a step further than just neutrality (e.g., by strict application of the consumption tax principle) and recommend preferential tax treatment for old-age pension provision.

The first argument applies to savings formation in general and its macroeconomic implications. The savings rate is low in many countries and requires large inflows of foreign capital to finance investments. An inadequately low savings rate leads to a high level of individual consumption in the short run but may also lead to a reduction in the productive investments required for a high level of long-term economic growth, which in turn permits higher consumption in the future.[5] It is difficult to define in practice how high the ideal savings rate should be. As long as the rate of return on capital continues to be higher than the growth in total wage income, however, an excessive savings rate has certainly not yet been reached.[6] This is the case in almost all OECD countries, including Germany (Abel et al. 1986). To achieve neutrality vis-à-vis the consumption of present and future generations, savings should be preferred to consumption as long as the rate of return on capital continues to be higher than the growth in total wage income.

The second set of arguments relies on human behavior and applies specifically to saving for retirement. The principal argument is that many people are simply shortsighted and only begin to make provision and to accumulate capital for their old age once it is already too late. Even if the paternalism implicit in this view—the state knows better than its citizens how to plan for the future—is unappealing in many respects, plenty of empirical evidence corroborates the observation that young people find it difficult to plan for their old age if this means deferring consumption. Tax relief might mitigate the negative effects of liquidity constraints. An additional factor is that most people have little intuitive grasp of interest and compound interest mechanisms and believe it is possible to compensate for the low contributions made during the first half of their working life by saving twice as much during the second half. Simple financial mathematics shows that this is not the case—in fact, individuals would need to save four times as much. As it is not possible for the individual citizen to rectify this mistake once it has been made, paternalistic logic suggests that the state should encourage saving. Whether people actually "undersave" is a matter of great controversy.[7]

The third argument concerns the transition. In those countries in which PAYG systems are gradually being supplemented by funded systems, tax allowances for old-age pension provision are used to accelerate the transition from one system to the other and to control the transition burden across generations.[8] The requisite tax concessions are self-financing to the extent that the PAYG contribution burden regarded by employees as "lost" drops, resulting in a boost in labor productivity, a reduction in moonlighting, and a rise in capital productivity as institutional investors increase their participation in capital markets (Börsch-Supan, Heiss, and Winter 2000).

The fourth argument addresses moral hazard. If retirement income falls below a certain threshold, most European countries provide social assistance; for example, by topping up inadequate incomes by supplementary payments. For individuals close to this threshold, saving for retirement will thus simply substitute for social benefits, and little incentive arises to save; phrased differently, there is moral hazard in exploiting the welfare state later rather than forgoing consumption now. The result is suboptimal because the farsighted end up subsidizing the shortsighted. In the Federal Republic of Germany, this would also result in federal side effects, as social assistance is financed from Länder (German states) and local authority resources. Whether subsidies for retirement saving now are actually more cost-effective than social assistance later is quite controversial, however (Coppola and Gasche 2011).

Finally, several more subtle reasons explain why efforts should be made to ensure that all citizens put aside savings to provide for their old age. One important argument in this context is what is known as adverse selection. This is based on the observation that people who believe they have an above-average life expectancy are more likely to convert funded old-age pension provisions into life annuities. Others prefer lump-sum payments. This means that personal life annuities are too expensive for most people (Walliser, Sauter, and Winter 1999). This adverse selection of "poor risks" can only be rectified by giving preferential tax treatment to life annuities relative to lump-sum payments, assuming that avoiding the instrument of compulsion and its negative incentive effects is desired. It is worth considering some of the side effects that would ensue if lump-sum payments were to be given inferior treatment, however; for example, in terms of paying off debts or moving into a smaller house.

8.4 Taxation Practice in Germany

This section describes the tax treatment of the nine most important social security and pension arrangements ("plans") in Germany in detail. It sketches the tax treatment before the 2005 reform, the complex transition rules between 2005 and 2040, and the final tax treatment that will be fully implemented after 2040.

Plan 1 is the mandatory public retirement insurance for all employees except civil servants and the self-employed. It covers roughly 85 percent of all workers and currently provides roughly 80 percent of their retirement income (Rentenversicherungsbericht 2014). Plan 2 is the self-contained system for civil servants. While the self-employed are largely free to self-insure or join other systems, Plan 3 describes the base system created for them in 2005.

Germany has a large number of different occupational pension plans, which were legally structured into five regimes (Durchführungswege) with essentially two different forms of taxation; they represent Plans 4 and 5.

Plan 6 is the Riester pension, the most prominent, highly subsidized form of voluntary private saving for retirement. Plans 7 through 9 are other private plans, including whole life insurance, traditionally used as a vehicle to generate retirement income.

Tables 8.2, 8.3, and 8.4 summarize these descriptions in tabular form, presenting their prereform status, the transition rules, and their final status after 2040, respectively. Section 8.5 computes after-tax returns and alternative measures for these plans in order to assess whether the goal of a level playing field was actually achieved by the 2005 reform.

Table 8.2
Prereform taxation in Germany (as of 2000).

Form of old-age pension provision	Contributions	Returns	Benefits
Public retirement insurance (GRV)	Various deduction rules, taxable share amounts to 44% of employee contributions.	No tax levied.	The profit share is taxed at the usual income tax rate.
Civil servants' pension	No tax levied.	No tax levied.	Subject to income tax. A special exemption of 40% of benefits, up to a maximum of €3000, is tax-deductible.
Occupational pension type I (direct pension and pension mutual fund)	80% of contributions subject to income tax. 20%, or €1700, of expenses are tax-exempt.	No tax levied.	The profit share is taxed at the usual income tax rate.
Occupational pension type II (pension promise and provident fund)	No tax levied.	No tax levied.	Subject to income tax. A special exemption of 40% of benefits, up to a maximum of €3000, is tax-deductible.
Capital sum life insurance	Subject to income tax. Fixed amounts are tax-deductible as special expenses.	No tax levied.	No tax levied.
AS pension investment funds	Included in taxable income and taxed accordingly.	Subject to income tax. €3000 or €6000 savers' tax-free amount and income-related expenses are deductible.	No tax levied.

Table 8.3
Transition rules and current taxation in Germany (as of 2015).

Form of old-age pension provision	Contributions	Returns	Transitional agreement for benefits	Benefits	Notes
Public retirement insurance (GRV)	80% of contributions are tax-deductible. In 2005, 60% of contributions were tax-free; percentage increases by 2% each year until 100% of contributions are tax-free in 2025.	No tax levied.	2005: taxable portion 50%, yearly increase by 2% until 2020, then by 1%. 2040: 100% subject to income tax.	In 2015, 70% of benefits were subject to income tax.	Contributions (transitional agreement): In 2005, 60% of contributions were tax-free; percentage increases by 2% each year until 100% of contributions are tax-free in 2025.
Rürup pension (basic pension)	Same as GRV.	No tax levied.	Same as GRV.	Same as GRV.	Transitional agreement as in GRV, but system is fully funded (not pay-as-you-go).
Civil servants' pension	No tax levied.	No tax levied.	Same as occupational pension type II, including an addition to the tax exemption (€900 in 2005, reduced yearly until 2040).	Same as occupational pension type II.	

(continued)

Table 8.3 (continued)

Form of old-age pension provision	Contributions	Returns	Transitional agreement for benefits	Benefits	Notes
Occupational pension type I (direct insurance, pension mutual fund, pension fund	No tax levied up to 4% of the income threshold; an additional tax-free contribution of €1800 can be made since 2005.	No tax levied.	No transitional agreement.	All benefits are subject to income tax.	Benefits of pension fund II are protected, unlike benefits of pension fund I and direct pension.
Occupational pension type II (pension promise and provident fund)	No tax levied.	No tax levied.	2005: taxable portion 60%, yearly increase by 1.6% until 2020, then by 0.8%. 2040: 100% subject to income tax.	In 2015, 76% of benefits are subject to income tax.	Benefits of pension promise and provident fund are protected.
Riester pension	No tax levied (maximum amount of €2100), supplementary state allowances.	No tax levied.	Same as occupational pension type II.	Same as occupational pension type II.	30% capital payment possible at start of retirement (subject to income tax).
AS pension investment fund	Included in taxable income and taxed accordingly.	No tax levied.	No transitional agreement.	Interest portion is subject to income tax, unless contract duration exceeded 11 years and pensioner enters retirement not before age 63.	Restrictions concerning risk and contract duration (contract duration of 18 years until pensioner reaches age 60).

Investment fund savings plan	Included in taxable income and taxed accordingly.	Taxable according to source tax on capital gains.	No transitional agreement.	Same as AS pension investment fund; interest portion is subject to age at start of retirement.	Fund consists of fixed-interest bonds (potential risk and return are limited).
Capital sum life insurance	Included in taxable income and taxed accordingly.	No taxation if contract duration exceeded 11 years and insured enters retirement at age 62.	No transitional agreement.	Same as AS-pension investment fund.	Advantageous conditions linked to age and contract duration.
Arbitrary investment	Included in taxable income and taxed accordingly.	Taxable according to source tax on capital gains.	No transitional agreement.	No tax levied.	

Table 8.4
Final taxation in Germany (as of 2040).

Form of old-age pension provision	Contributions	Returns	Benefits	Notes
Public retirement insurance (GRV)	No tax levied.	No tax levied.	All benefits are subject to income tax.	All earnings added up to determine taxable income.
Rürup pension (basic pension)	No tax levied.	No tax levied.	All benefits are subject to income tax.	Taxation same as GRV but system is fully funded (not pay-as-you-go).
Civil servants' pension	No tax levied.	No tax levied.	All benefits are subject to income tax.	
Occupational pension type I (direct insurance, pension mutual fund, pension fund)	No tax levied up to 4% of the income threshold; an additional tax-free contribution of €1800 can be made since 2005.	No tax levied.	All benefits are subject to income tax.	Benefits of pension fund type II are protected, unlike benefits of pension fund type I and direct pension.
Occupational pension type II (pension promise and provident fund)	No tax levied.	No tax levied.	All benefits are subject to income tax.	Benefits of pension promise and provident fund are protected.
Riester pension	No tax levied (maximum amount of €2100), supplementary state allowances.	No tax levied.	All benefits are subject to income tax.	30% capital payment possible at start of retirement (subject to income tax).

AS-pension investment funds	Included in taxable income and taxed accordingly.	No tax levied.	Interest portion is subject to income tax, unless contract duration exceeded 11 years and pensioner enters retirement not before age 63.	Restrictions concerning risk and contract duration (contract duration of 18 years or until pensioner reaches age 60).
Investment fund savings plan	Included in taxable income and taxed accordingly.	Taxable according to source tax on capital gains.	Same as AS pension investment fund, interest portion conforms to age at start of retirement.	Fund consists of fixed-interest bonds (potential risk and return are limited).
Capital sum life insurance	Included in taxable income and taxed accordingly.	No taxation if contract duration exceeded 11 years and insured enters retirement at age 62.	Same as AS-pension investment fund.	Advantageous conditions linked to age and contract duration.
Arbitrary investment	Included in taxable income and taxed accordingly.	Taxable according to source tax on capital gains.	No tax levied.	

8.4.1 Public Retirement Insurance (GRV)

Germany's PAYG public retirement insurance (Gesetzliche Rentenversicherung, or GRV, the equivalent of Social Security in the United States) underwent large changes during the past decade and a half. Significant reforms in 2001, 2004, and 2007 changed the entire system to make it resilient to demographic change. The tax reform in 2005 addressed the previous inconsistency in the taxation of pensions and introduced deferred taxation of public pensions, which came on top of these systemic reforms. The interactions between tax reforms and systemic reforms are subjects of controversial discussion; this chapter looks at the tax reform in isolation.

Until 2005, public pensions were subject to a mixture of partially immediate and partially deferred taxation, best characterized as "tEt," with the "t" referring to the small percentage actually resulting from taxation. The contributions by the employer (half of total contributions) were completely tax-free, while employee contributions could be deducted under several complex rules (Sonderausgabenabzug), which resulted in a taxable share of 44 percent of the contributions made by an average employee. Notional capital gains (i.e., current increases in pension benefits through increases in productivity and the number of workers) at stage 2 were entirely tax-free. On the benefit side, stage 3, only the so-called profit share (Ertragsanteil), deemed to be 27 percent for workers retiring at normal retirement age, was taxed at the individual income tax rate. As Börsch-Supan and Lührmann (2000, 2003) pointed out, this former tax treatment made the GRV more lucrative than other retirement income vehicles and significantly deviated from the tax treatment of civil servants (subsection 8.4.2).

This unequal treatment led to the 2005 reform resulting from the passage of the Retirement Income Act (Alterseinkünftegesetz). Following the German Federal Constitutional Court, which decided that the inconsistency of the taxation of pensions violated the principle of equality, the Bundestag almost completely followed the recommendations of the Reform Commission (see section 8.1) and introduced a complex set of transition rules that sought a balance between the dangers of double taxation and those of revenue loss (Commission to Reform the Taxation of Pension Contribution and Benefits 2003).

On the contribution side, to prevent revenue losses, the tax deductibility gradually increases to full deductibility in 2025. In 2005, 60 percent of employee contributions were tax-deductible, with a maximum amount of €20,000. This percentage will increase by 2 percent each year until, in 2025, contributions are entirely tax-deductible. Accordingly, in

2015, 80 percent of contributions were tax-deductible. Employer contributions will remain fully tax-exempt.

While no changes were made on the (notional) capital returns side, on the benefit side, all benefits (including any additional income) will become subject to pensioners' individual income tax rate. To prevent double taxation, another transitional agreement established a temporary tax allowance. In 2005, this tax allowance covered 50 percent of the public pension benefits. This percentage will decrease by 2 percent each year until 2020 and by 1 percent each year thereafter until, in 2040, all benefits will be subject to pensioners' individual income tax rate. The share of the tax-exempt amount during the transition period is determined at retirement for each pensioner and remains fixed for the entire retirement phase. For example, an individual retiring in 2015 will be granted a tax allowance of 30 percent (i.e., taxes must be paid on 70 percent of the benefits). The corresponding amount will remain constant for the entire duration of the retirement phase. Any benefit increases (e.g., generated via the benefit indexation formula through higher wages resulting from higher productivity) will thus be fully taxed. The intergenerational balance of the transition is thus strongly affected by economic performance (Fehr and Jess 2007).

In comparison to the regulations before the Retirement Income Act, the public retirement insurance (GRV) has become less lucrative for those pensioners who have a high retirement income, because all benefits will now be taxed instead of just the profit share. In turn, pensioners with a retirement income below the basic taxation threshold will be better off since they will pay no taxes at all. According to the simulations herein, the average pensioner will be very slightly better off after 2040, when the system of deferred taxation is fully implemented, while some extent of double taxation during the transition period will make the average pensioner slightly worse off during this time.

8.4.2 Civil Servants' Pensions

The civil servants' pension was already subject to the system of deferred taxation before the Retirement Income Act, with the proviso that individuals receiving a civil servants' pension were granted a special exemption of 40 percent of pension income up to a maximum of €3,000 annually (Versorgungsfreibetrag). This corresponds to a similar rule for occupational pensions of type II (subsection 8.4.5).

The 2005 reform therefore made very few changes. No changes at all were made on the contribution and capital return stages; both remain tax-exempt. The special exemption will be phased out, as it will be for occupational pensions of type II. Civil servants entering retirement in 2015 had a tax allowance of 40 percent (i.e., 60 percent of benefits were subject to the income tax) plus €900. Similar to those for the public pension, these rules will remain constant for the individual civil servant's retirement phase. Deferred taxation will be fully implemented in 2040, when 100 percent of civil servants' pensions will be subject to the income tax.

8.4.3 Rürup Pensions (Basisrente)

The third remaining group of workers besides employees and civil servants is the self-employed, who are largely free to self-insure or join other systems. Many are not eligible for subsidized personal pensions, however, especially Riester pensions. In 2005, Rürup pensions[9] were introduced to fill this gap. They are especially meant for those who cannot make use of the Riester pension as a supplement to the public PAYG system (e.g., self-employed individuals who are not required to pay into the GRV).

Unlike the supplementary Riester pensions, Rürup pensions have no effective contribution limit and can therefore serve as a fully supporting first-tier pension.[10] Unlike the GRV, which is financed on a PAYG basis, Rürup pensions are fully funded. Rürup pensions underlie several regulations and restrictions. Their main difference from other personal retirement income options is the requirement that benefits be annuitized (no option for a lump-sum payment) in exchange for deferred taxation (subsection 8.4.7).

Taxation of Rürup pensions corresponds exactly to that of the public PAYG pension system (subsection 8.4.1). On the contribution side, the same transitional agreement is in place as in the GRV, which gradually increases the tax-deductibility of contributions until 2025. In 2015, 80 percent of the contributions to Rürup pensions were tax-deductible.

Capital returns remain tax-free, and benefit payments are subject to the same transitional agreement as the GRV, with a gradual increase of the effective tax base until 100 percent is reached in 2040. All transitional details depend on the year in which the self-employed individual enters retirement. They remain fixed thereafter.

8.4.4 Occupational Pensions of Type I (Direktversicherung, Pensionskasse, Pensionsfond)

Germany features a complex, fragmented, and therefore somewhat nontransparent system of occupational pensions. The system has grown historically. Occupational pension plans were often created as a result of the initiative of a single employer or specific sectors, which explains part of the fragmentation. Lawmakers have tried to put structure into this jungle and have imposed five categories of occupational pensions, but resistance to the creation of a more unified system is strong. Since 2001, an employer must offer at least one pension plan out of those five categories if requested by an employee.

While great differences arise in the liability rules, investment regulations, and (partially implicit) subsidies across the five categories, only two different tax regimes exist, both of which are variants of deferred taxation. The first group of occupational pensions includes direct insurance (Direktversicherung), the pension mutual fund (Pensionskasse), and the pension fund (Pensionsfond). For the purpose of this chapter, their tax treatments are summarized under the label of occupational pensions of type I.

Direct insurance is technically a life insurance contract the employer makes with a licensed German insurer for the employee. It is subject to financial supervision by the state, which explains and leads to secure and conservative investments. The pension mutual fund functions as a legally independent institution within the occupational pension system. One of its main purposes is protection against a loss of income as a result of old age, disability, or death; it is also subject to financial supervision by the state and strict investment rules, such as a limit on risky assets. For both the direct insurance and (in most cases) the pension mutual fund, the benefits are not protected by a third party against insolvency of the employer.[11] Liability for benefits rests solely with the insurance company or the independent mutual fund. Pension benefits must be annuitized.

The pension fund introduced in 2002 is based on the idea that employees can gain from the potential profits that can be made in the capital market (this kind of retirement insurance has long been popular in the United States and the United Kingdom). Unlike the previous two options, the pension fund is not subject to financial supervision by the state. Thus, theoretically, all contributions can be invested in less conservative and potentially more lucrative options such as stocks. Another special characteristic is that the pension fund benefits can be paid out as a lump-sum payment or as an annuity. The choice can be made at retirement by the retiree. Another difference from the previous two occupational pension categories is that the benefits are insured by Germany's pension insurance association (Pensions-Sicherungs-Verein) against an employer's insolvency.

Before the 2005 Retirement Income Act, about 80 percent of contributions to an occupational pension plan of type I was subject to the income tax, while 20 percent up to a maximum amount of €1,700 was tax-exempt. Capital returns remained tax-exempt during the accumulation stage. On the benefit side, only the profit share was subject to taxation.

Since the reform, taxation has been essentially deferred. Contributions are tax-free up to 4 percent of the GRV contribution threshold[12] (i.e., up to about €2,900 in West Germany and €2,500 in East Germany). Furthermore, an additional tax-free contribution of €1,800 can be made unless this amount has already been exhausted as part of other pension or health insurance contributions. No taxes are levied on capital returns. Benefits are subject to the income tax in their entirety.

8.4.5 Occupational Pensions of Type II (Unterstützungskasse, Direktzusage)

The second type of occupational pension includes the provident fund (Unterstützungskasse) and the pension promise (Direktzusage).

The provident fund is a legally independent institution and, similar to the pension fund, is not subject to financial supervision by the state. Accordingly, it is unrestricted with regard to capital investments. The pension promise is a traditional defined benefit plan in which an employer commits to granting certain benefits out of its own resources to the employee or, in the instance of the employee's death, to his or her surviving dependents, after the employment relationship ends. This can be in the form of a lump-sum payment, in predefined installments, or as an annuity. There is no requirement that the employer prefund the promised benefits. They are, however, insured by Germany's pension insurance association against the insolvency of the employer.

Contributions to and capital gains by this second type of occupational pension plan are entirely tax-free; no changes were made here as a result of reforms. Benefits are subject to income taxation. Until 2005, 40 percent of the benefits were tax-exempt up to a maximum amount of about €3,000 annually (Versorgungsfreibetrag; subsection 8.4.2). A transitional agreement in place from 2005 to 2040 increases the taxable part of benefits by 1.6 percentage points each year until 2020 and subsequently by 0.8 percentage points, until 100 percent of benefits are subject to income taxation in 2040. In parallel, a gradually decreasing tax exemption is granted, starting with €900 in 2005 and decreasing by €36 each year until 2020 and thereafter by €18, until it vanishes in 2040.[13] These numbers remain constant for the length of the retirement and correspond to the tax treatment of civil servants.[14]

8.4.6 Riester Pensions

Named after former German minister for labor Walter Riester, Riester pensions were introduced in 2002. These voluntary personal pension plans are based on individual accounts and were designed to fill the "pension gap" created by the sustainability reforms of the public PAYG retirement insurance.[15] Riester pensions are highly subsidized. Households up to a certain income and depending on the number of children receive a state allowance that can cover as much as 90 percent of total contributions for the lowest-income decile. In addition, Riester pensions enjoy preferential tax treatment. Since their introduction, the taxation of Riester pensions has been deferred. A full implementation of deferred taxation will be achieved in 2040.

The individual's own contributions to the Riester pension are tax-exempt up to 4 percent of the individual's gross income for the previous year, capped at €2,100 per year minus the following allowances. Individuals receive a general allowance of €154, and a child allowance of €185 per child born before 2009 and €300 for children born after 2009. Capital returns are tax-exempt during accumulation. On the benefit side, individuals profit from an exemption (Altersentlastungsbetrag) that resembles the transitional agreements of the occupational pension type II. In 2005, 40 percent of benefits were tax-free (with a maximum amount of €1,900), which means that 60 percent were subject to the individual income tax. This exemption decreases by 1.6 percentage points each year until 2020, and subsequently by 0.8 percentage points until 2040, when all benefits from a Riester pension will be liable to income taxation. In 2015, 76 percent of Riester pension benefits were taxable.

8.4.7 Pension Investment Funds (Altersvorsorge Sondervermögen, AS)

Deferred taxation was marketed by the Reform Commission as a tax advantage in exchange for restrictions on how the savings can be used. Examples of such restrictions are that such savings cannot be dissolved before retirement (or disability); they must be annuitized; they cannot be bequeathed; and there must be a guarantee for at least the nominal value of the accumulated contributions. The commission's philosophy is that all other savings should be taxed immediately at income generation. One may argue that savings in general should be taxed at consumption rather than at income generation (section 8.2), but given the practical problems delineated in section 8.3, this is impractical in many cases.

This mixture of philosophy and pragmatism largely guided the tax treatment of the many other personal savings instruments that can be used to finance retirement consumption. In general, taxation is deferred if any use other than for retirement consumption can safely be excluded *ex ante*; otherwise taxation is immediate.

The AS pension investment fund, a savings vehicle introduced in 1988, is a case for this approach but also an example of the many deviations from the general principle. AS pension investment funds are funds with several investment restrictions that are likely to reduce the return on capital. For example, at least 51 percent of the capital must be invested in the capital market, the remainder can be held as a cash reserve, and the share consisting of stocks must be between 21 and 75 percent. Capital gains, interest, and dividends must be fully reinvested. Furthermore, the investment company must offer savings plans in addition to lump-sum investments. In the case of the former, the duration of the contract offered must be at least 18 years, and the investor must reach the age of 61 before receiving payouts. The reissue of AS pension investment funds was prohibited in 2013 to reduce the number of preferentially treated savings vehicles and increase transparency.

Contributions are part of taxable income; the system of deferred taxation is not applied. Capital returns have been taxed according to the source tax on capital gains (Abgeltungssteuer) since 2009. Since the individual's own contributions have already been taxed, on the benefit side only the profit share is subject to the income tax, taking account of the already paid source tax on capital gains. If, however, the contract has existed for at least 12 years and did not end before the investor turned 63, only 50 percent of the profit share must be taxed (the "50% rule").

8.4.8 Whole Life Insurance

Until recently, whole life insurance was tax-preferred and a common savings vehicle for old-age consumption, with many side benefits, such as term insurance. It could also be used to finance other consumption, such as buying owner-occupied housing.[16]

Contributions to capital sum life insurance are part of taxable income; here again, the system of deferred taxation does not apply. However, before 2005, capital returns were tax-free and benefits were potentially tax-free as well. The latter was the case if the benefits were paid out as a one-time payment and the contract duration was at least 12 years, during which contributions were made for at least 5 years. If these conditions were not met, the profit share of the benefits had to be taxed.

Since 2005, capital returns have been subject to the source tax on capital gains, unless the contract duration exceeded 11 years and the insured person reached age 62 before receiving payments. In this case, capital returns are tax-free. On the benefit side, the profit share is taxable. However, the 50% rule can apply if the conditions described in subsection 8.4.7 with regard to the AS pension investment funds are met.

8.4.9 General Pension Funds

Germany also features pension funds that are accessible by individuals outside of the system of occupational pensions. This type of pension fund mainly invests in fixed-interest bonds, such as government or mortgage bonds. These funds are generally considered to be very secure, with low fluctuations in their value, but are also less likely to yield high returns. The capital here is not fixed but rather can be bought or sold at any time.

Contributions are taxed, since they are made from after-tax income. Since 2009, capital returns must be taxed at the rate of the source tax on capital gains. On the benefit side, the profit share must be taxed unless the 50% rule takes effect (under the same conditions as previously mentioned).

8.5 Simulations

The institutional breadth of public retirement insurance and private old-age pension provision, and the various forms and levels of taxation imposed on them, have significant monetary effects. These are calculated in table 8.5 in a strictly comparable but highly stylized scenario based on the average worker contributing €3,510 per year to the public PAYG pension system during a working life of 45 years. This corresponds to a contribution rate of 9.5 percent of the average gross income of employees in the public pension system. It is assumed that a constant income tax rate of 22 percent applies throughout the individual's entire working life; this is the average tax rate for households with at least one employed household member. After retirement, the tax rate is substantially lower (15 percent), reflecting Germany's progressive tax system. All figures are in real terms, and the distorting effects of inflation are abstracted away (section 8.3), thus implicitly assuming that taxes are routinely adjusted for inflation.

Table 8.5
Comparison of the simulated effects of different taxation rules in Germany.

	(1)	(2)	(3)	(4)	*(5)*	(6)	*(7)*	(8)	(9)	(10)	(11)	(12)
	GRV2000	GRV2015 (%)	GRV2040 (%)	Civil servants (%)	*Occup I 2000 (%)*	Occup I 2040 (%)	*Occup II 2000 (%)*	Occup II 2040 (%)	Riester (%)	Rürup (%)	Whole life (%)	AS funds (%)
Pretax contributions	*100%*	100	100	100	*100*	100	*100*	100	100	100	100	100
Tax	*9%*	4	0	0	*18*	0	*0*	0	0	0	22	22
After-tax contributions	*91%*	96	100	100	*82*	100	*100*	100	100	100	78	78
Pretax capital returns	*102%*	105	112	112	*92*	112	*112*	112	112	112	88	78
Tax	*0%*	0	0	0	*0*	0	*0*	0	0	0	0	17
After-tax capital returns	*102%*	105	112	112	*92*	112	*112*	112	112	112	88	61
Pretax benefits	*192%*	200	212	212	*175*	212	*212*	212	212	212	166	139
Tax	*8%*	30	32	32	*7*	32	*19*	32	32	32	0	0
After-tax benefits	***184%***	**170**	**180**	**180**	***168***	**180**	***193***	**180**	**180**	**180**	**166**	**139**
Implicit rate of return	*2.47%*	2.17	2.39	2.39	*2.11*	2.26	*2.65*	2.26	2.39	2.39	2.06	1.37

This same scenario is applied to all other forms of retirement savings and pensions: civil servants', Rürup pensions for the self-employed, the two types of occupational pensions, Riester pensions, whole life insurance, AS funds, and general pension funds. The calculation is simplified to the extent that no account is taken of maximum tax-allowance amounts. In other words, it is assumed that the contributions to the various retirement schemes are as large as the applicable maximum tax-allowance amounts. To keep the figures comparable, the results are expressed as a percentage of lifetime contributions.

Finally, an identical rate of return of 3 percent is assumed for all investments, including the PAYG scheme. This is clearly counterfactual. Because of the low interest rate on government bonds, Riester pensions and whole life insurance create real returns that are slightly below this, and the public retirement insurance has a substantially lower implicit rate of return (closer to 1.5 percent for married couples). To isolate the effects of differential taxation, however, a common rate of return is used.

Table 8.5 expresses the results as a percentage of pretax lifetime contributions. The key results are in the penultimate row, which depicts after-tax benefits as a percentage of pretax lifetime contributions, and in the bottom row, which shows the implicit rate of return after taxes.

Table 8.5 shows the substantial differences before the 2005 reform (columns 1, 5, and 7). Public pensions created after-tax benefits slightly higher than those for occupational pensions of type I and substantially higher than for whole life insurance and AS investment funds. Only occupational pensions of type II were more advantageous. With a higher tax rate at retirement, these differences would be even larger. After the reform (columns 3, 4, 6, 8, 9, and 10), the playing field is almost level, with the exception of whole life insurance and general purpose investment funds, and, to a lesser extent, occupational pensions. In this respect, the 2005 reform broadly reached its goals and pretty much fulfilled the requirements of the 2002 Federal Constitutional Court decision.

Comparing column 3 of table 8.5 with columns 2 and 4 shows that the reform creates a significant amount of double taxation in the public pension system during the transition period. The figure shown here represents the average across all cohorts involved in the transition. Comparing columns 2 and 4 shows that the deferred taxation is slightly less advantageous than the prereform status; this would, however, change if an even lower tax rate were applied during retirement.

Ruland (2004) and, more recently, Siepe and Siepe (2016) computed the burden of double taxation and arrived at similar results. Both studies agree that employees who enter retirement in 2040 after 45 years of employment will face the highest burden of double taxation. For the "standard employee," defined by 45 years of average earnings, the income to be taxed twice amounts to between €46,000 (as estimated by Siepe and Siepe) and €53,000 (as estimated by Ruland).

8.6 Conclusions

The tax treatment of German retirement benefits and pensions has been very complex. One reason is that Germany provides many different pension subsystems, including public pension insurance, which covers about 85 percent of the German workforce, and a separate pension system for civil servants, who comprise about 5 percent of the German workforce. The remaining 10 percent of the workforce are self-employed and have a variety of old-age provisions. In addition, various types of occupational and personal pensions exist. The different pension subsystems have not been treated equally under the law. Capital market regulations (such as liquidity and liability rules) are different, and, relevant for this chapter, so is taxation.

The main aim of the 2005 reform initiated by the German Federal Constitutional Court was to produce a level playing field among the many instruments generating retirement income in Germany. As a general principle, the reform introduced an EET system of taxation that exempts contributions and capital returns during the accumulation phase and then taxes retirement benefits like any other income in old age. Because of the complex initial state of the German retirement system in 2005, the reform requires an equally complex transition regime until the new equilibrium is reached in 2040.

The first part of the chapter outlined principles for the taxation of retirement benefits and pensions and compared these with the current practice in Germany. The chapter then described and analyzed the tax treatment of the nine most important pension plans in Germany before, during, and after the reform. Finally, the chapter simulated the taxes due for a standardized contribution history before, during, and after the reform. It concluded that the 2005 reform flattened the playing field but that many deviations still keep it from being completely level. Public pensions, civil servants' pensions, and Riester pensions achieve exactly the same after-tax rate of return, given identical pretax returns.

Hence, a level playing field was achieved among these three most prominent pension instruments. However, occupational pensions and private pension funds face higher taxation and thus lower after-tax returns.

Moreover, substantial transition costs arise in the form of double taxation. For the "standard employee," defined by 45 years of average earnings, the income subject to double taxation is estimated to be between €46,000 and €53,000. Whether such double taxation will survive an appeal in the courts is uncertain.

Notes

Paper prepared for the CEPAR-CESifo workshop "Taxation of Pensions," Munich, September 3–4, 2015.

1. "Retirement benefits and pensions" refers to all income arising from provisions made for old age. Retirement benefits include PAYG-funded public retirement insurance schemes as well as the life annuities from funded private provision. Pensions include funded occupational pensions as well as PAYG-funded civil servant pensions.

2. An English version appeared in 2003.

3. As suggested in subsection 8.3.4, the state may also wish to encourage benefit payments in the form of life annuities more than lump-sum payments, on paternalistic and other grounds.

4. See Börsch-Supan, Härtl, and Leite (2017) for salient references.

5. The United States provides an example for the first part of the argument. Whether the second part holds is a matter of controversy.

6. The underlying argument is about the dynamic efficiency of an economy.

7. See Börsch-Supan, Härtl, and Leite (2017) for a review of the divergent opinions and the underlying theoretical models and empirical results.

8. Examples may be found in the United Kingdom and Hungary (Palacios and Rocha 1998).

9. Named after the economist Bert Rürup; see Kommission für die Nachhaltigkeit in der Finanzierung der Sozialen Sicherungssysteme (2003).

10. Hence the official name Basisrente in German.

11. Specifically, Germany's pension insurance association (Pensions-Sicherungs-Verein).

12. In 2015, the threshold amounted to €72,600 in West Germany and €62,400 in East Germany.

13. This is intended to substitute for the Versorgungsfreibetrag.

14. Note, however, that occupational pensions are supplemental pensions, while civil servants' pensions are tier 1 base pensions.

15. See Börsch-Supan, Coppola, and Reil-Held (2012) for a precise definition of the rules and regulations and the development of coverage. See Gasche et al. (2013) for the costs of the German individual account system.

16. Owner-occupied housing has both a consumption and an investment character.

References

Abel, Andrew, N. Gregory Mankiw, Lawrence H. Summers, and Richard J. Zeckhauser. 1986. "Assessing Dynamic Efficiency: Theory and Evidence." Working Paper No. w2097, National Bureau of Economic Research, Cambridge, MA.

Barr, Nicholas, and Peter Diamond. 2006. "The Economics of Pensions." *Oxford Review of Economic Policy* 22 (1): 15–39.

Börsch-Supan, Axel. 2004. "Mind the GAP: The Effectiveness of Incentives to Boost Retirement Saving in Europe." *OECD Economic Studies* 39 (2): 111–144.

Börsch-Supan, Axel, Tabea Bucher-Koenen, Michela Coppola, and Bettina Lamla. 2015. "Savings in Times of Demographic Change: Lessons from the German Experience." *Journal of Economic Surveys* 29 (4): 807–829.

Börsch-Supan, Axel, Michela Coppola, and Anette Reil-Held. 2012. "Riester Pensions in Germany: Design, Dynamics, Targeting Success and Crowding-in." Working Paper No. w18014, National Bureau of Economic Research, Cambridge, MA.

Börsch-Supan, Axel, Klaus Härtl, and Duarte Nuno Leite. 2017. "Social Security and Public Insurance." In *Handbook of the Economics of Population Aging*, edited by John Piggott and Alan Woodland, 781–863. Amsterdam: Elsevier.

Börsch-Supan, Axel, Florian Heiss, and Joachim K. Winter. 2000. "Pension Reform, Capital Markets, and the Rate of Return." Paper for the workshop "Reforming Old-Age Pension Systems," Herbert-Giersch-Stiftung, Magdeburg, May 25–26.

Börsch-Supan, Axel, and Melanie Lührmann. 2000. *Prinzipien der Renten- und Pensionsbesteuerung*. Bad Homburg: Frankfurter Institut.

Börsch-Supan, Axel, and Melanie Lührmann. 2003. "Retirement Benefit and Pension Taxation Principles." In *Pension Policy in an Integrating Europe*, edited by Onorato Castellino and Elsa Fornero, 152–174. Cheltenham: Edward Elgar.

Börsch-Supan, Axel, and Christina Benita Wilke. 2005. "The German Public Pension System: How It Will Become an NDC System Look-alike." In *Pension Reform—Issues and Prospects for Non-financial Defined Contribution (NDC) Schemes*, edited by Robert Holzmann and Edward Palmer, 573–610. Washington, DC: World Bank.

Brall, Natalie, Gesa Bruno-Latocha, and Albert Lohmann. 2003. "Eine Bewertung des Vorschlags zur Neuordnung der Rentenbesteuerung." *Wirtschaftsdienst* 83 (7): 445–452.

Bundesverfassungsgericht. 2002. Urteil des Zweiten Senats vom 6. März 2002, 2 BvL 17/99. http://www.bundesverfassungsgericht.de/SharedDocs/Entscheidungen/DE/2002/03/ls20020306_2bvl001799.html.

Commission to Reform the Taxation of Pension Contribution and Benefits. 2003. "Abschlussbericht." Bundesministerium der Finanzen, Berlin, http://www.sozialpolitik

-aktuell.de/tl_files/sozialpolitik-aktuell/_Politikfelder/Alter-Rente/Dokumente/Abschlussbericht-der-Sachverstaendigenkommission.pdf.

Coppola, Michela, and Martin Gasche. 2011. "Die Riester-Förderung—Mangelnde Information als Verbreitungshemmnis." *Wirtschaftsdienst* 91 (11): 792–799.

Coppola, Michela, and Anette Reil-Held. 2009. "Dynamik der Riester-Rente: Ergebnisse aus SAVE 2003 bis 2008." Report No.195-2009, Mannheim Research Institute for the Economics of Aging, Mannheim.

Diamond, Peter A. 2009. "Taxes and Pensions." *Southern Economic Journal* 76 (1): 2–15.

Fehr, Hans, and Heinrich Jess. 2007. "Who Benefits from the Reform of Pension Taxation in Germany?" *Fiscal Studies* 28 (1): 73–101.

Gasche, Martin, Tabea Bucher-Koenen, Marlene Haupt, and Simon Angstmann. 2013. "Die Kosten der Riester-Rente im Vergleich." MEA Discussion Paper Series No. 04-2013, Max-Planck-Institute for Social Law and Social Policy, Munich.

Grub, Martin. 2004. "Reform der Rentenbesteuerung." *Wirtschaftsdienst* 84 (5): 299–308.

Kambeck, Rainer, and Hans D. von Löffelholz. 2003. "Nachgelagerte Besteuerung von Renten: Stellungnahme zum Entwurf eines Alterseinkünftegesetzes." Publ. No. 6, RWI Materialien, Essen.

Kommission für die Nachhaltigkeit in der Finanzierung der Sozialen Sicherungssysteme. 2003. "Abschlussbericht." Bundesministerium für Gesundheit und Soziale Sicherheit, Berlin. http://www.bmgs.bund.de/deu/gra/themen/sicherheit/kommission/index.cfm.

Krause-Junk, Gerold. 2006. "Der Übergang zur nachgelagerten Rentenbesteuerung: Überlegungen zum Urteil des Bundesfinanzhofs." *Wirtschaftsdienst* 86 (5): 343–348.

Palacios, Robert, and Roberto Rocha. 1998. "The Hungarian Pension System in Transition." Social Protection Discussion Paper Series No. 9805, World Bank, Washington, DC.

Rentenversicherungsbericht. 2014. Bundesministerium für Arbeit und Soziales, Berlin, http://www.bmas.de/SharedDocs/Downloads/DE/Thema-Rente/rentenversicherungsbericht-2014-kabinettvorlage.pdf?__blob=publicationFile.

Ruland, Franz. 2004. "Zur Neuordnung der steuerrechtlichen Behandlung von Altersvorsorgeaufwendungen und Altersbezügen." In *Staat, Wirtschaft, Finanzverfassung. Festschrift für Peter Selmer zum 70.* Geburtstag. Berlin: Verlag Duncker und Humblot.

Schnabel, Reinhold. 1998. "Rates of Return of the German Pay-As-You-Go Pension System." *FinanzArchiv/Public Finance Analysis* 55 (3): 374–399.

Schnabel, Reinhold. 2004. "Die nachgelagerte Besteuerung der Altersvorsorge: Wirkung und Handlungsalternativen." Deutsches Institut fur Altersvorsorge, Bonn.

Scholtz, Hellmut D. 2013. "Werden die Renten der gesetzlichen Rentenversicherung sachgerecht besteuert?" *Deutsches Steuerrecht* 51 (3): 75–80.

Siepe, Günter, and Werner Siepe. 2016. "Rentenbesteuerung erneut auf dem Prüfstand: Zweifachbesteuerung ab Rentenbeginn in 2016." Studie für die Versicherungsberatergesellschaft mbH, Berlin-Reinickendorf, January.

Walliser, Jan, Nicolas Sauter, and Joachim Winter. 1999. "Tax Incentives, Bequest Motives and the Demand for Life Insurance: Evidence from Germany." Discussion Paper No. 99-28, Sonderforschungsbereich 504, University of Mannheim.

Wernsmann, Rainer. 2012. "Die steuerliche Förderung der zusätzlichen kapitalgedeckten Altersvorsorge." In *Handbuch der gesetzlichen Rentenversicherung SGB VI*, 2nd ed., edited by Eberhard Eichenhofer, Herbert Rische, and Winfried Schmähl, 783–795. Berlin: Hermann Luchterhand Verlag.

World Bank. 1999. "The Tax Treatment of Funded Pensions." *World Bank Pension Reform Primer 2.3*. Washington, DC: World Bank.

9 The Taxation of Pensions in the United Kingdom

Carl Emmerson and Paul Johnson

9.1 Introduction

The pension system in the United Kingdom can be thought of as consisting of three pillars. The first pillar is a relatively low state pension that, going forward at least, will effectively be paid at the same flat rate to all those over state pension age who have been resident in the United Kingdom for a long enough period. The second pillar is a system of occupational pension schemes organized by employers with contributions from employees and employers. These have traditionally been provided on a "defined benefit" basis but, outside of the public sector, are now, for younger generations, available almost exclusively only on a "defined contribution" basis. The third pillar consists of individual private pension provision.

This chapter focuses on the occupational and private pension pillars, the taxation of which has been subject to substantial reform in the last few years. Further changes appear to be likely in the near future. Indeed, in July 2015 the UK government launched a consultation about fundamental reform—moving from the long-established system in which contributions to pensions are exempt from tax and income from pensions is taxed to a system in which savings are made out of taxed income and withdrawals are free of tax (Her Majesty's Treasury 2015). For long-term savings vehicles such as pensions, this degree of change and uncertainty clearly has the potential to be damaging.

This chapter looks briefly at the tax regime for the main forms of savings in the United Kingdom but focuses on the taxation of private pensions, looking at the current structure, recent reforms, and proposals for more change. Section 9.2 briefly describes the principles for taxing pensions and savings, while section 9.3 examines the specific taxation mechanisms for pensions and savings in the United Kingdom. Section 9.4 highlights the scope and incidence of UK pension tax relief. Section 9.5 discusses some options for future reform, and section 9.6 offers concluding remarks.

9.2 Principles

The three obvious points where pension savings (or any other form of savings) could be subject to personal taxation are (1) when income is first received (i.e., before or at the point at which it is paid into a pension), (2) as the returns (interest, capital gains, or distributable profit) accrue, and (3) when funds are withdrawn from the pension. In addition, both corporation tax and stamp duties on purchases of shares and property can affect pension returns, so consideration needs to be given to whether the tax treatment of pensions at the personal level should reflect this.[1]

Very broadly (exceptions are noted later), private pensions in the United Kingdom are subject to an expenditure tax (or EET regime) as far as income tax is concerned. That is, contributions to the pension are exempt (E) from income tax, accruals in the pension fund are again exempt (E), but the pension payment is taxed (T). By contrast, savings in ordinary bank and building society accounts and direct holdings of shares were traditionally subject to an income tax (TTE) where savings are made from taxed income (T), returns are taxed (T), and no further tax is collected upon withdrawal (E). Savings in tax-privileged Individual Savings Accounts (ISAs) are subject to TEE taxation—savings are made from taxed income (T), but no tax is charged on returns (E) or at withdrawal (E).

The EET regime is the most common tax treatment of private pension saving at the individual level across industrialized countries (Yoo and de Serres 2004, table 1). It broadly achieves neutrality between consumption now and consumption in the future. It ensures that, at the individual level, normal returns to saving are not taxed. However, any returns in excess of this normal return are subject to tax (in contrast with the TEE regime applied to ISAs in the United Kingdom). If higher returns are generated, more tax will be paid on the eventual pension income.

In the face of a progressive tax system, some individuals will be subject to a higher rate of income tax during part of their working life but subject to the basic rate of income tax during their retirement. The EET regime allows them to smooth their income so that they need not end up paying more tax over their lifetime than an otherwise equivalent individual who receives the same lifetime income in a less variable way. Essentially, an EET regime allows tax-rate smoothing so that changes in the marginal income tax rate can be evened out over the individual's lifetime. Such a system has been advocated by, among others, the 1978 Meade Committee (Meade 1978).

Ideally, taxes on corporate profits and transaction taxes would be well designed so that they need not be a consideration for how pensions (or any other savings) should be taxed at the individual level.[2] But faced with a system for taxing corporate profits, share transactions, and property purchases that harshly taxes certain investments, the issue is whether this should be reflected in the way the personal tax regime treats returns on funds held in pensions. Specifically, (1) should investments made from funds in private pensions be exempt from any stamp duties, and (2) should returns that accrue on investments held in private pensions be given a repayable credit to compensate for the fact that tax will have been paid on normal returns at the corporate level? Doing so could help ensure that a significant proportion of overall UK wealth—that held in private pensions[3]—is treated by the overall tax system in a way that is neutral between saving and spending.

In principle, one might want the taxation of all forms of savings to be subject to an EET regime. In practice, this is more generous than the treatment of most forms of savings in the United Kingdom. Some additional tax incentive for pension saving specifically may also be appropriate to encourage people to lock their savings away for long periods.

9.3 Taxation of Pensions and Savings in the United Kingdom

While this chapter's focus is the taxation of private pensions in the United Kingdom, it is important to put this in the context of the taxation of pensions and savings more broadly.

The United Kingdom's first pillar, the basic state pension, is in principle contributory, but it can be thought of as a universal payment largely unrelated to any contributions made. An earnings-related element, introduced in 1978, was gradually phased out, leaving a single-tier, flat-rate pension. It is subject to income tax in the normal way. As with all nonearned income, and indeed all income received by those over pension age, no National Insurance contributions (NICs) are levied.

A variety of treatments exist for savings held in forms other than pensions, and these have been subject to major reforms in recent years. Most importantly:

1. Savings held in ordinary bank and building society accounts historically had been saved out of taxed income, with income tax then levied on interest received: a TTE regime. But as of April 2016, basic-rate taxpayers can receive £1,000 of interest free of income tax, while higher-rate taxpayers (the 20 percent or so with incomes over £42,700) can receive £500 free of income tax. So, for the vast majority of savers, savings in an ordinary interest-bearing account will be subject to a TEE regime.
2. ISAs are long-standing tax-exempt (TEE) savings vehicles that allow investment in equities (or cash) up to an annual maximum every year with returns free of income tax and capital gains tax. Recent reforms raised the annual maximum from £10,000 to £15,000, and to £20,000 as of April 2017, and liberalized rules restricting the amount of cash that can be held in an ISA (though this has been replaced by the more recent changes to the treatment of interest on cash deposits described earlier).
3. Owner-occupied housing is effectively subject to a TEE regime. The property is bought out of taxed income (and there is no relief for mortgage interest), but there is no tax on imputed income from owner occupation and no tax on any capital gain made. Given the very high excess returns earned on housing over recent decades, this TEE treatment will have been more generous *ex post* than an EET treatment (but there is a substantial tax on transactions, stamp duty, formally incident on the purchaser).

For most people, the pension regime is more generous than any of these treatments. Something rather more generous than an EET regime is applied, since a tax-free lump sum can be taken and contributions, formally from the employer, can be made free of NICs.

Table 9.1 provides a sense of the importance of different elements of wealth for two segments of the population—those aged 50 and over and those under 50. It illustrates the overwhelming importance of owner-occupied housing and private pensions—the two most tax-favored elements. (The same data cannot be used to calculate state pension wealth, but Banks et al. [2013] suggest that levels of state and private pension

Table 9.1
Composition of household wealth in the United Kingdom, 2010–2012.

	Aged less than 50		Aged 50 and over		All	
Total net wealth (£)	184,105	(% of total)	470,662	(% of total)	340,888	(% of total)
Of which:						
Primary housing	72,203	39.2%	168,643	35.8%	124,968	36.7%
Buy-to-let and other houses	9,542	5.2%	16,046	3.4%	13,100	3.8%
Other property	5,825	3.2%	7,374	1.6%	6,673	2.0%
Net current and savings accounts	8,320	4.5%	20,107	4.3%	14,769	4.3%
ISAs (cash and investment)	4,307	2.3%	15,283	3.2%	10,312	3.0%
Shares (excl. employee shares)	1,741	0.9%	8,777	1.9%	5,591	1.6%
Other net financial wealth	8,766	4.8%	24,560	5.2%	17,407	5.1%
Private pension wealth	73,402	39.9%	209,872	44.6%	148,068	43.4%

Source: Authors' calculations using data from the Wealth and Assets Survey (2010–2012).
Note: Total net wealth is the sum of the components listed (i.e., it excludes state pensions and physical wealth). Other net financial wealth includes fixed-term investment bonds, unit and investment bonds, employee shares, overseas gilts, UK gilts, insurance products, other investments and national savings products less formal loans, hire purchase arrears, loan arrears, outstanding value of loans, household bill arrears, outstanding value on credit cards, outstanding value of hire purchases, outstanding value of mail orders, and outstanding value of store cards. Private pension wealth includes value of retained rights in defined benefit schemes, value of Additional Voluntary Contributions, value of retained rights in employer defined contribution pensions, value of retained rights in personal pensions, outstanding value of pensions currently being drawn down, value of pensions of former spouse or partner, value of current employer defined benefit schemes, and value of current employer defined contribution schemes.

wealth are very similar among the over-50 population.) A number of important complications and deviations from a simple EET regime are described next.

9.3.1 Tax-Free Lump Sum

One-quarter of the accumulated pension balance in a defined contribution scheme can be withdrawn as a lump sum free of income tax. (A roughly equivalent, though somewhat more generous, rule works for defined benefit schemes, too.) The result is that one-quarter of contributions are effectively subject to a very generous EEE treatment for income tax purposes. This means that someone who accumulated £1 million in a private pension (the maximum on which tax relief is granted since April 2016) would be able to receive £250,000 that had escaped income tax altogether: it would be taxed neither when it was earned nor when it was withdrawn from the pension.

9.3.2 Contribution Limits

Tax relief is given on private pension contributions (both individual and employer) up to an annual limit, known as the annual allowance. This is currently set at £40,000; it was £255,000 until 2011, when it was reduced to £50,000. It was cut again to £40,000 in 2014. Individuals are allowed to make use of any unused allowance from the previous three years, as long as they were a member of a pension scheme in those years. This means that, for many, the annual allowance will eventually effectively become a £160,000 limit over a rolling four-year window.

Clearly, the annual allowance only affects relatively well-off individuals. However, the way that pension rights accrue in final salary defined benefit schemes also means that high-sounding annual allowances can affect people who are well off but perhaps not quite as rich as one might imagine. For example, an employee earning £38,000 a year with 30 years' membership in a final salary pension scheme and saw his pay rise to £55,000 in four years' time could be affected by the £40,000 limit, but defined benefit schemes that operate on a final salary basis are becoming increasingly rare. In the private sector, they have almost entirely been replaced by defined contribution schemes; just 8.4 percent of private sector employees were members of a defined benefit scheme in 2012, and this percentage has fallen rapidly in recent years.[4] Defined benefit schemes are still prevalent in the public sector but, following the recommendations of Lord Hutton's Independent Public Service Pensions Commission review, for future accruals these will operate on a career average rather than a final salary basis.[5] Career average defined benefit pensions typically accrue more gradually over an individual's lifetime than final salary pensions, making it less likely that individuals will be constrained by a given level of annual allowance in the future.

A cap on the total amount that can be accumulated in a private pension, known as the lifetime limit, also exists. This is set to fall from £1.25 million in 2015 to £1 million in 2016 (it was £1.8 million until 2012). To get a feel for how big a £1million pension pot is, note that a single man aged 65 with a pension pot that size could, at current annuity rates, take a tax-free lump sum of £250,000 and receive a retail price index (RPI)-linked annual pension of about £24,000—a sum close to average earnings (or an annual pension fixed in cash terms of about £38,000).[6] For someone in a defined benefit pension arrangement, a £250,000 lump sum and an annual RPI-linked pension of £37,500—some 50 percent higher than the maximum defined contribution pension—are deemed to be equivalent to a pension pot of £1 million (since defined benefit pension schemes are deemed to have a pot size 20 times larger than the annual pension).

Finally, a new and complex addition to the rules on contributions was introduced as of April 2016. From that date, the maximum annual contribution will be tapered from £40,000 for anyone earning up to £150,000 (including pension contributions) to just £10,000 for anyone earning £210,000 or more. In other words, the maximum contribution will be reduced by £500 for every additional £1,000 earned between £150,000 and £210,000. It is hard to think of any reasonable justification to allow someone earning £150,000 to put £40,000 into a pension but allow anyone earning over £210,000 to put in only £10,000. This will also significantly increase the effective marginal tax rates faced by high earners.

9.3.3 National Insurance Contributions

The NIC regime for pensions is quite different from the income tax regime. The treatment of pension contributions formally made by an individual is broadly sensible: there is no NIC relief on contributions, and no NICs are payable on pension income either (so, using the terminology set out here, these are subject to TEE treatment[7]). However, *employer* pension contributions are treated extremely generously: they are excluded from earnings for both employer and employee NICs—total NIC relief of 22.7 percent for those earning below the upper earnings limit[8]—while the pension income they generate is not subject to NICs either. Employer pension contributions are the only major form of employee remuneration that escapes NICs entirely, and these make up roughly three-quarters of all pension contributions.

9.3.4 Corporation Tax and Stamp Duty

The current UK corporation tax does, in part, tax the normal rate of return. In addition, stamp duty is levied at a rate of 0.5 percent on all purchases of UK shares, while stamp duty land tax applies to any property purchases. At the moment, the personal tax system does not compensate pension saving either for the tax paid on the normal return at the corporate level or for the presence of stamp duties. However, versions of both forms of compensation have existed in the past. Before April 1993, repayable dividend tax credits on UK (not global) shareholdings were paid at a rate equal to the basic income tax rate, which in 1992–1993 was 25 percent. This was reduced to 20 percent in 1993 and then abolished completely in July 1997.[9]

9.3.5 Annuitization

Historically, tax relief for pension savings was available in full only on the presumption that the accumulated pot of savings was used to purchase an annuity (with the exception of the tax-free lump sum). Those with defined benefit schemes would receive an annual pension related to their final earnings and years of employment. Beyond the lump sum, withdrawal other than via an annuity was subject to a penal rate of tax (55 percent).

By 2014, the rules had been liberalized in a number of ways. People could avoid annuitization by "drawing down" income from their accumulated pension savings. The amount that could be withdrawn was limited to 120 percent of what they would have received from an annuity. Those who could show they had a secure annual income of £20,000 from other sources did not need to annuitize, nor did those with very small amounts in defined contribution pensions. Otherwise, annuitization was compulsory by age 75. In practice, the large majority bought an annuity.

In 2014, a further liberalization was announced, effectively offering complete freedom over how and when to take money accumulated in a defined contribution pension (subject to being 55 or older). As of April 2015, any money withdrawn is taxed at the individual's normal marginal rate of income tax—0 percent, 20 percent, 40 percent, or

45 percent. Additional changes will allow those inheriting accumulated pension pots to access them and pay income tax only at their own marginal rate.

The behavioral consequences of these changes are hard to predict. Purchases of annuities during 2014 fell substantially in anticipation of the changes. Cannon, Tonks, and Yuille (2016) found evidence of an immediate 75 percent reduction in the demand for annuities. The government expects the change to bring in significant additional revenues of up to £1 billion per year in the next few years as people take their money earlier than otherwise, with lower revenues later on. These changes will substantially alter the nature of pension savings. Savings in a defined contribution pension will become much more similar to savings made through any other savings vehicle, with the exception of the rule preventing access to the savings before age 55.

9.3.6 Means-Tested Benefits

The discussion so far has ignored the existence of means-tested benefits and tax credits. To the extent that accumulated savings reduce entitlement to benefits, the incentive to save is reduced. On the other hand, if contributions to savings products are deducted from income in assessing entitlement to benefits, then incentives to save are enhanced. The way in which the benefit system in the United Kingdom takes account of savings is complex and inconsistent. Entitlements to means-tested benefits are reduced at high marginal rates in the face of income from private pensions. Entitlement to Pension Credit (a means-tested benefit available to pensioners with low incomes), for example, is reduced by 40p for every pound of pension income, and Housing Benefit entitlement is reduced by 65p for every £1. Significant numbers of pensioners are entitled to some form of means-tested benefit.

For pension savings, it also matters how contributions are treated when calculating benefits or tax credit entitlements. Pension contributions are in fact not counted as part of the income on which the tax credit entitlement is calculated, just as they are excluded from income when calculating the tax due. This potentially provides a significant saving incentive for tax credit recipients, since it effectively costs a tax credit recipient only 41p in lost income to save £1 in a pension.

The potential impact of tax credits and the Pension Credit, along with different income tax rates, on the incentive to save in a pension is illustrated in table 9.2, which shows how much one would need to contribute to a pension to match the returns from saving £1 under a

Table 9.2
Employee contribution to pension (10-year investment) required to match £1 contribution to TEE vehicle for different combinations of working-life and retirement tax rates.

Tax rate in work	Tax rate in retirement	Required contribution (p)
Basic rate (20%)	Basic rate (20%)	94
Higher rate (40%)	Higher rate (40%)	86
Higher rate (40%)	Basic rate (20%)	71
Basic rate (20%)	Pension credit taper (40%)	114
Tax credit taper (59%)	Basic rate (20%)	48
Tax credit taper (59%)	Pension credit taper (40%)	59

Source: Wakefield (2009).
Note: Assumes 3 percent annual real rate of return and 2 percent inflation.

TEE regime. The differences are dramatic. The last two rows show the effect of receiving means-tested tax credits while working. Even in the case where such a person would receive means-tested benefits (Pension Credit) in retirement, the incentive to save is very strong, and is even stronger in the more likely event that they end up simply paying basic-rate income tax in retirement. On the other hand, a strong disincentive to pension saving arises for basic-rate taxpayers expecting to end up on the Pension Credit taper (fourth row of the table).

As set out in the Mirrlees Review (Mirrlees et al. 2011), no easy reform presents itself. Standard approaches to the taxation of savings are problematic when it comes to means testing, for two reasons. First, little correlation exists between receiving any particular benefit when saving and when withdrawing the savings. Second, unlike a standard progressive tax schedule, means testing implies higher effective tax rates on those with lower incomes. Because means testing is an implicit tax on income received, a contradiction arises between a TEE income tax system and means testing. To quote the Mirrlees Review (Mirrlees et al. 2011, 329–330):

> A TEE-type regime makes little sense in the context of means-testing. If Pension Credit, for example, were not reduced in the face of higher private pension income, it would no longer be a means-tested benefit. One could conceive of a system in which a saver sacrifices Pension Credit now in order to enjoy the benefits of that saving, and of Pension Credit, in the future. But that is not consistent with the usual pattern of behaviour: almost nobody saves in a pension while in receipt of Pension Credit.
>
> An EET regime suffers from the mirror-image problem. Many of those on means-tested tapers when they withdraw the savings (receive a pension) will

have been facing just the basic tax rate when saving (in work). They will face the "T" without ever having benefited from the "E". And because means-testing involves higher effective tax rates when incomes are lower, saving to smooth consumption will result in an overall higher level of tax paid than would have occurred in the absence of saving. This is the opposite effect of an EET regime in the face of a tax system with rising marginal rates. In this case, as we have already seen, saving when income (and the tax rate) is higher and consuming when income is lower allows the overall tax paid to be smoothed, at least to some extent, to reflect income over a longer period.

There is no easy way around the issue of means-testing and savings. Obviously, less reliance on means-testing would help. But that can only be achieved either by reducing the generosity of benefits or by increasing universal benefits. The first makes poor people worse off; the second requires increases in taxes to pay for the benefits. Another path is to make some level of saving compulsory. If this leads to very small increases in eventual incomes because of the action of means-testing, then it has much the same effect as an increase in direct taxes on those affected.

9.4 The Scope and Incidence of UK Pension Tax Relief

The UK tax system currently treats pensions more generously than it treats other forms of savings. It is often argued that a substantial cost is associated with this, and many proposals for reform are predicated on the belief that the costs are large and the benefits inequitably distributed. Indeed, large costs and inequities are present in the system. They are just not those usually referred to.

The appropriate way of calculating the total cost of tax support for pension saving, and how much different types of individuals benefit, would require one to work out, for each individual, the total amount of tax they would pay on pension saving over their entire lifetime under the current UK tax system. This could then be compared with how much would be paid under an alternative system. Clearly, the choice among alternatives matters.

Her Majesty's Revenue and Customs (HMRC) produces an official estimate of the annual cost of tax relief given to private pension savings by the income tax and NIC systems. This estimate thus excludes the impact of capital gains tax, corporation tax, and stamp duties. The methodology HMRC employs looks at the amount of tax relief given in a particular year and compares this with the amount of tax collected on pension income in the same year. This compares the gross cost of giving tax relief to today's working-age population and the revenue raised from taxing the pensions of today's retirees. This method will tend to overstate the cost of tax relief for two reasons. First, real growth in per capita national income means that today's working-age individuals are likely, on average, to have higher pension incomes than today's retirees. Second, demographic change means that the current working-age population will, upon retirement, be more numerous at each age than the current retiree population. In addition, HMRC chooses to compare the current tax treatment of pension savings in the United Kingdom with a system with a TTE regime.

With these important caveats in mind, the HMRC estimates for 2011–2012 are presented in table 9.3. Because it looks at how income tax and NIC treatment compares with a TTE system, and because it uses the tax paid by today's pensioners as a proxy for the tax that will be paid on today's pension contributions when that income is drawn, HMRC looks at the "cost" of up-front relief and nets off the tax received on pension income. It also counts as relief the "cost" of not subjecting returns on funds held in private pensions to income tax (but not the "cost" of not subjecting them to capital gains tax). In 2011–2012, total up-front income tax and NIC relief on pension contributions was costed at £43.2 billion and income tax relief on returns at £6.8 billion, giving a gross cost of £50 billion. Income tax on pension income in that year raised £11.5 billion, giving an estimated net cost of £38.3 billion.

HMRC also publishes estimates of the proportion of income tax relief that is given to individuals in different income bands based on their individual pension contributions. Since these data only show individual contributions—and not those made on individuals' behalf by their employers—they only include about one-quarter of the total estimated

Table 9.3
HMRC estimates of the cost of pension tax relief, 2011–2012.

	£ billion
Income tax relief on contributions from employees	5.6
Income tax relief on contributions from self-employed	0.9
Income tax relief on contributions from employers	21.7
National Insurance relief on contributions	15.0
Income tax relief on returns	6.8
Gross tax relief	**49.9**
Income tax received on pension income	11.5
Net tax relief	**38.3**

Source: Table PEN6 of http://www.hmrc.gov.uk/statistics/pension-stats.htm.

up-front cost of income tax relief on pension contributions (and they also ignore relief from NICs on employer contributions). The calculation makes no allowance for the amount of tax that will eventually be paid on the pension income. Not surprisingly, these calculations suggest that a lot of the "cost" of tax relief is focused on higher-income individuals. Indeed, these numbers suggest that over 60 percent of tax relief accrues to higher-rate taxpayers, with more than one-fifth going to the 1 percent of income tax payers with incomes over £150,000.[10] It is often claimed that these numbers demonstrate that a disproportionate amount of pension tax relief goes to high-income individuals (Pensions Policy Institute 2013), but as well as getting an estimated 22 percent of the value of the tax relief, the top 1 percent of income tax payers accounted for 24 percent of all income tax revenue.[11] These numbers, of course, take no account of the taxes this group will pay on their pensions in retirement. Nor do they account for either income tax or National Insurance relief on employer contributions.

The lack of employer or employee NICs on pension contributions made on individuals' behalf by their employer, and the fact that up to one-quarter of a pension pot can be withdrawn entirely free of income tax, mean that the personal tax system does, overall, treat private pension savings generously. A good estimate of how much this relief costs would be useful. It is certainly not equal to £38 billion, which is the HMRC estimate relative to a TTE benchmark.

A better estimate would be the cost of NIC relief—estimated by HMRC at £15 billion—plus the cost of the tax-free lump sum, for which HMRC no longer publishes an estimate but which it previously estimated at £2.5 billion per year.[12] This suggests that the "true" cost of income tax and NIC relief, while still very substantial, could be less than half the official HMRC estimate.

9.5 Options for Reform

9.5.1 Rationale for Reform

In July 2015, the UK Treasury published a consultation on reform of pension tax relief (Her Majesty's Treasury 2015). The centerpiece of the consultation was the following statement:

> It has been suggested that a fundamental reform of the system so that pension contributions are taxed upfront (a "Taxed-Exempt-Exempt" system like ISAs), and then topped up by the government, may allow individuals to better understand the benefits of contributing to their pension. (para 3.12)

A number of commentators, including Michael Johnson of the right-leaning Centre for Policy Studies, have argued for this change. In addition to arguments about the apparent cost and inequity of the current system, Johnson argues that the recent abolition of the requirement to annuitize removes one of the fundamental justifications for the current tax treatment (Johnson 2015).

Certainly the removal of the annuitization requirement makes saving in a pension look much more like saving in any other form; the only additional restriction is that savings cannot be accessed before age 55. The 2015 Treasury consultation also suggested that problems of complexity, high charges, and lack of effective competition in the pension market might be related to the current system of taxation. In addition, of course, moving from an EET to a TEE system of taxation would have the very big attraction to the Treasury of moving a very large amount of revenue forward, reducing the deficit in the short term. Johnson refers to this as "The Great Trade to-do."

There are clear attractions to all this. In addition, one could use the opportunity of such radical reform to eliminate some of the anomalies alluded to earlier—the excessively generous treatment of employer contributions within the National Insurance system and the generous and poorly targeted tax-free lump sum. Some of the money spent on these subsidies could be used to fund the "top-up" mentioned in the Treasury consultation, presumably intended to provide an additional reward for those who do not access the accumulated savings until a particular age. Three substantial downsides to such a dramatic change (beyond any difficulties in transition) would arise, however, possibly explaining why the change was never implemented.

First, the apparent improvement in public finances would be largely illusory, bringing tax revenues forward rather than adding to them. If politicians could be relied on to bank this temporary windfall, then that would be fine, but the temptation to use a stronger headline fiscal position to justify tax cuts or spending increases in the short run would surely be hard to resist. Long-term fiscal sustainability would therefore be put at risk. Related to that, the EET system has the nice feature of reducing the sensitivity of public finances to population aging: while a population growing older will weaken public finances because of additional spending on the National Health Service and social care, taxing pension income when it is received will offset this to some extent. This makes it easier for the government to manage public finances appropriately. Moving to a TEE regime would make that more difficult.

Second, a TEE regime does not allow the sort of tax smoothing that is possible under the current EET regime. A progressive income tax system, in which tax liability is based on annual income, takes more tax from people whose incomes are volatile than from people with the same lifetime income but whose incomes are stable. The current system provides 40 percent relief for higher-rate taxpayers to save in a pension, but many will pay 20 percent tax on income when payment is received. In effect, such individuals are simply smoothing their taxable income between high-income and low-income periods, undoing the "unfairness" that an annually assessed progressive tax schedule creates.

Third, a TEE regime allows excess returns to go untaxed—in the presence of greater-than-normal returns, TEE is more generous than EET. The government would not get to share in any excess returns. The reverse would be true if returns were low. This feature of a TEE regime explains why the Mirrlees Review favored a "Rate of Return Allowance" regime, which would be a TEE regime with a tax on any excess return, or a rebate on below-normal returns.

To these issues might be added the political economy risk that if very large sums of money end up being withdrawn from pensions free of tax (although tax will have been paid on contributions), future governments might be tempted to renege on the deal with the taxpayer and attempt to impose an additional tax at a later date. Under the current system, the taxpayer has at least banked his tax relief up front.

In fact, the outcome of the process of consultation and policy development, announced in the March 2016 budget, was to refrain from making this change. Instead, the scope of ISAs was extended in two ways. First, it was announced that the maximum amount that can be saved in an ISA would increase in April 2017 to £20,000 annually. Second, a new product, the Lifetime ISA (LISA), was announced. Like an ISA, a LISA allows any returns to be free of tax, but in addition it will attract a 25 percent government top-up on contributions of up to £4,000 a year; however, this will only be available to those aged between 18 and 40 in April 2017, although once begun, top-ups will be available until contributors reach age 50. For the first time, this means that a savings product is available, currently only for a limited amount of saving, that is clearly more tax-advantaged for most people than saving in a pension.

So, while the headline reform of a move to TEE was not carried out, steps have been taken to encourage more TEE savings alongside tightening up on tax-free limits to pension savings. Whether this presages a longer-term change and eventual phase out of EET vehicles, to be replaced with TEE, remains to be seen.

In any case, other reforms to the current pension tax regime are needed. They should involve (1) abandoning the complex plans to taper away tax relief from high earners as described here and (2) possibly reversing at least some of the cuts to annual and lifetime allowances. They should also involve two significant reductions in the generosity of the current system—in the treatment of the tax-free lump sum and in the National Insurance treatment of employer contributions.

9.5.2 Capping the Tax-Free Lump Sum

The argument that is usually made for the tax-free lump sum (under which up to one-quarter of a pension pot can escape income tax altogether) is that it is compensation for the fact that pensions are constructed to be a highly inflexible form of savings, available only after a certain age. If, for reasons of public policy, the government wants people to lock money away for long periods, it is likely to have to provide them with a good reason for doing so.

That is a strong argument, but it has its limits. At the moment, the size of the lump sum that can be taken tax-free is limited only by the lifetime limit on the size of a pension pot: with a £1 million lifetime allowance, £250,000 can be taken tax-free. There may be a good case for introducing a cash limit on the amount that can be taken as a tax-free lump sum, at a level considerably below this.[13] Unfortunately, no reliable current estimate exists of the revenue that this would raise.[14]

With the end of rules compelling annuitization, the case for an additional "bonus" becomes weaker. The money saved is still tied up until at least age 55, but access otherwise becomes much more flexible.

9.5.3 Levy NICs on Employer Contributions

Employer pension contributions are the only major form of employee remuneration that escapes NICs entirely, and they did so at an estimated cost to the government of £15.0 billion in 2011–2012. This is a big incentive and creates a large bias toward contributions coming (formally) from employers rather than employees: a pension contribution that costs an employer £100 to make would cost nearly £130 if it came instead from an employee earning below the upper earnings limit.[15] This no doubt helps to explain why HMRC records income tax relief on employer contributions as more than three times as great as that on employee contributions (table 9.3).

The obvious solution would be to start charging NICs on employer pension contributions, so that they are treated like any other form of remuneration. Employer NICs are already virtually flat-rate (other than the earnings threshold) and could readily be charged at a flat rate on any contributions made by the employer. This solution would, however, be harder to implement with respect to charging *employee* NICs on *employer* pension contributions. The non–flat-rate structure of employee NICs would require employer contributions to be allocated to individuals; that is difficult for defined benefit pension schemes. But even if only employer NICs were charged, this would be an improvement on the current system and would raise an estimated £10 billion in 2015–2016 (Her Majesty's Revenue and Customs 2015).

Doing so would get rid of an expensive anomaly. Perhaps even better would be to move toward providing NICs relief on all pension contributions and levying NICs on all pension income, so that NICs treat pensions in the same way as income tax does (with the added advantage of moving further toward the integration of income tax and NICs) (Mirrlees et al. 2011, 339–340). This change would need to be introduced gradually both to avoid retrospective double taxation—levying NICs on pension income despite having already levied them on employee contributions to that pension—and to avoid undermining the legitimate expectations of those who have saved up to now. A long transition could create political risk (and would mean that while the reform generated significant revenue in the long run, it would actually cost money up front).

A simple alternative would be to start charging NICs on income received from pensions at a relatively low rate now and to increase this gradually over time. Each 1 percentage point charged would raise an estimated £350 million (Adam, Browne, and Johnson 2012, 29).

Such a change could help to spread fiscal consolidation more evenly across generations. Tax and benefit reforms announced to date have reduced the incomes of pensioners by less than those of working-age individuals (Browne 2013, slide 23). Starting to charge some NICs on pension income would also do something to unwind some of the, almost certainly unintended, consequences of the shift from income tax to NICs that has occurred over recent decades. This has meant that less tax on pension income will be paid by today's pensioners than they

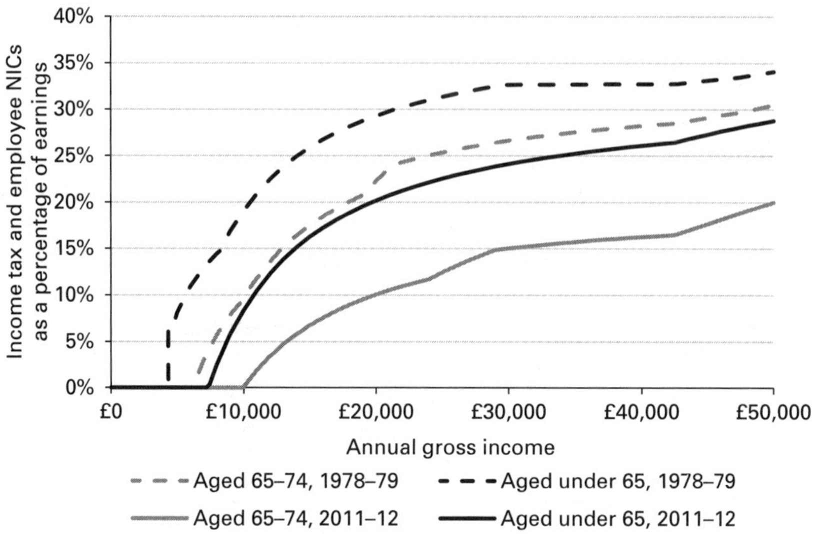

Figure 9.1
Income tax and employee NIC rates by income, 1978–1979 and 2011–2012. *Source*: Figure 2.9 of Adam, Browne, and Johnson (2012). *Note*: Assumes single man, no children, no income other than earnings for individual aged under 65, one job, contracted into the State Earnings-Related Pension Scheme / State Second Pension.

might have expected when they were saving for retirement. As shown in figure 9.1, the period between 1978–1979 and 2011–2012 saw a fall in the combined rates of income tax and employee NICs across the income distribution (compare the dashed lines with the solid lines). They fell by more for those aged 65 to 74 (the grey lines) than they did for those younger than 65 (the black lines), because income tax rates fell by more than NIC rates, and the latter do not apply to those aged 65 and over.

9.6 Conclusions

As the UK government has engaged in an unprecedented program of austerity measures since 2010, it is perhaps not surprising that the apparently generous tax treatment of private pensions has come under some scrutiny and been subject to reform. The amount that can be contributed tax-free each year, and over a lifetime, to a pension has been reduced substantially. The capacity to make pension contributions at all is being substantially withdrawn from high earners. This series of reforms will raise around £6 billion per year for the government, at the cost of creating complexity, uncertainty, and further incoherence in the pension tax system. Rather than raising money by tackling the genuinely generous aspects of the current system—exemption from NICs and availability of a tax-free lump sum—the reforms reduced the scope of the neutral EET tax treatment.

At the same time, rules requiring annuitization of defined contribution pensions were removed, making pension saving look more like saving in other forms, and taxation of other forms of saving moved in the other direction. Most people with money in interest-bearing accounts will now receive interest free of tax, and the amount of money that can be contributed to tax-free ISAs has doubled: since April 2017, individuals are able to contribute £20,000 a year. Further reforms now allow the first £12,000 of any dividend income to be received free of tax.

So this has been a period of substantial reform, reducing the scope for saving in EET pension vehicles but increasing the scope for saving with TEE treatment. These circumstances have led to calls to change the tax treatment of pensions altogether and to move from an EET treatment to a TEE treatment. The Treasury has recently consulted on possible reforms, including changes as radical as this.

From the point of view of achieving neutrality between consuming now and in the future, allowing risk sharing between savers and government, and allowing tax-rate smoothing over time, an EET system has clear advantages, but the UK system in place now is not a pure EET system. It is more generous in some respects but also increasingly constrained and circumscribed by a complex set of limits. Recent policy changes favor TEE savings through ISAs and the more generous LISA. The future direction for policy remains entirely unclear.

Notes

1. Inheritance tax—for example, how funds held in a private pension, and how pension payments that provide survivor benefits, are treated at death—can also affect the incentive to save, but this is outside the scope of this chapter. For a discussion of whether inheritances should be taxed at all and, if so, how the UK system of inheritance taxation could be improved, see chapter 15 of Mirrlees et al. (2011) and Boadway, Chamberlain, and Emmerson (2010).

2. A well-designed corporation tax would only tax returns in excess of the normal rate of return. The Institute for Fiscal Studies–led Mirrlees Review set out proposals for introducing an Allowance for Corporate Equity into a corporation tax that would achieve this objective (see 421–425 in chapter 17 and 446–448 in chapter 18 of Mirrlees et al. 2011). Furthermore, transaction taxes—stamp duty on shares and stamp duty land tax on

property transactions—would not exist, since both discourage individuals from making mutually beneficial trades at no detriment to the rest of society. It is argued that some trades take place that use real resources and yet do not have any real economic value, but rather than have a broad-based transaction tax, a better policy response would be to target regulation and/or taxes at these specific activities.

3. Estimated by the Office for National Statistics at almost half of net household wealth. Figure from the 2008–2010 wave of the Wealth and Assets Survey; source: figure 2 on page 3 of Office for National Statistics (2012a).

4. Source: Table 2.1 of Office for National Statistics (2012b).

5. See Independent Public Service Pensions Commission (2011).

6. Source: http://pluto.moneyadviceservice.org.uk/annuities. The calculation is based on a nonsmoking, single man born in 1948 living in Ipswich.

7. While this means that excess returns in a private pension are not subject to NICs, this is also true of excess returns more widely, as NICs only apply to earned income.

8. If an employer pays out £100 in pension contributions, that is the amount that goes into the employee's pension. A salary payment that costs the employer the same amount would leave the employee with only £77.32, or 22.7 percent less: paying a nominal wage of £87.87 would cost the employer £100 because of 13.8 percent employer NICs on top of the £87.87, while the employee would lose 12 percent of the £87.87 in employee NICs, leaving only £77.32 [22.7 percent is employee NICs of 12 percent plus employer NICs of 13.8 percent divided by total employer cost of (100 percent + 13.8 percent)].

9. The March 1993 budget measure is scored by the Treasury as boosting revenues in 1995–1996 by an estimated £900 million. The July 1997 budget measure is scored as increasing revenues in 1999–2000 by £5.4 billion. The latter is often described as a £5 billion pension "raid." However, only £3.5 billion of the £5.4 billion came from pension funds, while the remainder came from other exempt taxpayers such as charities. In addition, the concurrent cut in the main corporate tax rate from 33 percent to 31 percent, and a further cut to 30 percent in 1999, would have boosted the incomes of pension funds by up to £1 billion, reducing the net cost to pension funds to £2.5 billion or less. For analysis of the impact of the July 1997 budget, see Bond, Devereux, and Klemm (2005).

10. See House of Commons, *Daily Hansard—Written Answers*, February 20, 2012, column 643W, http://www.publications.parliament.uk/pa/cm201212/cmhansrd/cm120220/text/120220w0006.htm#12022110000486.

11. Source: Authors' calculations using data from HMRC Statistics, table 2.5, https://www.gov.uk/government/statistics/income-tax-liabilities-by-income-range.

12. See note 14.

13. To prevent charges of retrospective taxation, the government could consider exempting pension savings already in place that would exceed the cap. The last Labour government did the equivalent when it introduced the new lifetime cap on pension savings but did not apply the new cap to existing pension funds whose value exceeded it.

14. The government previously estimated the total cost of the tax-free lump sum at around £2.5 billion (it was formerly in HMRC Statistics table 7.9, as cited in, for example, footnote 20 of Lloyd and Nicholson (2011), but HMRC no longer produces an estimate. Note that this £2.5 billion figure assumed that no one would change their behavior in

response to the reform and that the tax-free lump sums would otherwise be taxed at 20 percent. Based on this £2.5 billion figure, Lloyd and Nicholson (ibid.) estimated that restricting the tax-free lump sum to the then higher-rate threshold of £42,475 would raise £0.5 billion per year.

15. For an employee to contribute £100 to a pension requires earnings of £113.64 (since 12 percent employee NICs are taken out of the £113.64), which costs the employer £129.32 (since 13.8 percent employer NICs are levied on the £113.64).

References

Adam, Stuart, James Browne, and Paul Johnson. 2012. "Pensioners and the Tax and Benefit System." IFS Briefing Note No. 130. http://www.ifs.org.uk/bns/bn130.pdf.

Banks, James, Rovena Crawford, Thomas Crossley, and Carl Emmerson. 2013. "Financial Crisis Wealth Losses and Responses among Older Households in England." *Fiscal Studies* 34 (2): 231–254. http://onlinelibrary.wiley.com/doi/10.1111/j.1475-5890.2013.12004.x/epdf.

Boadway, Robin, Emma Chamberlain, and Carl Emmerson. 2010. "Taxation of Wealth and Wealth Transfers." In *Dimensions of Tax Design*, edited by James A. Mirrlees, Stuart Adam, Timothy Besley, Richard Blundell, Stephen Bond, Robert Chote, Malcolm Gammie, Paul Johnson, Gareth Myles, and James Poterba, 737–836. Oxford: Oxford University Press for Institute for Fiscal Studies. http://www.ifs.org.uk/mirrleesreview/dimensions/ch8.pdf.

Bond, Stephen, Michael Devereux, and Alexander Klemm. 2005. "Dissecting Dividend Decisions: Some Clues About the Effects of Dividend Taxation from Recent UK Reforms." IFS Working Paper No. 05/17. http://www.ifs.org.uk/publications/3422.

Browne, James 2013. "Autumn Statement Policy Measures." IFS Post Autumn Statement Briefing, December 6. http://www.ifs.org.uk/budgets/as2013/as2013_james.pdf.

Cannon, Edmund, Ian Tonks, and Rob Yuille. 2016. "The Effects of the Reform to Compulsion on Annuity Demand." *National Institute Economic Review* 237 (1): R47–54.

Her Majesty's Revenue and Customs (HMRC). 2015. https://www.gov.uk/government/uploads/system/uploads/attachment_data/file/487119/Dec15_expenditure_reliefs_Final.xlsx.pdf.

Her Majesty's Treasury. 2015. "Strengthening the Incentive to Save: A Consultation on Pensions Tax Relief." https://www.gov.uk/government/uploads/system/uploads/attachment_data/file/442159/Strengthening_the_incentive_to_save_consultation_print_.pdf.

House of Commons. 2012. *Daily Hansard—Written Answers*, February 20, column 613W, http://www.publications.parliament.uk/pa/cm201212/cmhansrd/cm120220/text/120220w0006.htm#12022110000486.

Independent Public Service Pensions Commission. 2011. *Final Report*. https://www.gov.uk/government/publications/independent-public-service-pensions-commission-final-report-by-lord-hutton.

Johnson, Michael. 2015. "Time for TEE—the Unification of Pensions and ISAs." Centre for Policy Studies. http://www.cps.org.uk/blog/q/date/2015/04/07/time-for-tee-the-unification-of-pensions-and-isas/.

Lloyd, Mark, and Cris Nicholson. 2011. "A Relief for Some: How to Stop Lump Sum Tax Relief Favouring the Wealthy." Centre Forum Report. http://www.centreforum.org/assets/pubs/a-relief-for-some.pdf.

Meade, James 1978. *The Structure and Reform of Direct Taxation: Report of a Committee Chaired by Professor J. E. Meade.* London: George Allen & Unwin for Institute for Fiscal Studies. http://www.ifs.org.uk/publications/3433.

Mirrlees, James A., Stuart Adam, Timothy Besley, Richard Blundell, Stephen Bond, Robert Chote, Malcolm Gammie, Paul Johnson, Gareth Myles, and James M. Poterba, eds. 2011. *Tax by Design: The Mirrlees Review—Volume 2.* Oxford: Oxford University Press.

Office for National Statistics (ONS). 2012a. *Total Wealth, 2008/10.* http://www.ons.gov.uk/ons/dcp171776_271539.pdf.

Office for National Statistics (ONS). 2012b. *Annual Survey of Hours and Earnings Pensions Tables*, 2012 edition. http://www.ons.gov.uk/ons/rel/ashe/annual-survey-of-hours-and-earnings-pension-tables/index.html.

Pensions Policy Institute. 2013. *Tax Relief for Pension Saving in the UK.* http://www.pensionspolicyinstitute.org.uk/default.asp?p=12&publication=0347&.

Wakefield, Matthew. 2009. "How Much Do We Tax the Return to Saving?" IFS Briefing Note No. BN82. https://www.ifs.org.uk/bns/bn82.pdf.

Yoo, Kwang-Yeol, and Alain de Serres. 2004. "Tax Treatment of Private Pension Savings in OECD Countries." *OECD Economic Studies* 39:73–110.

10 The US Tax Preference for Retirement Savings

Gary Burtless and Eric Koepcke

10.1 Introduction

The private retirement system in the United States consists of employer-based retirement savings programs and Individual Retirement Accounts (IRAs). The public retirement system consists of mandatory social insurance—Social Security—and a small means-tested program known as Supplemental Security Income (SSI). Using one yardstick, the private system now provides substantially more resources than the public system to support Americans' old-age consumption. In 2015, benefit payouts and taxable withdrawals from the private system amounted to more than US$1.45 trillion (table 10.1). In the same year, benefit payments from the three main public programs—Social Security, Railroad Retirement, and SSI—totaled less than US$1 trillion. The financial dominance of the private retirement system represents a marked departure from US experience in the earlier post–World War II period. In 1995, payouts from the public and private systems were approximately equal, while in 1990, total public retirement benefits substantially exceeded payouts from the private system.

The increasing accumulation of household claims in the private retirement system is stunning. According to the Federal Reserve, in 1980, private retirement assets accumulated by workers and retirees accounted for just 16 percent of the net worth of the household and nonprofit sector (figure 10.1).[1] By 2015, this share had more than doubled to almost one-third of net worth. If unfunded liabilities of private and government employee defined benefit pension plans are subtracted from this total, in 1980 the private pension system held less than 10 percent of the net worth of households and nonprofit organizations. In 2015, it held tangible assets amounting to over 27 percent, or US$23.7 trillion. In comparison,

Table 10.1
Payouts of US pension and retirement savings system, by source, 1990–2015.

	Billions of 2015 dollars					
	1990	1995	2000	2005	2010	2015
Source of payout						
Public pensions	**$435.3**	**$521.3**	**$581.6**	**$665.1**	**$808.4**	**$940.7**
Supplemental Security Income, federal and state	27.1	39.7	41.8	45.5	53.0	56.7
Social Security and Railroad Retirement pensions	408.1	481.6	539.8	619.6	755.3	884.0
Employer-sponsored pensions	**369.8**	**465.1**	**715.3**	**746.2**	**896.3**	**1,209.0**
Private company DB plan benefit payments and withdrawals	107.8	122.1	168.0	162.2	182.7	262.4
Public employer DB plan benefit payments and withdrawals	154.1	191.8	238.2	294.4	362.9	426.4
Private and public DC plan benefit payments and withdrawals	107.8	151.2	309.1	289.6	350.6	520.2
Individual Retirement Account (IRA) flows: Taxable distributions	**28.5**	**53.5**	**130.4**	**133.3**	**209.4**	**267.9**
Total benefit payments, withdrawals, and taxable distributions	**$833.6**	**$1,039.9**	**$1,427.3**	**$1,544.5**	**$1,914.0**	**$2,417.6**
Percentage of US personal income	*10.5*	*11.5*	*12.5*	*12.3*	*14.2*	*15.6*

Sources: US Department of Commerce, Bureau of Economic Analysis, National Income and Product Accounts (October 2016 release); US Department of the Treasury, Statistics of Income (accessed November 2016); and authors' estimates.
Notes: Estimates converted to 2015 constant dollars using the chained personal consumption expenditure deflator. DB = defined benefit; DC = defined contribution.

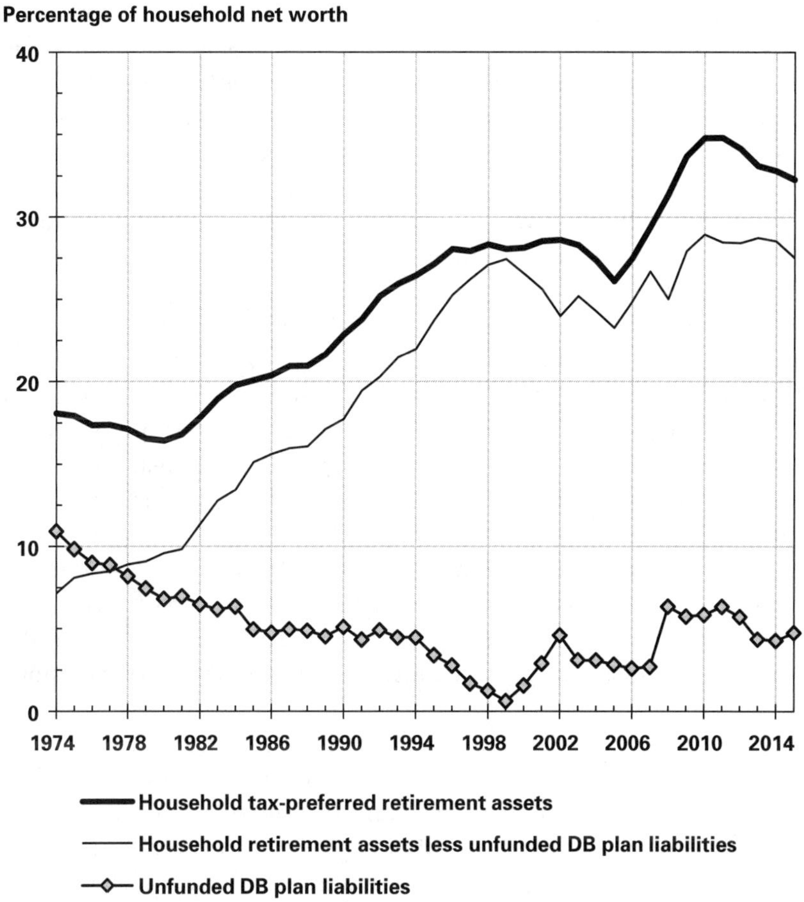

Figure 10.1
Pension assets, excluding social security, as percentage of household and nonprofit sector net worth, 1974–2015. *Sources*: Authors' tabulations using Board of Governors of the Federal Reserve System, "Financial Accounts of the United States," release, September 16, 2016; and Investment Company Institute, *The U.S. Retirement Market, Second Quarter 2016*.

households' net equity in real estate, including owner-occupied homes, amounted to just US$12.1 trillion.

The growth of the private retirement system was spurred by a generous tax preference for saving inside pension accounts. For most qualified retirement plans, taxation of labor earnings that are contributed to the plan is deferred until benefits are paid out in retirement. Workers who expect to be in a lower tax bracket when retired thus derive an important advantage from saving in a qualified plan. In addition, in all tax-preferred retirement plans, the investment income earned on assets in the plan is not counted in workers' current taxable income. In traditional retirement plans, investment earnings are only taxable when they are withdrawn from the plans in retirement.

US tax law provides a wide variety of qualified retirement savings options for individual workers, for the self-employed, and for firms that wish to provide retirement plans to their workers. However, private employers are under no legal obligation to offer a retirement savings program. Many of them, especially smaller firms, do not offer any retirement plan. Furthermore, in many workplaces, workers' participation in defined contribution retirement plans is voluntary. As a result, overall participation in the workplace retirement system is well below 100 percent, especially in private establishments. For private employers with fewer than 50 workers, the offer rate of workplace pensions is below 50 percent (US Bureau of Labor Statistics 2016). If workers do not hold jobs in a workplace where retirement contributions are automatically made on their behalf, their tax-preferred retirement savings will probably be low, even though the tax code permits them to make individual tax-preferred contributions into IRAs.

This chapter considers the evolution of asset holdings in the private retirement system and the generosity of the tax preference offered to savings accumulated therein. Section 10.2 presents the organization and evolution of the US retirement savings system. Section 10.3 develops the value of the retirement savings tax preference. Section 10.4 estimates the value of the tax preference to individual workers. Section 10.5 discusses the limitations of tax preferences as a policy tool, and section 10.6 presents conclusions.

10.2 Organization and Evolution of the US Retirement Savings System

For many years, the US retirement system was described as a three-legged stool, consisting of compulsory social insurance, employer-sponsored pensions, and private household savings. The most important government component of the public system is Social Security, known formally as Old-Age, Survivors, and Disability Insurance (OASDI). This federal program provides compulsory social insurance coverage to all private sector workers, including the self-employed, as well as to most government employees. In addition, the public system includes a much smaller and less costly program called SSI, aimed at guaranteeing modest monthly income to aged Americans who have little income and virtually no wealth.

10.2.1 Public Retirement Programs

Both Social Security and the precursor of today's SSI program were established during the Great Depression. Before that, only about 15 percent of industrial workers were covered by a company pension. Just 5 percent of the aged collected a pension (Social Security Administration 2016b). One response to the crisis was to create means-tested programs for the indigent, including the low-income elderly, and to establish social insurance for the provision of future pensions to industrial workers.

Collection of payroll contributions for OASDI is closely coordinated with collection of the US personal income tax. Wage earners covered by Social Security pay 6.2 percent of their pretax salaries to the program, up to an annual maximum taxed salary of US$127,200 in 2017.[2] A worker's income tax liabilities are calculated based on total wages, including the contribution to Social Security. Employers contribute an identical annual amount, so the combined contribution is 12.4 percent of taxed wages. For equivalent amounts of labor income, self-employed workers pay the same combined tax to Social Security as wage earners.

From the inception of Social Security until 1983, Social Security benefit payments were excluded from the federal income tax base. Since 1984, a portion of benefits has been included in taxable income, with the fraction that is included tied to the pensioner's total income. For lower-income pensioners, Social Security benefits continue to be wholly excluded from taxable income. Up to 85 percent of benefits are now included in taxable income for moderate- and high-income taxpayers.

Employer and employee contributions to traditional workplace retirement plans are not considered currently taxable income under the income tax to the employee. Instead, these contributions will be included in workers' taxable income when they withdraw the funds in retirement. Unlike employer contributions, however, worker contributions into a retirement plan are considered currently taxable earnings for purposes of calculating the Social Security and Medicare payroll tax. The combined employee and employer payroll tax for Social Security and Medicare in 2017 is 15.3 percent on wages below US$127,200 and 2.9 percent on wages above that amount. Given the high payroll tax on employee contributions to defined contribution plans, it may seem surprising that workers and employers would establish a workplace savings plan partly funded with worker contributions. If instead workplace retirement benefits were fully funded with employer contributions, both the employer and the worker could avoid paying the payroll tax on the employee's contribution. However, a large share of defined contribution plans established in the past four decades included the option of voluntary contributions from participating workers. In many of these plans, workers' voluntary contributions may account for most or even all of the plans' funding.[3]

10.2.2 The Private Retirement System

Most of the growth in employer pension coverage has occurred since World War II, when the great majority of workers began to pay income taxes. Not surprisingly, the development of workplace pensions was heavily influenced by the provisions of pension and income tax law and employers' eagerness to ensure their plans legally qualify for tax preferences.

The two broad types of workplace retirement plans are defined benefit and defined contribution pensions. Both obtain the same basic tax preference, but the regulatory oversight of defined benefit plans, for which benefits are partly guaranteed by the government, is more complicated than that of defined contribution plans, for which no such guarantee is provided. When the government offers a guarantee of future private defined benefit pension benefits, it needs to assure taxpayers that assets accumulated in each plan will be sufficient to pay for the promised future benefits. If the sponsoring firm should go bankrupt and leave the plan with too few assets, the federal Pension Benefit Guaranty Corporation (PBGC) is responsible for paying the portion of the pension benefit that is guaranteed under law. Consequently, a costly regulatory and oversight regime is needed to assure that pension plan reserves are large enough to cover expected benefits. In addition, the federal government must calculate and collect insurance premiums from covered defined benefit plans.

Regulatory oversight of defined contribution plans is more straightforward. In these plans, employers, employees, or both make regular contributions into employees' pension accounts. The money accumulated in each account is invested in assets selected by the employer or by the worker, and the accumulation is credited with the return earned on the assets. The employee receives the total accumulation in the account upon retirement, where the amount of the accumulation depends on the employer's and the worker's previous contributions and the returns earned. Because neither the employer nor the government offers any guarantee of investment performance, the risk of poor investment returns is borne by workers. This contrasts with the distribution of risk under defined benefit plans, where the sponsoring employer bears the financial risk if assets held in the pension fund experience poor returns. In some defined contribution retirement plans, retiring workers can convert part or all of their accumulation into an annuity that lasts for the life of the worker and a surviving spouse. However, many defined contribution plans do not have that option, so workers who wish to annuitize their accumulation must purchase annuities in the private insurance market. By contrast, most defined benefit plans specify their pension promise in terms of a level income payment for life, usually determined by the employee's average or final pay and years of creditable service under the plan.

To obtain the income tax preference for qualified pension plans, whether defined benefit or defined contribution, private sector employers must maintain plans that pass a nondiscrimination test showing that the benefits of the plan are broadly distributed across the relevant workforce and not concentrated on highly compensated employees.[4] Recognizing that it may be costly or burdensome for smaller employers to demonstrate that their plan passes such a test, Congress established alternative retirement savings arrangements with straightforward rules specifically for firms with fewer than 100 workers; for example, SIMPLE-IRAs. The administrative cost of establishing and maintaining these arrangements is modest.

In addition to employer-organized retirement plans, US law encourages retirement saving in IRAs. Contributions to an IRA, investment income in the account, and IRA withdrawals receive the same tax treatment as in traditional defined contribution plans. Created by the Employee Retirement Income Security Act (ERISA) in 1974, IRAs serve two main functions. First, they permit workers not covered by an employer-sponsored retirement plan to make tax-advantaged contributions into a retirement investment account. Second, IRAs offer a mechanism for workers who are leaving a pension-covered job to preserve the tax preference on retirement savings accumulated in that job. Workers who withdraw their retirement savings from a tax-preferred plan before the calendar year in which they reach 59½ years old ordinarily face a 10 percent penalty tax on the withdrawal. In addition, they must count the withdrawal as current (taxable) income in the year in which the withdrawal is made. However, if the funds from the qualified plan are transferred within 60 days into another qualifying retirement plan, including an IRA, the withdrawal is treated as a tax-free rollover.

10.2.3 Evolution of Coverage under Defined Benefit and Defined Contribution Plans

In the past four decades, the percentage of US workers covered by an employer-sponsored retirement plan changed relatively little, but the fraction covered by traditional defined benefit plans fell sharply. The workers most likely to be offered and to participate in employer plans are prime-age, full-time employees who have more than a year or two of job tenure.

All available data sources show a major decline in the proportion of pension-covered workers who are enrolled in a defined benefit plan and a corresponding rise in the proportion covered by defined contribution plans. The trend is especially strong in the private sector, where 84 percent of US payroll jobs are concentrated. The Employee Benefits Security Administration (EBSA) in the US Department of Labor collects annual informational returns about pension plans sponsored by private employers. In 1979, 84 percent of pension-covered workers in the private sector were enrolled in a defined benefit plan, possibly in combination with a supplemental defined contribution plan.[5] In that same year, 62 percent of pension-covered workers were enrolled solely in a defined benefit plan; only 16 percent of pension-covered workers were enrolled solely in a defined contribution plan. By 2011, the fraction of pension-covered workers enrolled solely in a defined contribution plan had risen to 69 percent, while the fraction enrolled solely in a defined benefit plan fell to just 7 percent. Twenty-four percent of pension-covered workers were enrolled in both types of plans, implying that only about 31 percent of all pension-covered workers were enrolled in a defined benefit plan, usually in combination with a defined contribution plan. The typical pension available to covered workers in the private sector is now a defined contribution pension rather than a defined benefit pension. In contrast, public employees of the federal government and state and local governments continue to receive pension coverage mainly under traditional defined benefit plans.

10.2.4 Preferences for Defined Contribution versus Defined Benefit Plan Design

Private employers may see several reasons for preferring a defined contribution plan over a defined benefit plan. First, the regulatory and administrative burden of ensuring that a defined benefit plan is adequately funded drives up the cost. Part of the regulatory burden is the required payment of insurance premiums to the PBGC. The burden of defined contribution plan administration is less costly, and sponsoring employers are not liable for insurance premiums.

Second, the government's requirement that defined benefit pension commitments be adequately funded imposes financing obligations on a firm that are variable and hard to predict. The obligations would be more predictable if pension reserves were invested in very safe, low-return assets. Of course, holding reserves in very safe assets increases required contributions to the plan in most years and may raise the cost of funding the pension commitment from the perspective of company managers and investors who have a moderate tolerance for risk. In practice, many companies that sponsor defined benefit plans find their required plan contributions rise sharply during and after recessions, when the price of risky assets in their portfolios falls and their plans become underfunded. These are also circumstances in which companies' cash flow and borrowing capacity fall. In contrast, companies' funding obligations for defined contribution plans are much easier to predict.

Finally, workers may have different tastes for retirement income. Some potential employees may be attracted by a generous plan, while others might prefer a pay package that emphasizes current cash wages over deferred compensation. Modern defined contribution pension plans can easily accommodate these differences in worker preferences.

Although risk-averse business owners may have good reasons for preferring defined contribution pensions over defined benefit ones, it is widely assumed—though not necessarily among economists—that rational workers should prefer a defined benefit plan. The case for traditional defined benefit pensions usually rests on the distribution of financial risks. Since most employers have deeper pockets and better access to credit than their employees, many worker advocates assume that the risks of poor financial market returns should be borne by employers. In addition, advocates of defined benefit pensions note that these assets are managed by experts, whereas investments in defined contribution plans are likely to be selected by workers themselves, few of whom know much about asset selection or allocation. Investment experts also can calculate with tolerable accuracy the annual contribution needed to pay for the promised benefit. Many workers cannot calculate the savings rate they need to support a comfortable old-age income. Finally, defined benefit plans offer the option of annuity payouts, which insures retirees against the risk of outliving their savings.

Except for the distribution of financial market risk between employers and employees, defined contribution plans could in principle enjoy all of these defined benefit plan advantages. Workers' contributions could be pooled and professionally managed; actuaries could calculate contribution rates to produce comfortable old-age incomes; and accumulations could be converted at retirement into life annuities. However, in most modern-day defined contribution plans in the United States, the total contribution rate, the selection of assets (usually from a menu of options chosen by the plan sponsor), and asset allocation are decisions made by individual workers rather than by experts. Annuitization of the worker's final defined contribution fund balance is not even an option offered in most defined contribution plans.

In one respect, modern defined contribution plans have a key advantage. Workers who accumulate contributions under a defined contribution plan can ordinarily keep them even if their tenure is interrupted by a dismissal. All of the employee's own contributions plus the investment income on those contributions are immediately vested; that is, owned by the worker. An employer's contribution to the employee account may not fully vest immediately, but by law it must become vested within a specified period. Thus, a worker's accumulation in a defined contribution plan is transparent and easily portable. When the employee leaves the company, the assets can be left in the sponsoring employer's defined contribution plan, rolled over into the defined contribution plan of a later employer, or rolled over into the worker's IRA.

The situation under a traditional defined benefit plan is usually more hazardous to participating workers. Workers employed for a full career under a traditional defined benefit plan ordinarily become entitled to a pension that replaces a predictable percentage of the worker's final career wage. When a worker quits or is laid off, the ultimate replacement rate can fall far short of the replacement rate advertised in the pension plan formula. One reason is that the financial value of a worker's pension rights under traditional defined benefit plans is often highly nonlinear in relation to the worker's job tenure (Burtless

2009). During the first few years of tenure, the value of pension rights may be small and grow very slowly. As workers approach the early or standard retirement age under the plan or attain the tenure requirement for an immediate pension, their pension rights become much more valuable. Under traditional defined benefit plan schedules, workers with short or even intermediate job tenures may not accumulate pension rights with much current value if they are dismissed from their job. Furthermore, except in cash balance defined benefit plans, it may be difficult to make the pension rights in the defined benefit plan portable. Thus, many workers enrolled in traditional plans face the risk that their pension rights will have little tangible value if their years of service are interrupted well before retirement age.

On balance, it is unclear whether the risks facing participants in a traditional defined benefit plan are greater than or less than those facing defined contribution plan participants. The types of risks in the two kinds of plans differ. The welfare consequences of the two kinds of risks are uncertain and undoubtedly vary across industries, occupations, and individual employers.

10.3 The Value of the Retirement Savings Tax Preference

An important goal of the tax preference for retirement saving is to increase the attractiveness of such saving and thereby increase the percentage of old-age consumption financed out of worker and employer savings rather than public transfers. The following analysis evaluates alternative savings options in terms of their effects on workers' capacity to pay for their old-age consumption.[6] It distinguishes between two basic savings options offered under the federal tax code: saving in an ordinary investment account and saving in a tax-preferred pension account, such as an employer-provided pension plan or an IRA. It then considers investments in two basic asset classes, bonds and corporate stock (equities), since the tax treatments of these two assets, if held outside a tax-preferred account, differ.

10.3.1 Theoretical Model

Under federal tax law, ordinary labor and capital income is subject to income tax in the year it is received. Workers who save part of their current gross wage earnings, say the sum S, in an ordinary investment account in year a will be able to consume the following amount in a future year, b:

$$C_b^1 = S \cdot (1 - \tau_{wa}) \prod_{i=a+1}^{b} [1 + r(1 - \tau_{ki})], \tag{10.1}$$

where C_b^1 = consumption in year b out of a standard investment account; S = amount set aside from pretax earnings for savings; r = gross annual rate of return on savings; τ_{wi} = marginal tax on ordinary income in year i; τ_{ki} = marginal tax on capital income in year i; a = age at which the contribution is made; and b = age when savings are consumed.

The portion of gross earnings set aside in a standard investment account is taxed in the year it is earned, say at age a, leaving only $S \cdot (1 - \tau_{wa})$ for initial investment in the account. In years between the initial investment and the year savings are consumed, say at age b, the investment earnings in the account are subject to annual income taxes at rate τ_{ki}, the income tax rate applied on capital income in year i. The annual after-tax return on investments held in the account is therefore $r \cdot (1 - \tau_{ki})$.

The US income tax code has long provided partial relief from capital income taxation when investment returns are accrued inside a pension account. The worker's labor earnings and investment income on savings held in the account are only subject to income tax when money is withdrawn in retirement. Thus, consumption from savings set aside in the pension account, C_b^2, will be

$$C_b^2 = S \cdot (1 - \tau_{wb}) \cdot (1 + r)^{b-a}. \tag{10.2}$$

In a Roth retirement savings arrangement, after-tax labor income is deposited in the retirement account and investment income in the account, and withdrawals from the account are never taxed again. Consumption from savings set aside in a Roth account, C_b^3, will thus be

$$C_b^3 = S \cdot (1 - \tau_{wa}) \cdot (1 + r)^{b-a}. \tag{10.3}$$

If the worker's tax rates in the contribution and consumption years are identical, $\tau_{wa} = \tau_{wb}$, the worker's retirement consumption is identical under the two arrangements. The Roth arrangement is more advantageous if $\tau_{wa} < \tau_{wb}$, whereas the standard retirement plan yields higher retirement consumption when $\tau_{wa} > \tau_{wb}$. The remainder of this chapter focuses on the tax preference provided to workers who enroll in standard retirement plans, since an overwhelming share of retirement savings has been accumulated under the standard tax preference.[7]

In comparison with accumulating savings in an ordinary investment account, the proportional consumption gain from saving in a qualified pension plan is

$$\frac{C_b^2}{C_b^1}=\frac{(1-\tau_{wb})\prod_{i=a+1}^{b}(1+r)}{(1-\tau_{wa})\prod_{i=a+1}^{b}[1+r(1-\tau_{ki})]}. \tag{10.4}$$

When $\tau_{wa}\equiv\tau_{wb}\equiv\tau_{ki}\equiv\tau$ for all i, then

$$\frac{C_b^2}{C_b^1}=\left[\frac{1+r}{1+r(1-\tau)}\right]^{b-a}. \tag{10.4a}$$

The proportional advantage of saving in a pension account as opposed to a standard (not tax-preferred) savings account rises with increases in the marginal tax rate, the rate of return on savings, and the number of years during which money is held in the savings account. If $\tau_{wa}\equiv\tau_{ki}\equiv\tau$ but $\tau_{wa}\neq\tau_{wb}$, then

$$\frac{C_b^2}{C_b^1}=\left(\frac{1-\tau_{wb}}{1-\tau_{wa}}\right)\left[\frac{1+r}{1+r(1-\tau_{wa})}\right]^{b-a}. \tag{10.4b}$$

Normally, the tax rate while working is expected to be higher than the rate after retirement, $\tau_{wa}>\tau_{wb}$. This increases the consumption gain from accumulating savings in a pension account rather than a standard savings account. If instead workers expect to face a higher tax rate in retirement than when they are employed, it may be advantageous to accumulate savings outside a pension plan; that is, to pay taxes on labor income before it is deposited in a savings account rather than when it is withdrawn in retirement.

10.3.2 Assessing the Value of the Pension Tax Preference

Every year, the US Office of Management and Budget and congressional Joint Committee on Taxation (JCT) offer estimates of the aggregate value of the federal tax preference for pensions. The estimates account for two components of the total tax expenditure on this preference: the failure of the government to collect income taxes on current labor compensation placed in worker pension accounts and the failure to collect taxes on the investment income earned inside pension accounts.

After estimating these two items, budget analysts subtract income taxes collected on money that is withdrawn from tax-preferred pension accounts. Measured in this way, total tax expenditures for the exclusion of pension contributions and pension investment income represent one of the most expensive tax preferences in the income tax code. According to an analysis of JCT estimates, the tax preference for retirement plans was the third-largest single tax preference in 2014, amounting to about US$89 billion (Marples 2015). In comparison, direct federal outlays on the Social Security Old-Age and Survivors Insurance program (OASI) amounted to US$714 billion in 2014.

The annual cash-flow estimate of revenue loss from the pension tax preference does not provide a meaningful estimate of the value to retirement savers of the tax reduction they receive as a result of saving in a qualified retirement account rather than an ordinary investment account. Instead, it shows the difference in revenue between what is raised this year under the current law and what would have been raised if the preference had never been part of tax law but pension contributions, account balances, and withdrawals were nonetheless the same.

The analysis that follows shows how the economic value to workers of the retirement saving incentives varied over time with changes in tax laws and depending on workers' wages and the types of assets held in qualified accounts. It is often assumed that, in the absence of the pension tax preference, retirement savers would hold fully taxable assets. In fact, most retirement savers hold assets that enjoy some tax preferences of their own, such as corporate equities. Relaxing the assumption that pension assets would have otherwise been held in fully taxable accounts reduces the value of the tax preference and affects estimates of how it has changed over time. When a financial asset is held inside an ordinary investment account, capital gains earned when the asset is sold are customarily taxed at a rate below the marginal rate assessed on other household income.[8] Although the amount of the capital gains tax concession has varied over time, some concession has been provided in the US tax code nearly every year since 1921. For example, in 2015, taxpayers paid 40–100 percent less on their long-term capital gains than they would have if the gains were taxed at taxpayers' marginal income tax rate. Furthermore, since 2003, the income tax code has provided concessionary tax rates on "qualified" dividends paid by US corporations and many foreign ones. In 2015, these concessionary tax rates were identical to those imposed on long-term capital gains.

Whatever the theory behind the special tax treatment of dividends and capital gains, there is no distinction within qualified pension accounts between holding bonds and stocks; both accrue free of income tax. So the value of the pension tax concession per dollar of pretax income is typically smaller if individuals hold stocks than if they hold bonds. If the concessionary tax rate on capital gains and dividends is low enough, workers may gain little benefit from building up stock market wealth inside pension funds. To see this, consider the ratio of retirement consumption out of a pension account and out of an ordinary investment account in equation (10.4). Assume the marginal tax on investment income is constant throughout the worker's career and is below the ordinary income tax rate ($\tau_{ki} \equiv \tau_k$ and $\tau_k < \tau_{wi}$ for all i). Then

$$\frac{C_b^2}{C_b^1} = \left(\frac{1-\tau_{wb}}{1-\tau_{wa}}\right)\left[\frac{1+r}{1+r(1-\tau_k)}\right]^{b-a}. \tag{10.4c}$$

Whether it is advantageous to hold assets in a pension account clearly depends on the relationship among τ_k, τ_{wa}, and τ_{wb}. For workers who face an ordinary marginal tax rate of 10 percent or 15 percent, the 2015 tax on investment income from stocks paying qualified dividends was 0 percent. When $\tau_k = 0$, the choice of investing in a pension or ordinary investment account depends only on the worker's marginal tax rate when the wage is earned and when the money will be withdrawn for consumption. If $\tau_{wb} < \tau_{wa}$, it is advantageous to hold stocks inside a pension account; if $\tau_{wb} > \tau_{wa}$, it is advantageous to hold stocks in an ordinary investment account; and if $\tau_{wb} = \tau_{wa}$, the worker's retirement consumption is identical regardless of where the investment is held. As changes in the tax code increase the preference for investment income from assets held outside pension accounts, they reduce the financial advantages of accumulating those assets inside pension accounts.

10.4 Value of the Tax Preference to Individual Workers

To assess the value of the pension tax preference for a given worker, it is assumed that the worker first chooses an asset class in which to invest and then determines the investment account alternative that offers the highest consumption payoff in retirement. The value of the tax preference can then be measured as the reduction in the lifetime present value of income taxes collected on the worker's contribution to the account compared with the taxes that would be owed if the investment occurred outside a pension. To operationalize this concept, workers must forecast the marginal tax they will face, both on ordinary income and on the investment income they would receive if assets were held outside the pension account. This forecast must cover each year from the year wage income is originally earned to the year the money is withdrawn for consumption. Obviously, this kind of forecast requires a large amount of very uncertain information that few workers are likely to possess. This analysis assumes, unrealistically, that workers believe the current tax rules and schedule will remain unchanged over the remainder of their lives and those of their spouses. A worker must also forecast future taxable income. The worker's marginal tax rate in a particular future year will be determined by the tax schedule in that year and the worker's taxable income.

Calculations were performed for representative workers under five different tax laws in effect between 1985 and 2015. The differences across the tax laws may indicate the kinds of tax changes that workers can anticipate over a career. The 1985 law had high top marginal tax rates but contained generous rules that sharply reduced the percentage of long-term capital gains included in taxable income. A major congressional overhaul of the tax code in 1986 drastically reduced the number of tax brackets and cut the top marginal tax rate from 50 percent to 28 percent. Equally important, the 1986 tax reform eliminated the tax preference for long-term capital gains. All capital income, regardless of its form, was subject to the same marginal income tax rate, and this rate was the same as that applied to the taxpayer's wage income. Between 1988 and 2000, a variety of provisions in the tax code were changed, reversing some of the reforms passed in 1986. By 2000, the top marginal tax rate had been raised from 33 percent to 39.6 percent. Long-term capital gains were once again subject to a lower tax rate than that imposed on ordinary income. Starting in 2001, the marginal tax rate schedule was lowered once again, and the tax concession for long-term capital gains was modestly increased. The 2003 tax law was the first one in which qualified stock dividends were subject to a special concessionary rate below the rate applied on ordinary income. In 2013, tax provisions of the Affordable Care Act raised the payroll tax rate on top earners and, more importantly, imposed an additional 3.8 percent tax on the investment income earned by top income recipients. In the same year, the top marginal income tax rate was restored to 39.6 percent.

These variations in the tax code affect the value of the pension tax preference, though in some cases only for a small number of retirement savers. The basic structure of the pension tax preference remained unchanged over the entire period. The limits on total annual contributions to most types of pension accounts, such as IRAs and 401(k) plans, also varied during the period analyzed. Our analysis only considers the decision of workers to contribute a modest sum, say US$100, to a pension account. New investments this small are not affected by the changes in contribution limits.

10.4.1 Representative Workers

Our analysis focuses on the tax preference available to a handful of representative workers. Lifetime earnings profiles estimated with individual earnings records in the Social Security files are used to forecast workers' current and future labor income. The Social Security Administration publishes earnings estimates, by year of age from 21 through 64, of the relative earnings of four representative workers (Clingman and Nichols 2007). Workers are classified as having "very low," "low," "medium," or "high" lifetime earnings, and their earnings at each age are measured relative to the economy-wide average wage in that year. All of the lifetime earnings profiles show the familiar humpback pattern that characterizes the typical age-earnings profile. In addition, workers' earnings change every year because of economy-wide growth in average earnings. The career-average earnings of the four workers are similar to those of earners at the twelfth, twenty-fifth, fifty-sixth, and eighty-first percentiles of the lifetime US earnings distribution. Each worker in the simulation is assigned one of these four lifetime earnings profiles.

To calculate taxable income and hence marginal tax rates at a given age, it is necessary to predict other components of family income besides the worker's wages. For married workers, the most important additional source of family income is usually their spouse's labor income. Four alternative tax situations are simulated for married workers. A married worker may have a spouse who is a nonearner; who earns one-half of the annual wage of the worker; who earns exactly the same annual wage; or who earns twice the annual wage of the worker. Our analysis simulates the tax positions of workers with four career earnings patterns (very low, low, medium, and high) and in five possible family situations (single, married / zero-earnings spouse, married / spouse with one-half of own earnings, married / spouse with equal earnings, and married / spouse with twice own earnings).

The procedures, described more fully in Burtless and Toder (2010), allow predictions of earners' taxable incomes for every age of a working career (ages 21 through 64) and the first year of retirement (age 65). Taxable income at 65 includes the taxable portion of retirees' Social Security benefits, assumed to be first claimed at that age. If it is assumed that all of the worker's private retirement nest egg is consumed at age 65, it is straightforward to calculate the relevant marginal tax rates that would apply to earned income, interest income, dividends, and long-term capital gains at successive ages up through 65. Also considered are the taxes workers face if they choose to convert their savings into a level annuity that begins at age 65 and continues until they die. Workers who accumulate their retirement savings in a pension account convert their accumulation into an annuity contract held inside their retirement plan. Only the annual annuity payments are taxed, and they are fully taxable. Workers who accumulate savings outside a pension account purchase their annuities with after-tax dollars, and their annuity withdrawals are subject to special tax rules, which are taken into account. It is assumed that when single workers retire, they convert their accumulation into a nominal, single-life, level annuity. Married workers purchase joint survivor annuities. The annuity makes level monthly payments until the longer-lived spouse dies. In all these calculations, it is assumed that both workers and their spouses survive to their sixty-fifth birthday. After that age, retirees face a rising probability that they and their spouse will die in successive future years. Social Security Administration mortality estimates are used to calculate the probability of death at successive ages (Bell and Miller 2005) and to calculate the price of an annuity.

10.4.2 Income Flows from Assets

An overwhelming share of US tax-preferred retirement savings is invested in equities, bonds and other interest-bearing assets, and insurance contracts (table 10.2). A modest percentage of pension holdings is invested in real estate. To compare the taxes that workers pay on a marginal contribution into either a tax-preferred pension account or an alternative investment account, the investment flows produced by different assets must be defined. The analysis is simplified by assuming that both equities and bonds generate a steady rate of return over time. Bonds are assumed to generate an annual nominal return of 5 percent, and stocks are assumed to produce annual returns of 8 percent. Because it is assumed that workers forecast future price inflation to be an average of 2.8 percent, this is equivalent to assuming that real bond returns will average 2.2 percent and real stock returns

Table 10.2
Asset allocations of investments held in IRAs and public and private pension funds, 2006–2014.

	Percentage of total assets					*2006–2014 average*
	2006	2008	2010	2012	2014	
Bonds or other interest-bearing assets	30	41	36	38	34	*36*
Equities of US and foreign companies	59	47	53	51	56	*53*
Insurance contracts	7	7	7	7	6	*7*
Real estate and other	4	5	4	5	4	*5*

Sources: Authors' calculations based on Board of Governors of the Federal Reserve System, Financial Accounts of the United States, and Investment Company Institute (various years).

will average 5.2 percent over the worker's remaining investment horizon. The stock return forecast is close to the geometric mean real return on large-capitalization stocks between 1965 and 2015. The bond return is close to the average post–World War II real return on a bond portfolio equally split between investment-quality corporate bonds and 10-year Treasury securities. To simplify the analysis, it is assumed that all returns on a bond portfolio are received as taxable interest payments; bond investors do not obtain any capital gains on their investments.

If equities are held inside a pension fund, it does not matter how equity returns are split between dividends and equity price appreciation. However, when stocks are held in an ordinary investment account, the split between dividend and capital gains returns can have an appreciable impact on after-tax returns. Long-term capital gains historically have been taxed more lightly than dividends. In addition, savers who own stocks in an ordinary investment account can choose when to realize capital gains, delaying realizations when their marginal tax rate is high and realizing capital gains when their tax rate is low. To reflect the important difference between the two kinds of equity returns, the tax preference for pensions is estimated when investments are made in (1) stocks with high capital gains and no dividends, (2) stocks with no capital gains and high dividends, and (3) stocks that provide a 2.5 percent annual dividend and generate enough capital gains to produce a total nominal annual return of 8.0 percent. In each case, the total nominal return on stocks is 8.0 percent.

Even if capital gains are heavily favored in the tax code, the tax law still provides an incentive for investors who hold stocks outside a pension to defer their realization of capital gains as long as possible. Since many retirement savers hold stocks in mutual fund accounts, this may not be practical. Most mutual fund managers periodically realize some capital gains income to achieve the fund's investment objectives. In this case, retirement savers who hold the mutual fund outside a pension or insurance account must report the capital gains income on their income tax returns and pay capital gains taxes. In addition, some investors outside mutual funds will realize gains to rebalance their portfolios. This simulation assumes that one-third of past unrealized capital gains are realized each year and that investors who hold assets in ordinary investment accounts pay the long-term capital gains tax on these realizations.

10.4.3 Estimated Tax Preferences under a Single Tax Law

The change in the present discounted value of the tax liability on the gross wage contribution invested in the account is reported herein. It equals the sum of the initial tax on the wage, the present value of taxes on future investment income from any portion of the wage that is saved, and the present value of taxes on future withdrawals from accumulated assets. The retirement saver has the option of directing US$100 of gross wage income into alternative investment accounts. If the contribution out of gross wages is invested in a standard investment account, the worker must pay the relevant marginal tax rate on the US$100 before it is invested in the selected asset. If instead the contribution is placed in a tax-preferred pension account, all of the US$100 is available for initial investment. Thereafter, the investment income is subject to the special tax rules pertaining to the particular asset and to the particular type of investment account selected; recall equations (10.1)–(10.3). All lifetime tax payments are discounted to the age when the contribution out of wage income is made. Future tax payments are discounted using the long-term predicted return on the asset in which contributions are invested. This means that future taxes on a bond investment are discounted at 5 percent per year, while future taxes on an equity investment are discounted at 8 percent per year.[9] Once savers convert their retirement nest egg into an annuity at age 65, the discount rate is reduced to reflect the lower expected rate of return on the assets that back the annuity. Since insurance companies are assumed to hold only the safest bonds, mostly Treasury securities, to back their annuities, the assumed discount rate after age 65 matches the lower interest rate on these very safe securities, or 4.5 percent.

The tax savings enjoyed by pension investors under the 2015 tax law are illustrated in figure 10.2. The top panel shows the cumulative effective tax rate on a worker's gross earnings depending on whether funds are placed in an ordinary investment account or in a tax-preferred pension account. In each case, the worker's savings are invested in bonds that yield a 5 percent pretax return. To calculate the tax rate that applies to gross wages, it is assumed that the worker earns the medium wage and is married to someone who earns twice the medium wage. The cumulative marginal tax rate is computed under the assumption that the 2015 tax rules remain in effect throughout the worker's lifetime. The cumulative effective tax rate is shown for contributions made at successive ages from 21 through 64.

The top panel in figure 10.2 has four lines: two show the cumulative tax rates on contributions when all the accumulation at age 65 is withdrawn and immediately consumed, and two show cumulative tax rates when the accumulation is converted into an annuity. In the case of bonds held inside a standard investment account, conversion of savings into an annuity increases the cumulative tax burden compared with the situation where all private retirement savings are consumed at age 65. Even though withdrawals from an annuity purchased with after-tax dollars are more lightly taxed than withdrawals purchased from an annuity purchased with before-tax earnings, all of the tax payments after age 65 represent an additional tax burden on the worker above and beyond the burden the worker would bear if savings in the account were entirely consumed at age 65.[10] In contrast, when the worker's savings are held inside a pension account, the tax deferral on wage and investment income is extended for a number of years, reducing the present discounted value of taxes paid. In addition, since the worker's marginal tax rate may decline during retirement, tax payments are further reduced.

Note that the cumulative tax on the gross wage contribution is the same, regardless of the age at contribution, in the case of investments made into a pension account. The contribution is simply taxed at the marginal tax rate on ordinary income when the retired worker is 65 or older. When gross earnings are allocated to the ordinary (not tax-preferred) account, the earnings are taxed in the year they are earned as well as in all later years. The jump in the cumulative tax rate on contributions made at age 28 compared with age 27 is because the rise in

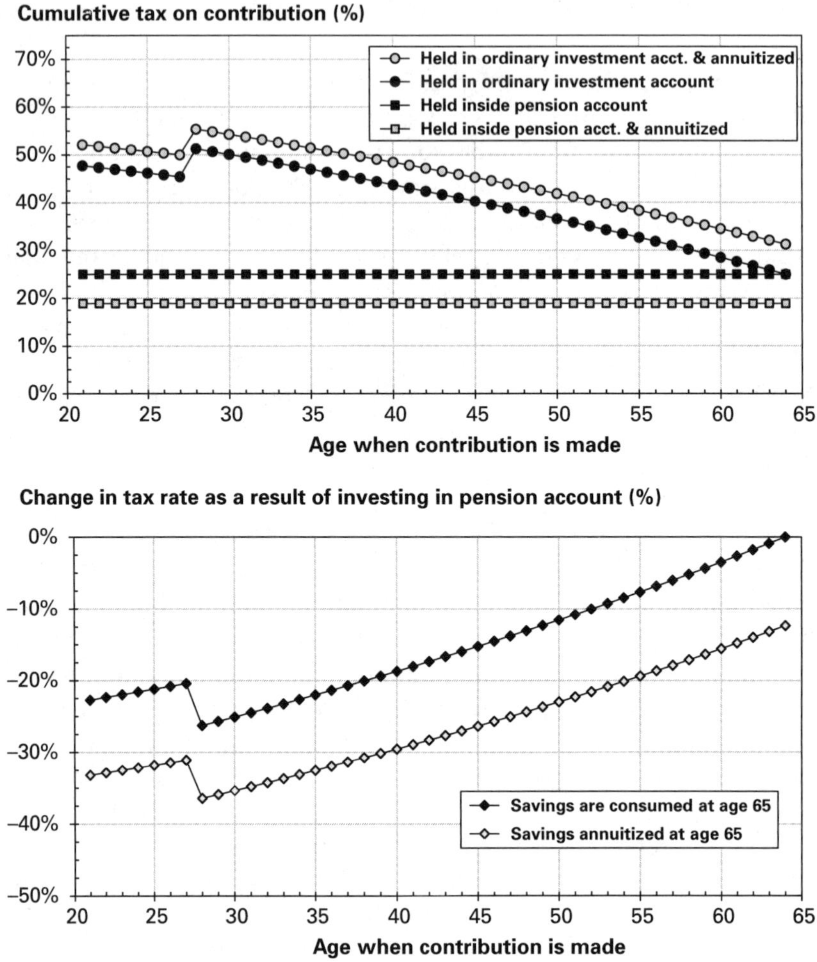

Figure 10.2
Cumulative tax on earned income invested in alternative types of bond investment accounts under 2015 tax law by worker's age at contribution.

earnings between those two ages pushes the worker into a higher marginal tax bracket, increasing the first-year tax taken out of the gross earnings contribution. When money is placed in an ordinary investment account, it is not taxed when it is withdrawn, but the investment income is subject to tax every year after the year of contribution until all funds are removed from the account.

The lower panel of figure 10.2 shows the size of the tax preference for pension investments compared with bond investments held in a non–tax-preferred account. For 30-year-old workers choosing where to place their retirement savings, the choice is straightforward. In the case of workers who consume their retirement nest egg at age 65, the cumulative tax rate will be 25 percentage points lower in the pension account than in the ordinary investment account. For older workers who plan to set aside part of their wages for retirement savings, the tax preference for accumulating savings in a pension account is smaller. At older ages, workers can take advantage of fewer years of tax-deferred investment earnings in the pension account.

10.4.4 Tax Savings with Equity Investments under the 2015 Law

Equity investment offers savers an opportunity to obtain a tax preference, even if the investment occurs in a standard investment account. For most taxpayers in 2015, this tax preference was not as generous as the one provided to savers who invested in a pension account. Figure 10.3 shows that the tax reduction workers obtain on their gross wage income depends on what type of equity they own and where they place their equity investment. The chart shows the cumulative tax that savers pay on their gross wages for three kinds of investments.[11] The flat line shows the tax paid on purchases of any kind of equity if it is held inside a pension account. The tax rate is identical to the one shown in figure 10.2 for the pension savings account containing bonds when pension savings are converted into an annuity. The three other lines in figure 10.3 refer to the cumulative tax paid on equities held in an ordinary investment account. The pension tax preference for holding equities is obviously smaller in the case of stocks with high capital gains compared with dividend-paying stocks. If the investor realized a smaller percentage of cumulative capital gains each year, the tax preference would be even smaller for these stocks.

Compared with the tax collected on an all-dividend stock, the cumulative tax on an all-capital-gains stock investment is generally lower, though the difference shrinks as workers approach retirement age. The relative tax preference for stocks generating large capital gains was even more noticeable before 2003, when the tax concession for qualified stock dividends was introduced into the tax code. Even so, workers whose tax position is illustrated in the chart would be better off locating their retirement savings inside a pension account, especially at ages immediately after 28, when a higher marginal tax rate on earnings applies.

The results in figures 10.2 and 10.3 refer to a worker who earns the medium lifetime wage and is married to a spouse who earns double

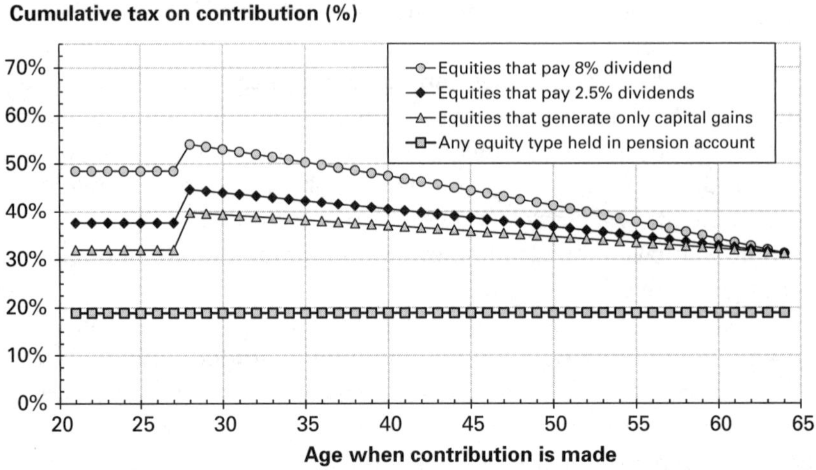

Figure 10.3
Cumulative tax on earned income invested in different kinds of equities held inside and outside pension accounts under 2015 tax law by age of worker's contribution to the account. *Source*: Authors' calculations. *Note*: Worker is assumed to convert retirement savings into a joint survivor annuity at age 65.

that wage. The tax preference varies, of course, with the worker's wage and family circumstances as well as the worker's age. The tax preference is typically larger for workers who earn higher wages (or who are married to a high-earning spouse) and can anticipate facing higher marginal tax rates over their careers. A typical finding is that the pension tax preference is considerably smaller for equity investments than it is for bond investments. Not surprisingly, the gap is particularly small in the case of stocks that generate most of their income through capital gains (Poterba, Shoven, and Sialm 2001; Dammon, Spatt, and Zhang 2004). The gap also tends to be wider for contributions made early in a worker's career; it is modest near the end of a career.

10.4.5 Tax Preferences under Successive Tax Laws

Table 10.3 shows estimates of the net tax preference for pension savings compared with the tax that would be paid on the same kind of asset if held in a standard (not tax-preferred) investment account. The increase in the tax rate on gross wage income that the worker would incur if the asset were shifted from a pension account into an ordinary investment account is calculated. The top section of the table shows the increased tax rate workers face on bonds held in an ordinary account.

Table 10.3
Tax increase if worker saves in an ordinary investment account rather than in a pension account: rate increases under alternative tax laws and at different contribution ages (annuity distribution).

Age at time of contribution	Percentage points / Calendar year of contribution					Change, 1985 to 2015
	1985	1988	2000	2007	2015	
Bonds						
29	41	38	37	36	36	–5
39	39	32	31	30	30	–9
49	35	25	24	23	24	–11
59	18	18	17	16	16	–1
Equities: No dividends / All capital gains						
29	23	37	30	26	21	–2
39	27	33	27	24	18	–8
49	28	28	23	20	16	–12
59	16	19	17	15	14	–2
Equities: 2.5% dividend						
29	34	41	36	29	25	–8
39	34	35	31	25	22	–12
49	32	29	25	21	18	–14
59	17	20	18	16	14	–3
Equities: All dividends / No capital gains						
29	51	47	46	34	35	–17
39	47	40	39	29	29	–18
49	40	31	30	23	23	–17
59	20	20	19	16	16	–4

Source: Authors' calculations.
Note: The calculations refer to a married worker who earns a medium lifetime wage and is married to a spouse who earns twice the medium wage. Both spouses are the same age and expect to retire and claim a Social Security benefit at age 65. All money in the investment account, after payment of taxes, is converted into a level, joint survivor annuity at age 65 (see the text).

The bottom three panels show the tax increase workers face if three kinds of equities were located in a standard investment account as opposed to a pension account. All cases assume that the worker earns the medium lifetime wage and has a spouse who earns double that wage. The tax rate is calculated under the assumption that the net withdrawals from the investment or pension account are converted into a level, joint survivor annuity after retirement at age 65. Calculations are performed at four ages (29, 39, 49, and 59) and under the tax rules and schedules in effect in five years (1985, 1988, 2000, 2007, and 2015).

For the tax situations presented in table 10.3, changes in the tax code since 1985 on balance reduced the tax preference available to pension savers. The biggest decline occurred in the case of dividend-paying equities. The decline was smaller in the case of equities where all of the saver's investment income was derived from long-term capital gains. The net tax preference for holding taxable bonds in a pension account also declined.

Table 10.3 also sheds light on the effects of individual tax laws. For example, the pension tax preference for bond investments and investments in all-dividend equities fell between 1985 and 1988, primarily because of the reduction in marginal tax rates. In contrast, the tax preference for equities that yield large capital gains increased noticeably. Because this kind of stock lost an important tax preference if held in regular investment accounts as a result of the 1986 Tax Reform Act, the pension tax preference became more valuable. Changes in tax laws after 1988 did not have an important effect on the value of the pension tax preference for bond holdings, but they substantially reduced the pension tax preference for equity holdings.

10.4.6 Calculations for a Cross Section of Workers

The estimates just described can be performed for workers with varying age-earnings profiles and in a variety of family situations. To calculate the tax preference for a composite worker with a given level of lifetime wages, say one with a "high" earnings profile, the relevant population weights of high-wage workers at different ages and in different family circumstances must be estimated. To obtain these weights, the public-use version of the Census Bureau's Current Population Survey (CPS) annual income supplement files for 2008 was tabulated. Interviews conducted in early 2008 obtained information on each worker's age, marital status, earnings in 2007, and the spouse's earnings, if any, in 2007. These data permit calculation of the percentage of 2007 earners in population cells defined by broad earnings level, age, marital status, and ratio of spouse's earnings to own earnings.[12] For workers with a combination of age and earnings level that places them in the "high" lifetime wage group, it is straightforward to calculate the percentage of high earners in different age, marital status, and spouse earnings ratio groups. With this information, approximate weights can be assigned to each tax situation covered by the analysis.

Under the 1985 tax law, for example, earners with high lifetime earnings on average faced a 47 percent cumulative tax on their gross earned income if savings out of wages were invested in bonds and placed in an ordinary investment account. In contrast, they faced a cumulative tax rate of just 19 percent if the same bond investment was placed in a pension account. The 28 percentage point difference in tax rates represents the tax advantage for locating bond investments in a pension account rather than an ordinary investment account. This difference reflects the weighted average of the estimates for high lifetime earners in all tax situations covered by the analysis.[13] Using the same set of weights to estimate the tax preference, the pension preference for bond investment fell to 26 percentage points under the 2000 tax law and to 24 percentage points under the 2007 tax law. At the other end of the earnings scale, the tax preference for pension savings among very low earners increased sharply between 1985 and 2000 and then fell modestly between 2000 and 2015. Workers with low and medium lifetime earnings saw only small changes in the pension tax preference when they invested in bonds.

Results like these can provide rough estimates of the tax preference obtained by workers 21 to 64 years old if they hold assets in a pension account rather than in a standard investment account. The approximation weights the pension tax preference obtained by very low, low, medium, and high earners by the population proportions in each age group. In the 2008 CPS files, the estimated proportions in the four earnings groups were 21 percent, 25 percent, 23 percent, and 31 percent, respectively. The approximation is imprecise for a couple of reasons. First, detailed information about the past and future tax situations of workers in the CPS samples is lacking, so the estimates are based on stylized representations of the circumstances of workers in broad earnings groups. Second, the estimates are based on the unrealistic assumption that taxpayers will face the same tax laws from the time they make retirement savings contributions until all their savings are withdrawn from their accounts. The calculations may nonetheless be informative about broad trends in the value of the pension tax preference for different kinds of assets.

Table 10.4 shows the workforce-average pension tax preference for bond and equity investments held in pension plans rather than in a standard investment account. The table shows the weighted-average increase in taxes on gross earnings workers experience if their investments are placed in an ordinary investment account rather than in a pension account. The top panel shows estimates of the pension tax preference when all savings in the accounts are consumed immediately

Table 10.4
Weighted tax increase if workers save in an ordinary investment account rather than a pension account: rate increases under alternative tax laws.

Asset	Percentage points / Calendar year of contribution					Change, 1985 to 2015
	1985	1988	2000	2007	2015	
	Account savings consumed at age 65					
Bonds						
Held in ordinary investment account	13.7	15.9	15.4	14.8	14.5	0.8
Equities						
No dividends / All capital gains	5.9	15.6	10.9	7.2	3.9	–2.0
2.5% dividend	10.8	17.9	14.8	8.6	4.8	–6.0
All dividends / No capital gains	19.9	22.5	22.1	11.5	6.7	–13.2
	Account savings converted into an annuity at age 65					
Bonds						
Held in ordinary investment account	20.3	22.7	22.7	20.5	20.2	–0.1
Equities						
No dividends / All capital gains	13.1	22.4	18.5	13.4	10.4	–2.7
2.5% dividend	17.6	24.5	22.1	14.6	11.2	–6.4
All dividends / No capital gains	26.1	28.8	28.9	17.3	12.9	–13.2

Source: Authors' calculations.
Note: Population weights reflect all persons aged 21–64 with positive labor earnings in 2007 (see the text).

after retirement at age 65. The lower panel shows tax rate increases when savings accumulated in an account are converted to a level annuity starting at age 65. For reasons mentioned earlier, the pension tax preference is nearly always greater if workers convert their savings into an annuity rather than consume all of their savings immediately after retirement.

The results in table 10.4 contain a couple of lessons about the value of the pension tax preference from the perspective of individual workers. First, the value of the tax preference for holding assets in a pension account is complicated and varies considerably depending on the asset. For obvious reasons, savers have always been well advised to hold bonds and other interest-bearing securities inside a pension account. However, the value of the tax preference for equities varies considerably depending on how the income flow from equities is taxed in standard investment accounts. This in turn varies depending on how equity returns are paid out to investors. Different forms of equity returns received widely different tax treatments under US law over the past 30 years, producing variation in the value of the pension tax preference for savers who held equities in their retirement savings accounts. The estimates in table 10.4 suggest that little change occurred between 1985 and 2015 in the value of the pension tax preference for equities that generate returns in the form of capital gains income. However, the similarity of the tax preferences in 1985 and 2015 disguises the fact that the value of the pension tax preference increased sharply between 1985 and 1988, when long-term capital gains income lost preferential treatment in the income tax code. The pension tax preference provided to dividend-paying stocks fell sharply between 1985 and 2015 primarily because qualified stock dividends received a generous tax preference in the regular tax code.

A second lesson from table 10.4 is that the pension tax preference continues to be economically significant for typical US workers, even if it is highly unpredictable in light of frequent changes in other income tax laws. Compared with accumulating retirement savings in a pension account, workers can expect to pay noticeably higher lifetime taxes on their gross earnings if they save for retirement outside a pension account. Even though the cumulative tax saving is now smaller than it was in the mid-1980s, it is still substantial for most workers.

10.5 Limitations of Tax Preferences as a Policy Tool

Saving inside a pension account should be financially attractive to all but a small fraction of American workers. It is clear from pension participation statistics, however, that the attractiveness of the incentive does not by itself guarantee that workers will accumulate much workplace savings by the time they retire. All analysts agree that participation varies by employer size and by workers' earnings levels. For example, Dushi, Iams, and Lichtenstein (2015) analyzed private employers' offers of retirement plans and workers' takeup of those plans using information from three waves of the SIPP surveys supplemented with information from workers' tax records. Their findings, displayed in figure 10.4, show the percentage of private sector employees 21 to 64 years old who are offered a retirement plan. Firms with 100 or more employees are very likely to offer workers a retirement plan, while workers in companies with fewer than 25 employees have less than a

50 percent chance of being offered a plan. If workers are offered a plan, they are very likely to enroll in it, regardless of employer size. This should not be surprising in defined benefit plans or in a defined contribution plan where employees are automatically enrolled. It seems more surprising in defined contribution plans where enrollment is voluntary and requires an employee contribution. Many small companies, including accounting firms, physician practices, and law partnerships, employ well-paid professional workers who have a keen interest in minimizing taxes on their compensation. The relatively few small firms that offer company pensions may be concentrated in these well-paid fields.

Offer rates and takeup rates for employer pension plans are strongly linked to workers' wages. As a result, participation in employer plans is powerfully correlated with worker pay, especially in the private sector. Figure 10.5 shows worker participation rates estimated in the 2016 Employee Benefits Survey, an annual survey of employers conducted by the US Bureau of Labor Statistics (BLS). The BLS divides occupations into six wage categories based on the average wage in the occupation. Based on employer reports of participation, just 15 percent

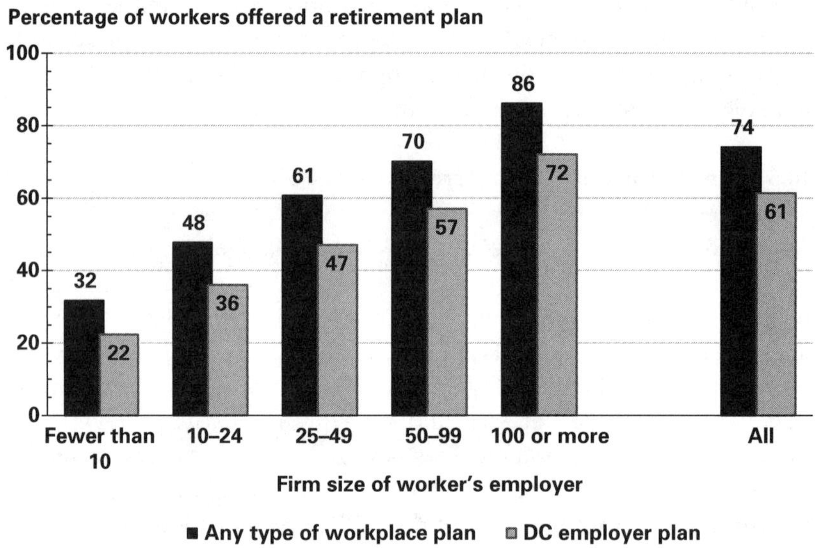

Figure 10.4
Offer rate of retirement plans among private sector workers, 2006–2012. *Sources*: Dushi, Iams, and Lichtenstein (2015, tables 1 and 2); tabulations of SIPP survey files supplemented with matched W-2 records; and authors' calculations. *Note*: Sample consists of private sector employees aged 21–64 in the 2006, 2009, and 2012 SIPP interview years.

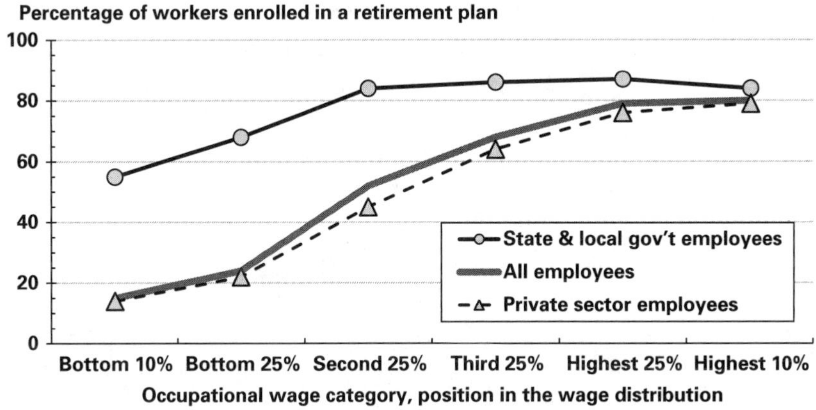

Figure 10.5
Participation in workplace retirement plans among US workers by occupational earnings, 2016. *Source*: US Bureau of Labor Statistics, Employment Benefits Survey, March 2016. https://www.bls.gov/ncs/ebs/benefits/2016/benefits_retirement.htm (accessed December 2016). *Note*: Estimates derived from a survey of employers in private nonfarm business and in state and local government. Federal government agencies, the military, and agricultural enterprises are not included in the survey.

of employees in the lowest-paying occupations are enrolled in a company retirement plan. The fraction who participate rises to 80 percent among employees in occupations in the top tenth of the wage distribution. Low participation among employees in poorly paid occupations occurs both because their employers are less likely to offer a plan and because workers are less likely to enroll even if a plan is offered.

Low-wage employees fail to enroll in an offered plan for several reasons. Some low-pay workers are unwilling to reduce their current earnings in exchange for higher consumption in the distant future because they apply a high discount rate to future consumption. Also, under a progressive tax system, low-wage workers ordinarily derive a smaller financial benefit from saving in a pension plan compared with workers who earn higher pay. Finally, nearly all US workers, regardless of their pay, participate in Social Security. The OASDI pension formula provides a much higher benefit replacement rate to low-wage contributors than to high-wage contributors.

Figure 10.6 shows Social Security Administration estimates of the replacement rate obtained by eligible workers with very low, low, medium, high, and very high career earnings profiles. For workers who claim benefits at age 66, the youngest age at which to claim a full retirement

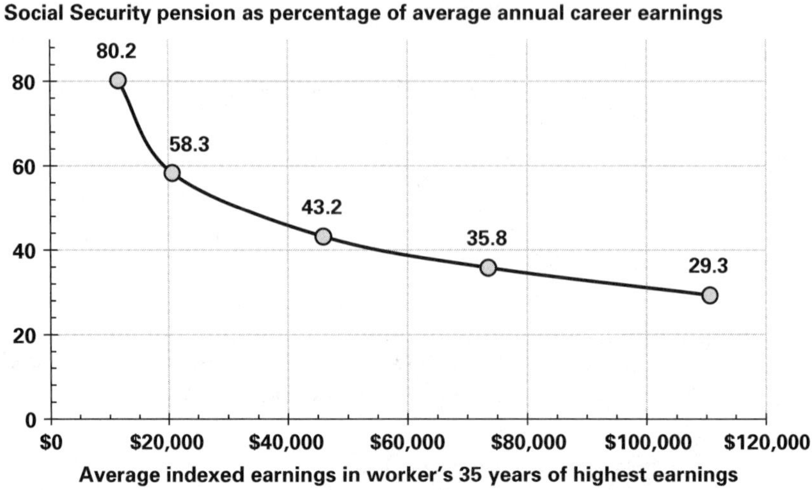

Figure 10.6
Social Security replacement rates for US workers born in 1945, by workers' career-average earnings. *Source*: Clingman, Burkhalter, and Chaplain (2014); Office of the Chief Actuary, Social Security Administration; authors' calculations. *Note*: Replacement rates for workers who claim benefits at age 66. Earnings measured in 2015 dollars.

pension, replacement rates for the five types of workers range from 80 percent for the very low lifetime earner to 29 percent for the very high career earner. For workers in the two lowest earnings groups, the annual Social Security benefit at age 66, if it is the retiree's sole source of income, would be too low to be taxable under the US income tax. Consequently, these workers' after-tax replacement rates are likely to be higher than the levels indicated in the chart. (The figure shows retirees' pretax replacement rates.) Under the life cycle consumption model, workers who expect to obtain a high after-tax replacement rate under the compulsory retirement program have little reason to sacrifice consumption when young for higher consumption when old.

A second reason for low participation is that many workers do not receive the offer of a retirement plan at work. Less than one-third of workers in companies with fewer than 10 employees are offered a workplace pension, and more than one-quarter of all private sector workers receive no offer of a company retirement plan (figure 10.4). Private employers report to the BLS that just 44 percent of workers in low-paying occupations receive the offer of a workplace retirement plan. Of those offered a plan, slightly more than half of workers in these occupations participate in it (US Bureau of Labor Statistics 2016). This suggests that many low-wage workers would participate in such plans if a plan were offered to them. Workers can, of course, set aside tax-preferred retirement savings in an IRA. The problem is that many workers do not get around to opening or making regular contributions to such a plan. The current US tax preference makes it attractive for workers to save in qualified retirement plans, but many workers are unlikely to make contributions unless their employers make it easy to do so.

Employers can take steps to boost retirement savings, even if they do not wish to contribute much to the plan. If a firm has fewer than 100 employees, it can establish a SIMPLE-IRA. Larger employers can adopt equally straightforward but somewhat more costly safe harbor 401(k) or 403(b) defined contribution plans. These simple plan designs are relatively inexpensive to manage and offer clear tax benefits to all or most employees. Abundant evidence suggests that workers' participation in and contributions to workplace savings plans are heavily influenced by the plan's defaults (Beshears et al. 2009). If the plan requires voluntary contributions for employee participation, employers can boost participation by making enrollment in the plan the default option when workers meet the tenure requirement for participation. Worker and matched employer contributions could be calculated at a default rate. Workers would be free to decline enrollment or to raise or lower their contribution rate, but these changes would require affirmative action on the part of each employee.

Despite the persistent and sizable holes in participation, the private retirement system accumulated massive assets over the past four decades. The assets owned by workplace retirement plans soared from about one-quarter of gross domestic product (GDP) in 1974 to 1.33 times GDP in 2015, more than a fivefold increase (figure 10.7). Household claims on the private retirement system are now more than 150 percent of US GDP, though almost one-seventh of these claims represent unfunded liabilities of defined benefit pension plans. The assets held by the private retirement system in the United States represent a higher multiple of GDP than is the case in the great majority of rich countries (OECD 2015, 7).

The benefits of the US system are very unequally distributed across the population, however. Tabulations from the Census Bureau's CPS annual income supplement show that only about 3 percent of the income received by retirees past age 65 who are in the bottom one-fifth of the retiree income distribution is derived from a pension or annuity. In the middle one-fifth of the retiree income distribution, the income

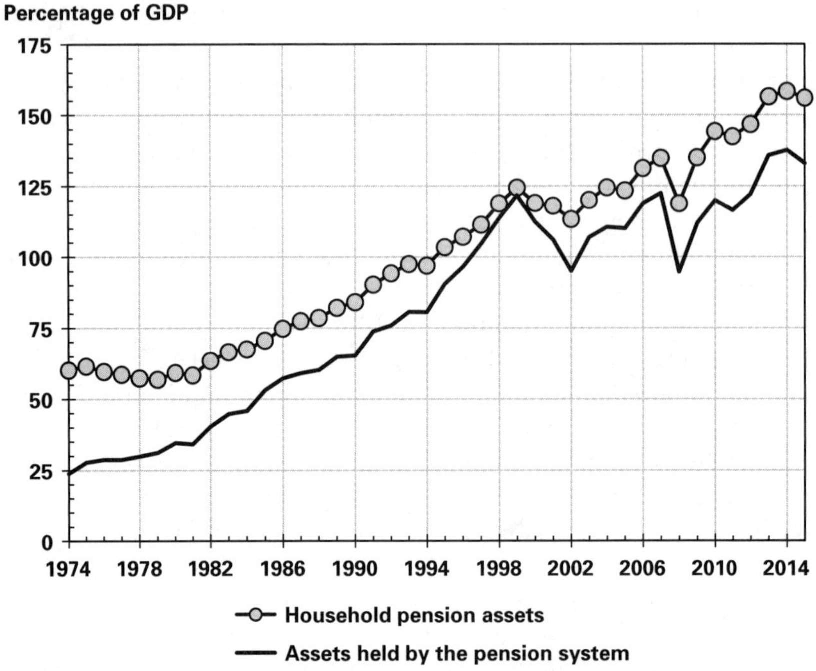

Figure 10.7
Assets of the private retirement system as percentage of US GDP, 1974–2015. *Source*: Board of Governors of the Federal Reserve System, "Financial Accounts of the United States," release, September 16, 2016; Investment Company Institute, *The U.S. Retirement Market, Second Quarter 2016*; and US Department of Commerce, Bureau of Economic Analysis, NIPA data, release, December 22, 2016.

share derived from pensions is just 13 percent. These income shares are only slightly higher than they were in the mid-1970s, when the private retirement system's holdings were far smaller. In contrast, among retirees in the top one-fifth of the retiree income distribution, the pension share of retirement income increased from 32 percent to 43 percent over the same time span (Brady and Bogdan 2013, tables 3, 5, and 7). It is very likely that income flows from the private retirement system are underreported in most household surveys (Bosworth, Burtless, and Anders 2007). However, there is little reason to think that the low-income elderly derive a sizable percentage of their income from the private retirement system.

Federal Reserve economists used the Survey of Consumer Finances (SCF) to estimate the retirement wealth of families headed by an employed person between 53 and 62 years old in 2013, the year of the most recent survey. Private retirement wealth consists of the present value of expected defined benefit pensions plus a family's accumulated savings in defined contribution and IRA accounts. After dividing families into three groups based on their usual annual incomes, the median retirement wealth holdings of families in each group were calculated. Private retirement wealth holdings for families in the bottom half of the income distribution were very low. The median amount in 2013 was just US$6,500, about 17 percent of families' usual annual income (Devlin-Foltz, Henriques, and Sabelhaus 2016, 77). Obviously, an accumulation this small will not finance much retirement consumption. Families with incomes between the 50th and 95th income percentiles accumulated more retirement savings, about US$288,000. This amount represents about 2.78 times the median annual income of families in the group and would support a larger flow of retirement consumption. Families in the top 5 percent of the income distribution accumulated US$716,000 in retirement-account assets. Though the amount is large, it is only about 1.5 times the families' median usual income.

These numbers show that private retirement wealth is very unequally distributed. As a result, the retirement income that can be supported out of private retirement wealth will also be very unequal. Devlin-Foltz, Henriques, and Sabelhaus (2016) point out, however, that family wealth held outside retirement accounts is more unequally distributed than wealth held inside retirement accounts. If Social Security wealth is included in retirement wealth, low-income families' relative wealth position improves, especially compared with the wealthiest families. When private and Social Security wealth are summed, the median retirement wealth to income ratio is 5.3 for families in the bottom half of the income distribution, 6.1 for families in the next 45 percent of the distribution, and just 2.3 for families in the top 5 percent of the distribution.

10.6 Conclusions

Fueled by a generous tax preference, the US private retirement system grew faster over the past four decades than publicly funded retirement programs. Not only does the private system now disburse more resources to support old-age consumption than the public system, the financial assets accumulated within the private system represent more than one-quarter of the net worth of US households and nonprofit organizations. Only a handful of OECD countries have private retirement systems that are as large relative to the size of their economies. This chapter's analysis shows that the financial incentive provided by the tax preference varied widely over time, especially for retirement savings held in the form of corporate equities. Stock market holdings constitute the most important asset held by the private retirement system, and the tax treatment of equities held outside pension accounts has varied considerably. When legislators make the tax preference for equity returns more generous, they cut the financial reward to holding equities inside a qualified pension account. The results also show that the value of the pension tax preference depends on changes in future tax rules, which are difficult to predict. An allocation of retirement savings to a qualified pension account that seems advantageous today may be far less attractive under tax rules adopted later. Nonetheless, over the entire period analyzed, workers' potential retirement consumption was higher if they set aside retirement savings inside rather than outside a qualified pension account.

Saving in a pension account is a financially attractive choice for all but a handful of American workers, so participation in the private retirement system should be nearly universal. Because participation requires voluntary action, however, this is far from the reality. The accumulation of private retirement savings is highly unequal, across both employers and employees. It is unequal across workplaces because of differences between the plans offered by different employers and because many offer no plan at all. Additionally, as the private retirement system continues to shift toward 401(k)-type plans, workers are increasingly obliged to make voluntary contributions to their own retirement accounts. Wide differences in employees' elective contributions mean that retirement savings vary among workers within a given workplace, too. Workers in the top half of the income distribution accumulate disproportionately more retirement savings than workers further down in the distribution. Thus, US policies to encourage private retirement savings are redistributive in the opposite direction from what is ordinarily expected. Notably, though, private retirement system accumulations are distributed less unequally than Americans' wealth holdings outside the retirement system. Moreover, when workers' public retirement system wealth is included, the total retirement wealth distribution is far less unequal than the distribution of nonretirement wealth.

The glaring flaw of the tax preference for US retirement saving is that coverage and publicly subsidized contributions under the system are so unequal. Some contributors, especially those with high incomes, derive outsized net benefits, while millions of potential contributors, because of bad luck or inattention, derive no benefit at all. If voters and policy makers want to make the private retirement system more egalitarian, they can either place lower limits on workers' annual contributions to tax-preferred plans or introduce compulsory elements to the current system. At a minimum, Congress should require private employers to offer a workplace retirement plan that offers automatic payroll withholding for tax-preferred retirement savings, even if worker contributions are not compulsory. The effects of this measure would be magnified if legislators phased in a requirement that workers or their employers contribute at least a minimum percentage of pretax earnings to a qualified retirement account. In the absence of these kinds of reforms, the private retirement system will continue to provide very unequal income supplementation to Americans' publicly funded retirement benefits.

Notes

The research reported here was partially supported under a grant from the US Social Security Administration funded as part of the Retirement Research Consortium (RRC). We are grateful to Eric Toder and Maria Ramrath for earlier research collaboration in developing the simulation model. The findings and conclusions are solely those of the authors and do not represent the views of the Social Security Administration, the RRC, or the Brookings Institution.

1. The Federal Reserve no longer tracks separately all the assets and liabilities of the household and nonprofit sectors. However, it did so between 1987 and 2000. In those 14 years, the approximate net worth of nonprofits ranged between 13 percent and 15 percent of the aggregate net worth of households and nonprofit organizations. If nonprofits owned the same share of aggregate net worth in 2015, nearly 38 percent of household net worth in 2015 would have consisted of claims against the private retirement system, including IRAs.

2. The maximum taxed salary amount is indexed to average wage growth. In recent years, about 94 percent of wage earners had salaries below the maximum taxed amount (Social Security Administration 2016a, table 4.B4). Workers with higher wages only pay OASDI taxes on their earnings below the ceiling.

3. In 2014, 60 percent of contributions into private sector defined contribution plans were made by employees and 40 percent were made by their employers. In the same year, just 1 percent of contributions into private defined benefit plans were made by employees and 99 percent were made by employers (US Department of Labor, Employee Benefits Security Administration 2016, table A4).

4. For a description of the test as applied to different kinds of plans, see Employee Benefit Research Institute (2009, chapter 13).

5. These estimates and those that immediately follow were made by the Employee Benefit Research Institute based on a combination of administrative reports of the EBSA and the Pension Benefit Guaranty Corporation as well as household interview responses

in the Current Population Surveys. See www.ebri.org/publications/benfaq/index.cfm?fa=retfaqt14fig2 (accessed September 10, 2016).

6. This section and the next borrow heavily from and extend the analysis in Burtless and Toder (2010).

7. In 2015, just 9 percent of the assets accumulated in IRAs were held in Roth IRA accounts (Investment Company Institute 2016, table 8). In employer-sponsored retirement plans, the asset share held in Roth accounts is even smaller.

8. Under 2015 income tax law, the asset must be held for a year for the capital gain to qualify for the concessionary tax treatment.

9. Bear in mind that the higher expected return on equities provides compensation to investors for the added risk they accept when investing in a riskier asset. To reflect this additional risk, the future returns must also be discounted at a higher rate.

10. This reflects the fact that with capital income taxable, the present value of taxes on this year's wage rises the longer consumption from the wage is deferred. Annuities raise the present value of taxes compared with lump-sum distributions that are consumed, because they extend the time period over which consumption is deferred.

11. The saver once again is assumed to earn the medium lifetime wage and to have a spouse who earns twice the medium wage. The worker and spouse are assumed to convert their retirement savings into a level, joint survivor annuity at age 65.

12. All 21–64-year-olds with 2007 earnings were classified in one of seven broad annual earnings groups (US$1 to US$9,999; US$10,000 to US$19,999; US$20,000 to US$29,999; US$30,000 to US$39,999; US$40,000 to US$49,999; US$50,000 to US$59,999; and US$60,000 and higher), nine age groups (age 21–24, 25–29, 30–34, 35–39, 40–44, 45–49, 50–54, 55–59, and 60–64), two marital status groups, and, for married earners, four spouse-earnings groups, depending on the ratio of a spouse's earnings to the individual's own earnings.

13. The population weights used to obtain the estimate reflect the number of high earners who face different tax rates as a result of differences in their age, marital status, own earnings, the earnings of a spouse (if any), and the imputations of the earner's other taxable income. As noted, the relative weight of each kind of earner was calculated using CPS interview data covering 2007.

References

Bell, Felicitie C., and Michael L. Miller. 2005. *Life Tables for the United States Social Security Area 1900–2100*. Office of the Chief Actuary, Actuarial Study No. 120. Baltimore: Social Security Administration.

Beshears, John, James J. Choi, David Laibson, and Brigitte C. Madrian. 2009. "The Importance of Default Options for Retirement Saving Outcomes: Evidence from the United States." In *Social Security Policy in a Changing Environment*, edited by Jeffrey Brown, Jeffrey Liebman, and David A. Wise 167–195. Chicago: University of Chicago Press.

Board of Governors of the Federal Reserve System. 2016. "Financial Accounts of the United States," release, September 16.

Bosworth, Barry P., Gary Burtless, and Sarah Anders. 2007. "Capital Income Flows and the Relative Well-Being of America's Aged Population." Working Paper No. 2007-21, Center for Retirement Research, Boston College, Chestnut Hill, MA.

Brady, Peter, and Michael Bogdan. 2013. "A Look at Private-Sector Retirement Plan Income after ERISA in 2012." Investment Company Institute, Washington, DC. http://www.ici.org/info/per19-08_data.xls.

Burtless, Gary. 2009. "Expanding Participation in America's Workplace Retirement System." In *Pensions, Social Security, and the Privatization of Risk*, edited by M. Orenstein. New York: Columbia University Press.

Burtless, Gary, and Eric Toder. 2010. "The Shrinking Tax Preference for Pension Savings: An Analysis of Income Tax Changes, 1985–2007." Working Paper No. 2010-3, Center for Retirement Research, Boston College, Chestnut Hill, MA.

Clingman, Michael, Kyle Burkhalter, and Chris Chaplain. 2014. "Replacement Rates for Hypothetical Retired Workers." Actuarial Note No. 2014.9 (July), Office of the Chief Actuary, Social Security Administration, Baltimore, MD.

Clingman, Michael, and Orlo Nichols. 2007. "Scaled Factors for Hypothetical Earnings Examples under the 2007 Trustees Report Assumptions." Actuarial Note No. 2007.3 (September), Office of the Chief Actuary, Social Security Administration, Baltimore, MD.

Dammon, Robert M., Chester S. Spatt, and Harold H. Zhang. 2004. "Optimal Asset Location and Allocation with Taxable and Tax-Deferred Investing." *Journal of Finance* 59 (3) (June): 999–1037.

Devlin-Foltz, Sebastian, Alice Henriques, and John Sabelhaus. 2016. "Is the U.S. Retirement System Contributing to Rising Wealth Inequality?" *Russell Sage Foundation Journal of the Social Sciences* 2 (6) (October): 59–85.

Dushi, Irena, Howard Iams, and Jules Lichtenstein. 2015. "Retirement Plan Coverage by Firm Size: An Update." *Social Security Bulletin* 75 (2) (May): 41–55.

Employee Benefit Research Institute. 2009. *EBRI's Fundamentals of Employee Benefit Programs*. Washington, DC: Employee Benefit Research Institute. http://www.ebri.org/publications/books/?fa=fundamentals.

Investment Company Institute. 2016. *The U.S. Retirement Market, Second Quarter 2016*. Washington, DC: Investment Company Institute. www.ici.org/info/ ret_16_q2_data.xls.

Investment Company Institute. Various years. *Investment Company Fact Book: A Review of Trends and Activity in the Investment Company Industry*. Washington, DC: Investment Company Institute.

Marples, Donald J. 2015. *Tax Expenditures: Overview and Analysis*. Washington, DC: Congressional Research Service, April.

OECD (Organisation for Economic Co-operation and Development). 2015. *Pension Markets in Focus*. Paris: OECD Publishing.

Poterba, James, John Shoven, and Clemens Sialm. 2001. "Asset Location for Retirement Savers." In *Private Pensions and Public Policies*, edited by W. Gale, John Shoven, and M. Warshawsky, 290–331. Washington, DC: Brookings Institution.

Social Security Administration. 2016a. *Annual Statistical Supplement to the Social Security Bulletin, 2015*. Baltimore, MD: Social Security Administration.

Social Security Administration. 2016b. *Historical Background and Development of Social Security*. Baltimore, MD: Social Security Administration. https://www.ssa.gov/history/briefhistory3.html.

US Bureau of Labor Statistics. 2016. *National Compensation Survey: Employee Benefits in the United States, May 2016.* Bulletin No. 2787 (September). Washington, DC: US Department of Labor.

US Department of Labor, Employee Benefits Security Administration. 2016. *Private Pension Plan Bulletin Abstract of 2014 Form 5500 Annual Reports* (September; Version 1.0). Washington, DC: US Department of Labor, Employee Benefits Security Administration. https://www.dol.gov/sites/default/files/ebsa/researchers/statistics/retirement-bulletins/private-pension-plan-bulletins-abstract-2014.pdf.

11 Tax Expenditures on Pensions: Concepts, Concerns, and Misconceptions

Rafal Chomik and John Piggott

11.1 Introduction

Tax expenditures occur when the tax treatment favors a certain activity. The forgone tax is thought to be analogous to spending and can thus attract commensurate attention. This concept was first articulated some 50 years ago by Stanley Surrey of the US Treasury Department (Surrey 1969), but exemptions to tax are as old as tax itself.[1,2]

As governments around the world look at ways to balance their budgets, tax expenditures will increasingly and justifiably come under scrutiny. This is particularly the case in countries with expanding funded pensions that seek to encourage self-provision for retirement or to maintain neutrality between current and future consumption. Such arrangements can make the tax costs appear large and skewed toward the rich, while the benefits, which are far in the future, seem unsubstantiated.

However, much of the criticism of tax arrangements is based on inadequate analysis. This chapter contributes to the debate by explaining the basic concepts and practice, tackling concerns related to the scale and fairness of tax expenditures and presenting a policy reform that can improve fairness. This is done by way of illustrative examples of savings over the life cycle and across the earnings distribution, using the Australian retirement income system as a test case. The Australian system is a good subject for analysis because tax expenditures on pensions are prominent in the policy debate and because their scale is particularly large.

Indeed, in few countries do tax expenditure estimates garner as much media and public attention as in Australia. A key reason is the large amount of prefunding that takes place through superannuation—the main income-replacement pillar in Australia's retirement income system.[3] As other countries expand their funded pension arrangements, they, too, will face similar concerns about the scale and equity of tax expenditures.

Under the current estimation methodology, tax expenditures on superannuation are generated because contributions and investment returns are exempt from personal income tax and are taxed at a flat rate (which is generally lower than the marginal rate), or not at all in the case of investment returns in the withdrawal phase. The lower rates compared to income tax generate perceptions about fiscal costs. In addition, the flat-rate nature of the taxing regime results in concerns about the overly generous treatment of high-income earners, who benefit from the lower tax rates of superannuation compared to their high marginal tax rates.[4] Both concerns are not atypical in discussions of tax expenditures in other jurisdictions.[5]

The added transparency hoped for in the Tax Expenditure Statement[6] has instead generated confusion. For example, the methodology for official estimates overstates the scale of tax revenues by ignoring behavior (see subsection 11.4.2), interactions with other tax expenditures (subsection 11.4.3), broader fiscal and economic impacts (subsections 11.4.5 and 11.4.6), and sensitivity to the benchmark (subsections 11.4.4 and 11.4.7). That a high share of tax expenditures accrues to high-income earners is unsurprising; it reflects a highly progressive tax system in which high-income earners pay a greater share of tax, which is only partly the result of disproportionate contribution tax concessions across the earnings distribution (subsection 11.4.7).

Australia's Commonwealth Treasury notes in its Tax Expenditure Statement several caveats and limitations of the estimates, but the exact methodology is not entirely transparent, the definition of the benchmark is subjective, and the caveats are demonstrably insufficient. In a recent review of the Tax Expenditure Statement by the House of Representatives Standing Committee on Tax and Revenue (2015, 45), the committee noted that the public misuses and misunderstands the estimates, suggesting that "the warnings in the document are not sufficiently clear to inform enough of its users."

These criticisms are not new. In 1992, when mandatory superannuation was first introduced, Bateman and Piggott (1992, 48) wrote that "in the debate over appropriate tax treatment of superannuation saving, there is perhaps no issue which generates more confusion than that of revenue costs."

With this background and motivation, section 11.2 explains the concepts and practice of measuring tax expenditures. Section 11.3 covers concerns often raised in relation to tax expenditures on pensions. Section 11.4 addresses flaws in these concerns, using novel illustrative examples. Section 11.5 discusses what a sensible equity-enhancing reform could look like. Section 11.6 presents our conclusions.

11.2 Concepts and Application

11.2.1 What Are the Options for Taxing Savings?

Saved income can be taxed at three points: (1) when it is saved, (2) when investment returns are generated, and/or (3) when it is withdrawn.

In theory, which of these three points attracts tax depends on whether an income tax or an expenditure tax is believed more appropriate. If income is chosen, defined as any consumption plus any increase in net wealth, then the comprehensive income tax would apply.[7] Under this concept, all forms of income, including the amounts saved and accrued through investment, would be taxed as if in the hands of the saver, while the income withdrawn is tax-free. In the context of retirement savings, this is known as a TTE system—contributions are taxed (T), investment returns are taxed (T), and benefits are exempt (E).

If consumption—the amount effectively devoted to spending—is chosen, then the expenditure tax would apply. That is, only income that is withdrawn is taxed. This is known as an EET system—contributions are exempt (E), investment returns are exempt (E), and benefits are taxed (T). It is also possible to prepay the expenditure tax by only taxing income at the point when it is saved (i.e., a TEE system). With a proportional tax rate, no excess returns on some investments, and no inflation, EET and TEE are equivalent, as are TTE and ETT (Bateman, Kingston, and Piggott 1993).[8]

11.2.2 What Is the Practice of Taxing Savings?

In practice, most advanced economies have a mixed system of taxation and aspire to neither a comprehensive income tax nor an expenditure tax base. Rather, taxation design plays out as a pragmatic mix, trading off issues of price distortion against equity and revenue accrual. With respect to pensions, an EET system is more often deployed; that is, a "deferred" or "postpaid" expenditure tax approach.

Often, even a TEE or EET system attracts further reductions relative to the prevailing tax schedule. For example, in the United Kingdom, contributions and returns are exempt, and while benefits are taxed, a quarter of these benefits can be taken tax-free, which would be described as EET* (Johnson and Emmerson 2016).

Various permutations are in use in different countries.[9] Over the last few decades, Australia's superannuation scheme experienced almost every combination of exemption and taxation among the three possible taxing points (see Bateman, chapter 7, this volume).

Australian superannuation is taxed as a T*T*E system: employer contributions into a superannuation fund (up to a cap) are taxed at 15 percent for most workers (30 percent for those earning above A$300,000, which roughly corresponds to the top 1 percent of earners) and 15 percent for the investment returns within the fund (though the actual tax on returns is lower because of a discount on capital gains on assets held longer than 12 months and the operation of dividend imputation, which effectively credits tax on net-of-tax dividends of corporations).

But not all savings are taxed the same. In Australia, as in most countries, owner-occupied housing is taxed as TEE: a home is purchased using after-tax income, and the imputed rent and receipts from the home's sale are tax-exempt. Like the EET setup, a TEE arrangement is a form of expenditure tax because the tax accrues when income is spent. Bank account savings are made from after-tax income, returns incur tax at the marginal rate, but withdrawals are tax-free—a TTE arrangement. Other assets, such as shares or investment property, are taxed in line with a TT*E approach (capital gains are taxed at half the marginal rate).

11.2.3 How Is the Benchmark Decided?

To measure the extent to which each of these tax treatments departs from a given benchmark, one needs to decide on the benchmark. Should it align with the comprehensive income tax or the expenditure tax? Which other provisions of the existing tax structure should be included? The choice is subjective. It is also the most controversial part of any discussion of tax expenditures, since it leads to very different estimates (see subsection 11.4.4).

Two rules of thumb can guide the choice. First, one can ask what the ideal tax treatment of a given activity or taxpayer should be. A sensible tax treatment is likely to lead to sensible policy. It sounds like a normative question about "what ought to be" that needs to be answered by a political process, but it can be tackled by appealing to criteria from first principles of basic economics.

With savings, a reasonable criterion is neutrality between present and future consumption. That is, investment returns that represent the time value of money would be left untaxed, as is the case in a prepaid or postpaid expenditure tax.[10] Subsection 11.4.6 presents a further discussion of the economics of this.

The second option is to look at the most common tax treatment that currently applies to similar types of activity or taxpayers. This approach seems pragmatic, but it is ultimately idiosyncratic. In Australia, more household savings are held in assets that are taxed under an expenditure base than under a comprehensive income base (figure 11.1). Superannuation makes up 16 percent of household assets. By contrast, owner-occupied housing is the largest form of savings, making up 43 percent of all household assets, or 51 percent of nonsuperannuation assets. Since both the tax treatment and the benchmark for owner-occupied housing align with a consumption tax, the conclusion would be that superannuation assets' taxes should also be set against an expenditure tax benchmark.

The approach of looking at how other activities are taxed is purportedly taken by Australia's Commonwealth Treasury, yet it reaches the opposite conclusion and determines that a comprehensive income base should apply. Its rationale is that financial savings vehicles such as bank accounts are the best reference point and that "saving through owner-occupied housing is not comparable to superannuation, since the former is not simply a savings vehicle but also provides current consumption (i.e. a place to live)" (Commonwealth Treasury 2016, 5). This conclusion came in spite of the fact that few Australians accumulate any substantial fraction of their retirement income by saving in a bank account.

A recent report by the Standing Committee on Tax and Revenue (2015) recommended that the comprehensive income benchmark remain, basing its view on the review of Henry et al. (2009, 731), who recommended aligning savings taxation with an expenditure tax, and with respect to reporting said that "benchmarks should allow an objective evaluation of the effects of government policy, rather than represent that policy." Yet, an alternative interpretation of the Henry Tax Review is that tax expenditure reporting should objectively measure the departure of a T*EE treatment from a TEE benchmark.

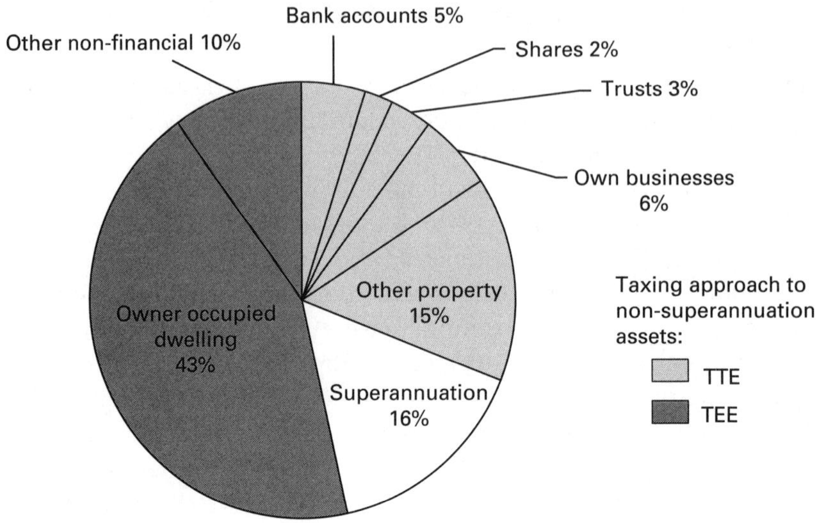

Figure 11.1
Composition of household assets in Australia (in percent) by taxing approach, 2011–2012.
Source: Authors' analysis of Australian Bureau of Statistics (2013).

11.2.4 Combining the Tax Treatment and Tax Benchmark

Table 11.1 summarizes how tax expenditures arise for different savings vehicles and under each benchmark. For example, under the comprehensive income tax benchmark, current superannuation taxation appears concessional and generates tax expenditures.

Under the expenditure tax, concessional tax at the contribution stage is a tax expenditure, while taxing investment returns is a negative tax expenditure (i.e., a tax penalty). Thus, the official use of a comprehensive income tax benchmark for superannuation results in considerable revenue costs, while the use of an expenditure tax benchmark for owner-occupied housing does not.

11.3 Common Concerns

Early analyses by Surrey and others (Surrey 1969; Surrey and McDaniel 1980) deemed tax expenditures to be inferior policy instruments and advocated their repeal or replacement with direct expenditures. While various tax expenditure provisions are now a more accepted part of the tax system, some concerns persist and fuel calls for reform (Smith 2003; Xynas and Jaynes 2013; Ingles and Dennis 2009). Two of the most

Table 11.1
Tax on savings and tax expenditure that would apply under a given benchmark.

	Tax expenditures under pure comprehensive income tax benchmark			Tax expenditures under pure expenditure tax benchmark		
	Contributions	Returns	Benefits	Contributions	Returns	Benefits
TEE (e.g., owner-occupied housing in Australia; Roth 401(k) in US; ISAs in UK)	Taxed	Exemption counted as tax expenditure	Exempt	Taxed	Exempt	Exempt
EET (e.g., pension schemes in most OECD countries)	Exempt	Exemption counted as tax expenditure	Taxed	Taxed	Exempt	Taxed
TTE (e.g., personal saving accounts in Australia)	Taxed	Taxed	Exempt	Taxed	Taxed: Counted as negative tax expenditure	Exempt
T*T*E (e.g., superannuation in Australia)	Partial exemption counted as tax expenditure	Partial exemption counted as tax expenditure	Exempt	Partial exemption counted as tax expenditure	Partial exemption	Exempt
	Partly taxed	Partly taxed		Partly taxed	Part taxed counted as negative tax expenditure	

Source: Authors' compilation.
Note: Dark shading indicates a tax expenditure under a given benchmark (less than the specified norm is being taxed); grey shading indicates a negative tax expenditure (more than the specified norm is being taxed).

prominent concerns relate to fiscal sustainability and equity. Consistent with the rest of the chapter, the following discussion relies primarily on the Australian debate, institutions, and statistics to unravel these issues. In broad terms, though, the analysis is applicable to other jurisdictions.

11.3.1 Significant Fiscal Implications

According to official estimates, tax expenditures in Australia are large. If summed together and compared to those of other countries, as was done recently in a report by the International Monetary Fund (IMF) (Tyson 2014), Australian tax expenditures (at approximately 8 percent of gross domestic product—GDP) are the largest among developed countries. Similarly, according to the Organisation for Economic Co-operation and Development (OECD), Australian tax breaks for private pensions appear large, at approximately 2 percent of GDP, or A$30 billion (figure 11.2, panel A). The tax treatments of superannuation contributions and earnings are the third- and fourth-largest tax expenditures according to the Tax Expenditure Statement, following two tax expenditures related to capital gains taxation.[11]

International comparisons are inherently flawed, however, since they are the outcome of radically different methodologies—a point made by the IMF and OECD. Indeed, no international consensus exists for calculating tax expenditures, which in itself is a warning about being wedded to a single approach. For example, working tax credits are counted as tax expenditures in France but as direct spending in Germany. New Zealand does not tax capital gains and deems such treatment a part of its tax benchmark rather than a departure. Some countries, such as Belgium and the Scandinavian countries, tax capital income but do so within a dual taxation system that recognizes lower tax rates on capital as part of the benchmark. Australian reporting ignores subnational tax expenditures, which is not the case in Austria and Italy. Australian estimates focus on superannuation tax expenditures from current workers, unlike the United Kingdom and the United States, where EET pension arrangements incur tax expenditures on the exempt contributions and returns from current workers but reduce these amounts by tax receipts on benefits of current pensioners. Some countries tax public pension income, presumably spending more on it than if it was tax-exempt; in Australia, public pension income is less than the tax-free threshold for a senior citizen, which lowers outlays but results in tax expenditures. Whereas Australia includes the Medicare Levy as part of its tax benchmark, the United Kingdom does not include National Insurance Contributions—yet both are unhypothecated and act as a tax (Polackova Brixi, Valenduc, and Swift 2004; Minarik 2009; OECD 2010; New Zealand Treasury 2015).

The upward trend is apparent when comparing Tax Expenditure Statement estimates over time (figure 11.2, panel B). Increases can be expected since tax parameters lack indexation, so nominal wage increases drag taxpayers into higher brackets and create greater gaps between marginal income taxes and superannuation taxes. The Temporary Budget Repair Levy, in place from 2014–2015 to 2016–2017, had a similar effect. Furthermore, recent and expected increases are also the result of a maturing superannuation system: a worker with a full career on the former full rate of contributions of 9 percent of earnings is not expected to retire until the late 2040s; a worker subject to the new full rate of 12 percent (expected by 2025) is not expected to retire until the 2070s.

11.3.2 Significant Equity Implications

General concerns about the inequity of tax expenditures are longstanding in Australia and elsewhere (International Fiscal Association 1976). The benefit of tax exemptions can be magnified by the higher tax base and/or marginal tax rates of high earners. The absolute value of tax expenditures increases steeply with income, but arguably more important is whether there is an increase as a proportion of the tax base. This can happen when the rate of tax concession increases with income.

For example, in Australia, the largely flat-rate superannuation taxes are divorced from the personal income tax schedule (figure 11.3, panel A). This means that workers earning 300 percent of average earnings receive a concession of 30 percent compared to the marginal tax rate (plus 2 percent exemption from the Medicare Levy and 2 percent exemption from the Temporary Budget Repair Levy). Workers earning about 25 percent of average earnings are effectively penalized by paying higher tax rates on superannuation contributions than they would on labor income. Counting tax expenditures on investment returns yields similar results, though the effective tax rate on super returns is below 15 percent. The overall outcome is that benefits, measured as a departure from a comprehensively levied income tax, accrue disproportionately to those with higher incomes (figure 11.3, panel B). For example, in 2011–2012, the top decile of earners (i.e., those earning above about 180 percent of the average) accounted for over 37 percent of total superannuation tax expenditures.[12,13]

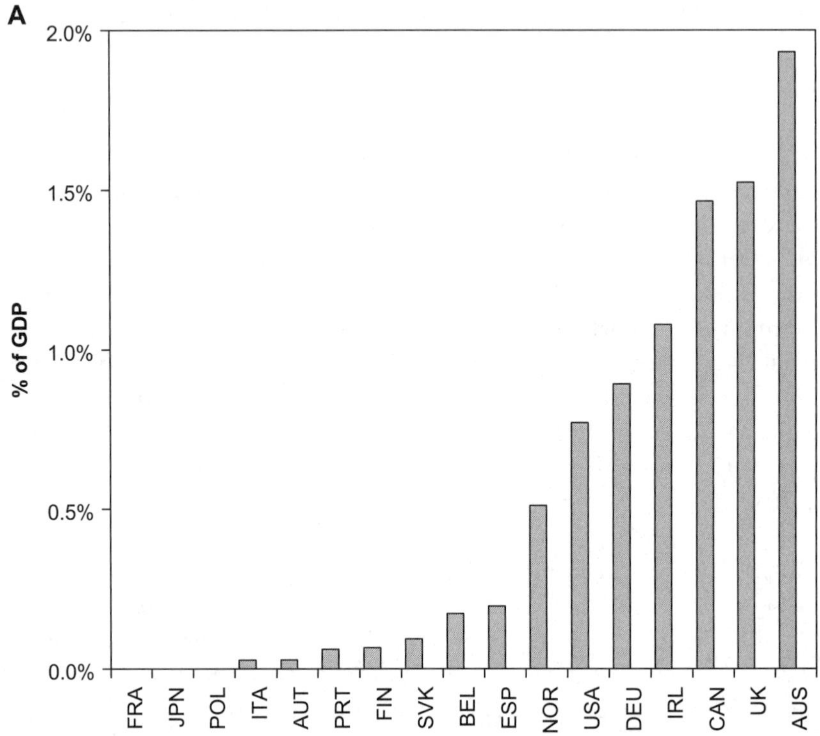

Figure 11.2
Australian tax expenditures on pensions appear large and increasing. *Sources*: (A) OECD (2015); (B) Authors' analysis based on Commonwealth Treasury (various years), Commonwealth of Australia (2015), and Australian Bureau of Statistics (2015). *Note*: As discussed in the text, comparability of estimates between countries and over time is problematic because of the radically different methodologies and nonadditivity of different tax expenditures and over time.

The regressive nature of these tax arrangements was recognized in the Henry Tax Review (Henry et al. 2009), which proposed linking contribution taxes with the marginal tax rate but with a constant level of concession or rebate (e.g., 15–20 percent), designed to reflect retirees' lower income in retirement. The Henry Tax Review also recommended reductions in the superannuation returns tax that effectively transitioned superannuation to a prepaid expenditure tax.

These recommendations have not been acted on, but two ad hoc policy changes were made: the Low Income Superannuation Contribution (LISC), which offsets the contribution tax penalty for those in the bottom two tax brackets (i.e., by crediting the superannuation accounts so that their contribution tax becomes zero), and the doubling of the

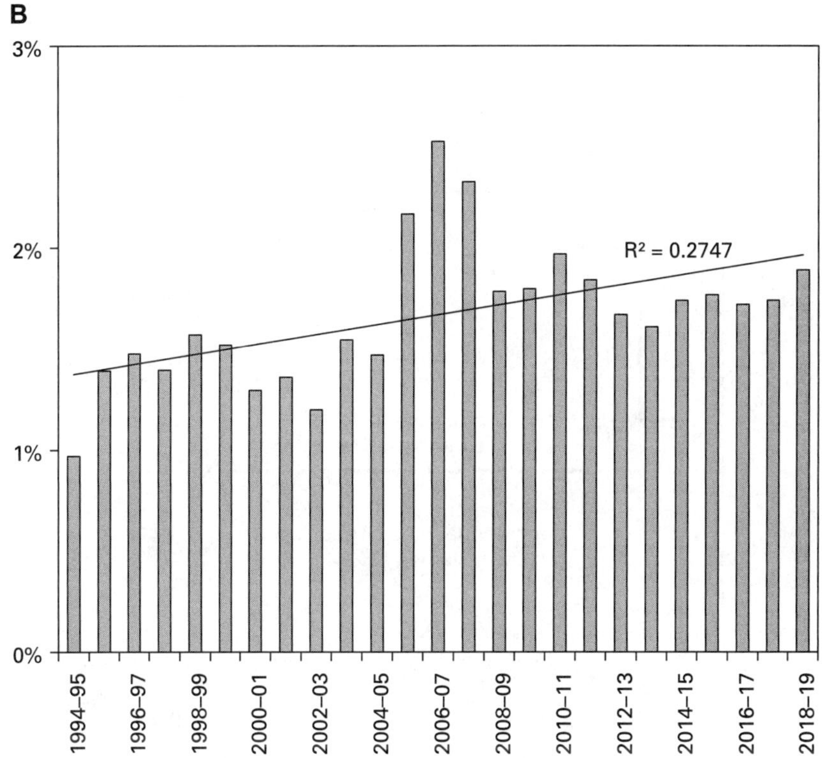

Figure 11.2 (*continued*)

contribution tax for very high earners (i.e., they pay contribution taxes of 30 percent on total income above A$300,000). Once this income exceeds by A$300,000 the amount of superannuation contributions, all contributions are taxed at 30 percent. Both are shown in figure 11.3 (panel A).

However, each measure came with design flaws. The Low Income Superannuation Contribution was implemented as a spending program, which made it easier to unwind by a subsequent fiscally conservative government, since its abolition was seen as cutting spending rather than increasing taxes on the poor. More recently, it was reintroduced as an offset. Also, the high-earner contribution rate added some progressivity, but it affected few people—only the top 1.2 percent in 2012–2013 (Shorten 2013). The more recent proposal is to reduce the threshold at which this takes effect.[14]

More generally, there have been calls for regular reporting of distributional effects of tax expenditures, including from Henry et al. (2009) and more recently from the Australian National Audit Office (2013) and

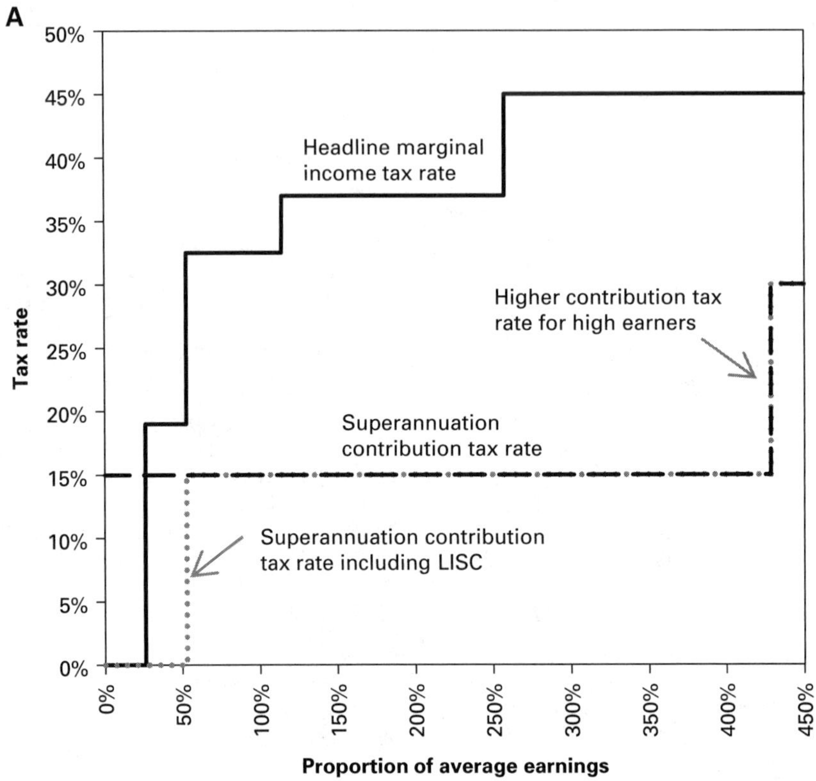

Figure 11.3
Commonly reported trend and distribution of Australian tax expenditures on pensions. *Sources*: (A) Authors' compilation; (B) Commonwealth Treasury (2014). *Note*: (A) Excludes Low Income Tax Offset and Medicare Levy. LISC denotes Low Income Superannuation Contribution. (B) Relates to pretax contributions and in-fund returns.

the Standing Committee on Tax and Revenue (2015). The point of such analyses would be to take account of the progressivity of the tax-benefit system as a whole, not look at specific parts of it in isolation.

11.4 Challenging the Basis of Concerns

The following sections seek to challenge and address concerns about the scale and inequity of tax concessions as measured by tax expenditure methodology. The common pitfalls are demonstrated by presenting a number of modeled examples of saving over the life cycle and across the earnings distribution. In some sense, tax expenditures are taken on their own terms, so illustrative calculations embody assumptions not necessarily supported by the authors.

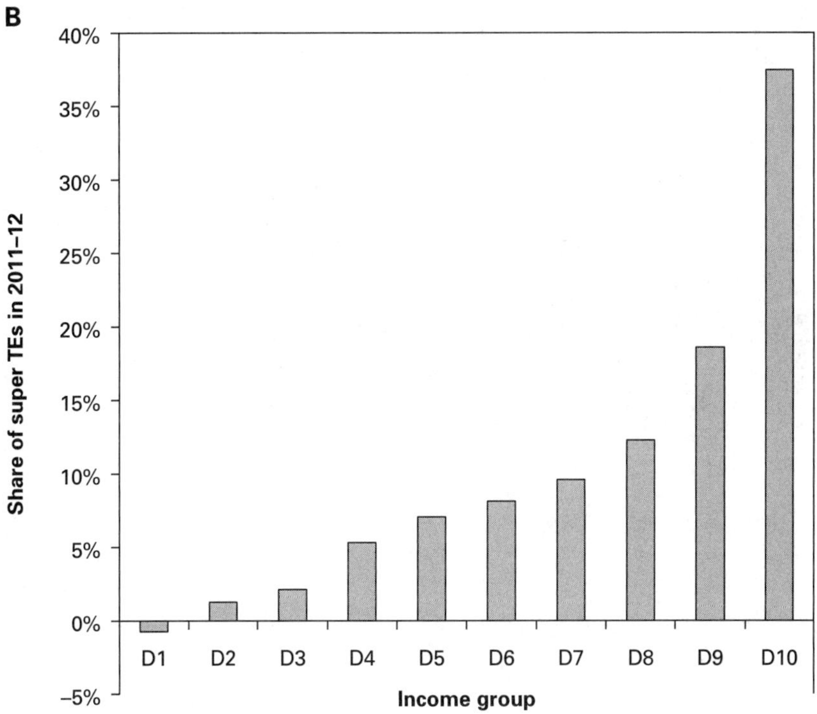

Figure 11.3 (*continued*)

11.4.1 Modeling Used in Illustrative Examples

The modeling is based on legislated superannuation and pension rules (including Age Pension means-test changes) as of late 2016. It follows hypothetical and stylized savers across the earnings distribution, from when they enter the labor force in 2017 at age 20, through a full career, retirement at age 67, and death at age 95. This includes superannuation saving at the mandatory level and subject to a cap. The modeling makes standard assumptions about inflation (2.5 percent), real wage growth (1.5 percent), and real investment returns during accumulation (4.5 percent) and during the (annuitized) pension phase (1.5 percent). Pension and tax thresholds are necessarily assumed to be indexed with wage growth, and results are in today's wage terms. The income tax benchmark is in line with the personal income tax schedule (figure 11.3, panel A).[15]

The analytical exercise accounts for total tax expenditures mechanically ascribed to an individual at a given earnings level, as shown for an average earner over the life cycle in figure 11.4 (panel A) and in the

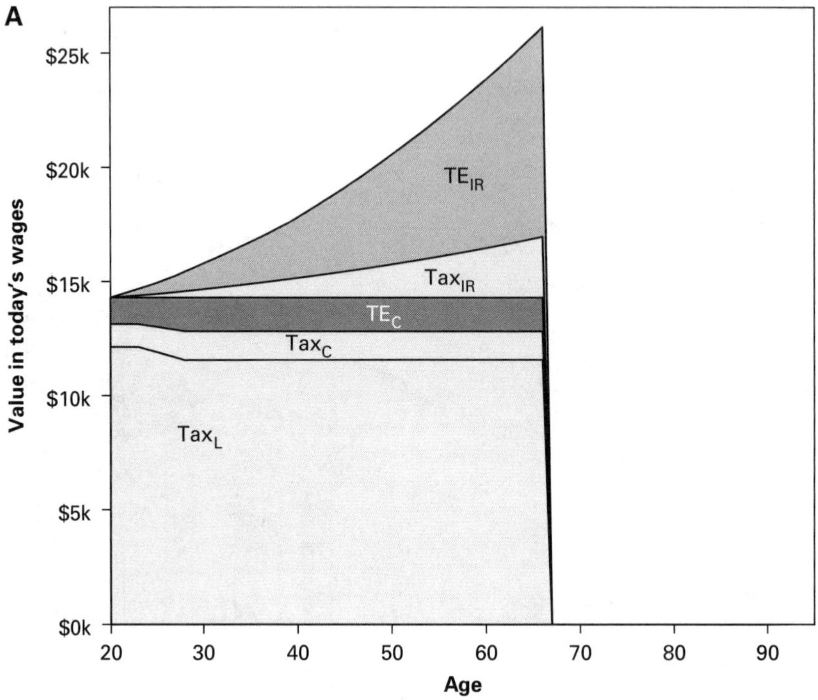

Figure 11.4
Modeling over life cycle and in single year. *Source*: Authors' analysis. *Notes*: Tax_L, Tax_C, and Tax_{IR} denote tax paid on labor, contributions, and investment returns, respectively. TE_C and TE_{IR} denote tax expenditures on contributions and investment returns, respectively. τ_y, τ_C, and τ_{IR} denote the personal income tax, contribution tax, and investment return tax functions, respectively. τ_{IR} assumes the tax rate is reduced by the operation of capital gains discounts and imputed tax. Y, C, and IR denote the amounts, in a given year, of total income (labor income before contributions plus investment income), contributions, and investment income, respectively. Panel B refers to the last year of work.

final year of work (panel B). The calculations are expressed over the life cycle by the formulas

$$TE_{IR}(y) = \sum_{n=20}^{66} (\tau_y(y_n) - \tau_y(y_n - IR_n) - \tau_{IR}(IR_n)) \tag{11.1}$$

and

$$TE_C(y) = \sum_{n=20}^{66} (\tau_y(y_n - IR_n) - \tau_y(y_n - IR_n - C_n) - \tau_C(C_n)), \tag{11.2}$$

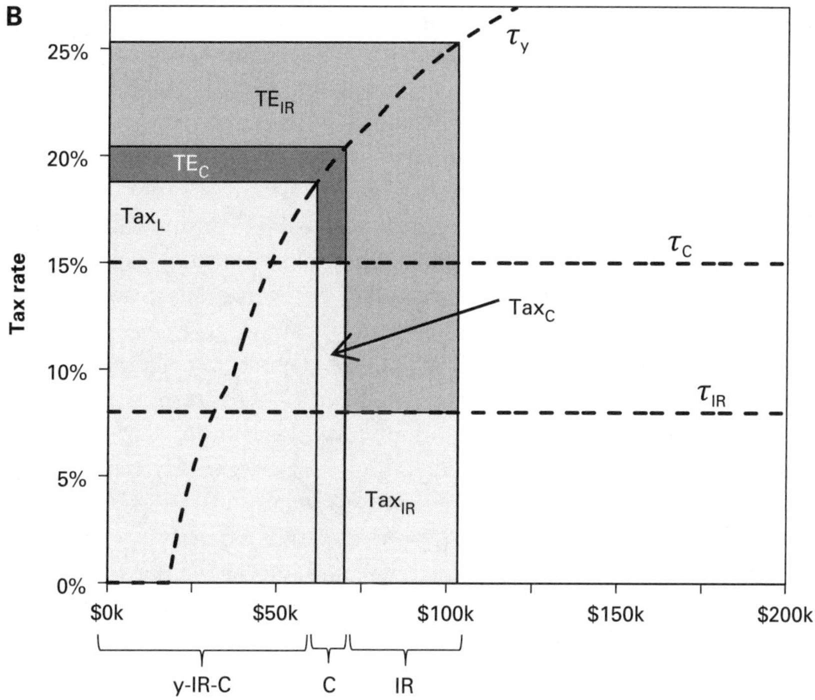

Figure 11.4 (*continued*)

where TE_C and TE_{IR} denote tax expenditures on contributions and investment returns, respectively; τ_y, τ_C, and τ_{IR} denote the tax functions for personal income, contributions, and investment returns, respectively; and y, C, and IR denote the amounts, in a given year, of total income (labor income before contributions plus investment income), contributions, and investment returns, respectively.

The intuition is that TE_{IR} equals the tax that would have been notionally paid had all income been taxed at the individual's marginal rate (the largest rectangle in panel B), minus the tax that would have been paid on precontribution labor income (second-largest rectangle), minus the tax actually paid on investment returns.[16]

In turn, TE_C equals the tax that would have been paid on precontribution labor income (second-largest rectangle), minus the tax actually paid on labor income and contributions.

At the outset, it is important to note that this strawman mechanical approach mimics the way that tax expenditures are currently conceived, but subsequent sections will expose flaws in the methodology (e.g., behavioral change, nonadditivity, and benchmark specification).

11.4.2 Fiscal Implications Can Change with Behavior

Intuitively, it would seem that when government abolishes a given program, the fiscal savings will equal the costs of that program. This is not always the case. For example, cuts to the Age Pension can result in a greater number of people seeking a disability pension, which offsets the original savings. Tax provisions may be even more prone to such behavioral effects.

For superannuation, behavioral effects depend on alternative tax-preferred options, mandated rates, and elasticity of the response. Abolishing tax advantages of superannuation would leave a number of low-tax options to redirect savings into, including trusts, negatively geared property (where rent is lower than interest repayments, allowing tax offsets), owner-occupied housing (which is purchased out of net-of-tax income but is thereafter not taxed at all in Australia), and international investments.

The majority of workers receive only the mandatory superannuation contribution (currently 9.5 percent of earnings), but additional contributions occur as part of remuneration packages or salary sacrifice arrangements. Surveys suggest that in addition to mandatory savings, about 10 percent of workers make pretax contributions via salary sacrifice and 20 percent make personal after-tax contributions. Such participation increases with age and income (Feng, Gerrans, and Clark 2014).[17]

The potential behavioral impact of abolishing tax expenditures is illustrated by comparing a scenario where workers contribute an additional 5 percent of earnings to one with only mandatory contribution rates (figure 11.5, panel A). This hypothetical behavioral change results in a decline in tax expenditures attributable to an average earner (under a comprehensive income benchmark) of 44 percent, to about A$240,000 over the life cycle, or A$5,000 over an average working year. Someone earning twice the average earnings sees a life cycle decline of 42 percent, to about A$570,000.

The behavioral impact can have other fiscal effects, such as an increase in the cost of the Age Pension (see subsection 11.4.5). Here, 5 percentage points less saving can more than double the total cost of the Age Pension for an average earner and more than triple it for an earner making twice the average earnings (figure 11.5, panel B).

The example shows how dramatically the fiscal implications can change with behavior. Since only a small proportion of workers make an additional contribution, aggregate impacts would be smaller.

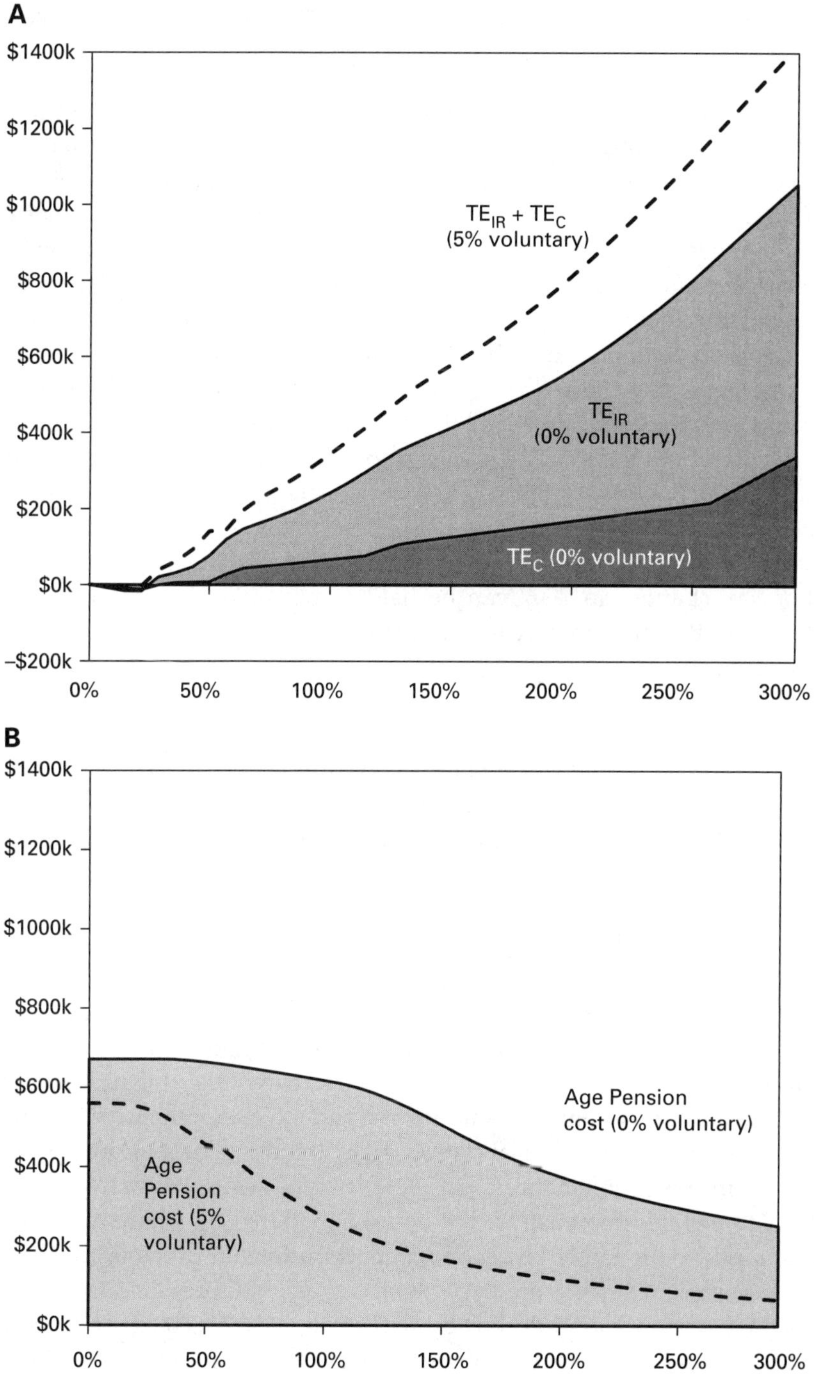

Figure 11.5
Effect of reducing voluntary pretax superannuation contributions by 5 percent. *Source*: Authors' calculations. *Note*: Top earners receive considerable Age Pension because no other savings or income is assumed, contributions are restricted up to the contributory cap, and all super savings are drawn down by the age of death.

Since 2009–2010, the Commonwealth Treasury has published figures incorporating behavioral effects, in which all voluntary superannuation contributions are assumed to be redirected to alternative investments. These "revenue gain" estimates are published alongside the main, "revenue forgone" estimates, but they receive less public attention. Since revenue gain estimates were first reported for superannuation, they have been between 4 percent and 31 percent lower than the revenue forgone numbers (Commonwealth Treasury, various years).

Revenue gain figures are an improved way to understand the fiscal impact of tax expenditures, but these, too, are uncertain. Indeed, empirical evidence of behavioral savings responses to tax incentives is mixed (OECD 2007; Johansson et al. 2008; New Zealand Treasury 2010; Chetty et al. 2014; Feng, Gerrans, and Clark 2014). This is not to say that tax-minimization efforts can be ignored. For example, major superannuation tax changes in 2007 can be held responsible for a doubling in contributions in a single year (Australian Prudential Regulation Authority 2016).

11.4.3 Fiscal Implications Are Not Additive

Unlike direct expenditures, tax expenditures cannot be added to each other and over time. This is because they represent independently calculated hypotheticals. As discussed earlier, the removal of a tax expenditure in superannuation would likely increase the utilization of tax expenditures on other tax-preferred savings but not symmetrically. In fact, since 2012, the Tax Expenditure Statement no longer reports aggregate figures.

The interactions can become more confounding over time. If government were to tax contributions at the marginal rate to reduce tax expenditures, there would be fewer funds on which to calculate the subsequent tax expenditure on investment returns (under a comprehensive income benchmark). Such technical flaws render trend analysis of official tax expenditures problematic.

This effect is demonstrated in figure 11.6 (panel A), where funds are adjusted by the lower levels of net contributions in previous periods. For example, over the life cycle, total tax expenditures credited to an average worker would decline by 16 percent to A$200,000; for a worker earning twice the average earnings, the decline is 20 percent, to A$455,000. Revenue gain estimates attempt to account for such interactions (presumably over the four years of reported projections).[18]

Despite the warnings, commentators continue to refer to the aggregate superannuation figure of approximately A$30 billion. A recent review by the Standing Committee on Tax and Revenue (2015) asked that Treasury consider offering an overall sum of tax expenditures. Such estimates, as one response to the review noted, could "adopt a targeted approach, investigating the interactions for large tax expenditure items when it is likely to make a material difference to the estimate or for items that generate significant public interest." One option is for this to also be taken up in the proposed periodic reviews, which would look at interactions over extended periods, as done illustratively here.

11.4.4 Fiscal Implications Change with the Benchmark

The current choice of benchmark can be considered arbitrary. By contrast, sensible arguments exist that an expenditure tax benchmark is superior since it respects intertemporal and interasset neutrality (see subsection 11.4.5). But what is the effect of using an expenditure benchmark?

This is demonstrated in figure 11.6 (panel B). Since an expenditure benchmark embodies zero taxation of investment returns, the taxation receipts recorded over the individual's lifetime are counted as a negative tax expenditure, or tax penalty. When netted out against the concessionary treatment of contributions, it reveals tax expenditures much lower than shown in the charts so far. For example, total expenditures attributable to an average earner become relatively trivial, at about 6 percent of the tax expenditures under a comprehensive income tax benchmark; for a worker earning twice the average earnings, the figure is 11 percent of the comprehensive income tax benchmark result.[19]

The 2013 Tax Expenditure Statement reported experimental estimates under an expenditure tax benchmark compared to the income tax benchmark. While tax expenditures on contributions were A$16 billion in both cases, tax expenditures on investment returns were shown to be A$–4.7 billion under the former, compared to A$16.1 billion under the latter. Unfortunately, this reporting has not been continued.

11.4.5 Fiscal Implications Change When Interactions with Transfers Are Included

Tax expenditure estimates are not designed to take account of interactions with the transfer system. As a result, they do not capture the actual impacts on current or future budgets. The obvious example is

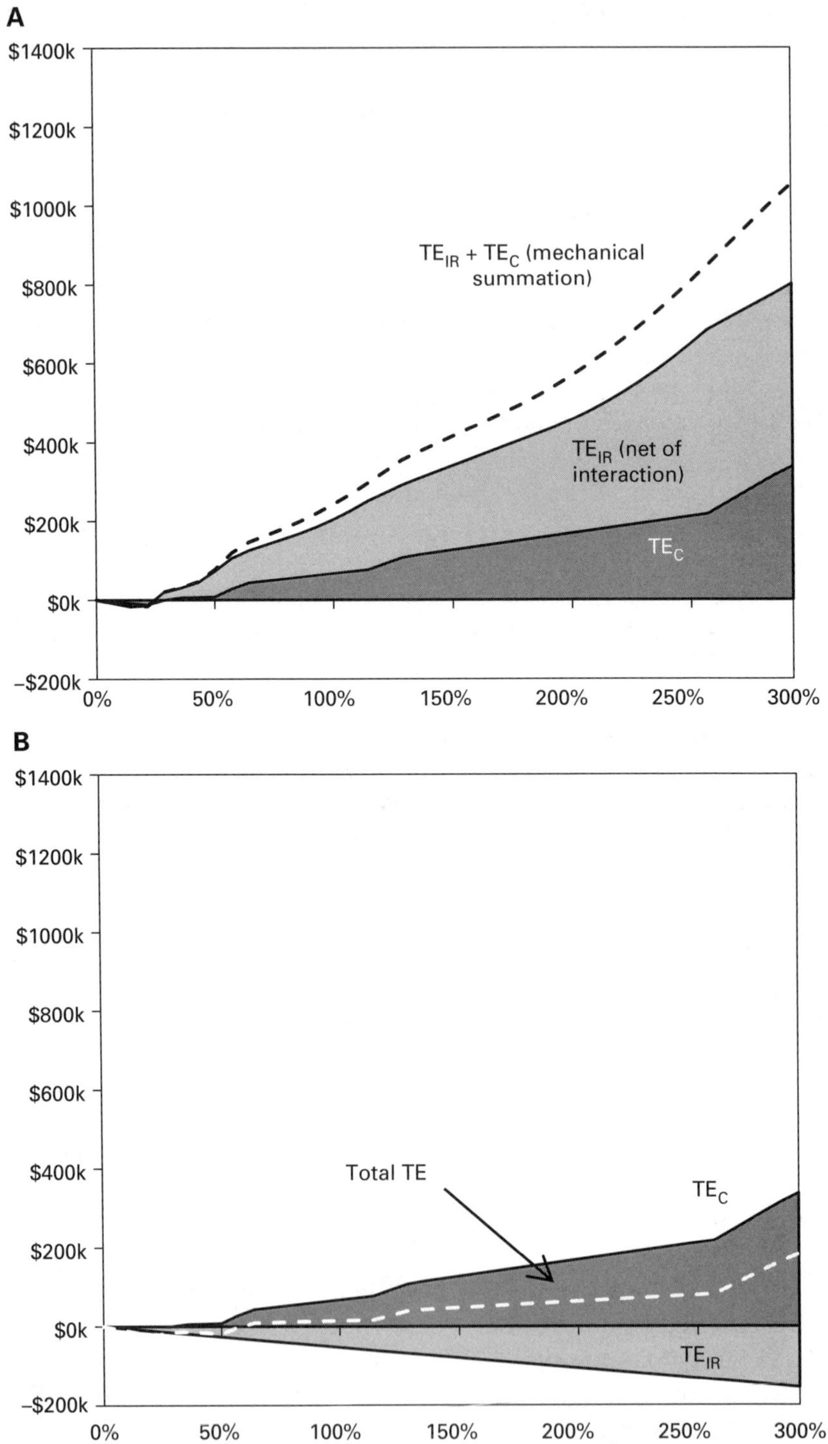

Figure 11.6
Accounting for interactions and different benchmarks. *Source*: Authors' calculations.

that higher taxes on superannuation would lead to lower self-funded retirement incomes and higher spending on Australia's means-tested Age Pension (already mentioned with respect to additional, voluntary contributions in subsection 11.4.2).

Figure 11.7 shows the impact of measuring tax expenditures net of Age Pension costs. Under a comprehensive income tax benchmark (panel A), the additional inclusion of Age Pension costs reduces tax expenditures by about one-fifth for an average worker and by about one-half for someone earning twice the average wage. Under the expenditure tax benchmark (panel B), including Age Pension costs reduces tax expenditures to nearly zero for an average worker and makes them negative for someone earning twice those earnings.

While standard tax expenditure reporting does not take account of the net effects of superannuation policy, occasional analyses do (Commonwealth Treasury 2013). Such total costings are helpful when evaluating policy effectiveness, though admittedly few programs are ever subject to them. For example, how health spending early in life reduces health spending in old age is rarely taken account of. Both Henry et al. (2009) and the Standing Committee on Tax and Revenue (2015) recommended that the Treasury publish regular reports on the long-run economic effects of tax expenditures, including interactions with the Age Pension.

11.4.6 Official Estimates Ignore Economic Efficiency Implications

In addition to fiscal impacts, it is important to take account of broader economic impacts. Any assessment of the efficacy of a major part of the tax system, such as the taxation of savings, needs to recognize how it influences prices and consequently economic outcomes. Two important price distortions are associated with savings taxation and especially pension taxation.

First, a comprehensive income tax benchmark for lifetime savings, or retirement savings, distorts the price of present consumption relative to future consumption. This was first formalized nearly a century ago by Pigou (1928). Taxing the return to net-of-tax savings under the income tax regime is sometimes termed the "double taxation" of savings. This is often cited as an argument in favor of an expenditure tax benchmark.

However, an expenditure tax can also cause distortions, since it affects the choice between labor and leisure, so the argument is not clear-cut. But consumption through working life and consumption in

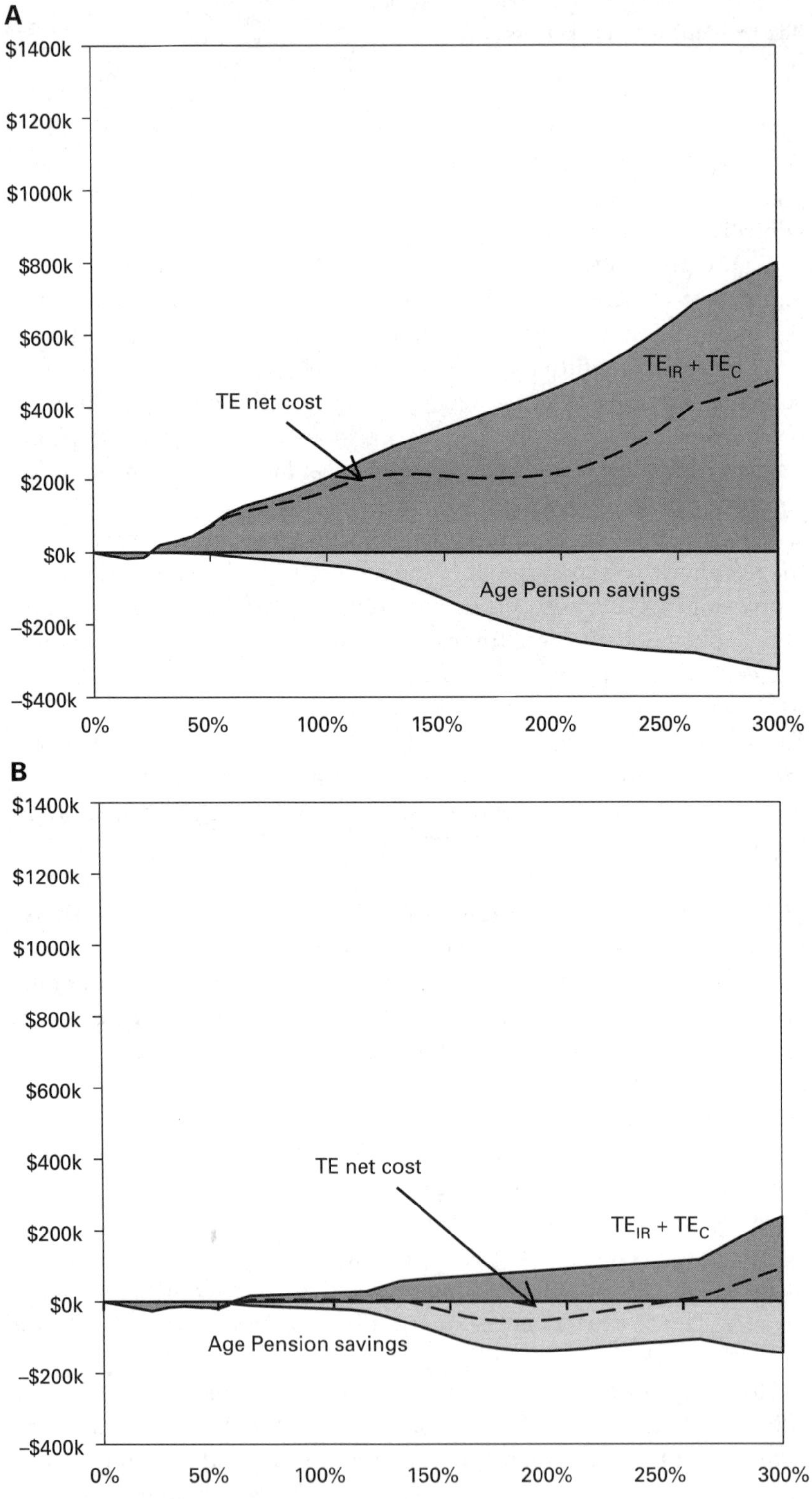

Figure 11.7
Taking account of interactions with the Age Pension. *Source*: Authors' calculations.

retirement can be seen as two major commodity bundles, and introducing a major price distortion that alters their relative prices will likely have negative consequences for economic efficiency.

Another reason why the argument is not clear-cut is that intertemporal neutrality could be delimited to the individual life cycle, wherein consumption during work is treated as equal to consumption during retirement. It may not necessarily apply over multiple life cycles, wherein bequests are used to pass on untaxed capital to future generations. The existence of bequests justifies some capital taxation (Piketty and Saez 2013), for example, via inheritance tax or a reasonable lifetime limit on capital exemption, but this is an argument in favor of limits on tax-preferred saving.

Second, and perhaps more pragmatic, is how differential taxation of assets distorts the relative prices of those assets. It is sometimes argued that many developed economies with income taxes at the center of their fiscal systems are already partway to a consumption tax system. Owner-occupied housing, which constitutes a major slice of privately held wealth and is accumulated over a lifetime, is typically taxed under what is effectively an expenditure tax regime (as is the case in Australia; recall figure 11.1). Pension accumulations are often given a similar tax preference. While capital taxation applies elsewhere, these two key channels of tax-preferred saving are seen as a partial move toward expenditure taxation, albeit through specific savings deductions from an income tax base, and therefore constitute a welfare improvement since they limit interasset distortions.

If an income tax benchmark is adopted, the pursuit of minimizing interasset distortions would suggest that income tax treatment should apply to both owner-occupied housing and pension savings. While such a position has its advocates, this reform is not seriously on the policy agenda. There is therefore an argument born of political constraint that would support the expenditure tax treatment of superannuation savings.[20]

11.4.7 Fairness Implications Change with the Progressivity of the Personal Income Tax

The fact that a large amount of tax expenditures go to high earners should not in itself be a cause for reform. A good deal of the apparent inequity is in fact a result of the progressive nature of the tax system. This can be demonstrated by considering tax expenditures under alternative tax schedules. If a proportional tax system were to apply (such as in the Czech Republic), then tax expenditures would be smaller and have a flatter gradient as earnings increased.

Figure 11.8 (panel A) shows the results under a 20 percent rate across all earners above the zero tax bracket. This less progressive system results in a more equal distribution of tax expenditures. In the base Australian system, someone earning twice the average earnings receives 2.3 times the tax expenditures of an average earner, compared to a proportional system where the earner receives exactly twice the tax expenditure level.

By contrast, increasing the progressivity of the current system (figure 11.8, panel B) makes tax expenditures appear "less fair," despite the fact that such a change would see more overall taxes levied on top earners.[21] Furthermore, such changes to the base would not affect Age Pension spending, since actual super contributions and returns are unaffected.

The analysis emphasizes that the progressivity of the benchmark has a considerable impact on the calculation of tax expenditures, but a remaining concern is that the separation of superannuation tax rates from the personal income tax schedule creates contribution tax penalties for low earners and excessive concessions for high earners. Section 11.5 addresses this.

11.5 What Would a Sensible Reform Look Like?

In seeking to address basic principles of tax neutrality and equity, a sensible reform would align the tax treatment of most savings, including pensions, with an expenditure tax (either TEE or EET) and offer any concessions (either T*EE or EET*) on at least a proportional basis.

This was the recommendation for superannuation taxation reform of the Henry Tax Review (Henry et al. 2009), which suggested a system with a rebate for contributions that was of the same proportional value across the earnings distribution (i.e., so that the contribution tax was effectively the personal income tax rate minus a 15 percent or 20 percent rebate) in addition to low taxation of returns (effectively zero after imputed tax and capital gains discounts). Such a reform would do two things: avoid higher tax advantages to those with higher marginal tax rates and espouse an expenditure tax approach by avoiding taxation of investment returns.

The effect of such a reform is shown in figure 11.9, where the contribution tax is 15 percentage points lower than the marginal rate and

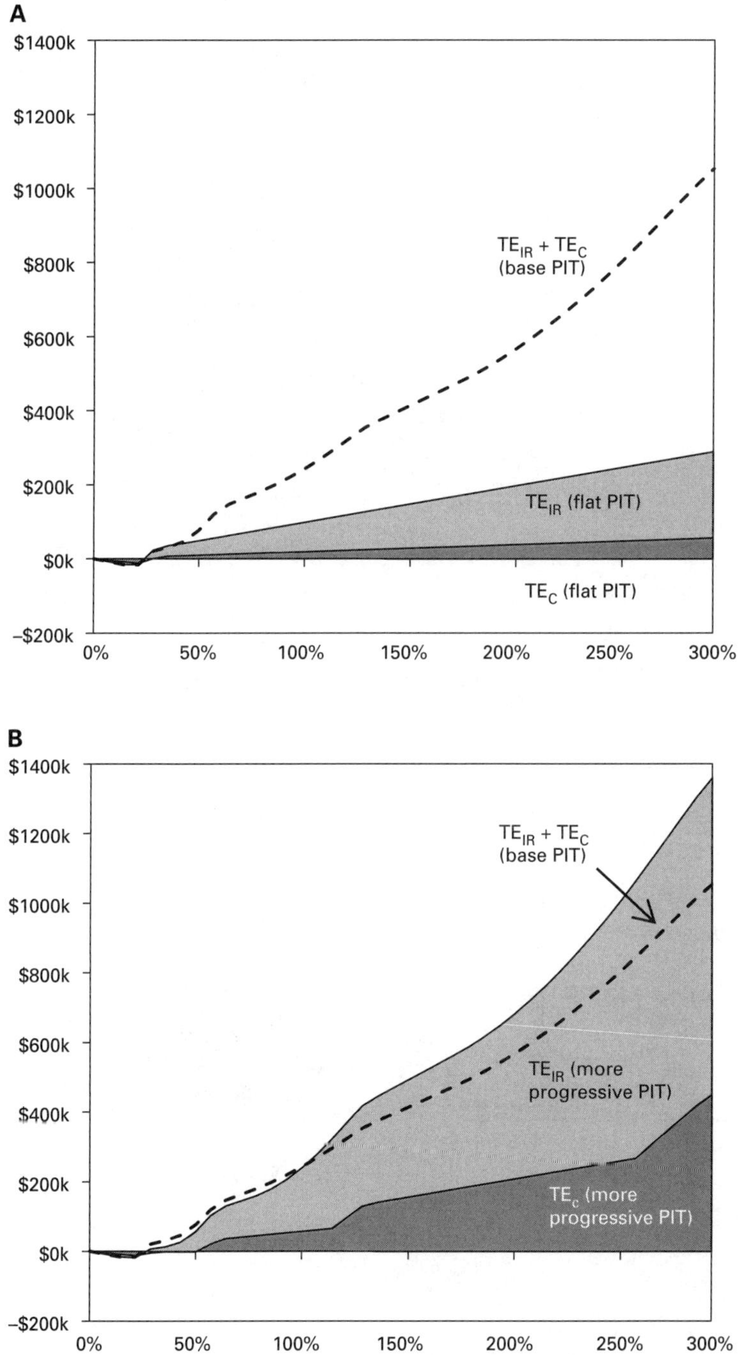

Figure 11.8
The more progressive a tax system, the more tax expenditures. *Source*: Authors' calculations. *Note*: PIT denotes personal income tax, negative TE not shown, comprehensive income tax benchmark, interactions not accounted for. (A) Tax of 20 percent. (B) Tax bracket changes, from top to bottom bracket (in percentage points): +10, +5, –2.5, –5.

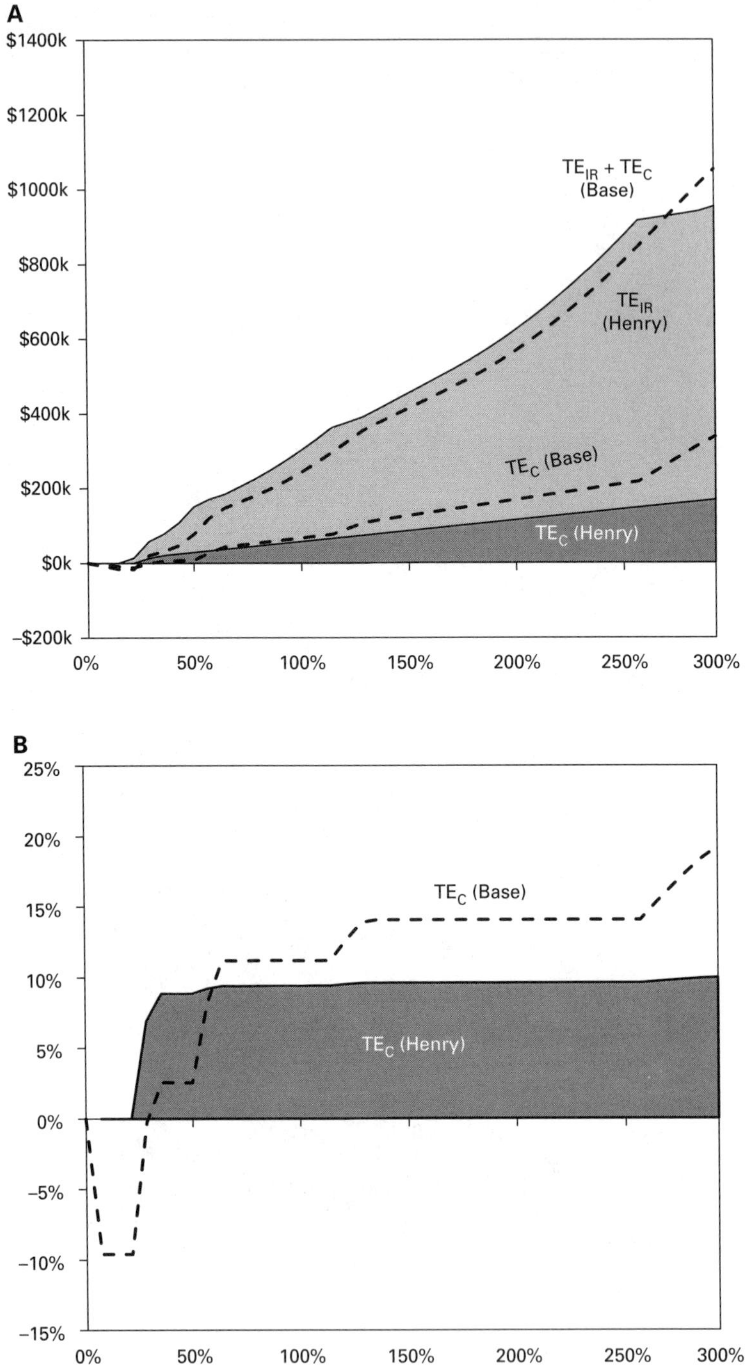

Figure 11.9
Contribution tax linked to personal income tax with a 15 percent concession and no effective tax on investment returns. *Source*: Authors' calculations. *Note*: The Henry Tax Review assumes a 15 percent rebate to all taxpayers. Gross savings consists of present value of total super accumulation and taxes paid on contributions.

the investment tax is effectively zero. Panel A shows that against an income tax benchmark, the reform causes tax expenditures on contributions to be lower and flatter, those on returns to be higher, and tax expenditures overall (though not accounting for interactions) to be higher, except for top earners.

More importantly, panel B illustrates the effect under an expenditure tax benchmark as a proportion of gross savings. Whereas the current system is shown to be regressive, the reform results in a proportional allocation of concessions, thereby restoring the progressivity of the personal income tax scale.[22]

11.6 Conclusions

The concept of tax expenditures was developed in the mid-twentieth century. Since then, estimates of these expenditures have been produced by a range of governments, and to some degree by international organizations. In the absence of more sophisticated tax evaluation instruments, they provide a readily calculable means of measuring the degree of arbitrary or politically motivated erosion of standard taxation bases.

Fundamental to the usefulness and validity of these estimates is their basis of calculation. Rather than being considered on their merits, in much public debate the choice of base has become a kind of ideological battleground. This serves to give greater prominence to the estimates of tax expenditures than they deserve in a mature policy discussion. As noted in a recent review in Australia, "the fact that Treasury's estimates of tax expenditure are often used inappropriately in public debates as a proxy for the budget impact of tax concessions points to a significant unmet demand in the community" (Public Budget Office 2015).

This chapter contributes to the debate by explaining the concepts and concerns via illustrative examples of savings over the life cycle and across the earnings distribution, using the Australian retirement income system as the basis for analysis.

The chapter demonstrates that policy makers in countries with large and/or expanding prefunded private pensions should be cautious about the methodology of calculating tax expenditures and comparing them between countries and over time. Public debates in which tax expenditure estimates are quoted are liable to overstate the scale of tax revenues forgone by ignoring behavior, interactions with other tax expenditures and transfers, and economic efficiency, as well as the sensitivity of results to the benchmark used.

Indeed, official tax expenditure reporting should only be a starting point for good tax-benefit policy design. Additional analysis should include more comprehensive taxation modeling that casts behavior and the impact of tax imposts on choice within a holistic economic modeling structure. Prioritized reviews, meaningful aggregates of tax expenditures, and longer-term costs and benefits of tax treatment of pensions should be developed along the way.

In Australia at least, and probably elsewhere, the debate also focuses on the inequity of pension taxation rather than considering the equity of the overall system. In fact, the high share of tax expenditures that accrues to top earners mostly reflects a progressive tax system in which those earners pay a greater share of tax. Nonetheless, in instances such as Australia's, the proportional nature of contribution taxes can result in concessions that are regressive when compared to the personal income tax schedule. The chapter presents an example of a reform that reverses this regressivity by linking contribution taxes with the progressive personal income tax schedule, along the lines suggested in the Henry Tax Review (Henry et al. 2009).

Addressing basic tax principles of intertemporal neutrality is important for ensuring that consumption today is treated equally to consumption in the future. Broadly speaking, pension tax structures in developed countries are approximated by an expenditure tax regime. This can be given effect by taxing either contributions or benefits (but not both) under the personal income tax and exempting fund investment earnings from taxation—taxation patterns that have earned the acronyms TEE and EET, respectively. This structure is prevalent despite these same jurisdictions taxing savings held for shorter time periods. The details of pension taxation are complex, however, including various limits and thresholds. Tax expenditure calculations that take this widely held structural design as given, and focus on anomalies within this structure, would highlight the need for more detailed, specific analysis of particular features of these regimes.

But how far should intertemporal neutrality extend? While an economic argument for neutrality exists when capital is transferred from working age to retirement, this breaks down when untaxed capital is transferred to the next generation via bequests. In the absence of an inheritance tax or capital transfer tax, it would be justifiable to implement reasonable lifetime limits on the amount of capital exempt from the tax base—probably a better policy reform than annual contribution limits. This would serve to limit the exploitation of retirement income structures for estate management purposes.

Notes

This chapter was prepared for two CEPAR CESifo workshops on "Pension Taxation, Population Ageing and Globalisation," first in Sydney on November 13–14, 2014, and then in Munich on September 3–4, 2015. The chapter benefited from comments by the participants of the workshop and reviewers Robert Holzmann and Bernd Genser. The chapter also benefited from discussions with Robert Holzmann, for which the authors are particularly grateful. Responsibility for any errors of omission or commission remains with the authors.

1. The Rosetta Stone, for example, records that in ancient Egypt priests and some nobles were exempt from taxes on labor and grains (Adams 2001).

2. Departures from a benchmark tax can take several forms, including (1) exemptions, which exclude certain items from the tax base, (2) deductions, which reduce an amount of the assessable tax base before the tax rate is applied, (3) concessions, which reduce the tax rate, (4) offsets, which reduce tax payable by a given amount after the tax rate is applied, and (5) deferrals, which delay the tax calculation or liability to a later period.

3. The system is made up of a large means-tested public pillar; the mandatory, defined contribution superannuation pillar; and voluntary superannuation contributions.

4. Not all tax expenditures related to retirement incomes are considered regressive. For example, the Seniors and Pensioners Tax Offset effectively reduces tax liabilities related to the means-tested Age Pension.

5. For example, see Joint Committee on Taxation (2015) and Emmerson (2014) on policy debates in the United States and the United Kingdom.

6. First published in 1980, detailed estimates are now a legislative requirement, with the express purpose of informing policy making and public debate.

7. This is the Schanz-Haig-Simons definition of income.

8. In some situations, equivalence will only be approximate; for example, when a tax schedule is progressive and replacement rates are below 100 percent. That is, higher income at the time of contribution compared to the time of withdrawal can result in more tax (or tax expenditure) being ascribed to prepaid (TTE and TEE) systems than to postpaid (ETT and EET) systems. Prepaid and postpaid systems will also not be equivalent when the nominal return or tax brackets are not adjusted for inflation. Equivalence will also be compromised where investments benefit from excess returns (e.g., resource rents), where the rate of return differs significantly from the discount rate.

9. For example, see Polackova Brixi, Valenduc, and Swift (2004), OECD (2010), and other chapters in the present volume.

10. Separately, concessions that incentivize savings may offset behavioral biases such as myopia and hyperbolic discounting, which is consistent with maintaining intertemporal neutrality.

11. In addition to the two main tax expenditures on pensions, others relate to retirement provision. Only two-thirds of any nominal capital gain made from a capital gains tax

event occurring on or after September 21, 1999, is included in the assessable income of a fund, provided the fund has held the asset for at least 12 months. According to Commonwealth Treasury (2016), in 2015–2016, the tax revenue forgone from this measure was worth A$580 million. Senior Australians also benefit from a tax expenditure related to the means-tested, public Age Pension, which is effectively provided tax-free via the Senior Australians' and Pensioners Tax Offset, worth A$720 million in 2015–2016.

12. Note that caps on contributions from gross income act to limit excessive regressivity.

13. It is worth recognizing that overall, probably because of the influence of nonlabor income, about 50 percent of income tax in Australia is paid by those in the top decile (Phillips and Stewart 2015). This underlines the point that equity needs to be considered as a whole, not necessarily with every possible element of the tax-benefit system.

14. Since then, others have called for reforms in line with the Henry recommendations (e.g., Australian Council of Social Service 2012; Deloitte as reported in Martin and Bourke 2015). The ACOSS proposal went further by suggesting a budget-neutral, capped, two-tiered rebate that was higher for those on low incomes.

15. The analysis excludes the Low Income Tax Offset, affecting those in the first two tax brackets, and the Medicare Levy of 2 percent, which applies separately to most taxpayers' taxable income. The tax rate on investment returns is assumed to be 8 percent, so tax expenditures under the comprehensive income benchmark will include an amount attributable to dividend imputation and capital gains discounts.

16. As part of the annuitization, the small tax expenditures associated with investment returns in the pension phase are ignored. Inclusion would not change results for average earners, since their taxable income ends up in the zero tax bracket. For a worker earning twice the average earnings, tax expenditures under a comprehensive income tax benchmark would be 5 percent higher.

17. High earners, who have more discretionary income and more to gain from superannuation tax arrangements, have tended to invest in Self-Managed Superannuation Funds, which make up about one-third of total superannuation assets (Australian Prudential Regulation Authority 2016) and on average have balances 14 times higher than for standard member accounts (Australian Tax Office 2016).

18. In addition to these technical calculation flaws, comparisons over time can be problematic because of methodological changes. Australia's Commonwealth Treasury notes that "estimates may change between editions as benchmarks are modified, tax expenditures are modified, revised or new data becomes available, or changes in modelling methodology are made" (Commonwealth Treasury 2016, 5). Which changes were made between different editions is not clear.

19. For comparability, calculations under both benchmarks ignore the types of interactions introduced earlier.

20. A related issue is how the Age Pension means test compounds the tax system's differential treatment of assets (Chomik and Piggott 2016).

21. This would have been the effect of the Temporary Budget Repair Levy of 2 percent on the incomes of those in the top tax bracket between 2014–2015 and 2016–2017.

22. As noted previously, a proposal by the Australian Council of Social Service (ACOSS) went further by suggesting a two-tiered rebate that was higher for those on low incomes. Such a measure could also be designed to provide a negative tax to those in the zero tax bracket.

References

Adams, Charles. 2001. *For Good and Evil: The Impact of Taxes on the Course of Civilisation.* Lanham, MD: Madison Books.

Australian Bureau of Statistics (ABS). 2013. "Household Wealth and Wealth Distribution, Australia, 2011–12." Cat. No. 6554, Australian Bureau of Statistics, Canberra.

Australian Bureau of Statistics (ABS). 2015. "Australian National Accounts: National Income, Expenditure and Product." Cat. No. 5206.0, Australian Bureau of Statistics, Canberra.

Australian Council of Social Service (ACOSS). 2012. "Building Super on a Fair Foundation: Reform of the Taxation of Superannuation Contributions." ACOSS Paper No. 185, Australian Council of Social Service, Locked Bag, New South Wales.

Australian National Audit Office (ANAO). 2013. "Preparation of the Tax Expenditures Statement." Audit Report No. 34, 2012–13, Commonwealth of Australia, Canberra.

Australian Prudential Regulation Authority (APRA). 2016. "Quarterly Superannuation Performance." Commonwealth of Australia, Canberra.

Australian Tax Office (ATO). 2016. "Self-Managed Super Funds: A Statistical Overview 2013–14." Commonwealth of Australia, Canberra.

Bateman, Hazel, Geoffrey Kingston, and John Piggott. 1993. "Taxation, Retirement Transfers and Annuities." *Economic Record* 69:274–284.

Bateman, Hazel, and John Piggott. 1992. "Superannuation Guarantee Charge—What Do We Know About Its Aggregate Impact?" In *Economic and Social Consequences of Australia's Ageing Population—Preparing for the 21st Century*, edited by the Economic Planning Advisory Council, Background Paper No. 23: 41–55. Canberra: Australian Government Publishing Service.

Chetty, Raj, John N. Friedman, Søren Leth-Petersen, Torben Heien Nielsen, and Tore Olsen. 2014. "Active vs. Passive Decisions and Crowding-Out in Retirement Savings Accounts: Evidence from Denmark." *Quarterly Journal of Economics* 129 (3): 1141–1219.

Chomik, Rafal, and John Piggott. 2016. "A Note on the Treatment of Assets in the Australian Age Pension Means Test." CEPAR Working Paper, ARC Centre of Excellence for Population Ageing Research, University of New South Wales, Sydney, Australia.

Commonwealth of Australia. 2015. "Mid-year Economic and Fiscal Outlook 2015–16." Commonwealth of Australia, Canberra.

Commonwealth Treasury. 2013. "A Super Charter: Fewer Changes, Better Outcomes." Commonwealth of Australia, Canberra. http://www.treasury.gov.au/Policy-Topics/SuperannuationAndRetirement/supercharter/~/media/Treasury/Policy%20Topics/Superannuation/supercharter/Downloads/PDF/super_charter_report.ashx.

Commonwealth Treasury. 2014. "Financial System Inquiry: Final Report." Commonwealth of Australia, Canberra.

Commonwealth Treasury. (Various years). "Tax Expenditure Statement." Commonwealth of Australia, Canberra.

Emmerson, Carl. 2014. "Taxation of Private Pensions." In *IFS Green Budget 2014*, edited by Carl Emmerson, Paul Johnson, and Helen Miller, 221–239. London: Institute for Fiscal Studies.

Feng, Jimmy, Paul Gerrans, and Gordon Clark. 2014. "Understanding Superannuation Contribution Decisions: Theory and Evidence." Working Paper, CSIRO-Monash Superannuation Research Cluster, Project 3: Better Superannuation Outcomes, http://www.superresearchcluster.com.

Henry, Ken, Jeff Harmer, John Piggott, Heather Ridout, and Greg Smith. 2009. "Australia's Future Tax System: Report to the Treasurer." Commonwealth of Australia, Canberra.

Ingles, David, and Richard Denniss. 2009. "The Great Superannuation Tax Concession Rort." Research Paper No. 61, The Australia Institute, Manuka.

International Fiscal Association (IFA). 1976. *Tax Incentives as an Instrument for Achievement of Government Goals*, Studies in International Fiscal Law 61a. Dordrecht: Kluwer for the International Fiscal Association.

Johansson, Åsa, Christopher Heady, Jens Arnold, Bert Brys, and Laura Vartia. 2008. "Tax and Economic Growth." Economics Department Working Paper No. 620, OECD, Paris.

Johnson, Paul, and Carl Emmerson. 2016. "The Taxation of Private Pensions in the UK." CEPAR Working Paper No. 2016/10, ARC Centre of Excellence in Population Ageing Research, University of New South Wales, Sydney, Australia.

Joint Committee on Taxation. 2015. "Estimates of Federal Tax Expenditures for Fiscal Years 2015–2019." Congress of the United States of America, Washington, DC.

Martin, Peter, and Latika Bourke. 2015. "Superannuation 'Circuit Breaker' Would Save Budget $6b per Year." *Sydney Morning Herald*, October 26, http://www.smh.com.au/federal-politics/political-news/superannuation-circuit-breaker-would-save-budget-6b-per-year-20151025-gkhy11.html.

Minarik, Joe. 2009. "Tax Expenditures in OECD Countries." Presentation at Meeting of Senior Budget Officials, OECD, Paris, June 4–5, 2009.

New Zealand Treasury. 2010. "The Effect of Tax Incentives on Retirement Savings." New Zealand Treasury Savings Working Group Working Paper, New Zealand Treasury, Wellington, New Zealand.

New Zealand Treasury. 2015. "2015 Tax Expenditure Statement." New Zealand Government, Wellington, New Zealand.

OECD (Organisation for Economic Co-operation and Development). 2007. *Encouraging Savings through Tax-Preferred Accounts*. Tax Policy Studies No. 15. Paris: OECD Publishing.

OECD (Organisation for Economic Co-operation and Development). 2010. *Tax Expenditures in OECD Countries*. Paris: OECD Publishing.

OECD (Organisation for Economic Co-operation and Development). 2015. *Pensions at a Glance*. Paris: OECD Publishing.

Phillips, Ben, and Miranda Stewart. 2015. "FactCheck: Is 50% of All Income Tax in Australia Paid by 10% of the Working Population?" *The Conversation*, https://theconversation.com/factcheck-is-50-of-all-income-tax-in-australia-paid-by-10-of-the-working-population-45229.

Pigou, Arthur. 1928. *A Study in Public Finance*. London: Macmillan.

Piketty, Thomas, and Emmanuel Saez. 2013. "A Theory of Optimal Inheritance Taxation." *Econometrica* 81 (5): 1851–1886.

Polackova Brixi, Hana, Christian Valenduc, and Zhicheng Swift. 2004. *Tax Expenditures—Shedding Light on Government Spending through the Tax System: Lessons from Developed and Transition Economies*. Washington, DC: World Bank.

Public Budget Office (PBO). 2015. "Submission to the Standing Committee on Tax and Revenue Inquiry into the Tax Expenditures Statement." Commonwealth of Australia, Canberra.

Shorten, Bill. 2013. "2012–13 Budget—Superannuation Reforms." Press Release No. 024, Minister for Financial Services and Superannuation, Commonwealth of Australia, Canberra.

Smith, Julie. 2003. "Tax Expenditures: The $30 Billion Twilight Zone of Government Spending." Department of the Parliamentary Library, Information and Research Services, http://apo.org.au/files/Resource/03rp081.pdf.

Standing Committee on Tax and Revenue. 2015. "The Tax Expenditures Statement." House of Representatives, Commonwealth of Australia, Canberra.

Surrey, Stanley. 1969. "Excerpts from Remarks Before the Money Marketeers on The U.S. Income Tax System: The Need for a Full Accounting, November 15, 1967." In *Annual Report of the Secretary of the Treasury on the State of the Finances for the Fiscal Year Ended June 30, 1968*, 322. United States Department of the Treasury. Washington, DC: Government Printing Office.

Surrey, Stanley, and Paul McDaniel. 1980. "The Tax Expenditure Concept and the Legislative Process." In *The Economics of Taxation*, edited by H. Aaron and Michael Boskin, 123. Washington, DC: Brookings Institution Press.

Tyson, Justin. 2014. "Reforming Tax Expenditures in Italy: What, Why, and How?" IMF Working Paper No. WP/14/7, International Monetary Fund, Washington, DC.

Xynas, Lidia, and Steve Jaynes. 2013. "From Tax Expenditures to Rebates: An 'Output Based Equity' Approach for Australia's Retirement Policies." *Revenue Law Journal* 22 (1): 1–51.

III Country-Calibrated OLG/CGE Models

12 Aging, Taxes, and Pensions: Switzerland

Christian Keuschnigg

12.1 Introduction

Demographic change poses a challenge to Switzerland's welfare state. With current levels of benefits and a much larger dependent population, contribution rates and social spending will grow to unprecedented levels. Social spending is already a main driver of public sector growth in Switzerland. Given the projected rise in the dependency ratio, this trend is bound to accelerate over several decades if current policies remain unreformed. The burden of labor taxes and social security contributions will have to grow substantially to sustain current levels of benefits, with negative consequences for labor market performance, or benefits will have to be cut to much smaller levels.

The financing of social security and labor market behavior are interrelated in important ways. Aging necessitates higher taxes and contributions, with negative effects on labor earnings and growth. Lower earnings, in turn, require further increases in contribution rates and taxes. This chapter focuses on the incentive effects on five aspects of labor supply in general equilibrium.

First, employees can adjust intensive labor supply, consisting of hours worked or effort on the job. This incentive is measured by the effective tax rate on wage income, which includes not only the income tax but also contributions to social security as well as consumption taxes. In principle, the contributions to social security are a nondistorting price for individual insurance. However, insurance benefits are typically worth less than contribution payments. As pointed out by Feldstein and Samwick (1992) long ago, part of the statutory contribution rate is an implicit tax that adds to tax distortions.

Second, employees may invest in education and lifetime training. The Swiss government often subsidizes current training costs. On the other hand, a progressive income tax discourages training, since the extra tax on higher future earnings is larger than the present tax savings when the individual gives up income to devote more time to training. In an aging society, postponed retirement is needed to balance pension systems by raising labor force participation among older workers. This obvious adjustment also strengthens incentives for training among younger employees, as they can expect to reap the returns to training over a longer working period.

Third, taxes and benefits affect labor market participation among prime-age workers. The larger the earnings from a job net of tax relative to social assistance benefits, the larger the incentive to (re)enter the labor market. Fiscal incentives are captured by "participation tax rates," which are typically large, since they consist of the sum of tax and contribution rates plus the replacement rate when out of the labor force.

Fourth, incentives to search for jobs are diminished by taxes and contributions as well as forgone social benefits when leaving unemployment.

Finally, an individual's retirement date reflects another participation decision. When continuing to work instead of retiring, a person pays taxes and social security contributions over a longer period and, at the same time, may have to give up an eligible pension. Again, the participation tax on continued work tends to be very high since it consists of the sum of taxes and forgone benefits. However, incentives for early retirement can be greatly reduced if the system includes significant pension discounts when retiring earlier and supplements when retiring later.

This chapter uses an overlapping-generations model to replicate demographic projections and quantifies the fiscal and economic consequences of aging in Switzerland. The model captures in detail the interactions between taxes, social security, and the labor market. The base case scenario simulates the effects of a passive fiscal strategy that merely adjusts labor taxes and contribution rates to balance budgets. Economic consequences turn out to be rather discouraging, leading to an increase in total labor taxes of 21 percentage points and a reduction in per capita income of roughly 20 percent. The next scenario turns to a comprehensive reform that implements six policy measures, ranging from structural reform of the pay-as-you-go (PAYG) pillar to an increase in the statutory retirement age. Raising the retirement age by four years is by far the most important measure. Simulation results show that the reform can limit the increase in the tax burden to 4 percent of the value-added tax (VAT) rate and the decline in per capita income to less than 6 percent in the long run.

The key message is that a large part of the negative consequences of aging can be offset by a comprehensive reform to boost the quantity and quality of labor supply and thereby the contribution base of social security. The tax system already allows for deferred taxation of pension income and is thereby in line with the goals of mandatory pension savings. It also includes tax incentives for voluntary incremental pension savings. Tax reform is thus not part of the policy scenario.

This chapter relates to extensive literature on aging and social security reform.[1] The demographic effects on the financing of pensions and on the economy are discussed in Miles (1999) and Bovenberg and Knaap (2005), for example. Important survey articles include Feldstein and Liebman (2002), Bovenberg (2003), and Lindbeck and Persson (2003). A particular problem is the trend toward early retirement. Retirement incentives are extensively analyzed in the theoretical and empirical literature; see, for example, Gruber and Wise (2004), who summarized results for a wide range of industrial countries. Jaag, Keuschnigg, and Keuschnigg (2010) analyzed aging and pension reform in Austria. Recently, the debate in the United States has focused on either assigning a more important role to capital funding (Kotlikoff 1997; Feldstein 2005a, 2005b) or reforming the existing PAYG system (Diamond 2004; Diamond and Orszag 2005). Holzmann (2013) offered a review of worldwide trends in pension reform, while the OECD (2014) provided an extensive analysis of aging and offered policy recommendations for Switzerland. Börsch-Supan et al. (2015) reviewed the effects of aging and pension reform on savings. Recent work with state-of-the-art quantitative models has focused on aging and human capital formation (Kindermann 2015; Vogel, Ludwig, and Börsch-Supan 2017) and on fiscal costs under alternative reforms (Kitao 2014, 2015).

The present analysis is one of the most detailed in assessing the potential labor market effects of aging and social security reform. Most of the literature does not institutionally model the coexistence of PAYG and capital-funded pillars and limits attention to only one or two aspects of labor supply. This chapter quantitatively demonstrates that all five employment aspects are important determinants of the economic response to aging and pension reform. Another novel contribution is the rigorous analysis of the different labor market consequences of the PAYG and funded pension systems in a unified framework. Agents separately contribute to the PAYG and funded pillars and accumulate private savings to provide for old-age consumption. Retirement income stems from private savings on top of separate PAYG and funded pensions. The analysis here explicitly shows how the three pillars of the Swiss pension system together with labor taxation, unemployment insurance, and social assistance add to the effective tax rates on labor supply. To compute these effective tax rates is in itself a novel contribution.

The chapter proceeds as follows. Section 12.2 presents the model. Section 12.3 documents demographic changes, develops a comprehensive pension reform scenario, and discusses the taxation of pensions in Switzerland. Section 12.4 presents quantitative results, and section 12.5 offers conclusions.

12.2 A Model of Aging and the Labor Market

The analysis uses a dynamic general equilibrium model with overlapping generations, a rich institutional model of the public sector and social security, and five aspects of employment L^D. For the sake of transparency, the main identities and behavioral equations are presented to intuitively explain the key transmission channels for policy effects.[2] Maybe the most important channel for labor market effects is endogenous retirement, which determines the physical labor force N^W via the participation decisions of older persons. Prime-age workers respond in four additional areas: a participation decision determining the participation rate $\overline{\delta}$, where the bar stands for an average among age groups; job search, which, together with job creation by firms, results in an unemployment rate $\bar{u}$ for the active labor force; hours worked or on-the-job effort of employed workers $\overline{l}$; and lifetime training affecting the skill level $\overline{\theta}$. Aggregate employment is

$$L_t^D = \overline{\theta}_t \cdot \overline{l}_t \cdot (1 - \overline{u}_t) \cdot \overline{\delta}_t \cdot N_t^W. \quad (12.1)$$

12.2.1 Demographic Change

An overlapping-generations model with a period length of one year is applied. A limited number of age states, $a \in \{1, \ldots, A\}$, is assumed to exist, each associated with life cycle characteristics, such as earnings, employment risk, and mortality. The calibrated model distinguishes five active and three retired groups with size N_t^a.[3] At each date, an individual faces three possible events: (1) death with probability $1 - \gamma^a$; (2) survival without aging (i.e., keeping all life cycle characteristics), remaining in the same age state with probability $\gamma^a \omega^a$; or (3) surviving, aging, and belonging to group $a+1$ in the next period with probability $\gamma^a (1-\omega^a)$. Individuals in the last state have exhausted the aging process ($\omega^A = 1$) and either survive with probability γ^A or die with probability $1-\gamma^A$, as in Blanchard's (1985) model of perpetual youth. After aggregation, the demographic system is

$$N_{t+1}^1 = \gamma^1 \omega^1 \cdot N_t^1 + n_{t+1}^0, \quad N_{t+1}^a = \gamma^a \omega^a \cdot N_t^a + \gamma^{a-1}(1-\omega^{a-1}) \cdot N_t^{a-1}. \tag{12.2}$$

The total population remains constant only when the inflow of newborns n^0 equals the outflow caused by mortality in all age groups.

Retirement choice occurs in an intermediate state, corresponding to people 60 to 69 years old. Retirement leads to an endogenous fraction $0 < x^m < 1$ of still active workers in the "mixed" group, while a share $1-x^m$ are retired and collect pension benefits. Noting $x^a = 1$ for prime-age workers, $a < m$, and $x^a = 0$ for fully retired people, the physical labor force N^W as stated in (12.1) is $N^W = \Sigma_{a \le m} x^a N^a$, while the number of retirees is $N^R = \Sigma_{a \ge m}(1-x^a)N^a$. The economic dependency ratio N^R / N^W depends on retirement choice in group m.

12.2.2 Life Cycle Labor Supply and Consumption

12.2.2.1 Earnings Prime-age workers are equipped with skill units of labor θ^a so that work per unit of time pays a gross wage $w^a \theta^a$. Training shifts life cycle earnings profiles. Active agents can be in one of three different labor market states: nonparticipating; participating and unemployed; or participating and working. Denoting the participation rate by δ^a and the unemployment rate by u^a, the average wage-related income per unit of skill amounts to

$$\bar{y}_t^a = \delta_t^a \cdot y_t^a + (1-\delta_t^a) \cdot s_t^a, \quad y_t^a = (1-u_t^a) \cdot l_t^a w_t^{n,a} + u_t^a \cdot b_t^a. \tag{12.3}$$

When nonparticipating, agents obtain social assistance and other benefits equal to s^a. If participating but unemployed, they are entitled to unemployment benefits $b^a = b^U \cdot l^a w^{n,a}$, which are indexed to net wage earnings with a replacement rate b^U. The net wage is reduced by employee contribution rates t^E and t^F to the PAYG and funded pillars, and by wage tax rates $t^{w,a}$. While contributions are proportional, the wage tax is progressive and implies varying tax rates over the life cycle, reflecting the typical hump-shaped pattern of life cycle earnings. Since social security contributions are tax-deductible, net wages amount to $w^{n,a}=(1-t^{w,a})\,(1-t^{E}-t^{F})\,w^{a}$.

Participation incentives reflect the income gap between replacement income s^a and expected income y^a when joining the labor force. If participating, an agent either finds employment with probability $1-u^a$ and earns net wages or ends up unemployed with probability u^a and collects benefits. The employment probability itself is determined by incentives for job searching that are often undermined by the welfare system. The unemployment rate $u^a=1-\zeta^a\cdot f$ in life cycle group a depends on the search effort ζ^a and on the state of the market given by the matching probability f. High taxes and benefits reduce the income gap between work and unemployment, discourage job searching ζ^a, and result in larger unemployment, which, in turn, reduces expected income y^a and feeds back negatively on labor market participation.

12.2.2.2 Savings Four ways to provide for the future are distinguished: (1) private savings and asset accumulation A^a; (2) contributions to earnings-linked pensions, accumulating (implicit) future pension claims $A^{E,a}$; (3) contributions to the funded pillar, accumulating assets $A^{F,a}$ in an individual account; and (4) skill accumulation by devoting time to training. Skills become obsolete with rate $1-\delta^h$. Agents must thus engage in training to prevent a depreciation of skills. New skills are acquired with technology $F(\cdot)$ using teaching resources I^a and training time as inputs. When people are employed, they allocate time to training e^a and hours of work l^a, adding up to e^a+l^a. Training is on the job. Effective training rises with higher participation and employment rates, while nonparticipation and unemployment lead to a loss of skills:

$$\begin{aligned}
\gamma^a G A^a_{t+1} &= R_{t+1}\left[A^a_t + \text{net earnings} - (1+t^c_t)C^a_t\right],\\
\gamma^a G A^{F,a}_{t+1} &= R^F_{t+1}\left[A^{F,a}_t + \text{contributions} - \text{pensions}\right],\\
G A^{E,a}_{t+1} &= R^E_{t+1}\left[A^{E,a}_t + m^a\cdot(\text{earnings})\right],\\
G\theta^a_{t+1} &= F(\text{training}, I^a_t)\theta^a_t + \delta^h\theta^a_t.
\end{aligned} \tag{12.4}$$

The factor G is one plus the growth rate and reflects exogenous productivity growth, while γ^a enters by the assumption of reverse life insurance, as in Blanchard (1985) for financial assets, applied to each group separately. When accidental bequests are distributed among surviving agents via this implicit insurance contract, individuals' effective return on savings is augmented by the factor $1/\gamma^a$. In the first equation of (12.4), new savings consist of earnings net of tax minus consumption spending $(1+t^c)C^a$ including tax at rate t^c. In a small open economy, the interest factor $R=1+r$ is fixed on world markets.

The second equation of (12.4) shows the accumulation of financial assets $A^{F,a}$ in the individual account of the mandatory funded pillar. In any period, contributions by workers and firms at rates t^F and $t^{F,F}$, respectively, add to existing assets and build up a person's financial wealth until retirement, when it is converted into a pension annuity. The contribution rates apply to gross wage earnings of employed workers. Unemployment and nonparticipation result in lower contributions and reduce pensions after retirement. It is assumed that the funded system generates a return on assets that is possibly below the market return. The return differential captures costly investment regulations and high administrative costs, making savings via the funded system only an imperfect substitute for private savings.

The third equation of (12.4) models the accumulation of implicit pension claims $A^{E,a}$ in the earnings-linked PAYG pillar. At any date, new pension claims are added that are equal to the fraction m^a of the pension assessment base, which normally would consist of earnings of an employed worker. In Switzerland, unemployment benefits received during periods of joblessness fully raise the assessment base.[4] Other countries often apply similar rules. The factor m^a captures the tax-benefit link. If it is zero, future benefits are independent of current earnings, making the contribution rate a full tax. If it is positive, agents anticipate that higher earnings today will translate into higher benefits in the retirement period so that contributions are perceived less as a tax. At the date of retirement, the starting pension is equal to accumulated claims.

12.2.2.3 Lifetime utility Anticipating consequences later in life, agents optimally choose consumption and work-related activities C_t^a, l_t^a, e_t^a, ζ_t^a, δ_t^a, and x_t^m to maximize expected lifetime utility. Preferences in recursive form (Weil 1990; Gertler 1999) are

$$V_t^a = \max\left[(Q_t^a)^\rho + \gamma^a \beta (G\bar{V}_{t+1}^a)^\rho\right]^{1/\rho}, \tag{12.5}$$

where β is a discount factor and $\sigma = 1/(1-\rho)$ is the intertemporal elasticity of substitution. Instantaneous utility $Q_t^a \equiv C_t^a - \bar{\varphi}_t^a$ is assumed separable in consumption C_t^a and effort costs $\bar{\varphi}_t^a$, which are convex, increasing in job-related activities. Separability excludes income effects of labor supply. Expected utility in the next period, $\bar{V}_{t+1}^{a} = \omega^{a} V_{t+1}^{a} + (1-\omega^{a}) V_{t+1}^{a+1}$, takes account of the fact that, with probability $1-\omega^{a}$, the agent may switch to the next age state, $a+1$.

Given four ways to provide for future consumption, five aspects of labor market activity, and a multitude of policy instruments, the solution of the household decision is necessarily complicated.[5] However, behavior reflects the same intuition known from stylized models. Households smooth consumption over income states and life cycle periods. The level of the consumption profile exhausts lifetime resources so that, at any date, consumption net of effort costs is a fraction of lifetime wealth, consisting of financial assets, discounted future earnings (human wealth), pension wealth, and the present value of transfers. The marginal propensity to consume rises with higher mortality rates in later stages of life.

12.2.2.4 Work and training Fiscal incentives are captured by effective tax rates. The effective tax on intensive labor supply is reduced by the deductibility of social security contributions, reflecting the consumption tax treatment of pension savings. It is further reduced by wage indexation of unemployment benefits. When a worker is employed, working more hours not only raises earnings but also raises benefits when the worker becomes unemployed. Hence, benefit indexation reduces the effective wage tax on work effort. Intensive labor supply is also discouraged by the effective pension contribution tax. This implicit tax is greatly reduced if there is a strong tax-benefit link m^{a}. Higher earnings today add to the pension assessment base and raise benefits after retirement. The present value of these extra benefits reduces the tax character of the statutory contribution rate. Strengthening the tax-benefit link thereby boosts the intensive labor supply. Finally, the implicit contribution tax to the funded pillar is very low, even zero under ideal conditions. When an individual pays into her individual account at the statutory rate t^{F}, the contribution will earn interest, much like private savings. At retirement, the individual gets a pension annuity with a present value equal to the value of the accumulated assets. All this would just replicate private savings if $R^{F}=R$. The contribution would be a perfect substitute for private savings and would not be perceived as a tax at all, giving an implicit tax rate of zero. If $R^{F}<R$, pension fund savings yield a lower return and contain a tax component.

The general principle is that an effective tax rate rises when higher earnings lead to paying more tax or giving up social benefits (e.g., unemployment and social assistance) but declines with a stronger tax-benefit link (i.e., when higher earnings today contribute to higher retirement income). The choice of intensive labor supply on the job (equivalently, hours worked or work effort) balances the marginal increase in earnings net of effective tax rates and the marginal utility cost of work. When employed, agents allocate time $l^a + e^a$ on training and work, creating an effort cost. More training comes at the expense of working time, but the acquired skills shift up future earnings. Training is optimal when the marginal return is equal to the common opportunity cost of productive time. Importantly, postponed retirement boosts training incentives since the additional earnings accrue over a longer working life. The effect should be more important for persons close to retirement, where an increase in the retirement age means a disproportionately large extension of the remaining working life.

12.2.2.5 Job search Job search is conditional on labor market participation. A person's probability of employment, $1 - u^a = \zeta^a \cdot f$, depends on search intensity ζ^a and market tightness as reflected by the matching rate f. More search effort raises employment prospects. The gains from a search consist of the increase in lifetime welfare when a person switches from unemployment into a job. Equating this to marginal effort cost yields the optimal search. The effective tax on the job search summarizes fiscal incentives. When an unemployed person switches into a job, she incurs a double cost, paying wage taxes (reduced by the deductibility of social security contributions) and forfeiting benefits. Given tax rates and a replacement rate of around 50 percent, the effective tax is substantial. Search incentives are also undermined by the implicit contribution taxes for pensions. Switzerland allows periods of unemployment to add to pension claims by crediting the replacement income toward the assessment base. This rule weakens the negative consequences of unemployment for future pension income. By allowing unemployment benefits to add to the pension assessment base, the system significantly raises the effective tax on the job search.

12.2.2.6 Participation When more individuals join the labor force, the participation rate δ^a rises. The gains from participation consist of expected earnings y^a arising from wages and unemployment benefits as a result of a job search. Another benefit is the increase in future income arising from job-related training. These gains are partly offset by utility costs, which consist of the forgone utility from household production of a nonparticipating person and the effort costs of a job search, training, and on-the-job effort. Optimal participation equates the marginal utility cost of participation, reflecting a general preference for leisure and nonmarket activities, with the increase in expected income net of utility costs of job-related activities and net of the participation tax. This effective tax consists of the sum of the wage tax plus the replacement rate in forgone social assistance (Immervoll et al. 2007). Furthermore, a higher replacement rate of wage-indexed unemployment insurance reduces the participation tax. More generous unemployment benefits encourage participation by strengthening income in the event of an unsuccessful job search. The implicit pension contribution taxes also discourage participation, but less so if there is a tight tax-benefit link. Finally, the consumption tax discourages participation by reducing real earnings but not utility benefits from nonparticipation.

12.2.2.7 Retirement In an aging society, retirement is arguably the most important dimension of labor supply.[6] The retirement date in the time span of ages 60 to 69 can be mapped one-to-one into a participation rate $x \in [0, 1]$ in the cross section of people aged 60 to 69. In the next group, representing people aged 70 and older, this ratio is zero, as all people are retired. Agents in the mixed group split time between work and retirement, where the shares determine average income:

$$Y_t^a = x_t \cdot \bar{y}_t^a \theta_t^a + (1 - x_t) \cdot (1 - t_t^{w,a}) \sum_j P_t^{j,a}. \tag{12.6}$$

Agents collect three types of pensions, $j \in \{E, F, L\}$: earnings-linked PAYG, funded, and lump sum. The flat-rate pension is not linked to past earnings and contributions.[7] Postponing retirement leads to an income gain of $dY^a/dx = \bar{y}^a \theta^a - (1 - t^{w,a}) \sum_j P_t^{j,a}$. However, for physical and psychological reasons, individuals find it increasingly burdensome and costly to postpone retirement, which is captured by a progressively rising disutility, $\varphi_R(x)$. Thus, the instantaneous utility denoted in (12.5) is expanded to $C^a - x \cdot \bar{\varphi}^a - \varphi_R(x)$ in the mixed group.

In the earnings-linked and funded pillars, the starting levels of pensions depend on three factors: accumulated entitlements, expected remaining lifetime, and supplements for late retirement and discounts for early retirement. Fiscal disincentives for continued work are summarized by an effective tax rate τ^R. Intuitively, first take the simplest case, with full participation of workers, no unemployment, no training, and no other public program beyond the PAYG system. The retirement choice then reduces to $\varphi_R'(x)=\left[\left(1-\tau^R\right)l^a w^a-\varphi_L^a\right]\theta^a$, where the effective old-age participation tax $\tau^R=t^{E,a}+\frac{P^a}{w^a\theta^a l^a}-\frac{1-x}{\theta w l}\frac{\partial P}{\partial x}$ is the sum of the contribution and replacement rates minus the pension supplement $\frac{\partial P}{\partial x}$.[8] Retiring at the statutory age $x=x^R$ yields a normal PAYG pension, while retiring later, $x>x^R$, entitles one to a higher pension. In general, the effective tax τ^R measures the total fiscal cost of remaining active. A higher replacement rate in unemployment insurance and better protection of an active worker with social assistance encourages prolonged work since it strengthens the expected income from staying active. The flat basic pension with fixed benefits $\left(\frac{\partial P}{\partial x}=0\right)$ raises the effective tax and discourages late retirement. The tax is greatly reduced, however, if the system includes incentives for late retirement, $\frac{\partial P}{\partial x}>0$. The entire benefit stream until the end of life shifts up but is paid over a shorter remaining time period.

The funded pillar rewards postponed retirement in a forward-looking way to satisfy the intertemporal budget constraint of the individual account, independent of the actual retirement date. Postponing retirement means more contributions and savings in pension payments. The resulting surplus to the system is fully returned to the individual by raising the starting level of the pension until the account is balanced again. Under ideal conditions, funded pensions are fully neutral with respect to retirement choice and other aspects of labor supply. If the pension fund offers exactly the same interest as is available to private households, $R^F=R$, savings via contributions to the pension fund are perfect substitutes for private savings, without any implicit tax. In this case, the capital-funded system does not distort retirement behavior or any other dimension of labor supply. A deviation from these conditions, however, such as high administrative costs leading to $R^F<R$ or the presence of wage taxes, makes the capital-funded pillar distortive also in a minor way.

12.2.3 General Equilibrium

12.2.3.1 Production and the labor market Unemployment results from search friction in a matching labor market where workers searching for a job meet firms wanting to fill vacancies. Using the notation in (12.3) and (12.6), there are x^aN^a active households in age group a, who participate at rate δ^a and spend time ζ^a per person on job searching. These activities add up to a total supply of $L^M = \Sigma_a \zeta^a \delta^a x^a N^a$ effective job searchers. Firms post v vacancies in total. Market friction results in $f \cdot L^M = q \cdot v$ matches. Only a fraction f of search units and a fraction q of vacancies are matched. These matching rates are taken as given by individual agents.[9]

A firm with a vacancy finds a suitable worker with probability q, who belongs to age group a with probability ϕ^a, has skills θ^a, and supplies work effort l^a. Hiring thus results in an effective labor force $L_t^D = \Sigma_a l_t^a \theta_t^a \cdot \phi_t^a q_t v_t$. Firms produce output $F(K, L^D)$ using capital K and labor. They maximize firm value equal to the present value of dividends by choosing job vacancies and the rate of investment to accumulate the capital stock. Value maximization results in a simple condition for long-run capital demand, $F_K - \delta^K = r/(1-t^k)$, where t^k is a source tax on corporate profits and δ^K is the depreciation rate. In a small open economy, the capital to labor ratio is thus entirely determined by the world interest rate.[10] Posting a vacancy costs κ units of output, leading to recruitment costs κv. Firms post vacancies until the marginal cost of hiring additional workers is equal to the expected return on hiring, $\kappa = (\text{job rent}) \cdot q_t$. The firm's job rent per efficiency unit is proportional to the gap $F_L - (1 + t^{E,F} + t^{F,F})w^a$ between the marginal product and the gross wage cost, where $t^{E,F}$ and $t^{F,F}$ are employer contributions to the PAYG and funded pillars.

When a firm and a worker are matched, they bargain over a wage to divide the total job rent relative to their outside options, which define reservation wages. The worker's reservation wage is the minimum gross wage $w_{R,t}^a$ per hour that makes the worker indifferent between accepting or rejecting the offer. A gross wage in excess of this leaves a strictly positive rent. However, a higher wage reduces the firm's surplus. The firm's reservation wage is the maximum wage that leads to a nonnegative firm rent, $F_L/(1 + t^{E,F} + t^{F,F}) \geq w^a$. If the wage were higher, the firm would have a loss. The wage per hour resulting from bargaining over the joint surplus is

$$w_t^a = \xi \cdot F_L / \left(1 + t_t^{E,F} + t_t^{F,F}\right) + (1 - \xi) \cdot w_{R,t}^a, \tag{12.7}$$

where ξ measures the worker's bargaining power. A strong position (high ξ) pushes up the wage.

Bargaining leads to tax shifting. Employers' contributions, $t^{E,F}$ and $t^{E,F}$, are a pure factor tax that reduces the firm's reservation wage and are partly shifted to workers. The consumption tax erodes purchasing power. To compensate, workers demand a higher reservation wage so that consumption taxes get partly shifted to firms. Similarly, higher wage taxes and social contributions boost the reservation wage, leading workers to insist on higher wages. Employment raises future pensions, both in the earnings-linked and capital-funded pillars, which squeezes implicit contribution taxes and reduces wage demands of workers. A higher replacement rate in unemployment insurance clearly drives up wages. When unemployment benefits are added to the assessment base, unemployment becomes less detrimental since it still creates pension claims. This also strengthens the worker's fallback position and wage.

12.2.3.2 General equilibrium Aggregation is in two stages: (1) analytical aggregation of agents in the same age state a, but with different life cycle histories, into a common age group; and (2) aggregation across groups, giving macroeconomic variables such as $A \equiv \Sigma_a A^a$. Reverse insurance redistributes accidental bequests from the deceased to surviving persons, which eliminates γ^a in aggregate private asset accumulation as in (12.4):

$$GA_{t+1} = R_{t+1}\left[A_t + Y_t + Z_t - (1+t_t^c)C_t\right], \tag{12.8}$$

where $Y \equiv \Sigma_a Y^a$ and $Y^a = x^a \cdot \bar{y}^a \theta^a + (1-x^a)\cdot(1-t^{w,a})\Sigma_j P^{j,a}$. Note that $x^a = 1$ for prime-age workers and $x^a = 0$ for fully retired persons.

An equilibrium is found when private behavior is optimal, budget constraints are fulfilled, and markets clear. The public sector includes unemployment insurance and social assistance on top of other redistributive and consumption spending, plus the PAYG and funded pension pillars. The model allows for accumulation of government debt D^G. Taxes and spending must thus fulfill an intertemporal constraint. In capital market equilibrium, assets of households and pension funds are invested in domestic equity V, government debt, and international bonds D^F:

$$A_t + A_t^F = V_t + D_t^G + D_t^F. \tag{12.9}$$

The economy accumulates net foreign assets $GD^F_{t+1} = R_{t+1}(D^F_t + T^B_t)$, where T^B is the trade surplus. The current account reflects the savings investment identity.

12.3 Aging Policies

This section summarizes demographic change in Switzerland, develops a comprehensive pension reform, and finally discusses how it relates to the taxation of pensions.

12.3.1 Demographic Change in Switzerland

The Swiss Federal Statistical Office projects that Switzerland's population will grow from 7.2 million in 2005 to 8.1 million in 2050. This increase is not the result of immigration or higher birthrates but rather results from higher life expectancy. Lower mortality rates result in more old people. The dependency ratio, measured as the number of people older than 65 divided by those aged 20 to 64, must inevitably rise. The share of the population consisting of those over 65 years old is expected to reach 28 percent, compared to 16 percent in 2005. The dependency ratio will almost double by 2050 (figure 12.1).

Mortality and life expectancy, birthrates, and migration determine demographic developments. Three scenarios exist with respect to life expectancy in Switzerland (Bundesamt für Statistik 2006). An intermediate scenario assumes that better prevention and medical advancements raise life expectancy at birth to 85.0 years for men and 89.5 years for women in 2050, compared to 78.6 and 83.7 years in 2005. The average birthrate was 1.4 children per woman in 2005. The intermediate scenario assumes that rising public awareness of the economic and social importance of families leads to increased support. As a result, the currently low birthrate is expected to rise somewhat. Finally, the intermediate scenario assumes that current trends in net migration will be extended into the future. The free movement of persons will yield only transitory effects on net immigration from new EU member states.

A restriction when using a model of balanced growth is that simulations must assume that the economy starts from a stationary state. Neither the economy nor the population is in a steady state at any point in time, so data must be averaged over time. However, the key macro and demographic indicators, such as the current dependency ratio, are correctly implemented. The old-age dependency ratio is expected to double and eventually reach a ratio of roughly 0.5. Aging implies that

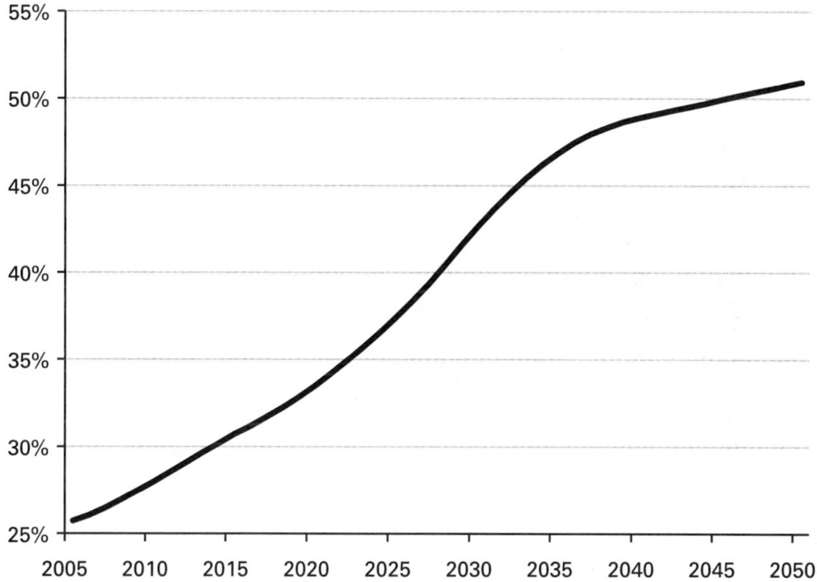

Figure 12.1
Old-age dependency ratio in Switzerland, 2005–2050.

survival rates rise already in earlier stages of the life cycle. A 60-year-old person will more probably reach the age of 70, a 70-year-old is more likely to live until the age of 80, and so on. Lower mortality rates at younger ages imply that a much larger share of people reach the age of 90–99.

For a given inflow of newborns, lower mortality rates change both the structure and the size of the population. Keeping the inflow of newborns constant, the size of the older population grows when mortality declines. Figure 12.2 shows how the share of older age groups rises while the share of younger cohorts shrinks. The bars illustrate the relative weights. The long-run age composition is determined exclusively by survival and mortality rates. A lower permanent inflow of new generations, brought about by a lower birthrate or as a result of immigration, cannot change the demographic structure in the long run but can only scale down total population. The inflow in the model is set such that population size grows by 10 percent in the long run, roughly in line with the abovementioned demographic projections for Switzerland.

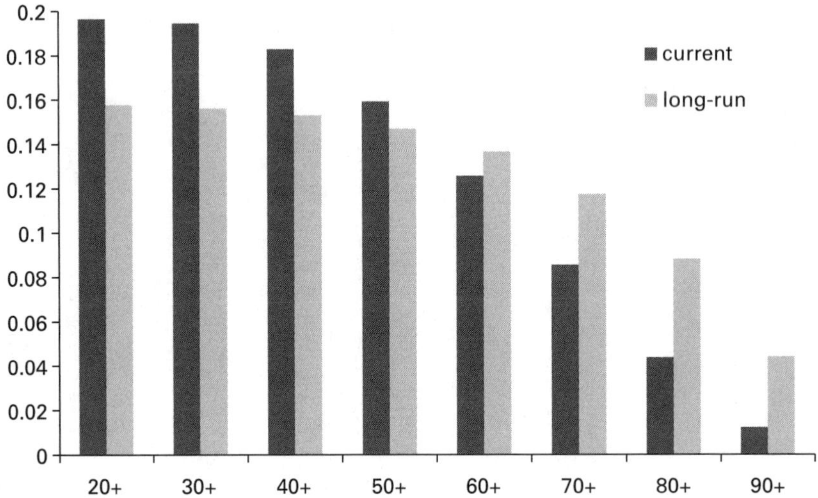

Figure 12.2
Long-run and current population structure in Switzerland.

12.3.2 Pension Reform

In Switzerland, the average labor market participation rate is currently 74 percent. The average retirement age of 64 is relatively high compared with that of other nations. Approximately 40 percent of Swiss workers 60–69 years old are still active in the labor market. The 60–69-year-olds represent about 13 percent of the population. The dependency ratio (the ratio of retirees to workers) is currently 28 percent. Keuschnigg (2016, table A.1) shows effective tax rates for the first group, which corresponds to the 20–29-year-olds. The effective tax on hours worked mirrors the wage tax burden of 26 percent on average. It is also inflated by the tax component of PAYG contributions and the consumption tax. The effective rate is about 22 percent for the youngest workers. Finally, the participation tax on retirement choice is 51 percent, relatively low by international standards. The Swiss PAYG pillar includes pension supplements for each year of postponed retirement, equal to 6.8 percent. The funded pillar involves only a low effective tax rate by construction.

The model captures the characteristics of the Swiss pension system with three pillars: the mandatory PAYG and funded pillars, and voluntary private savings with preferential tax treatment as a third pillar. PAYG pension spending represents 6.6 percent of gross domestic product (GDP), of which about three-quarters is covered by contributions. The gross replacement rate in the PAYG pillar is 40 percent. Only 60 percent of PAYG pensions are earnings linked. The flat component results from the fact that the tax-benefit link is eliminated for minimum pensions of low-income households and maximum pensions of people with earnings in excess of an upper income threshold. The division into a flat and a variable part is important for the size of the implicit tax: the larger the share of the flat part, the higher the contribution tax. The total effective average employee and employer contribution is about 8.3 percent, yielding an implicit tax rate of about 2 percent in the youngest age group.

Adding mandatory PAYG and funded pensions yields a gross replacement rate of about 60 percent of wage earnings. Of total pension income, 65 percent stems from the PAYG and 35 percent from the funded pillar. Funded pensions reflect not only accumulated contributions but also earned interest. The tax component of funded pillar contributions is clearly lower but remains positive because of administrative costs. Overhead costs are assumed to consume 1 percent of the return on pension assets. Hence, pension funds generate an effective return of 2.5 percent, which is lower than the long-run market interest rate of 3.5 percent in the calibrated model. Total pension assets amount to 125 percent of GDP.

As demographic change proceeds, the pension system must adjust substantially to remain sustainable. The effects of aging on the financing of social security can be offset in three ways: reduced benefits, higher contributions, or an increase in the retirement age. Simple analytics imply that increased longevity can be offset by a "neutral" increase in the retirement age that keeps the pension system balanced without raising contributions or cutting pension replacement rates. Intuitively, if agents spend three-quarters of their adult life in work and one-quarter in retirement, then each additional year of life extension should be divided in the same way. The argument implies that an increase in retirement age is a central policy response to prevent large increases in tax rates or declining replacement rates.

The analysis combines improvements in the pension system with complementary labor market reform and suggests a comprehensive policy scenario consisting of six elements:

1. raising the retirement age;
2. eliminating the upper income threshold so that PAYG pensions become earnings linked also for incomes in excess of this ceiling;

3. eliminating unemployment benefits from the contribution base so that unemployment no longer adds to pension entitlements;

4. taking measures to reduce administrative costs in the funded pillar by half a percentage point;

5. tightening active labor market policy to limit rising unemployment;

6. pushing lifelong training to strengthen the contribution base but also to improve the employability of older workers and facilitate the rise in retirement age.

In all cases, the VAT is raised by 4 percentage points. The VAT is considerably less harmful to incentives for an extensive labor supply than wage taxes because it taxes income in both active and inactive states, while the wage tax reduces only employed income. Wage tax and contribution rates are adjusted to continuously assure fiscal balance. The higher VAT limits these tax increases so that financing of social security becomes less damaging to labor market performance. It is also argued that the taxation of pensions in Switzerland does not require reform.

12.3.3 Taxing Pensions

The three-pillar pension system contributes to consumption smoothing by extending labor earnings into the retirement period. Households can shift present earnings to future life cycle periods via private savings, the pension system, and human capital and housing investments. The Swiss tax system is rather consistent in treating alternative ways of long-term saving and adopts, with exceptions, an expenditure (consumption) tax treatment. First, human capital investments are largely tax-exempt, since forgone earnings reduce current wage tax liability while increased future earnings are subject to tax. Home ownership is largely treated like investment income. Imputed rental income is subject to the personal income tax after allowances for a number of costs. There is a general allowance of 30 percent of imputed rental income, leaving only 70 percent to be taxed at the personal income tax rate. In addition, and most importantly, households can deduct interest on housing credit. They also can deduct expenses for repair and maintenance costs, either a lump sum or actual costs.

Mandatory pension savings get consumption tax treatment. Contributions to the PAYG and funded pillars as well as (notional) interest on accumulated pension wealth are tax-exempt, while pension payouts are subject to wage taxation, under an EET regime: savings exempt (E), interest exempt (E), consumption taxed (T). Voluntary private pension savings in the third pillar are tax-favored but not fully exempt: (1) people can deduct from tax new savings up to an upper limit, (2) interest is taxed at the normal income tax rate, but (3) drawdowns of accumulated funds in old age are not taxed [tTE regime: savings partly exempt (t), interest taxed (T), consumption exempt (E)]. Taxation of other private savings follows the TTE system and is thus subject to double taxation [see Genser (2015) and Cremer and Pestieau (2016, chapter 2, this volume) on alternative ways of taxing pensions].

The pension system is meant to correct for at least two market failures that can arguably rationalize deferred taxation of mandatory pension savings. Given incomplete private annuity markets, the system provides valuable insurance for longevity risk. In addition, evidence points to shortsightedness and myopia, leading to underestimation of long-term needs and insufficient and belated savings for retirement. Preventing insufficient preparation for retirement and outright poverty in old age is the very reason for forced savings via mandatory pension insurance. Taxing insufficient private retirement savings would thus be particularly distortive, thereby justifying intertemporal neutrality by adopting deferred taxation with the EET system. Deferred taxation is a natural complement to postponed private consumption. The government gives up instant tax revenue in favor of taxing retirement income later in life. Young households are often credit constrained, and pension savings are in sharp rivalry with urgent current needs, such as spending on children as well as housing and education investments. Finally, not only private households but also policy makers with limited tenure are subject to a bias for present spending and might thus neglect long-term needs. One might argue that deferred taxation, shifting tax revenue to the future when it is most needed in an aging society, might partly address the bias toward immediate government spending. A TEE system would run counter to the need to stimulate long-term saving when individuals as well as policy makers are shortsighted.

The arguments for deferred taxation seem to be particularly relevant for the mandatory part of pension savings covering the basic needs in retirement. They are less convincing for voluntary private pension savings in the third pillar. They vary according to individual tastes for topping up pension income in excess of basic needs that are already provided by the mandatory system. Clearly, tax privileges for these supplementary pension savings cannot be justified in terms of correcting shortsightedness and preventing old-age poverty. It thus seems appropriate to impose upper limits on tax deductions for voluntary private pension savings. With regard to other forms of private savings, good reasons exist to subject them to income taxation, although generally at a separate and lower rate than labor income (for a review, see Banks and Diamond 2011). Tax practice in Switzerland by and large conforms to these principles and does not call for a substantial reform. Changing the taxation of pensions is thus not part of the comprehensive pension reform outlined here.

12.4 Quantitative Analysis

12.4.1 Long-Run Effects of Aging

The analysis first quantifies the long-run economic impact of aging. The scenario consists of three elements: (1) the dependency ratio roughly doubles as a result of increased longevity, (2) the total population rises by 10 percent in the long run, and (3) the working-age population declines by about 6 percent. As a benchmark, the government is assumed to follow a passive strategy, leaving current benefit rules unchanged and merely adjusting wage taxes and contribution rates to balance budgets. The long-run effects are reported in the "Age" column of table 12.1. Contribution rates and wage tax rates must strongly increase, and the pure demographic effect implies a large decline in per capita income. The higher tax and contribution rates strongly discourage labor supply, leading to a further reduction in per capita income beyond the demographic and mechanical budget effects.

Table 12.1 shows a large long-run impact of aging on public finances and the economy. Fiscal balance requires adding 7.1 percentage points to the wage tax schedule over the entire income range. On top of that, contribution rates to the PAYG pillar of both employees and employers must also be raised by the same amount. Altogether, the statutory labor tax burden rises by 21 percentage points. Contributions only partly count as a tax. The effective tax on hours worked thus rises by roughly 10 percentage points, and the participation tax rises similarly. Aggregate labor supply shrinks because of fewer hours worked and lower participation by prime-age workers. The effective tax rate on job searching rises to a lesser extent since unemployment benefits are partly indexed to net wages so that higher wage tax rates reduce not only the value of work but also the value of unemployment. Still, the tax distortion rises substantially from an already high level and leads to an increase in the unemployment rate from 3.6 percent in the absence of

Table 12.1
Aging and comprehensive social security reform.

	ISS	Age	Late	Ceil	Un	Adm	Mon	Train
Absolute changes								
Tax increase[a]	0.000	0.071	0.019	0.015	0.012	0.005	0.004	0.001
Implicit PAYG tax[b]	0.016	0.075	0.025	0.007	0.005	0.001	0.001	–0.002
Effective tax on hours[b]	0.223	0.320	0.243	0.224	0.223	0.213	0.216	0.211
Effective participation tax[b]	0.280	0.382	0.303	0.283	0.282	0.272	0.274	0.270
Effective tax on search[b]	0.651	0.700	0.663	0.653	0.625	0.621	0.620	0.618
Effective retirement tax	0.510	0.556	0.514	0.400	0.394	0.365	0.367	0.361
Pension replacement ratio	0.600	0.557	0.582	0.567	0.559	0.561	0.562	0.558
Retirement date	0.400	0.348	0.801	0.811	0.811	0.814	0.814	0.815
Participation rate	0.740	0.722	0.726	0.729	0.729	0.731	0.731	0.732
Unemployment rate	0.036	0.055	0.042	0.039	0.032	0.030	0.025	0.024
Percentage changes								
Labor force		–6.952	1.744	1.933	1.945	1.999	1.990	2.027
Gross wage		–5.076	–1.535	–1.314	–1.619	–1.074	–1.739	–1.534
Hours worked		–1.584	–1.223	–0.957	–0.962	–0.792	–0.850	–0.811
Labor productivity		0.735	1.291	1.301	1.324	1.325	1.317	2.637
Labor demand		–11.762	–0.746	0.455	1.254	1.954	2.318	3.962
GDP per capita		–19.939	–9.944	–8.854	–8.129	–7.494	–7.164	–5.672
Wealth per capita		11.231	1.025	2.036	2.381	1.475	0.957	–0.198

Notes: ISS = initial steady state. Columns report cumulative effects. [a]Financing by higher wage tax and PAYG contributions. In the reform scenarios, 4 percentage points of VAT are added. [b]Tax rate for 20–29-year-olds; Age: aging without reform (no use of VAT financing); Late: increase in retirement age; Ceil: eliminate pension ceiling in PAYG pillar; Un: no accumulation of pension entitlements of unemployed; Adm: reduction of administrative costs in funded pillar; Mon: monitoring of the unemployed; Train: investment in training.

aging to 5.5 percent. This large effect also results as inflated wage costs discourage firms from creating jobs.

This scenario induces a tendency for early retirement. Increased longevity leads to a large cut in funded pensions, which, other things being equal, encourages postponed retirement. In contrast, rising taxes favor early retirement. Although higher wage taxes reduce both wages and pensions, higher contribution rates exclusively diminish active income and make work relatively less attractive compared to retirement. This second effect dominates and induces early retirement. The participation rate among 60–69-year-olds shrinks from 40 percent to 35 percent. This scenario implies diverse training incentives for different life cycle groups, which overall results in moderately higher average labor productivity. With this exception, all labor market responses work to magnify substantially the demographically induced reduction of the workforce. Total employment thus falls by 11.8 percent in absolute terms. Since aging has no consequences for long-run capital intensity in a small economy with a fixed interest rate, GDP shrinks by the same percentage. However, GDP is divided over a 10 percent larger population so GDP per capita falls by 20 percent. Asset wealth per capita rises strongly, by 11 percent, since individuals must save much more to complement pension income over a longer retirement period.

12.4.2 A Comprehensive Policy Approach

This section reports the quantitative effects of implementing the comprehensive pension reform proposed in subsection 12.3.2. The columns in table 12.1 present the cumulative impact. The last column shows the total impact of aging and policy reform.

12.4.2.1 Raising retirement age Keeping older workers in the labor force is the centerpiece of the reform package. Raising the statutory retirement age by three years means that the regular pension will not be received until the age of 68 instead of at 65, with no additional compensation and an unchanged replacement rate. The column "Late" in table 12.1 reports the long-run effects. Comparing this to the column "Age" shows the differential impact of the reform, while comparing it to the ISS (initial steady state) gives the total impact of aging and the higher retirement age. The (exogenous) long-run expected retiree to worker ratio as a result of aging is close to 0.50, almost twice as much as today's ratio of 0.27. Raising the retirement age reduces the number of pensioners and augments the active workforce, leading to a much smaller increase in the dependency ratio, to 0.38. Still, the number of retirees is 40 percent higher than for the status quo. Hence, not only is the VAT rate up by 4 percent, but the wage tax and contribution rates to the PAYG pillar also have to rise by 1.9 points each to finance the large increase in pension spending resulting from longer life spans.

Postponing retirement turns the 6.9 percent decline in the labor force into a gain of 1.7 percent relative to the ISS. Effective tax rates are still higher for all aspects of labor supply, although much less than in the pure aging scenario. Effective rates shrink considerably, which boosts incentives for job searching and reduces the unemployment rate from 5.5 percent to 4.2 percent. Investments in training become more profitable since the returns accrue over a longer working life. Average labor productivity improves significantly, by 1.3 percent, up from 0.7 percent in the aging scenario. To sum up, raising the retirement age provides strong fiscal relief, allows for a lower tax burden, and strengthens incentives in all aspects of labor supply. The measure thus offsets a large part of the negative economic incentives created by aging. Consequently, the decline in total labor demand is reduced to 0.7 percent, a huge improvement relative to the loss of 12.0 percent in the aging scenario. While the level of GDP is down by a moderate 0.7 percent, GDP per capita still declines by around 10.0 percent, since GDP must be divided among more people. The loss in per capita GDP as a result of aging is halved. Finally, a higher retirement age strongly reduces life cycle savings and wealth per capita since individuals need to save for a shorter remaining retirement period.

12.4.2.2 Strengthening the tax-benefit link In Switzerland, the PAYG pillar limits benefits to a maximum amount so that contributions above an upper income threshold (equal to SFr 84,240 per year) no longer augment individual pensions. This income ceiling implies that pensions on incomes in excess of this threshold are no longer linked to individual earnings. In this upper income range, contributions are perceived as a full tax that adds to the general income tax and discourages labor market behavior. Currently, out of all pension payments from the PAYG pillar, 2 percent refer to minimum pensions, 60 percent to regular earnings-linked pensions, and 38 percent to maximum pensions above the income ceiling. In the simulation model, 40 percent of pensions in the status quo are flat and 60 percent are earnings linked. This scenario specifically assumes that the share of earnings-linked PAYG pensions is raised to 90 percent by adjusting upward the parameter m^a in (12.5) and that the flat pension is reduced to 10 percent rather than to 2 percent. This conservative assumption should allow for somewhat higher minimum pensions to cushion other negative distributional effects such as the reduction of the real pension value as a result of a higher VAT rate. Finally, to avoid an increase in pension levels when a larger part of income enters the benefit assessment, the scenario also assumes a moderate reduction of the replacement rate.

Column "Ceil" reports the total long-run impact, where the differential effect is seen by comparing this column to column "Late." The measure reduces the tax component in PAYG contributions to reap efficiency gains by strengthening the tax-benefit link. The required increase in wage tax and contribution rates is reduced from 1.9 percent to 1.5 percent. Effective tax rates fall on all margins of labor supply, and rather strongly in the case of the effective retirement tax, because of a somewhat lower replacement rate. Consistent with the empirical evidence, retirement becomes much less sensitive to incentives when the retirement age is already very high. Hence, the old-age participation rate rises only moderately. The reform stimulates labor supply on other aspects as well, but these effects (relative to column "Late") remain limited. Total employment expands by more than 1 percentage point, turning a loss of 0.7 percent into a gain of 0.4 percent. GDP per capita now shrinks by 8.8 percent instead of 9.9 percent. Strengthening the tax-benefit link by eliminating the income ceiling yields an income gain of roughly 1 percentage point of GDP.

12.4.2.3 Eliminating unemployment benefits from the contribution base The PAYG pillar includes unemployment benefits in the pension assessment base. The problem with this rule is that it alleviates the consequences of unemployment and weakens job search incentives. Presumably, this rule is intended to prevent old-age poverty. Such a goal, however, is already addressed by the existence of minimum pensions, which are raised as part of the preceding policy initiative. By eliminating this rule, pensions become linked exclusively to employment. Denying new pension entitlements during unemployment strengthens search incentives and favorably affects the unemployment rate. As column "Un" in table 12.1 shows, the effective tax rate on job searching is reduced by 3 percentage points, leading to a significant reduction in unemployment, from 3.9 percent to 3.2 percent. Lower unemployment saves spending on social benefits and allows a small reduction in wage tax and contribution rates, from 1.5 percent down to 1.2 percent. The gross wage falls more strongly, since the reform cuts the workers' fall-back option in wage bargaining. With higher job rents, firms expand labor demand by placing more vacancies, making possible the substantial reduction in the unemployment rate. The slight cut in the wage tax rate has positive side effects on other aspects of labor supply. Therefore, effective employment and the level of GDP now expand by 1.3 percent, where the differential effect amounts to almost 1 percentage point. Accordingly, the loss in GDP per capita is reduced from 8.8 percent to 8.1 percent.

12.4.2.4 Reducing administrative costs of the funded pillar The fragmentation and complexity of the funded pillar with numerous pension funds and low returns have been criticized. Better supervision, more competition, and more freedom of choice might yield a higher return. As the precise magnitude of the gains cannot be quantified, it is assumed, somewhat arbitrarily, that administrative costs can be cut from 1 percent to 0.5 percent of assets. The return in the second pillar thus rises from 2.5 percent to 3 percent, while the net interest rate in the capital market remains at 3.5 percent. The contribution rate to the funded pillar is kept constant, but contribution capital earns higher interest and results in a larger pension. To keep the total pension replacement rate fixed, the PAYG pension is scaled down to offset the increase in private pensions. Budget savings are used to cut wage tax rates as well as employee and employer contributions to the PAYG system. Column "Adm" in table 12.1 reports that in long-run equilibrium these rates can be cut in total by roughly 2 percentage points ($3 \times (1.2 - 0.5)$ on the first line of table 12.1). Effective tax rates are moderately reduced, which stimulates all aspects of labor supply. The unemployment rate drops further, to 3 percent. Altogether, effective employment and per capita GDP expand by another 0.7 percent.

12.4.2.5 Tighter monitoring of the unemployed Sanctions against shirking a job search and monitoring of unemployed job seekers are often-used instruments of active labor market policy. It is assumed that unemployment also yields some leisure utility and that monitoring and sanctions in the case of observed inactivity can reduce the value of being unemployed by a monetary equivalent of 5 percent of benefits. These activities are assumed to be covered at no extra cost out of the existing budget for labor market policy. Column "Mon" in table 12.1 shows the quantitative impact. The intervention not only boosts search incentives; in eroding the fallback option, it also squeezes the reservation wage and thereby augments the total job rent. Wage bargaining splits the larger surplus between workers and firms so that the gross wage rate falls (by 1.7 percent instead of 1.1 percent), which in turn boosts the job rent of firms. As a result, workers search more intensively, and firms find it more profitable to create jobs. The unemployment rate shrinks from 3 percent to 2.5 percent. The repercussions on wage taxes and on other dimensions of labor supply are basically insignificant. Overall, the effect on employment and GDP is an additional 0.4 percentage points, leading to a level effect of 2.3 percent relative to the ISS. The loss in GDP per capita is further reduced to 7.2 percent.

12.4.2.6 Incentives for lifelong training Training may be an important means of compensating, at least partly, for the decline in labor supply resulting from a reduced inflow of young workers. Skill accumulation rests on households' willingness to reallocate time from work to training and on public spending. The modeling scenario assumes that government raises the public input per trainee (teachers, learning materials, classrooms, and other resources) by 1 percent. Since the number of trainees rises, the government must spend about 2.7 percent more on training. However, this item amounts only to roughly 5 percent of tax revenue, so the effect on the public budget is rather limited. Households respond by using more time for training, incurring an opportunity cost in terms of forgone earnings. As a result of more training, average labor productivity rises by an additional 1.3 percent and ends up 2.6 percent higher than in the ISS. The higher quality of the workforce boosts effective employment by an extra 1.6 percent. All in all, the levels of effective employment and GDP are 4 percent higher than under the status quo. The loss in per capita income is limited to 5.7 percent, down from 7.2 percent. Other dimensions of aggregate labor supply are not much affected. To conclude, training seems an important policy area for cushioning the economic impact of aging.

12.4.3 Life Cycle Incidence

Aging and structural reform of social security may have an uneven impact on the life cycle. Figure 12.3 reveals that strengthening training may disproportionately benefit older workers in the long run. As workers respond to better incentives, the effects accumulate over the entire working life. Postponed retirement also stimulates training, since returns accrue over a longer time period. The strongest effect is prob-

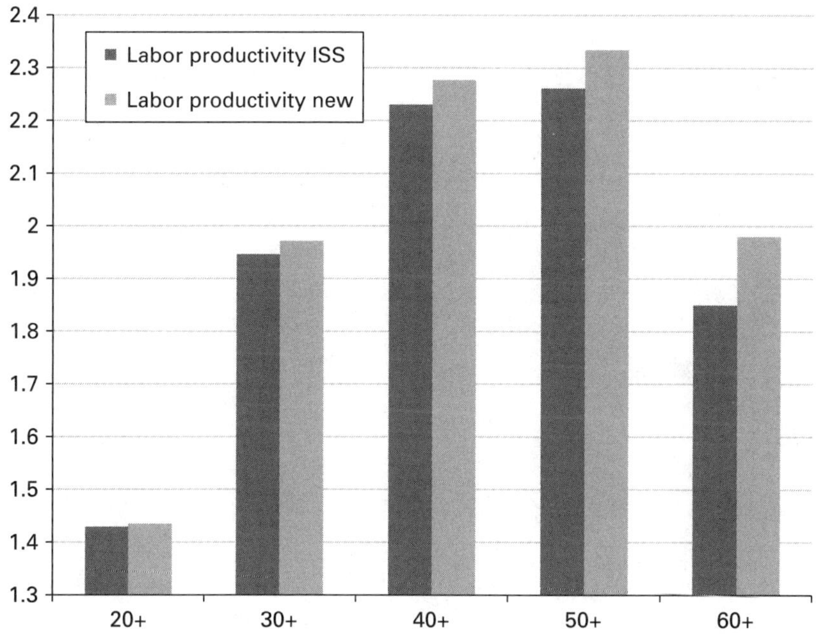

Figure 12.3
Life cycle productivity.

ably on persons near retirement. The skills of older workers are also of special interest, since they affect workers' employability. Many observers are concerned that raising the retirement age could be ineffective because older workers may be difficult to employ. However, the simulations show that postponed retirement disproportionately favors training incentives and skills of older workers, which enhances their employability.

The life cycle pattern in figure 12.4 points to the different unemployment incidences for young and old workers. Unemployment among younger workers falls quite sharply, by 1.5 percentage points for 20–29-year-olds. The main reason is the elimination of unemployment benefits from the contribution base as well as stronger monitoring as part of active labor market policy. A stronger tax-benefit link also encourages job searching and reduces unemployment. Unemployment among older workers, in contrast, is hardly affected at all. Delaying actual retirement by about four years amounts to a strong increase in the labor supply, which prevents a more significant reduction in the unemployment rate. Compared with other countries around the world, old-age

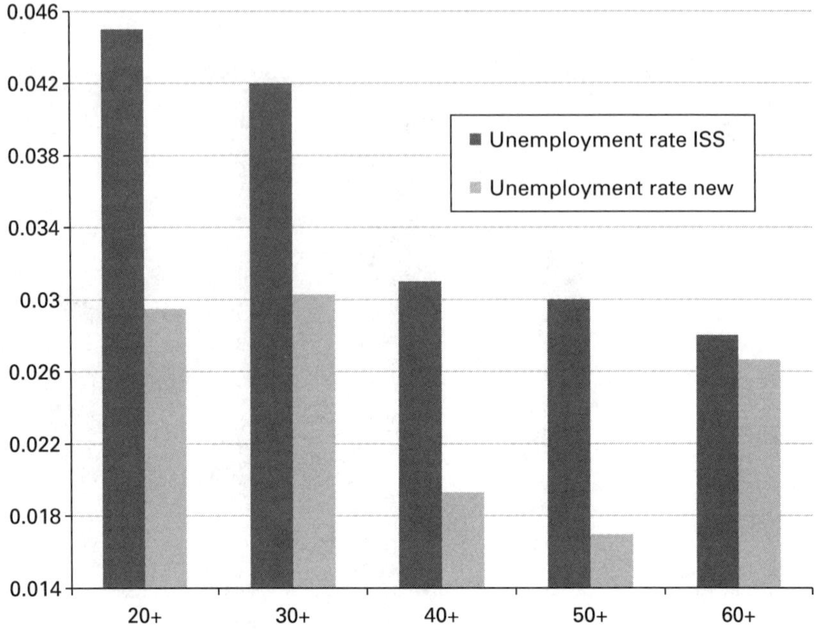

Figure 12.4
Life cycle unemployment.

unemployment in Switzerland still remains very low. The present framework does not lend support to the view that postponing retirement is ineffective because older workers might be difficult to employ.

12.4.4 Transitional Adjustment

Table 12.1 reports long-run values. However, short- and medium-run effects are of special interest to policy makers. Given that demographic change is a slow process extending over several decades, policy measures also should be introduced at roughly the same speed. Hence, the model scenario gradually implements reform according to $y_t = y_\infty + (y_0 - y_\infty) \times 0.95^t$, where y is an element of the policy package with value y_0 in the initial equilibrium and y_∞ after complete implementation. The adjustment speed 0.95 implies a half-life of $t_{0.5} \approx 13.5$ years; that is, half of the policy change is completed within 13.5 years, half of the remaining part takes another 13.5 years, and so on. The analysis refrains from any more elaborate transition strategies. Public debt and real public spending are kept constant in per capita terms. The response to policy shocks and aging can easily lead to nonmonotonic adjustment, since demographic

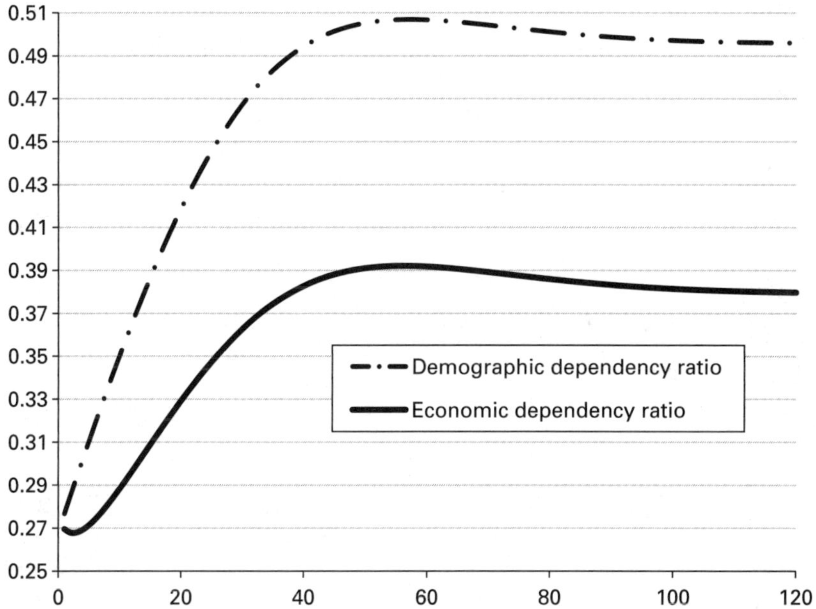

Figure 12.5
Demographic and economic dependency ratios.

change with overlapping generations, economic adjustment such as savings, investment, and skill formation, and gradual policy implementation occur at different speeds. Figure 12.5 shows that the old-age dependency ratio may take up to six decades to fully adjust. The horizontal axis measures time (in years) after the reform.

The economic dependency ratio is the ratio of retired persons to active workers and is rather more important for fiscal balance and economic performance than the demographic dependency ratio, which is the ratio of persons older than 65 to younger ones. As figure 12.5 illustrates, the large increase in retirement age adds additional workers, shrinks the number of retired persons, and thereby squeezes the economic dependency ratio by about 12 percentage points in the long run. The values for tax rates and employment gains in figure 12.6 converge to the long-run values listed in table 12.1. Given the delayed implementation, no policy change occurs at all in period zero, but the anticipation of improved labor market incentives in future periods leads to an immediate, endogenous increase in the retirement age and old-age participation rate from 40 percent to 43 percent. Together with other labor supply

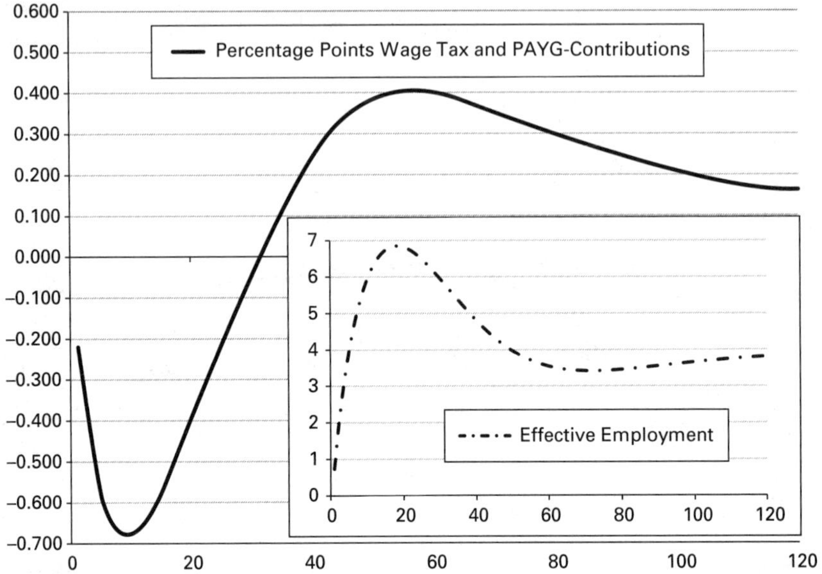

Figure 12.6
Wage tax, PAYG contributions, and employment.

responses, effective employment jumps up by 0.7 percent, allowing an instantaneous cut in the wage tax rate and employer plus employee contribution rates to the PAYG pillar by 0.2 percentage points.

When the policy changes set in slowly, the retirement age rises and ultimately boosts the participation rate among 60–69-year-olds to 81 percent, up from 40 percent initially. Accordingly, the economic dependency ratio in figure 12.5 rises much less dramatically than the demographic ratio. Although policy changes are phased in gradually, they are still "too fast" to some extent, boosting labor market incentives by more than what would be required to prevent a change in tax and contribution rates. Accordingly, tax rates significantly fall in the first phase to a maximum of 0.7 percentage points in period 9, or a total of 2.0 percentage points if the wage tax rate and the employer and employee contribution rates to the PAYG pillar are added up. The employment rate thus overshoots, leading to a maximum gain of 6.8 percent in period 18 before the economy approaches a long-run equilibrium with more moderate employment gains, as reported in table 12.1. In general, it is difficult to devise a phase-in policy that would completely avoid any nonmonotonic or overshooting adjustment in labor market behavior resulting from overly fast or too slow policy implementation. In principle, it would be possible to use debt policy to smooth tax rates over time and to distribute employment gains more evenly across generations.

12.5 Conclusions

Increased longevity induces a large demographic change. It thereby creates difficult challenges in financing social security and could substantially reduce per capita income. In Switzerland, the old-age dependency ratio will approximately double by 2050, and the population is expected to grow by 10 percent until then. A large shock must have large consequences. This chapter used a rich computational model of life cycle labor supply, unemployment, and retirement, explicitly including the separate PAYG and funded pillars of the Swiss pension system, to quantify the potential impact of aging. When benefit rules are kept constant and the government follows a passive policy of raising wage taxes and social security contributions, the consequences are rather bleak. Simulations show that the labor tax burden needs to rise by 22 percentage points and that per capita income could fall by roughly the same amount.

Such a scenario is neither politically realistic nor reasonable but serves as a reference point. The analysis found that a comprehensive policy approach can largely alleviate the unfavorable consequences of aging on per capita income. The financing of social security with largely the same replacement rates as today might require only a moderately higher tax burden. By far the most important measure is an increase in the retirement age by about four years so that longer-lived future generations roughly split their extended total lifetime between work and retirement in the same way as present generations must do.

The comprehensive policy approach investigated in this chapter includes further structural reform of the pension system and other measures to stimulate training. All in all, the results show that this reform package could limit the increase in the tax burden to 4 percentage points of VAT and keep the loss in per capita income to a moderate 6 percent. To put this number in perspective, a period of zero growth over three to four years relative to the continued trend growth would yield the same decline in per capita income.

Notes

The paper was presented at the CEPAR and CESifo workshop "Taxation of Pensions" held September 3–4, 2015, in Munich. I thank Viktor Steiner, the discussant, and seminar participants for stimulating comments. I am also grateful to the editor, Robert Holzmann, for helpful advice.

1. The empirical literature on the labor market impact of taxes and social security is surveyed in subsection 12.3.1.

2. Refer to Keuschnigg, Keuschnigg, and Jaag (2011) for a detailed formal presentation of the model.

3. The calibration details are presented in the appendix to the complete discussion paper, available at www.alexandria.unisg.ch/249760.

4. In the funded pillar, in contrast, benefits depend only on actual contributions paid.

5. Details are in Keuschnigg, Keuschnigg, and Jaag (2011), and separate appendices are available upon request.

6. Fisher and Keuschnigg (2010) show how retirement interacts with labor supply in younger age.

7. In part, the flat pension reflects social policy to prevent old-age poverty among low-income persons. It also captures the fact that, in Switzerland, earnings in excess of an income ceiling do not create pension entitlements.

8. Similar to that in Cremer and Pestieau (2003), the problem

$$\max_x \; [(1-t^E)\, wl - \varphi_L\,]\theta \cdot x + P(x) \cdot (1-x) - \varphi_R\,(x)$$

yields the optimality condition

$$\varphi_R'(x) = \left[(1-t^E)wl - \varphi_L\right]\theta - P(x) + (1-x)\frac{\partial P}{\partial x},$$

leading to the definition of τ^R. The term $1-x$ stands for the "remaining retirement period," which is reduced by a higher retirement age x.

9. The most common matching function $M = M_0 \cdot (L^M)^\eta\, v^{1-\eta}$ is used and yields matching rates $f = M_0 \Theta^{1-\eta}$, $q = M_0 / \Theta^\eta$, and $f = \Theta \cdot q$, where $\Theta = v/L^M$ measures labor market tightness.

10. Adjustment costs lead to slow transitional investment dynamics in the small open economy.

References

Banks, James, and Peter Diamond. 2011. "The Base for Direct Taxation." In *Dimensions of Tax Design: The Mirrlees Review*, edited by The Institute for Fiscal Studies, 548–648. Oxford: Oxford University Press for The Institute of Fiscal Studies (Oxford).

Blanchard, Olivier J. 1985. "Debt, Deficits and Finite Horizons." *Journal of Political Economy* 93:223–247.

Börsch-Supan, Axel, Tabea Bucher-Koenen, Michela Coppola, and Bettina Lamla. 2015. "Savings in Times of Demographic Change: Lessons from the German Experience." *Journal of Economic Surveys* 29 (4): 807–829.

Bovenberg, Lans A. 2003. "Financing Retirement in the European Union." *International Tax and Public Finance* 10:713–734.

Bovenberg, Lans A., and Thijs Knaap. 2005. "Ageing, Funded Pensions and the Dutch Economy." CESifo Working Paper No. 1403, CESifo, Munich.

Bundesamt für Statistik. 2006. *Szenarien zur Bevölkerungsentwicklung in der Schweiz.* Neuchâtel, Switzerland: Bundesamt für Statistik.

Cremer, Helmuth, and Pierre Pestieau. 2003. "The Double Dividend of Postponing Retirement." *International Tax and Public Finance* 10:419–434.

Cremer, Helmuth, and Pierre Pestieau. 2016. "Theoretical Foundations of the Taxation of Pensions." CESifo Working Paper No. 5930, May, CESifo, Munich.

Diamond, Peter A. 2004. "Social Security." *American Economic Review* 94:1–24.

Diamond, Peter A., and Peter R. Orszag. 2005. "Saving Social Security." *Journal of Economic Perspectives* 19:11–32.

Feldstein, Martin. 2005a. "Rethinking Social Insurance." *American Economic Review* 95:1–24.

Feldstein, Martin. 2005b. "Structural Reform of Social Security." *Journal of Economic Perspectives* 19:33–55.

Feldstein, Martin, and Jeffrey B. Liebman. 2002. "Social Security." In *Handbook of Public Economics*, vol. 4, edited by Alan Auerbach and Martin Feldstein, 2245–2324. Amsterdam: Elsevier.

Feldstein, Martin, and Andrew Samwick. 1992. "Social Security Rules and Marginal Tax Rates." *National Tax Journal* 45:1–22.

Fisher, Walter H., and Christian Keuschnigg. 2010. "Pension Reform and Labor Market Incentives." *Journal of Population Economics* 23:769–803.

Genser, Bernd. 2015. "Towards an International Tax Order for the Taxation of Retirement Income." Working Paper No. 2015-13, University of Konstanz, Konstanz, Germany.

Gertler, Mark. 1999. "Government Debt and Social Security in a Life-Cycle Economy." *Carnegie-Rochester Conference Series on Public Policy* 50:61–110.

Gruber, Jonathan, and David A. Wise, eds. 2004. *Social Security Programs and Retirement around the World: Micro-estimation.* Chicago: University of Chicago Press.

Holzmann, Robert. 2013. "Global Pension Systems and Their Reform: Worldwide Drivers, Trends and Challenges." *International Social Security Review* 66:1–29.

Immervoll, Herwig, Henrik J. Kleven, Claus T. Kreiner, and Emmanuel Saez. 2007. "Welfare Reform in European Countries: A Microsimulation Analysis." *Economic Journal* 117:1–44.

Jaag, Christian, Christian Keuschnigg, and Mirela Keuschnigg. 2010. "Pension Reform, Retirement and Life-Cycle Unemployment." *International Tax and Public Finance* 17:556–585.

Keuschnigg, Christian. 2016. "Aging, Taxes, and Pensions in Switzerland." Working Paper, November 23, University of St. Gallen, School of Economics and Political Science, St. Gallen, Switzerland. https://www.alexandria.unisg.ch/publications/249760.

Keuschnigg, Christian, Mirela Keuschnigg, and Christian Jaag. 2011. "Aging and the Financing of Social Security in Switzerland." *Swiss Journal of Economics and Statistics* 147:181–231.

Kindermann, Fabian. 2015. "Earnings Related Pension Schemes and Human Capital Formation." *Journal of Pension Economics and Finance* 14:19–54.

Kitao, Sagiri. 2014. "Sustainable Social Security: Four Options." *Review of Economic Dynamics* 17:756–779.

Kitao, Sagiri. 2015. "Fiscal Costs of Demographic Transition in Japan." *Journal of Economic Dynamics and Control* 54:37–58.

Kotlikoff, Laurence J. 1997. "Privatizing Social Security in the United States: Why and How." In *Fiscal Policy: Lessons from Economic Research*, edited by Alan J. Auerbach, 213–248. Cambridge, MA: MIT Press.

Lindbeck, Assar, and Mats Persson. 2003. "The Gains from Pension Reform." *Journal of Economic Literature* 41:74–112.

Miles, David. 1999. "Modelling the Impact of Demographic Change upon the Economy." *Economic Journal* 109:1–36.

OECD (Organisation for Economic Co-operation and Development). 2014. *Alterung und Beschäftigungspolitik: Schweiz 2014*. Paris: Bundesamt für Sozialversicherung and OECD.

Vogel, Edgar, Alexander Ludwig, and Axel Börsch-Supan. 2017. "Aging and Pension Reform: Extending the Retirement Age and Human Capital Formation." *Journal of Pension Economics and Finance* 161 (1): 81–107.

Weil, Philippe. 1990. "Nonexpected Utility in Macroeconomics." *Quarterly Journal of Economics* 105:29–42.

13 Longevity and Taxation of Public Pensions: Finland

Jukka Lassila and Tarmo Valkonen

13.1 Introduction

The decline in mortality rates in recent decades has been concentrated among older people in developed countries of the West. The increased longevity has caused severe financing problems for typical public pension schemes, which are based on pay-as-you-go (PAYG) financing and the defined benefit principle. Continuously increasing the pension contribution rate is not considered a viable solution because of its negative influence on labor supply. Moreover, the actual growth in longevity has often exceeded predictions, and the amount of future increase needed in the pension contribution rate is not well known, given the uncertainty related to future mortality rates.

Recent pension reforms in countries of the Organisation for Economic Co-operation and Development (OECD) have introduced two ways out of this problem. The first, life expectancy adjustment of monthly pensions, is more well known and is largely in use under nonfinancial defined contribution pension schemes. However, because this adjustment may endanger the adequacy of pensions, it has been emphasized that people should recognize this risk and react to it by working longer. Experience in Sweden, where life expectancy adjustment has affected benefits since 2001, shows that providing information about future pensions is not an adequate response to the problem, however. A Swedish committee thus suggested that the lowest eligibility age for pensions should also be linked to life expectancy (Slutbetänkande av Pensionsåldersutredningen 2013). Finland introduced a similar two-way link to life expectancy in its statutory earnings-related pension scheme that commenced in 2017 (Reipas and Sankala 2015).

The second option is taxation of public pensions, which reallocates resources between working lives and retirement years, but also between cohorts, when mortality rates change. The extent of this reallocation depends on the details of the tax system and of the pension scheme. Longevity affects the development of both pension expenditures (which is the tax base under an EET[1] regime but not under a TEE[2] regime) and pension contributions (which are deductible under EET but not under TEE).

This chapter illustrates the connections among pension tax regimes, longevity, and pension policies using Finland's earnings-related, first-pillar pension scheme as an example. Currently, the tax regime is EET. The chapter studies how a gradual switch to a TEE regime would affect the economy, public finances, firms, and households representing various birth cohorts in the future, when longevity will likely increase and pension policies may or may not take this increase into account. It also studies how longevity risks are shared between household generations and between the pension scheme and taxpayers under the two tax regimes.

The analysis combines three branches of the previous literature on the subject:

- Studies that use stochastic population projections as inputs in economic models to simulate the influence of pension policies on intergenerational risk sharing and public finances under demographic uncertainty (Alho, Hougaard Jensen, and Lassila 2008).
- Recent pension policy papers that simulate different options for adjusting public pension schemes to account for higher longevity (Sánchez Martín 2010; Fehr, Kallweit, and Kindermann 2012; Staubli and Zweimüller 2013; Lassila, Määttänen, and Valkonen 2014). The results point out the efficiency of increasing the eligibility ages for old-age pensions and early retirement benefits in terms of both improved public finances and higher retirement incomes.
- Papers that analyze the taxation of fully funded second- or third-pillar pension schemes. For example, Kudrna and Woodland (2012) simulated a transition from the current flat-rate taxation regime to either the EET or the TEE taxation regime under the Australian superannuation pension scheme. The idea is to limit the adverse intragenerational redistribution under the current tax rules. Fehr, Habermann, and Kindermann (2008) studied the savings and growth effects of introducing a new taxed EET scheme for private pension saving to increase private savings in order to compensate for the expected decline in the replacement rates of public pensions.

This chapter is mostly related to a study of intergenerational risk sharing by Chen et al. (2016). The policy options in that study are changes in pension contribution rates, indexation, and taxes. The restrictions are set in terms of the minimum and maximum public debt and the solvency of the pension fund. The pension fund investments are risky. Under the EET taxation regime, the government participates in sharing the investment risk more when there is more room for the debt to change. Individuals can also benefit from risk premiums, but the tax rates may vary more. Under the TEE regime, the government can reduce the debt but earns only the risk-free rate on this operation. Therefore, a regime shift is not preferred.

Section 13.2 describes the main features of the Finnish pension system and the principles of pension taxation. Section 13.3 explains and analyzes the tax switch around a base demographic projection. Tax-switch aspects related to future longevity, as well as how the pension schemes react to longevity, are considered in section 13.4. section 13.5 presents conclusions.

13.2 Taxation of Pensions in Finland

Savings for old age are commonly tax-favored. The aims of tax allowances are to avoid the cumulative distortions of capital income taxation, compensate for the restricted liquidity, and promote long-term savings by shortsighted individuals (Diamond 2009). Preferential tax treatment has also been applied to public pension schemes, in which the statutory pension contributions are typically deductible in earned income taxation and pensions are taxed. This section extends the discussion of tax regime neutrality to PAYG-financed pensions and illustrates the interaction of tax regimes and the incidence of employees' and employers' pension contributions (i.e., who bears the economic burden in contrast to who actually pays the contribution). It also describes the main features of the taxation of the Finnish pension system.

13.2.1 Taxation of a PAYG-Financed Defined Benefit Pension Scheme

The taxation of fully funded, defined contribution pension schemes provides savings neutrality if certain conditions are met. The neutral tax regimes are TEE, EET, and TtE.[3] These regimes are identical if the tax rates applied to deductions and pensions are the same and if there are no risks related to the rate of return. Even if the pension funds are invested in risky assets, EET and TtE regimes can generate identical outcomes if the saved deductions in the EET regime are invested in riskless assets. In that case, the government participates in sharing the yield risk and receives positive expected tax revenue as a reward. If the deductions are invested in risky assets, the outcomes of TEE and EET regimes become identical, and the government does not participate in sharing the yield risk.

Incentives for savings are not relevant to mandatory PAYG pension schemes, but it is illustrative to discuss the lifetime neutrality of the tax regimes in this context as well. The commonly used EET tax regime is not neutral, for several reasons. The tax rates applied to deductions and pensions are different, and the implicit yield of the pension contributions is, on average, below the yield of savings. In the case of employees' contributions, the disparity between the tax rates applied results from the progressivity of earned incomes and possibly also because of specific rules applied in the taxation of pensions. If employees invest the money saved from the tax deduction in financial markets, they are likely to receive higher returns on their contributions under the EET regime than under the TEE regime, where there is no deduction but pensions are tax-free.

The interaction between employers' contributions and tax revenues is more complicated. The contributions can be deducted from taxable profits under the EET regime. If the deduction is on labor, deductibility lowers labor costs, allowing higher wages and increased employment. Even if the government loses corporate income tax revenues because of EET, it receives more earned income taxes, since the total wage bill is larger. If the deduction is on capital, the government receives less corporate income tax revenue but more capital income tax revenue from firms' owners because after-tax profits are higher as a result of the deduction.

In short, employees benefit more under the EET regime the higher their contribution rate, the higher the marginal tax rate of wages relative to the marginal tax rate of pensions, and the larger the difference between the yield of savings and the implicit yield of the defined benefit pension scheme. If the deduction is on labor, the benefit from EET is greater the higher the employers' contribution rate and the corporate income tax rate.[4] The tax relief improves the incentives to supply labor but weakens the redistributive effects of progressive taxation. Since EET will likely reduce tax revenues, the final effect also depends on how the government balances its budget.

13.2.2 Finnish Pension System

The Finnish public pension system consists of a zero-pillar, means-tested national pension and a complementary guarantee pension, and a first-pillar statutory earnings-related pension. In addition to providing old-age lifetime pensions, the system covers risks related to family earners' disabilities and death.

The flat-rate national pension and the guarantee pension provide a minimum income when the earnings-related pension is insufficient. Access to the national pension requires that a person has lived for three years in Finland after turning 16, while access to the guarantee pension requires permanent residence. The eligibility age for the full pension is 65 years. The pension expenditure was 1.2 percent of gross domestic product (GDP) in 2015. Both pension schemes are tax-financed. Because of the specific pension income deduction, these pensions are in practice tax-free for the pensioner.

Under the earnings-related scheme, every year's earnings affect the future pension without a ceiling. The earliest eligibility age for old-age pensions is 63, but pensions accrue at an accelerated rate until the age of 68 if they are not withdrawn while the recipient is working. After a person turns 68, no new pension rights are accrued, but a yearly increase is applied if withdrawal is deferred.[5] Moreover, a longevity adjustment is applied to pensions. The size of the adjustment is calculated by comparing the observed life expectancy of the cohort at age 62 to the average of that number from 2003 to 2007. A tight link between earnings and benefits[6] and the longevity adjustment of pensions imply that even though the pension scheme follows the defined benefit principle, it reacts to earnings risks and longevity risks quite similarly to a defined contribution scheme.

The scheme has collected substantial funds to smoothen the contribution increases resulting from the aging of the population. The size of the pension expenditure was 12.1 percent of GDP in 2015, and the size of the prefunded amount was 87.3 percent of GDP at the end of 2015. Taxation of earnings-related pensions applies the EET principle. The tax regime supports the scheme rather strongly because of the highly progressive earned income tax.

The lack of a pension ceiling under the earnings-related scheme explains why voluntary group pensions financed by employers and individual pensions have a limited role in Finland. Contributions to these schemes amounted to only 0.3 percent of GDP in 2015. The total sum of accrued funds was 8.5 percent of GDP at the end of 2015.

Voluntary pensions are taxed based on the EET principle. Voluntary group pensions are taxed similarly to the earnings-related, first-pillar pensions. In contrast, the tax deductions of the contributions of individual pensions are calculated by using the almost flat capital income tax rate, and the pensions are taxed as capital income. The maximum yearly contribution eligible for this capital income tax regime is €5,000. Contributions above the ceiling are double-taxed by partially applying the TET[7] regime, which in practice rules out single-premium pension insurance. Significant increases in the lowest eligibility age and the transition from the earned income tax regime to the less generous capital income tax regime heavily reduced the popularity of individual pensions in recent years.

13.3 Pension Tax Reform

Consistent implementation of a shift from an EET to a TEE tax regime is rather complicated in a partially funded PAYG scheme, since historical accruals should still be taxed using the EET regime. The tax reform simulations herein use an overlapping-generations (OLG) model, which allows accurate allocation of the taxes to the right periods of time and to the right generations. This section illustrates the implementation of the tax regime shift, presents the main details of the OLG model, and discusses the main driving forces of the simulation results for a traditional defined benefit pension scheme.

13.3.1 Design of the Reform

Under the Finnish earnings-related pension scheme, all paid work increases the individual's future pension. Thus, the monthly benefit is a sum of accruals from different working years. The move from the EET regime to the TEE regime is assumed to be gradual whereby, in the future, the portions of the pension benefits that are based on accruals from 2013 onward are not taxed. The benefits based on accruals before 2013 are taxed, yielding tax revenues until all pensioners who have even a small accrual from before 2013 are dead.

Earnings-related pensions are financed by pension contributions paid by both employers and employees. Under the current EET taxation, employer contributions are accepted as expenses when corporate taxes are set, and employee contributions can be deducted from wage income when income taxes are calculated. In the gradual move from the EET to the TEE regime, it is assumed that contributions financing pension benefits based on accruals from 2013 onward are not tax-deductible, whereas contributions financing benefits based on accruals before 2013 are deductible. The tax regime switch thus ensures generational tax consistency. If benefits are taxed, the contributions that finance such benefits are tax-deductible, and if benefits are not taxed, the corresponding contributions are not tax-deductible.

Generational tax consistency has different implications for different types of pension systems. In a fully funded pension system, a gradual move from the EET to the TEE regime would be generationally tax-consistent in the sense here if benefits based on contributions paid from the switch date onward become tax-free and the tax-deductibility of contributions is removed at the beginning of the switch. The reason is that future contributions are used to finance future pension accruals only. In a PAYG-financed system, generational tax neutrality requires a more complicated treatment of contributions because future contributions are used to finance benefits based on both old and new accruals.

Whereas EET can be described as "postponed taxation" when the pension system is fully funded, it can be described as "postponed deduction" when PAYG financing is applied. This may sound counterintuitive since all contributions have been tax-deductible since day one of the PAYG pension system. However, the PAYG system can be thought of as a fully funded system with debt (and a different inner yield). The debt accumulated because there were "missing contributions," and when the debt is paid from a portion of future contributions, the deductions can be carried out. Nonfinancial defined contribution systems usually show this debt explicitly. The debt may never be fully paid; it is just rolled over, but specific portions of the debt are related to individual pension rights and are fully paid when the individual ceases to receive benefits.

The Finnish earnings-related pension scheme is partially funded and partially PAYG. In the switch from the EET to the TEE regime, contributions that are funded for future benefits based on accruals from 2013 onward cease to be tax-deductible, similar to a fully funded system. Contributions that finance the PAYG portion of benefits will be tax-deductible if benefits are based on accruals before 2013 and not deductible otherwise.

The quantitative effects of the tax switch will obviously depend on how the population ages and how the pension scheme copes with this. This section assumes that future demographics follow Statistics Finland's 2012 population forecast. Life expectancies are also predicted to grow in the future. As noted earlier, longer lifetimes would increase pension expenditures unless some pension policy measures prevent this. Two popular measures are automatic benefit adjustment and higher eligibility ages. In Finland, the first has been in use since 2010; based on observed mortality rates, the longevity adjustment of future monthly benefits is done when the cohort reaches the age of 62. The second measure is included in the 2017 reform, where the earliest old-age retirement age will be gradually raised to 65 and, after 2029, linked to life expectancies.

For the pension scheme, two extremes are considered. The rigid pension scheme is a traditional defined benefit, where there is neither a longevity adjustment of benefits nor longer work careers when people live longer. This was the case in Finland before 2005.The adjusting pension scheme has both longevity adjustment of benefits and longer work careers, which are partially the result of a link between retirement age and longevity, as is the case in Finland after 2017. Otherwise, both pension schemes follow the rules of the current statutory Finnish earnings-related pension scheme, with minor exceptions (see the Appendix).

13.3.2 The Overlapping-Generations Model

The population projection is used as an input in an economic model. This analysis uses a perfect foresight, numerical OLG model of the type created by Auerbach and Kotlikoff (1987). It is modified to describe a small open economy and is calibrated to the Finnish economy. The FOG (Finnish Overlapping Generations) model consists of five sectors and three markets. The sectors are households, enterprises, the government, two pension funds, and a foreign sector. Markets for labor, goods, and capital are competitive, and prices balance supply and demand period by period. No money or inflation exist in the model. The unit period is five years, and the model has 16 adult generations living in each period. The model is described in more detail by Lassila and Valkonen (2007).

The driving forces of the model economy are the transitions in the demographic and educational structures of the population and the growth trend of labor productivity. The population is aging because of longer lifetimes, low birthrates, and the transition of baby boomers from working age to retirement.

Labor input is determined partly by exogenous assumptions and partly by endogenous adjustments in the model. The exogenous factors are the growth trend of labor productivity, demographic trends, educational gains, and the unemployment rate. Real wages adjust to equalize the value of the marginal product of labor and labor costs in the production of private goods and services. The rest of the workers, who provide tax-funded services produced in the private and public sectors, earn the same wages.

Public expenditures have a strong connection to the age of individuals. The provision of public services is allocated mainly either to the early part of the life cycle (daycare and education) or to the last 10 years (health care and old-age care). Similarly, income transfers are distributed mainly to either young families or retired individuals. It is for this reason that the changes in the demographic structure are so important. It is assumed that all income transfers (except the earnings-related pensions) are fully indexed to wages because any other assumption would have dramatic consequences for income distribution in the long-term analysis. Expenditures other than age-related ones are assumed to grow at the same rate as GDP.

The main subsectors of the national government, such as the municipal sector, public and private sector pension funds, and the national social security institute, have their own budgets, which are balanced by either social security contributions or earned income taxes. The only exception is the state budget, which is balanced by a lump-sum tax/transfer. Earned income tax brackets are adjusted with the growth of the economy. The pension funds follow their current prefunding plans, and pension contributions are endogenous. Households react to the income and substitution effects of taxation and social security contributions. The current rules of the earnings-related pension scheme are described in detail in the Appendix.

13.3.3 How the Tax Reform Operates

The main mechanisms expected from the tax reform are discussed first. As described earlier, the simulation model includes detailed descriptions of the subsectors of the Finnish public sector and the main rules of taxation and social security, which somewhat complicates the results but makes them more realistic. The quantitative effects are also influenced by the fact that Finland is a Nordic welfare state and thus uses a lot of tax revenue to finance the extensive provision of income transfers and public services. The regime shift described in what follows is implemented assuming that the rigid pension scheme is in place.

13.3.3.1 Firms and labor market Firms pay a major share of the pension contributions. In Finland, firms pay around 18 percent of wages, compared to employees' 6 percent share. After the reform, these employers' contributions will gradually become nondeductible in corporate income taxation, which currently applies a flat tax rate of 20 percent. Abolishing the deductibility of contributions would therefore initially reduce net profits by 3.6 percent of wages and increase the public sector's tax revenues by the same amount. As the after-tax marginal productivity of the labor input falls, the demand for labor and wages also decreases. After the adjustment period, the after-tax yield on capital returns to the initial level.

13.3.3.2 Households For households, the tax reform means that the average and marginal tax rates of wages gradually become higher and the tax rate of pensions eventually declines to zero. Since the first effect is larger, the lifetime taxation of labor income will be tightened. Since wages also decline, the incentives to work weaken, and households supply fewer hours. Savings decrease significantly because after-tax income diminishes during working life and increases during the retirement years.

13.3.3.3 Local and central governments For public finances, the net outcome consists of three elements:

- The increase in tax revenue resulting from the tightening of wage taxation.
- The decrease in tax revenue because of lower wages, capital incomes, and consumption.
- The decline in public expenditures as a result of the lower wage rate, which cuts down public sector labor costs and income transfers indexed to wages.

The local government (municipalities) taxes incomes at a flat rate. Abolishing the deductibility of employees' pension contributions increases revenues from taxing wages, but the reduction in the wage bill and the abolition of the tax on pensions scale down the tax revenues. Municipalities also receive a portion of the increased corporate income tax revenues from the government. On the expenditure side, the decrease in public sector workers' wages and pensions supports the finances. The negative effects dominate, so municipalities have to raise the income tax rate to balance the budget.

The central government taxes incomes with a strongly progressive scale. Therefore, abolition of the deduction of the employees' contribution rate has a much larger effect than in municipal taxation. The positive effect of the tax reform on the earned income tax revenues is amplified by the fact that the average state tax rate on pensions is low. In practice, approximately 70 percent of pensioners do not pay any state tax on their pensions in Finland. The central government also collects a major share of the strongly increasing revenues from the corporate income tax. These factors outweigh the negative influences on tax revenues caused by the abolished tax on pensions, the lower wage bill and profits, less savings, and reduced consumption. The overall improvement in state revenues allows a reduction in the lump-sum tax that is used in the simulations to balance the state budget.

13.3.3.4 Earnings-related pension scheme The tax regime shift also influences the pension scheme, but not significantly, under the assumption that the rules determining the size of benefits are not changed even though pensions become tax-free. The decrease in the wage rate lowers earned pension rights and index adjustments of the accrued pension rights and the pensions. Therefore, pension expenditures diminish. On the other hand, the lower wage bill reduces the amount of contribution revenues raised. Thus, no major changes in the contribution rate are expected.

13.3.4 Summary

How can all these mechanisms be summarized? The tax reform succeeds in improving public finances but at the expense of lower wages, employment, private consumption, and household wealth (table 13.1). A measure that reduces lump-sum taxation (the balancing element in the state budget) and increases the taxation of wages and corporate incomes weakens the efficiency of the economy and will likely cause a welfare loss.

The general equilibrium price effects in the small almost open economy are rather limited. The real interest rate does not rise although savings decrease, which restricts the decline in investment. Domestic production somewhat diminishes because of the negative labor supply reaction, but since private consumption is reduced even more, the equilibrium in the markets for domestic goods requires a decrease in producer prices.

Table 13.1
Effects of the tax regime shift under the rigid pension scheme.

	Year				Long term
	2023	2043	2063	2083	
Wage, %	–4.65	–4.60	–4.35	–4.33	–5.6
Private employment, %	–0.10	–0.52	–1.39	–2.00	–1.2
Household wealth, %	–7.17	–19.05	–28.85	–36.14	–52.0
Private consumption, %	–0.68	–0.97	–1.60	–2.69	–6.2
Public expenditure/GDP, pp	–0.89	–1.01	–0.94	–0.86	–1.0
Total taxes/GDP, pp	–0.24	–0.16	0.49	0.82	0.6

Note: pp = percentage points.

13.4 Longevity Risk and Pension Tax Reform

Section 13.3 showed that the main drivers of the economic outcomes of the tax regime shift are the higher costs of financing the pensions and decreased lifetime savings of households. Both are sensitive to how long people live. Therefore, the future mortality rate at an old age obviously has an important connection with the results of tax reform. However, the history of mortality projections indicates that they have not been accurate in the relevant time horizon of pension systems, which comprises several decades.

Therefore, a stochastic approach is adopted in the following tax reform analysis. The idea is to provide a probability-based assessment of the reform's outcomes. This section first presents the stochastic mortality projection used. Next, it discusses the interaction between longevity risk and pensions on the one hand and the interaction between longevity risk and taxation of pensions on the other hand. Finally, the simulation results are presented and evaluated.

13.4.1 Stochastic Population Projections

Demographic uncertainty is dealt with by using stochastic population projections. Many researchers have developed statistical methods for expressing demographic uncertainty (Alho and Spencer 2005). These methods quantify uncertainty probabilistically, based on analyses of past demographic data and experts' views. Fertility, mortality, and migration are considered stochastic processes. The parameters of these processes are fitted to match the errors of past forecasts (Alho, Hougaard Jensen, and Lassila 2008). Thereafter, sample paths for the future population by age group are simulated. In this study, stochastic population projections are produced by a computer program called PEP (Program for Error Propagation). As a descriptor of the length of life, a period life expectancy at 30 is used as an average of men and women. It is expressed as total life expectancy; that is, 30 years plus the remaining life expectancy at age 30. Over the next 50 years, this life expectancy is expected to rise to an unprecedented level in Finland. However, it is very hard to state exactly how high it will go. For this reason, stochastic simulations are used that are based on statistical analysis of past demographics and forecasting errors. According to Alho (2002, 8), "The analysis of uncertainty was based on the relative error of the naive forecast with data for 5-year age-groups for 1900–1994. In the case of mortality, the naive forecast assumed that the recent past decline in mortality continues indefinitely. As discussed in Alho (1990) and Lee and Miller (2001), the naive method and related extrapolation methods perform typically equally well as (or better than!) the judgmental official forecasts."

Figure 13.1 shows the predictive distribution of total life expectancy at 30 for the next 50 years. The median increases by 7.5 years. The 50 percent probability interval is about 3.5 years in the 2060s, and the 80 percent interval is 7.0 years. The predictive distribution is calculated

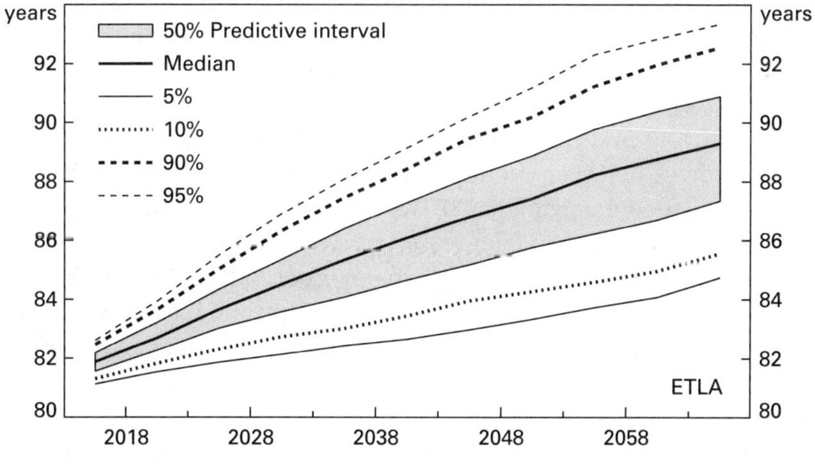

Figure 13.1
Predictive distribution of total life expectancy at 30 in Finland.

from a stochastic population projection produced by Alho in 2013 using PEP.[8] This stochastic projection is built around Statistics Finland's 2012 projection.

This OLG model analysis first makes a constant-mortality version of the 2012 population forecast. The constant-mortality population starts from the age structure in the beginning of 2013 and assumes a constant inflow of persons below 20 years old in the future, no net migration, and the 2012 age-specific mortality rates in all future periods. This population evolves so that new generations are all of the same size, and cohorts are diminished in time by constant mortality rates.

To get stochastic mortality paths, the analysis starts from the constant-mortality projection but allows future mortalities to deviate from that. These deviations follow the assumptions used in the stochastic population projection. Five hundred simulated population paths are used and differ only because of different mortality developments. The constant-mortality path is not used further.

13.4.2 Longevity Risk and Pension Schemes

According to Määttänen's (2014) estimates, an additional three years in the life expectancy of 30-year-old individuals would extend working lives by six months, assuming that any health problems are likewise postponed for three years. This information is used in the FOG model in such a way that the change in life expectancy automatically affects the length of working life at the ratio depicted, even if pension rules are unchanged.

Linking retirement age to life expectancy, as in the adjusting scheme, affects the length of working life. Based on the model used by Määttänen (2014), raising the eligibility age for the pension, the unemployment pathway, and the part-time pension by two years would extend working lives by seven months. Extending working lives is included in the FOG model, starting in 2018 exogenously through the pensioner proportion, since the model does not contain labor supply decisions in the extensive margin (i.e., to participate or not in the labor markets).

The interaction of pension schemes and uncertain life expectancy in the EET tax regime is illustrated in figure 13.2; the pension contribution rate rises with future longevity under the rigid pension scheme but stays flat under the adjusting pension scheme. The outcomes are created with the FOG model. Each dot represents one realization of the 500 stochastic mortality projections.

Figure 13.3 depicts a similar pattern for the pension expenditure relative to the wage bill, except that the adjusting scheme generates a

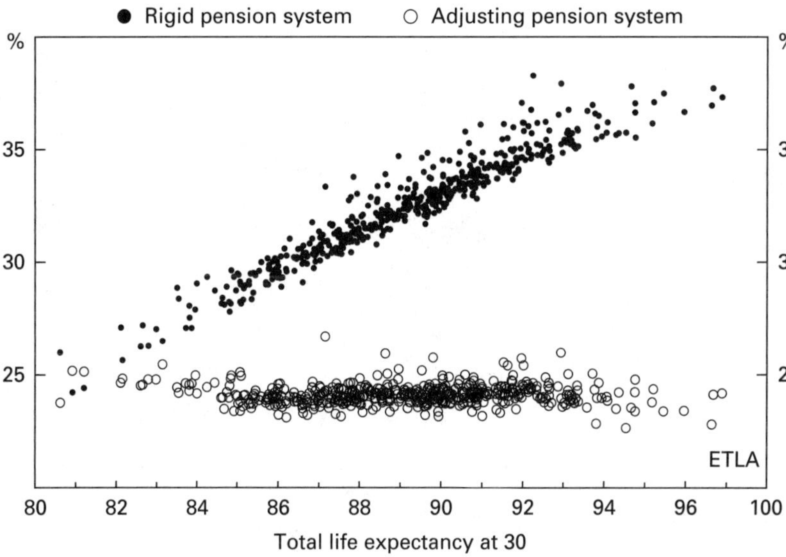

Figure 13.2
Pension contribution rates in 2063–2067, with varying longevities.

slightly negative trend. Longevity is measured in both figures by the total life expectancy of a 30-year-old in 2063–2067.

If lifetimes become continuously longer, the contribution rate under the rigid pension scheme will be too low to finance the future pensions of the current working-age generations because it is based on realized pension expenditures and mortality rates. The adjusting pension scheme aims to allocate the higher expenditures to the right generations. The allocation is not perfect, because it is based on life expectancy near retirement age, which does not consider the changes in mortality rates during the retirement years.

Households react to longer lifetimes by working more and saving more for old age (figure 13.4). The scale of the reaction depends strongly on the details of the pension scheme. The higher pension contributions under the rigid scheme decrease wages. Thereby, they also reduce incentives to work and the ability to save for old age. The lower pensions and higher retirement age under the adjusting scheme extend working lives and increase savings for old age. The substantial increase in working hours has a negative effect on wages, but private consumption can still be sustained at a considerably higher level. The public finances are also more resilient against lower mortality rates.

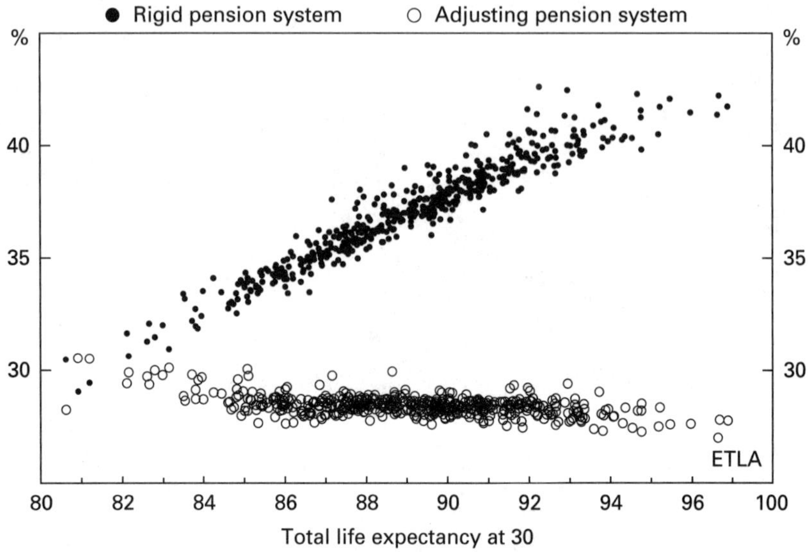

Figure 13.3
Pension expenditures as percent of wage bill in 2063–2067, with varying longevities.

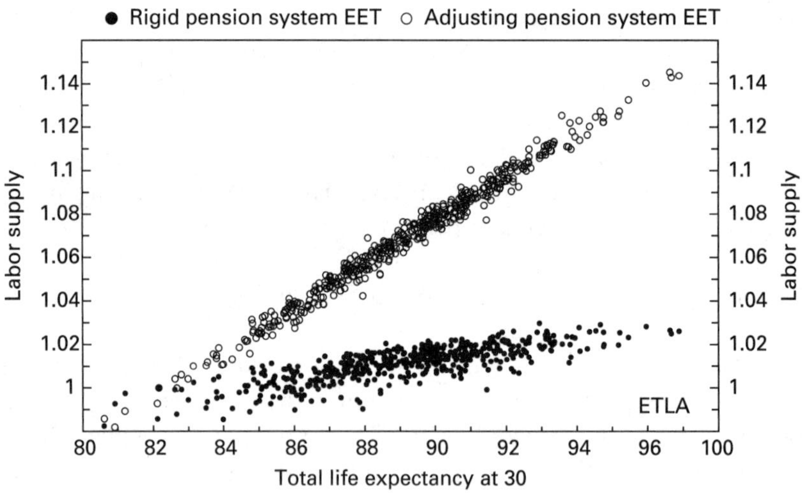

Figure 13.4
Labor supply (index 2013 = 1) in 2063–2067, with varying longevities.

13.4.3 Longevity and Taxation of Pensions

13.4.3.1 Rigid pension scheme As noted, longer lifetimes increase the number of pensioners as well as the pension expenditures and contribution rates under the rigid pension scheme. The tax revenues of the national government decline because the higher employer contributions lower wages.

If the taxation of the pension scheme follows EET rules, the tax deductions from wages and profits will be larger because of higher contributions, which will worsen the loss in tax revenues. Although the amount of taxed pensions will also be larger, overall tax revenues will drop, since the average tax rate of pensions will be low. In the TEE regime, the higher contributions resulting from longer lifetimes are not deductible, limiting the direct loss in tax revenues. On the other hand, wages and profits decrease more in reaction to higher labor costs.

13.4.3.2 Pension scheme adjusted to longevity Adjusting pensions to life expectancy means that at the time of retirement the accrued pension rights are divided by the expected number of retirement years. The monthly benefit becomes lower the more life expectancy increases. On the other hand, the needed increase in the contribution rate is also smaller. With this kind of adjustment, sharing the longevity risk under a defined benefit pension scheme operates in a manner similar to that under a defined contribution scheme.

If longevity adjustment is applied in the EET regime, higher life expectancy does not generate as much taxable pension income, but the needed increase in the contribution rate is also smaller, as are the deductions of the contributions from taxable wages and profits. The public finances are also less sensitive to longer lifetimes under the TEE tax regime, since the smaller increase in pension contributions means the decrease in wages and profits is limited as well.

Adjusting the eligibility age for old-age pensions to life expectancy operates in another way, but the beneficial public finance outcomes are comparable. Longer lifetimes strongly increase labor supply. The larger tax base for pension contributions, together with the reduced number of retirement years, diminishes the pressure to increase the contribution rate generated by longer lifetimes. The choice of tax regime again becomes less important.

Under the adjusting pension scheme, both the pension benefit and retirement age adjustments to higher life expectancy are used. However, the life expectancy adjustment is moderated to avoid an excessive cut in the ratio of paid contributions to received benefits.

13.4.4 Tax Regime Shift under Longevity Uncertainty

13.4.4.1 Rigid pension scheme A surprise policy reform is simulated in which the new employees' and employers' contributions under the rigid defined benefit pension scheme are no longer tax-deductible, and newly accrued pension rights are tax-exempt. The old pension rights will still be taxed as soon as they are realized as paid pensions. This reform is simulated 500 times using different realizations of the stochastic mortality projection. The results are shown in figures 13.5 and 13.6 and in table 13.2.

Shifting the taxation of pensions from the retirement years to the working years has profound impacts on the decisions of households and on public finances. Moreover, under the rigid pension scheme, these impacts become greater the longer the lifetime. This is because the main driver of the tax reform results, the amount of pension contributions to be deducted during taxation, is directly linked to the length of the retirement period.

The Finnish earnings-related pension scheme is financed mainly by employers' contributions, which means that most of the labor market adjustments depend on the incidence of corporate taxes and the contributions. As the economy is small and open, the effect is mostly on labor.

The second-largest driver of the results is the reduced need to save for old age after the tax reform. The longer the lifetime, the more people save. Therefore, the amount of additional savings needed is cut by the tax reform more strongly in high-longevity scenarios.

The third marked driver of the results is the tightening of labor income taxation, which becomes stronger the longer the lifetime. The longer the retirement period, the more households need to work, but taxation increasingly distorts the decision.

Figures 13.5 and 13.6 show the effects of the regime shift on total taxes/GDP and public expenditures/GDP, respectively. This tax measure excludes the lump-sum tax used to balance the state budget. The policy reform has a consistent influence under the rigid pension scheme. The higher the life expectancy, the higher the tax rate, although public expenditures also diminish. The main effect is caused by increasing pension contributions, which cannot be deducted when taxing income

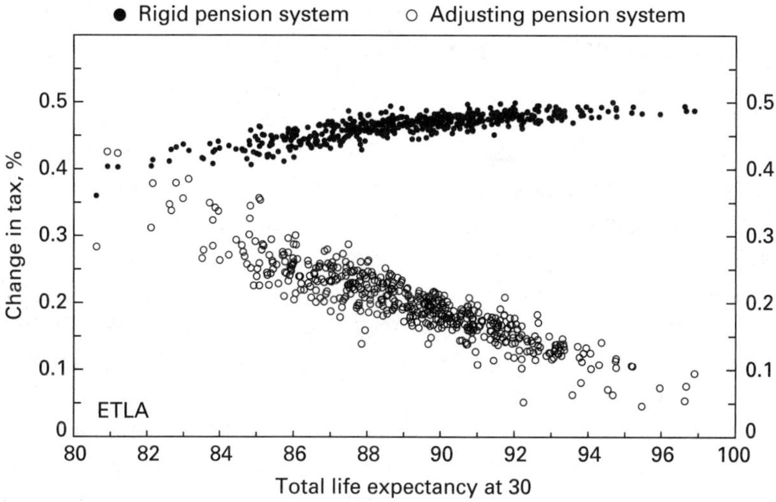

Figure 13.5
Tax-switch effects on total taxes/GDP (%) in 2063–2067, with varying longevities.

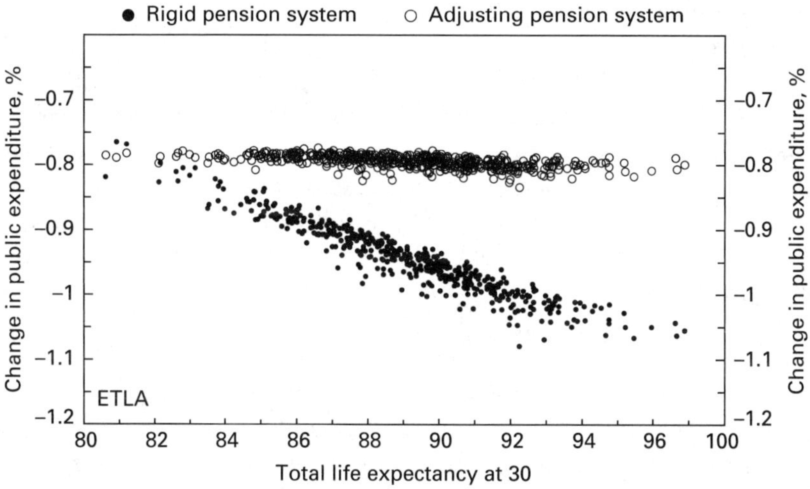

Figure 13.6
Tax-switch effects on public expenditures/GDP (%) in 2063–2067, with varying longevities.

after the reform. Public expenditures decline more in high-longevity scenarios because the tax regime shift cuts public sector wages more.

13.4.4.2 Adjusting pension scheme In the second set of simulations, the tax reform is implemented in an economy that has longevity adjustments in both pensions and the retirement age under the earnings-related pension scheme. With such a scheme, the reduction in old-age mortality rates has three separate effects on the total amount of pensions paid and thus the tax base for pension taxation: it lowers monthly pensions as a result of the life expectancy adjustment, increases monthly pensions as a result of the higher number of pension accrual years, and shortens the pension entitlement period.

Compared to the rigid scheme, the adjusting scheme shifts the aggregate longevity risk from contributions to benefits and reduces the variation in the deducted amount but increases the variation in revenues from taxing pensions. The overall variation in the net tax revenues under longevity uncertainty is smaller under the adjusting scheme than under the rigid scheme, as is the role of the government as a sharer of the aggregate longevity risk.

The regime shift itself still increases the labor costs of firms and lowers wages in all mortality realizations. Private savings, wealth, and consumption also decline considerably but will still be markedly larger than in the case of the rigid scheme, since the contribution rate does not react as much to the increase in life expectancy.

Under the adjusting pension scheme, individuals compensate for the decrease in monthly pensions by their longer lifetimes and by working and saving more. Therefore, private consumption also remains at a higher level. The links among longevity, pension contributions, tax revenues, and public sector wages as expenditures are much weaker, and the public finances are more resilient to longevity risks. In other words, from the perspectives of public finances and longevity risk sharing, introducing life expectancy adjustments of pensions and retirement age seems to serve as a substitute for the transition from the EET regime to the TEE regime.

13.4.5 Patterns in Variation

Table 13.2 also includes standard deviations of variables in each longevity quadrant. Some patterns can be observed.

First, the variation is often larger in the first and fourth quadrants (Q1 and Q4) than in the middle quadrants (Q2 and Q3). This is because

Table 13.2
Selected economic variables under different pension and tax systems, by life expectancy quartiles.

Total life expectancy at 30 in 2063 (TLE)	Q_1 TLE < 87.3		Q_2 87.3 < TLE < 89.3		Q_3 89.3 < TLE < 90.9		Q_4 90.9 < TLE	
	Mean	*Std*	Mean	*Std*	Mean	*Std*	Mean	*Std*
Pension expenditure/wage bill (%), 2063–2067								
Rigid scheme, EET	34.07	1.338	36.42	0.744	37.80	0.696	39.64	1.019
Rigid scheme, TEE	34.28	1.365	36.68	0.763	38.10	0.711	39.99	1.047
Adjusting scheme, EET	28.63	0.602	28.45	0.300	28.29	0.280	28.14	0.425
Adjusting scheme, TEE	28.75	0.608	28.58	0.307	28.42	0.287	28.27	0.436
Policy effects, Rigid	0.22	0.030	0.27	0.022	0.30	0.019	0.35	0.031
Policy effects, Adjusting	0.12	0.012	0.13	0.011	0.13	0.010	0.14	0.015
Pension contribution rate (%), 2063–2067								
Rigid scheme, EET	29.45	1.413	31.83	0.821	33.28	0.724	35.23	1.066
Rigid scheme, TEE	29.63	1.430	32.04	0.834	33.51	0.735	35.50	1.087
Adjusting scheme, EET	24.17	0.500	24.19	0.378	24.18	0.381	24.25	0.515
Adjusting scheme, TEE	24.28	0.508	24.30	0.385	24.29	0.388	24.37	0.525
Policy effects, Rigid	0.18	0.018	0.21	0.015	0.23	0.013	0.27	0.022
Policy effects, Adjusting	0.11	0.009	0.12	0.008	0.12	0.008	0.12	0.011
Wage rate, 2063–2067 (2008–2012 = 1)								
Rigid scheme, EET	1.037	0.006	1.032	0.005	1.030	0.005	1.030	0.005
Rigid scheme, TEE	0.994	0.006	0.987	0.005	0.985	0.004	0.984	0.005
Adjusting scheme, EET	1.045	0.008	1.037	0.006	1.032	0.006	1.027	0.007

(continued)

Table 13.2 (continued)

Total life expectancy at 30 in 2063 (TLE)	Q_1 TLE < 87.3		Q_2 87.3 < TLE < 89.3		Q_3 89.3 < TLE < 90.9		Q_4 90.9 < TLE	
	Mean	*Std*	Mean	*Std*	Mean	*Std*	Mean	*Std*
Adjusting scheme, TEE	1.004	0.008	0.996	0.006	0.991	0.006	0.986	0.007
Policy effects, Rigid	–4.15	0.095	–4.30	0.057	–4.39	0.050	–4.51	0.063
Policy effects, Adjusting	–3.92	0.025	–3.95	0.025	–3.97	0.023	–4.00	0.025
Labor supply, 2063–2067 (2008–2012 = 1)								
Rigid scheme, EET	1.002	0.006	1.010	0.005	1.014	0.004	1.019	0.005
Rigid scheme, TEE	0.993	0.006	1.000	0.005	1.004	0.004	1.008	0.005
Adjusting scheme, EET	1.032	0.015	1.060	0.007	1.079	0.005	1.103	0.014
Adjusting scheme, TEE	1.025	0.015	1.053	0.007	1.071	0.005	1.095	0.014
Policy effects, Rigid	–0.94	0.047	–1.02	0.032	–1.06	0.030	–1.13	0.041
Policy effects, Adjusting	–0.70	0.042	–0.69	0.030	–0.68	0.029	–0.67	0.042
Household wealth/GDP (%), 2067								
Rigid scheme, EET	123.55	7.196	135.74	5.052	142.84	3.668	152.06	5.632
Rigid scheme, TEE	87.02	5.491	96.35	4.025	101.62	2.888	108.41	4.333
Adjusting scheme, EET	132.18	8.936	146.60	5.362	154.53	4.161	164.41	5.757
Adjusting scheme, TEE	102.14	8.669	116.05	5.014	123.68	3.914	133.19	5.513
Policy effects, Rigid	–36.52	1.844	–39.39	1.247	–41.22	1.017	–43.65	1.427
Policy effects, Adjusting	–30.04	0.383	–30.55	0.388	–30.85	0.286	–31.22	0.285
Private consumption, 2063–2067 (2008–2012 = 1)								
Rigid scheme, EET	0.978	0.014	0.955	0.009	0.941	0.008	0.922	0.011
Rigid scheme, TEE	0.962	0.014	0.940	0.009	0.926	0.008	0.907	0.011

Adjusting scheme, EET	1.001	0.007	0.990	0.007	0.983	0.006	0.974	0.007
Adjusting scheme, TEE	0.984	0.007	0.973	0.007	0.967	0.006	0.957	0.007
Policy effects, Rigid	–1.65	0.049	–1.62	0.050	–1.61	0.038	–1.59	0.036
Policy effects, Adjusting	–1.72	0.030	–1.70	0.026	–1.70	0.023	–1.71	0.026
Consumer prices, 2063–2067 (2008–2012 = 1)								
Rigid scheme, EET	0.988	0.002	0.989	0.002	0.990	0.002	0.991	0.002
Rigid scheme, TEE	0.988	0.002	0.989	0.002	0.990	0.002	0.992	0.002
Adjusting scheme, EET	0.984	0.002	0.981	0.002	0.979	0.001	0.977	0.002
Adjusting scheme, TEE	0.983	0.002	0.980	0.001	0.978	0.001	0.976	0.002
Policy effects, Rigid	0.00	0.010	0.02	0.008	0.03	0.007	0.04	0.011
Policy effects, Adjusting	–0.07	0.009	–0.08	0.006	–0.08	0.005	–0.09	0.007
Total taxes/GDP (%), 2063–2067								
Rigid scheme, EET	46.46	0.621	47.43	0.448	48.06	0.394	48.99	0.552
Rigid scheme, TEE	46.90	0.628	47.89	0.446	48.54	0.393	49.47	0.555
Adjusting scheme, EET	44.84	0.244	45.02	0.283	45.15	0.281	45.41	0.308
Adjusting scheme, TEE	45.10	0.235	45.24	0.271	45.34	0.274	45.55	0.303
Policy effects, Rigid	0.44	0.017	0.46	0.011	0.47	0.009	0.48	0.009
Policy effects, Adjusting	0.26	0.046	0.22	0.025	0.18	0.019	0.14	0.031
Public expenditures/GDP, 2063–2067								
Rigid scheme, EET	40.36	0.714	41.43	0.555	42.16	0.498	43.24	0.672
Rigid scheme, TEE	39.48	0.684	40.50	0.536	41.19	0.482	42.23	0.649
Adjusting scheme, EET	38.42	0.295	38.49	0.341	38.57	0.338	38.80	0.370
Adjusting scheme, TEE	37.63	0.290	37.70	0.333	37.78	0.331	38.00	0.363

(continued)

Table 13.2 (continued)

Total life expectancy at 30 in 2063 (TLE)	Q_1 TLE < 87.3		Q_2 87.3 < TLE < 89.3		Q_3 89.3 < TLE < 90.9		Q_4 90.9 < TLE	
	Mean	*Std*	Mean	*Std*	Mean	*Std*	Mean	*Std*
Policy effects, Rigid	–0.88	0.032	–0.93	0.020	–0.96	0.018	–1.01	0.025
Policy effects, Adjusting	–0.79	0.006	–0.79	0.008	–0.80	0.008	–0.80	0.009
Sustainability gap (%)								
Rigid scheme, EET	2.74	0.359	3.28	0.270	3.65	0.242	4.173	0.314
Rigid scheme, TEE	1.89	0.341	2.40	0.258	2.75	0.231	3.248	0.299
Adjusting scheme, EET	1.06	0.094	1.03	0.104	1.02	0.094	1.04	0.089
Adjusting scheme, TEE	0.29	0.090	0.26	0.101	0.26	0.091	0.28	0.085
Policy effects, Rigid	–0.85	0.018	–0.88	0.012	–0.90	0.011	–0.92	0.014
Policy effects, Adjusting	–0.77	0.005	–0.76	0.004	–0.76	0.004	–0.76	0.005

of the property of the stochastic mortality simulations that longevity itself varies less in the middle quadrants. The ranges of Q2 and Q3 are 2.0 years and 1.5 years, respectively, whereas the range of Q1 is about 7 years and the range of Q4 is 6 years. These differences are also reflected in the economic variables.

Second, the variation is often larger in the first quadrant (Q1) than in the fourth quadrant (Q4). Again, longevity itself varies more in the first quadrant, and generally the variation is larger at lower life expectancies (figure 13.1). This is explained by the fact that the longevity measure is a multiplicative statistic of survival values that are between zero and one. The larger variation among low life expectancies can also be seen in figures 13.5 and 13.6, where it generates more variation in the results of the tax regime shift in the scheme that includes adjustment rules related to life expectancy.

Third, the variation in the effects of the tax switch is larger in the rigid pension scheme than in the adjusting pension scheme. The fiscal flows caused by the tax shift depend on the size of the pension expenditure and the amount of contributions, both of which are larger under the rigid scheme than under the adjusting scheme. Variation in these pension variables is also larger under the rigid scheme, so the higher variation in policy effects is not surprising. The only exception to this pattern is that the variation in total taxes (not including the lump-sum tax that balances the state budget) is smaller under the adjusting scheme.

13.4.6 Generational Effects

For an intergenerational measure of policy effects, relative compensated variations are used for each cohort. They are calculated as $100(\ln E(c) - \ln E(s))$, where E denotes discounted consumption expenditure during the rest of a lifetime, s refers to the simulation run, and c is the consumption necessary to achieve the baseline utility at simulation prices.

Two main factors causing the losses are the declines in wages (both gross and net) and in labor supply. The gains come from decreased lump-sum taxes. As noted earlier, gross wages decline almost immediately to a new, lower level. The decline is real because consumer prices remain practically unchanged. Furthermore, wage income is effectively taxed with a higher rate since employees' contributions cease to be deductible. Labor supply declines gradually, reflecting how the weakening incentives affect a larger share of working careers as time progresses.

The distribution of the gains depends on how the improvement in the central government's finances is used. In the simulations described earlier, it is used to decrease lump-sum taxes. The decrease is shared equally with each household in every period. This assumption causes the rather significant generational redistribution revealed in table 13.3. The government could of course choose some other rule to smoothen the welfare outcomes, but the losses would dominate in any case.

For those who are already retired, the lump-sum tax effects dominate. The decline in wages lowers pension benefits, which are partly indexed to wages, but this effect is rather small. On the other hand, the lump-sum effects are initially also small, so the welfare effects remain small. Those who are already working usually suffer a little. The wage decline hits them fully, and lump-sum effects do not compensate enough.

Cohorts who enter the labor force when the tax switch is made or 5 to 10 years later gain a little. They benefit from the lump-sum tax effects that grow during their lifetimes, and the tax increase does not hit them fully in their early working years. Under the rigid scheme, the largest lifetime consumption increases amount to around 1.5 percent. Under the adjusting scheme, the gains are smaller. Future generations lose from the reform, and the losses grow from one generation to the next. Over the long term, the losses amount to around 5 percent under the rigid scheme and close to 3 percent under the adjusting scheme.

Table 13.3
Relative gains and losses from the pension tax switch.

	Birth year of the cohort						Long term
	1933	1953	1973	1993	2013	2033	
Rigid scheme							
90%	0.7	0.0	−0.5	2.0	0.5	−1.1	−4.1
Median	0.6	−0.1	−0.6	1.5	0.3	−1.3	−4.7
10%	0.5	−0.2	−0.8	1.1	0.0	−1.5	−5.1
Adjusting scheme							
90%	0.5	−0.5	−1.1	1.0	−0.2	−1.2	−2.6
Median	0.5	−0.6	−1.2	0.8	−0.3	−1.3	−2.8
10%	0.5	−0.6	−1.3	0.7	−0.4	−1.3	−2.9

Note: Compensated variation as percentage of discounted consumption expenditure during remaining lifetime.

Under the rigid scheme, the losses are smaller, and the gains are larger with longer lifetimes. Under the adjusting scheme, the differences are negligible.

13.4.7 Effects on Fiscal Sustainability

The sustainability gap estimates in table 13.2 are based on 100-year evaluations. The gap is larger under the rigid scheme than under the adjusting scheme. This is easily understandable because under the latter scheme monthly pension benefits are adjusted downward if longevity increases, and work careers also become longer, bringing more tax revenues. Under the rigid scheme, none of this happens. The gap also grows more with longevity under the rigid scheme than under the adjusting scheme, for the same reasons that affect the average gap size. The effects of the tax switch grow very slightly with longevity under the rigid scheme. No clear pattern related to longevity arises under the adjusting scheme, but, on average, the effects are slightly smaller than under the rigid scheme.

13.5 Conclusions

This chapter aimed at limiting the problematic consequences of continuously increasing longevity on public finances by introducing a tax regime shift from EET to TEE in Finland's earnings-related, first-pillar pension scheme. A shift to TEE taxation of pensions broadens the tax base both in wage income and corporate income taxation by abolishing the entitlement to deduct employees' and employers' contributions. It also abolishes taxation of pension benefits. The net effect is expected to increase tax revenues in progressive taxation because of the differences in timing and the tax rates used.

The chapter studied the connections between pension tax regimes, longevity, and pension policies using the Finnish earnings-related pension scheme as an example. Uncertainty in longevity is considered using a large number of sample paths (500) from a stochastic mortality projection in an economic simulation model that is an open economy version of the Auerbach-Kotlikoff OLG model. Three levels of results were presented: how the economy reacts to the tax regime shift, how longevity and the two pension schemes interact, and how the outcomes of the tax regime shift change with longevity.

Abolishing deductibility of pension contributions has strong indirect effects on tax bases. Since the Finnish earnings-related pension scheme is financed mainly by employers' contributions, firms' reaction to the increase in labor costs dominates the outcomes. Wage rates and demand for labor fall, which decreases income and consumption, but the total tax rate increases because of tightened taxation of profits and labor income. Moreover, lower wages decrease public sector wages and income transfers indexed to wages. Therefore, the regime shift improves public finances as expected, but at the expense of a less efficient tax structure and lower consumption.

Several first-pillar pension schemes have already adopted rules that adjust pensions or pension eligibility ages to life expectancy. Therefore, two extremes were considered. A rigid pension scheme has neither longevity adjustment of benefits nor a higher eligibility age for pensions when people live longer. In this scheme, longer lifetimes increase pension expenditures and contribution rates and reduce tax revenues. An adjusting pension scheme has both longevity adjustment of benefits and longer work careers that are partially the result of a link between retirement age and longevity. Increasing longevity slightly reduces pension expenditures relative to wages. The net tax revenues related to the pension scheme increase.

Under the rigid pension scheme, the effects of the tax regime switch on wages, employment, household wealth, pension variables, and public finances are stronger than in the adjusting scheme. The difference is larger in projections where lifetimes grow more.

The stochastic longevity simulations show that the effects of switching from an EET to a TEE regime change in different ways in the two pension schemes when longevity changes. Under the rigid scheme, the effects are larger the more longevity increases, but if longevity does not greatly affect pension expenditures or pension financing, as in the adjusting scheme, the effects of the tax switch do not change much with changes in longevity. In this automatically adjusting pension scheme, the tax regime shift is not so efficient, but more importantly, not so necessary either.

Appendix: Modeling the Tax Regime Shift in Finland's Earnings-Related Pension Scheme

Finland's earnings-related pension scheme aims to provide sufficient retirement income to cover consumption comparable to levels enjoyed during working years and comparable to current workers' consumption. It covers risks related to old age, disability, and death of family earners. In cases where the earnings-related pension is absent or insufficient, the national pension guarantees a minimum income. Both of these first-pillar schemes are mandatory. Voluntary pensions are still of minor importance in Finland but are becoming more common. The private sector earnings-related scheme is described here as it is since the 2005 reform. A new reform took place in 2017, but it is not essential for this study. Public sector pension schemes are becoming similar, except that funding is different and there are long transition periods from old benefit rules.

Pensions consist of both disability pensions and old-age pensions. Every year's earnings and accrual rates directly affect the future pension. The accrual rate is 1.5 percent per year between the ages of 18 and 53 and 1.9 percent between the ages of 53 and 62. Between the ages of 63 and 68, the accrual is 4.5 percent per year, aiming to reward later retirement in a cost-neutral way. Earnings-related pensions are financed by pension contributions paid by both employers and employees. The scheme has collected substantial funds that smoothen the development of contribution rates over time.

Two things happen in the gradual move from an EET regime to a TEE regime. First, pension benefits gradually become tax-free. Second, the tax-deductibility of pension contributions gradually ends. These things are connected: if benefits are taxed, the contributions that finance such benefits are tax-deductible, and if benefits are not taxed, the corresponding contributions are not tax-deductible.

The regime shift starts at 2013. After that, those parts of pension benefits that are based on accruals from 2013 onward will not be taxed. Benefits based on accruals before 2013 are taxed, yielding tax revenues until all pensioners that have even a small accrual from before 2013 are dead.

13.A.1 Regime Shift in Benefits

Since every year's earnings and accrual rates directly affect the future pension, the part of the benefit that has accrued before a certain date can be separated from the part that accrues after that date. This can also be done in the pension part in the OLG model.

Both pension rights and benefits are index linked, with 80/20 weights on wages and consumer prices, respectively, during working years and 20/80 weights after retirement, irrespective of retirement age. In the model, function $I(t, u, \lambda)$ states that the change in wages w from period t to period u is weighted by λ and the change in consumer prices p is weighted by $1-\lambda$. Employees' contributions e are deducted from wages in this calculation.

$$I(t,u,\lambda)=\left(\frac{w(u)(1-e(u))}{w(t)(1-e(t))}\right)^{\lambda}\left(\frac{p(u)}{p(t)}\right)^{1-\lambda}. \tag{13.1}$$

Accruals are denoted by $k(x)$, where x refers to age. Thus, the pension benefit b for an individual i in age group x who retired at age $z+1$ and had earned wage income denoted by y is in two parts, the first accrued before z_0 and the second after z_0,

$$b_i(t,x,z)=b_i^{1}(t,x,z)+b_i^{2}(t,x,z) \tag{13.2}$$

where

$$b_i^{1}(t,x,z)=A\sum_{s=18}^{z_0}k(s)y_i(t-x+s)(1-e(t-x+s))I(t-x+s,t-x+z,0.8)\\ I(t-x+z,t,0.2)$$

$$b_i^{2}(t,x,z)=A\sum_{s=z_0+1}^{z}k(s)y_i(t-x+s)(1-e(t-x+s))I(t-x+s,t-x+z,0.8)\\ I(t-x+z,t,0.2)$$

For each household, $b_i^1(t,x,z)$ is taxable income and thus subject to state and municipal income taxation if it exceeds minimum levels. $b_i^2(t,x,z)$ is tax-free. The term A represents the cohort-wise longevity adjustment, described next.

13.A.2 Longevity Adjustment

Pensions are adjusted for increasing life expectancy simply by taking increasing longevity into account in the value of the annuity. The adjustment coefficient is a ratio of two present values of a unit pension, calculated at two different periods. The present value of a unit pension (A), which begins in period t and is calculated forward from age 62, is

$$A(t,62)=\sum_{s=63}^{100}S(t-1,62,s)/(1.02)^{s-62}. \tag{13.3}$$

The present value of a unit pension is a discounted sum of terms generated during various retirement years. The terms have two parts.

The first term, S, expresses the survival probability from age 62 to age s, and the first argument of the term demonstrates that the probability is evaluated using information available in period t, when the latest observed mortalities are from period $t-1$. The survival probabilities are actually five-year moving averages. The second term is the discount factor, where the discount rate is 2 percent per year. In the model, individuals die at the age of 100 at the latest.

The pension of a person born in period $t-62$ is multiplied by the longevity adjustment coefficient $E(t, 62)$ after age 62. The coefficient is a ratio of two A-terms as follows:

$$E(t, 62) = A(2009, 62) \,/\, A(t, 62). \tag{13.4}$$

13.A.3 Regime Shift in Contributions

In the switch from EET to TEE, contributions that are funded for future benefits based on accruals from 2013 onward cease to be tax-deductible. Contributions that finance the PAYG part of benefits will be tax-deductible if benefits are based on accruals before 2013 and not deductible otherwise. Since the pension scheme is partially funded, a part of those pension benefits that are based on rights accrued before the tax shift are paid from the pension fund. The rest, which is tax-deductible, is paid from current contributions. To find the deductible part, funding rules must be examined.

Finnish private sector pension funding is collective but based on individual pension rights. Individual pension benefits do not depend on the existence or yield of funds. Funds only affect contributions. When a person receives a pension after the age of 65, his or her funds are used to pay that part of the pension benefit that was prefunded. The rest comes from the PAYG part.

Equation (13.5) describes new funding for an individual i. The labor income y creates a pension right for each year in old age. A share g of the present value of the pension right accruing in period t to workers in the age range 18–54 is put in the funds. The present value includes all old-age pension years, from 65 to a maximum age, assumed to be 100. Discounting includes both the so-called fund rate of interest q, which is administratively set, and survival probability S. For prefunding purposes, the magnitude of the pension right is evaluated ignoring all future changes resulting from wage or price developments. Thus, the value of the pension right is simply k times the labor income, without the employee contribution part, for each retirement year.

Thus, the amount h funded for an individual i in age group x is

$$h_i(t,x) = g\sum_{s=65}^{100} k(x)y_i(t)(1-e(t))S(t-1,x,s)/(1+q)^{s-x}, \tag{13.5}$$

where $x = 18,\ldots, 54$.

Equation (13.6) states that for a retired person the amounts prefunded earlier (when the current pensioner was between the ages of 18 and 54) for period t's pension, with the interest accrued to the person with rate r and leading to a total amount v, are used to pay a part of the person's pension.

$$\begin{aligned} v_i(t,x) = \sum_{s=18}^{54} & gk(s)y_i(t-x+s)(1-e(t-x+s)) \\ & S(t-x+s-1,x-s,x)(1+q)^{s-x}(1+r)^{x-s} \end{aligned} \tag{13.6}$$

where $x = 65,\ldots, 100$.

Assume that the tax regime shift starts when the individual is at age X, where $18 < X < 54$. Then the amount related to the taxable part of the benefit and paid from the fund is

$$\begin{aligned} v_i^1(t,x) = \sum_{s=18}^{X} & gk(s)y_i(t-x+s)(1-e(t-x+s)) \\ & S(t-x+s-1,x-s,x)(1+q)^{s-x}(1+r)^{x-s}. \end{aligned} \tag{13.7}$$

In paying the benefit for an individual i in age group x, the deductible amount of contributions is

$$b_i^1(t,x,z) - v_i^1(t,x). \tag{13.8}$$

Aggregating (13.8) over all individuals yields the total amount of deductible contributions in period t. Expressing this total amount as a share of total contributions in period t, each household can then deduct this share of the contributions it has paid, and firms can deduct the same share of the employer's contributions.

13.A.4 The Time Path of Contribution Rates

The time path of the contribution rates is given by equation (13.9). Let $n(t, x)$ be the number of workers and $\overline{h}(t,x)$ be the average amount of new funding per worker of age x in period t. The total amount of new funding in period t is obtained by multiplying the average individual funding in age group x by the number of workers in the age group and summing over all age groups where funding takes place. Analogously, $m(t,x)$ is the number of retired persons and $\overline{v}(t,x)$ is the average amount withdrawn from the funds per retiree in each age group, and the total amount withdrawn from the funds is obtained by multiplying the average withdrawals by the number of retirees and summing over the relevant age groups. Three other aggregates are defined in a similar fashion: the total wage bill from which the pension contributions are collected, denoting the average wage income at age x by $\overline{y}(t,x)$; the total amount of earnings-related pension expenditures, denoting the average pension of retired persons by $\overline{b}(t,x)$; and the total amount of other transfers from the pension sector, denoting the average transfer per person by $\overline{s}(t,x)$.

Not only employees but also employers must pay contributions, denoted by $c(t)$, based on the wage bill. The left-hand side of equation (13.9) is the total amount of contributions. That must be sufficient to cover that part of the pension expenditure (first term on the right-hand side) that does not come from withdrawals from the funds (second term), plus new funding (third term), plus transfers (the final term):

$$\left[c(t)+e(t)\right]\sum_{x=18}^{64} n(t,x)\overline{y}(t,x)=\sum_{x=18}^{100} m(t,x)\overline{b}(t,x)-\sum_{x=65}^{100} m(t,x)\overline{v}(t,x)$$
$$+\sum_{x=18}^{54} n(t,x)\overline{h}(t,x)+\sum_{x=18}^{100}\left[n(t,x)+m(t,x)\right]\overline{s}(t,x) \tag{13.9}$$

The contribution rate refers to the sum of the employer and employee contribution rates, where the latter is weighted using the age-dependent rates with corresponding revenue shares.

13.A.5 The Rigid and Adjusting Pension Schemes

The rigid pension scheme is the Finnish scheme described earlier, except that the longevity adjustment is not applied. Another noteworthy feature is that the earliest eligibility age for an old-age pension is kept constant, and the average effective retirement age does not change even if people live longer.

In the adjusting pension scheme, a longevity adjustment is applied, but it is mitigated, cutting monthly pensions to a lesser degree than the current longevity indicator does. The mitigated longevity indicator is also applied to the earned part of the disability pension.

Besides longevity adjustment, the adjusting pension scheme reacts to longevity shocks in accord with retirement age. The earliest eligibility age for an old-age pension is tied to adulthood life expectancy (adulthood begins at age 18) so that the retirement age divides the adulthood life expectancy in the same proportion each year. When the link is introduced, the retirement age is raised by 10 months. If the life expectancy of a 63-year-old grows by an ample six years over a period of 50 years, the retirement age is raised by four years as a result of making this link. The earliest eligibility age for a part-time pension and the unemployment pathway to retirement are raised in the same manner. If a person continues to work past the earliest eligibility age for old-age retirement, the pension will accrue at 1.9 percent of earnings. The start year of the 1.9 percent accrual rate will change from the current 53 years by three-quarters of a year for each year of change in retirement age.

Linking retirement age to life expectancy affects the length of working life. Based on the model used by Määttänen (2014), raising the eligibility ages for the pension, the unemployment pathway, and the part-time pension by two years would extend working lives by seven months. These relations, from life expectancy to earliest eligibility age and from the eligibility age to working lives, are used in the stochastic simulations. Extending working lives is included in the OLG model exogenously, starting in 2018, through the pensioner proportion, since the model does not contain pensionable age as a variable. For a more detailed description, see Lassila (2014).

Notes

We thank Robert Holzmann, Viktor Steiner, and other participants of the CEPAR CESifo workshop "Taxation of Pensions," and Niku Määttänen, for their useful comments. We also thank Eija Kauppi for efficient assistance. This study was funded by the European Commission's Seventh Framework Programme under grant FP7-SSH-2012-1/No 320333.

1. Contributions are tax-exempt (E), yearly accrued yields are tax-exempt (E), and pensions are taxed (T).

2. Contributions are taxed (T), yearly accrued yields are tax-exempt (E), and pensions are tax-exempt (E).

3. Contributions are taxed (T), yearly accrued yields corresponding to the riskless rate of return are tax-exempt (t), and pensions are tax-exempt (E).

4. The size of the deduction is $t \times l \times wL$, where t is the corporate income tax rate, l is the employers' pension contribution rate, and wL denotes total wages.

5. Starting in 2018, the lowest eligibility age for old-age pensions will increase gradually by two years and will be linked thereafter to life expectancy. The same increases will also be applied to the access ages of early-retirement schemes and the upper age limit of accruing pensions.

6. Actually, the means testing of the national pension and the pensioner's housing supplement against earnings-related pensions weakens the link between earned income and pensions. However, this kind of implicit taxation is also common in countries that apply defined contribution pension schemes.

7. Contributions are taxed (T), yearly accrued yields are tax-exempt (E), and pensions are taxed (T).

8. For a probabilistic interpretation of stochastic population simulations, visit http://www.stat.fi/tup/euupe/sf_interpretation.html.

References

Alho, Juha M. 1990. "Stochastic Methods in Population Forecasting." *International Journal of Forecasting* 6:521–530.

Alho, Juha M. 2002. "The Population of Finland in 2050 and Beyond." Discussion Paper No. 826, The Research Institute of the Finnish Economy, Helsinki.

Alho, Juha M., Svend E. Hougaard Jensen, and Jukka Lassila, eds. 2008. *Uncertain Demographics and Fiscal Sustainability*. Cambridge: Cambridge University Press.

Alho, Juha M., and Bruce D. Spencer. 2005. *Statistical Demography and Forecasting*. New York: Springer.

Auerbach, Alan J., and Lawrence J. Kotlikoff. 1987. *Dynamic Fiscal Policy*. Cambridge: Cambridge University Press.

Chen, Damiaan, H. J. Roel Beetsma, Eduard Ponds, and Ward E. Romp. 2016. "Intergenerational Risk-Sharing through Funded Pensions and Public Debt." *Journal of Pension Economics and Finance* 15 (2): 127–159.

Diamond, Peter. 2009. "Taxes and Pensions." Center for Retirement Research Working Paper No. 2009-12, Center for Retirement Research, Boston College, Boston, MA.

Fehr, Hans, Christian Habermann, and Fabian Kindermann. 2008. "Tax-Favored Retirement Accounts: Are They Efficient in Increasing Savings and Growth?" *FinanzArchiv: Public Finance Analysis* 64 (2): 171–198.

Fehr, Hans, Manuel Kallweit, and Fabian Kindermann. 2012. "Pension Reform with Variable Retirement Age: A Simulation Analysis for Germany." *Journal of Pension Economics and Finance* 11 (3): 389–417.

Kudrna, George, and Alan Woodland. 2012. "Progressive Tax Changes to Private Pensions in a Life-Cycle Framework." Working Paper No. 2012-09, ARC Centre of Excellence in Population Ageing Research (CEPAR), Australian School of Business, University of New South Wales, Sydney.

Lassila, Jukka. 2014. "Linking Retirement Age to Longevity: Economic Assessment." In *Linking Retirement Age to Life Expectancy—What Happens to Working Lives and Income*

Distribution?, edited by Jukka Lassila, Niku Määttänen, and Tarmo Valkonen, 14–15. ETLA B 260. Helsinki: Taloustieto.

Lassila, Jukka, and Tarmo Valkonen. 2007. "The Finnish Pension Reform of 2005." *Geneva Papers on Risk and Insurance* 32 (1): 75–94.

Lee, Ronald D., and Timothy Miller. 2001. "Estimating the Performance of the Lee-Carter Method for Forecasting Mortality." *Demography* 38:537–549.

Määttänen, Niku. 2014. "Pension Reforms, Careers and Income Distribution." In *Linking Retirement Age to Life Expectancy—What Happens to Working Lives and Income Distribution?*, edited by Jukka Lassila, Niku Määttänen, and Tarmo Valkonen, 10–11. ETLA B 260. Helsinki: Taloustieto.

Reipas, Kaarlo, and Mikko Sankala. 2015. "Effects of the 2017 Earnings-Related Pension Reform: Projections Based on the Government Bill." Report No. 08/2015, Finnish Centre for Pensions, Helsinki.

Sánchez Martín, Alfonso R. 2010. "Endogenous Retirement and Public Pension Scheme Reform in Spain." *Economic Modelling* 27 (1): 336–349.

Slutbetänkande av Pensionsåldersutredningen (SOU). 2013. "Åtgärder för ett längre arbetsliv." Statens offentliga utredningar, SOU 2013:25. Stockholm.

Staubli, Stefan, and Josef Zweimüller. 2013. "Does Raising the Early Retirement Age Increase Employment of Older Workers?" *Journal of Public Economics* 108:17–32.

14 Progressive Tax Changes to Superannuation in a Life Cycle Framework: Australia

George Kudrna and Alan Woodland

14.1 Introduction

Private pension pillars around the world benefit from concessional tax treatments that aim to increase private retirement incomes and household savings. As shown in table 14.1, most countries tax their private pensions under the "Exempt-Exempt-Taxed" (EET) regime, in which contributions and fund income are exempt from any taxation but benefits are treated as ordinary income and taxed progressively. An alternative approach is the "Taxed-Exempt-Exempt" (TEE) regime, which allows no deductions of contributions from gross income but then applies no further tax. By contrast, the existing tax treatment applied to Australia's superannuation (Australia's term for private pensions) features a flat tax rate on contributions and fund income, with benefits generally tax-free. As the statutory rate of this flat tax on contributions and fund income is 15 percent,[1] the system is concessional for most income earners compared to progressive personal income taxation.[2] The concessions, however, flow largely to high-income earners, as demonstrated by Ingles and Denniss (2009) and Australia's Future Tax Structure (AFTS) (2008, 2010). For instance, AFTS (Australia's Future Tax Structure 2008, 22) estimates that over 37 percent of concessional contributions go to only those Australians whose incomes are in the top 5 percent.

Given concerns regarding the vertical equity of Australia's superannuation tax arrangements, this chapter provides a quantitative analysis of hypothetical replacements of the existing superannuation taxation regime with traditional EET and TEE taxation regimes. Under both reforms, the existing flat tax rates on contributions and fund earnings that are currently paid by superannuation funds are abolished and either the withdrawals or the contributions are treated as ordinary

Table 14.1
Taxation of private pensions in selected countries.

EET				TTE	
EEt[a]	EET	TEE	ETT	tTE	ttE
France	Canada	Hungary	Denmark	New Zealand	Australia
Germany	Finland	Luxembourg	Italy		
Ireland	Greece	United States	Sweden		
Japan	Iceland	(Roth IRA)			
Korea	Netherlands				
Slovakia	Norway				
Spain	Poland				
Turkey	Switzerland				
United Kingdom	United States				
Belgium	Austria				
Portugal	Brazil				
Chile					

Sources: Yoo and de Serres (2004); OECD (2015).
Notes: E=exempt; T=taxed under personal income tax; t=concessional tax or partial exemption.
[a] Partial exemptions apply mainly to lump sums, with income streams often taxed as ordinary income; some countries, such as the United Kingdom, also impose limits on lump-sum payouts.

income and taxed progressively at households' marginal tax rates. The chapter also examines the effects of a variant of the TEE regime recommended by AFTS (Australia's Future Tax Structure 2010, 84–85) that, in addition to the progressive taxation of contributions, includes (1) a flat-rate tax offset such that the majority of taxpayers do not pay more than 15 percent tax on their contributions, and (2) a reduction of the statutory tax on fund earnings to 7.5 percent.

It is well known that under certain conditions the EET and TEE approaches are equivalent; that is, a shift to either the EET or TEE regime would have the same effect on the present value of superannuation tax revenues and the lifetime behavior of utility-maximizing households (Kingston and Piggott 1993; Creedy and Guest 2008a). However, there would be no general equivalence for a pension or tax policy change that would be unanticipated by households and where tax rates would differ over the life cycle (e.g., progressive taxation), some of the aspects incorporated in the modeling herein.

Australia's superannuation and its taxation arrangements underwent many changes over the last decade. Probably the most significant change to superannuation taxation was the abolition of the superannuation benefit tax for people aged 60 years and older, implemented in July 2007. While this change made superannuation taxation simpler, it adversely affected the vertical equity of the system (Bateman and Kingston 2007). The fiscal effects of this reform were examined by the Institute of Actuaries Australia (IAA) (2006) and Davidson and Guest (2007). Both employed microsimulation models that projected low fiscal costs for this benefit tax removal because of already highly preferential tax treatments of superannuation benefits in the prereform system.

Before the 2007 superannuation changes, many retirement income commentators and industry experts called for a move toward a traditional EET regime (Australian Superannuation Fund Association 1998; Doyle, Kingston, and Piggott 1999), and some proposed abolishing the flat tax on contributions (Clare 2006). Horne (2002) applied a microsimulation model to assess the ASFA (Australian Superannuation Fund Association 1998) proposal, with the key finding that it would increase savings and improve vertical equity. The microsimulation study of the shift to the EET regime by Doyle, Kingston, and Piggott (1999) showed only a small net loss in tax revenues, since the revenue loss from abolition of contribution and earnings taxes is partly offset by imposing marginal income tax rates on superannuation benefits. Atkinson, Creedy, and Knox (1999), also using a microsimulation model, found that the traditional EET regime scored better in terms of intragenerational equity and overall progressivity than the concessional TTT regime in Australia at that time.

The theoretical basis for analysis of a policy change to the taxation of private pensions was provided by Creedy and Guest (2008a). Their three-period utility-maximization model studied the behavioral effects of various superannuation tax changes and showed that, for example, abolition of the benefit tax would reduce savings and increase the labor supply. Creedy and Guest (2008b) employed a computable overlapping-generations (OLG) model to examine macroeconomic and welfare impacts of the 2007 abolition of benefit taxation in Australia. Their simulations found that this policy change favors middle-aged and older workers more than younger workers and reduces national savings. To address the "equity" issue, their policy recommendation was to increase marginal tax rates on those with higher incomes. To address the reduced national savings, their recommendation was to increase public saving through lower transfers.

A large body of international literature has used computable OLG models to examine the economic effects of voluntary, tax-deferred retirement savings accounts (Imrohoroglu, Imrohoroglu, and Joines 1998; Fehr, Habermann, and Kindermann 2008; Nishiyama 2011; Armstrong, Davis, and Ebell 2015). In general, these studies found positive effects on national wealth, capital stock, and long-run welfare, although these effects vary greatly mainly because of different assumptions about government budget-balancing policy instruments. Fehr, Habermann, and Kindermann (2008) assessed not only the effects of tax-deferred or front-loaded accounts taxed under the EET regime but also the implications of tax-exempt or back-loaded accounts taxed under the TEE regime. They showed that increases in national wealth are significantly greater with front-loaded (EET) accounts, which burden old (and benefit young) rich households more than back-loaded (TEE) accounts.

This chapter's quantitative analysis of the superannuation taxation reforms builds on these computable OLG models. It uses an extended version of the small open economy OLG model developed by Kudrna and Woodland (2011a, 2011b), with a more detailed disaggregation of households into income quintiles and gradual withdrawals of superannuation savings in retirement. Compared to Creedy and Guest's (2008b) model, this model includes intragenerational household heterogeneity, life span uncertainty, endogenous retirement, and a richer structure of Australia's fiscal and retirement income systems. While Creedy and Guest (2008b) examined the effects of eliminating the concessional tax rates on contributions, fund earnings, or benefits, this chapter evaluates the effects of replacing these concessional superannuation tax rates with progressive income taxation applied to either benefits or contributions. Compared to Fehr, Habermann, and Kindermann (2008), who assessed the introduction of voluntary tax-favored retirement accounts, this chapter analyzes the reforms to the concessional taxation of already established mandatory superannuation. The chapter's main goal is to assess how these progressive tax reforms to superannuation affect the welfare and net income of households of different income classes (vertical equity) and of different ages (intergenerational equity).

The simulation results indicate that the reforms to superannuation taxation examined improve vertical equity and reduce income inequality, as shown by (1) greater relative gains in welfare and net income shares for lower-income households and (2) a lower Gini coefficient. These findings provide support for the proposal by ASFA (Australian Superannuation Fund Association 1998) to apply progressive income taxation to superannuation benefits and for the proposals by Australia's Future Tax System (2010) and Ingles and Denniss (2009) to tax the mandatory contributions as ordinary income. The reforms also have important intergenerational implications. Specifically, under the EET taxation regime, older generations suffer from large welfare losses, as their private pensions are now taxed at marginal income tax rates. Compared to the two other taxation reforms, the shift to the EET regime, however, leads to greater long-run welfare gains for all income types because of significant reductions in the assumed budget-balancing consumption tax or income tax rates. The model also shows the reforms' positive long-run effects on domestic assets and reduced public pension expenditures, which are significant especially for the shift toward the EET regime. Similar effects on national wealth were obtained by Fehr, Habermann, and Kindermann (2008) for the introduction of voluntary front-loaded (EET) accounts in Germany.

Section 14.2 provides a technical description of the model. Section 14.3 reports on the calibration of the model and compares the benchmark steady-state equilibrium solutions with Australian data. Section 14.4 presents the simulation results for the three reforms to superannuation taxation, concentrating on equity and macroeconomic implications. Section 14.5 is devoted to a sensitivity analysis of the long-run effects of the reforms on a higher mandatory contribution rate and on an aging demographic. Finally, section 14.6 offers some concluding remarks and suggestions for future research.

14.2 The Model

A computable general equilibrium model with overlapping generations is constructed to analyze the superannuation taxation reforms. The model builds on Kudrna and Woodland (2011a, 2011b) and is extended to (2) include a detailed disaggregation of households into income quintiles based on the ABS (Australian Bureau of Statistics 2007) data and (2) allow for gradual withdrawals of superannuation savings rather than assuming lump-sum payouts.[3]

The model is essentially a small open economy type of Auerbach and Kotlikoff's (1987) OLG model, variants of which have been used worldwide by many researchers to analyze various tax and pension policy reforms. In Australia, Kulish, Smith, and Kent (2010) used a closed economy model to analyze macroeconomic consequences of population aging, and Creedy and Guest (2008b) applied an open economy model to simulate changes to the superannuation taxation regime. Computable OLG models with stochastic incomes were employed by Tran and Woodland (2014) and by Cho and Sane (2013) to study the effects of policy changes on Australia's means-tested pension. Compared to the aforementioned models, this model specifically includes major aspects of Australia's superannuation, the means-tested Age Pension and progressive income taxation, which, combined with household heterogeneity in both age and income type, is crucial for the analysis of the investigated superannuation tax reforms' distributional effects.

14.2.1 Households

Consider a model economy populated by sequences of cohorts distinguished by age a and income type i. In particular, 70 generations of single-person households aged 21 to 90 years exist at any time t, with each generation consisting of the lowest, second, third, fourth, and highest quintiles. Every year, a new generation aged 21 years enters the model structure and faces random survival with a maximum further life span of 70 years, while the oldest generation, aged 90 years, dies. Random survival is given by conditional survival probabilities denoted by s_a. This benchmark model uses a stationary demographic setup with a constant rate of population growth, n, that together with survival probabilities gives time-invariant cohort shares, $\mu_a = [s_a/(1+n)]\mu_{a-1}$.

Each i-type household beginning economic life at time t is assumed to optimally choose consumption, c, and leisure, l, at each age and when to retire from the workforce to maximize the expected lifetime utility function given by

$$\max_{\{c^i_{t+a-21},\, l^i_{t+a-21}\}} \frac{1}{1-1/\gamma} \sum_{a=21}^{90} S_a \beta^{a-21} u\left(c^i_{t+a-21}, l^i_{t+a-21}\right)^{1-1/\gamma}, \tag{14.1}$$

subject to the within-period budget constraint written as

$$\begin{aligned} A^i_{a,t} &= (1+r)A^i_{a-1,t-1} + w_t e^i_a(1-l^i_{a,t}) + AP^i_{a,t} + SB^i_{a,t} \\ &\quad + ST^i_a + B^i_{a,t} - T(y^i_{a,t}) - (1+\tau^c)c^i_{a,t}, \end{aligned} \tag{14.2}$$

where γ is the intertemporal elasticity of substitution, $u(c,l)$ denotes annual utility, with any future utility discounted by the subjective discount factor, β, and the unconditional survival probability, $S_a = \Pi_{j=21}^{a} s_{j-1}$.

In the per-period budget constraint (14.2), $A_{a,t}^{i}$ denotes the stock of ordinary private assets for type i households at the end of age a and time t, which equals the assets at the beginning of the period, plus the sum of interest income, $rA_{a-1,t-1}^{i}$, labor earnings, $w_t e_a^i(1-l_{a,t}^i)$, Age Pension, $AP_{a,t}^i$, superannuation pension, $SB_{a,t}^i$, social transfer payments, ST_a^i, and bequest receipts, $B_{a,t}^i$, minus the sum of income taxes paid, $T(y_{a,t}^i)$, and consumption expenditures, $(1+\tau_t^c)c_{a,t}^i$.[4] Labor earnings are the product of labor supply, $1-l_{a,t}^i$, and the hourly wage, $w_t e_a^i$, where w_t is the market wage rate for a person with unit efficiency and e_a^i is the age- and income-specific earnings ability variable. Labor supply is required to be nonnegative, $1-l_{a,t}^i \geq 0$. Taxable income or income tax base, $y_{a,t}^i = w_t e_a^i(1-l_{a,t}^i)+rA_{a-1,t-1}^i + AP_{a,t}^i$, comprises labor earnings of working agents, investment income, and Age Pension payments. Given the uncertain survival, the assets of persons who die are aggregated within each income type and are assumed to be equally redistributed as accidental bequests, $B_{a,t}^i$, to all surviving i-type persons aged 45–65 years.[5] This means that the bequests received by higher-income types are significantly larger than those received by lower-income types.

Persons are assumed to be born with no wealth and to exhaust all accumulated wealth at the maximum age of 90 years, so that $A_{20,t}^i = A_{90,t+70}^i = 0$.[6] Borrowing constraints are imposed by requiring $A_{a,t}^i \geq 0$ to prevent younger workers from borrowing against their superannuation payouts, as the Superannuation Guarantee legislation prohibits such borrowing.

14.2.2 Private and Public Pensions

Australia has a three-pillar retirement income system: the targeted, publicly provided Age Pension; the mandatory and fully funded Superannuation Guarantee scheme; and other long term private savings, including housing and voluntary superannuation. The model incorporates the main aspects of the two publicly stipulated pillars—Age Pension and mandatory superannuation. The analysis begins with compulsory superannuation, as the superannuation assets and the incomes they generate affect the Age Pension payments through means testing.

The Superannuation Guarantee currently mandates that employers contribute 9 percent of gross wages into employees' superannuation fund.[7] It is assumed that mandatory contributions are made on behalf of all workers at the contribution rate, cr, from their gross labor earnings, $w_t e_a^i(1-l_{a,t}^i)$. These contributions net of the contribution tax, $\tau^s cr$, are added to the stock of superannuation assets, $SA_{a,t}^i$, which earns fund income at the after-tax interest rate, $(1-\tau^r)r$. Superannuation assets are assumed to be kept in the fund until workers reach age 60. Workers aged 60 and older can draw down their superannuation savings as pensions, $SB_{a,t}^i$, which become part of the per-period budget constraint defined in (14.2). The stock of superannuation assets accumulates in the fund according to

$$SA_{a,t}^i = \left[1+(1-\tau^r)r\right]SA_{a-1,t-1}^i + (1-\tau^s)cr \cdot w_t e_a^i(1-l_{a,t}^i) - SB_{a,t}^i, \tag{14.3}$$

where τ^r is the effective earnings tax rate and τ^s denotes the statutory contribution tax rate. If eligible workers decide to collect superannuation pensions, $SB_{a,t}^i$, then these pensions are subject to the maximum and minimum withdrawal limits.[8]

The Age Pension, $AP_{a,t}^i$, is paid to single-person households aged 65 and older provided that they satisfy the means test. The means test comprises the income test and the asset test, with the test that results in lower pension payments (i.e., the binding test) applied. The means testing of the Age Pension can be expressed as

$$\begin{aligned} AP_{a,t}^i &= \min\{APi_{a,t}^i, APa_{a,t}^i\}, \\ APi_{a,t}^i &= \max\{\min\{p, p-\theta(\hat{y}_{a,t}^i - IT)\}, 0\}, \\ APa_{a,t}^i &= \max\{\min\{p, p-\phi[(A_{a,t}^i + SA_{a,t}^i) - AT)]\}, 0\}, \end{aligned} \tag{14.4}$$

where p is the single rate of the maximum Age Pension, θ is the income taper rate, ϕ represents the annual asset taper (reduction) rate, IT denotes the income threshold, and AT is the asset threshold. The private income assessed under the income test of the Age Pension, $y_{a,t}^i = r(A_{a-1,t-1}^i + SA_{a-1,t-1}^i) + 0.5 \times w_t e_a^i(1-l_{a,t}^i)$, consists of interest earnings generated from superannuation and non-superannuation assets and half of labor earnings.[9]

14.2.3 The Rest of the Model

In addition to the household and pension sectors, the general equilibrium model includes the production, government, and foreign sectors.

The production sector comprises a single producer that represents a large number of perfectly competitive firms. This representative producer maximizes the present value of all future profits discounted at the world interest rate, r, specified by

$$\max \sum_{t=0}^{\infty} D_t \left[(1-\tau^f)(F(K_t, L_t) - C(I_t, K_t) - I_t - (1+cr)w_t \, L_t) \right], \tag{14.5}$$

by choosing capital, K_t, labor input, L_t, and net investment, I_t, subject to the (per capita) capital accumulation equation of the form

$$(1+n)K_{t+1} = I_t + (1-\delta)K_t, \tag{14.6}$$

where $D_t = (1+n)^t/(1+r)^t$ accounts for discounting and population growth, τ^f stands for the corporate tax rate, $F(K_t, L_t)$ represents the production of gross output, $C(I_t, K_t)$ gives the adjustment cost function, and the term $(1+cr)w_t \, L_t$ denotes the total wage bill, which also includes mandatory contributions.

The government is assumed to maintain a balanced budget, which includes pension expenditures, AP_t, social transfers, ST, and public consumption, G, on the expenditure side, and the tax revenues from household income, TR_t^Y, consumption, TR_t^C, superannuation, TR_t^S, and firms' profits, TR_t^F, on the income side. The per capita pension expenditures and tax receipts from households and firms in period t are given by

$$\begin{aligned}
AP_t &= \sum\nolimits_{i=1}^{5} \omega_i \sum\nolimits_{a=65}^{90} \mu_a \, AP_{a,t}^i, \\
TR_t^Y &= \sum\nolimits_{i=1}^{5} \omega_i \sum\nolimits_{a=21}^{90} \mu_a \, T(y_{a,t}^i), \\
TR_t^C &= \sum\nolimits_{i=1}^{5} \omega_i \sum\nolimits_{a=21}^{90} \mu_a \, \tau_t^c \, c_{a,t}^i, \\
TR_t^S &= \sum\nolimits_{i=1}^{5} \omega_i \sum\nolimits_{a=21}^{60} \mu_a \left[\tau^s \cdot cr \cdot w_t e_a^i (1 - l_{a,t}^i) + \tau^r \cdot rSA_{a-1,t-1}^i \right], \\
TR_t^F &= \tau^f (Y_t - \delta q_t K_t - (1+cr) w_t L_t),
\end{aligned} \tag{14.7}$$

which are the weighted averages of each component across households, with weights given by the intragenerational shares, ω_i, and cohort shares, μ_a.[10] In the per capita corporate tax revenue expression, Y_t is output net of adjustment costs and $\delta q_t K_t$ represents depreciation of the value of the capital stock. The government budget is assumed to be balanced in every time period by adjusting the consumption tax rate, τ_t^c, or through proportional changes to the personal income tax schedule, $T(y_{a,t}^i)$.

The foreign sector is represented by the international budget constraint. The constraint equates capital flows with the current account and can be written in per capita terms as

$$(1+n)FD_{t+1} - FD_t = TB_t - rFD_t, \tag{14.8}$$

where FD_t is per capita net foreign debt at the beginning of time t, TB_t is the trade balance (or net export), and rFD_t represents the interest payments on net foreign debt. The domestic interest rate, r, is exogenous in this small open economy model and is equal to the world interest rate.

The endogenous variables of the model are determined such that all agents optimize their objective functions subject to any constraints and such that all markets clear in every period. The clearing conditions for labor, capital, and output markets are

$$\begin{aligned} L_t &= \sum_{i=1}^{5} \omega_i \sum_{a=21}^{90} e_{a,t}^{i} \left(1 - l_{a,t}^{i}\right) \mu_a, \\ q_t K_t &= \sum_{i=1}^{5} \omega_i \sum_{a=21}^{90} \left(A_{a,t}^{i} + SA_{a,t}^{i}\right) \mu_a - FD_t, \\ Y_t &= \sum_{i=1}^{5} \omega_i \sum_{a=21}^{90} c_{a,t}^{i} \mu_a + I_t + G_t + TB_t, \end{aligned} \tag{14.9}$$

where q_t is the price of capital (i.e., Tobin's q), obtained by solving the firm's profit maximization problem.

14.3 Calibrating the Model

The model is calibrated to the key Australian aggregates averaged over the five-year period ending in June 2010. It assumes a stationary demographic environment with the constant population-growth rate, n, set to the current rate of 1.8 percent per year. The rate of population growth together with the male survival probabilities, s_a, taken from the 2007–2009 life tables (Australian Bureau of Statistics 2010a), generates the existing old-age dependency ratio of 0.2. The intragenerational shares, ω_i, are equal to 0.2 for each income class because of the income quintiles used by the Australian Bureau of Statistics (2007). This section discusses intragenerational differences among households, presents the per-period utility and production functions, and reports the values for the model parameters. It also compares the model-generated solutions with Australian data for some variables.

14.3.1 Income Heterogeneity among Households

The model considers five income types of households in each generation that differ by their exogenously given earnings ability and social transfer payments (which exclude the Age Pension).

The earnings ability (or labor productivity) profile is the potential wage at each age earned with all the time endowment allocated to work.

The approach used by Fehr, Jokisch, and Kotlikoff (2008) is followed to derive these profiles for each of the five income types. Specifically, using the estimated lifetime wage function for men who completed high school from Reilly, Milne, and Zhao (2005) and the income distribution shift parameter, ζ^i, the earnings ability variable, e_a^i, is constructed as

$$e_a^i = \zeta^i \times e^{2.235 + 0.04(a-17) - 0.00067(a-17)^2},$$

where ζ^i is set to 0.26 for the lowest quintile, 0.55 for the second quintile, 1.00 for the third quintile, 1.52 for the fourth quintile, and 2.63 for the highest quintile. These values are the ratios of the private incomes of lower and higher quintiles to the private income of the third quintile, calculated from the Australian Bureau of Statistics (2007, table 7, p. 22). Hence, the earnings ability profile for middle-income households (i.e., those in the third quintile) is taken from Reilly, Milne, and Zhao (2005), and the profiles for lower- and higher-income quintiles are shifted down and up, respectively, to approximate the distribution of private income in Australia.[11]

To account for a changing income distribution over the working years and also to approximate the distribution in gross income, workers are assumed to receive social transfers, denoted by ST_a^i in equation (14.2). These payments, assumed to be constant and received by workers younger than 65 years (except for those in the highest quintile), are calculated as follows. First, the Australian Bureau of Statistics (2007) data are used to derive the share of social transfers in gross income for each eligible quintile. These shares are 0.44 for the lowest quintile, 0.30 for the second quintile, 0.15 for the third quintile, and 0.06 for the fourth quintile. Second, the value of social transfers for eligible households is calculated such that these payments together with the endogenous Age Pension yield the aforementioned shares in their lifetime gross income. These income-specific social transfers have a particularly significant income effect on the labor supply of lower-income households, resulting in labor earnings profiles that are relatively flat for lower-income types compared to those of higher-income types.[12]

14.3.2 Preferences and Technology

The annual utility and production functions and parameter values chosen are standard in the literature. The per-period utility function takes the constant elasticity of substitution (CES) form

$$u(c, l) = \left[c^{(1-1/\rho)} + \alpha l^{(1-1/\rho)}\right]^{1/(1-1/\rho)},$$

where the intratemporal elasticity of substitution, ρ, is set to 0.9 and the value for the leisure distribution parameter, α, is 1.4. The remaining parameters in the lifetime utility (14.1) are the intertemporal elasticity of substitution, $\gamma=0.4$, and the discount factor, $\beta=0.99$, with its value chosen to generate the capital output ratio of 3 (Australian Bureau of Statistics 2010b).

The technology is described by the standard CES production function

$$F(K_t, L_t) = \kappa\left[\varepsilon K_t^{(1-1/\sigma)} + (1-\varepsilon)L_t^{(1-1/\sigma)}\right]^{[1/(1-1/\sigma)]},$$

where the technology constant, $\kappa=0.88$, is calibrated to reproduce the market wage rate that is normalized to 1 in the benchmark steady-state equilibrium. The elasticity of substitution in production, $\sigma=0.87$, and the capital intensity parameter, $\varepsilon=0.45$, are calibrated via the producer's first-order conditions to match the interest rate and national account data for factor shares. The exogenous interest rate is set to 4 percent, the same rate used in Creedy and Guest (2008b). Following Fehr (2000), the adjustment cost function is assumed to be quadratic in net investment, given by

$$C(I_t, K_t) = 0.5\psi(I_t/K_t - (n+\delta))^2 K_t.$$

The value for the depreciation rate, δ, which is set to target the investment to capital ratio of 0.09 (Australian Bureau of Statistics 2010b), is 7.2 percent, and the adjustment cost parameter ($\psi=10$) is taken from Auerbach and Kotlikoff (1987). The model is also calibrated to target the net foreign debt to capital ratio of 0.195, reflecting net foreign ownership of about 19.5 percent of Australia's capital stock (Australian Bureau of Statistics 2010b).

14.3.3 Policy Parameters

Table 14.2 reports the values for taxation and retirement income policy parameters. The values for the Age Pension and superannuation parameters are those applicable in September 2009. The Age Pension eligibility age is 65 years. The consumption tax rate is set to the statutory Goods and Services Tax (GST) rate of 10 percent. The "tax base" parameter is then computed to replicate the average ratio of this tax revenue to gross domestic product (GDP), which was 0.0389 over the five-year period ending in June 2010 (Commonwealth of Australia 2011). The product of the statutory tax rate and the computed tax base parameter

Table 14.2
Values of policy parameters in benchmark steady-state model.

Symbol	Description	Value	Source
$\overline{\tau}^c$	Statutory consumption tax rate (GST)	0.1	Data
τ^f	Statutory corporation tax rate	0.3	Data
υ^c	Consumption tax base parameter	0.694	Calibrated[a]
p	Single rate of maximum pension (annual)	A\$17,469	Data
IT	Income test threshold (annual)	A\$3,976	Data
θ	Asset test threshold	A\$307,000	Data
AT	Income reduction (taper) rate	0.5	Data
ϕ	Asset reduction (taper) rate (annual)	0.039	Data
cr	Superannuation contribution rate	0.09	Data
τ^s	Superannuation contribution tax rate	0.15	Data
τ^r	Superannuation earnings tax rate	0.071	Data[b]

[a] The product of this tax base parameter and the statutory Goods and Services Tax (GST) rate of 10 percent gives the effective consumption tax rate of 6.94 percent that appears in the households' budget constraint.
[b] This rate is roughly the value for the effective tax rate on superannuation earnings.

gives the effective tax rate on consumption, $\tau^c = 6.94$ percent. The corporate tax rate is set to the statutory rate of 30 percent, and the government budget is assumed to be balanced with no government debt.

The model incorporates a differentiable approximation function for the Australian progressive personal income tax schedule in 2009–2010. The approximation income tax function of taxable income, $T(y)$, takes the form

$$T(y) = t_5(y) - t_5(yt_1)\exp\left(\sum_{z=1}^{M-1} -(0.1)^z v_z \times \frac{y^z}{z}\right),$$
$$z = 1, \ldots, M-1, t_5(y) = m_5(y - yt_5) + tax_5,$$

where $v_z = (v_1, v_2, v_3, v_4)$ is a parameter vector, M denotes the number of tax brackets ($M = 5$), yt_1 and yt_5 are the lowest and highest tax thresholds ($yt_1 = 0$ and $yt_5 = 180$, expressed in A\$1,000),[13] m_5 is the top marginal tax rate ($m_5 = 0.45$), and tax_5 is the tax payable at the highest threshold ($t = 54.55$, expressed in A\$1,000). The parameter vector $v_z = (v_1, v_2, v_3, v_4)$ is estimated by nonlinear least squares using the Stata software. A grid of equally spaced incomes in the range [0, 200.5] is constructed, and the corresponding income taxes payable are based on the 2009–2010 Australian tax schedule, with both variables expressed in units of A\$1,000. The parameter estimates obtained are $v_z = (0.1446, 0.0160, -0.0049, 0.0003)$.

Note that since the model is assumed to be populated with single-person households, the tax, superannuation, and Age Pension parameters are those applicable to individuals rather than households. While the progressive income tax applies to the individual taxable income and superannuation is accumulated by individuals, the Age Pension policy rules distinguish between higher pension rates for single pensioners and lower pension rates for couples. As the proportion of pensioners in the 65–69 age group receiving the couples rate of the maximum pension is around 60 percent (and then declines to less than 30 percent for those aged 80 and older), the model somewhat overestimates average pension payments in the early years of receiving the Age Pension. The model also somewhat overestimates income tax receipts from lower-income and middle-aged households, as it abstracts from any income tax offsets and tax benefits to families with children that are means tested in Australia. However, the choice to model the life cycle behavior of single-person households seems appropriate for the analysis of tax changes to superannuation that is accumulated by individuals (and not by households). In addition, the single-person household model is standard in the related literature (Altig et al. 2001; Creedy and Guest 2008b; Fehr, Habermann, and Kindermann 2008; Tran and Woodland 2014; Armstrong, Davis, and Ebell 2015).[14]

14.3.4 Computation and Benchmark Steady-State Solution

After specifying the parameter values, the GAMS software is used to compute the solutions for the benchmark steady-state and transition path equilibria. The algorithm applies the iterative Gauss-Seidel computational method suggested by Auerbach and Kotlikoff (1987). The steps carried out to solve for the steady states and the transition paths are listed in Kudrna and Woodland (2011a). This section briefly outlines how to deal with the nonconvexity of the household budget set caused by the Age Pension means test. It follows Altig et al. (2001) to handle the kinked household budget constraints and identifies households that choose to locate at the kinks in particular periods by evaluating their income assessable under the pension income test. If their assessable income is close to the income threshold of the pension income test, this income is set exactly to that threshold. Doing so puts such households at exactly the kinks in each period in which being at a kink is optimal.

Table 14.3 shows the results for the key macroeconomic ratios and household net income variables generated by the benchmark steady-

Table 14.3
Benchmark model and Australian data comparison.

Variable	Benchmark model	Australia[a]
Expenditures on GDP (percentage of GDP)		
Private consumption	56.12	56.22
Investment	27.01	27.38
Government consumption	15.58	17.88
Trade balance	1.29	–1.3
Government indicators (percentage of GDP)		
Age Pension expenditure	2.89	2.7
Personal income taxes	12.31	11.49
Corporation taxes	5.08	5.27
Consumption taxes (GST revenue)	3.89	3.89
Superannuation taxes	1.05	0.8
Targeted calibration ratios		
Capital to output (*K/Y*)	3	3
Investment to capital (*I/K*)	0.09	0.09
Foreign debt to capital (*FD/K*)	0.195	0.195
Net income share		
Lowest quintile	0.069	0.075
Second quintile	0.121	0.125
Third quintile	0.184	0.171
Fourth quintile	0.243	0.229
Highest quintile	0.384	0.401
Gini coefficient	0.336	0.326

Source: Authors' simulations; Commonwealth of Australia (2011); Australian Bureau of Statistics (2010b, 2011).
[a] These are five-year averages over the period ending in June 2010.

state solution of the model and provides a comparison with the actual data. The distribution of net incomes across household quintiles and the Gini coefficient match the actual data very closely. The comparison of model-generated and actual macroeconomic indicators also indicates that the model replicates the Australian economy fairly well. The components of domestic aggregate demand are close to their actual values expressed as a percentage of GDP. The exception is the trade balance; its positive value is implied by the calibration target for the net foreign debt to capital ratio. Similar conclusions can be drawn for the government indicators displayed, apart from government revenues from the superannuation taxes. The difference between the model-generated and actual revenues from the superannuation tax is caused by the full maturity of the superannuation system assumed in the model.[15]

14.4 Dynamic Simulations of Superannuation Tax Reforms

This section numerically evaluates three hypothetical reforms to superannuation taxation: (1) a shift to an EET taxation regime, (2) a shift to a TEE taxation regime, and (3) implementation of the AFTS proposal.

Under the shift to the EET regime, the existing concessional tax rates on superannuation contributions and fund earnings paid by the superannuation fund are abolished, with the superannuation withdrawals added to ordinary taxable income and taxed progressively at marginal income tax rates. The second reform—the shift to the TEE regime—also eliminates the existing concessional superannuation taxes, but it is the mandatory superannuation contributions that are included in ordinary taxable income and taxed progressively at marginal income tax rates. The third reform examined—the AFTS proposal—follows the TEE regime by treating superannuation contributions as ordinary taxable income. In addition, the proposal includes a 15 percent tax offset to contributions for all households and a reduction of the statutory tax on fund earnings to 7.5 percent.[16]

These reforms are expected to have implications for the government budget. As mentioned, adjustments are made to either the consumption tax or income tax rate to maintain a balanced government budget. Specifically, the consumption tax rate is adjusted under the consumption tax adjustments, and proportional changes are made to the progressive income tax schedule (thus proportionally raising or lowering average and marginal income tax rates) under the income tax adjustments.

The following discussion of the simulation results concentrates on the equity and macroeconomic implications of the three superannuation tax reforms. An overview of the key results is presented first, after which the results are discussed in more detail.

14.4.1 Overview

All three examined reforms to superannuation taxation basically consist of two parts. The first part is to abolish the concessional 15 percent tax rate on mandatory contributions and either fully eliminate the effective fund earnings tax of 7.1 percent for the EET and TEE regimes or partially eliminate this tax for the AFTS proposal. These changes greatly favor the superannuation assets that households can draw down from the age of 60 onward. The resulting increases in national wealth, saving, and interest incomes upon reaching the eligibility age of 60 for the Age Pension mean that the income and/or asset tests become more binding for potential Age Pension recipients and hence that government expenditures on the Age Pension decline. In that sense, a substitution occurs between the Age Pension and superannuation as retirement income supports, which is especially significant under the shift toward the EET taxation regime.[17]

The second part of the simulated reforms is to treat either the withdrawals (for the EET regime) or the contributions (for the TEE regime and the AFTS proposal) as ordinary taxable income. Consequently, the average income tax base increases, thus generating larger revenues from income taxation and allowing for budget-balancing reductions in the consumption tax rate or average income tax rate.[18] Under the EET regime, the budget-balancing tax instruments are lower over the entire transition path because of the increased labor supply of younger cohorts, yielding positive effects on their ordinary non-superannuation assets. The decrease in the consumption tax or income tax rate is shown to be only temporary for the two other taxation reforms, with the refundable superannuation tax offset paid under the AFTS proposal implying higher budget-balancing tax rates relative to those under the TEE reform.

The progressive income tax treatment of superannuation benefits or contributions is behind improvements in vertical (or intragenerational) equity and reductions in income inequality, which are demonstrated by greater gains (or smaller losses) in welfare and net income shares for lower-income households and lower values of the Gini coefficient. In terms of intergenerational implications, older generations experience significant welfare losses under the EET regime, as their superannuation pensions are taxed at marginal income tax rates. This contrasts with higher welfare losses or only small welfare gains and losses under the TEE regime and the AFTS proposal, respectively, for older cohorts, who are affected only indirectly through the budget-balancing tax changes. In the long run, however, the shift to the EET regime generates larger average welfare compared to the other policy reforms.

14.4.2 Equity Effects

To examine the equity effects of the superannuation taxation reforms, the analysis uses the concepts of equivalent variation, net income shares for household quintiles, and the Gini coefficient calculated using net incomes. The first equity measure—equivalent variation—provides the distributional welfare effects across the five income types of households (i.e., measuring the effects on vertical equity) and across different generations (i.e., measuring the effects on intergenerational equity). In particular, equivalent variation for the given generation measures the percentage increase or reduction in this generation's wealth, which brings about a proportional increase or reduction in consumption and leisure in each year of remaining life needed in the benchmark scenario to produce the realized remaining lifetime utility in the reform scenario (Auerbach and Kotlikoff 1987, 87).[19]

The distributional welfare effects of the superannuation taxation reforms examined are reported in table 14.4. These effects are presented as percentage changes in remaining utility for generations of different ages at the time of the reform and for three income types of households, assuming either consumption tax or income tax adjustments to balance the government budget.[20,21]

Two main observations can be drawn for the intragenerational implications. First, under the consumption tax adjustments, the key result is that all three reforms improve intragenerational or vertical equity, depicted by larger or smaller gains or losses in welfare for lower-income types of households relative to those for higher-income households. For instance, the shift to the EET taxation regime generates a welfare loss of 0.89 percent for lower-income households where the person is age 80 at the time of the reform, but the welfare loss for higher-income types of the same age is 5.52 percent. In the long run, lower-income households gain in welfare by about 0.49 percent, compared to a 0.27 percent gain for higher-income types. Under the shift to the TEE regime, future-born generations of lower-income quintiles gain in welfare by 0.22 percent, while higher-income types attain a welfare loss of about 0.18 percent. These improvements in vertical equity result from the progressive taxation of the benefits or the contributions, and this outweighs the elimination of the concessional tax on fund earnings, which favors higher-income types.

Second, the choice of budget-balancing tax instruments also has intragenerational implications. In particular, reduced budget-balancing income tax rates are more beneficial for welfare of higher-income types and increased rates less so, while reduced budget-balancing consumption taxes are more beneficial for welfare of lower-income types and increased rates less so. For example, under the shift to the EET regime with reduced income tax rates, the long-run welfare gain for higher-

Table 14.4
Welfare implications of superannuation tax reforms
(percentage changes in welfare from initial steady-state solution).

	Consumption tax adjustments				Income tax adjustments			
Age in 2010	Lower income[a]	Middle income[b]	Higher income[c]	Average welfare[d]	Lower income[a]	Middle income[b]	Higher income[c]	Average welfare[d]
Shift to the EET taxation regime								
80	–0.890	–3.036	–5.519	–3.171	–1.009	–3.083	–5.450	–3.200
40	0.048	–0.330	–0.845	–0.385	–0.107	–0.362	–0.692	–0.392
20	0.405	0.310	0.141	0.280	0.266	0.289	0.301	0.285
–80	0.492	0.408	0.267	0.385	0.375	0.444	0.529	0.451
Shift to the TEE taxation regime								
80	0.228	0.220	0.213	0.220	0.114	0.068	0.037	0.074
40	0.339	0.161	0.005	0.170	0.259	0.166	0.119	0.185
20	0.317	0.101	–0.101	0.107	0.264	0.108	–0.010	0.123
–80	0.216	0.003	–0.175	0.017	0.226	0.000	–0.195	0.012
Shift to the AFTS proposal								
80	–0.039	–0.117	–0.160	–0.103	–0.036	–0.118	–0.164	–0.103
60	–0.184	–0.343	–0.506	–0.344	–0.161	–0.309	–0.465	–0.312
20	0.315	0.125	–0.045	0.133	0.365	0.136	–0.092	0.137
–80	0.248	0.059	–0.090	0.075	0.325	0.032	–0.259	0.033

Notes: Standard equivalent variation measures in percent.
[a] Average value for lowest and second quintiles.
[b] Value for third quintile.
[c] Average value for fourth and highest quintiles.
[d] Average value across all income quintiles.

income types is 0.53 percent, compared to the gain of 0.27 percent for higher-income types under the consumption tax adjustments with the reduced consumption tax rate. On the other hand, the long-run welfare gain for lower-income types under the AFTS proposal with increased income tax rates is 0.36 percent, compared to the long-run gain of 0.25 percent for these income types under the AFTS proposal with the increased consumption tax rate.

Table 14.4 also shows large differences in intergenerational equity implications among the superannuation taxation reforms. Under the EET taxation regime, older generations receiving (or close to the age of receiving) the superannuation benefits experience welfare losses, with the average welfare loss for generations aged 80 years at the time of the reforms being 3.18 percent (or 3.20 percent with income tax adjustments). In contrast, future-born generations gain in welfare, with a long-run welfare gain of 0.39 percent (or 0.45 percent with income tax adjustments). The long-run gains indicate that the resulting decreases in budget-balancing consumption or income tax rates and significantly larger assets offset the negative effects of increased marginal income tax rates applied to superannuation withdrawals. On the contrary, the shift to the TEE regime increases older generations' welfare because of initially reduced consumption or income tax rates. In the long term, the average welfare gain is smaller under this policy because of lower welfare for higher-income households, who bear most of the burden of the progressive income tax applied to their superannuation contributions.[22]

The two other equity measures for which results are provided are the net income shares for five household types and the Gini coefficient. The percentage changes in net income shares and in the Gini coefficient are presented in table 14.5. Similar to the distributional welfare implications, all three reforms increase net income shares for lower- income types and reduce them for higher-income types, thus reducing the Gini coefficient. Under the shift to the EET regime, the Gini coefficient falls by 0.94 percent (or by 0.48 percent with income tax adjustments) upon impact and by 1.13 percent (or by 0.69 percent with income tax adjustments) in the long run. The improvements in vertical equity during the transition path result from the transitional increases in the net income shares for lower-income types. The opposite transitional effects on vertical equity result from the shift to the TEE regime and also from adopting the AFTS proposal with consumption tax adjustments, with the decreases in the Gini coefficient being larger in the short term than in

Table 14.5
Effects of superannuation tax reforms on income shares and Gini coefficient (percentage changes in net income shares and Gini coefficient from initial steady-state solution).

	Consumption tax adjustments				Income tax adjustments			
Period	Lower income[a]	Middle income[b]	Higher income[c]	Gini coefficient	Lower income[a]	Middle income[b]	Higher income[c]	Gini coefficient
Shift to the EET taxation regime								
2010	0.855	0.220	–0.365	–0.935	0.400	0.118	–0.216	–0.482
2015	0.926	0.193	–0.347	–0.936	0.480	0.091	–0.202	–0.485
2030	1.174	0.462	–0.433	–1.308	0.967	0.404	–0.367	–1.081
Long run	1.007	0.414	–0.370	–1.126	0.601	0.306	–0.245	–0.686
Shift to the TEE taxation regime								
2010	2.128	0.187	–0.652	–1.899	1.710	0.120	–0.517	–1.504
2015	2.156	0.145	–0.638	–1.908	1.792	0.098	–0.524	–1.569
2030	1.865	–0.026	–0.473	–1.618	1.893	–0.013	–0.474	–1.673
Long run	1.717	–0.042	–0.456	–1.390	1.743	–0.041	–0.464	–1.412
Shift to the AFTS proposal								
2010	1.686	0.066	–0.508	–1.431	1.530	0.023	–0.456	–1.266
2015	1.713	0.049	–0.501	–1.457	1.607	0.017	–0.466	–1.341
2030	1.690	–0.015	–0.443	–1.451	1.853	–0.019	–0.488	–1.583
Long run	1.455	–0.096	–0.379	–1.133	1.664	–0.085	–0.440	–1.311

[a] Average value for lowest and second quintiles.
[b] Value for third quintile.
[c] Average value for fourth and highest income quintiles.

the long run. For example, under the TEE regime, the Gini coefficient falls by about 1.9 percent (or by 1.5 percent with income tax adjustments) upon impact and by 1.39 percent (or by 1.41 percent with income tax adjustments) in the long run.

14.4.3 Macroeconomic Effects

Macroeconomic or aggregate variables are obtained as weighted averages of optimal household behavior, where the weights are the constant cohort and income type shares. The macroeconomic effects of the superannuation tax reforms are displayed in table 14.6 as percentage changes in the selected per capita variables in the selected years of the transition from the benchmark steady-state solution. Note that the reforms are assumed to be implemented in 2010, with the results for that year depicting the immediate effect of the reforms. The results for 2030 and the long-run effects of the policy reforms are also presented. The discussion of the macroeconomic results concentrates on the implications for asset accumulation and capital, the goods market, the labor market, and the main government indicators.

Removal of the superannuation contribution tax rate, combined with full elimination (under both the EET and TEE regimes) or partial elimination (under the AFTS proposal) of the fund earnings tax implies larger superannuation assets, which generate the reported increases in total domestic assets. The magnitude of these increases, however, differs greatly among the three reforms. Similar differences in the effects on national wealth arising from the introduction of voluntary front- and back-loaded retirement accounts were derived by Fehr, Habermann, and Kindermann (2008). Under the EET regime, the long-run increase in total wealth is 21.78 percent (or 24.84 percent with income tax adjustments), which results from greater superannuation assets and also from increased private non-superannuation assets. Increased private assets are the result of lower consumption expenditures and an initially higher labor supply. As for the TEE regime and the AFTS proposal, the increases in total domestic assets are moderated by decreases in private assets, which are affected by higher income taxes faced by younger generations.[23] While the total wealth increases, the effects of the superannuation taxation reforms on the capital stock per capita (not displayed) are negative. In the short and medium terms, the capital stock decreases are caused by lower capital prices (not displayed), but in the long term these negative effects are entirely driven by lower labor input. Hence, the increases in household savings are not invested in the

Table 14.6
Macroeconomic implications of superannuation tax reforms
(percentage changes in selected per capita variables from initial steady-state solution).

	Consumption tax adjustments			Income tax adjustments		
Variable	EET	TEE	AFTS	EET	TEE	AFTS
Domestic assets						
2010	0.00	0.00	0.00	0.00	0.00	0.00
2030	19.05	3.03	3.64	20.82	4.10	3.09
Long run	21.79	4.37	4.85	24.84	4.16	3.00
Labor supply						
2010	1.92	−0.53	−0.11	2.98	0.39	0.18
2030	−1.81	−0.81	−0.63	−1.54	−0.94	−1.09
Long run	−2.24	−1.10	−0.84	−1.76	−1.14	−1.15
Output (GDP)						
2010	1.17	−0.33	−0.06	1.81	0.24	0.11
2030	−1.72	−0.81	−0.61	−1.41	−0.91	−1.03
Long run	−2.24	−1.10	−0.84	−1.76	−1.14	−1.15
Gross national product (GNP)						
2010	1.17	−0.28	−0.04	1.77	0.25	0.14
2030	0.37	−0.41	−0.18	0.81	−0.39	−0.61
Long run	0.16	−0.56	−0.28	0.89	−0.62	−0.74
Consumption						
2010	−3.64	−0.48	−0.44	−3.55	−0.46	−0.43
2030	−1.23	−1.15	−0.83	−0.67	−0.96	−1.09
Long run	−0.57	−0.89	−0.54	0.29	−0.96	−1.08
Pension expenditure						
2010	0.63	0.02	0.03	0.57	0.01	0.04
2030	−2.84	−0.49	0.01	−3.15	−0.61	0.09
Long run	−4.52	−0.93	−0.67	−5.11	−0.89	−0.29
Income tax revenue						
2010	13.67	12.33	6.90	8.19	8.39	6.19
2030	11.30	9.32	4.44	8.58	9.00	6.76
Long run	12.16	8.77	3.90	7.98	9.11	6.69
Tax rate[a]						
2010	−16.43	−11.14	−1.66	−5.63	−4.26	−0.88
2030	−7.63	−0.84	6.45	−3.12	−0.34	2.80
Long run	−11.33	0.93	7.55	−4.85	0.40	3.29

[a] These are percentage changes in either the consumption tax rate or income tax imposed on taxable income that includes superannuation benefits (the EET regime) or contributions (the TEE regime and AFTS proposal).

domestic capital stock but instead are exported abroad, leading to substantial reductions in net foreign debt.

The policy changes to superannuation taxation examined have significant implications for household labor supply. As shown in table 14.6, the effects of the TEE regime and the AFTS proposal on per capita labor supply are negative over the entire transition path. The lower average labor supply results from reduced working hours of middle-aged and older working households that face increased income tax rates as contributions are now subject to progressive income taxation. The relatively more favorable outcome for per capita labor supply arising from the AFTS proposal is caused by the uniform 15 percent tax offset to superannuation contributions, which effectively reduces income tax rates (relative to the rates under the TEE regime). On the other hand, the shift to the EET regime leads initially to a higher per capita labor supply, which in 2010 increased by 1.92 percent with consumption tax adjustments or by 2.98 percent with income tax adjustments. This is because the current middle-aged and older working households supply more labor to boost their superannuation savings. In the succeeding years of the transition, the increases in average labor supply disappear, with the average labor supply falling by 2.24 percent (or by 1.76 percent with income tax adjustments) in the long term, mainly because of the dominating income effect of significantly larger asset holdings.[24]

Output (or GDP) is produced using the capital stock and labor supply, so the effects of the reforms on output follow the changes in these two inputs to production. Table 14.5 indicates that only under the shift to the EET regime in the short and medium terms does output increase, because of a higher average labor supply. The effects on national income (or gross national product, GNP), which equals output less the interest payments on foreign debt, are more favorable because of lower foreign debt. In fact, the national income is higher over the entire transition and in the long term as a result of the shift to the EET regime. The largest component of output is consumption, which is measured in per capita terms, as are all the other macroeconomic variables. As shown, all three reforms have negative effects on per capita consumption. Under the EET regime, average consumption decreases significantly, by about 3.6 percent upon impact, caused by lower consumption for the current elderly, who now have their superannuation benefits taxed as ordinary income. However, per capita consumption improves during the transition because of greater accumulated assets. By contrast, the shift to the TEE regime and the AFTS proposal generate relatively higher consumption in the short run than in the long run, driven mainly by the budget-balancing changes in the consumption tax or income tax rates over the course of the transition.[25]

The simulation results also show that all three reforms reduce the elderly's reliance on the publicly provided Age Pension. This is because larger accumulated assets and asset incomes in retirement imply reduced Age Pension benefits because the means test is more strictly binding. The decline in Age Pension expenditures is especially significant for the shift to the EET regime, generating a long-run fall in pension costs of 4.52 percent with consumption tax adjustments or 5.11 percent with income tax adjustments. As expected, the receipts from the income tax increase under all three reforms, as either benefits or contributions are treated as ordinary taxable income. Assuming consumption tax rate adjustments to balance the government budget, the effects on income tax receipts are quite similar for both the EET and TEE regimes in the short run, but during the transition the shift to the TEE regime leads to greater decreases in income tax revenues. This is caused by the higher income tax rates faced by middle-age households, which lower their labor supply, private assets, and asset income. In the short run, the consumption tax rate declines under all three reforms examined. However, relative to the immediate effects, the consumption tax rate increases, and is 0.93 percent and 7.55 percent higher for the TEE regime and the AFTS proposal, respectively. These increases are caused partly by declining intakes from personal income taxation, corporate taxation (which largely follows the effects on per capita output), and declining average consumption, which affects overall consumption tax revenues. The relatively higher consumption taxes or income taxes for the AFTS proposal result from the uniform 15 percent contribution tax offset.

14.5 Sensitivity Analysis

To investigate the sensitivity of the results, the model now considers the long-run effects of the three superannuation taxation reforms under two alternative assumptions. The first alteration involves a higher 12 percent mandatory superannuation contribution rate; the second modification accounts for a more aged demographic environment.[26]

14.5.1 Higher Superannuation Contributions

In 2010, the Australian government announced that the mandatory contribution (or Superannuation Guarantee) rate would be gradually increased, reaching 12 percent of gross wages by July 2019. The macroeconomic and welfare effects of the gradual increases in the Superannuation Guarantee rate were examined by Kudrna and Woodland (2013). Long-run effects similar to those in Kudrna and Woodland (2013) are reported in the column "ttE" of table 14.7, which shows the long-run percentage changes of the increased Superannuation Guarantee rate with the existing concessional tax rates on superannuation contributions and fund earnings. The policy change increases superannuation assets; the resulting increases in total assets and interest income upon reaching pension eligibility age reduce overall reliance on the Age Pension support in retirement. Although the government's pension expenditures fall as a result of the increased Superannuation Guarantee rate, income tax revenues decrease (because of lower labor earnings) and have to be compensated by an increase in the consumption tax rate, or alternatively by an increase in the average income tax rate. In terms of the welfare effects, the increased Superannuation Guarantee rate increases the welfare of higher-income types, whereas lower-income types with no preferential tax treatment of their superannuation suffer welfare losses because of a reduced wage rate and increased consumption tax or income tax rates that compensate for higher superannuation tax concessions.

The long-run effects of the superannuation taxation reforms with the 12 percent Superannuation Guarantee rate are reported in table 14.7 as percentage changes in the selected variables from the new (long-run) steady-state solution with the higher contribution rate. A comparison with the long-run effects of the superannuation taxation reforms under the lower 9 percent Superannuation Guarantee rate presented in section 14.4 reveals that the long-run effects presented here, although different quantitatively, are broadly the same qualitatively, with the same direction of change in most macroeconomic and welfare variables. That is, the examined superannuation taxation reforms with the higher 12 percent Superannuation Guarantee rate continue to yield greater domestic assets, lower pension expenditures, improved intragenerational equity, and reduced income inequality. The only exception occurs for the shift to the EET regime with income tax adjustments, where the long-run welfare gains are greater for higher-income types compared to the gains for lower-income types (i.e., vertical equity worsens). This is because of the budget-balancing reduction in income tax rates, which favors higher-income types. The larger long-run increases in domestic assets compared to those reported in section 14.4 result from smaller superannuation offsets (i.e., reductions in ordinary non-superannuation assets).

Table 14.7

Long-run effects of superannuation tax reforms with 12% Superannuation Guarantee rate
(percentage changes in selected variables from new steady-state solution with 12% Superannuation Guarantee rate).

	Consumption tax adjustments				Income tax adjustments			
Variable	ttE[a]	EET	TEE	AFTS	ttE[a]	EET	TEE	AFTS
Macro implications								
Domestic assets	9.90	23.48	12.76	10.41	7.59	26.99	14.12	11.00
Labor supply	–0.15	–2.43	–2.23	–1.56	–0.52	–1.69	–2.42	–2.24
Consumption	0.77	–0.40	–1.29	–0.74	0.11	0.78	–1.40	–1.51
Pension expenditure	–2.44	–5.43	–2.41	–1.47	–2.02	–5.51	–2.25	–1.29
Income tax revenue	–6.14	17.87	13.11	6.18	–2.79	10.52	12.31	9.19
Tax rate[b]	8.94	–12.07	0.75	7.55	4.55	–7.85	–0.82	3.06
Welfare effects								
Lower income[c]	–0.14	0.72	0.35	0.36	–0.05	0.49	0.31	0.45
Middle income[d]	0.08	0.55	0.09	0.14	0.06	0.50	0.06	0.12
Higher income[e]	0.37	0.36	–0.20	–0.08	0.17	0.72	–0.21	–0.28
Average welfare[f]	0.11	0.54	0.08	0.14	0.06	0.58	0.05	0.09
Income shares								
Lower income[c]	–0.53	1.45	1.96	1.58	–0.25	0.88	1.93	1.83
Middle income[d]	–0.35	0.53	–0.01	–0.11	–0.32	0.30	–0.01	–0.05
Higher income[e]	0.34	–0.51	–0.56	–0.43	0.26	–0.29	–0.54	–0.52
Gini coefficient	0.54	–1.53	–1.55	–1.16	0.28	–0.92	–1.54	–1.42

[a] Long-run results for increased contributions with existing concessional tax rates on contributions and earnings.
[b] Percentage changes either to consumption tax rate or income tax rate.
[c] Average value for lowest and second quintiles.
[d] Value for third quintile.
[e] Average value for fourth and highest quintiles.
[f] Average value across all income quintiles.

As mentioned, the increased Superannuation Guarantee rate results in larger superannuation savings, which offset (displace) other savings. Additional increases in the superannuation assets arising from the superannuation taxation reforms then lead to smaller superannuation offsets and thus larger increases in total assets compared to those with the 9 percent Superannuation Guarantee rate.

14.5.2 Aging Demographic

To examine the long-run effects of the superannuation taxation reforms in an aging environment, the medium population projections by the Productivity Commission (2013) are used. In particular, the model uses their age-specific survival rates in 2050 and calculates the annual rate of population growth to generate an old-age dependency ratio of 0.38, taken from their projections for 2050. The long-run steady-state effects of this aging demographic with increased longevity and reduced population growth are presented in the column "ttE" of table 14.8, which shows the percentage changes in selected variables in the new steady state with aging (but with the existing superannuation tax treatment) from the initial steady state in 2010.

Similar to the results of Kudrna, Tran, and Woodland (2015), the results show increased domestic assets (because of increased longevity and the proportion of older households with large asset holdings), reduced labor supply (because of a reduced proportion of working-age population), and significant increases in either consumption tax or income tax rates needed to fund higher Age Pension expenditures. The welfare effects of population aging are negative across all income types because of the increased tax rates. However, income inequality declines—as measured by the impacts on income shares and on the Gini coefficient. In the simulation herein, where increased pension expenditures are financed by tax hikes, income inequality falls, partly because the higher tax rates more negatively affect those households with higher incomes and partly because of a more binding pension means test for higher-income households, which accumulate more assets as a result of increased longevity.

The results for the three superannuation taxation reforms are presented in table 14.8 as percentage changes in the selected macroeconomic and welfare variables between the two new steady states (one with the tax reform and aging demographic and the other with the aging demographic only). As reported for the effects of the tax reforms with the 12 percent contribution rate, the macroeconomic implications

Table 14.8
Long-run effects of superannuation tax reforms with aging demographic
(percentage changes in selected variables in long-run steady state with aging demographic).

	Consumption tax adjustments				Income tax adjustments			
Variable	ttE[a]	EET	TEE	AFTS	ttE[a]	EET	TEE	AFTS
Macro implications								
Domestic assets	41.45	19.59	0.38	1.45	14.46	44.81	5.01	4.34
Labor supply	–9.68	–2.27	–0.52	–0.46	–11.44	–0.64	–1.99	–1.64
Consumption	–0.94	1.52	–0.49	–0.20	–6.85	7.10	–1.36	–1.09
Pension expenditure	53.77	–6.39	–1.30	–0.86	60.44	–8.71	–1.11	–0.65
Income tax revenue	–2.70	22.16	6.71	2.66	18.02	2.18	7.13	4.50
Tax rate[b]	52.18	–32.69	2.78	4.07	32.16	–22.69	–0.19	0.43
Welfare effects								
Lower income[c]	–4.90	1.34	0.12	0.25	–4.66	1.03	0.16	0.31
Middle income[d]	–5.23	1.18	–0.08	0.07	–5.83	1.74	–0.11	0.02
Higher income[e]	–5.25	0.97	–0.24	–0.08	–7.09	2.72	–0.48	–0.34
Average welfare[f]	–5.11	1.16	–0.06	0.08	–5.87	1.85	–0.15	–0.01
Income shares								
Lower income[c]	1.68	0.92	1.03	0.96	4.14	–1.33	1.22	1.11
Middle income[d]	–0.84	0.46	–0.22	–0.14	–0.42	0.30	–0.02	–0.11
Higher income[e]	–0.23	–0.30	–0.17	–0.22	–0.98	0.28	–0.38	–0.33
Gini coefficient	–0.74	–1.29	–0.88	–0.80	–3.15	1.12	–1.01	–0.87

[a] Long-run results for an aging economy with existing concessional tax rates on contributions and earnings.
[b] Percentage changes either to consumption tax rate or income tax rate.
[c] Average value for lowest and second quintiles.
[d] Value for third quintile.
[e] Average value for fourth and highest quintiles.
[f] Average value across all income quintiles.

in this aging economy are also broadly the same qualitatively as those derived in section 14.4. The magnitude of the change in some macroeconomic variables, however, differs greatly between the two demographic assumptions. For instance, the reductions in either consumption tax or income tax rates in this aging environment are significantly larger under the shift to the EET regime. This is simply a result of comparing the results of this tax reform with the new higher-aging steady state, which requires significantly higher tax rates to fund the increased pension expenditure. Table 14.8 also indicates that vertical equity—measured by the long-run effects on welfare and income inequality—improves under all the superannuation tax reforms in this higher-aging environment, except for the shift to the EET regime with the progressive income tax adjustments. As discussed, this reform allows for a large income tax cut that favors higher-income households, generating relatively larger welfare gains and net income shares compared to those of lower-income households.

14.6 Conclusions

This chapter examined three progressive tax reforms to superannuation (i.e., private pensions) by using a computable OLG model that incorporates essential features of Australia's retirement income and taxation policy settings. These hypothetical reforms are: (1) a shift to an EET taxation regime, (2) a shift to a TEE regime, and (3) adoption of the AFTS proposal on the taxation of superannuation. The first two reforms comprise replacement of the existing concessional superannuation taxation with the taxation regimes commonly applied to private pensions in other countries, where either benefits or contributions are treated as ordinary income and taxed progressively. The third reform is a variant of the shift to the TEE regime but also includes a 15 percent refundable contribution tax offset and a halving (but not full elimination) of the effective tax rate on investment earnings by the superannuation fund.

The major objective of the chapter was to assess whether, and to what extent, the reforms would improve vertical equity of the superannuation system, which currently provides tax concessions mainly to wealthy households, with lower-income households deriving little or no benefit (Australia's Future Tax System 2010). The simulation results indicate that all three reforms generate positive effects on vertical equity in the short, medium, and long terms, supporting proposals to impose progressive income taxes on either superannuation contributions or benefits (Australian Superannuation Fund Association 1998; Ingles and Denniss 2009; Australia's Future Tax System 2010). The welfare gains are greater and losses smaller for lower-income households relative to those experienced by higher-income households. The net income shares for lower-income households also improve, while the shares for higher-income households are smaller. The Gini coefficient declines under all the reforms examined. To rank the reforms in relation to their impact on the Gini coefficient, the most effective reform for reducing income inequality—which has been steadily increasing in Australia, with the current Gini coefficient up by 10 percent since the 1990s (Australian Bureau of Statistics 2011)—is the TEE regime, followed by the AFTS proposal and the EET regime.

The chapter also examined the intergenerational implications of the reforms and showed that the effects obtained from the shift to the EET taxation regime differ greatly from those caused by the TEE regime and the AFTS proposal. Under the shift to the EET regime, older generations suffer from large welfare losses, as their private pensions are now taxed at potentially higher marginal tax rates under progressive income taxation. However, future generations gain more in welfare under the EET regime than under the two other tax reforms, because of significantly higher income tax revenue, which allows lower tax rates. The macroeconomic implications are that removal of the existing concessional taxes on mandatory contributions and fund earnings generates larger superannuation assets, household savings, and overall domestic assets. The increased assets and asset incomes in retirement are assessed under the Age Pension means test, reducing average Age Pension payments and overall pension expenditures by the government. Therefore, the reforms (especially the shift to the EET regime) increase self-funding for retirement and reduce reliance on the public pension for many pensioners. Most of these macroeconomic and welfare effects are robust to modifications of the model to account for a higher mandatory superannuation contribution rate and a more aged population.

While the simulated impacts of the investigated changes to the taxation of superannuation are in accordance with economic intuition, they vary in numerical size and importance. Broadly, the implications of the superannuation tax reforms are relatively small for macroeconomic variables such as output, labor supply, and inequality as measured by the Gini coefficient. On the other hand, they are much larger quantitatively for other variables such as assets, tax revenues, Age Pension expenditures, and the budget-balancing tax rates. This is especially true under the policy change that replaces the current superannuation taxation arrangements with the EET taxation regime.

Any modeling analysis like that employed here is subject to limitations. First, the simulation of the superannuation tax reforms is undertaken in the environment of an assumed fully mature superannuation system, while the existing system is still in a transition toward maturity. Accordingly, if the current values for superannuation assets and superannuation tax revenues were targeted in the benchmark model, the effects generated by the reform would change to some extent from those presented here. For example, eliminating the concessional superannuation tax rates would require smaller increases in other taxes. Similarly, the shift to the EET regime is likely to lead in the short run to smaller increases in income tax revenues than those presented, as the actual superannuation balances are not as large as those predicted by the model. Second, the choice by households to make voluntary superannuation contributions was not modeled. Although aggregate voluntary contributions to superannuation are quite small compared to mandatory contributions, higher-income and older individuals make more significant voluntary contributions, and their voluntary choice of contributions is likely to be impacted by the superannuation tax reforms examined. Third, the present model abstracts from uncertainty for households regarding labor productivity over the life cycle and from precautionary savings during the working years. These extensions are left for future research.

Notes

We would like to thank Viktor Steiner, Robert Holzmann, and participants of the CEPAR-CESifo workshops on "Taxation of Pensions" in Sydney and in Munich for comments and feedback. This research was supported by the Australian Research Council Centre of Excellence in Population Ageing Research (CEPAR) under grant CE110001029.

1. Note that the effective fund earnings tax rate is about 7.1 percent, which is because of imputation credits on dividend income and the capital gains tax discount (Yoo and de Serres 2004).

2. The Australian personal income taxation system is progressive, with five tax brackets. In the financial year of 2009–10, the marginal tax rates range from zero to 45 percent (excluding the Medicare Levy).

3. Phased withdrawals of superannuation savings are assumed in the model because in 2009 the value of superannuation benefits paid as phased withdrawals exceeded for the first time the value of lump sums received (Bateman and Piggott 2011).

4. The social transfer payments are assumed to be paid to persons in the lowest to the fourth income quintiles aged younger than 65 years (see section 14.3 for details).

5. The bequest range of 46–64 years reflects intergenerational transfers from parents to children, as childbearing occurs largely between 25 and 35 years of age and the probability of death is particularly high in the 80+ age group.

6. The model abstracts from planned bequests, based on Gokhale et al. (2001), who documented a number of studies that found strong empirical evidence against intergenerational altruism.

7. The initial decision by the Australian government was to increase the rate to 12 percent by July 2019, but this was delayed by a subsequent government to 2025.

8. The maximum limit of 10 percent of the superannuation balance applies only to working households. The minimum limits are age based. These limits are 4 percent of the balance for persons younger than 65, 5 percent for those aged 65–74, 6 percent for those 75–79, 7 percent for those 80–84, 9 percent for those 85–89, and 11 percent for those 90 years old.

9. The model closely follows the pension means-testing rules in relation to assessing the superannuation assets at retirement (Department of Families, Community Services and Indigenous Affairs 2009). The superannuation assets that pensioners hold are assessed in full under the asset test of the Age Pension; the interest earnings generated by superannuation assets (similar to income generated by non-superannuation assets) are subject to the income test of the Age Pension, reflecting the means-testing rules applied to short-term income streams.

10. Government consumption and social transfers are assumed to be constant, with per capita social transfers equal to $ST = \Sigma_{i=1}^{4}\omega_i \, \Sigma_{a=21}^{64} \mu_a \, ST_a^i$.

11. The earnings ability for each income class after age 65 is also assumed to decline at a constant rate to reach zero at age 90, as Reilly, Milne, and Zhao (2005) considered only workers aged 15–65 years.

12. The effects of the superannuation tax reforms are also analyzed using alternative labor productivity profiles that differ not only in their level but also in their shape among the five income types (see section 14.5 for more details).

13. All figures are in Australian dollars unless otherwise specified.

14. Similar to the models in the articles listed, the behavior of self-employed workers (i.e., entrepreneurs) is not explicitly modeled. Although they are not required to contribute toward their superannuation, they are encouraged to do so through generous tax concessions. Importantly, self-employed workers account for only about 8 percent of the Australian workforce. It is also very likely that at some stage during their working years, those reported as self-employed workers were (or will be) employed and accumulated (will accumulate) superannuation through employers' mandatory contributions.

15. Note that compulsory superannuation (i.e., Superannuation Guarantee) was introduced in 1992 with initial 3 percent contributions, which were gradually increased to the existing rate of 9 percent in 2002. The model assumption of the 9 percent mandatory contributions paid to workers over their whole working life also generates higher ratios of superannuation assets to GDP and to total assets. Thus, the superannuation tax reforms are examined in the environment of a fully mature superannuation system.

16. The effective fund income tax rate is reduced from 7.1 percent to 3.55 percent under this policy change.

17. The policy simulations of eliminating concessional tax rates on either contributions, fund earnings, or benefits by Creedy and Guest (2008b) assume universal Age Pension benefits and thus are incapable of capturing the effects of a superannuation tax policy on the publicly provided Age Pension.

18. The income tax base (i.e., taxable income) increases for older households under the EET regime and for younger and middle-aged households under the two other reforms. These households then face higher average and marginal income tax rates. The budget-balancing reduction or increase under the income tax adjustments is made to these increased income tax rates.

19. The welfare effect for an *i*-type household of generation aged *a* at the time of the superannuation tax reform is calculated as $W_g^i = \left[\left(\hat{U}_g^i / \bar{U}_g^i\right)^{1/(1-1/\gamma)}\right] - 1] \times 100$, where $\hat{U}_g^i$ is the value of the remaining lifetime utility after the reform and $\bar{U}_g^i$ is the value of the remaining lifetime utility in the benchmark scenario.

20. The youngest generation at the time of the reforms is aged 21, which is the assumed entry age in the model. All the generations aged 20 and younger are those born in the succeeding transitional years. The results for the generation of those aged –80 in year 2010 (i.e., the generation born in 2090) approximate the long-run welfare effects.

21. The model assumes five income types of households. The welfare effects on lower-income, middle-income, and higher-income households in table 14.4 are presented as the average effect for the lowest and second quintiles, the effect on the third quintile, and the average effect for the fourth and highest quintiles, respectively.

22. Similar intergenerational welfare effects were obtained by Fehr, Habermann, and Kindermann (2008) for the policy introducing voluntary front-loaded and back-loaded accounts. The differences in their results between the two types of tax-preferred accounts come mainly from the general equilibrium effects on the assumed budget-balancing policy instrument rather than from direct effects on households from the taxation applied to these voluntary accounts.

23. Recall that borrowing constraints are imposed on all households so they cannot borrow against their superannuation assets. Removing the borrowing constraints would generate a larger superannuation offset (i.e., reduction in private non-superannuation assets) and smaller increases in total wealth for all three reforms examined. Creedy and Guest (2008b) allowed for borrowing, which partly explains the lower savings generated by their policy simulation of removing the concessional tax rate on benefits.

24. The wage rate (not displayed) is unchanged in the long run in this small open economy model, but during the transition it moves in the opposite direction from the changes in average labor supply.

25. The effects on the other components of aggregate demand are not displayed. In brief, government or public consumption is kept constant over the entire transition, and the policy effects on investment demand are similar to those in the capital stock. The external demand or net export balances output supply with domestic demand, and under all three reforms it decreases in the long run as output falls more than domestic demand.

26. To evaluate the sensitivity of the results to a relaxation of the assumption that the productivity profiles for the five income types of households have the same shape, dif-

fering only in level, the long-run effects of the superannuation tax reforms are also examined, using alternative labor productivity profiles. These alternative profiles assume different years of schooling among the income types. In particular, the third quintile is assumed to have the same number of years of schooling as in the benchmark model (12 years), but the two lower-income types have only 10 years of schooling and the two higher-income types have 15 years of schooling. This assumption generates labor productivity profiles, e_a^i, that are relatively flat for the two low-income types and relatively steep for the two high-income types. Given that the results are not significantly different from those presented in section 14.4, they are not reported here. Results are available from the authors upon request.

References

Altig, David, Alan Auerbach, Laurence Kotlikoff, Kent Smetters, and Jan Walisser. 2001. "Simulating Fundamental Tax Reform in the United States." *American Economic Review* 91:574–595.

Armstrong, Angus, Philip Davis, and Monique Ebell. 2015. "An Economic Analysis of Pension Tax Proposal." National Institute of Economic and Social Research, Cambridge, MA.

Atkinson, Margaret, John Creedy, and David Knox. 1999. "Some Implications of Changing the Tax Basis for Pension Funds." *Fiscal Studies* 20:189–203.

Auerbach, Alan, and Laurence Kotlikoff. 1987. *Dynamic Fiscal Policy*. Cambridge: Cambridge University Press.

Australian Bureau of Statistics (ABS). 2007. "Government Benefits, Taxes and Household Income." Cat. No. 6537.0, Australian Government Publishing Service, Canberra.

Australian Bureau of Statistics (ABS). 2010a. "Life Tables, Australia 2007–2009." Cat. No. 3302.0.55.001, Australian Government Publishing Service, Canberra.

Australian Bureau of Statistics (ABS). 2010b. "Australian System of National Accounts 2009–10." Cat. No. 5204.0, Australian Government Publishing Service, Canberra.

Australian Bureau of Statistics (ABS). 2011. "Household Income and Income Distribution 2009–10." Cat. No. 6523.0, Australian Government Publishing Service, Canberra.

Australian Superannuation Fund Association (ASFA). 1998. "Blue Skies: ASFA's Blueprint for a National Retirement Incomes Policy." ASFA Research Centre, Sydney.

Australia's Future Tax System (AFTS). 2008. "Retirement Income Consultation Paper." Commonwealth of Australia, Canberra.

Australia's Future Tax System (AFTS). 2010. "Final Report." Commonwealth of Australia, Canberra.

Bateman, Hazel, and Geoffrey Kingston. 2007. "Superannuation and Personal Income Tax Reform." *Australian Tax Forum* 22 (3): 137–163.

Bateman, Hazel, and John Piggott. 2011. "Too Much Risk to Insure? The Australian (non-) Market for Annuities." In *Securing Lifelong Retirement Income*, edited by Olivia S. Mitchell, John Piggott, and Noriyuki Takayama, 81–105. Oxford: Oxford University Press.

Clare, Ross. 2006. "The Benefits, Revenue Cost, and Implications for Individuals and the Economy of Abolishing the Contributions Tax." ASFA Research Centre, Sydney.

Cho, Stanley, and Renuka Sane. 2013. "Means-Tested Age Pension and Homeownership: Is There a Link?" *Macroeconomic Dynamics* 17:1281–1310.

Commonwealth of Australia. 2011. "Budget Strategy and Outlook 2010–11." Budget Paper No. 1, Commonwealth of Australia, Canberra.

Creedy, John, and Ross Guest. 2008a. "The Labour Supply and Savings Effects of Superannuation Tax Changes." *Australian Economic Papers* 47:1–14.

Creedy, John, and Ross Guest. 2008b. "Changes in the Taxation of Private Pensions: Macroeconomic and Welfare Effects." *Journal of Policy Modelling* 30:693–712.

Davidson, Sinclair, and Ross Guest. 2007. "Superannuation Tax Reform: Fiscal Consequences." *Agenda* 14:5–16.

Department of Families, Community Services and Indigenous Affairs (FaCSIA). 2009. "Retirement Income Streams." Commonwealth of Australia, Canberra.

Doyle, Suzanne, Geoffrey Kingston, and John Piggott. 1999. "Taxing Super." *Australian Economic Review* 32:207–218.

Fehr, Hans. 2000. "Pension Reform during the Demographic Transition." *Scandinavian Journal of Economics* 102:419–443.

Fehr, Hans, Christian Habermann, and Fabian Kindermann. 2008. "Tax-Favored Retirement Accounts: Are They Efficient in Increasing Savings and Growth?" *FinanzArchiv: Public Finance Analysis* 64 (2): 171–198.

Fehr, Hans, Sabine Jokisch, and Laurence Kotlikoff. 2008. "Fertility, Mortality and the Developed World's Demographic Transition." *Journal of Policy Modeling* 30:455–473.

Gokhale, Jagadeesh, Laurence Kotlikoff, James Sefton, and Martin Weale. 2001. "Simulating the Transmission of Wealth Inequality via Bequests." *Journal of Public Economics* 79:93–128.

Horne, Jocelyn. 2002. "Taxation of Superannuation in Australia: An Assessment of Reform Proposals." Working Paper, Macquarie University, Sydney, Australia.

Imrohoroglu, Ayse, Selahattin Imrohoroglu, and Douglas Joines. 1998. "The Effect of Tax-Favored Retirement Accounts on Capital Accumulations." *American Economic Review* 88:749–768.

Ingles, David, and Richard Denniss. 2009. "The Great Superannuation Tax Concession Rort." Research Paper No. 61, Australia Institute, Manuka.

Institute of Actuaries of Australia (IAA). 2006. "Taxation of Superannuation in Australia: A Future Revenue Problem?" http://www.actuaries.asn.au.

Kingston, Geoffrey, and John Piggott. 1993. "A Ricardian Equivalence Theorem on the Taxation of Pension Funds." *Economics Letters* 42:399–403.

Kudrna, George, Chung Tran, and Alan Woodland. 2015. "The Dynamic Fiscal Effects of Demographic Shift: The Case of Australia." *Economic Modelling* 50:105–122.

Kudrna, George, and Alan Woodland. 2011a. "An Intertemporal General Equilibrium Analysis of the Australian Age Pension Means Test." *Journal of Macroeconomics* 33:61–79.

Kudrna, George, and Alan Woodland. 2011b. "Implications of the 2009 Age Pension Reform in Australia: A Dynamic General Equilibrium Analysis." *Economic Record* 87:183–201.

Kudrna, George, and Alan Woodland. 2013. "Macroeconomic and Welfare Effects of the 2010 Changes to Mandatory Superannuation." *Economic Record* 89:445–468.

Kulish, Mariano, Kathryn Smith, and Christopher Kent. 2010. "Ageing, Retirement and Savings: A General Equilibrium Analysis." *B.E. Journal of Macroeconomics* 10 (1): n.p. https://doi.org/10.2202/1935-1690.1808.

Nishiyama, Shinichi. 2011. "The Budgetary and Welfare Effects of the Tax-Deferred Retirement Saving Accounts." *Journal of Public Economics* 95:1561–1578.

OECD (Organisation for Economic Co-operation and Development). 2015. *Pension at a Glance: OECD and G20 Indicators*. Paris: OECD Publishing.

Productivity Commission. 2013. "An Ageing Australia: Preparing for the Future." Research Report, Productivity Commission, Canberra.

Reilly, Robert, William Milne, and Shiji Zhao. 2005. "Quality-Adjusted Labour Inputs." ABS Research Paper No. 1351.0.55.010, Australian Bureau of Statistics, Canberra.

Tran, Chung, and Alan Woodland. 2014. "Trade-offs in Means Tested Pension Design." *Journal of Economic Dynamics and Control* 47:72–93.

Yoo, Kwang-Yeol, and Alain de Serres. 2004. "The Tax Treatment of Private Pension Savings in OECD Countries and the Net Tax Cost per Unit of Contributions to Tax Favoured Schemes." OECD Working Paper No. 406, OECD, Paris.

IV Cross-Border Taxation of Pensions

15 The Taxation of Internationally Portable Pensions: Fiscal Issues and Policy Options

Bernd Genser and Robert Holzmann

15.1 Introduction

Recent developments in old-age pensions in countries of the Organisation for Economic Co-operation and Development (OECD) are reflected in several characteristic features. First, old-age income consists of a mix of public, occupational, and private retirement incomes whose components have become more diversified and variable across countries. Second, to motivate employers and individuals to compensate for lower public generosity, countries have increased their support for occupational and private retirement savings via various forms of tax preferences or direct subsidies. Third, mandatory as well as voluntary pension savings are typically subject to income tax, but tax rules deviate from the general principle of comprehensive income taxation within and between countries. Finally, a rising number of individuals spend some part of their working life or their retirement period abroad, a circumstance facilitated by improved portability of pension claims between OECD countries but also within key migration corridors (e.g., France and Morocco; Germany and Turkey).

As a result of these developments, individuals increasingly acquire pension and other retirement income claims from institutions inside and outside their country of residence, and benefits from these claims differ in their tax treatments within and across countries. This has two main economic consequences:

1. Taxation provokes efficiency losses because of planned tax arbitrage or unplanned exposure to tax distortions, as individuals are motivated to either move between countries (or are prevented from doing so) or to restructure their retirement income portfolio with little effect on overall retirement saving.

2. Taxation infringes on equity principles at both the individual and country levels. At the individual level, the application of different tax rules for retirement benefits and savings instruments by different countries violates horizontal equity and is a source of interpersonal fiscal unfairness. At the country level, different, inconsistent, and uncoordinated taxation rules for retirement income risk creating fiscal unfairness between countries and motivate tax competition.

A glimpse of the scope and dynamics of pensions paid abroad and received from abroad is provided for Germany in table 15.1. The total number of pensioners living abroad on a German pension reached 1.7 million in 2013 (or 6.85 percent of all pensioners with a German pension). While the share of pensions paid to non-Germans living abroad is decreasing, the share paid to Germans living abroad is increasing. Non-German pensioners living in Germany may also receive a pension for premigration insurance periods in their country of origin (as do 1.1 million pensioners, or 4.21 percent of all pensioners with a German pension). Adding both together gives a total number of 2.8 million (or 11.1 percent of all pensioners) potential recipients of a cross-border pension. Yet these numbers of current pensioners reflect past labor mobility and do not include the effects of higher pan-European labor mobility since the 1990s. Estimates for the European Union (EU) of the likely share of pensions paid abroad to the current workforce in the future are in the range of 15–25 percent (Holzmann 2015).

Table 15.1
Recipients of statutory German pensions—in Germany and abroad.

Number of pensioners in millions (% of total pensioners)	2013	2010	2005
Total non-German pensioners	2.562 (100%)	2.367 (100%)	2.032 (100%)
living in Germany	1.059 (41.3%)	0.944 (39.9%)	0.774 (38.1%)
living outside Germany	1.503 (58.7%)	1.423 (60.1%)	1.258 (61.9%)
Total German pensioners	22.602 (100%)	22.646 (100%)	22.452 (100%)
living outside Germany	0.222 (0.98%)	0.206 (0.91%)	0.170 (0.76%)
Total pensioners	25.164 (100%)	25.013 (100%)	22.484 (100%)
living outside Germany	1.725 (6.85%)	1.629 (6.51%)	1.427 (5.83%)
non-German pensioners living in Germany	1.059 (4.21%)	0.944 (3.77%)	0.774 (3.44)
potential recipients of cross-border pensions	2.784 (11.1%)	2.573 (10.3%)	2.201 (9.8%)

Sources: Eurostat Online Database (June 2015); authors' calculations.

The traditional instruments for addressing inequity issues in taxation are (1) an appropriate income tax reform at the national level and (2) renegotiation of double-taxation treaties at the international level. It is doubtful that these unilateral and bilateral approaches are promising strategies for reducing the international complexity in income taxation of pensions and other retirement income. In particular, bilateral negotiations will be blocked by the fundamental belief that any assignment of taxing rights that supports interpersonal equity among migrating pensioners will generate inequity among national treasuries facing income tax revenue losses, particularly from tax-exempt retirement savings in the pension accumulation stage.

On the other hand, the international complexity in pension taxation indicates that normative economics does not offer clear advice on how to tax old-age income consistently and is even less informative on the taxation of internationally portable pensions. Nevertheless, to overcome lengthy and ineffective bilateral negotiations dominated by tax lawyers and to support a coordinated international approach on the taxation of internationally portable pensions, a convincing conceptual framework based on a good economic foundation is urgently needed. This is terra incognita.

Against this background, this chapter is organized as follows. Section 15.2 offers an overview of the current state of taxation of the main forms of retirement income provision in and between OECD countries. Section 15.3 explains why the taxation of pensions has become so complex in OECD countries and why characteristic differences prevail between countries. Section 15.4 argues that international coordination of pension taxation is desirable, and it explores three possible blueprints for tax regimes that replace the current dominant but not omnipresent approach of deferred pension taxation with a front-loaded approach to income tax liability that can be combined with different payment patterns of income tax due over the contribution, return, and disbursement cycles of pension wealth. Section 15.5 offers some conclusions.

15.2 The State of Pension Taxation within and between OECD Countries

In all OECD countries, old-age income from pensions and other retirement savings[1] can be attributed to three pension pillars: statutory, occupational, and personal. The magnitude of these three tiers varies markedly between countries and between social groups within a country. Moreover, remarkable differences characterize the tax treatment of these pension pillars within and between countries.

Before exploring the diversity and complexity of tax treatment, this section offers some indicators on the importance of each pillar and the effects of taxation. Since no OECD- or EU-wide database is available to quantify the fiscal importance of the three tiers for pensioners across countries, the available coverage rates and gross replacement rates across the three pillars are used as proxies, as well as the gross versus net replacement rates for the public pillar in EU member states and some other OECD countries (table 15.2).

The data in table 15.2 confirm that countries with high net replacement rates in statutory pension benefits make less use of occupational pensions, whereas countries with a broad enrollment in occupational pensions grant substantially lower net replacement rates in statutory pensions. This is seen in countries where the tradition of high statutory pensions is still the dominant social policy goal, such as Germany, Austria, France, Italy, Spain, Portugal, Finland, and Slovenia, whereas a pronounced multipillar strategy of statutory and occupational pensions can be found in Denmark, Estonia, the Netherlands, Sweden, Ireland, Norway, and Switzerland, as well as in Australia, Canada, and the United States. This assessment is confirmed by the size of pension funds as a percentage of gross domestic product (GDP) across these countries (OECD 2015b; Towers Watson 2016). For the 19 countries in the world with the largest pension fund assets, these assets on average amounted to 80 percent of their GDP at the end of 2015.

The net pension income replacement rates under the mandated scheme are determined by national pension law and also by national income tax law. The effects of income taxation on pension income can be approximated by comparing gross and net pension replacement rates; that is, by comparing the gross pension to the gross income before retirement and the corresponding net values after deducting income taxes, respectively.[2] If the income tax rates on earned income and pension benefits are the same, both replacement rates will coincide. If the income tax burden on pension benefits is lower than that on earned income before retirement, then the numerator of the gross replacement rate is reduced by less than the denominator and the net pension replacement rate will be higher than the gross replacement rate. Table 15.3 shows this is true for all OECD countries except Denmark and Sweden, which exhibit a negative replacement gap. Since OECD countries apply a progressive income tax schedule for which the degree of progressivity

Table 15.2
Coverage and pension income replacement rates by pillar for OECD countries, 2015.

Country	Statutory	Occupational	Personal	Country	Statutory	Occupational	Personal
Austria	100 (76.6)	17.7 (n.a.)	18.0	Luxembourg	100 (87.1)	3.0 (n.a.)	n.a.
Belgium	100 (40.1)	45.2 (n.a.)	17.5	Netherlands	100 (29.5)	91.0 (61.1)	28.3
Bulgaria	100 (84.3)	98.0	n.a.	Poland	100 (48.8)	94.0 (n.a.)	4.7
Czech Republic	100 (51.3)	0	93.0	Portugal	100 (54.7)	3.3 (n.a.)	5.1
Germany	100 (57.1)	22.5 (n.a.)	40.0	Romania	100 (65.0)	n.a.	n.a.
Denmark	100 (35.2)	n.a.	n.a.	Sweden	100 (55.6)	n.a. (22.6)	n.a.
Estonia	100 (27.4)	75.0 (24.8)	7.0	Slovenia	100 (39.2)	47.0 (n.a.)	n.a.
Spain	100 (80.1)	9.0 (n.a.)	34.0	Slovakia	100 (n.a.)	n.a.	n.a.
Finland	100 (58.3)	6.4 (n.a.)	19.1	United Kingdom	100 (32.0)	46.0 (n.a.)	n.a.
France	100 (58.8)	16.5 (n.a.)	5.4	Switzerland	100 (32.0)	70.5 (23.1)	n.a.
Greece	100 (53.9)	0.2 (n.a.)	n.a.	Norway	100 (45.7)	68.1 (6.8)	23.2 (11.3)
Hungary	100 (76 3)	n.a.	18.9	Australia	100 (13.6)	68.5 (38.7)	19.9
Ireland	100 (36.7)	31.0 (n.a.)	12.0	Canada	100 (56.2)	33.4 (33.9)	32.8
Italy	100 (n.a.)	14.2 (n.a.)	n.a.	New Zealand	100 (40.6)	77.1 (14.1)	n.a.
Lithuania	100 (48.0)	78.1	n.a.	United States	100 (38.3)	41.6 (37.8)	22.0
Latvia	100 (47.0)	89 (n.a.)	11.6				

Source: Allianz International Pensions (2015).
Notes: Replacement rates are in brackets. These estimates refer to employees (= 100%) and not total population; n.a. = not available.

Table 15.3
Gross versus net pension replacement rates for median-income earners in OECD countries in 2014 (or nearest available year).

Country	Replacement rates		Difference	Country	Replacement rates		Difference
	Gross	Net	(net-gross)		Net	Gross	(net-gross)
Argentina	71.6	87.5	15.9	Italy	69.5	79.7	10.2
Australia	44.5	58.0	13.5	Japan	35.1	40.4	5.3
Austria	78.1	91.6	13.5	South Korea	39.3	45.0	5.7
Belgium	46.6	60.9	14.3	Luxembourg	76.8	88.6	11.8
Brazil	69.5	76.4	6.9	Mexico	25.6	28.4	2.8
Canada	32.6	42.9	10.3	Netherlands	90.5	95.7	5.2
Chile	32.8	37.7	4.9	New Zealand	40.1	43.0	2.9
People's Republic of China	74.0	80.5	6.5	Norway	49.8	60.2	10.4
Czech Republic	49.0	63.8	14.8	OECD	52.7	63.0	10.3
Denmark	67.8	66.4	–1.4	Poland	43.1	52.8	9.7
Estonia	50.5	59.8	9.3	Portugal	73.8	89.5	15.7
EU28	59.0	70.9	11.9	Russia	75.2	86.4	11.2
Finland	55.8	63.5	7.7	South African Republic	59.6	65.4	5.8
France	55.4	67.7	12.3	Slovakia	62.1	80.6	18.5
Germany	37.5	50.0	12.5	Slovenia	38.4	57.4	19
Greece	46.2	54.1	7.9	South Africa	10.5	11.8	1.3
Hungary	58.7	89.6	30.9	Spain	82.1	89.5	7.4
Iceland	69.2	76.7	7.5	Sweden	64.4	63.6	–0.8
India	96.5	109.7	13.2	Switzerland	40.2	46.9	6.7
Indonesia	13.0	13.8	0.8	Turkey	75.7	104.8	29.1
Ireland	34.7	42.2	7.5	United Kingdom	29.7	38.6	8.9
Israel	61.0	68.8	7.8	United States	35.2	44.8	9.6

Sources: OECD (2015a); https://data.oecd.org/pension.

shrinks with rising income, the replacement gap would also be expected to be large if the gross replacement rate is low and to be smaller if the gross replacement rate is high. In effect, this pattern characterizes the majority of OECD countries, but noteworthy exceptions arise. Whereas in New Zealand and a couple of developing countries the replacement gap is low despite a gross replacement rate well below 50 percent, some Eastern EU countries and Turkey have a high replacement gap although the gross replacement rate is high as well.

Average replacement gaps emphasize the importance of income taxation on the average purchasing power of pensioners in a country, but they do not capture distribution effects across those pensioners. For disaggregated national replacement gaps, one would expect that progressive income taxation would tend to favor high-income pensioners, whose gross replacement rates are usually lower than those of low-income pensioners. Empirically, however, these effects are fairly small. Besides preferential tax treatment of low-income pension earners, this finding may be related to changes in the composition of gross pension income along the income scale. For high-income pensioners, the share of statutory pension benefits will usually be smaller than the share of occupational and personal pensions, which are typically taxed differently under national income tax law.

Before exploring the actual modalities of taxation of pensions and other retirement savings within and between countries, an appropriate benchmark must be established. Tax policy makers in most countries agree that the basic guideline of their income tax system is the Schanz-Haig-Simons (SHS) principle of comprehensive income taxation. Perhaps not surprisingly, income taxation of old-age pensions in almost all OECD countries is characterized by a deviation from the SHS standard. This benchmark would require that individual entitlements to pension benefits accrued during citizens' working lives represent individual pension wealth for which the economic value can be calculated. Annual increments of pension wealth increase individuals' ability to pay and should therefore be taxed under a comprehensive income tax.

To compare national tax practices with the SHS benchmark, it is useful to distinguish three different forms of pension taxation, corresponding to the different phases of pension wealth accumulation and disbursement. Phase 1 is the establishment of pension claims through individuals' contributions (and contributions on their behalf) or voluntary pension saving. Phase 2 is the explicit or implicit return on individual pension wealth by capital market or social security institutions. Phase 3 is the disbursement of pension wealth when benefits are paid out. All three phases affect individual pension wealth and are relevant under a comprehensive income tax. The three phases overlap along an individual's life cycle since payment of contributions and returns on pension wealth occur in each year of earning and returns on pension wealth are incurred when pension benefits are paid out after retirement.

Technically, comprehensive income taxation of pensions can be characterized by a TTE income tax, where T is the individual income tax rate and E indicates that an income flow is tax-exempt. The triplet TTE implies that (1) individual contributions are not deductible from the tax base because they increase pension wealth (phase 1), (2) accruals to pension claims stemming from financial or notional returns during pension wealth holding in the working and retirement years are taxable (phase 2), and (3) pension benefits paid out are neutral with respect to comprehensive income because they transform pension wealth into cash holdings and are therefore exempt (phase 3). Moreover, lowercase "t" is used to indicate that a reduced tax rate $t<T$ is applied according to the income tax code.

A review of pension taxation over the pension wealth cycle reveals a very complex picture of deviations from the principle of comprehensive income taxation across OECD countries. No country in the sample applies TTE taxation to statutory pensions (table 15.4); all of them provide tax relief either by deferring income taxation or by subjecting income to lower tax rates. Slovakia is the only country that fully exempts income that is invested in pension savings and withdrawn after retirement.

The picture for income taxation of occupational pensions is similar and exhibits an even greater scope of complexity (table 15.5), although no country fully exempts occupational pensions from income tax. Two countries in the sample, Denmark and the United States, codify comprehensive income taxation, at least for some forms of occupational pensions.

Personal pensions[3] are granted particular tax preferences that differ for specific pension savings vehicles (table 15.6). None of the OECD countries in the sample offers expenditure taxation for personal pension savings. Despite the complexity in personal pension taxation, this finding seems to reflect a distinct dividing line in tax policy between taxing statutory and occupational pensions on the one hand and personal pensions on the other.

The complexity of the tax treatment of pensions is further increased if pensions are accumulated or disbursed across borders. The avoid-

Table 15.4
Income taxation of statutory pensions in OECD countries.

Tax regime	Country	Characterization of tax regime
TTE	None	Comprehensive income taxation (CIT)
tET	Canada, France, Ireland, Malta, Netherlands, United Kingdom	Deferred CIT with double-taxation relief
EET	Austria, Belgium, Cyprus, Czech Republic, Denmark, Estonia, Finland, Greece, Italy, Latvia, Luxembourg, Poland, Portugal, Slovenia, Spain, Sweden, Switzerland	Fisher/Kaldor expenditure tax, "deferred income taxation"
TEE	Lithuania	Prepaid expenditure tax
tEt	Germany, United States	Partially deferred prepaid expenditure tax
tEE	Hungary	Reduced prepaid expenditure tax
EEE	Slovakia	Full income tax exemption

Sources: Wellisch et al. (2008, table 2, p. 27); International Bureau of Fiscal Documentation (2015).

ance of international double taxation of cross-border pensions is codified in bilateral double-taxation treaties. Although these treaties usually follow the recommendations of the OECD model treaty, those that have been signed exhibit differences for a specific residence country whose residents receive pensions from different source countries. Differences also arise when a specific source country pays out pensions to pensioners in different residence countries. Nevertheless, the general tendency in bilateral treaties is to assign tax competences in line with the residence principle. On the other hand, none of the treaties in the sample applies exemption with progression (i.e., keeps the foreign pension untaxed but subjects the residential pension to the hypothetical average tax rate of foreign plus residential retirement income).

A closer look at the bilateral network of double-taxation treaties of Germany and Switzerland reveals fundamental complexities of cross-border pension taxation, as both countries signed treaties that tax their residents' cross-border pension benefits differently depending on the source country and type of pension benefit (tables 15.7 and 15.8). Thus, a pensioner residing in Germany faces different tax rules for statutory, occupational, and personal pension benefits based on whether they are

Table 15.5
Income taxation of occupational pensions in OECD countries.

Tax regime	Country	Characterization of tax regime
TTE	Denmark, United States	Comprehensive income taxation (CIT)
tTt	Italy, Sweden	CIT with partially deferred savings taxation
TET	Canada, Malta	CIT with deferred return taxation
ETT	Denmark, Germany, Portugal, United States	CIT with deferred savings taxation
tET	Austria, Belgium, Cyprus, Estonia, Finland, France, Ireland, Latvia, Slovenia, United Kingdom	Deferred CIT with double-taxation relief
EET	Austria, Canada, Germany, Greece, Luxembourg, Netherlands, Slovenia, Switzerland	Fisher/Kaldor expenditure tax, deferred income taxation
TEE	Poland	Prepaid expenditure tax
tEt	Austria, Germany, Hungary, Lithuania, Portugal, Slovakia, Spain, United States	Partially deferred prepaid expenditure tax
tEE	Austria, Cyprus, Greece, Hungary, Lithuania, Luxembourg	Reduced prepaid expenditure tax
EEE	None	Full income tax exemption

Sources: Wellisch et al. (2008, table 3, p. 29); International Bureau of Fiscal Documentation (2015).

received from France, Italy, the Netherlands, Austria, Denmark, Belgium, or Canada.

Moreover, the double-taxation treaties reveal that tax rules for pension benefits from the same source country (e.g., Canada) are codified differently in the treaty between Canada and Germany as well as in the treaty between Canada and Switzerland.

While it is true that negotiations between two treaty partners generate results that are determined by the initial positions of, and the economic interdependencies between, the two countries, it is amazing that bilateral bargaining for an equitable assignment of tax revenue has generated such a complex and uncoordinated multicountry pattern. This is particularly incomprehensible for OECD countries, which share basic principles of market economics, legality, and political governance and take account of recommendations by international institutions such as the United Nations, OECD, International Monetary Fund (IMF), and EU Commission, all of which strive for a more transparent and

Table 15.6
Income taxation of personal pensions in OECD countries.

Tax regime	Country	Characterization of tax regime
TTE	Denmark, Sweden	Comprehensive income taxation (CIT)
tTt	Italy	Partially deferred CIT
TET	France, Malta	CIT with deferred return taxation
ETT	Denmark	CIT with deferred savings taxation
tET	Belgium, Canada, Cyprus, Estonia, Finland, France, Ireland, Latvia, Luxembourg, Slovenia, Switzerland, United Kingdom	CIT with deferred savings and partially deferred savings taxation
TEt	Germany, Finland, France, Malta, Spain	CIT with deferred preferential savings taxation
EET	None	Fisher/Kaldor expenditure tax
TEE	Portugal, United States	Prepaid expenditure tax
tEt	Austria, Czech Republic, Germany, Hungary, Latvia, Lithuania, Luxembourg, Netherlands, Portugal, Slovakia, Spain, Switzerland, United States	Partially deferred prepaid expenditure tax
tEE	Austria, Cyprus, Greece, Hungary, Latvia, Lithuania	Reduced prepaid expenditure tax

Sources: Wellisch et al. (2008, table 4, p. 30); International Bureau of Fiscal Documentation (2015).

coordinated international tax system. These countries must be aware that the status quo of international pension taxation is not fair and sustainable and opens the door for strategic tax competition. Section 15.3 offers explanations for this disarray and provides considerations to guide the policy options described in section 15.4.

15.3 Explaining the Diversity, Complexity, and Inconsistency of Approaches for Taxing Internationally Portable Pensions

Hardly any other field in public finance or international economics exhibits such a level of diversity, complexity, and inconsistency within and across countries as the taxation of internationally portable pensions. Before offering possible policy solutions in design and implementation, it is useful to identify likely reasons for such conceptual and operational turmoil as well as analyze them to establish a

Table 15.7
Tax assignment of cross-border pension benefits in German double-taxation treaties.

Tax assignment	Statutory	Occupational	Personal
Residence country exclusively	Canada, Czech Republic, Estonia, Finland, Greece, Hungary, Ireland, Italy, Luxembourg, Portugal, Slovenia, Spain, Sweden, Switzerland, United Kingdom, United States	Austria, Belgium, Czech Republic, Estonia, Finland, France, Greece, Hungary, Ireland, Italy, Luxembourg, Malta, Netherlands, Poland, Slovenia, Spain, Sweden, Switzerland, United Kingdom, United States	Austria, Belgium, Czech Republic, Denmark, Estonia, Finland, France, Greece, Hungary, Ireland, Italy, Luxembourg, Malta, Netherlands, Poland, Portugal, Slovenia, Spain, Sweden, Switzerland, United Kingdom, United States
Source country exclusively	Austria, Belgium, Denmark, France, Italy (citizens), Malta, Netherlands, Poland, Sweden	France (mandatory)	
Tax credit in residence country		Canada, Denmark	Canada, Denmark (rental income)
Exemption with progression			

Source: Wellisch et al. (2008).

common understanding against which alternative policy solutions can be judged.

Four interrelated elements help explain the turmoil: (1) the diversity of ways to tax national pensions, (2) the lack of fiscal fairness across countries as a result of double-taxation treaties that do not appropriately address taxation of internationally portable pensions, (3) the coordination dilemma of bilateral double-taxation treaties, and (4) the separation of social and fiscal policy responsibilities at the national and international levels. The main arguments of each of the four explanatory elements are sketched in the following subsections.

15.3.1 The Diversity of Taxing National Pensions

For the diversity of national pension taxation, we offer three explanations: a simple, legalistic one that emphasizes the difference in pension funding; a more complex one that reflects the critical view of economists

Table 15.8
Tax assignment of cross-border pension benefits in Swiss double-taxation treaties.

Tax assignment	Statutory	Occupational	Personal
Residence country exclusively	Canada, Czech Republic, Estonia, Spain, Finland, Greece, Hungary, Ireland, Italy, Luxembourg, Portugal, Slovenia, Sweden, Switzerland, United Kingdom, United States	Austria, Belgium, Czech Republic, Estonia, Finland, France, Greece, Hungary, Ireland, Italy, Luxembourg, Malta, Netherlands, Poland, Slovenia, Spain, Sweden, Switzerland, United Kingdom, United States	Austria, Belgium, Czech Republic, Denmark, Estonia, Finland, France, Greece, Hungary, Ireland, Italy, Luxembourg, Malta, Netherlands, Poland, Portugal, Slovenia, Spain, Sweden, Switzerland, United Kingdom, United States
Source country exclusively	Austria, Belgium, Denmark, France, Italy (citizens), Malta, Netherlands, Poland, Sweden	France (mandatory)	
Tax credit in residence country		Canada, Denmark	Canada, Denmark (rental income)
Exemption with progression			

Source: Wellisch et al. (2008).

on consumption-oriented income taxation of retirement savings within a comprehensive income tax system; and a third one which accounts for the varying scope and composition of tax preferences within countries.

1. One common argument for taxing unfunded and funded pensions differently is the legalistic classification of statutory and certain forms of occupational pensions as deferred labor income and payouts from funded pensions as capital income. Hence, unfunded pension are cash-flow taxed in the same way as labor income when pension benefits are paid out. Accordingly, employer and employee contributions are considered vehicles for withholding labor income and are deducted from the labor income base. These pensions are therefore taxed EET. In contrast, contributions to funded occupational pensions, particularly personal pensions, are regarded as capital investments and are therefore not deductible. Returns on pension wealth are regarded as capital income

and are taxed upon accrual. In line with the principle of comprehensive income taxation, these pensions are taxed TTE.

However, both funded occupational pensions and personal retirement savings are quite often granted preferential tax treatment for various reasons; for example, to counterbalance biased individual preferences, to reap positive externalities of higher retirement savings, or to give way to lobbying pressure from trade unions or the financial sector. Preferential treatment ranges from full or partial tax deferral of income spent on pension savings and of returns on accumulated pension wealth to reduced tax rates and full tax exemption of disbursements.

2. An alternative explanation for taxing pensions differently is related to the dispute on comprehensive versus consumption-oriented income taxation. For almost 100 years, the comprehensive income tax approach has been the worldwide guideline for rational income tax design. The SHS principle of income taxation offers tax policy makers two key advantages: (a) a broad definition of income allows collection of the required amount of tax revenue with a lower tax rate on a larger tax base; and (b) the application of the same (marginal and average) tax rates to all forms of a taxpayer's annual income simplifies tax compliance, tax administration, and tax audits.

However, for taxation of retirement income, the approach has a number of pitfalls that have contributed to its punctuation and partial demise: comprehensive income taxation according to a progressive schedule is equitable with respect to annual ability to pay but penalizes individuals whose annual income fluctuates over their life cycle. Furthermore, comprehensive income taxation distorts intertemporal consumption decisions, as income spent on savings is subject to double taxation—once when parts of the income are saved and again when these savings earn returns. Economic recommendations to avoid these distortions by switching from comprehensive income taxation to consumption-oriented income taxation (Fisher 1930; Kaldor 1955) were largely ignored and rejected by tax policy makers and their advisers. On the other hand, tax policy makers were willing to deviate from the principle of comprehensive income taxation by deferring tax payment on unrealized capital returns and offering tax preferences on realized capital gains.

The theory of optimal tax policy in the 1970s brought an important change in the view on whether income or consumption was the superior tax base. Second-best tax policy models showed that political constraints and fundamental deviations from perfect market assumptions have important effects on optimal tax design that cannot be reduced to the decision of using either comprehensive income or personal consumption as the appropriate income tax base. A general result was that the principle of comprehensive income taxation, which requires that labor and capital income be taxed at the same rate, could not be an optimal tax rule. The theoretical and institutional proposals in the 1970s suggested that a cash-flow approach that avoids double taxation by exempting normal returns to capital is operationally feasible (Atkinson and Stiglitz 1976; Institute for Fiscal Studies 1978; US Department of Treasury 1977).

Despite the conceptual advantages of expenditure taxation, no industrialized country in the world has ever tried to replace the traditional comprehensive income tax by an expenditure tax (Auerbach 2009). Yet, with regard to retirement income, a limited and variable consumption-type income tax treatment of contributions, returns, and payouts has taken hold in most countries.[4] This expenditure tax treatment of retirement savings became the typical benchmark for tax lawyers and pension economists (including Whitehouse 1999; Robalino et al. 2005; and Huang 2008), although the SHS standard remains the guiding principle of income taxation.

3. A third explanation for differences in taxing pensions is politically motivated tax preferences. These vary between countries with respect to the type of participation (mandated or voluntary) in pension schemes, the type of funding (nonfinancial or financial), the benefit type (defined contribution or defined benefit), and socioeconomic characteristics (such as family size and composition). Essentially three reasons explain the diversity of arrangements. First, the diversity of arrangements reflects differences in efficiency and equity concerns by governments across countries that may change over time. For example, the mostly unlimited deductibility of contributions to a mandated first- or second-pillar scheme is consistent with governments' objective of providing income replacement within pension floors and ceilings that are related to lower and upper limits of statutory contributions. For voluntary schemes—occupational and personal—the limits are typically much tighter and more variable over time. Second, not only are the objectives of government and individuals reflected in the tax treatment of retirement provisions, but so are those of the financial industry, which is powerful and influential in most countries. Finally, changing tax preferences over time

reflect the degree of fiscal pressure on government policy. When retirement savings contracts become unsustainable but cannot be adjusted for old contract holders, one possibility for coping with growing fiscal pressure is to change tax preferences for new contracts only. This need for transitional arrangements has contributed to tax systems' complexity.

15.3.2 The Lack of Fiscal Fairness across Countries

No general consistent rule in double-taxation treaties defines how portable pensions should be taxed. This is due to the fact that Article 18 of the OECD model convention treaty only deals with the taxation of pension benefits and assigns the right to tax them to the residence country. An escape clause allows the source country (Article 19/2) to retain the right to tax income from public pensions paid directly by public authorities or by public funds (unless the pensioner is a citizen of the residence country). Thus, Article 18 recommends the residence principle on statutory pensions for employees outside the public sector, as well as on occupational and personal pensions, but offers room for bilateral negotiations on taxing pension rights that are related to services rendered to the public sector.

However, the model convention does not address pension taxation in the contribution and accumulation phases. Indeed, two problems arise that violate either equity between individuals or fiscal fairness across countries.

If a double-taxation treaty assigns the right to tax pension benefits to the residence country, which is the typical case for statutory and unfunded pensions, then pensioners will be overtaxed if they were already taxed in the source country during the contribution or accumulation phase; this is because tax credits are restricted to income taxes paid on the identical tax base in the same year. If retirement savings and/or pension accumulation were tax-exempt in the source country, then EET taxation implies that all income tax on pensions goes to the residence country, and the source country cannot recoup tax revenue losses resulting from exempting earned income spent on pension savings.

For nonresident civil servants, the OECD model convention allows pensions to be taxed in the country of disbursement. If this rule is included in a double-taxation treaty, then the residence country has to forgo any income tax revenue from those pensions as well as from notional returns accrued after retirement.

Table 15.9
Equity effects of tax principles and taxation assignment rules.

Residence country	Source country	
	TEE	EET
TEE	I: Taxed once in source country	I: Untaxed in both countries
	C: Tax revenue only in source country	C: No tax revenue in any country
EET	I: Double taxation	I: Taxed once in residence country
	C: Tax revenue in both countries	C: Tax revenue only in residence country

Source: Holzmann (2015).
Note: I = individual; C = country.

Attempts by EU countries to unilaterally override fiscally unfair treaty rules and to recoup tax losses from pension tax preferences on occupational and private retirement savings upon migration were ruled discriminatory and thus illegal by the European Court of Justice because they hamper free mobility (for details, see Wellisch et al. 2008, 48ff).

Yet even the application of either front- or back-loaded consumption taxation (TEE or EET) in both countries does not guarantee fiscal fairness between national treasuries. Table 15.9 presents the fiscal impact of different taxation principles in the source and residence countries. The results range from no taxation to double taxation and reveal that interpersonal equity and fiscal fairness require a fundamental extension of the OECD model treaty.

Extended double-taxation treaties seem particularly necessary to ensure that residence countries of pensioners are capable of providing migrated retirees with public goods and services that are typically age dependent. On the other hand, it is desirable to curb strategic or opportunistic behavior by countries that voluntarily forgo taxing pensions of resident retirees to attract high-income pensioners and expect revenue through indirect taxation (such as Portugal; see Bravo 2016, chapter 6, this volume).

15.3.3 The Coordination Dilemma of Bilateral Double-Taxation Treaties

The standard instrument for settling tax-assignment issues among countries is a bilateral tax treaty. The primary objective of such a treaty historically was avoidance of international double taxation of natural or legal entities, but recent renegotiations increasingly have tried to limit strategic shifting of taxable income across national borders, particularly by multinational corporations (OECD 2013). Model treaties by the OECD and the United Nations led to a coordination of bilateral treaties, and six Scandinavian countries did sign a multilateral treaty. Nonetheless, the present international network still offers ample room for strategic tax arbitrage and treaty shopping.

Besides the complexity and inconsistency of this international network, further problems arise as bilateral tax assignments leave national tax autonomy unchanged. Yet the treaty network may trigger national tax reform measures that enable countries to benefit from strategic cross-border flows of tax bases and from the international redistribution of revenue. Tax revenue shifts across national borders reflect differences in national law (tax law, business law, pension law), in the international structure of taxable units, and in the strength of national tax administrations and tax audits.

Renegotiations of bilateral treaties are under way, but multilateral treaty coordination is nevertheless poor because negotiations start out from the traditional treaty concept; they remain bilaterally focused; political bargaining over country-specific taxation topics results in case-by-case agreements; and the model treaties still lack convincing global rules to grant international equity, although the OECD has tried to support treaty revisions via regular adjustments of its model treaty. Moreover, renegotiations of bilateral double-taxation treaties have proven to be too slow and casuistic to keep pace with rapid economic and demographic developments.

Against this background, it is very unlikely that bilateral revisions of the treaty network will help reduce the diversity, complexity, and inconsistency in international taxation of pension income. A successful approach for a treaty network reform with respect to global pension taxation requires three necessary conditions: (1) multilateral consent on fair revenue sharing of income taxation on cross-border pensions, (2) a consistent conceptual framework that can be implemented in the model treaty to provide transparent information on prepaid income taxes in the national pension wealth accumulation cycle, and (3) some readiness to listen to economic recommendations for a coordinated tax and pension policy within and across countries.

15.3.4 Separation of Social and Fiscal Policy Responsibility Nationally and Internationally

The complaint about the lack of conceptual and administrative coordination between social and fiscal policy is not new and was reiterated in the Mirrlees Review (Mirrlees 2011).

In most countries, social policy and tax policy are assigned to different ministries, with few coordination requirements or little overall government guidance. Consequently, there is little readiness to look for economic trade-offs in the use of the most appropriate tax and pension policy instruments, as from a parochial perspective no gains exist. It remains to be seen whether the Mirrlees Review's call for a concerted policy design that simultaneously considers taxes and transfers will be taken up in the United Kingdom (or elsewhere).

The situation is similar at the EU Commission, where pension issues are split across a number of Directorates General (namely, the DGs for Employment, Social Affairs and Inclusion; Financial Stability, Financial Services and Capital Markets Union; and Economic and Financial Affairs) and separated from income taxation issues handled by the DG Taxation and Customs Union. These DGs seem to have had little motivation to engage in cross-sectoral issues such as equity and fiscal fairness of portable pensions in the internal market.

To the best of the authors' knowledge, no international organization has used its mandate to explore, analyze, and guide pension design and pension taxation coherently at the national and international levels. The International Labour Organization (ILO), historically in the forefront of social policy and retirement income considerations, has never dealt with pension taxation issues. For many decades, the IMF's Fiscal Affairs Department (FAD) was the leader on taxation issues (micro and macro) and explored aging and pension issues at the macro level, but these topics were never brought together, let alone in a transcountry perspective. The World Bank established itself as a leader in the international pension discussion with the 1994 publication "Averting the Pension Crisis" and the ensuing knowledge management on pension issues. The World Bank was never strong on taxation issues, though, and often had to rely on advice from the IMF/FAD. Finally, the OECD hosts substantive pension work and taxation work under one roof but in different departments that often do not interact with one another, as their work programs are determined by committees that reflect the schedule of responsibilities of the national ministerial divisions (bringing the discussion full circle).

15.4 Policy Options for Streamlining Taxation of Internationally Portable Pensions

The current approach of taxing internationally portable pensions is not only complex and distortionary but is also unfair and fiscally unsustainable. With rising labor migration between countries within the EU and elsewhere in the world, a residence-based taxation approach leads to increasing tax revenue losses for the source country. It is rather unlikely that countries can solve the issue at the national level or through renegotiation of existing bilateral double-taxation treaties. A globally sustainable solution requires consent on key objectives of an internationally fair tax revenue distribution and on implementable options to transfer individual equity in intertemporal taxation to a global setting with migrating workers and pensioners.

Efficiency and fairness in a tax regime for internationally portable pensions can only be achieved if national and international objectives are considered simultaneously. The following principles seem relevant in shaping an appropriate tax design. First, a consumption-type treatment of mandated retirement savings is justified, as it aims at contributing to intertemporal neutrality for consumption decisions and also inasmuch as contributions to mandatory pension systems are perceived as "social security taxes" rather than savings. Second, (limited) consumption-tax treatment of private pension savings can be motivated because voluntary old-age pensions complement mandatory statutory and occupational pensions, which are regarded as insufficient to smooth intertemporal consumption in an aging society. Third, national as well as international double taxation of old-age pensions should be avoided. Fourth, revenue from income taxation over the life cycle must be allocated fairly among the states involved. Finally, pension taxation should not distort the migration decisions of individual workers or pensioners.

The problem with the current state of pension taxation in many OECD countries, and in particular in the EU, is that these institutions concentrated on specific objectives by recommending portability of pension entitlements and EET taxation of statutory and mandatory occupational pensions but left the solution of the other objectives to individual countries. It is not surprising that countries focused on national fiscal revenue by using or extending existing double-taxation treaties.

The key problem of fairness among national budgets is that, under the current design, the initial income tax exemptions for migrant laborers cannot be recouped by the usual double-taxation treaty measures in a simple and transparent way. Negotiations on any form of source taxation of cross-border pension income suffer from a lack of transparency on previous income tax losses induced by preferential income tax treatment of pension savings. A temporary extension of unlimited income tax liability in the source country will only work if pensioners migrate after they start receiving pension payments. Codifying a reimbursement scheme by which residence countries compensate source countries for migration-induced income tax losses seems an impossible political venture under the current circumstances.

This section sketches a new set of pension tax policy options that directly address the double equity dilemma of cross-border pensions and proposes solutions that require modifications of pension tax liability calculations at the national level but work efficiently within the current treaty network. The three pension tax options presented have one common feature, namely the front-loaded calculation of pension tax liability, but they differ in the tax payment pattern across an individual's pension cycle. Subsection 15.4.2 presents a regime of front-loaded pension taxation and immediate tax payment (i.e., taxes have to be paid in the year when contributions are made and returns accrue). In subsection 15.4.3, the tax payment of the front-loaded pension tax liability is delayed to the migration stage or the retirement period. Finally, in subsection 15.4.4, the payment of the front-loaded pension tax liability is phased over the stages of contribution payment, receipt of returns, and benefit disbursement.

Before presenting these options, and to characterize different pension tax regimes in a transparent way, it is useful to define them unambiguously in a stylized life cycle model of a representative agent economy. Numerical simulations will help explain and compare different tax regimes and reform options in subsequent subsections.

15.4.1 A Simple Life Cycle Model of Pension Benefits, Saving, and Taxation

In this model, the agent earns labor income in period 1 that is spent on consumption, contributions to a mandatory pension regime, income taxes, and savings. In retirement, period 2, the agent's consumption is financed from pension benefits and accumulated savings net of income taxes levied on pension benefits and returns on savings.

Endogenous labor supply h_1 earns a constant wage rate w, and gross labor income in period 1 amounts to $y_1 = h_1 w$. Gross labor income is the assessment base for statutory old-age pension contributions, levied at the rate β, and for the income tax, levied at the rate τ_y. Pension contributions may, however, be deductible from the income tax base. Statutory pension contributions reduce the personal income tax burden by $\tau_d\beta y_1$, while personal pension contributions reduce the income tax burden by $\tau_s s_1$. Full deductibility is granted for tax rates $\tau_s=\tau_y$, and $\tau_d=\tau_y$, and nondeductibility applies for tax rates $\tau_d=0$ and $\tau_s=0$.

Net labor income in the working period 1 is therefore $y_1{}^n=h_1w(1-\tau_y)-\beta h_1w+\tau_d\,\beta h_1w+\tau_s s_1$. The budget constraint for the representative agent in period 1 is

$$c_1+s_1=h_1w(1-\tau_y)-\beta h_1w(1-\tau_d)+\tau_s s_1=h_1w[(1-\tau_y)-\beta(1-\tau_d)]+\tau_s s_1. \quad (15.1)$$

Gross income in the retirement period consists of the pension benefit b and savings inclusive of earned interest $s_1(1+r)$. Net income after the deduction of income tax on pension benefits τ_p and the income tax on interest τ_r becomes $y_2{}^n=(1-\tau_p)\ [b+s_1[1+r(1-\tau_r)]]$.

Disregarding bequests, the budget constraint for retirement period 2 is

$$c_2=(1-\tau_p)[b+s_1[1+r(1-\tau_r)]]. \quad (15.2)$$

For a rational consumer, the optimal labor/consumption plan is the solution to the problem

$$\max\ u(c_1,h_1)+v(c_2)/(1+\rho), \quad (15.3)$$

subject to constraints (15.1) and (15.2), with u and v as the period-specific utility functions and ρ the subjective rate of time preference.

With λ and η as the Lagrange parameters, the Lagrangian function is

$$L=u(c_1,h_1)+v(c_2)/(1+\rho)-\lambda[h_1w[(1-\tau_y)-\beta(1-\tau_d)]-c_1-s_1]$$
$$-\eta[(1-\tau_p)[b+s_1[1+r(1-\tau_r)]]-c_2].$$

The optimal consumption/savings plan is determined by the four marginal conditions

$$\partial L/\partial c_1=u_c+\lambda=0, \quad (15.4a)$$

$$\partial L/\partial s=\lambda(1-\tau_s)-\eta(1-\tau_p)[1+r(1-\tau_r)]=0, \quad (15.4b)$$

$$\partial L/\partial c_2=v_c/(1+\rho)+\eta=0, \quad (15.4c)$$

$$\partial L/\partial h_1=u_h-\lambda w[(1-\tau_y)-\beta(1-\tau_d)]=0, \quad (15.4d)$$

and the two budget constraints (15.1) and (15.2). Substituting out the two Lagrange parameters, the marginal conditions for the optimal consumption/leisure choice in period 1 and the optimal intertemporal consumption choice are

$$u_h/u_c = -w[1-\tau_y-\beta(1-\tau_d)], \tag{15.5a}$$

$$u_c/v_c = (1-\tau_p)[1+r(1-\tau_r)]/(1+\rho)(1-\tau_s), \tag{15.5b}$$

and reflect the standard tax effects: the marginal utility of leisure is reduced by the income tax and the net contribution rate of the mandatory pension system; the marginal utility of retirement consumption is reduced by the income tax on earned interest and the net of tax income ratio of retirement income taxation and tax relief is reduced by the deductibility of savings.

This simple representative citizen model suffices to characterize the basic features of different pension tax regimes as well as the pension tax proposals sketched in subsections 15.4.2 to 15.4.4. The appropriate choice of tax parameters allows capture of the popular tax regimes, as summarized in table 15.10.

Inserting the tax parameters of the second column into (15.5a) and (15.5b) immediately reveals how a comprehensive income tax TTE distorts the leisure/consumption choice as well as intertemporal consumption:

$$u_h/u_c = -w[1-\tau_y-\beta(1-\tau_d)] = -w[1-(\tau_y+\beta)], \tag{15.6a}$$

$$u_c/v_c = (1-\tau_p)[1+r(1-\tau_r)]/(1+\rho)(1-\tau_s) = [1+r(1-\tau_r)]/(1+\rho). \tag{15.6b}$$

Inserting the tax parameters of the third or fourth column into (15.5b) shows that deferred expenditure taxation and prepaid expenditure taxation do not distort intertemporal consumption because for both tax regimes the marginal condition becomes

Table 15.10
Tax parameters for standard tax systems.

Model tax parameters	TTE	EET	TEE
τ_y	>0	>0	>0
τ_d	0	τ_y	0
τ_s	0	τ_y	0
τ_r	τ_y	0	0
τ_p	0	0	0

$$u_c/v_c = (1+r)/(1+\rho). \tag{15.7}$$

However, under both expenditure regimes, the leisure/consumption choice remains distorted because of the price wedge of the income tax and the mandatory pension contribution.

Whereas this simple model allows identification of basic properties of the different tax regimes, it is not elaborate enough to serve as a building block in a normative optimal tax design analysis. For this purpose, important extensions incorporate heterogeneity of agents, multiperiod decisions, endogenous retirement, and labor market and survival risks. Moreover, the intertemporal budget constraints for the various pension schemes and the government sector must be considered.

15.4.2 Intertemporally Neutral Front-loaded Pension Taxation

Deferred income taxation of old-age pensions has been adopted as an attractive tax regime by many OECD countries, although it drives a wedge between regular saving and pension saving. Recent criticism of deferred taxation, however, does not concern the uneven playing field for taxing returns from savings but instead complains about international income tax revenue shifts when workers or pensioners migrate. Countries that lose income tax revenue through labor migration call for amendments or revisions of bilateral double-taxation treaties to find an acceptable balance between source and residence country taxation of old-age pensions.

This chapter proposes a promising alternative solution to the double equity dilemma inherent in the deferred income taxation of pensions. If the back-loaded EET regime is replaced by an appropriate front-loaded tax regime, then international equity can be regained without major changes to the existing network of bilateral double-taxation treaties (see Genser 2015). Source countries will not suffer from income tax revenue losses if income taxes are already paid when individuals migrate as workers or retirees.

It is true that comprehensive income taxation would serve this purpose and can even be justified if pension contributions are qualified as investments in a defined contribution system rather than deductible "social security taxes" that finance a subsistence-covering defined benefit scheme. However, TTE taxation of pension savings instead of deferred EET taxation also implies taxing the annual nominal growth of individual "pension wealth" and distorting intertemporal consumption.

Intertemporal neutrality in consumption can be achieved not only by a Fisher-Kaldor-type deferred-consumption-oriented income tax, however. It can also arise from a front-loaded TtE income tax that exempts pension benefits withdrawn from accumulated pension wealth but taxes income spent on pension savings when contributions are made as well as annual returns on pension wealth that exceed normal capital returns. In line with Kaldor's terminology, EET designates an expenditure tax regime and TtE a prepaid expenditure tax regime.[5] Restricting the tax base on capital returns to excess returns has been proposed as a "Rate of Return Allowance" regime for the Nordic countries (Sørensen 2010) and for the United Kingdom (Mirrlees 2011, chapter 14), and has already been implemented in Norway (Alstadsæter and Fjærli 2009).

Using the simple model sketched in subsection 15.4.1, the equivalent tax effects of EET and TtE tax regimes can be illustrated for a representative pension saver who earns a fixed wage income y_1 while working, saves $ßy_1$ in a mandatory pension scheme and σy_1 voluntarily, earns excess returns on pension savings $r > \rho$, and is subject to an income tax rate τ_y. Table 15.11 reveals the tax burden differences for such a representative pension saver in a defined contribution system. The income tax is highest for a comprehensive income tax; it is lower for a deferred consumption-oriented income tax (i.e., an expenditure tax), which is equivalent in present value terms to a prepaid consumption tax (i.e., an earnings tax, following the terminology of the Mirrlees Review) with taxable excess returns; and it is lowest for a prepaid consumption tax that leaves excess returns untaxed. Of course, EET and TtE regimes impose the same total tax burden on a pensioner in present value terms only if the marginal income tax rate is the same over the whole pension cycle and if positive and negative income tax bases are treated symmetrically.[6,7]

Whereas EET taxation and TtE taxation are intertemporally neutral, with equal amounts of present value taxes paid by the taxpayer and received by the tax authority in a closed economy, the situation changes in an open economy setting. National tax authorities are no longer indifferent between the two tax regimes, as their revenue situation changes if taxpayers migrate. According to the assumptions in table 15.11, the present value of the migrant's tax burden is 40.8 under both regimes (i.e., 30 percent of the discounted tax base of 136), but the emigration country's revenue, which is 36 under the TtE regime, shrinks to 21.6 under the EET regime.

Table 15.11
Consumer choice under comprehensive income and expenditure taxation ($y_1 = 120$, $s_1 = 24$, $r = 1.0$, $\rho = 0.5$, $\tau_y = \tau_r = 0.3$, $\beta = 0.2$).

	Tax regime											
	TTE			EET			TtE			TEE		
Wage income	120	0	120	120	0	120	120	0	120	120	0	120
Pension contributions	24	0	24	24	0	24	24	0	24	24	0	24
Pension benefits	0	48	32	0	48	32	0	48	32	0	48	32
Personal savings	24	0	24	24	0	24	24	0	24	24	0	24
Savings benefits	0	48	32	0	48	32	0	48	32	0	48	32
Income tax base	120	48	152	72	96	136	120	24	136	120	0	120
Income tax	36	14.4	45.6	21.6	28.8	40.8	36	7.2	40.8	36	0	36
Consumption	36	81.6	90.4	50.4	67.2	95.2	36	88.8	95.2	36	96	100

Source: Authors' calculation.
Note: The three columns of each tax regime represent the monetary values for each variable in periods 1 and 2 and the present value of the total lifetime sum over periods 1 and 2.

The important advantage of applying TtE rather than EET is that pensioners' migration no longer violates international equity among treasuries. Since pension benefits are pretaxed when contributions to pension systems are not deductible in the country of residence, no recovery of income tax relief is required to restore equity among countries' budgets. On the other hand, double taxation is avoided if the residence country applies TtE as well and exempts cross-border old-age pension benefits. An open question, however, is the assignment of tax revenue from excess returns that go to the residence country under EET. In the two-period model, this is also the case under TtE. In a multiperiod model with annual taxation of excess returns, this revenue remains in the emigration country before migration and goes to the immigration country in the years after migration. Even if a residence country abstains from implementing a TtE regime, double taxation can be avoided by the traditional treaty instruments of exemption (with or without progression) and foreign tax credits (unlimited or limited).

Another important point of discussion for every tax regime is administrative efficiency, which for a TtE tax depends crucially on a transparent and simple determination of excess returns on pension wealth. One attractive feature of TtE taxation is that its administration is largely in line with capital income taxation under a comprehensive income tax regime. Under both regimes, pension savings are not deductible, but a difference exists in the treatment of returns to pension wealth W. While under a comprehensive income tax the total annual returns on pension wealth rW are taxable income, TtE requires that only excess returns be taxable. The appropriate calculation of excess returns requires a political decision on the rate of normal returns to pension wealth. A theoretical benchmark for such a rate is a risk-free interest rate marked up by an actuarial risk premium. Scandinavian countries use such a normal rate of return ρ to run their dual-income tax systems. Basically this rate must be fixed for each tax year and is binding for the taxpayer and the tax authority. Once this normal rate of return ρ is fixed, the allowance ρW can be calculated for each taxpayer, and the respective tax base is $(r-\rho)W$. Instead of using $(r-\rho)W$ as a component of the individual income tax base, TtE income taxation refers to a simple transformation by defining a reduced income tax rate t, which when applied to total returns rW raises the same amount of income tax, $trW=T(r-\rho)W$. The reduced tax rate t is thus defined by $t=(1-\rho/r)T$. The tax rate decrement $(T-t)=(\rho/r)T$ reveals the "tax preference" that is implicitly incorporated in the EU recommendation to defer pension taxation rather than taxing pension savings as comprehensive income.

A final advantage in administering TtE in contrast to EET is that no control of correct deductions for pension savings is required. Administration and compliance are greatly simplified, as old-age pension contributions and pension savings do not reduce the income tax base. Excess returns on pension wealth are calculated in the pension accounts of financial institutions that accumulate pension wealth or in pension agencies that administer notional defined contribution schemes. Monitoring of appropriate tax payments by tax authorities can thus focus on a small number of pension funds and other agencies managing old-age pensions; further audits of millions of individual income tax returns are no longer necessary. Since old-age pension benefits to pensioners are tax-free, filing an income tax return is not required even if pension benefits are received from several sources. This final advantage will not be reaped if not all pension savings vehicles are pretaxed, although no mix of EET and TtE taxation for different types of old-age pensions jeopardizes intertemporal neutrality or interpersonal equity.

15.4.3 Deferred Payment of Front-loaded Pension Tax Liabilities

While deferred and front-loaded consumption tax regimes generate the same income tax burden and the same consumption in an aggregate lifetime perspective (see the last two rows in table 15.11), they nevertheless differ in the staging of their tax payments, which leaves the consumption path unchanged but impacts the saving path (Holzmann 2015). Table 15.12 demonstrates the consequences of strategic pension saving and reveals the equivalence of deferred and front-loaded income taxation with respect to period consumption if the capital market is perfect (i.e., $r=\rho$) and no excess returns can be earned. Without excess returns, the TtE and TEE regimes must of course be identical (see the last six columns in table 15.12).

Although the intertemporally aggregated income tax revenue is the same under the EET and TtE regimes, substantial revenue differences arise between the single periods, which affect the corresponding government budgets. Moreover, the revenue effects are intensified dramatically if pensioners migrate because the distribution of income tax revenue between the emigration and the immigration countries is fundamentally changed. Rather than solving the tax revenue allocation problem by revising the bilateral network of double-taxation treaties,

Table 15.12
Consumption smoothing under different pension tax regimes ($y_1=120$, $r=\rho=0.5$, $\tau_y=\tau_r=0.3$, $\beta=0.2$).

	Tax regime											
	TTE			EET			TtE			TEE		
Wage income	120	0	120	120	0	120	120	0	120	120	0	120
Pension contributions	24	0	24	24	0	24	24	0	24	24	0	24
Pension benefits	0	36	24	0	36	24	0	36	24	0	36	24
Personal savings	20.2	0	20.2	36	0	36	18	0	18	18	0	18
Savings benefits	0	30.3	20.2	0	54	36	0	27	18	0	27	18
Income tax base	120	22.1	134.7	60	90	120	120	0	120	120	0	120
Income tax	36	6.6	40.4	18	27	36	36	0	36	36	0	36
Consumption	39.8	59.7	79.6	42	63	84	42	63	84	42	63	84

Source: Authors' calculation.
Note: The three columns of each tax regime represent the monetary values for each variable in periods 1 and 2 and the present value of the total lifetime sum over periods 1 and 2, respectively.

a legal separation of individual tax liability and individual tax payments must be considered.

The first tax policy option for such a separation is to postpone payment of the pension tax liability under a TtE regime until pension benefits are paid out. For nonmigrating pensioners, this deferred tax payment option largely parallels the current deferred income tax regime EET. For migrating pensioners, the accumulated tax liability is well defined at the emigration date. Rather than becoming due as an "emigration tax," the liability can be turned into a tax annuity that must be paid to the tax administration after retirement in line with the payout of the monthly pension benefit. If pension wealth is portable across borders and pension benefits are paid out by a pension fund in the immigration country, the possibility exists for a revenue-sharing arrangement between the tax administrations of the emigration and immigration countries that grants that the tax annuity payable to the emigration country is withheld when the monthly pension benefit is paid out.

Conceptually, such an approach is greatly simplified if both unfunded and funded pensions are defined contribution schemes in which at retirement or upon migration the accumulated notional or actual amounts of pension wealth and income tax liability are well defined and both can be turned into an annuity using the same parameters (e.g., conditional cohort life expectancy).

What are the possible advantages of such a deferred TtE tax payment option over the immediate TtE tax payment regime proposed in subsection 15.4.2? Five considerations are offered.

First, the approach combines a formal front-loading of income taxation (TtE) that supports political credibility of tax policy and simplifies tax assessment in the contribution phase with a material back-loading, as tax payments are only due when benefits are disbursed. Thus, the downward pressure on private saving to avoid disposable income cuts will be mitigated and should not jeopardize overall societal saving, capital accumulation, and economic growth.

Second, as most countries currently operate retirement tax regimes that are close to EET, the transition toward a TtE regime with deferred tax payments should create less havoc. It avoids higher immediate tax revenue, which would offer incentives for higher government spending and diminishing expenditure reform efforts.

Third, while exit taxation on accumulated pension wealth upon migration meets resistance under the current EU ruling and is not addressed in most double-taxation treaties, the existence of an open income tax liability upon migration should be more easily accepted. Furthermore, moving to a new country of residence before or after retirement need not trigger immediate payment of the tax liability, if the deferred monthly tax payments are withheld when pension benefits are paid out in the source country and transferred directly to the tax authority. Such a tax payment arrangement avoids the imposition of an exit tax on migrants and affords equal treatment to migrating and nonmigrating pensioners. Moreover, informing the new residence country about the gross and net annuity would allow tax authorities of the residence country to assess the overall tax liability of the retiree correctly under a progressive income tax.

Fourth, the recording of deferred tax liabilities, taxes already paid, and the net amount of pension wealth over an individual's life cycle should prove very useful and offer transparency on tax revenue claims, tax payments, and thus their distribution across individuals and groups. This is useful even if pension claims are not portable across borders, because this information facilitates evaluating and auditing fairness across individuals and countries.

Last but not least, the availability of aggregated pension and tax liability data at the national level would allow an easier assessment of gross versus net implicit public debt. By 2017, EU member countries have been required to publish data on implicit pension liabilities through System of National Accounts (SNA) satellite accounts.

15.4.4 Phased Payment of Front-loaded Pension Tax Liabilities

A natural extension of a front-loaded pension tax with deferred tax payment is to phase payments evenly across the whole life cycle by charging a constant "tax payment" rate t^* on income spent on contributions, income from pension wealth returns, and benefit payouts. Conceptually, this third tax payment option is again based on the TtE income tax liability and an appropriately chosen payment rate t^* that generates the net present value of tax payments to redeem the front-loaded expenditure tax liability.

Under the tax liability constraint, the tax rate t^* is an endogenous variable. This creates a problem because the tax rate has to be fixed before the actual returns on pension wealth are known, but given that the present value of contributions and pension wealth returns should cover the present value of pension benefits, an appropriate tax rate t^* can be determined. Table 15.13 assumes excess returns, and the model compares savings responses to the three tax payment options: immediate

Table 15.13
Front-loaded pension taxation with different tax payment options ($y_1 = 120$, $r = 1.0$, $\rho = 0.5$, $\tau_y = \tau_r = 0.3$, $\beta = 0.2$).

	Tax payment regimes								
	Immediate payment			Deferred payment			Phased payment		
	P1	P2	P1+2	P1	P2	P1+2	P1	P2	P1+2
Earnings	120	0	120	120	0	120	120	0	120
Contribution	24	0	24	24	0	24	24	0	24
Benefit	0	24	24	0	24	24	0	24	24
Saving	15.3	0	15.3	28.8	0	28.8	27.2	0	27.2
Dissaving	0	23.0	23.0	0	43.2	43.2	0	40.8	40.8
Tax base	120.0	7.7	127.7	120.0	14.4	134.4	120.0	13.6	133.6
on earnings	80.7	0	80.7	67.2	0	67.2	68.8	0	68.8
on savings	39.3	7.7	47.0	52.8	14.4	67.2	51.2	13.6	64.8
Tax liability	36.0	2.3	38.3	36.0	4.3	40.3	36.0	4.1	40.1
on earnings	24.2	0	24.2	20.2	0.0	20.2	20.6	0	20.6
on savings	11.8	2.3	14.1	15.8	4.3	20.2	15.4	4.1	19.4
Tax payment	36.0	2.3	38.3	20.2	20.2	40.3	22.0	18.0	40.1
on earnings	24.2	0	24.2	20.2	0	20.2	11.4	9.3	20.6
on savings	11.8	2.3	14.1	0	20.2	20.2	10.7	8.7	19.4
Consumption	44.7	44.7	89.4	47.0	47.0	94.1	46.8	46.8	93.5

Source: Authors' calculation.
Note: The three columns of each tax regime represent the monetary values for each variable in periods 1 and 2 and the present value of the total lifetime sum over periods 1 and 2, respectively.

tax payment in each period; deferred tax payment as a fixed percentage of pension benefits; and lifetime tax payment as a fixed percentage t^* of pension wealth accumulation and withdrawal flows. The results reveal that lifetime repayment of the pension tax liability generates the expected savings response, which increases personal pension saving and reduces the first-period income tax revenue payment compared to the benchmark case of immediate payment of income tax liabilities.

What are the possible advantages of a t^* payment option compared to a TtE regime with immediate tax payment or deferred tax payment in the withdrawal stage? Three main considerations are relevant.

First, t^* is much lower than the income tax rate T because tax payments become due along the whole accumulation and withdrawal phase of pension wealth. Although the present value of tax payments and therefore the lifetime income effect are the same, individuals may be induced to interpret t^* as the relevant income tax rate in adjusting their intertemporal consumption behavior and to regard pension taxation as less distortive. Such an effect can result from reduced liquidity constraints under a lower tax rate and phased tax payment.

Second, the t^* lifetime payment option should facilitate negotiations on fiscal fairness between countries under rising labor migration. For migrating workers, the pressure for any exit tax arrangement is reduced, as an appropriate share of the income tax due has already been paid in the emigration country. For migrating retirees, the new residence country may get access to a substantial share of the migrant's income tax liability if it is entitled to keep the tax payment after migration as an adequate benefit tax. In this sense, income tax payment determines an income tax sharing rule for migrants that lies between the residence-based EET regime (which is under attack because the emigration country suffers from a permanent loss of the exemption of income spent on pension saving) and an immediate front-loading regime, which would allocate almost all income tax on pension savings to the emigration country. Hence the t^* option may be welcome because it addresses the double equity dilemma directly without any further agreement on income tax revenue sharing between the emigration and immigration countries.

Third, expanding the base for pension tax payments introduces a new tax handle for revisions of double-taxation treaties. Proposed here is a lifetime payment option with a rate t^* that is unanimously determined by a TtE regime according to the national income tax code and the pension scheme. Newly designed double-taxation treaties might, however, take account of t^* and consider floors or ceilings to t^* to reallocate pension tax revenues of migrants between residence and source countries. It remains to be seen whether this new instrument will be regarded as a helpful tool in double-taxation treaty renegotiations.

15.5 Conclusions

The taxation of internationally portable pensions and other retirement savings is characterized by astonishing diversity, complexity, and inconsistency. This disarray reflects national autonomy in the taxation of retirement income but also room for specific bilateral rules in avoiding double taxation of different forms of old-age pensions. This conceptual and operational heterogeneity creates economic distortions and inequities among individual pensioners as well as fiscal distortions and revenue inequities between countries. In view of the rising share of individuals spending at least some part of their working life abroad and acquiring assets and pension rights in source countries away from their future retirement residence, the situation is unsustainable and must be corrected.

Addressing the issue requires a coordinated approach beyond bilateral tax treaties and an agreed general concept for the taxation of pensions that avoids or at least minimizes distortions at the individual and country levels; neither a benchmark for coordination nor a conceptual framework is currently at hand.

To initiate discussion toward such a conceptual framework of portable pension taxation, this chapter suggests three nested policy options that build on existing policy thinking and should facilitate consensus building. It also offers new perspectives that may help to overcome resistance to reform.

First, the analysis supports a consumption-type taxation of retirement savings but proposes a move from back-loaded to front-loaded consumption-oriented income taxation. Front-loaded consumption taxation does not distort intertemporal individual consumption and facilitates the solution of fiscal inequity problems between countries triggered by migration.

Second, the analysis proposes a separation of the tax assessment of a pension saver from the payment of the assessed income tax liability. Three policy options are offered that subject an individual to the same front-loaded income tax liability in present value terms but differ in the timing of settlement: (1) immediate payment of the income tax liability in the period in which it is created, (2) postponed settlement until emigration or until pension wealth is dispersed and liquidated (whichever comes first), and (3) a phased settling of income tax liability across the stages of contribution payment, receipt of returns, and benefit disbursement.

Third, implementation of any of these three tax policy options requires a multilateral approach, starting with, for example, a pan-European decision to move from back-loaded to front-loaded pension taxation, while the operational implementation of income tax payment can be left to a revision of bilateral treaties. The resistance to moving from back-loaded to front-loaded pension taxation may be limited, as a number of European and non-European countries affected by cross-border migration have already started a discussion about front-loading pension taxation.

Notes

The first version of this chapter was presented at the CEPAR-CESifo workshop "Taxation of Pensions" in Munich in September 2015; a revised version was presented at the IMF/FAD-EPD seminar in Washington in December 2016. We want to thank the participants, Hans Georg Ruppe, and John Piggott for critical and helpful comments; any remaining errors and shortcomings are ours. This research was conducted by the Australian Research Council Centre of Excellence in Population Ageing Research (project number CE110001029). The views expressed herein are those of the authors and are not necessarily those of the Australian Research Council.

1. A pension benefit paid as a lifetime annuity from retirement until death is the main but not the only form of retirement income. It is dominant but not omnipresent in mandated schemes; was dominant in occupational schemes at the time of defined benefit schemes, which were gradually replaced by defined contribution schemes, often with no obligation to buy a lifetime annuity at a certain age; and hardly exists for voluntary savings. The remainder of this chapter uses "pensions" and "retirement savings" interchangeably unless a differentiation is warranted.

2. Replacement rates are a tricky concept that lends itself to many definitions. The same applies to the extent that the net replacement rate covers all tax elements. This happens only if pure back-loaded taxation is considered. When some front-loaded tax elements are present, the net pension and contribution base need to be adjusted accordingly.

3. Personal pensions subsume private savings vehicles that exhibit an explicit retirement income objective and are subject to specific regulations and supervision.

4. Under standard model conditions, the back-loaded form of income taxation, EET, is equivalent to the front-loaded form, TEE, which therefore is regarded as a variant of expenditure taxation. This equivalence breaks down when excess returns on capital, progressive income taxes, or investments in risky assets are taken into account. Deviations from simple standard model assumptions usually create a rationale for further diversity in pension taxation (see Holzmann 2015).

5. A TEE regime should not be regarded as a prepaid expenditure tax regime, because excess returns remain untaxed under TEE, whereas they are taxed under an EET expenditure tax (table 15.11).

6. In a world of certainty, excess returns above a normal market return reflect market imperfections. In a world exposed to uncertainty and risk, excess returns are those that exceed the normal market return and the appropriate risk premium. Therefore, t does not charge a tax burden on the risk premium and should be zero in a world of perfect capital markets

7. The argument that equivalence between EET and TtE can never be attained for real intertemporal income paths under progressive tax schedules because annual pension benefits will be lower than annual earned income and thus taxed at a lower rate is true but not well targeted. The same argument can be raised against intertemporal horizontal equity, because a constant progressive annual income tax schedule will always generate different tax burdens for the same lifetime income in present value terms whenever annual tax bases fluctuate over time. Perfect horizontal equity would require an ex post tax assessment of lifetime incomes and an imputation of an average lifetime income for each tax year in present values, which would result in a constant marginal tax rate over time. Horizontal equity is regarded as a useful benchmark, although income tax policy

abstains from such an adjustment mechanism to attain lifetime equity. In the same sense, the assumption of a constant marginal tax rate over the pension cycle should therefore not be criticized as an untenable simplification.

References

Allianz International Pensions. 2015. *Allianz Country Factsheets 2015*. Munich: Allianz SE.

Alstadsæter, Annette, and Erik Fjærli. 2009. "Neutral Taxation of Shareholder Income? Corporate Responses to an Announced Dividend Tax." *International Tax and Public Finance* 4:571–604.

Atkinson, Anthony, and Joseph Stiglitz. 1976. "The Design of Tax Structure: Direct versus Indirect Taxation." *Journal of Public Economics* 6 (1–2): 55–75.

Auerbach, Alan. 2009. "Direction in Tax and Transfer Theory." In *Australia's Future Tax and Transfer Policy Conference: Proceedings of a Conference*, edited by the Melbourne Institute, 63–71. Melbourne: University of Melbourne.

Bravo, Jorge. 2016. "Taxation of Pensions in Portugal: Is there a Rationale for a Semi-dual Income Tax System?" CESifo Working Paper No. 5981, CESifo, Munich.

Eurostat. 2015. *Migration and Migrant Population Statistics*. Eurostat Data Base. http://ec.europa.eu/eurostat/statistics-explained/index.php/Migration_and_migrant_population_statistics.

Fisher, Irving. 1930. *The Theory of Interest*. New York: Macmillan.

Genser, Bernd. 2015. "Towards an International Tax Order for the Taxation of Retirement Income." CEPAR Working Paper No. 2015/25, ARC Centre of Excellence in Population Ageing Research, University of New South Wales, Sydney.

Holzmann, Robert. 2015. "Taxing Pensions of an Internationally Mobile Labor Force: Portability Issues and Taxation Options." CEPAR Working Paper No. 2015/22, ARC Centre of Excellence in Population Ageing Research, University of New South Wales, Sydney.

Huang, Jennifer. 2008. "Taxable and Tax-Deferred Investing: A Tax-Arbitrage Approach." *Review of Financial Studies* 21 (5): 2174–2207.

Institute for Fiscal Studies (IFS). 1978. *The Structure and Reform of Direct Taxation*. London: Allen and Unwin.

International Bureau of Fiscal Documentation (IBFD). 2015. *European Tax Handbook 2015*. Global Tax Series. Amsterdam: IBFD.

Kaldor, Nicholas. 1955. *An Expenditure Tax*. London: Allen and Unwin.

Mirrlees, James A., Stuart Adam, Timothy Besley, Richard Blundell, Stephen Bond, Robert Chote, Malcolm Gammie, Paul Johnson, Gareth Myles, and James M. Poterba, eds. 2011. *Tax by Design: The Mirrlees Review—Volume 2*. Oxford: Oxford University Press.

OECD (Organisation for Economic Co-operation and Development). 2013. *Action Plan on Base Erosion and Profit Shifting*. Paris: OECD Publishing.

OECD (Organisation for Economic Co-operation and Development). 2015a. *Pensions at a Glance 2015: OECD and G20 Indicators*. Paris: OECD Publishing.

OECD (Organisation for Economic Co-operation and Development). 2015b. *Pension Funds in Figures*. Paris: OECD Publishing.

Robalino, David, Edward Whitehouse, Anca Mataoanu, Alberto Musalem, Elisabeth Sherwood, and Oleksiy Sluchynsky. 2005. "Tax Treatment of Pension Systems." In *Pensions in the Middle East and North Africa: Time for Change*, edited by David Robalino, 211–216. Orientations in Development Series. Washington, DC: World Bank.

Sørensen, Peter B. 2010. "Dual Income Taxes: A Nordic System." In *Tax Reform in Open Economies*, edited by I. Claus, N. Gemmell, M. Harding, and D. White, 78–107. Cheltenham: Edward Elgar.

Towers Watson. 2016. *Global Pension Asset Study 2016*. February. https://www.willistowerswatson.com/en/insights/2016/02/global-pensions-asset-study-2016.

US Department of Treasury. 1977. *Blueprints for Basic Tax Reform*. Washington, DC: US Government Printing Office.

Wellisch, Diemar, Sven-Oliver Lenz, Kerstin Tiele, and Rasmus Gahl. 2008. *Besteuerung der Altersvorsorge: Ein internationaler Vergleich*. Baden-Baden: Nomos.

Whitehouse, Edward. 1999. "The Tax Treatment of Funded Pensions." Social Protection Discussion Paper Series No. 9910, World Bank, Washington, DC.

World Bank. 1994. *Averting the Old-Age Crisis: Policies to Protect the Old and Promote Growth*. Washington, DC: World Bank.

Contributors

Torben M. Andersen is a professor of economics in the Department of Economics and Business Economics, Aarhus University, and a research fellow at the Pension Research Centre (PeRCent), Center for Economic Studies & Ifo Institute (CESifo), Center for Economic Policy Research (CEPR), and Institute of Labor Economics (IZA). His research interests cover public economics, pension economics, and labor economics.

Spencer Bastani obtained his PhD from Uppsala University in 2012. Since 2016 he has been associate professor in the Department of Economics and Statistics of Linnaeus University (Sweden). His research interests are in the area of public and labor economics.

Hazel Bateman is a professor of economics in the School of Risk and Actuarial Studies at UNSW Sydney, and deputy director and a chief investigator with the ARC Centre of Excellence in Population Ageing Research (CEPAR). She has long-standing research interests in public and private provision for retirement, particularly behavioral retirement finance and the taxation and regulation of pension funds.

Sören Blomquist obtained his PhD from Princeton University in 1976 and is professor emeritus in the Department of Economics at Uppsala University (Sweden). His research is mainly in the field of public economics, in particular on taxation and the interaction between public expenditures and taxes.

Axel Börsch-Supan is director of the Munich Center for the Economics of Aging (MEA) at the Max-Planck-Institute for Social Law and Social Policy (MPISOC), Munich, Germany, professor at the Technical University of Munich (TUM), and a member of the National Bureau of Economic Research (NBER), Cambridge, Massachusetts. He publishes widely on issues of population aging, pensions, and public finance.

Jorge Miguel Bravo is a professor of economics and finance at NOVA IMS, Universidade Nova de Lisboa, and invited professor at Université Paris-Dauphine. He coordinates the Observatory of Biometric Risks of the Portuguese Insured Population at Associação Portuguesa de Seguradores and is a member of the BBVA Bank Pensions Institute. He holds a PhD and a BSc in Economics from the University of Évora.

Gary Burtless holds the Whitehead Chair in Economic Studies at the Brookings Institution, Washington, DC. He is a labor and public finance economist and a long-time student of public and private pensions.

Rafal Chomik is an economist and a senior research fellow at the ARC Centre of Excellence in Population Ageing Research (CEPAR). He has worked in public administration and policy analysis for over a decade, including for the British government and the Organisation for Economic Co-operation and Development (OECD).

Helmuth Cremer is a professor of economics at the Toulouse School of Economics, University of Toulouse Capitole. His main area of research is public economics, particularly the design of tax, social insurance, pension, health, and education policies.

Carl Emmerson is deputy director at the Institute for Fiscal Studies (IFS) and a member of the Social Security Advisory Committee and the advisory panel of the Office for Budget Responsibility. He has worked extensively on pensions, welfare, and public finances in the United Kingdom and served as a specialist adviser to the House of Commons Work and Pensions Select Committee.

Csaba Feher is a senior economist in the International Monetary Fund's (IMF's) Fiscal Affairs Department. He previously worked at the World Bank, the Fiscal Council, and the National Bank of Hungary and headed the Private Pension Guarantee Fund. His fields of expertise are social insurance, public and private pension regulations, disability insurance, and fiscal sustainability.

Bernd Genser is professor emeritus in public finance at the University of Konstanz and a research fellow at the Center for Economic Studies & Ifo Institute (CESifo). He holds an honorary doctorate at the University of Freiberg, Germany, and was editor of the Finanzarchiv / Public Finance Analyses between 2002 and 2010.

Robert Holzmann is a member of the Austrian Academy of Sciences, holds honorary positions at the University of New South Wales (Sydney) and University of Malaya (Kuala Lumpur), and is a research fellow at the ARC Centre of Excellence in Population Ageing Research (CEPAR), Center for Economic Studies & Ifo Institute (CESifo), and Institute of Labor Economics (IZA). He was an academic in Austria and Germany and held positions at the International Monetary Fund (IMF), the Organisation for Economic Co-operation and Development (OECD), and the World Bank.

Paul Johnson is director of the Institute for Fiscal Studies (IFS) and a visiting professor at University College London. He previously worked at the Financial Services Authority and at Her Majesty's Treasury, where he was deputy head of the UK Government Economic Service.

Alain Jousten is a professor at the University of Liege (Law Faculty, Tax Institute, and HEC-Liège), where he holds the chair in Public Finance and Economic Policy. He is a research fellow at the Institute of Labor Economics (IZA) and NETSPAR and serves as an expert for the Fiscal Affairs Department of the International Monetary Fund (IMF).

Christian Keuschnigg is a professor of economics at the University of St. Gallen and a research fellow at the Center for Economic Studies & Ifo Institute (CESifo) and ARC Centre of Excellence in Population Ageing Research (CEPAR). His research focuses on tax reform, aging, and social security, as well as the impact of capital market frictions on economic growth, and he is engaged in scientific policy advice.

Eric Koepcke, formerly a senior research assistant in economic studies at the Brookings Institution in Washington, DC, is now pursuing a PhD in economics at the University of California, Berkeley.

George Kudrna is a senior research fellow at the ARC Centre of Excellence in Population Ageing Research (CEPAR) and a research associate at the Centre for Applied Macroeconomic Analysis at the Australian National University. He holds a PhD in economics from the University of Sydney and has published on a broad range of pension-related topics, including means testing of public pensions, taxation of private pensions, and evaluation of international pension reforms.

Jukka Lassila is a research advisor at the Research Institute of the Finnish Economy (ETLA) and an adjunct professor in the Department of Politics and Economics at the University of Helsinki. He has coordinated several international research projects concerning population aging and its economic consequences and policy implications, and edited (with Juha M. Alho and Svend E. Hougaard Jensen) *Uncertain Demographics and Fiscal Sustainability*.

Luca Micheletto obtained his PhD from the University of Milan (Italy) in 2002 and since 2015 has been a professor of economics in its Department of Law. His research interests lie in the area of public economics.

Pierre Pestieau is a professor emeritus at the University of Liege, a member of CORE, Louvain-la-Neuve, an associate member of the Paris School of Economics, and a research fellow at the Center for Economic Studies & Ifo Institute (CESifo) and the Institute of Labor Economics (IZA). He received his master's degree in economics from the University of Louvain and his PhD from Yale University. His research focuses on public economics and population economics.

John Piggott is director of the ARC Centre of Excellence in Population Ageing Research (CEPAR) and Scientia Professor of Economics at the University of New South Wales. He is a Research Fellow with both CESifo and IZA. He has a long-standing interest in the economics of pensions, aging, and retirement, and has published widely on these issues. He has advised on pension reforms internationally and is actively engaged in the policy debate in Australia.

Christopher Quinn obtained his bachelor's degree at the College of the Holy Cross (Worcester, Massachusetts) and his master's degree in economics and philosophy at the University of Bayreuth (Germany). He is now Account Manager at Bloomberg LP, London.

Tarmo Valkonen works as a research advisor at the Research Institute of the Finnish Economy (ETLA), Helsinki. His research interests include population aging, pension systems, taxation, and sustainability of public finances.

Alan Woodland is a Scientia Professor of Economics at the University of New South Wales and a chief investigator with the ARC Centre of Excellence in Population Ageing Research (CEPAR). He is a fellow of the Econometric Society and of the Academy of the Social Sciences of Australia, and a recipient of the Distinguished Economist Award of the Economics Society of Australia. His research interests include taxation and pension issues in the context of population aging, applied econometrics, and international trade.

Index

Note: Figures and tables are indicated by "f" and "t" respectively, following page numbers.